SIXTH
EDITION

Drugs, Behavior, and Modern Society

Charles F. Levinthal

Hofstra University

Allyn & Bacon

Boston   New York   San Francisco

Mexico City   Montreal   Toronto   London   Madrid   Munich   Paris

Hong Kong   Singapore   Tokyo   Cape Town   Sydney

Editor: *Stephen Frail*
Editorial Assistant: *Kerri Hart-Morris*
Production Supervisor: *Beth Houston*
Manufacturing Buyer: *JoAnne Sweeney*
Cover Administrator: *Joel Gendron*
Editorial Production Service: *Andrea Cava*
Photo Researcher: *PoYee Oster*
Electronic Composition: *NK Graphics*

Library of Congress Cataloging-in-Publication Data

Levinthal, Charles F., 1945–
   Drugs, behavior, and modern society / by Charles F. Levinthal. —6th ed.
     p. cm.
   Includes bibliographical references and index.
   ISBN 0-205-66570-5 (alk. paper)
 1. Drugs.   2. Drug abuse.   3. Drugs—Physiological effect.   4. Psychotropic drugs.
5. Psychopharmacology.   I. Title.
   HV5801.L49 2010
   362.290973—dc22

                                    2008049767

10 9 8 7 6 5 4 3 2 1   13 12 11 10 09

Allyn & Bacon
is an imprint of

www.pearsonhighered.com

ISBN-10: 0-205-66570-5
ISBN-13: 978-0-205-66570-9

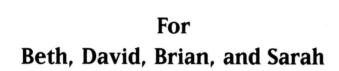

For
Beth, David, Brian, and Sarah

CONTENTS

CHAPTER 3
How Drugs Work in the Body and on the Mind   60

PART TWO   Legally Restricted Drugs in Our Society   90

CHAPTER 4
The Major Stimulants: Cocaine and Amphetamines   90

CHAPTER 5
Narcotics: Opium, Heroin, and Synthetic Opiates   117

In today's world, drugs and their use present a social paradox, combining the potential for good and for bad. As a society and as individuals, we can be the beneficiaries of drugs or their victims. This perspective continues to be the message of *Drugs, Behavior, and Modern Society*, Sixth Edition. As has been the case since the first edition was published in 1996, you will be introduced to the basic facts and the major issues concerning drug-taking behavior in a straightforward, comprehensive, and reader-friendly manner. A background in biology, sociology, psychology, or chemistry is not necessary. The only requirement is a sense of curiosity about the range of chemical substances that affect our minds and our bodies and an interest in the challenges these substances bring to our daily lives.

You are about to embark on a journey that began thousands of years ago. You will discover that drugs and drug-taking behavior have been around for a very long time, and you will find that present-day issues are really issues that society has had to confront for quite a while. In an important way, drugs and drug-taking behavior are consequences of a particular human need to feel stronger, more alert, calmer, more distant and dissociated from our surroundings, or simply good. The misuse and abuse of chemical substances that achieve these ends have resulted in massive problems in the United States and around the world.

To understand the complex issues surrounding drugs in our society, we need to recognize the enormous diversity that exists among drugs that affect the mind and the body. We must educate ourselves not only about illicit street drugs such as cocaine, amphetamines, heroin, hallucinogens, and marijuana but also about legally available drugs such as alcohol, nicotine, and caffeine. *Drugs, Behavior, and Modern Society*, Sixth Edition, has been designed to be the most comprehensive review of psychoactive drugs of all undergraduate college textbooks available today. It is particularly notable for the currency of the statistical information regarding drug use and abuse in America.

We also need to recognize that, like it or not, the decision to use drugs today is one of life's choices, regardless of our racial, ethnic, or religious background, how much money we have, where we live, how much education we have acquired, whether we are male or female, and whether we are young or old. The potential for misuse and abuse is a problem facing all of us.

Features of the Sixth Edition

The Sixth Edition of *Drugs, Behavior, and Modern Society* is built upon the strengths of earlier editions. Like the Fifth Edition, it is divided into five sections:

- Part One (Chapters 1–3): Drugs in Society/Drugs in Our Lives
- Part Two (Chapters 4–8): Legally Restricted Drugs in Our Society
- Part Three (Chapters 9–13): Legal Drugs in Our Society
- Part Four (Chapters 14–16): Medicinal Drugs
- Part Five (Chapters 17–18): Treatment, Prevention, and Education

As you will see, discussions of particular drugs have been grouped not in terms of their pharmacological or chemical characteristics but, rather, in terms of how readily accessible they are to the general public and societal attitudes toward their use. The last section of the book concerns itself with treatment, prevention, and education. In addition, several special features throughout the book will enhance your experience as a reader and serve as learning aids.

By the Numbers . . .

At the beginning of each chapter, a feature called By the Numbers . . . provides an often surprising and provocative insight into current viewpoints and research. It is presented in a brief format that draws the reader into the chapter itself and sets the stage for further exploration of the text.

Quick Concept Checks

Sometimes, when the material gets complicated, you want to have a quick way of finding out whether you understand the basic concepts being explained. I have included from time to time a Quick Concept Check, where you can see in a minute or two where you stand. Some of the Checks will be in a matching format; others will involve interpreting a graph or diagram. In some cases you will be asked to apply the principles you have learned to a real-world situation.

Portraits

The Portrait feature in each chapter takes you into the lives of individuals who either have influenced our thinking about drugs in our society or have been affected by drug use or abuse. Some of them are known to the public at large, but many are not. In any case, the Portraits add a human touch to the discussion of drugs and behavior. They remind us that throughout this book, we are dealing with issues that affect real people in all walks of life, now and in the past.

Drugs ... in Focus

There are many fascinating stories to tell about the role of drugs in our history and our present-day culture, along with the important facts and serious issues surrounding drug use. Some examples of Drugs ... in Focus features are the following:

- What Happened to the Coca in Coca-Cola? (Chapter 4, page 93)
- Paco: A New Cheap Form of Cocaine Floods Argentine Slums and Beyond (Chapter 4, page 101)
- Crack Babies Revisited: Is There an Adverse Effect? (Chapter 4, page 105)
- Methamphetamine across America (Chapter 4, page 109)
- The Secret and Dangerous Life of a (Heroin) Chipper (Chapter 5, page 132)
- Strange Days in Salem: Witchcraft or Hallucinogens? (Chapter 6, page 146)
- Hemp in America—Coming Full Circle (Chapter 7, page 186)
- Gene-Doping: Disqualified by DNA? (Chapter 8, page 195)
- Suspension Penalties for Steroid Use in Sports (Chapter 8, page 197)
- Visualizing the Pattern of Alcohol Consumption in the United States (Chapter 9, page 223)
- Alcohol, Security, and Spectator Sports (Chapter 9, page 235)
- Cigarette Purchases on the Internet (Chapter 11, page 278)
- Why There Are No (Live) Flies in Your Coffee (Chapter 12, page 302)
- Resistol and Resistoleros in Latin America (Chapter 13, page 324)
- Is There Any Truth Regarding "Truth Serum"? (Chapter 15, page 359)
- Abraham Lincoln, Depression, and Those "Little Blue Pills" (Chapter 16, page 383)
- A Test Kit for Drugs in the Home: Whom Can You Trust? (Chapter 18, page 433)

Health Line

Helpful information regarding the effectiveness and safety aspects of particular drugs, specific aspects of drug-taking behavior, and new medical applications can be found in Health Line features throughout the book. Here are some examples of Health Line features:

- Defining Drugs: Olive Oil, Curry Powder, and a Little Grapefruit? (Chapter 1, page 5)
- Effects of Psychoactive Drugs on Pregnant Women and Newborns (Chapter 2, page 45)
- Drug Craving and the Insula of the Brain (Chapter 3, page 82)
- Seven Rules for Cocaine Abusers Who Want to Quit (Chapter 4, page 102)
- Stimulant Medications as "Smart Pills" (Chapter 4, page 112)
- African Americans, Smoking, and Mentholated Cigarettes (Chapter 11, page 276)
- Ten Tips on How to Succeed When Trying to Quit Smoking (Chapter 11, page 291)
- Coffee, Genes, and Heart Attacks (Chapter 12, page 310)
- Mercury Poisoning: On Being Mad as a Hatter (Chapter 16, page 378)
- The Public Health Model and the Analogy of Infectious Disease Control (Chapter 18, page 421)
- Peer-Refusal Skills: Ten Ways to Make It Easier to Say No (Chapter 18, page 426)
- Alcohol 101 on College Campuses (Chapter 18, page 436)

Health Alert

Information of a more urgent nature is provided in the Health Alert features. You will find important facts that you can use to recognize the signs of drug misuse or abuse and ways you can respond to emergency drug-taking situations, as well as useful Internet web links where you can go for assistance. Examples of some Health Alert features are the following:

- Adverse Effects of Drug–Drug and Food–Drug Combinations (Chapter 3, page 68)
- Cocaine after Alcohol: The Risk of Cocaethylene Toxicity (Chapter 4, page 96)
- The Physical Signs of Possible Cocaine Abuse (Chapter 4, page 97)
- Emergency Guidelines for a Bad Trip on LSD (Chapter 6, page 151)

- MDMA Toxicity: The Other Side of Ecstasy (Chapter 6, page 158)
- The Symptoms of Steroid Abuse (Chapter 8, page 202)
- Emergency Signs and Procedures in Acute Alcohol Intoxication (Chapter 9, page 229)
- Signs of Trouble from Smokeless Tobacco (Chapter 11, page 285)
- Side Effects of Common Medications (Chapter 14, page 344)
- The Risks of Web Pharmacies/The Allure of Foreign Drugs (Chapter 14, page 352)
- In Case of a Barbiturate Overdose Emergency . . . (Chapter 15, page 360)
- The Dangers of Rohypnol as a Date-Rape Drug (Chapter 15, page 368)
- SSRI Antidepressants and Elevated Risk of Suicide among Children and Adolescents (Chapter 16, page 385)
- The Risks of Interactions between St. John's Wort and Prescription Drugs (Chapter 16, page 389)
- Coping with a Child's Abuse of Alcohol or Other Drugs: What Parents Should and Should Not Do (Chapter 17, page 410)

Point/Counterpoint Debates

Drug issues are seldom black or white, right or wrong. Some of the most hotly debated questions of our day involve the use, misuse, and abuse of drugs. These issues deserve a good deal of critical thought. This is the reason I have written a Point/Counterpoint debate at the end of each of the five sections of the book. I have taken five important controversies concerning drugs, collected the primary viewpoints pro and con, and simulated a debate that two hypothetical people might have on that question. I invite you to read these debates carefully and try to come to your own position, as an exercise in critical thinking. Along with a consideration of the critical thinking questions for further discussion that follow each feature, you may wish to continue the debate in your class.

New to This Edition

The Sixth Edition is marked by attention to major theoretical perspectives in the field of drug abuse and an expanded coverage of contemporary issues and concerns. Here are some examples:

- Continued emphasis on the Biopsychosocial Model throughout the book, conceptualizing drug-taking behavior as a complex interaction of biological, psychological, and social factors.
- Continued extensive coverage of important theoretical perspectives in drug abuse: the Family Systems Model (Chapters 1, 17, and 18), the Public Health Model (Chapters 1, 2, and 18), the Harm Reduction Model (Chapter 2), and positions opposing the Disease Model in alcoholism and other forms of drug abuse (Chapter 10).
- Totally revised and updated coverage of drug-related statistical information from the 2008 Monitoring the Future survey of the University of Michigan, 2006 Drug Abuse Warning Network (DAWN) survey, and the 2007 National Survey on Drug Use and Health.
- New or revised Drugs . . . in Focus features: Endorphins in our Lives: A Psychosocial Perspective (Chapter 3), Paco: A New Cheap Form of Cocaine Floods Argentine Slums and Beyond (Chapter 4), Is There Any Truth Regarding "Truth Serum"? (Chapter 15), and Penalties for Crack versus Penalties for Cocaine: New Developments in Criminal Prosecution (Chapter 17).
- New or revised Health Line features: Defining Drugs: Olive Oil, Curry Powder, and a Little Grapefruit? (Chapter 1), Drug Craving and the Insula of the Brain (Chapter 3), Defining Drugs: Nutmeg as a Spice and a Hallucinogen (Chapter 6), and African Americans, Smoking, and Mentholated Cigarettes (Chapter 11).
- New Health Alert feature: Sustained-Release Buprenorphine: Ushering in a New Era (Chapter 5).
- New or revised Portraits: Nicholas and the Dextromethorphan High (Chapter 1), Robert Downey, Jr.—Cleaning Up His Life after Cocaine (Chapter 4), and Scott Pecor and the Scotchgard High (Chapter 13).
- A "Where to go for assistance" web link included in all Health Alert features.
- New Point/Counterpoint feature: Should Cognitive Performance-Enhancing Drugs Be Used by Healthy People? at the end of Part Two.
- Expanded "Critical Thinking Questions for Further Discussion" at the end of all Point/Counterpoint features.
- New and expanded sections on major contemporary issues of public concern: Drug-taking behavior among children of parents who had been involved in drug use at an earlier time (Chapter 1); current trends in prescription and over-the-counter (OTC) drug abuse (Chapter 1); harm reduction as a national drug-abuse policy (Chapter 2); genetic contributions to an understanding of individual differences in drug-taking behavior (Chapter 3); current

status of anti-craving drugs for cocaine-abuse treatment (Chapter 4); prescription pain medication misuse and abuse (Chapter 5); current availability of high-potency marijuana grown in remote areas of Canada (Chapter 7); differential rates of law enforcement for marijuana possession among African American and Latino men (Chapter 7); steroid abuse, abuse of human growth hormone, and misuse of stimulant medication in major league baseball (Chapter 8); potential health benefits from a natural substance in red wine (Chapter 9); chronic alcohol abuse and alcoholism in the workplace (Chapter 10); extensive tobacco use among nations of the world and the global health crisis related to tobacco-related disease (Chapter 11); placebo effects of caffeine as a performance-enhancing drug (Chapter 12); soft-drink consumption and childhood obesity (Chapter 12); conservatism in recent FDA approvals of new drugs (Chapter 14); new recommendations for use of cough-suppressant products with children under the age of fourteen (Chapter 14); specialized drug courts in the criminal justice system (Chapter 17); the influence of popular music and the Internet on drug-taking behavior of young people (Chapter 18); and the current trend toward alcohol-free college fraternity and sorority houses (Chapter 18).

All told, this edition includes approximately 250 new reference citations of information published since 2007.

MyPsychKit

The companion web site for the book can be accessed at www.mypsychkit.com. This web site contains learning objectives, web links to relevant sites of interest, and online practice tests. These multiple-choice and true-false practice questions enable you to assess your mastery of the course content before you take an actual test.

An Invitation to Readers

I welcome your reactions to *Drugs, Behavior, and Modern Society*, Sixth Edition. Please send any comments or questions to the following address: Dr. Charles F. Levinthal, Department of Psychology, Hofstra University, Hempstead, NY 11549. You can also fax them to me at (516) 463-6052 or e-mail them to me at charles.f.levinthal@hofstra.edu. I hope to be hearing from you.

Acknowledgments

In the course of writing this edition of the book, as well as the previous editions, I have received much encouragement, assistance, and expert advice from a number of people. I have benefited from their generous sharing of materials, knowledge, and insights. I am particularly indebted to Dr. Patrick M. O'Malley, Institute for Social Research, University of Michigan, Ann Arbor, and Dr. Elizabeth Crane, Substance Abuse and Mental Health Services Administration, Rockville, MD.

I am very fortunate to have worked with a superb team at Pearson. I am especially indebted to my editor, Stephen Frail, and my production supervisor, Beth Houston. Their professionalism and friendship are greatly appreciated. I also want to acknowledge the efforts of Andrea Cava, project editor, and PoYee Oster, photo researcher, whose talents and expertise contributed so much to the production quality of this book. I appreciate the help of Meghan Brady in researching new information for this edition. A number of manuscript reviewers made invaluable suggestions as I worked on the Sixth Edition. I thank all of them for their help: Kevin Doyle, University of Virginia; Robert Hale, Shippensburg University; Michael Madson, University of Southern Mississippi; Terry Pettijohn, Ohio State University; Diane Spokus, Penn State; Robert E. Stewart, Washington and Lee University; and Christopher L. Vowels, Kansas State University.

On a more personal note, there are others who have given me their support over the years and to whom my appreciation goes beyond words. As always, I thank my mother, Mildred Levinthal, and my mother-in-law, Selma Kuby, for their encouragement and love.

Above all, my family has been a continuing source of strength. I will always be grateful to my wonderful sons David and Brian, and daughter-in-law Sarah, for their love and understanding. I am especially grateful to my wife, Beth, for her abiding love, support, and complete faith in my abilities.

Charles F. Levinthal

Photo Credits

Page 3, © Spencer Grant/Stock Boston; 9, © Victor Englebert/Photo Researchers; 10, © Bettmann/CORBIS; 12 left, Courtesy Everett Collection; 12 right, © Henry Diltz; 19, © JupiterImages/BananaStock/Alamy; 25, © Patrick McCarthy/Newsday; 35, © Chuck Nacke/Woodfin Camp & Associates; 39, © Eugene Richards/ Magnum Photos; 44, © Robert McElroy /Woodfin Camp & Associates; 53, © UPI- Bettmann/CORBIS; 54, © Hans Deryk/AP Images; 61, © Richard Lord/The Image Works; 63, © Robert Harbison; 71, © Bruce Ayres/Getty Images; 81, Courtesy of Brookhaven National Laboratory; 83, © Mitch Wojnarowicz/The Image Works; 84, Courtesy of Brookhaven National Laboratory; 92 top, © CORBIS; 92 bottom, © Bettmann/ CORBIS; 95, © Piotr Powietrzynski/Getty Images 99, © Spencer Grant/Photolibrary; 103, © Rune Hellestad/CORBIS; 108, © AP Images, 119, © Marcelo Salinas; 121, 122, 124, © Bettmann/CORBIS; 137 left, © 2001 Newsday. Reprinted with permission; 137 right, © Andy Molloy/Kennebec Journal; 138, © Darren McCollester/Getty Images; 147, © Gene Anthony/Stockphoto.com; 148, © Frank Capri/SAGA/Woodfin Camp & Associates; 149, © David Hoffman; 153, © Vaugh Fleming/Science Photo Library/Photo Researchers; 155, © Francois Gohier/Photo Researchers; 157, © Scott Houston/Sygma/CORBIS; 168, © Gene Anthony/Stockphoto.com; 170, © fl online/Alamy; 172, © Hulton Archive/Getty Images; 184, © AP Images; 185, Marijuana Policy Project Foundation www.MarijuanaPolicy.org; 186, © Kenneth Hayden/ Stockphoto.com; 194 both, © AP Images; 197, © Reuters New Media/ CORBIS; 198, © Catherine Karnow/Woodfin Camp & Associates; 202, NYT Graphics/NYT Pictures; 207, © Tribune Media Services, Inc. All Rights Reserved. Reprinted with permission; 209, © Blair Seitz/Photo Researchers; 218, Courtesy of the Print Collection, The Lewis Walpole Library, Yale University; 221 top, © George Steinmetz; 221 bottom, © Joe Raedle/Getty Images; 233, © Zuma Press/ZUMA/CORBIS; 234, Courtesy of Candace Lightner; 237, By permission of Mike Luckovich and Creators Syndicate, Inc.; 246, National Clearinghouse for Alcohol & Drug Information; 250, © Bettmann/CORBIS; 253 top, © Martin M. Rotker/Photo Researchers; 253 bottom, © Biophoto Associates/Science Source/Photo Researchers; 255, © George Steinmetz; 261, © Hank Morgan/Science Source/Photo Researchers; 262 top, Compliments of the Wilson House, East Dorset, VT; 272, © Bettmann/CORBIS; 274 left, © John Coletti/Photolibrary; 274 right, Gaslight Advertising Archives; 277, © Reuters News Media/CORBIS; 287 top, DOONESBURY ©1992 G. B. Trudeau. Reprinted with permission of UNIVERSAL PRESS SYNDICATE. All rights reserved; 287 bottom, © Richard Hutchings/Photo Researchers; 289, National Library of Medicine; 290, Yola Monakhov for The New York Times; 293 top, Courtesy of California Department of Health Services; 293 bottom, Design: Better World Advertising <www.socialmarketing.com>; 301, © Thad Samuels Abell/NGS Image Collection; 303, © Bettmann/CORBIS; 305, Used with permission of Hershey Corporation; 308, © Blair Seitz/Photo Researchers; 313, © Bob Daemmrich/Stock Boston; 319, © Bettmann/CORBIS; 323, © Reuters News Media/CORBIS; 325, © Barry C. Allen/The Palm Beach Post; 326, Courtesy of the National Inhalant Prevention Coalition, Austin, Texas, 800-269-4237; 335, © Spencer Grant/Stock Boston; 336, © UPI-Bettmann/CORBIS; 344, © Bob Daemmrich/Stock Boston; 348, © Steve Leonard/Stockphoto.com; 350, © 2003 Newsday. Reprinted with permission; 360, © Will McIntyre/Photo Researchers; 363, © Johnathan Kirn/Liaison/Getty Images; 371, © Amanda Friedman/Getty Images; 372, © Eric Risberg/AP Images; 377, © Grunnitus Studio/Photo Researchers; 379 left, © AP Images; 379 right, © Universal Pictures/Courtesy Everett Collection; 387, Courtesy of Dr. Lewis Baxter and Dr. Michael Phelps, UCLA School of Medicine; 399, © Eli Reed/Magnum Photos; 404, Courtesy of DAYTOP Village; 405, Courtesy of Partnership for a Drug-Free America; 410, © Sybil Shackman; 424, © Jim Pickerell; 431, Courtesy of Partnership for a Drug-Free America; 432, Courtesy of the Ad Council's and the U.S. Department of Health & Human Services' Substance Abuse & Mental Health Services Administration's Underage Drinking Prevention campaign. Designed by the Kaplan Thaler Group; 434, Native American Posters. Artwork courtesy of Blas E. Lopez; 435, A Matter of Degree, a partnership of the American Medical Association Office of Alcohol and Other Drug Abuse and The Robert Wood Johnson Foundation. All Rights Reserved. 437, Courtesy of Meredith Poulton/The Milford Daily News.

chapter 1

Drugs and Behavior Today

Mike was seventeen, a high school junior—an age when life can be both terrific and terrifying. He looked at me with amazement, telling me by his expression that either the question I was asking him was ridiculous or the answer was obvious. "Why do kids do drugs?" I had asked. "It's cool," he said. "That's why. Believe me, it's important to be cool. Besides, in my life, drugs just make me feel better. Smoking a little weed, chilling out with some Perks or a little Vicodin, spinning with some Addies—it's a way of getting away from stuff. You know that everybody does it. At least all of my friends do it. And it's easy to get them. That's the answer, if you want to know. It's easy and it's cool."

The conversation was over. But as he started to leave, Mike seemed to notice the concern on my face. "Don't worry about me," he said, "I can handle it. I can handle it just fine."

Today, more than ever, drugs affect our daily lives. It is difficult to pick up a newspaper or watch television without finding a report or program that concerns drug use or some issue associated with it. We are continually bombarded with news about drug-related arrests of major drug dealers and ordinary citizens, news about the most recent drug involvement among popular celebrities, news about drugs intercepted and confiscated at our borders and in the towns and cities of America.

More important, in your personal life, you have had to confront the reality of drugs. One-fourth of adults in the United States report that drugs have been a cause of trouble in their family. It may have happened to you. In school, you have been taught the risks involved in drug use. It is likely that you have had to contend with social pressure to share a drug experience with your friends or the possibility of drugs being sold to you. According to a national survey, about one in five males and about one in eight females between the ages of twelve and seventeen have been approached in the past month by someone selling drugs. For fifteen- or sixteen-year-old youths, the number is approximately one in four. These official statistics might appear to be an underestimate in light of your personal experience with drugs.[1]

It is not uncommon for high school students on a Monday morning to boast about how drunk they got over the weekend. For some, regular consumption of alcohol began in junior high school or earlier, in a society where twenty-one is the minimum legal age for obtaining alcoholic beverages. Binge drinking continues to be a significant problem on college campuses nationwide. Experimentation and, in some cases, regular use of stimulants, marijuana, inhalants from common household products, performance-enhancing agents to build muscle mass, and mind-altering substances of all sorts seem commonplace.

Cigarette smoking among young people continues to be a major societal problem, despite the fact that it is illegal for those younger than eighteen years old to purchase tobacco products. The public-health concern about underage cigarette smoking centers on the fact that approximately 82 percent of regular smokers in the United States, aged thirty to thirty-nine, smoked their first cigarette—and more than half had become regular smokers—*before they were eighteen years old.*[2]

Whether we like it or not, the decision to use drugs of all types and forms, legally sanctioned or not, has become one of life's choices in American society and in communities around the world.

Social Messages about Drug Use

Unfortunately, we live in a social environment that sends us mixed messages with respect to drug use. The appearance of Joe Camel, the Marlboro Man, and the Virginia Slims Woman in print advertisements for cigarettes may be increasingly distant memories, but at one time they were dominant images that conveyed the attractiveness of smoking to the public, particularly to young people. They are gone now as a result of federal regulations established in 1998. For decades, warning labels on cigarette packs and public service announcements have cautioned us about the serious health hazards of tobacco use. Yet cigarette smoking is often glamorized in movies. Beer commercials during telecasts of football games and other athletic events are designed to be entertaining and to associate beer drinking with a desirable lifestyle of friendship, sex, and romance, but we are expected to "know when to say when."

Prominent political figures, including a former U.S. president (Bill Clinton) and a former U.S. vice president (Al Gore) as well as a host of public officials on a local or national level, have admitted their experiences with marijuana earlier in their lives. Yet the position of the U.S. government on marijuana is that it is an illegal substance, officially classified since 1970 as a drug with a high potential for abuse and no accepted medical use, in the same category as heroin. Experiences with alcohol abuse and alcoholism abound, even as research studies show that moderate alcohol drinking (unless contraindicated) is actually beneficial to our health.

Anti-drug campaigns in the media are created to discourage young people from becoming involved with drugs. At the same time, we observe a continuing stream of sports figures, entertainers, and other high-profile individuals engaging in drug-taking behavior. Even though careers are frequently jeopardized and, in some instances, lives are lost as a result, powerful pro-drug-use messages continue to influence us. These messages come from the entertainment industry and traditional media sources, as well as web sites on the Internet.[3]

These facts, as confusing and often contradictory as some of them are, represent the present-day drug scene. The purpose of this book is to answer your questions in a straightforward and understandable manner, and to address your concerns about drugs and behavior in our society. In the chapters that follow, two general themes related to drugs will become clear.

The first theme is that the diversity in the types of available drugs is immense. A quick glance at the contents of this book will show you the wide range of substances that will be covered. Some of you will have expected to see only the "classic" street drugs: cocaine, amphetamines, heroin, LSD, and marijuana. The coverage of other substances may be surprising because they are so accessible and, in many cases, are legally available—inhalants in common household products, anabolic steroids, caffeine, prescription pain medications, and nicotine. You will see two chapters on the subject of alcohol, by far the most pervasive drug abuse problem in our society. As you will discover, communities in this country and around the world have had as many problems contending with legal drugs as with illegal ones.

The second theme is that drug use must be considered not as a "young people's issue" but rather as one that encompasses every segment of our society. The availability of drugs and the potential for drug abuse present a challenge for people of all ages, from the young to the elderly. The effects are being felt in the workplace and retirement communities as well as on street corners, in school yards, and on college campuses.

The personal and social problems associated with drugs extend in one way or another to men and women of all ethnic and racial groups, geographic regions, and socioeconomic levels. No group should believe themselves exempt from this scourge.[4]

As concerned as we may be about the dangers of drugs, however, we should not fail to recognize a more positive aspect of drug use today. You may know someone whose depression nearly led to suicide but who is now living a normal life as a result of taking antidepressant medication. You may know someone else who has been helped by a medication that controls anxiety. Millions of individuals in the United States and around the world

The problems associated with drug abuse and misuse in our society extend beyond the use of illegal drugs. We must also be concerned with the abuse and misuse of legally available substances such as alcohol, nicotine, and caffeine, as well as of prescription and over-the-counter medications.

who suffer from the torment of mental illness have benefited from drug treatment. The rapid pace in the development of new therapeutic drugs brings the prospect of increasingly effective ways to treat severe psychiatric disorders as well as behavior problems.

There is also a tremendous amount of excitement among researchers engaged in discovering new drugs for the treatment of drug abuse itself. The development of anti-craving medications, particularly with respect to cocaine abuse (see Chapter 4), is a hopeful sign that we can finally understand the biochemical basis for drug dependence.

Two Ways of Looking at Drugs and Behavior

In the chapters ahead, we will look at the subject of drugs and behavior in two basic ways. First, we will examine the biological, psychological, and sociological effects of consuming certain types of drugs. The focus will be on the study of specific substances that alter our feelings, our thoughts, our perceptions of the world, and our behavior. These substances are referred to as **psychoactive drugs**

psychoactive drugs: Drugs that affect feelings, thoughts, perceptions, or behavior.

because they influence the functioning of the brain and hence our behavior and experience. Examples that often receive the greatest amount of attention are officially defined in the United States as **illicit** (illegal) **drugs:** heroin, cocaine, and marijuana, as well as club drugs such as Ecstasy, LSD, PCP, ketamine, and GHB. Other equally important psychoactive substances, however, are **licit** (legal) **drugs,** such as alcohol, nicotine, and caffeine. In the cases of alcohol and nicotine, legal access carries a minimum-age requirement.

Second, we will focus on the complex interplay of circumstances in our lives that lead to drug-taking behavior. We will examine the possibility that drug use is, at least in part, a consequence of how we feel about ourselves in relation to our parents, to our friends and acquaintances, to events occurring around us, and to the community in which we live. We will also examine the biological factors that may predispose us to drug-taking behavior. An exploration into the reasons why some individuals engage in drug-taking behavior, whereas others do not, will be a primary topic of discussion.

Understanding the interplay between drug-taking behavior and society is essential when we consider the dangerous potential for drug use to become **drug dependence.** As many of us know all too well, a vicious circle can develop in which drug-taking behavior fosters more drug-taking behavior, in a spiraling pattern that is often extremely difficult to break. Individuals showing signs of drug dependence display intense cravings for the drug and, in many cases, require increasingly greater quantities to get the same, desired effect. They become preoccupied with their drug-taking behavior and eventually realize that their lives have gotten out of control (see Chapter 2).

Ultimately, an understanding of drug dependence requires an examination of both biological and sociological factors. First, the use of psychoactive drugs modifies the functioning of the brain, both at the time during which the drug is present in the body and later when the drug-taking behavior stops. Drug dependence, therefore, produces long-lasting brain changes. As Alan Leshner, former director of the National Institute on Drug Abuse (NIDA), has put it, a "switch" in the brain seems to be thrown following prolonged drug use. It starts as a voluntary behavior, but once that switch is thrown, a pattern of drug dependence takes over. Second, drug dependence is a result of a complex interaction of the individual and his or her environment. We cannot fully understand the problem of drug dependence without being aware of the social context in which drug-taking behavior occurs. As you will see in Chapter 17, the recognition that drug dependence can be defined in terms of biological *and* social components has important implications for treatment.[5]

Which drugs have the greatest potential for creating drug dependence? How can someone escape drug dependence once it is established? What factors increase or decrease the likelihood of drug-taking behavior in the first place? These are some of the important questions to be considered as we examine the impact of drugs and drug-taking behavior on our lives.

A Matter of Definition

Considering the ease with which we speak of drugs and drug use, it seems as if it should be relatively easy to define what we mean by the word **drug.** Unfortunately, there are significant problems in arriving at a clear definition.

The standard approach is to characterize a drug as *a chemical substance that, when taken into the body, alters the structure or functioning of the body in some way.* In doing so, we are accounting for examples such as medications used for the treatment of physical disorders and mental illnesses, as well as for alcohol, nicotine, and the typical street drugs. Unfortunately, however, this broad definition could also refer to ordinary food and water. Because it does not make much sense for nutrients to be considered drugs, we need to refine our definition, adding the phrase *excluding those nutrients considered to be related to normal functioning.*

Bear in mind that we may still be on slippery ground. We can now effectively eliminate the cheese in your next pizza from consideration as a drug, but what about some exotic ingredient in the sauce? Sugar is safely excluded, even though it has significant energizing and therefore behavioral effects on us, but what about the cayenne pepper that burns your tongue? Where do we draw the line between a drug and a nondrug? It is not an easy question to answer.

---

illicit drugs: Drugs whose manufacture, sale, or possession is illegal.

licit drugs: Drugs whose manufacture, sale, or possession is legal.

drug dependence: A condition in which an individual feels a compulsive need to continue taking a drug. In the process, the drug assumes an increasingly central role in the individual's life.

drug: A chemical substance that, when taken into the body, alters the structure or functioning of the body in some way, excluding those nutrients considered to be related to normal functioning.

We can learn two major lessons from this seemingly simple task of defining a drug. First, there is probably no perfect definition that would distinguish drugs from nondrugs without leaving a number of cases that fall within some kind of gray area. The best we can do is to set up a definition, as we have, that handles most of the substances we are likely to encounter. However, significant practical difficulties may still arise. As we will see in Chapter 14, the current nonregulation of dietary supplements in the United States has resulted from a governmental decision that these particular substances are not to be considered drugs in the same category as prescription or over-the-counter medications.

The second lesson is more subtle. We often make the distinction between drugs and nondrugs not in terms of their physical characteristics but rather in terms of whether the substance in question has been *intended to be used primarily as a way of inducing a bodily or psychological change.*[6] By this reasoning, if the pizza maker intended to put that spice in the pizza to make it taste better, the spice might not be considered a drug; it would simply be another ingredient in the recipe. If the pizza maker intended the spice to intoxicate you or quicken your heart rate, then it might be considered a drug (Health Line).

Ultimately, the problem is that we are trying to reach a consensus on a definition that fits our intuitive sense of what constitutes a drug. We may find it difficult to define pornography, but (as has been said) we know it when we see it. So it may be with drugs. Whether we realize it or not, when we discuss the topic of drugs, we are operating within a context of social and cultural values, a group of shared feelings about what kind of behavior (that is, what kind of drug-taking behavior) is right and what kind is wrong.

Health Line

Defining Drugs: Olive Oil, Curry Powder, and a Little Grapefruit?

An ever-increasing number of reminders about the blurriness of the distinction between drugs and nondrugs come from recent research on the chemical properties of specific foods we eat on a daily basis. For example, in 2005 it was found that freshly pressed olive oil contains large amounts of oleocanthal, a compound that inhibits the activity of cyclooxygenase enzymes in the identical manner as ibuprofen, a popular nonsteroid anti-inflammatory medication. Essentially, olive oil reduces inflammation in the body in a drug-like manner. By this definition, olive oil could be classified as a drug.

The discovery provides a biochemical clue toward understanding the well-documented but puzzling health benefits of a Mediterranean (olive-oil-based) diet, which leads to a lower risk of cancer, heart disease, and other chronic disorders, despite its heavy emphasis on fat and salt.

Another example is the understanding we have of the biologically active compounds in tumeric, a common ingredient in most commercial curry powders as well as the basis for the bright yellow color in many yellow mustards. The active ingredient of turmeric, called curcumin, has been credited with several medicinal benefits. Curcumin apparently has antioxidant, anti-inflammatory, antiviral, antibacterial, and antifungal properties with potential benefits in the treatment of cancer, diabetes, arthritis, Alzheimer's disease, and other chronic disorders. In 2005 alone, nearly 300 technical and scientific papers referenced the drug-like activity of curcumin, three times the number reported in 2000. If the regulatory hurdles established by the U.S. Food and Drug Administration with respect to long-term safety can be overcome, curcumin could provide an inexpensive alternative approach to several mainstream pharmaceuticals currently available as prescription drugs.

Still another example is the recent finding that a common flavonoid called naringenin, found in grapefruit, has a specific inhibitory effect on the secretion of hepatitis C virus from infected liver cells. Nontoxic amounts of naringenin reduced hepatitis C virus secretion by as much as 80 percent. The effects of the interaction of grapefruit with certain prescription medications will be covered in Chapter 3.

As we continue to learn more about the therapeutic effects of common foods and spices on the body, the customary exclusion of nutrients in a definition of drugs becomes increasingly problematic. In the future, we might be hearing someone say that they are taking olive oil, curry powder, or a little grapefruit extract for "medicinal reasons."

Source: Beauchamp, Gary K.; Keast, Russell S. J.; More, Diane; Lin, Jianming; Pika, Jana; Han, Qiang; Lee, Chi-Ho; Smith, Amos B.; and Breslin, Paul A. S. (2005). Phytochemistry: Ibuprofen-like activity in extra-virgin olive oil. *Nature, 437*, 45–46. Hampton, Tracy (2008, April 2). Grapefruit compound battles hepatitis C. *Journal of the American Medical Association*, 1532. Stix, Gary (2007, February). Spice healer. *Scientific American*, pp. 66–69.

The judgments we make about drug-taking behavior even influence the terminology we use when referring to that behavior. When we say "drug misuse" and "drug abuse," for example, we are implying that something wrong is happening, that a drug is producing some harm to the physical health or psychological well-being of the drug user or to society in general.

But what criteria do we use to decide whether a drug is being misused or abused? We cannot judge on the basis of whether the drug is legal or illegal, since the legality of a psychoactive drug often depends more on historical and cultural circumstances than on its chemical properties. Tobacco, for example, has deeply rooted associations in American history, dating to the earliest colonial days. Although it is objectionable to many individuals and harmful to the health of the smoker and others, tobacco is nonetheless legally available to adults. Alcohol is another substance that is legal, within the bounds of the law, even though it can be harmful to individuals who become inebriated and potentially harmful to others who may be affected by the drinker's behavior. The difficulty of using a criterion based on legality is further complicated by cultural differences around the world.

Instrumental and Recreational Use of Drugs

Given the great variability in attitudes toward drugs and drug-taking behavior across cultures and societies, it is useful to base our discussion on the answer to a simple but fundamental question: What is the intent or motivation on the part of the drug user with respect to this kind of behavior? Depending on the intent of the individual, drug-taking behavior can be classified as either instrumental or recreational.[7]

By **instrumental use,** we mean that a person is taking a drug with a specific socially approved goal in mind. The user may want to stay awake longer, fall asleep more quickly, or recover from an illness. If you

are a medical professional on call over a long period of time or a long-distance truck driver, your taking a drug with the goal of staying alert is considered acceptable by most people. Recovery from an illness and achieving some reduction in pain are goals that are unquestioned. *In these cases, drug-taking behavior occurs as a means toward an end that has been defined by our society as legitimate.*

The legal status of the drug itself is not the issue here. The instrumental use of drugs can involve prescription and nonprescription (over-the-counter) drugs that are licitly obtained and taken for a particular medical purpose. Examples include an antidepressant prescribed for depression, a cold remedy for a cold, an anticonvulsant drug to control epileptic seizures, and insulin to maintain the health of a person with diabetes. The instrumental use of drugs can also involve drugs that are illicitly obtained, such as an amphetamine or other stimulant drug that has been procured through illegal means to help a person stay awake and alert after hours without sleep.

In contrast, **recreational use** means that a person is taking the drug not as a means to a socially approved goal but for the purposes of acquiring the effect of the drug itself. The motivation is to enjoy a pleasurable feeling or positive state of mind. *Whatever happens as a consequence of the drug-taking behavior is viewed not as a means to an end, but as an end unto itself.* Drinking alcohol and smoking tobacco are two examples of licit recreational drug-taking behavior. Involvement with street drugs, in the sense that one's goal is to alter one's mood or state of consciousness, falls into the category of illicit recreational drug-taking behavior.

Although this four-group classification scheme, as shown in Figure 1.1, is helpful in understanding the complex relationship between drugs and behavior, there will be instances in which the category might be less than clear. Drinking an alcoholic beverage, for example, is considered recreational drug-taking behavior under most circumstances. If it is recommended by a physician for a specified therapeutic or preventive purpose (see Chapter 9), however, the drinking might be considered instrumental in nature. You can see that whether drug use is judged to be recreational or instrumental is determined in no small part by circumstances under which the behavior takes place.

Misuse and Abuse of Drugs

How do misuse and abuse fit into this scheme? **Drug misuse** typically applies to cases in which a prescription or nonprescription drug is used inappropriately. Many

---

instrumental use: Referring to the motivation of a drug user who takes the drug for a specific purpose other than getting "high."

recreational use: Referring to the motivation of a drug user who takes the drug only to get "high" or achieve some pleasurable effect.

drug misuse: Drug-taking behavior in which a prescription or nonprescription drug is used inappropriately.

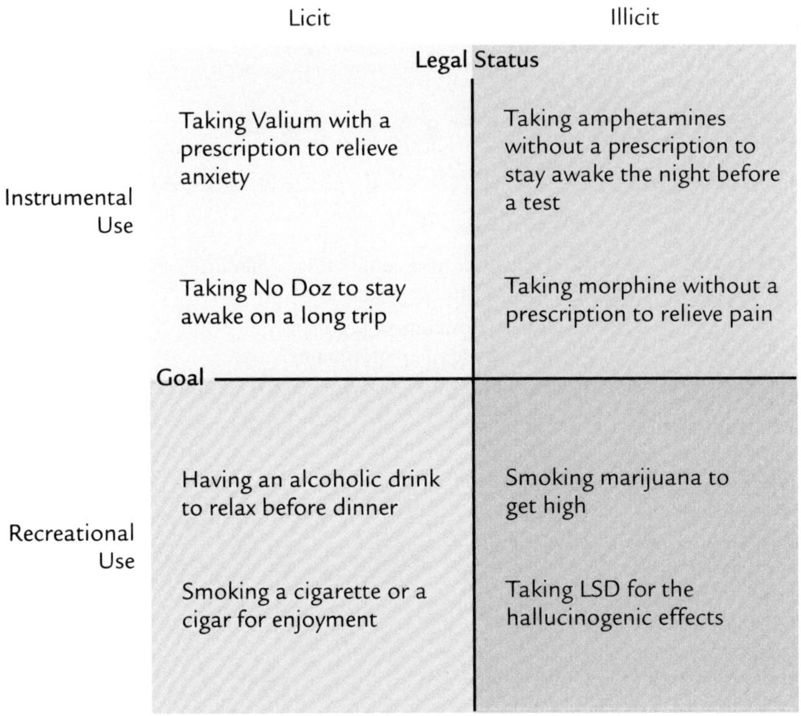

FIGURE 1.1

	Licit	Illicit
	Legal Status	
Instrumental Use	Taking Valium with a prescription to relieve anxiety	Taking amphetamines without a prescription to stay awake the night before a test
	Taking No Doz to stay awake on a long trip	Taking morphine without a prescription to relieve pain
Goal		
Recreational Use	Having an alcoholic drink to relax before dinner	Smoking marijuana to get high
	Smoking a cigarette or a cigar for enjoyment	Taking LSD for the hallucinogenic effects

Four categories of drug-taking behavior, derived from combinations of the user's goal and the drug's legal status.

Source: Expanded from Goode, Erich (2005). *Drugs in American Society* (6th ed.). New York: McGraw-Hill, p. 16.

instances of drug misuse involve instrumental goals. For example, drug doses may be increased beyond the level of the prescription in the mistaken idea that if a little is good, more is even better. Or doses may be decreased from the level of the prescription to make the drug supply last longer. Drugs may be continued past the time during which they were originally needed; they may be combined with some other drug; or a prescription drug might be shared by family members or lent to a friend.

Drug misuse can be dangerous and potentially lethal, particularly when alcohol is combined with drugs that depress the nervous system. Drugs that have this particular feature include antihistamines, antianxiety drugs, and sleeping medications. Even if alcohol is not involved, however, drug combinations can still represent serious health risks, particularly for the elderly, who often take a large number of separate medications. This population is especially vulnerable to the hazards of drug misuse.

In contrast, **drug abuse** is typically applied to cases in which a licit or illicit drug is used in ways that produce some form of physical, mental, or social impairment (Drugs . . . in Focus, page 8). The primary motivation for individuals involved in drug abuse is recreational. Drugs with abuse potential include not only the common street drugs but also legally available psychoactive substances such as caffeine and nicotine (stimulants), alcohol

and inhaled solvents (depressants), as well as a number of prescription drugs designated for medical purposes but used by some individuals exclusively on a recreational basis. In Chapter 5, we will examine concerns about the abuse of pain medications, known as narcotic analgesics, that contain synthetic opiates or opiate derivatives and are marketed under such brand names as Vicodin, OxyContin, Percodan, Demerol, and Darvon. In these particular cases, the distinction between drug misuse and drug abuse is particularly blurry. When there is no intent to make a value judgment as to the motivation or consequences of a particular type of drug-taking behavior, that behavior will simply be referred to as *drug use*.

Before examining the major role that drugs and drug-taking behavior play in our lives today, it is important to understand the historical foundations of drug use. We need to understand the reasons why drug-taking behavior has been so pervasive a phenomenon over the many centuries of human history and the reasons why drug-taking behavior remains so compelling for us in our society. We also need to understand the ways in

drug abuse: Drug-taking behavior resulting in some form of physical, mental, or social impairment.

Drugs...in Focus

Drug Abuse and the College Student: An Assessment Tool

In a study conducted at Rutgers University, a cutoff score of five or more "yes" responses to the following twenty-five questions in the Rutgers Collegiate Substance Abuse Screening Test (RCSAST) was found to distinguish problem alcohol and other drug users from nonproblem users in a college student population. More research, however, must be done to determine if a score of 5 represents the best cutoff. It is important to remember that the RCSAST does not by itself determine the presence of substance dependence or abuse (see Chapter 2). Rather, the RCSAST is designed to be used as one part of a larger assessment battery aimed at identifying which young adults experience problems due to substance use and specifically what types of problems a particular individual is experiencing.

1. Have you gotten into financial trouble as a result of drinking or other drug use?
2. Is alcohol or other drug use making your college life unhappy?
3. Do you use alcohol or other drugs because you are shy with other people?
4. Has drinking alcohol or using other drugs ever caused conflicts with close friends of the opposite sex?
5. Has drinking alcohol or using other drugs ever caused conflicts with close friends of the same sex?
6. Has drinking alcohol or using other drugs ever damaged other friendships?
7. Has drinking alcohol or using other drugs ever been behind your losing a job (or the direct reason for it)?
8. Do you lose time from school due to drinking and/or other drug use?
9. Has drinking alcohol or using other drugs ever interfered with your preparations for exams?
10. Has your efficiency decreased since drinking and/or using other drugs?
11. Do you drink alcohol or use other drugs to escape from worries or troubles?
12. Is your drinking and/or using other drugs jeopardizing your academic performance?
13. Do you drink or use other drugs to build up your self-confidence?
14. Has your ambition decreased since drinking and/or drug using?
15. Does drinking or using other drugs cause you to have difficulty sleeping?
16. Have you ever felt remorse after drinking and/or using other drugs?
17. Do you drink or use drugs alone?
18. Do you crave a drink or other drug at a definite time daily?
19. Do you want a drink or other drug the next morning?
20. Have you ever had a complete or partial loss of memory as a result of drinking or using other drugs?
21. Is drinking or using other drugs affecting your reputation?
22. Does your drinking and/or using other drugs make you careless of your family's welfare?
23. Do you seek out drinking/drugging companions and drinking/drugging environments?
24. Has your physician ever treated you for drinking and/or other drug use?
25. Have you ever been to a hospital or institution on account of drinking or other drug use?

Source: Bennett, Melanie E.; McCrady, Barbara S.; Frankenstein, William; Laitman, Lisa A.; Van Horn, Deborah H. A.; and Keller, Daniel S. (1992). The Rutgers Collegiate Substance Abuse Screening Test: Identifying young adult substance abusers. Presentation at the meeting of the American Psychological Association, August, Washington DC. Reprinted with permission of the authors of the RCSAST.

which our society has responded to problems associated with drug use. How have our attitudes toward drugs changed over time? How did people feel about drugs and drug-taking behavior one hundred years ago, fifty years ago, twenty years ago, or even ten years ago? These are questions that we will now address.

Drugs in Early Times

Try to imagine the circumstances under which a psychoactive drug might have been accidentally discovered. Thousands of years ago, perhaps a hundred thousand years ago, the process of discovery would have been as natural as eating, and the motivation as basic as simple curiosity. In cool climates, next to a cave dwelling may have grown a profusion of blue morning glories or brightly colored mushrooms, plants that produce hallucinogens similar to LSD. In desert regions, yellow-orange fruits grew on certain cacti, the source of the hallucinogenic drug peyote. Elsewhere, poppy plants, the source of opium, covered acres of open fields. Coca leaves, from which cocaine is made, grew on shrubs along the mountain valleys throughout Central and South America. The hardy cannabis plant, the source of marijuana, grew practically everywhere.

Some of this curiosity may have been inspired by observing the unusual behavior of animals as they fed on these plants. Within their own experience people made the connection, somewhere along the line, between the chewing of willow bark (the source of modern-day aspirin) and the relief of a headache, or the eating of the senna plant (a natural laxative) and the relief of constipation.[8]

Of course, some of these plants made people sick, and many of them were poisonous and caused death. Probably the plants that had the strangest impact on humans were the ones that produced hallucinations. Having a sudden vision of something totally alien to everyday living must have been overwhelming, like a visit to another world. Individuals with prior knowledge about such plants, as well as about plants with therapeutic powers, would eventually acquire great power over others in the community. The accumulation of knowledge about consciousness-altering substances would mark the beginning of **shamanism,** a practice among primitive societies, dating back by some estimates more than 40,000 years, in which an individual called a **shaman** acts as a healer through a combination of trances and plant-based medicines, usually in the context of a local religious rite. Shamans still function today in remote areas of the world, often alongside practitioners of modern medicine. As we will see in Chapter 6, hallucination-producing plants of various kinds play a major role in present-day shamanic healing.

With the development of centralized religions in Egyptian and Babylonian societies, the influence of shamanism gradually declined. The power to heal through a knowledge of drugs passed into the hands of the priesthood, which placed a greater emphasis on formal rituals and rules than on hallucinations and trances.

The most dramatic testament to the development of priestly healing during this period is a sixty-five-foot-long Egyptian scroll known as the **Ebers Papyrus,** named after a British Egyptologist who acquired it in 1872. This mammoth document, dating from 1500 B.C., contains

In a wide range of world cultures throughout history, hallucinogens have been regarded as having deeply spiritual powers. Under the influence of drugs, this modern-day shaman communicates with the spirit world.

more than eight hundred prescriptions for practically every ailment imaginable, including simple wasp stings and crocodile bites, baldness, constipation, headaches, enlarged prostate glands, sweaty feet, arthritis, inflammations of all types, heart disease, and cancer. More than a hundred of the preparations contained castor oil as a natural laxative; some contained "the berry of the poppy," which is now recognized as a reference to opium. Other ingredients were quite bizarre: lizard's blood, the teeth of swine, the oil of worms, the hoof of an ass, putrid meat with fly specks, and crocodile dung (excrement of all types being highly favored for its ability to frighten off the evil spirits of disease).[9]

How successful were these strange remedies? It is impossible to know because no records were kept on what happened to the patients. Although some of the ingredients, such as opium and castor oil, had true

shamanism: The philosophy and practice of healing in which diagnosis or treatment is based on trance-like states, either on the part of the healer (shaman) or the patient.

shaman (SHAH-men): A healer whose diagnosis or treatment of patients is based at least in part on trances. These trances are frequently induced by hallucinogenic drugs.

Ebers Papyrus: An Egyptian document, dated approximately 1500 B.C., containing more than eight hundred prescriptions for common ailments and diseases.

medicinal value, it may be that much of the improvement from these concoctions was psychological rather than physiological. In other words, improvements in the patient's condition resulted from the patient's *belief* that he or she would be helped, a phenomenon known as the **placebo effect.** Psychological factors have played a critical role throughout the history of drugs. Chapter 3 will examine in more detail the importance of the placebo effect as an explanation of some drug effects.

Along with substances that had genuine healing properties, some psychoactive drugs were put to other uses. In the early Middle Ages, Viking warriors ate the mushroom *Amanita muscaria*, known as fly agaric, and experienced a tremendous increase in energy, which resulted in wild behavior in battle. They were called Berserkers because of the bear skins they wore, and reckless, violent behavior has come to be called berserk. Later, witches operating on the periphery of medieval society created "witch's brews." They were said to induce hallucinations and a sensation of flying by consuming mixtures made of various plants such as mandrake, henbane, and belladonna. The toads that they included in their recipes did not hurt either: We know now that the sweat glands of toads contain a chemical related to DMT, a powerful hallucinogenic drug, as well as bufotenine, a drug that raises blood pressure and heart rate.[10]

Drugs in the Nineteenth Century

By the end of the nineteenth century, the medical profession had made significant strides with respect to medicinal healing. Morphine was identified as the active ingredient in opium, a drug that had been in use for at least three thousand years and had become the physician's most reliable prescription to control the pain of disease and injury. The invention of the syringe made it possible to deliver the morphine directly and speedily into the bloodstream. Cocaine, having been extracted from coca leaves, was used as a stimulant and antidepressant. Sedative powers to calm the mind or induce sleep had been discovered in bromides and chloral hydrate.

placebo (pla-CEE-bo) effect: Any change in a person's condition after taking a drug, based solely on that person's beliefs about the drug rather than on any physical effects of the drug.

patent medicine: A drug or combination of drugs sold through peddlers, shops, or mail-order advertisements.

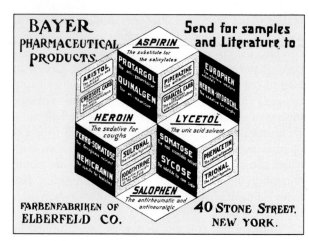

Around 1900, heroin was advertised as a completely safe remedy for common ailments, along with aspirin. No one knows the number of individuals who became dependent on heroin as a result.

The nineteenth century also saw the development of new drugs to be used for specific purposes or particular diseases. Anesthetic drugs had been discovered that made surgery painless for the first time in history. A few diseases could actually be prevented through the administration of vaccines, such as the vaccine against smallpox that had been introduced by Edward Jenner in 1796 and the vaccine against rabies introduced by Louis Pasteur in 1885. The discovery of new pharmaceutical products marked the modern era in the history of healing.[11]

The social picture of drug-taking behavior during this time, however, was more complicated. By the 1890s, prominent leaders in the medical profession had begun to call attention to social problems resulting from the widespread and uncontrolled access to psychoactive drugs. Remedies called **patent medicines,** sold through advertisements, peddlers, or general stores, contained opium, alcohol, and cocaine and were promoted as answers to every common medical or nonmedical complaint.

Opium itself was cheap, easily available, and completely legal. Most people, from newborn infants to the elderly, in the United States and Europe "took opium" during their lives. The way in which they took it, however, was a critical social factor. The respectable way was to drink it, usually in a liquid form called *laudanum.* By contrast, the smoking of opium, as introduced by Chinese immigrants imported for manual labor in the American West, was considered degrading and immoral. Laws prohibiting opium smoking began to be enacted in 1875. In light of the tolerant attitude toward opium drinking, the strong emotional opposition to opium smoking may be viewed as more anti-Chinese than anti-opium.[12]

Like opium, cocaine was also a drug in widespread use in Europe and North America and was taken quite casually in a variety of forms. The original formula for Coca-Cola, as the name suggests, contained cocaine until 1903, as did Dr. Agnew's Catarrh Powder, a popular remedy for chest colds. In the mid-1880s, Parke, Davis, and Company (since 2002, merged with Pfizer, Inc.) was selling cocaine and its botanical source, coca, in more than a dozen forms, including coca-leaf cigarettes and cigars, cocaine inhalants, a coca cordial, and an injectable cocaine solution.[13]

A Viennese doctor named Sigmund Freud, who was later to gain a greater reputation for his psychoanalytic theories than for his ideas concerning psychoactive drugs, promoted cocaine as a "magical drug." In an influential paper published in 1884, Freud recommended cocaine as a safe and effective treatment for morphine addiction. When a friend and colleague became heavily addicted to cocaine, Freud quickly reversed his position, regretting for the rest of his life that he had been initially so enthusiastic in recommending its use (Chapter 4).[14]

Drugs and Behavior in the Twentieth Century

By 1900, the promise of medical advances in the area of drugs was beginning to be matched by concern about the dependence that some of these drugs could produce. For a short while after its introduction in 1898, heroin (a drug derived from morphine) was completely legal and considered safe. Physicians were impressed with its effectiveness in the treatment of coughs, chest pains, and the respiratory difficulties associated with pneumonia and tuberculosis. This was an era in which antibiotic drugs were unavailable, and pneumonia and tuberculosis were among the leading causes of death.[15] Some physicians even recommended heroin as a treatment for morphine addiction. Its powerful addictive properties, however, soon became evident. The enactment of laws restricting access to heroin and certain other psychoactive drugs, including marijuana, would eventually follow in later years, a topic discussed further in Chapter 2.

At the beginning of the twentieth century, neither the general public nor the government considered alcohol to be a drug. Nonetheless, the temperance movement dedicated to the prohibition of alcohol consumption, led by the Women's Christian Temperance Union and the Anti-Saloon League, was a formidable political force. In 1920 the Eighteenth Amendment to the U.S. Constitution took effect, ushering in the era of Prohibition, which lasted for thirteen years.

Although successful in substantially reducing the rates of alcohol consumption in the United States as well as the number of deaths attributed to alcohol-related diseases, Prohibition also succeeded in establishing a nationwide alcohol distribution network dominated by sophisticated criminal organizations.[16] Violent gang wars arose in major American cities as one group battled another for control of the liquor trade.

By the early 1930s, whatever desirable health-related effects Prohibition may have brought were perceived to be overshadowed by the undesirable social changes that had come along with it. Since its end in 1933, the social problems associated with the era of Prohibition have often been cited as an argument against the continuing restriction of psychoactive drugs in general.

Drugs and Behavior from 1945 to 1960

In the years following World War II, for the first time, physicians were able to control bacteria-borne infectious diseases through the administration of antibiotic drugs. Although penicillin had been discovered in a particular species of mold by Alexander Fleming in 1928, techniques for extracting large amounts from the mold were not perfected until the 1940s. Also during that time, Selman Waksman found that a species of fungus had powerful antibacterial effects; it was later to be the source of the drug streptomycin.

In the field of psychiatry, advances in therapeutic drugs did not occur until the early 1950s, when quite accidentally a group of psychoactive drugs were discovered that relieved schizophrenic symptoms without producing heavy sedation. The first of these, **chlorpromazine** (brand name: Thorazine), reduced the hallucinations, agitation, and disordered thinking common to schizophrenia. Soon after, a torrent of new drugs were introduced not just for schizophrenia but for the whole range of mental illnesses. It was a revolution in psychiatric care, equivalent to the impact of antibiotics in medical care a decade earlier.

In the recreational drug scene in the post–World War II United States, a few features stand out. Smoking was considered romantic and sexy. It was the era of the

chlorpromazine (chlor-PRO-mah-zeen): An antipsychotic (antischizophrenia) drug. Brand name is Thorazine (THOR-a-zeen).

James Dean was one of many Hollywood actors and actresses in the 1950s whose smoking was part of their glamorous screen image. In some recent "sanitized" reproductions of this photograph, the cigarette has been airbrushed out.

The famous Woodstock Festival concert drew an estimated 500,000 people to a farm in upstate New York in the summer of 1969. According to historian David Musto, ". . . it was said that the (use of marijuana) at the gigantic Woodstock gathering kept peace—as opposed to what might have happened if alcohol had been the drug of choice."

two-martini lunch, when social drinking was at its height of popularity and acceptance. Cocktail parties dominated the social scene. There was little or no public awareness that alcohol or nicotine consumption constituted drug-taking behavior.

In contrast, the general perception of certain drugs such as heroin, marijuana, and cocaine was simple and negative: They were considered bad, they were illegal, and "no one you knew" had anything to do with them. Illicit drugs were seen as the province of criminals, the urban poor, and nonwhites.[17] The point is that a whole class of drugs were, during this period, outside the mainstream of American life. Furthermore, an atmosphere of fear and suspicion surrounded people who took such drugs. For the vast majority of Americans, drugs were not considered an issue in their lives.

Drugs and Behavior after 1960

During the 1960s, basic premises of American life—the beliefs that working hard and living a good life would bring happiness and that society was stable and calm—were being undermined by disturbing events: President John F. Kennedy assassinated in 1963, Dr. Martin Luther King, Jr., and Senator Robert Kennedy gunned down in 1968. We worried about the continuing Cold War, nuclear annihilation, and Vietnam.

College students, in particular, found it difficult to be as optimistic about the future as their parents had been. The reality of the Vietnam War represented to many of them all that had gone wrong with the previous generation. A prominent historian describes the disillusion this way:

> To the young the Vietnam War represented the return of all the rotten and useless in history, all the tyranny and horror that had diverted men from satisfying their best hopes and deepest faith. The war was viewed as the return of the dragon, the resuscitation of the old order.[18]

Many young people were searching for new answers to old problems, and their search led to experimentation with drugs that their parents had been taught to fear. The principal symbol of this era of defiance against the established order, or indeed against anyone over thirty years old, was marijuana. No longer was marijuana something foreign to middle America.

Marijuana, as well as other drugs such as LSD, "uppers," and "downers," became associated with sons and daughters in our own families and in our own neighborhoods. Along with the turbulence of this period came a disturbing increase in heroin abuse across the country. The issues surrounding drug abuse, once a problem associated with minority populations, inner cities, and the poor, were now too close to our personal lives for us to ignore.

One of the governmental responses to these events, particularly the increase in heroin dependence, was to finance basic research related to the effects of drugs on the brain. The timing could not have been better. During the early 1970s, a new branch of science, called **neuroscience,** was being established. Its intent was to bring together researchers from formerly separate scientific fields in a new collaborative effort to understand the relationship between brain functioning and human behavior. In the area of drug research, pharmacologists (those who specialize in the study of drugs) were joined by biochemists, psychologists, and psychiatrists, among others.

One of the important discoveries that emerged from this era was the identification of receptors in the brain that are tailored specifically for drugs taken into the body. The findings of neuroscience research will be discussed in Chapter 3 and several of the chapters that follow.

With the decade of the 1980s came significant changes in the mood of the country in the form of a social and political reaction to earlier decades. If the media symbol had formerly been the "hippie," now it was the "yuppie," a young, upwardly mobile professional. The political climate grew more conservative, in all age groups.

In the area of drugs, the concern about heroin dependence was being overshadowed by a new fixation: cocaine. At first, cocaine took on an aura of glamor and (because it was so expensive) became a symbol of material success. The media spotlight shone on a steady stream of celebrities in entertainment and sports who used cocaine. Not long after, however, the very same celebrities who had accepted cocaine into their lives were experiencing the consequences; many were in rehabilitation programs, and some had died from cocaine overdoses.

To make matters worse, in 1985, a smokable and cheap form of cocaine called *crack* succeeded in extending the problems of cocaine dependence to the inner cities of the United States, to segments of American society that did not have the financial resources to afford cocaine itself. In the glare of intense media attention, crack dependence soon took on all the aspects of a national nightmare. Fortunately, by the end of the 1990s, the extent of crack abuse had greatly diminished, and the urban violence and social upheaval associated with it had declined. Nonetheless, the legacy of this era continues to be felt to the present day.[19]

Quick Concept Check 1.1

Understanding the History of Drugs and Behavior

Check your understanding of the changes in drug-taking behavior over history by matching the statement (on the left) with the appropriate historical period (on the right).

1. Opium and castor oil are first documented as therapeutic drugs.
2. Marijuana use symbolizes a generation's defiance against establishment values.
3. Waksman discovers the antibacterial effects of streptomycin.
4. Opium use extends to all levels of Western society.
5. Cocaine use is at its peak as a symbol of glamor and material success.
6. Heroin is first introduced as a treatment for morphine addiction.
7. Widespread use of antischizophrenic drugs in mental hospitals begins.
8. Vaccines against smallpox and rabies are introduced.

a. approximately 1500 B.C.
b. late 1700s to late 1880s
c. late 1800s
d. late 1940s
e. mid-1950s
f. late 1960s to early 1970s
g. early 1980s

Answers: 1. a 2. f 3. d 4. b 5. g 6. c 7. e 8. b

Present-Day Attitudes toward Drugs

Attitudes toward drug-taking behavior in the twenty-first century are quite different from those that prevailed even as recently as twenty years ago. First, there is a far greater awareness today that a wide range of psychoactive drugs, whether they are licit or illicit, qualify as substances with varying levels of potential for misuse and abuse. The

neuroscience: The scientific study of the nervous system, undertaken as a collaborative effort among researchers from many scientific disciplines.

"war on drugs," declared officially in 1971 and still ongoing today in the United States, is no longer a war on a particular drug, such as heroin in the 1970s or cocaine in the 1980s. We are also aware of the need to address the widespread personal and social difficulties created by the abuse of alcohol, steroids, inhalants, and nicotine, as well as the misuse of prescription drugs and dietary supplements. In short, the battles being waged today are against a wide range of drug misuse and abuse, involving licit as well as illicit substances.

A second difference in attitude toward drug-taking behavior is related to the history of such behavior in our society since the late 1960s. It is important to recognize that in 1980, about two-thirds of high school seniors had reported illicit drug use (principally marijuana smoking) at some time in their lives. They were born toward the end of the "baby boom" generation (technically defined as those born between 1946 and 1964) and were the first group to have grown up during the explosion of drug experimentation. Now, as the parents of teenagers in the twenty-first century, they face the challenge of dealing with the present-day drug-taking behavior of their children.

What has been the effect, if any, on drug-taking behavior among children of parents who had been involved in drug use at an earlier time? With respect to marijuana use, studies have resulted in two major conclusions. First, parents of this particular generation have a more accepting attitude of drug use than an older generation and are more resigned to the idea that their own children would engage in illicit drug-taking behavior. Second, there is no evidence that the prior use of marijuana by parents is related to the extent of present marijuana use by their children. Indeed, the far stronger association lies between adolescent marijuana use and the adolescent's own personal attitude toward the lack of harm involved.[20]

Patterns of Drug Use in the United States

How is it possible to obtain information that would give us a statistical picture of drug-taking behavior today? Assuming that we cannot conduct large-scale random drug testing, the only alternative we have is simply to ask people about their drug-taking behavior through self-reports. We encourage honesty and arrange the data-collection procedure so as to convince the respondents that their answers are confidential, but the fact remains that any questionnaire is inherently imperfect because there is no way to verify the truthfulness of what people say about themselves. Nevertheless, questionnaires are all we have, and the statistics on drug use are based on such survey measures.

One of the best-known surveys, referred to as the Monitoring the Future study, has been conducted every year since 1975 by the University of Michigan. Typically, nearly fifty thousand American students in the eighth, tenth, and twelfth grades participate in a nationally representative sampling each year, as well as more than seven thousand college students and young adults between the ages of nineteen and forty-five.

The advantage of repeating the survey with a new sample year after year is that it enables us to look at trends in drug-taking behavior over time and compare the use of one drug relative to another. We can assume that the degree of overreporting and underreporting stays relatively constant over the years and does not affect the interpretation of the general trends.[21]

Survey questions concerning drug use have been phrased in four basic ways:

- Whether an individual has ever used a certain drug in his or her lifetime
- Whether an individual has used a certain drug over the previous year
- Whether an individual has used a certain drug within the previous thirty days
- Whether an individual has used a certain drug on a *daily* basis during the previous thirty days

You can see that these questions distinguish three important degrees of involvement with a given drug. The first question focuses on the extent of experimentation, including individuals who may have taken a drug only once or twice in their lives and who have stayed away from it ever since. The second and third questions focus on the extent of current but moderate drug use, while the fourth question focuses on the extent of heavy drug use. What do the numbers tell us?

Illicit Drug Use among High School Seniors

We are naturally concerned with any level of drug-taking behavior among U.S. high school seniors, but it is at least encouraging to know that 2008 statistics of drug use are lower than prevalence levels in the late 1990s and are substantially lower than they were at the end of the 1970s. In 2008, for example, 37 percent of high school seniors reported use of an illicit drug over the previous year, less than the 54 percent reporting such use in the peak year of 1979 (Figure 1.2). If we look specifically

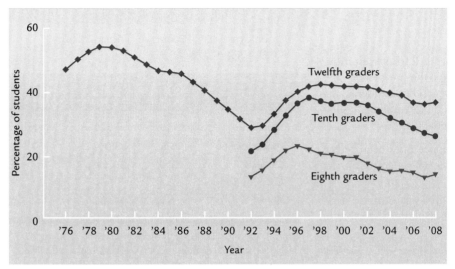

FIGURE 1.2

Trends in annual prevalence of illicit drug use among eighth, tenth, and twelfth graders.

Source: Johnson, Lloyd D.; O'Malley, Patrick M.; Bachman, Jerald G.; and Schulenberg, John E. (2008, December 11). Various stimulant drugs show continuing gradual declines among teens in 2008, most illicit drugs hold steady. University of Michigan News Service, Ann Arbor, Figure 1.

at marijuana use over the previous year, we find that the senior sample reported 32 percent, a reduction from a level of 51 percent in 1979. Cocaine use over the previous year for seniors was 4 percent, less than one-half the number reporting such behavior in the peak year of 1985. Recreational use of inhalants has held steady at between 3 and 5 percent since 2001, about one-half the number reporting such behavior in the mid-1990s.

Nonetheless, the absolute percentages in 2008 were still substantial. They indicate that about one out of every three high school seniors had used some form of illicit drug over the last twelve months, with by far the most prevalent drug being marijuana. About one in twenty-five had used cocaine, and about one in twenty-five had used inhalants on a recreational basis. In 2008, about one in twenty-five had used Ecstasy. One in forty seniors had used LSD, about one-fourth the prevalence rate in 1996, reflecting a downward trend in the use of hallucinogens in general.[22]

Illicit Drug Use among Eighth Graders and Tenth Graders

Since 1991, we also have had extensive survey information about illicit drug use among students as early as the eighth grade. As Figure 1.2 shows, the upward trend in the percentages of drug use among eighth and tenth graders from 1991 to 1996 paralleled a similar trend among high school seniors. At the time, the data from these two groups reflected a level of drug involvement that was quite disturbing. Drug-abuse professionals were left to speculate as to the negative effect on still younger children, as they observed the drug-taking behavior of their older brothers and sisters.

Fortunately, since 1996, the upward trend among the eighth graders in several categories has reversed its course substantially (Table 1.1), as has been the case among tenth graders to a somewhat lesser degree.[23] It is now expected that in the years ahead, as eighth graders progress through high school, their increasing disinclination toward drug use will be reflected in declining prevalence rates among older secondary school students.

TABLE 1.1

Percentage of drug use among eighth graders, 2008

	2008	CHANGE SINCE 1996
Been drunk in past year	12.7	36% down
Marijuana in past year	10.9	40% down
Cocaine in past year	1.8	40% down
Use of cigarettes in previous 30 days	6.8	68% down
Amphetamines in the past year	4.6	51% down
Daily use of cigarettes	3.1	70% down
Inhalants in past year	8.9	27% down

Source: Johnston, Lloyd D.; O'Malley, Patrick M.; Bachman, Jerald G.; and Schulenberg, John E. (2008, December 11). Various stimulant drugs show continuing gradual declines among teens in 2008, most illicit drugs hold steady. University of Michigan News Service, Ann Arbor, Tables 2, 3, and 4.

Illicit Drug Use among Adolescents, 1975–2008

Over the more than three decades during which the University of Michigan has tracked the prevalence rates of illicit drug use among secondary school students, the overall picture (Figure 1.2) ends up resembling a roller-coaster ride. Here are a few essential features:

- The historical peak in prevalence rates occurred in 1979. This was followed by a steep decline in the 1980s, ending in a historical low point in 1992.
- Prevalence rates started to climb again in the early 1990s, reaching another peak (smaller than that of 1979) in 1997.
- A gradual decline has occurred since 1997, particularly among eighth graders.
- In general, changes in the trend of prevalence rates among high school seniors have been preceded a year or two earlier by the shifting prevalence rates among eighth graders.

Drug Use among College Students and Young Adults

The University of Michigan survey also allows a look at drug use among college students and young adults. Compared to high school seniors, college students report somewhat lower annual prevalence rates in the use of illicit drugs in general (35 percent for college students versus 36 percent for high school seniors) and also lower rates for many drug categories, with the prominent exception of alcohol. Table 1.2 shows the lifetime, annual, and 30-day prevalence rates among college students with respect to five major illicit drugs.[24]

When you examine the drug-taking behavior of young adults (not necessarily college students) by tracking them at two-year intervals for as long as fourteen years after they graduate from high school, an interesting pattern emerges. Evidently, the new freedoms of young adulthood initially lead to an increase in substance use for some individuals. Not surprisingly, those young adults who frequently go out at night for fun and recreation are the ones who are most likely to drink heavily, smoke heavily, and use illicit drugs.

As these people grow older, however, these relationships weaken. The link between going out and cigarette smoking, for example, virtually disappears by the time they are in their late twenties and early thirties. On average, drug use at these ages drops substantially from levels reported in high school, as young adults begin making

TABLE 1.2			
Percentage of illicit drug use among college students, aged 19–22			
	EVER IN LIFETIME	**IN PAST TWELVE MONTHS**	**IN PAST THIRTY DAYS**
Marijuana	47.5	31.8	16.8
Hallucinogens	9.1	4.9	1.3
Cocaine	8.5	5.4	1.7
Crack cocaine	1.3	0.6	0.1
Heroin	0.5	0.2	0.1

Source: Johnston, Lloyd D.; O'Malley, Patrick M.; Bachman, Jerald, G.; and Schulenberg, John E. (2008). Monitoring the Future: National survey results on drug use, 1975–2007. Vol. II: College students and adults ages 19–45. Bethesda, MD: National Institute on Drug Abuse, Tables 2-1, 2-2, and 2-3.

personal commitments, marrying, and starting families. Not surprisingly, non-drug-using wives have a major influence in reducing their husbands' level of drug use. Personal setbacks such as divorces, however, produce an increase in drug use, often to the same levels as when they were in high school. In other words, in hard times, an individual will revert to old patterns of drug-taking behavior.[25]

Patterns of Alcohol Use

Not surprisingly, the prevalence percentages related to the use of alcohol are much higher than for illicit drugs. Whereas about 22 percent of high school seniors in 2008 reported use of illicit drugs in the previous month, almost half (43 percent) drank an alcoholic beverage, with 28 percent reporting at least one instance of *binge drinking*, defined as having five or more drinks in a row in the previous two weeks. These figures are down substantially from those found in surveys conducted in 1980, when 72 percent of high school seniors reported that they had consumed alcohol over the previous month, and 41 percent reported binge drinking.

A partial explanation for the decline from 1980 to the present lies in the reduced accessibility to alcohol for this age group, with all U.S. states now having adopted a twenty-one-years-or-older requirement. Despite the long-term downward trend and a suggestion of further decline in alcohol use in recent years, however, the present level of alcohol consumption among high school seniors remains a matter of great concern. Alcohol consumption on a regular basis is widespread for individuals in this age group despite the fact that it is officially illegal for any of them to purchase alcoholic beverages.

The drinking habits of college students, however, have shown relatively little change since the mid-1990s. In 2007, 67 percent of college students surveyed drank at least once in the previous month, and 41 percent reported an instance of binge drinking in the previous two weeks. Evidently, the "know when to say when" message, as promoted by major beer companies, has not gotten through.[26]

Patterns of Tobacco Use

Roughly 11 percent of high school seniors in 2008 had established a regular habit of nicotine intake by smoking at least one cigarette every day. In fact, nicotine remains the drug most frequently used on a daily basis by high school students, although present-day rates are substantially lower than those observed in 1977, when more than twice as many high school seniors (29 percent) smoked cigarettes. From the mid-1990s, there had been a steady decline in smoking rates in eighth and tenth graders as well as seniors, owing to the national attention directed toward cigarette smoking among young people. Nonetheless, in 2008, about 5 percent of seniors and 2 percent of tenth graders reported smoking at least a half-pack of cigarettes per day, a strikingly high level for these age groups, con-sidering the legal obstacles they face when attempting to obtain cigarettes.[27]

Somewhat fewer college students smoke cigarettes than high school seniors. The reason is not a matter of a change in smoking behavior from high school to college but, rather, a reflection of differences between the two populations. Non-college-bound seniors are about three times more likely to smoke at least a half-pack of ciga-rettes per day than college-bound seniors. Therefore, the difference in smoking rates between seniors to college students is chiefly a result of excluding the heavier smok-ers in the survey as students progress from secondary to postsecondary education. In 2007, about 9 percent of col-lege students smoked cigarettes on a daily basis, with about 4 percent smoking more than a half-pack per day.[28]

Drug Attitudes and Drug Use

To understand the changing patterns of drug use among young people over the years and what patterns might unfold in the future, it is helpful to look at their *perception of the risks involved in drug use* during the same span of time. A troubling trend reflected in the University of Michigan surveys during the 1990s was the steady *decline* in the percentages of high school students, college students, and young adults who regarded regular drug use as potentially dangerous. These responses con-trasted with reports beginning in 1978 that had shown a steady increase in such percentages (Figure 1.3).

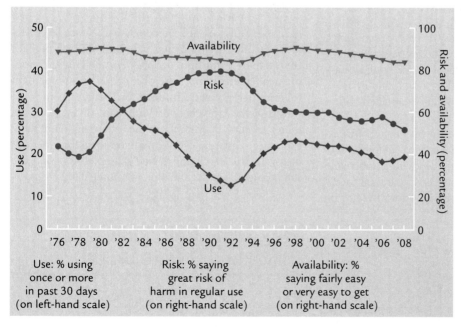

FIGURE 1.3

Trends in perceived availability, perceived risk of marijuana use, and prevalence of mari-juana use in the past month for high school seniors.

Source: Johnston, Lloyd D.; O'Malley, Patrick M.; Bachman, Jerald G.; and Schulenberg, John E. (2008). Various stimulant drugs show continuing gradual declines among teens in 2008, most illicit drugs hold steady. University of Michigan News Service, Ann Arbor, Tables 3, 7, and 13.

Use: % using once or more in past 30 days (on left-hand scale)

Risk: % saying great risk of harm in regular use (on right-hand scale)

Availability: % saying fairly easy or very easy to get (on right-hand scale)

A spokesperson for the 1996 Michigan survey offered one possible reason for this reversal:

> This most recent crop of youngsters [in 1996] grew up in a period in which drug use rates were down substantially from what they had been 10 to 15 years earlier. This gave youngsters less opportunity to learn from others' mistakes and resulted in what I call "generational forgetting" of the hazards of drugs.[29]

Also troubling during much of the 1990s were changes in the way our society dealt with the potential risks of drug use. Drug abuse prevention programs in schools were scaled back or eliminated due to a lack of federal funding, parents were communicating less with their children about drug use, anti-drug public service messages were less prominent in the media than they were in the 1980s, and media coverage in this area declined. At the same time, the cultural influences of the music and entertainment industry were, at best, ambivalent on the question of drug-taking behavior, particularly with respect to marijuana smoking (see Chapter 7). All these elements can be seen as having contributed to the upward trend in drug use during this period.

The reciprocal relationship between perceived risk of harm in regular drug use and the likelihood of drug use itself is shown in Figure 1.3, in the case of marijuana smoking trends across a span of more than thirty years. For the most part, the percentages who consider marijuana smoking as presenting a great risk form a mirror image to the percentages who report smoking marijuana at least once in the previous month.

The relationship between a decline in prevalence rates and an increase in the perception of risk is particularly striking in the case of Ecstasy use over recent years. Following a moderate increase in the percentages of high school seniors reporting "great risk in trying Ecstasy once or twice" from 2000 to 2001, a dramatic increase in risk perception from 2001 to 2005 coincided with a major decline in Ecstasy use.

From 2005 to 2008, however, an erosion in perceived riskiness associated with Ecstasy use among secondary school students had coincided with a noticeable increase in prevalence rates. Increases in annual prevalence rates were observed most prominently among seniors.[30]

Patterns of Illicit Drug Use in Adults Aged Twenty-Six and Older

A comprehensive examination of the prevalence rates of illicit drug use among Americans in several age groups across the life span has been accomplished by the

National Survey on Drug Use and Health (formerly the National Household Survey on Drug Abuse). Table 1.3 shows the estimated number of illicit drug users aged twenty-six or older in the United States. About 11 percent of this population (more than 20 million people) reported using an illicit drug over the past twelve months, about 7 percent (nearly 13 million people) used marijuana or hashish, and about 5 percent (more than 9 million people) engaged in the non-medical (recreational) use of a prescription-type pain reliever, tranquilizer, stimulant, or sedative. As with the results of the University of Michigan survey, however, there are some limitations on the interpretation of these estimates. Patients institutionalized for either medical or psychiatric treatment as well as homeless people are not included in the collection of sample data.[31]

Why Some Individuals Use Drugs and Others Don't

Why do students and other young people take drugs? What factors influence the drug-taking behavior that we see in all these statistics?

TABLE 1.3

Illicit drug use during the past year among persons in the United States aged 26 or older in 2007

	ESTIMATED NUMBERS OF USERS
Any illicit drug	20,102,000
Marijuana and hashish	12,953,000
Cocaine	3,271,000
Crack	1,137,000
Heroin	200,000
Hallucinogens	1,087,000
LSD	121,000
Ecstasy	770,000
Inhalants	561,000
Nonmedical use of any psychotherapeutic medication (not including over-the-counter drugs)	9,334,000
Pain relievers	6,815,000
Tranquilizers	3,077,000
Stimulants	1,447,000
Sedatives	580,000
Any illicit drug other than marijuana	11,860,000

Source: Substance Abuse and Mental Health Services Administration (2008). *Results from the 2007 National Survey on Drug Use and Health: Detailed tables.* Rockville, MD: Office of Applied Studies, Substance Abuse and Mental Health Services Administration, Tables 1.7A and 1.8A.

When high school seniors reported their personal reasons for taking drugs, the most frequently occurring responses among the classes of 1983 and 1984 were "to have a good time with my friends" (65 percent), "to experiment or see what it's like" (54 percent), "to feel good or get high" (49 percent), and "to relax or relieve tension" (41 percent). These responses were similar to reasons given by the class of 1976 in earlier surveys, and there is no reason to suspect significant differences today.[32]

Is there any way of predicting which individuals may be inclined to take drugs and which individuals are likely to stay drug-free? One way of thinking about predicting drug use is to consider any given person as having a certain degree of vulnerability to drug-taking behavior. This vulnerability seems to be shaped by two separate groups of factors in a person's life. The first are **risk factors**, which make it *more likely* that a person might be involved with drugs; the second are **protective factors**, which make it *less likely* that a person might be involved with drugs.

Together, risk factors and protective factors combine to give us some idea about the likelihood that drug-taking behavior will occur. The emphasis, however, should be on the phrase "some idea." We still would not know for certain which individuals would use drugs and which ones would not. An understanding of risk factors and protective factors in general and knowledge about which factors apply to a given individual are useful pieces of information in the development of effective drug abuse prevention programs (see Chapters 17 and 18).

Specific Risk Factors

Certain factors that may appear to be strong risk factors for drug-taking behavior in general (socioeconomic status, for example) turn out to have an association that is far from simple and may depend on the particular drug under discussion. The most reliable set of risk factors consists of psychosocial characteristics that reflect a tendency toward nonconformity within society. Young people who take drugs are more inclined to attend school irregularly, have poor relationships with their parents, or

Peer influence is a major factor in predicting the extent of drug-taking behavior during adolescence. It can represent either a risk factor or a protective factor for drug abuse.

risk factors: Factors in an individual's life that increase the likelihood of involvement with drugs.

protective factors: Factors in an individual's life that decrease the likelihood of involvement with drugs and reduce the impact that any risk factor might have.

TABLE 1.4

Major risk factors: Odds ratios for marijuana use over the past year among youths aged 12–17 as related to specific questions

RISK FACTOR	REPRESENTATIVE QUESTION	ODDS RATIO
Antisocial behavior	*"How many times have you gotten into a serious fight at school or at work?"*	7.10
Friends' marijuana use	*"How many friends would you say use marijuana?"*	6.25
Perceived prevalence of marijuana use in school	*"How many of the students in your grade in school would you say use marijuana?"*	4.78
Individual attitudes toward marijuana use	*"How would you feel (positively) about someone your age trying marijuana?"*	4.47
Friends' attitudes toward marijuana use	*"How do you think your close friends would feel (positively) about your trying marijuana?"*	4.37
Marijuana use in community	*"How many adults who you know personally would you say used marijuana?"*	4.14
Perceived risk of marijuana use	*"How (little) do you think people risk harming themselves physically and in other ways when they smoke marijuana?"*	3.48
Marijuana available in community	*"How easy would it be to get some marijuana, if you wanted some?"*	2.72
Lack of parental monitoring	*"How (seldom) have your parents checked on whether you did your homework?"*	2.60

Note: By definition, protective risk factors have odds ratios greater than 1. Behavior is more likely to occur if a risk factor is present, through a multiplier designated by the odds ratio. Risk factors related to multiple substance use/availability/attitudes tend to have higher odds ratios than risk factors related to use/availability/attitudes associated with marijuana alone.

Source: Wright, Douglas, and Pemberton, Michael (2004). *Risk and protective factors for adolescent drug use: Findings from the 1999 National Household Survey on Drug Use.* Rockville, MD: Office of Applied Studies, Substance Abuse and Mental Health Services Administration, Chapter 3 and Appendix A.

get into trouble in general. Sociologists refer to such individuals as members of a *deviant subculture.*[33]

The effects of being a participant in a socially deviant subculture are highlighted by the increased probability that an individual will display some level of drug-taking behavior. For example, the odds of youths aged twelve to seventeen using marijuana during the past year are more than six times greater among those who had at least a few close friends who tried or used marijuana than among those who did not have such friends (Table 1.4). However, it should be pointed out that, in the case of marijuana use, we are speaking of an increased *probability* that it will occur—not necessarily a cause-and-effect relationship.

The leading risk factors for marijuana use include the perceived prevalence of marijuana use by friends in and out of school and the perceived prevalence of use in the community. Individual attitudes toward marijuana smoking and, in particular, the attitude of friends toward marijuana smoking are also significant risk factors. The most significant risk factor, however, is the inclination toward delinquent (antisocial) behavior (Table 1.4). By contrast, economic deprivation, as measured by a household income under $20,000, fails to be a risk factor for marijuana use.[34]

Specific Protective Factors

Protective factors provide the basis for someone to have stronger resistance against the temptations of drugs, to have a degree of resilience against engaging in a drug-taking life-style, despite the presence of risk factors in that person's life.[35] It is important that we not see these protective factors as simply the inverted image, or the negation, of opposing risk factors. Rather, each group of factors operates independently of the other. One way of thinking about protective factors is to view them as a kind of insurance policy against the occurrence of some

TABLE 1.5

Major protective factors: Odds ratios for marijuana use over the past year among youths aged 12–17 as related to specific questions

PROTECTIVE FACTOR	REPRESENTATIVE QUESTION	ODDS RATIO
Sanctions against substance use in school	"How much trouble do you think a student in your grade would be in if he or she got caught using an illegal drug?"	0.28
Parents as sources of social support	"Would you select your mother or father as a source of social support?"	0.40
Commitment to school	"Do you like going to school?"	0.45
Religiosity	"How many times did you attend religious services?"	0.47
Extracurricular activities	"Have you participated in at least two extracurricular activities in or out of school?"	0.52
Parental encouragement	"How often did your parents let you know that you'd done a good job?"	0.59
Exposure to prevention messages in school	"Have you had a special class or some information in your school about drugs or alcohol?"	0.63
Exposure to prevention messages in the media	"Have you seen or heard any alcohol or drug prevention messages outside of school?"	0.70

Note: By definition (see text), risk factors have odds ratios less than 1. Behavior is less likely to occur if a protective factor is present, through a multiplier designated by the odds ratio.

Source: Wright, Douglas, and Pemberton, Michael (2004). *Risk and protective factors for adolescent drug use: Findings from the 1999 National Household Survey on Drug Use.* Rockville, MD: Office of Applied Studies, Substance Abuse and Mental Health Services Administration, Chapter 3 and Appendix A.

future event that you hope to avoid. The major protective factors are listed in Table 1.5.[36]

Protective factors can serve as a buffering element among even high-risk adolescents, allowing them to have a greater degree of resilience against drug-taking behavior and a higher resistance to drug use than they would have had otherwise. In one study, protective factors were examined in one thousand high-risk male and female adolescents in the seventh and eighth grades, and information was collected on their drug use later in high school. As the number of protective factors increased, the resistance of these students to drug use increased as well. With six or more such factors in their lives, as many as 56 percent of the high-risk adolescents showed a resistance to drug use three years later. In contrast, with three or fewer factors, only 20 percent of the youths were drug-free.[37]

Recently, the concept of protective factors has been taken a step further. In research by the Search Institute in Minneapolis, as many as forty protective factors have been identified, referred to collectively as *developmental assets.*[38] Similar to the protective factors listed in Table 1.5, these developmental assets have been found to increase resistance not only to drug-taking behavior (such as problem alcohol use and illicit drug use) but to other high-risk behaviors (such as sexual activity and violence) as well (Figure 1.4).

Looking to the Future and Learning from the Past

What does the future hold with respect to psychoactive drugs? Where should we direct our concerns? Predictions are always tricky to make, but with regard to drug-taking behavior there are historical patterns that can serve as guides.

Old Drugs, New Drugs

One certainty is that specific drugs will continue to come into and fall out of favor. New drugs will appear on the scene, and others may reappear like ghosts from the past, sometimes in new forms and involving new faces in the drug underground. As one researcher has pointed out, "There is always something old and something new in the U.S. drug scene."[39]

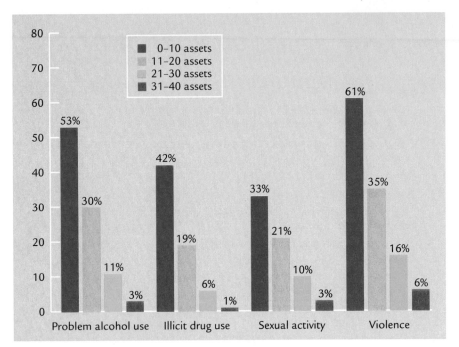

FIGURE 1.4

The percentages of four high-risk behaviors as a function of the number of developmental assets, based on responses of sixth- to twelfth-grade youth.

Source: Information courtesy of Search Institute, Minneapolis, Minnesota, 2000.

For example, as cocaine declined in popularity in the United States during the 1990s, heroin reemerged as a major drug of abuse. During this time, heroin was distributed not only in an injectable form, but also in a more potent blend that could be snorted like cocaine or smoked like crack. On the one hand, these new forms of drug-taking behavior circumvented the traditional need for a hypodermic syringe and the associated dangers of being infected by nonsterile needles. As a result, the possibility of becoming infected with hepatitis or the virus responsible for acquired immunodeficiency syndrome (AIDS) was avoided. On the other hand, new populations of people who had been turned off by heroin because of their fear of needles were introduced to it for the first time.[40]

LSD and other hallucinogens, once the darlings of the psychedelic generation in the 1960s, staged a comeback during this period of time as well. In recent years, as mentioned earlier, prescription painkillers—traditionally the primary medical option for pain management in the treatment of cancer, arthritis, and a host of other

physical disorders—have become increasingly popular drugs of abuse.[41]

Club Drugs

A serious concern in today's drug scene has been the popularity of "club drugs," a term referring to substances typically ingested at all-night dance parties ("raves"), dance clubs, and bars. Examples of club drugs include MDMA (Ecstasy), GHB, ketamine, Rohypnol, methamphetamine, and LSD. When used in combination with alcohol, as they often are, these drugs carry considerably increased health risks, beyond their own individual toxicities. Since many club drugs are colorless, tasteless, and odorless, they can be slipped unobtrusively into drinks by individuals who want to intoxicate or sedate others. The potential danger of sexual assault, therefore, is a major problem.[42] Drugs ... in Focus examines the major features of these six club drugs. A more detailed discussion will follow in Chapter 4 (methamphetamine), Chapter 6 (LSD, MDMA, and ketamine), and Chapter 15 (GHB and Rohypnol).

Dietary Supplements

Another phenomenon that has attracted considerable concern has been the increasing prominence of herbal and nonherbal products, packaged and marketed as **dietary supplements**, that purport to enhance mood,

dietary supplements: Commercial preparations derived from vitamins, amino acids, or herbal extracts. Dietary supplement manufacturers are permitted to claim that these products can help with certain physical conditions associated with different stages of life, but they cannot be used to diagnose, treat, cure, or prevent physical disease.

Drugs...in Focus

Facts about Club Drugs

MDMA (methylenedioxymethamphetamine)
- Street names: Ecstasy, XTC, X, E, Adam, Clarity, Lover's Speed, Hug Drug, Euphoria, M&M
- Variations: MDA (methylenedioxyamphetamine), MDEA (methylenedioxyethylamphetamine)
- Forms: Tablet or capsule
- Drug type: Stimulant and hallucinogen
- Behavioral effects: Appetite suppression, excitation, perceptual distortions
- Physiological effects: Increased heart rate and blood pressure, dehydration
- Length of effect: 3 to 6 hours
- Toxicity: Marked increase in body temperature; possible heart attack, stroke, or seizure (see Chapter 6)

GHB (gamma-hydroxybutyrate)
- Street names: Grievous Bodily Harm, G, Liquid X, Liquid Ecstasy, Georgia Home Boy, Goop Soup
- Variations: Gamma-butyrolactone (GBL)
- Forms: Clear liquid, tablet, capsule, or white powder
- Drug type: Depressant
- Behavioral effects: Intoxication, euphoria, sedation, anxiety reduction
- Physiological effects: Central nervous system depressant, stimulation of growth-hormone release
- Length of effect: Up to 4 hours
- Toxicity: Overdoses produce drowsiness, loss of consciousness, impaired breathing, coma, potential death. GHB greatly potentiates the sedative action of alcohol (see Chapter 15).

Ketamine
- Street names: K, Special K, Vitamin K, Ket
- Variations: None
- Forms: Liquid, white powder snorted or smoked with marijuana or tobacco, intramuscular injection
- Drug type: Hallucinogen
- Behavioral effects: Dream-like state of consciousness, hallucinations
- Physiological effects: Increased blood pressure, potential seizures, and coma
- Length of effect: 1 hour
- Toxicity: Impaired attention and memory, impaired motor coordination, disorientation (see Chapter 6)

Rohypnol (flunitrazepam)
- Street names: Roofies, Rophies, Roche, Rope, Forget-me pill
- Variations: None
- Forms: Tablet dissolvable in beverages
- Drug type: Antianxiety drug
- Behavioral effects: Sedation
- Physiological effects: Decreased blood pressure, visual disturbances, gastrointestinal disturbances
- Length of effect: 8 to 12 hours
- Toxicity: Anterograde amnesia (loss of memory for events experienced under its influence). Rohypnol effects are greatly potentiated by alcohol (see Chapter 15).

Methamphetamine
- Street names: Speed, Ice, Meth, Crystal, Crystal Meth, Crank, Fire, Glass, Ice, Rock Candy
- Variations: Amphetamines, with varying degrees of similarity
- Forms: Many forms; methamphetamine can be smoked, snorted, injected, or orally ingested.
- Drug type: Stimulant
- Behavioral effects: Increased alertness and energy
- Physiological effects: Increased heart rate and blood pressure, decreased appetite
- Length of effect: Several hours
- Toxicity: Possible heart attack or cardiovascular collapse, seizures, cerebral hemorrhage, and coma (see Chapter 4)

LSD (lysergic acid diethylamide)
- Street names: Acid, Boomers, Yellow Sunshines, Barrels, Blotters, Cubes, Domes, Lids, Wedges
- Variations: Hallucinogens, with varying degrees of similarity
- Forms: Crystalline material soluble in water
- Drug type: Hallucinogen
- Behavioral effects: Distortions of visual perceptions, distortions of time and space
- Physiological effects: Increased heart rate and blood pressure, sweating, tremors
- Length of effect: 30 to 90 minutes, though effects might last several hours
- Toxicity: Numbness, nausea (see Chapter 6)

Sources: Brands, Bruna, Sproule, Beth, and Marshman, Joan (1998). *Drugs and drug abuse: A reference text.* Toronto: Addiction Research Foundation. Ricaurte, George A., and McConn, Una D. (2005). Recognition and management of complications of new recreational drug use. *Lancet, 365,* 2137–2145.

energize the mind, or relieve feelings of anxiety. Although they are clearly not as problematic as illicit drugs such as heroin and hallucinogens or club drugs, the fact remains that these products need to be closely examined for their potential to create as well as resolve health problems. It is estimated that dietary supplements are used for medicinal purposes on a regular basis by 20 percent to 30 percent of the U.S. population. In the vast majority of cases, people are taking supplement preparations without any communication with a physician or other health professional. In addition, herb-based dietary supplements are now commercially available in products such as iced tea, soft drinks, fruit juices, and yogurts. Sales of food and drink products that promise benefits beyond basic nutrition presently exceed $40 billion each year.[43]

Since dietary supplements are not officially classified as drugs, governmental regulations for them are different from those that apply to prescription and over-the-counter medications. The Dietary Supplement Health and Education Act of 1994 does not require that dietary supplements have been tested for safety or effectiveness, although as of 2010 they must be determined to be free of contaminants, and the labels must accurately reflect the contents. Federal law requires that supplement labels contain the statement that any claims made by the manufacturer "have not been evaluated by the U.S. Food and Drug Administration." In effect, this disclaimer allows these products to be marketed and sold in the United States without the rigorous process of review and evaluation that assures the consumer that they are safe to take and effective for medicinal purposes. Some examples of such dietary supplements are creatine, ginkgo biloba, ginseng, and St. John's wort. We will examine the safety and effectiveness of these dietary supplements in Chapters 8, 14, and 16, in the context of presently available drugs and medications.

What medical claims can be made for these preparations? On the one hand, the 1994 law clearly prohibits manufacturers from making any claim that refers to a form of disease. On the other hand, a federal ruling in 2000 stipulated that certain common physical conditions associated with different stages of life such as aging, adolescence, pregnancy, and menopause are not diseases, and therefore dietary supplement claims for helping these conditions are allowed. Uncommon or more serious conditions associated with these life stages would still be considered diseases, and supplement labels are required to indicate that the products are not intended to "diagnose, treat, cure, or prevent" these particular conditions.

Unfortunately, the distinction between disease and non-disease can be difficult to make. For example,

"nutraceutical" manufacturers can now claim that certain supplements may be able to treat muscle pain but are prohibited from mentioning joint pain, because the latter is a symptom of arthritis. They can claim to treat "mild memory loss associated with aging" but not more severe memory problems associated with Alzheimer's disease. Federal officials admit that, at best, it is a difficult line to draw. At worst, there are serious concerns that consumer protections are being compromised. Science and common sense are far less influential in decisions regarding dietary supplement use than feelings of hope, publicity hype, or simple word of mouth. As a prominent nutritionist has expressed it, "A lot of the information about supplements is generated by the manufacturers or by personal testimonials. Someone at the machine next to you in the gym says, 'You've got to try this.'"[44]

Beyond the potential risks associated with the instrumental use of dietary supplements, however, are the risks associated with the use of these products (particularly the herbal varieties) for recreational purposes by those individuals seeking a so-called natural "herbal high." For example, a product that claims to increase alertness may also produce extreme euphoria, disorientation, and dangerous cardiovascular changes.

Prescription and Over-the-Counter (OTC) Drug Abuse

Although the prevalence rates among young people for several categories of illicit drugs have shown declines since their most recent peaks in the late 1990s, the recreational use of prescription and over-the-counter (OTC) drugs has remained at relatively high levels. Approximately 10 percent of high school seniors and 7 percent of tenth graders in 2008 reported using the prescription pain medication hydrocodone (brand name: Vicodin) for nonmedical reasons in the past year, and approximately 5 percent of high school seniors and 4 percent of tenth graders reported using the sustained-release form of oxycodone (brand name: OxyContin). From 2002 to 2008, recreational use levels in these age groups either remained steady or increased (Chapter 5). The use over the past year of sedative-hypnotic drugs such as barbiturates (Chapter 15) among high school seniors rose gradually from 3 percent in 1993 to 6 percent in 2008. In 2008, a major federal effort to educate parents about teen prescription drug abuse was launched, including the promotion of broadcast, print, and online advertising, community outreach, and new print and online resources.

In addition, approximately 6 percent of high school seniors reported in 2008 taking OTC cough-and-cold medications, such as Coricidin HBP Cough and Cold Tablets, Robitussin products, and NyQuil, containing the cough suppressant dextromethorphan (abbreviated DXM) in the past year for the purpose of getting high, a practice commonly referred to as "robo-tripping" or "skittling." In 2006, nearly one million individuals between twelve and twenty-five years of age were estimated to have misused OTC dextromethorphan products in the previous year. The alcohol content (up to 10 percent) in many of these products compounds the health-related problems. The easy availability of dextromethorphan for people of all ages and the increased risk of brain damage, seizure, and death associated with high doses of dextromethorphan are matters of great concern in today's drug scene (see the accompanying Portrait).[45]

Why Drugs?

If the history of drug-taking behavior teaches us anything, it is that there will always be an attraction to the drug experience. This certainty arises directly from the character of psychoactive drugs themselves, namely their ability to cause an alteration in consciousness. For a time, they can make us feel euphoric, light-headed, relaxed, or powerful, and there is little doubt that all this feels good. There may be other nonpharmacological ways of arriving at these states of mind, but drugs are easy and quick. They also seem to increase awareness of the environment and give the impression of a feeling that we are seeing or hearing things in a more intense way. No matter whether we are young or old, rich or poor, drugs can allow us to retreat from an uncomfortable environment, to feel no pain.

Unfortunately, in every generation there will be young people who are alienated from their families and the community of adults around them, who seek some form of temporary release from an unhappy existence. There will be a younger generation seeking some form of rebellion against traditional values. There will be adolescents who will use drugs in the context of having a good time with their friends.

Despite our best efforts to prevent it from happening, there will be young people who are simply willing to try anything new, including drugs. Their curiosity, to find out "what it's like," brings us full circle to the earliest times in human history, when we nibbled on the plants in the field just to find out how they tasted. In the modern era, drug experimentation is neither a new nor a singular phenomenon; it can involve an alcoholic drink, an inhaled solvent from some household product, a cigarette, or an illicit drug. Whether this experimentation leads to a more intense level of drug use or drug abuse is another question. The personal and social dangers of drug-taking behavior are examined in the next chapter.

PORTRAIT

Nicholas and the Dextromethorphan High

Nicholas, sixteen years old, began using dextromethorphan to get high in late 2006. At first, he took two Coricidin HBP Cough and Cold pills a day and later increased his intake to eight a day, then sixteen. When his lunch money allowance to pay for his drug supply ran out, he shoplifted. At one point, he began to experience hallucinations at school.

By early 2007, his mother (pictured) was desperate. She pleaded with local drugstores to keep the cold remedies away from her son and other teenagers who were engaged in dextromethorphan abuse. "My son is going to die from these pills," she said.

The day after Nicholas's mother had made her plea with drugstore managers, Nicholas was charged with petty larceny for allegedly stealing fourteen boxes of Coricidin, worth about $168. If he had been convicted, he would have faced up to a year in jail.

The case of Nicholas and other similar cases has spurred Suffolk County, New York, to ban the sale of medicines containing dextromethorphan to anyone eighteen years old or younger. This regulatory legislation has made the county the first New York municipality to impose a ban of this kind, placing it at the forefront of a nationwide movement to prevent minors to purchase these products and use them for recreational purposes.

In the meantime, Nicholas was released from custody and committed to a drug rehabilitation facility, after his mother declared her son a danger to himself.

Source: Schuster, Karla (2007, June 28). Cold remedy ban. *Newsday*, p. A50. Lam, Chau (2007, April 19). Sick over teen's use of medicine for high. *Newsday*, p. A2.

Summary

A Matter of Definition

- Psychoactive drugs are those drugs that affect our feelings, perceptions, and behavior. Depending on the intent of the individual, drug use can be considered either instrumental or recreational.

- Drug misuse refers to cases in which a prescription or nonprescription drug is used inappropriately. Drug abuse refers to cases in which a licit or illicit drug is used in ways that produce some form of impairment.

Drugs in Early Times

- Probably the earliest experiences with psychoactive drugs came from tasting naturally growing plants. Individuals with knowledge about such plants were able to attain great power within their cultures.

- Ancient Egyptians and Babylonians in particular had extensive knowledge of both psychoactive and non-psychoactive drugs. Some of these drugs had genuine beneficial effects.

Drugs in the Nineteenth Century

- Medical advances in the 1800s succeeded in the isolation of active ingredients within many psychoactive substances. For example, morphine was identified as the major active ingredient in opium.

- Psychoactive drugs were in widespread use, principally in the form of patent medicines. Only by the end of the century were the risks of drug dependence beginning to be recognized.

Drugs and Behavior in the Twentieth Century

- Increased concern about the social effects of drug dependence led to restrictive legislation regarding the use of morphine, heroin, cocaine, and marijuana.

- Social pressure from the temperance movement resulted in the national prohibition of alcohol consumption in the United States from 1920 to 1933.

- After 1945, important strides were made in the development of antibiotics and psychiatric drugs.

- By the 1940s and 1950s, illicit drugs such as heroin, cocaine, and marijuana were outside the mainstream of American life.

- In the 1960s and 1970s, the use of marijuana and hallucinogenic drugs spread across the nation, along with an increase in problems related to heroin.

- A decline in heroin abuse in the 1980s was matched by an increase in cocaine abuse and the emergence of crack as a cheap, smokable form of cocaine.

Present-Day Attitudes toward Drugs

- It is now recognized that a wide range of psychoactive drugs, licit or illicit, qualify as potential sources of misuse and abuse.

- Individuals born toward the end of the "baby boom" generation were the first group to have grown up during the explosion of drug experimentation in the 1960s and 1970s. Now, as the parents of teenagers at the beginning of the twenty-first century, they face the difficult challenge of dealing with the present-day drug-taking behavior of their children. Interestingly, there appears to be no relationship between prior marijuana use among the parents and marijuana use by their children.

Patterns of Drug Use in the United States

- Surveys of illicit drug use among high school seniors in 2008 have shown that one in every three seniors used an illicit drug over the last twelve months, one in three smoked marijuana, one in twenty used Ecstasy, and one in twenty used cocaine.

- During the 1990s, marijuana use among high school seniors rose significantly, as did the use of other illicit drugs. Since 1997, however, there has been a steady decline in illicit drug use among eighth and tenth graders.

- In 2007, more than 20 million Americans aged twenty-six or older had used an illicit drug of some kind during the past twelve months. Nearly 13 million Americans used marijuana or hashish, and nearly 7 million Americans engaged in the recreational use of a prescription pain reliever during this time period.

Why Some Individuals Use Drugs and Others Don't

- Risk factors for drug-taking behavior in adolescence include a tendency toward nonconformity within society and the influence of drug-using peers.

- Protective factors for drug-taking behavior include an intact home environment, a positive educational experience, and conventional peer relationships.

Looking to the Future and Learning from the Past

- Predictions regarding future drugs and drug-taking behaviors are largely founded on patterns from the past. New drugs will undoubtedly come on the scene; old drugs that are out of favor might regain popularity.

- A serious concern in recent years has been the emergence of a group of drugs referred to as club drugs. They include MDMA (Ecstasy), GHB, ketamine, Rohypnol, methamphetamine, and LSD.
- Herbal or nonherbal products, marketed as dietary supplements, have been under increasing scrutiny with respect to possible toxic effects. Since dietary supplements are not officially classified in the United States as drugs, governmental regulations for them are different from those that apply to prescription and over-the-counter medications.
- Relatively high prevalence rates for recreational use of prescription drugs and over-the-counter (OTC) drugs among young people have raised serious concerns. Examples of abused drugs in this category include pain medications such as Vicodin and OxyContin, sedative-hypnotic drugs such as barbiturates, and dextromethorphan in popular cough-and-cold remedies.

Key Terms

chlorpromazine, p. 11
dietary supplements, p. 22
drug, p. 4
drug abuse, p. 7
drug dependence, p. 4

drug misuse, p. 6
Ebers Papyrus, p. 9
illicit drugs, p. 4
instrumental use, p. 6
licit drugs, p. 4

neuroscience, p. 13
patent medicine, p. 10
placebo effect, p. 10
protective factors, p. 19
psychoactive drugs, p. 3

recreational use, p. 6
risk factors, p. 19
shaman, p. 9
shamanism, p. 9

Endnotes

1. Roper Center at the University of Connecticut (2003). Organization conducting the survey: The Gallup Organization. Substance Abuse and Mental Health Services Administration (2004, January 16). Availability of illicit drugs among youths. *The NSDUH Report*. Rockville, MD: Office of Applied Studies, Substance Abuse and Mental Health Services Administration, p. 2.

2. U.S. Department of Health and Human Services (1995). *Youth and tobacco: Preventing tobacco use among young people: A report of the surgeon general*. Washington, DC: U.S. Department of Health and Human Services, p. 49.

3. Forman, Robert F. (2003). Availability of opioids on the Internet. *Journal of American Medical Association, 290,* 889. Ifill, Gwen (1992, March 30). Clinton admits experiment with marijuana in 1960's. *New York Times*, p. A13. Levy, Clifford J. (2005, October 9). Drink, don't drink. Drink, don't drink. *New York Times*, p. 14. Primack, Brian A.; Dalton, Madeline A.; Carroll, Mary V.; Agarwal, Aaron A.; and Fine, Michael J. (2008). Content analysis of tobacco, alcohol, and other drugs in popular music. *Archives of Pediatrics and Adolescent Medicine, 162,* 169–175. Stern, Susannah R. (2005). Messages from teens on the big screen: Smoking, drinking, and drug use in teen-center films. *Journal of Health Communication, 10,* 331–346.

4. Butterfield, Fox (2002, February 11). As drug use drops in big cities, small towns confront upsurge. *New York Times*, pp. A1, A18. Substance Abuse and Mental Health Services Administration (2005, April 22). Substance use among older adults 2002 and 2003 update. *The NHSDA Report*. Rockville, MD: Office of Applied Statistics, Substance Abuse and Mental Health Services Administration.

5. Leshner, Alan I. (1998, October). Addiction is a brain disease—and it matters. *National Institute of Justice Journal*, 2–6.

6. Jacobs, Michael R., and Fehr, Kevin O'B. (1987). *Drugs and drug abuse: A reference text*. Toronto: Addiction Research Foundation, pp. 3–5.

7. Goode, Erich (2005). *Drugs in American society* (6th ed.). New York: McGraw-Hill College, pp. 15–21.

8. Caldwell, A. E. (1970). *Origins of psychopharmacology: From CPZ to LSD*. Springfield, IL: Charles C. Thomas, p. 3. Muir, Hazel (2003, December 20; 2004, January 9). Party animals. *New Scientist*, pp. 56–59.

9. Bryan, Cyril P. (1930). *Ancient Egyptian medicine: The Papyrus Ebers*. Chicago: Ares Publishers. De Feo, Vincenzo (2003). Ethnomedical field study in northern Peruvian Andes with particular reference to divination practices. *Journal of Ethnopharmacology, 85,* 243–256. Del Castillo, Daniel (2002, November 22). Just what the shaman ordered. *The Chronicle of Higher Education*, p. A72. Inglis, Brian (1975). *The forbidden game: A social history of drugs*. New York: Scribner, pp. 11–36. Metzner, Ralph (1998). Hallucinogenic drugs and plants in psychotherapy and shamanism. *Journal of Psychoactive Drugs, 30,* 333–341.

10. Grilly, David (2006). *Drugs and human behavior*. (5th ed.). Boston: Allyn and Bacon, p. 3.

11. Sneader, Walter (1985). *Drug discovery: The evolution of modern medicines*. New York: Wiley, pp. 15–47.

12. Levinthal, Charles F. (1988). *Messengers of paradise: Opiates and the brain*. New York: Anchor Press/Doubleday, pp. 3–25.

13. Bugliosi, Vincent (1991). *Drugs in America: The case for victory*. New York: Knightsbridge Publishers, p. 215.

14. Freud, Sigmund (1884). Über Coca (On Coca). *Central-blatt für die gesammte Therapie*. Translated by S. Pollak (1884). *St. Louis Medical and Surgical Journal, 47*.

15. Inciardi, James A. (2002). *The war on drugs III*. Boston: Allyn and Bacon, p. 24.

16. Aaron, Paul, and Musto, David (1981). Temperance and prohibition in America: A historical overview. In Mark H. Moore and Dean R. Gerstein (Eds.), *Alcohol and public policy*. Washington DC: National Academy Press, pp. 127–181.

17. Helmer, John (1975). *Drugs and minority oppression*. New York: Seabury Press. Schlosser, Eric (2003). *Reefer madness: Sex, drugs, and cheap labor in the American black market*. Boston: Houghton Mifflin, p. 245.

18. Cantor, Norman F. (1969). *Western civilization: Its genesis and destiny*. Vol. 2. New York: Scott, Foresman, pp. 845–846.

19. Courtwright, David (2001). *Forces of habit: Drugs and the making of the modern world*. Cambridge, MA: Harvard University Press. Egan, Timothy (1999, February 28). War on crack retreats, still taking prisoners. *New York Times*, pp. 1, 22–23.

20. Kandel, Denise B.; Griesler, Pamela C.; Lee, Gang; Davies, Mark; and Schaffsan, Christine (2001). *Parental influences on adolescent marijuana use and the baby boom generation: Findings from the 1976–1996 National Household Survey on Drug Abuse*. Rockville, MD: Office of Applied Studies, Substance Abuse and Mental Health Services Administration. Morrow, Lance, et al. (1996, December 9). Kids and pot. *Time*, pp. 26–30.

21. Johnston, Lloyd D.; O'Malley, Patrick M.; Bachman, Jerald G.; and Schulenberg, John E. (2008a). *Monitoring the Future: National survey results on drug use, 1975–2007. Vol. I: Secondary school students 2007*. Bethesda, MD: National Institute on Drug Abuse. Johnston, Lloyd D.; O'Malley, Patrick M.; Bachman, Jerald G.; and Schulenberg, John E. (2008b). *Monitoring the Future: National survey results on drug use, 1975–2007. Vol. II: College students and adults ages 19–45, 2007*. Bethesda, MD: National Institute on Drug Abuse.

22. Johnston, Lloyd D.; O'Malley, Patrick M.; Bachman, Jerald G.; and Schulenberg, John E. (2008c, December 11). Various stimulant drugs show continuing gradual declines among teens in 2008, most illicit drugs hold steady. University of Michigan News Service, Ann Arbor, Tables 2, 3, and 4.

23. Ibid.

24. Johnston, O'Malley, Bachman, and Schulenberg (2008b), *Monitoring the Future, Vol. II*, Table 2-2.

25. Bachman, Jerald G.; O'Malley, Patrick M.; Schulenberg, John E.; Johnston, Lloyd D.; Bryant, Alison L.; and Merline, Alicia C. (2002). *The decline of substance use in young adulthood: Changes in social activities, roles, and beliefs*. Mahwah, NJ: Lawrence Erlbaum Associates. Bachman, Jerald G.; Wadsworth, Katherine N.; O'Malley, Patrick M.; and Johnston, Lloyd D. (1997). *Smoking, drinking, and drug use in young adulthood: The*

impacts of new freedoms and new responsibilities. Mahwah, NJ: Lawrence Erlbaum Associates. Leonard, Kenneth E., and Homish, Gregory G. (2005, Spring). Changes in marijuana use over the transition into marriage. *Journal of Drug Issues*, 409–430.

26. Johnston, O'Malley, Bachman, and Schulenberg (2008b), *Monitoring the Future, Vol. II*, Tables 2-3 and 2-4. Johnston, O'Malley, Bachman, and Schulenberg (2008c), Various stimulant drugs show continuing gradual declines, Table 3.

27. Centers for Disease Control and Prevention (2006, June 9). Youth behavior surveillance, United States. *Mortality and Morbidity Weekly Report, 55*, 1–108. Johnston, Lloyd D.; O'Malley, Patrick M.; Bachman, Jerald G.; and Schulenberg, John E. (2008d, December 11). More good news on teen smoking: Rates at or near record lows. University of Michigan News Service, Ann Arbor, Table 1.

28. Johnston, O'Malley, Bachman, and Schulenberg (2008b), *Monitoring the Future, Vol. II*, pp. 26–27.

29. Johnston, Lloyd D. (1996, December 19). The rise in drug use among American teens continues in 1996. News release from the University of Michigan, Ann Arbor, pp. 6–7.

30. Johnston, O'Malley, Bachman, and Schulenberg (2008c), Various stimulant drugs show continuing gradual declines, Tables 2, 7, and 13.

31. Substance Abuse and Mental Health Services Administration (2008). *Results from the 2007 National Survey on Drug Use and Health: National findings*. Rockville, MD: Office of Applied Studies, Substance Abuse and Mental Health Services Administration. Substance Abuse and Mental Health Services Administration (2008). *Results from the 2007 National Survey on Drug Use and Health: Detailed tables*. Rockville, MD: Office of Applied Studies, Substance Abuse and Mental Health Services Administration, Tables 1.7A and 1.8A.

32. Johnston, Lloyd, and O'Malley, Patrick M. (1986). Why do the nation's students use drugs and alcohol? Self-reported reasons from nine national surveys. *The Journal of Drug Issues, 16*, 29–66.

33. Goode, *Drugs*, pp. 68–71.

34. Wright, Douglas, and Pemberton, Michael (2004). *Risk and protective factors for adolescent drug use: Findings from the 1999 National Household Survey on Drug Abuse*. Rockville, MD: Office of Applied Studies, Substance Abuse and Mental Health Services Administration, Chapter 3 and Appendix A.

35. Scheier, Lawrence M., Botvin, Gilbert J., and Baker, Eli (1997). Risk and protective factors as predictors of adolescent alcohol involvement and transitions in alcohol use: A prospective analysis. *Journal of Studies in Alcohol, 58*, 652–667.

36. Wright and Pemberton, *Risk and protective factors*, Chapter 3 and Appendix A.

37. Smith, Carolyn; Lizotte, Alan J.; Thornberry, Terence P.; and Krohn, Marvin D. (1995). Resilient youth: Identify-

ing factors that prevent high-risk youth from engaging in delinquency and drug use. In J. Hagan (Ed.), *Delinquency and disrepute in the life course.* Greenwich, CT: JAI Press, pp. 217–247.

38. Scales, Peter C., and Leffert, Nancy (1999). *Developmental assets: A synthesis of the scientific research on adolescent development.* Minneapolis: Search Institute. Search Institute (2001, February). *Profiles of student life: Attitudes and behavior.* Minneapolis: Search Institute.

39. Inciardi, *War on drugs,* p. 69.

40. Hernandez, Daisy (2003, March 23). Heroin's new generation: Young, white, and middle class. *New York Times,* p. 34. Office of National Drug Control Policy (1998, Winter). *Pulse check: Trends in drug abuse, January–June 1998,* Washington DC: Office of National Drug Control Policy. Sabbag, Robert (1994, May 5). The cartels would like a second chance. *Rolling Stone,* pp. 35–37. Wilkinson, Peter (1994, May 5). The young and the reckless. *Rolling Stone,* pp. 29, 32.

41. Substance Abuse and Mental Health Services Administration (2004, September). Narcotic analgesics. *The DAWN Report, 2002 update.* Rockville, MD: Office of Applied Studies, Substance Abuse and Mental Health Services Administration, pp. 1–8.

42. Substance Abuse and Mental Health Services Administration (2004, July). Club drugs, 2002 update. *The DAWN Report.* Rockville, MD: Office of Applied Studies, Substance Abuse and Mental Health Services Administration, pp. 1–4.

43. Barnes, Julian E., and Winter, Greg (2001, May 27). Stressed out? Bad knee? Relief promised in a juice. *New York Times,* pp. 1, 18. Brody, Jane E. (2003, February 4). Herbal and natural don't always mean safe. *New York Times,* p. F7. De Smet, Peter (2002). Herbal remedies. *New England Journal of Medicine, 347,* 2046–2056. Straus, Stephen E. (2002). Herbal medicines—What's in the bottle? *New England Journal of Medicine, 347,* 1997–1998.

44. F.D.A. approves vitamin rules (2007, June 23). *New York Times,* p. A8. Fontanarosa, Phil B., Rennie, Drummond, and DeAngelis, Catherine D. (2003). The need for regulation of dietary supplements—Lessons from ephedra. *Journal of the American Medical Association, 289,* 1568–1570.

45. Johnston, O'Malley, Bachman, and Schulenberg (2008c). Various stimulant drugs show continuing gradual declines, Table 2. Substance Abuse and Mental Health Services Administration (2008). *The abuse of prescription and over-the-counter drugs.* Rockville, MD: Substance Abuse and Mental Health Services Administration. Substance Abuse and Mental Health Services Administration (2007, January 10). Misuse of over-the-counter cough and cold medications among persons aged 12 to 25. *The NSDUH Report,* pp. 1–4. Reynolds, Gretchen (2007, March). Give us this day our daily supplements. *Play,* pp. 24, 26. Quotation by Kathleen Laquale, p. 24.

chapter 2

Drug-Taking Behavior: The Personal and Social Concerns

It doesn't seem to matter whether you're on or off crack . . . you're crazy both times. If you're high, you think someone's goin' ta do something to you, or try an' take your stuff. If you're comin' down or are waiting to make a buy or just get off, you seem to get upset easy. . . . A lot of people been cut just because somebody looked at them funny or said somethin' stupid.[1]

—A seventeen-year-old crack cocaine abuser

After you have completed this chapter, you will understand

- The personal and social dangers of drug abuse

- Effective and lethal dose-response curves as indices of drug toxicity

- The DAWN statistics as measures of drug-related medical emergencies

- Drug tolerance and the problems it causes for drug abusers

- The distinction between physical and psychological dependence

- The impact of drug abuse on pregnancy and AIDS

- The relationship between drug abuse and violent crime

- U.S. drug enforcement policy as an attempt to regulate drug-taking behavior

Ask someone whether drugs present a major problem in the United States today, and you will get a loud, clear, affirmative answer. This is probably the only aspect of drug-taking behavior on which our opinions are unanimous. On a consistent basis, Americans rank drug abuse among the most important problems facing the nation, as reported by the Gallup Poll and other major opinion surveys. It is clear that drug abuse seriously undermines America's family life, economy, and public safety.[2]

Yet, an agreement that we have a problem is only the first step. The next step is to focus on a more tangible issue. What are the specific problems that drugs present to us as individuals and as members of society?

This is more than an academic question. If we are to expend our energies as well as our public funds on ways to reduce "the drug problem," it is important to know or at least reach some degree of consensus as to where the problems are and which problems are most deserving of our efforts. Here is where people disagree and controversy exists. This chapter will concern itself with the various aspects of drugs that are known to present significant problems for individuals and for society in general. It will then explore the response our society has made to these problems, in the form of governmental policy.

At the outset, it can be argued that the real culprits are not the drugs per se but rather certain forms of drug-taking behavior. If a drug, for example, were totally without any redeeming value (let us say it was extremely poisonous), most people would simply avoid it. It would be a "non-issue." It would have no street value (other than perhaps to a terrorist), and no one would object to measures that restricted access to it. It would be a totally "bad" drug, but in terms of drug use few people would care about it at all.

When we characterize heroin and cocaine as "bad drugs" we are essentially saying that society has balanced the perceived risks of heroin or cocaine *use* against any potential social benefits. Heroin as well as other opiates such as opium and morphine are excellent painkillers and have been used medically in many countries of the world. Cocaine is an excellent local anesthetic and has been used in a large number of medical procedures in the United States. Nonetheless, society has decided that these positive applications in medicine are outweighed by the negative consequences for the general public, on both a personal and a social level.

The advantage of focusing on drug-taking behavior rather than simply on drugs themselves can be highlighted by a bizarre but true story from the mid-1970s. At that time, a number of male patients were being treated for alcoholism in a Veterans Administration hospital in California. In one ward, a patient was observed moving his bed into the men's room. Shortly afterward, several of his fellow patients, one by one, did the same.

What was behind this curious behavior? Evidently, these men, deprived of alcohol after years of alcohol abuse, had discovered that drinking enormous amounts of water, more than seven gallons a day, produced a "high" by altering the acid-to-base balance of their blood. They had found a medically dangerous but psychologically effective way of getting drunk. The fact that they were also urinating approximately the same amount of water each day accounted for their decision to move into the men's room.[3] The point of the story is that, in this case, water had become a psychoactive substance without technically being a drug (recall the definition from Chapter 1). Once again, it is useful to place the focus on specific behavior and its consequences rather than on the substance itself.

In this chapter, our examination of the personal and social problems associated with drug-taking behavior will focus on three broad questions:

- What are the potential risks to one's physical health and to the health of others?
- What are the potential risks for psychological and physiological dependence?
- What is the connection between drug-taking behavior and violence and crime?

by the numbers...

28	Percentage of drug-related emergency department visits in the United States in 2006 due to the non-medical use of prescription or OTC drugs alone. Use of illicit drugs alone accounted for 31 percent.
1,889,810	Drug-law arrests in the United States in 2006, 82% of them for drug possession alone

Sources: Federal Bureau of Investigation (2008). *Uniform Crime Reporting Program.* Washington, DC: U.S. Department of Justice. Substance Abuse and Mental Health Services Administration (2008). *Drug Abuse Warning Network, 2006: National estimates of drug-related emergency department visits.* Rockville, MD: Office of Applied Studies, Substance Abuse and Mental Health Services Administration, Table 1.

Drug Toxicity

When we say that a drug is toxic, we are referring to the fact that it may be dangerous, poisonous, or in some way interfering with a person's normal functioning. Technically, any substance, no matter how benign, has the potential for **toxicity** if the **dose,** the amount in which the substance is taken, is high enough. The question of a drug's safety, or its relative safety when compared to other drugs, centers on the possibility that it may be toxic at relatively low doses. We certainly do not want people to harm themselves accidentally when taking the drug in the course of their daily lives. When there is a possibility that the *short-term* effects of a particular drug will trigger a toxic reaction, then this drug is identified as having some level of **acute toxicity.**

To understand the principle of toxicity in general, we need to examine an S-shaped graph called the **dose-response curve** (Figure 2.1a). Let us assume we have the results of data collected from laboratory tests of a hypothetical sleep-inducing drug. Increases in the dose level of the drug are producing the desired sleep-inducing effect in an increasingly large percentage of a test population of mice. At 10 milligrams (mg), 50 percent of the population has fallen asleep; at 50 mg, 100 percent has done so.

toxicity (tox-IS-ih-tee): The physical or psychological harm that a drug might present to the user.

dose: The quantity of drug that is taken into the body, typically measured in terms of milligrams (mg) or micrograms (μg).

acute toxicity: The physical or psychological harm a drug might present to the user immediately or soon after the drug is ingested into the body.

dose-response curve: An S-shaped graph showing the increasing probability of a certain drug effect as the dose level rises.

effective dose (ED): The minimal dose of a particular drug necessary to produce the intended drug effect in a given percentage of the population.

lethal dose (LD): The minimal dose of a particular drug capable of producing death in a given percentage of the population.

therapeutic index: A measure of a drug's relative safety for use, computed by the ratio of the lethal dose for 50 percent of the population over the effective dose for 50 percent of the population.

margin of safety: The ratio of a lethal dose for 1 percent of the population to the effective dose for 99 percent of the population.

There is always some variability in individual reactions to any drug; some mice may be internally resistant to the drug's effect, while others may be quite susceptible. Any one animal may fall asleep with an extremely low dose or a dose of 50 mg, so we have to think of the **effective dose (ED)** of a drug on a test population in terms of probabilities, from 0 percent to 100 percent.

For example, the ED50 of a drug refers to the effective dose for 50 percent of the population; ED99 refers to the effective dose for 99 percent of the population. In this case, the ED numbers refer to the drug's effect of producing sleep. The same drug may be producing other effects (muscular relaxation, for instance) at lower doses; these drug effects would have their own separate dose-response curves. It is a good idea to remember that we are looking at the properties of a specific drug *effect* here, not the overall properties of the drug itself.

Now we can look at Figure 2.1b, where the effective dose-response curve is represented along with another S-shaped dose-response curve, also gathered from laboratory testing, in which the "response" is death. It makes sense that the second curve should be shifted to the right because the **lethal dose (LD)** generally involves greater amounts of a drug than the amounts necessary to produce a nonlethal effect.

Emphasis should be placed on the word "generally" because the lethal dose-response curve overlaps with the effective dose-response curve in this example. While a 100 mg dose has to be taken to kill 50 percent of the test population, it can be seen that a dose of as little as 50 mg (or less) is lethal for at least a few of them. The LD50 of a drug refers to the lethal dose for 50 percent of the population; LD1 refers to a relatively lower dose that is lethal for 1 percent of the population.

It is necessary to combine the effective and lethal doses of a drug in a ratio to arrive at some idea of that drug's toxicity. The ratio of LD50/ED50 is called the **therapeutic index.** If the LD50 for a drug is 450 mg and the ED50 is 50 mg, then the therapeutic index is 9. In other words, you would have to take nine times the dose that would be effective for half of the population to incur a 50 percent chance of dying.

It can be argued, however, that a 50 percent probability of dying represents an unacceptably high risk even for a drug that has genuine benefits. To be more conservative in the direction of safety, the ratio of LD1/ED99 is often calculated. Here we are calculating the ratio between the dose that produces death in 1 percent of the population and the dose that would be effective in 99 percent. Naturally, this second ratio, called the **margin of safety,** should be as high as possible. As

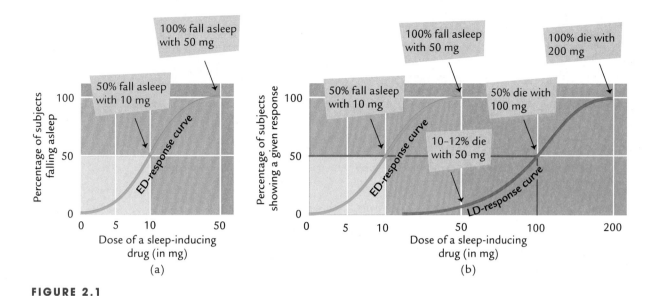

FIGURE 2.1

(a) An effective dose-response curve, and (b) an effective dose-response curve (left) alongside a lethal dose-response curve (right).

before, the higher the ratio, the safer, or less toxic, the drug. It can be seen that the margin of safety for the hypothetical drug examined in Figure 2.1 would present serious toxicity problems.

The therapeutic index or the margin of safety is very helpful when considering the toxicity of drugs that are manufactured by recognized pharmaceutical companies and regulated by the U.S. Food and Drug Administration (FDA), keeping in mind the possibility that a person might intentionally or unintentionally take a higher-than-recommended dose of the drug. But what about the toxicity risks in consuming illicit drugs? The reality of street drugs is that the buyer has no way of knowing what he or she has bought until the drug has been used, and then it is frequently too late.

Few if any illicit drug sellers make a pretense of being ethical businesspeople; their only objective is to make money and avoid prosecution by the law. Frequently, the drugs they sell are diluted with either inert or highly dangerous ingredients. Adulterated heroin, for example, may contain a high proportion of milk sugar as a harmless filler and a dash of quinine to simulate the bitter taste of real heroin, when the actual amount of heroin that is being sold is far less than the "standard" street dosage. At the other extreme, the content of heroin may be unexpectedly high and may lead to a lethal overdose, or else it may contain animal tranquilizers, arsenic, strychnine, insecticides, or other highly

toxic substances.[4] Cocaine, LSD, marijuana, and all the other illicit drugs that are available to the drug abuser, as well as look-alike drugs that are unauthorized copies of popular prescription medications, present hidden and unpredictable risks of toxicity. Even if drugs are procured from a friend or someone you know, these risks remain. Neither of you is likely to know the exact ingredients. The dangers of acute toxicity are always present.

Given the uncertainty that exists about the contents of many abused drugs, what measure or index of acute toxicity can we use to evaluate their effects on individuals in our society? The natural tendency is to look first to the news headlines; think of all the well-known public individuals who have died as a direct consequence of drug misuse or abuse (Drugs...in Focus, page 34).

Such examples, however, can be misleading. Celebrities are not necessarily representative of the drug-using population in general, and the drugs prevalent among celebrities, because of their expense, may not represent the drugs most frequently encountered by the rest of society. To have some idea of the toxic effects of psychoactive drugs in a broader context, we have to turn to the institutions that contend with drug toxicity on a daily basis: the emergency departments of hospitals around the country. As we will see, the drugs involved in hospital emergencies are not necessarily the ones that are associated with *illicit* drug use.

Drugs...in Focus

Acute Toxicity in the News: Drug-Related Deaths

The following famous people have died either as a direct consequence or as an indirect consequence of drug misuse or abuse.

Name	Year of Death	Age	Reasons Given for Death
Marilyn Monroe, actress	1962	36	Overdose of Nembutal (a sedative-hypnotic medication); circumstances unknown
Lenny Bruce, comedian	1966	40	Accidental overdose of morphine
Judy Garland, singer and actress	1969	47	Accidental overdose of sleeping pills
Janis Joplin, singer	1970	27	Accidental overdose of heroin and alcohol
Jimi Hendrix, singer and guitarist	1970	27	Accidental overdose of sleeping pills
Elvis Presley, singer and actor	1977	42	Cardiac arrhythmia suspected to be due to an interaction of antihistamine, codeine, and Demerol (a painkiller), as well as Valium and several other tranquilizers
John Belushi, comedian and actor	1982	33	Accidental overdose of heroin combined with cocaine
David A. Kennedy, son of U.S. senator Robert F. Kennedy	1984	28	Accidental interaction of cocaine, Demerol, and Mellaril (an antipsychotic medication)
Len Bias, college basketball player	1986	22	Cardiac-respiratory arrest from accidental overdose of cocaine
Don Rogers, professional football player	1986	23	Cardiac-respiratory arrest from accidental overdose of cocaine
Abbie Hoffman, antiwar and political activist	1989	52	Suicide using phenobarbital combined with alcohol
River Phoenix, actor	1993	23	Cardiac-respiratory arrest from accidental combination of heroin and cocaine
Jonathan Melvoin, keyboardist for the Smashing Pumpkins rock band	1996	34	Accidental overdose of heroin
Chris Farley, comedian and actor	1998	33	Accidental overdose of heroin and cocaine
Dee Dee Ramone, bassist for the Ramones rock band	2002	49	Accidental overdose following an injection of an undisclosed drug of abuse
Steve Bechler, Baltimore Orioles pitcher	2003	23	Multiple organ failure due to heatstroke, suspected to be related to the use of Xenadrine RFA-1, a weight-control dietary supplement containing ephedra
Bobby Hatfield, singer, the Righteous Brothers	2003	63	Heart failure following overdose of cocaine
Mitch Hedberg, comedian	2005	37	Heart failure due to "multiple drug toxicity," including heroin and cocaine
Anna Nicole Smith, model and actress	2007	39	Accidental overdose of sedative-hypnotic chloral hydrate, with intestinal flu and bacterial infection being contributing factors
Heath Ledger, actor	2008	28	Acute intoxication from combined use of six prescription medicines for pain, anxiety, insomnia, and nasal congestion

Note: Celebrities whose drug-related deaths have been attributed to the toxicity of alcohol alone or nicotine, tars, or carbon monoxide in tobacco products are not included in this listing.

Sources: Various media reports.

Understanding Dose-Response Curves

Check your understanding of dose-response curves and the toxicity of drugs by answering the following question.

The following three sets of dose-response curves show the effective and lethal responses to three drugs, A, B, and C.

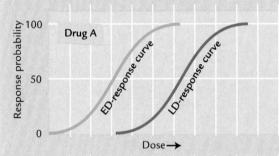

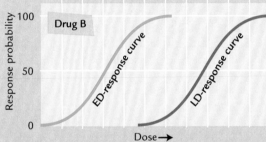

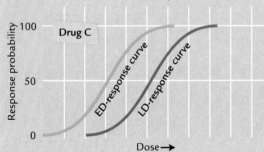

Which of the three drugs would be considered the least toxic? Which would be considered the most toxic?

Answer: The second set of curves (B) refers to the least toxic drug. The third set of curves (C) refers to the most toxic drug.

The DAWN Reports

The U.S. government currently gathers data concerning drug-related medical emergencies in major metropolitan hospitals through a program called the **Drug Abuse Warning Network (DAWN).** Two basic types of information are reported. The first concerns the number of times an individual visits an emergency department (ED) for any reason that is connected to recent drug use. These **drug-related ED visits** involve a wide range of drug-related situations: suicide attempts, malicious poisoning, overmedication, and adverse reactions to medications, as well as the use of illicit drugs, the use of dietary supplements, and the nonmedical use of prescription or over-the-counter (OTC) drugs. The second type of information concerns the number of drug-related deaths, as determined by a coroner or medical examiner.[5]

Approximately one out of seven ED visits in the United States in 2006 was associated with either drug misuse or abuse. Nearly one-third (31 percent) of all *drug-related* ED visits involved illicit drugs only, while 28 percent involved prescription or OTC medications alone, and 8 percent involved a combination of illicit drugs and medications (Figure 2.2).[6]

The proportion of drug-related ED visits involving alcohol use shown in Figure 2.2 requires some explanation. First, statistics about ED visits *related to the use of*

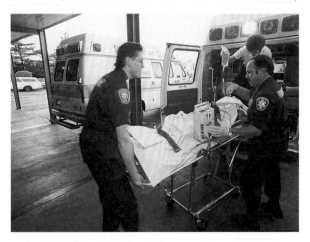

Emergency medical service (EMS) crews frequently have to deal with drug-related cases.

Drug Abuse Warning Network (DAWN): A federal program in which metropolitan hospitals report the incidence of drug-related lethal and nonlethal emergencies.

drug-related ED visit: An occasion on which a person visits an emergency department (ED) for a purpose that is related to recent drug use.

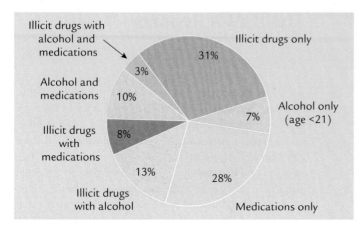

FIGURE 2.2
_____

Distribution of drug-related ED visits in 2006 by type of drug involvement.

Source: Substance Abuse and Mental Health Services Administration (2008). *Drug Abuse Warning Network, 2006:* National estimates of drug-related emergency department visits. Rockville, MD: Office of Applied Studies, Substance Abuse and Mental Health Services Administration, Table 1.

alcohol alone are restricted in the DAWN reporting system to such use by individuals younger than twenty-one years of age. In other words, such medical emergencies are resulting, by definition, from underage drinking.

DAWN statistics are not collected for ED visits involving alcohol use alone by individuals who are twenty-one years or older. There is a very good reason for this exclusion. If all emergencies related to alcohol use alone were reported, the numbers would far exceed those related to any other drug. Considering the fact that more than 700,000 individuals in the United States are injured in alcohol-related automobile accidents and more than 1 million incur alcohol-related personal injuries each year (see Chapter 9), the examination of ED visits related to other circumstances would be obscured if all alcohol-related ED visits were included.

Second, an important message in the ED-visit statistics is the considerable toxicity resulting from *alcohol-in-combination.* This term refers to the use of alcohol in conjunction with another drug, regardless of one's age. About one-fourth (26 percent) of drug-related ED visits in 2006 involved some use of alcohol in combination with an illicit drug, with a prescription or OTC medication, or with an illicit drug and a medication. As Figure 2.3 shows, a large number of alcohol-in-combination ED visits involved either cocaine or marijuana or a combination of the two together. A much smaller proportion involved heroin, stimulants (principally methamphetamine), and alprazolam (brand name: Xanax), which are used in the

treatment of anxiety. The remainder, more than 50 percent of the total, were spread among a wide variety of illicit drugs or medications, including OTC medications such as acetaminophen (brand name: Tylenol) and ibuprofen (brand names: Advil, Motrin, among others).[7]

Emergencies Related to Illicit Drugs

What types of illicit drugs are most likely to result in an ED visit? In 2006, of the approximately 958,000 illicit-drug-related ED visits, the largest number of cases involved cocaine, followed by marijuana, heroin, and stimulants (principally methamphetamine), in that order. The use of MDMA (Ecstasy), PCP, LSD, and other hallucinogens each accounted for a considerably smaller number of cases. In general, patients in 2006 were twice as likely to be male than female in ED visits involving illicit drugs.[8]

Drug-Related Deaths

Current DAWN statistics on instances of drug-related deaths in the United States are not reported on a nationwide basis but instead in terms of individual metropolitan areas. Because the population levels of

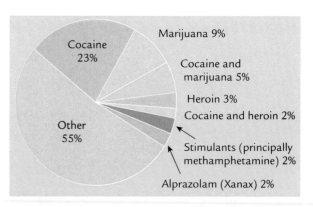

FIGURE 2.3
_____

Relative frequency of drugs reported in alcohol-in-combination ED cases in 2006.

Note: More than 340 drugs are represented in the "Other" category of alcohol-in-combination ED cases.

Source: Substance Abuse and Mental Health Administration (2008). *Drug Abuse Warning Network, 2006: National estimates of drug-related emergency department visits.* Rockville, MD: Office of Applied Studies, Substance Abuse and Mental Health Administration, pages 8, 29, and Table 6.

these areas vary widely, overall interpretations of these statistics have to be made with great care. For example, the almost identical level of opiate-drug involvement in drug-related deaths in Washington DC and San Diego in 2004, with their respective populations approaching a ratio of 2:1, was indicative of a relatively greater opiate-drug problem in San Diego rather than an equivalent concern in these two cities. In addition, each metropolitan area had a somewhat different drug problem "profile." Cocaine use, for example, was prominently reported in drug-related deaths in most metropolitan areas surveyed in the DAWN report but played a relatively minor role in drug-related deaths in Louisville, Kentucky.

Yet, despite these problems in examining drug-related deaths across metropolitan areas in the United States, a number of generalizations can be made.

- In nearly all metropolitan areas surveyed in the DAWN report, opiate drugs (predominantly heroin but also including morphine and methadone) and cocaine are the two most frequently reported drugs. Alcohol (chiefly alcohol in combination with some other drug but also including alcohol ingested by someone younger than twenty-one years old) is commonly in third place.

- Typically, medications used to treat anxiety and depression are either the fourth or fifth most frequently reported drugs in drug-related death cases. However, the presence of these categories of licit drugs in the "top five" listing should be interpreted carefully. The amounts ingested in these circumstances either far exceed the recommended dosage levels or have been combined with one or more other drugs.

- In general, it is far more common for drug-related deaths to be a result of multiple-drug (polydrug) use than from single-drug use. In the cases of alcohol, antianxiety medication, and antidepressant medication, it is extremely unusual for a death to result from the use of any of these drugs alone.

- Marijuana is far less prominent in drug-related deaths and, when there are reports of its involvement, it is almost exclusively in the context of multiple-drug rather than single-drug use.

- Methamphetamine use as a cause of a drug-related death is largely underestimated in the DAWN statistics, due to the emphasis on reports from large metropolitan areas rather than smaller, rural areas in the United States, where methamphetamine has been a significant public health concern (see Chapter 4).[9]

Judging Drug Toxicity from Drug-Related Deaths

The finding that the use of heroin (and other opiate drugs) or cocaine alone is frequently involved in drug-related deaths is particularly striking when you consider the fact that heroin and cocaine users constitute a relatively small proportion of the total number of illicit drug users, and certainly in terms of the general population. The fact that there are more instances of heroin use in drug-related deaths than instances of cocaine use underestimates the potential lethality of heroin, since there are far fewer heroin users than cocaine users in the United States. In contrast, the rare association of marijuana with drug-related deaths is actually overstating its potential lethality, given its widespread use within a much larger group of people.

In short, a judgment about the relative toxicity of illicit drugs requires an understanding of how frequently a particular drug is used in the general population. All other facts being equal, if one illicit drug produces twice as many deaths as a second drug but the number of users of the first drug is twice that of the second, then the toxicity levels of the two drugs should be considered equivalent.

Demographics and Trends

By examining DAWN statistics from 1980 to 2006, we can arrive at some idea of the changes that have taken place in the frequency of medical emergencies over recent years. For example, a dramatic increase in the number of cocaine-related emergencies occurred in the 1980s as a result of the rise of cocaine abuse and crack cocaine abuse. A decade later, an upturn in heroin-related emergencies took place during the 1990s, as the purity of available heroin increased and the availability of heroin use without a needle injection caused heroin-related emergency rates to rise.

In the mid-1990s, significant concerns emerged about the increase in ED visits arising from the use of two classes of drugs. The first consisted of illicit club drugs that included Ecstasy, GHB, ketamine, LSD, and methamphetamine. The second class of drugs that raised health concerns during this period included opiate-based prescription pain medications, also known as *narcotic analgesics*. The two principal medications of this type are oxycodone (brand name: Percodan) and hydrocodone (brand name: Vicodin).[10]

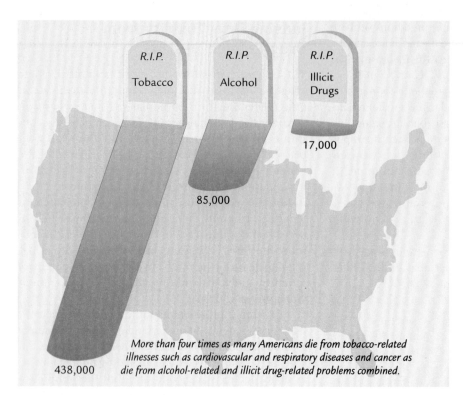

FIGURE 2.4

U.S. deaths per year from tobacco, alcohol, and illicit drug use.

Sources: Centers for Disease Control and Prevention (2005, July 1). Annual smoking-attributable mortality, years of potential life lost, and productivity losses —United States, 1997–2001. *Morbidity and Mortality Weekly Report.* Atlanta: Centers for Disease Control and Prevention. Mokdad, Ali H.; Marks, James S.; Stroup, Donna F.; and Gerberding, Julie L. (2004). Actual causes of death in the United States, 2000. *Journal of the American Medical Association, 291,* 1238–1245.

More than four times as many Americans die from tobacco-related illnesses such as cardiovascular and respiratory diseases and cancer as die from alcohol-related and illicit drug-related problems combined.

From Acute Toxicity to Chronic Toxicity

Through the DAWN reports, we can appreciate the extent of acute toxicity involved in the ingestion of a particular drug, but we are unable to get an illuminating picture of the negative consequences of using a particular drug over a long period of time. Examples of **chronic toxicity** can be found in a wide range of psychoactive drugs, either legally or illegally obtained. Ironically, it is the chronic use of alcohol and tobacco, both of which are legally available in our society, that causes by far the greatest adverse health effects. As we will see in Chapters 10 and 12, the number of people who die each year as a result of drinking alcohol or smoking tobacco far outstrips the number of fatalities from the abuse of illicit drugs (Figure 2.4).

A number of important issues with respect to drug-taking behavior will be examined in the chapters ahead. What exactly are the problems associated with *chronic* drug use? What is the most productive way of looking at drug dependence in general? How has our

chronic toxicity: The physical or psychological harm a drug might cause over a long period of use.

society responded to the problems of drug-taking behavior over the years? How successful have we been in dealing with these problems? What new strategies are there to handle drug-related problems in a more effective way?

Behavioral Tolerance and Drug Overdose

Legend has it that in the first century B.C., King Mithridates VI of Pontus, a region of modern-day Turkey near the Black Sea, grew despondent following a series of defeats by the Romans and decided to commit suicide by poison. The problem was that no amount of poison was sufficient, and the grim task had to be completed by the sword. It turned out that Mithridates, having lived in fear of being poisoned by his rivals, had taken gradually increasing amounts of poison over the course of his life to build up a defense against this possibility. By the time he wanted to end his life by his own hand, he could tolerate such large doses that poisoning no longer presented any threat to his life. This royal case is the first recorded example of drug tolerance. In fact, the phenomenon originally was called *mithridatism,* and several celebrated poisoners of history, including the notorious Lucretia Borgia in the early sixteenth century, were later to use the same defensive strategy.[11]

The concept of **tolerance** refers to the capacity of a drug dose to have a gradually diminished effect on the user as the drug is taken repeatedly. Another way of viewing tolerance is to say that over repeated administrations a drug dose needs to be increased to maintain an equivalent effect.

A common illustration of drug tolerance is the effect of caffeine in coffee. When you are first introduced to caffeine, the stimulant effect is usually quite pronounced; you might feel noticeably "wired" after a 5-ounce cup of coffee, containing approximately 100 mg of caffeine. After several days or perhaps a few weeks of coffee drinking, the effect is greatly diminished; you may need to be on the second or third cup by that time, consuming 200 to 300 mg of caffeine, to duplicate the earlier reaction. Some individuals who drink coffee regularly have developed such high levels of tolerance to caffeine that they are able to sleep comfortably even after several cups of coffee, while individuals with more infrequent ingestions of caffeine end up awake through the night after a single cup.

The danger that the tolerance effect presents is the possibility of death by drug overdose, frequently the cause of drug-related deaths listed in the DAWN reports. Individuals involved in drug abuse are often taking drug doses that are precariously close to the LD-response curve amounts, as described earlier. These dosage levels may be sustainable by a drug abuser who has grown tolerant to the drug over repeated administrations but quite lethal to an individual being introduced to the drug for the first time.

In understanding the possibility of drug overdose, it is useful to look at the *interaction* between the actual amount of the drug taken and other factors involved in the drug-taking behavior. Although, as already noted, the number of previous times the drug has been used is crucial, an important factor is the setting within which the drug-taking behavior occurs. There is strong evidence that tolerance effects are maximized when the drug-taking behavior occurs consistently in the same surroundings or under the same set of circumstances.[12] We speak of this form of tolerance as **behavioral tolerance.**

To have a clear idea of behavioral tolerance, we first have to understand the basic facts of Pavlovian conditioning, upon which behavioral tolerance is based. Suppose you consistently heard a bell ring every time you had a headache. Previously, bells had never had any negative effect on you. The association between the ringing bell and the pain of the headache, however, would become

Having overdosed on pure heroin, the driver in the car has already died and the passenger would die soon afterward. The police found a needle injected through the driver's pants leg. The two men had just cashed their paychecks and bought the drugs.

strong enough that the mere ringing of a bell would now give you a headache, perhaps less painful than the ones you had originally but a headache nonetheless; this effect is Pavlovian conditioning at work.

A pioneering study by the psychologist Shepard Siegel showed a similar phenomenon occurring with drug-taking behavior. In his experiment, one group of rats was injected with doses of morphine in a particular room over a series of days and later tested for tolerance to that dose in the same room. Predictably, they displayed a lessened analgesic effect as a sign of morphine tolerance. A second group was tested in a room other than the one in which the injections had been given. No tolerance developed at all. They reacted as if they had never been given morphine before, even though they had received the same number of repeated injections as the first group.

In a more extreme experiment, Siegel tested two groups of rats that were administered a series of heroin injections with increasingly higher dosages. Eventually both groups were surviving a dosage level that would have been lethal to rats experiencing the drug for the first time. The difference in the groups was related to the

tolerance: The capacity of a drug to produce a gradually diminished physical or psychological effect upon repeated administrations of the drug at the same dose level.

behavioral tolerance: The process of drug tolerance that is linked to drug-taking behavior occurring consistently in the same surroundings or under the same circumstances. Also known as *conditioned tolerance.*

environment in which these injections were given. One group received these injections in the colony room where they lived. When the second group were receiving their injections, they were in a room that looked quite different and were hearing 60-decibel "white noise." Siegel then administered a single LD100 dose of heroin, normally a level that should have killed them all. Instead, rats administered this extremely high dosage in the same room in which they had received the earlier heroin injection series showed only a 32 percent mortality rate. When the room was different, however, the mortality rate doubled (64 percent). In both groups, more rats survived than if they had never received heroin in the first place, but the survival rate was influenced by the environment in which the heroin was originally administered.

Siegel explained the results of his studies by assuming that environmental cues in the room where the initial injections were given elicited some form of effect *opposite* to the effect of the drug. In the case of heroin, these compensatory effects would partially counteract the analgesic effect of the drug and protect the animal against dying from potentially high dosage levels.

The phenomenon of behavioral tolerance, also referred to as *conditioned tolerance* because it is based on the principles of Pavlovian conditioning, explains why a heroin abuser may easily suffer the adverse consequences of an overdose when the drug has been taken in a different environment from the one more frequently encountered or in a manner different from his or her ordinary routine.[13] The range of tolerated doses of heroin can be enormous; amounts in the 200 to 500 mg range may be lethal for a first-time heroin abuser, while amounts as high as 1800 mg may not even be sufficient to make a long-term heroin abuser sick.[14] You can imagine how dangerous it would be if the conditioned compensatory responses a heroin abuser had built up over time were suddenly absent.

Behavioral tolerance also helps to explain why a formerly drug-dependent individual is strongly advised to avoid the surroundings associated with his or her past drug-taking behavior. If these surroundings provoked a physiological effect opposite to the effect of the drug through their association with prior drug-taking behavior, then a return to this environment might create internal changes that only drugs could reverse. In effect, environmentally induced withdrawal symptoms would increase the chances of a relapse. The fact that conditioning effects have been demonstrated not only with respect to heroin but with alcohol, cocaine, nicotine, and other dependence-producing drugs as well makes it imperative that the phenomenon of behavioral tolerance be considered during the course of drug abuse treatment and rehabilitation.[15]

Another perspective on drug tolerance, based on physiological changes that occur as result of repeated drug administrations, will be discussed in Chapter 3.

Physical and Psychological Dependence

When we refer to the idea of dependence in drug abuse, we are dealing with the fact that a person has a strong compulsion to continue taking a particular drug. Two possible models or explanations for why drug dependence occurs can be considered. The first is referred to as physical dependence, and the second is referred to as psychological dependence. The two models are not mutually exclusive; the abuse of some drugs can be a result of both physical and psychological dependence, while the abuse of others can be a result of psychological dependence alone.

Physical Dependence

The concept of **physical dependence** originates from observations of heroin abusers, as well as of those who abuse other opiate drugs, who developed strong physical symptoms following heroin withdrawal: a runny nose, chills and fever, inability to sleep, and hypersensitivity to pain. For barbiturate abusers in a comparable situation, symptoms include anxiety, inability to sleep, and sometimes lethal convulsions.[16] For chronic alcoholics, abstention can produce tremors, nausea, weakness, and tachycardia (a rapid heart rate). If severe, symptoms may include delirium, seizures, and hallucinations.[17]

While the actual symptoms vary according to the drug being withdrawn, the fact that we observe physical symptoms at all suggests very strongly that some kind of physical need, perhaps as far down as the cellular level, has developed over the course of drug abuse. It is as if the drug, previously a foreign chemical, has become a normal part of the nervous system, and its removal and absence become abnormal.

From this point of view, it is predictable that the withdrawal symptoms would involve symptoms that are opposite to effects the drug originally had on the body. For example, heroin can be extremely constipating, but eventually the body compensates for heroin's intestinal effects. Abrupt abstinence from heroin releases the processes that have been counteracting the constipation and the result of withdrawal is diarrhea. You may have noticed a strong resemblance between the action-counteraction phenomena of withdrawal and the processes Siegel has hypothesized as the basis for behavioral tolerance.

Psychological Dependence

The most important implication of the model of physical dependence, as distinct from psychological dependence, is that individuals involved in drug abuse continue the drug-taking behavior, at least in part, *to avoid the feared consequences of withdrawal*. This idea can form the basis for a general model of drug dependence only if physical withdrawal symptoms appear consistently for every drug considered as a drug of abuse. It turns out, however, that a number of abused drugs (cocaine, hallucinogens, and

marijuana, for example) do not produce significant physical withdrawal symptoms, and the effects of heroin withdrawal are more variable than we would expect if physical dependence alone were at work.

It is possible that drug abusers continue to take the drug not because they want to avoid the symptoms of withdrawal but because they crave the pleasurable effects of the drug itself. They may even feel that they need the drug to function at all. This is the way one heroin abuser has expressed it:

> *I'm just trying to get high as much as possible. . . . If I could get more money, I would spend it all on drugs. All I want is to get loaded. I just really like shooting dope. I don't have any use for sex; I'd rather shoot dope. I like to shoot dope better than anything else in the world.*[18]

Many heroin abusers (between 56 percent to 77 percent in one major study) who complete the withdrawal process after abstaining from the drug experience relapse.[19] If physical dependence were the whole story, these phenomena would not exist. The withdrawal symptoms would have been gone by that time, and any physical need that may have been evident before would no longer be present.

When we speak of **psychological dependence,** we are offering an explanation of drug abuse based not on the attempt of abusers to avoid unpleasant withdrawal symptoms but on their continued desire to obtain pleasurable effects from the drug. Unfortunately, we are faced here with a major conceptual problem: The explanation by itself is circular and tells us basically nothing. If I were to say, for example, that I was taking cocaine because I was psychologically dependent on it, then I could as easily say I was psychologically dependent on cocaine because I was abusing it. Without some *independent* justification, the only explanation for the concept of psychological dependence would be the behavior that the concept was supposed to explain!

Fortunately, there is independent evidence for the concept of psychological dependence, founded chiefly upon studies showing that animals are as capable of

---

physical dependence: A model of drug dependence based on the idea that the drug abuser continues the drug-taking behavior to avoid the consequences of physical withdrawal symptoms.

psychological dependence: A model of drug dependence based on the idea that the drug abuser is motivated by a craving for the pleasurable effects of the drug.

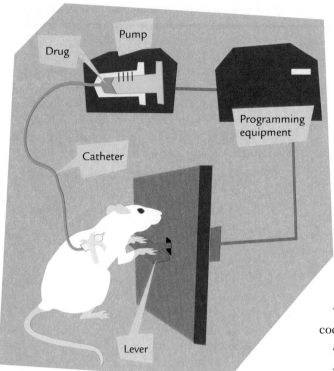

FIGURE 2.5

A simplified rendition of how drugs are self-administered in rats. The rat's pressure on a lever causes the pump to inject a drug through a catheter implanted into its vein.

self-administering drugs of abuse as humans are. Using techniques developed in the late 1950s, researchers have been able to insert a **catheter** into the vein of a freely moving laboratory animal and arrange the equipment so that the animal can self-administer a drug intravenously whenever it presses a lever (Figure 2.5). It had been well known that animals would engage in specific behaviors to secure rewards such as food, water, or even electrical stimulation of certain regions of the brain. These objectives were defined as positive reinforcers because animals would learn to work to secure them. The question at the time was whether animals would self-administer drugs in a similar way. Could drugs be positive reinforcers as well?

The experiments showed clearly that animals would self-administer drugs such as cocaine and other

catheter (CATH-eh-ter): A device to deliver intravenous injections of a drug in a free-moving human or animal.

stimulants, despite the fact that these drugs would not ordinarily produce physical symptoms during withdrawal. In one study, rats pressed the lever as many as 6,400 times for one administration of cocaine; others were nearly as eager for administrations of amphetamines.[20] Interestingly, a number of other drugs were aversive, judging from the reluctance of animals to work for them. Hallucinogens such as LSD, antipsychotic drugs, and antidepressant drugs were examples of drugs that animals clearly did not like.[21]

By connecting the concept of psychological dependence to general principles of reinforcement, it is possible for us to appreciate the powerful effects of abused drugs. When presented with a choice of pressing levers for food or for cocaine, cocaine wins hands down even to the point of an animal starving to death.[22] When comparing the effects of heroin with cocaine, the differences are dramatic:

> *Those rats that self-administer heroin developed a stable pattern of use, maintained their pretest weight, continued good grooming behavior, and tended to be in good health. Their mortality rate was 36 percent after thirty days. Those self-administering cocaine . . . exhibited an extremely erratic pattern of use, with "binges" of heavy use alternating with brief periods of abstinence. They lost 47 percent of their body weight, ceased grooming behavior, and maintained extremely poor physical health. After thirty days, 90 percent were dead.[23]*

In the final analysis, from the standpoint of treating individuals who abuse drugs, it might not matter if there is physical dependence or psychological dependence going on. According to many experts in the field, the distinction between physical and psychological dependence has outgrown its usefulness in understanding the motivation behind drug abuse. Whether the discontinuation of an abused drug does induce major physical withdrawal symptoms (as in the case of heroin, alcohol, and barbiturates) or does not (as in the case of cocaine, amphetamines, and nicotine), the pattern of compulsive drug-taking behavior in all instances is remarkably similar. If the pattern of behavior is the same, then there can be common strategies for treatment. Chapter 3 will examine the current understanding that most, if not all, drugs of abuse are linked together by virtue of common physiological processes in the brain.

Psychiatric Definitions

Most health professionals use guidelines provided by the American Psychiatric Association as an official standard for defining problems associated with drug-taking behavior. Generally speaking, these problems, which range from the ingestion of a drug of abuse (including alcohol) to the experience of side effects of a medication, are collectively referred to as *substance-related disorders*. The fourth edition (text revision) of the association's *Diagnostic and Statistical Manual of Mental Disorders* (DSM-IV-TR or simply DSM-IV, for short), published in 2000, identifies two specific behavioral conditions: **substance dependence** and **substance abuse** (Table 2.1).

substance dependence: A diagnostic term used in clinical psychology and psychiatry that identifies an individual displaying significant signs of a dependent relationship with a psychoactive drug.

substance abuse: A diagnostic term used in clinical psychology and psychiatry that identifies an individual who continues to take a psychoactive drug despite the fact that the drug-taking behavior creates specific problems for that individual.

TABLE 2.1

Criteria for substance dependence and substance abuse, according to the DSM-IV-TR

SUBSTANCE DEPENDENCE	SUBSTANCE ABUSE
At least three out of the following must apply within a 12-month period:	At least one of the following must apply within a 12-month period:
1. Tolerance. The person has to take increasingly large doses of the drug to get the desired effect. Or else the person experiences a diminished effect from the same amount of the drug.	1. Recurrent substance use resulting in a failure to fulfill major role obligations at work, school, or home. Examples include repeated absences from work, suspensions or expulsions from school, or neglect of children or one's household.
2. Withdrawal. When the drug is stopped, there are psychological or physiological withdrawal symptoms. Or else the substance is taken to relieve or avoid these symptoms.	2. Recurrent drug use in situations in which use is physically hazardous.
3. Unintentional overuse. The person often takes more of the drug or takes it over a longer period of time than he or she intended.	3. Recurrent substance-related legal problems, such as an arrest for disorderly conduct or drug-related behavior. Symptoms of the disturbance must have persisted for more than a month or occurred over a longer period of time.
4. Persistent desire or efforts to control drug use. The person tries to quit and repeatedly relapses into further drug use.	4. Continued drug use despite the knowledge of persistent social, occupational, psychological, or physical problems that would be caused or made more difficult by the use of the drug.
5. Preoccupation with the drug. The person spends a great deal of time in activities necessary to obtain the substance, use it, or recover from its effects.	*Important:* The person must have never met the criteria for substance dependence for this particular drug.
6. The reduction or abandonment of important social, occupational, or recreational activities in order to engage in drug use. A person quits a job, neglects a child, or gives up other important activities.	
7. Continued drug use despite major drug-related problems. A person repeatedly arrested for drug possession still maintains the drug habit, or a person with serious lung disease continues to smoke cigarettes, for example.	
Symptoms of the disturbance must have persisted for more than a month or occurred repeatedly over a longer period of time.	

Source: Adapted from the *American Psychiatric Association: Diagnostic and statistical manual of mental disorders, Text Revision* (4th ed.). Washington DC: American Psychiatric Association. Reprinted with permission from the *Diagnostic and statistical manual of mental disorders* (4th ed.). Copyright 2000 American Psychiatric Association, pp. 191, 197, and 199.

Two features of the DSM-IV guidelines are worth noting. First, the guidelines consist of a listing of behavioral criteria to be used for the diagnosis (identification) of substance dependence or substance abuse. There is no discussion of why these problems have arisen or what circumstances produced them, only their behavioral features. The position of the American Psychiatric Association is that a judgment of whether a person has a problem of dependence or abuse should depend on the behavior of that person, not the chemical that is being consumed. Second, the broader term "substance" has been substituted for the word "drug" in the guidelines, primarily because there is often confusion in the public mind in deciding what is defined as a drug and what is not, particularly in the instance of alcohol or nicotine use.[24]

Special Problems in Drug Abuse

The discussion so far has dealt with drug-abuse problems, specifically the problems of acute and chronic toxicity, that affect only the drug user. Unfortunately, other people are frequently involved as well. Consider two special circumstances related to drug abuse that require discussions of their own: the problems of drug abuse in pregnancy and in association with AIDS.

Drug Abuse in Pregnancy

Prior to the 1960s, doctors and scientists regarded the placenta joining the bloodstream of a pregnant woman with that of the developing fetus as a natural barrier protecting the fetus from toxic substances in the mother. We now know that the idea of a "placental barrier" is clearly wrong. During gestation, almost all drugs cross the placenta and affect the unborn child.

Approximately 16 percent of pregnant women in the United States report having smoked cigarettes in the past month, about 12 percent report having consumed some alcohol (4 percent report binge drinking), and 5 percent report having used some form of illicit drug.[25] These percentages should be viewed as underestimates of the actual picture of drug-taking behavior and pregnancy, because women are frequently reluctant to admit such behaviors.

It is clear that women who do engage in the consumption of licit or illicit drugs during pregnancy are at increased risk for obstetrical complications and for premature labor and delivery. They are also more likely

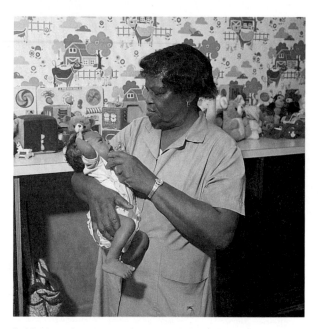

Babies born to women who abused drugs during their pregnancy require special health care during their early months of development.

to suffer loss of the fetus through spontaneous abortions (miscarriages) and stillbirths than are women who abstain from drugs. The greater the extent of drug-taking behavior, the more likely there will be adverse consequences.

The timing of drug use during a pregnancy has a great deal to do with the specific risks to the fetus. Drug use during the early weeks of pregnancy, from the fourth to the eighth week following conception, is more likely to increase the risks of spontaneous abortions and physical malformations in the newborn than drug use later in the pregnancy. Drug use after the eighth month of pregnancy is frequently associated with growth retardation, prematurity and low birth weight, and neurological damage to the infant.[26] These warnings are generalizations, cutting across many categories of psychoactive substances. Health Line examines the specific risks associated with specific categories of drugs.

Drug Abuse and AIDS

One of the hazards associated with drug use by injection is the spread of disease when needles are shared. In the past, the contamination has primarily involved infectious hepatitis, a serious liver disease. Since the late 1970s, however, attention has turned to the potential spread of the human immunodeficiency virus (HIV) responsible for acquired immunodeficiency syndrome

Health Line

Effects of Psychoactive Drugs on Pregnant Women and Newborns

In addition to the adverse effect of psychoactive drugs on fetal development and pregnancy in general, a number of such drugs carry very specific risks. Here is a review of these effects.

Alcohol
- Fetal effects: Impairment in the supply of fetal oxygen and stimulation of excess prostaglandins possibly causing fetal malformations.
- Pregnancy effects: Risk of miscarriage during the second trimester of pregnancy if the mother consumed only one or two drinks a day.
- Newborn effects: Signs of alcohol withdrawal upon birth if the mother drank heavily. Fetal alcohol syndrome involving retardation of postnatal growth and nervous system, abnormal craniofacial features, numerous organ abnormalities.

Tobacco
- Fetal effects: Reduced oxygen supply compounded by carbon monoxide that interferes with the blood's ability to carry oxygen throughout the body.
- Pregnancy effects: Increased frequency of spontaneous abortions and fetal death.
- Newborn effects: Increased risk of physical defects, lower birth weight. Also a higher risk that infants born to mothers who smoke will die before their first birthday.

Marijuana
- Fetal effects: Increased carbon monoxide levels in mother's blood, particularly in the last trimester, resulting in reduced oxygen in fetal blood.
- Pregnancy effects: Inconsistent findings, although there is a tendency for more males to be conceived than females if either parent is a heavy marijuana smoker.
- Newborn effects: Some evidence for abnormal sleep and arousal patterns if mothers have used marijuana.

Cocaine or Crack Cocaine
- Fetal effects: Constriction of blood vessels, which reduces normal fetal blood flow and causes urogenital malformations.
- Pregnancy effects: High rates of spontaneous abortion and early separation of the placenta from the uterine wall, resulting in increased numbers of stillbirths. Increased risks of early onset of labor and preterm delivery.
- Newborn effects: Increased risk of intrauterine growth retardation: lower birth weight and smaller length and head circumference. Tendency to be jittery and easily startled. Fewer discernible withdrawal symptoms than in newborns exposed to heroin or other narcotics in utero.

Methamphetamine
- Fetal effects: Unknown but likely to be similar to effects of cocaine.
- Pregnancy effects: Increased risk of premature birth, fetal distress during delivery
- Newborn effects: Growth retardation, lethargy, increased difficulty to arouse and, once aroused, increased autonomic reactivity. Long-term effects largely unknown.

Heroin or Morphine
- Fetal effects: Reduced oxygen supply to the fetus, as well as reduced pancreatic, liver, and intestinal functioning.
- Pregnancy effects: In 10 to 15 percent of pregnant women using heroin, development of toxemia, a poisoning of the blood between the mother and the fetus.
- Newborn effects: Retardation of intrauterine growth. Likelihood of lung problems, brain hemorrhages, and respiratory distress. Risk for perinatally transmitted HIV infection and the development of AIDS. Dramatic withdrawal symptoms usually beginning forty-eight to seventy-two hours after delivery.

Prescription Drugs
- Accutane (isoretinoin): Major birth defects associated with this antiacne medication and Vitamin A derivative.
- Tetracycline antibiotics: Possibility of permanent discoloration of a child's teeth.
- Salicylates (aspirin products): Possibility of bleeding in the mother or fetus and of delay in delivery if taken close to term or prior to delivery.
- Dilantin (phenytoin): Increased risk of heart malformations, cleft lip, and mental retardation associated with this and other anticonvulsants.
- Antianxiety drugs: Possible depression of respiration in newborn when taken during labor. Fourfold increase in cleft palates and malformations of the heart and limbs when taken during early pregnancy.
- Paxil (paroxetine): Increased risk of birth defects when this antidepressant is taken during the first trimester of pregnancy.
- Barbiturates: Birth defects resembling fetal alcohol syndrome associated with long-acting barbiturates such as phenobarbital. Withdrawal symptoms in the newborn four to seven days after delivery.

Sources: Cook, Paddy S., Peterson, Robert C., and Moore, Dorothy T. (1990). *Alcohol, tobacco, and other drugs may harm the unborn.* Rockville, MD: Office of Substance Abuse Prevention. U.S. Food and Drug Administration, 2009. Smith, Lynne M., et al. (2008). Prenatal methamphetamine use and neonatal neurobehavioral outcome. *Neurotoxicology and Teratology, 30,* 20–28.

TABLE 2.2

HIV infections among three at-risk populations in the 96 largest cities in the United States

RISK GROUP	ESTIMATED NUMBER IN RISK GROUP	ESTIMATED PERCENT TESTED HIV-POSITIVE	ESTIMATED NUMBER OF HIV-POSITIVE INDIVIDUALS
Injecting drug users	1.5 million	14.0	315,000
Men who have sex with men	1.7 million	18.3	311,100
At-risk heterosexuals*	2.1 million	2.3	48,300

*Men and women who are at risk because they have sex with injecting drug users and/or bisexual or gay men.

Source: Department of Health and Human Services (1999). *Drug abuse and addiction research: 25 years of discovery to advance the health of the public. The sixth triennial report to Congress from the Secretary of Health and Human Services.* Washington DC: Department of Health and Human Services.

(AIDS). Since HIV-infected individuals may not show discernible AIDS symptoms for a considerable period of time (the median interval being ten years), there is unfortunately ample opportunity for contaminating others, either through sexual contact or via some direct exchange of bodily fluids.

At the beginning of the 1990s, almost 60 percent of injection-drug users (IDUs) in New York tested HIV-positive, and the prevalence levels were even higher in some regions of Asia.[27] While the percentage of IDUs with HIV infection has declined since that time, this form of drug-taking behavior remains a significant risk factor. Table 2.2 shows the incidence of HIV infection among three at-risk populations in major U.S. cities.[28]

In an effort to reduce the risk of HIV infection among injecting drug users, needle-exchange programs, in which addicts have the opportunity to trade in their used needles for sterile ones, have been operating successfully in several countries, including England, Canada, Australia, Sweden, and the Netherlands. In the United States, however, the idea of providing sterile needles to heroin users has met with considerable political and social resistance. Nonetheless, such programs do exist in dozens of U.S. communities, either officially sanctioned or operating underground.

It has been estimated that needle-exchange programs can reduce new cases of HIV infection by one-third. In 1998, the U.S. Department of Health and Human Services

officially endorsed needle-exchange programs as an effective part of a comprehensive strategy to reduce the incidence of HIV transmission, having received no evidence that they encourage the use of illicit drugs. Nonetheless, the use of federal funds for needle-exchange programs remains restricted, and such programs are still officially illegal in many regions of the United States.[29]

Drugs, Violence, and Crime

Important questions often end up being the most complicated ones to answer. Consider the question of whether illicit drugs cause violence and crime. We can look at the news headlines reporting acts of social violence linked to the world of illicit drugs and the impact of those acts on our society: innocent children killed in the cross fire of rival drug gangs, thousands of crimes against individuals and property to pay for a continuing pattern of drug abuse, terrorization of whole communities by drug dealers. Illicit drugs and crime are bound together in a web of greed and callous disregard for human life.

The association clearly exists. Figure 2.6 shows the results from ten representative large and small cities studied in the **Arrestee Drug Abuse Monitoring (ADAM) Program,** conducted by the U.S. Department of Justice, in which individuals arrested for a serious offense are tested for various drugs through urinanalysis. It is evident that a large proportion of arrestees test positive for illicit drugs. Summarizing across thirty-nine metropolitan areas participating in the program, approximately two out of three adult male arrestees were found to have recently used at least one of five drugs: cocaine, marijuana, heroin, methamphetamine, or PCP. Marijuana was the

Arrestee Drug Abuse Monitoring (ADAM) Program: A reporting system, administered by the U.S. Department of Justice, that identifies the presence of alcohol or illicit drugs in the system of individuals who have been arrested for a serious offense.

	Percentage Testing Positive for Any of Five Major Illicit Drugs	Methamphetamine	Cocaine	Heroin	Marijuana	Multiple Drugs
Birmingham, AL	66	1	34	8	45	20
Cleveland, OH	75	0	39	5	49	25
Denver, CO	66	5	38	7	42	23
Minneapolis, MN	65	3	28	6	48	65
New York, NY	70	0	36	15	43	22
Phoenix, AZ	74	38	23	4	41	28
Portland, OR	72	25	30	15	38	30
San Diego, CA	67	36	10	5	41	24
San Jose, CA	63	37	13	3	35	25
Tulsa, OK	70	17	20	5	52	24

FIGURE 2.6

Prevalence of drug use (alcohol and nicotine excluded) among male adult arrestees in ten U.S. cities in 2003. Percentages for cocaine, heroin, multiple drugs, and any drug are generally much higher among adults than juveniles; percentages for marijuana are generally higher among juveniles than adults.

Source: National Institute of Justice (2005). *Drug and alcohol use and related matters among arrestees 2003.* Washington DC: Arrestee Drug Abuse Monitoring Program, U.S. Department of Justice, Tables 3, 5, 6, 7, and 8.

most commonly used drug, with the incidence ranging from 35 to 52 percent. The second most commonly used drug was cocaine (between 10 and 39 percent) and methamphetamine shows the greatest variation by geographical region (between 0 percent in the eastern U.S. cities and 38 percent in some areas of the West).[30]

It is important to be careful, however, when we draw conclusions from ADAM statistics or other studies that point to a correlation between illicit drug use and criminal activity. Do drugs actually *cause* violent behavior and crime? If they do, which drugs have a greater responsibility than others? Are illicit drugs necessarily more problematic with respect to violent behavior and crime than licit drugs such as alcohol? As we will see, the question of the relationship between drugs and societal problems such as violence and crime needs to be broken down into three specific issues.

Pharmacological Violence

Pharmacological violence refers to an act of violence committed by an offender who is under the direct influence of a psychoactive drug. The implication is that a specific drug caused violent or criminal behavior while the drug was actually present in the individual's system. Although the ADAM statistics reflect the fact that a large proportion of people have some illicit drug in their system at the time of arrest, it is difficult to say whether the offense was committed as a direct result of the influence of that drug. The main criticism of pharmacological explanations is that the detection period in a standard urinalysis test for an illicit drug can range from a matter of several hours to two days in the case of cocaine and several days to two months in the case of marijuana (see Table 8.3 on page 208). Therefore, testing positive for a drug at the time of arrest indicates only that the individual *might* have become violent or have been motivated to commit a crime while under the influence of the drug, assuming that the drug has the potential for creating a violence-producing or crime-producing effect in the first place.

In some instances, the physiological nature of the drug itself makes the possibility of pharmacological violence quite unlikely. Marijuana by itself, for example, makes the user more passive than active, in effect quite mellow in circumstances in which there may be some interpersonal conflict. Heroin produces a passive state of mind that reduces the inclination toward violent behavior. In fact, as rates of heroin abuse rise, the incidence of crimes against individuals (as opposed to crimes against property) declines.[31]

pharmacological violence: Violent acts committed while under the influence of a particular psychoactive drug, with the implication that the drug caused the violence to occur.

Psychoactive stimulants such as amphetamines and cocaine or the hallucinogenic PCP (known as angel dust), however, produce an on-edge manner and a social paranoia that can lead to violent behavior, although there is no current evidence that these drugs specifically stimulate violent behavior. Yet, even in such cases, we need to be careful in the interpretation of studies reporting violent behavior in unselected populations. For example, in a study conducted at an Atlanta medical center, more than half of all patients being treated for acute cocaine intoxication were reported to be aggressive, agitated, and paranoid just prior to and at the time of hospital admission. It is impossible to determine whether these patients were mentally unstable to begin with, prior to their taking cocaine. People who have long-standing psychological problems may be overrepresented in any population of cocaine abusers.[32]

Crack cocaine has the dubious reputation of making the crack smoker irritable, suspicious, and inclined to lash out at another person at the slightest provocation.[33] Whether these effects are due to being under the influence of the drug, however, is unclear. Tendencies toward violence are observed during times of *crack withdrawal* as well as crack intoxication.

Of all the psychoactive drugs we could consider, the one with the most definitive and widely reported links to violent behavior is alcohol. In this case, the violence is clearly pharmacological, since the effects of being drunk from the ingestion of alcohol are apparent almost immediately. On a domestic level, males involved in spouse abuse commonly report having been drinking or having been drunk during many of the times that abuse has occurred. Moreover, violent crime outside the home is strongly related to alcohol intoxication. The more violent the crime, the greater the probability that the perpetrator of the crime was drunk while committing it. Studies show at least a majority of homicides and sexually aggressive acts (rapes and attempted rapes) are committed while the offender is drunk (Figure 2.7).[34]

Does the chronic, long-term use of drugs cause individuals to engage in criminal behavior in general? There is little evidence that drugs *cause* an increase in one's general inclination toward antisocial behavior. In other words, it is not true that drugs alone are capable of changing the personality of the user, turning him or her from being some kind of upstanding pillar of the community into a social menace. As discussed in Chapter 1,

economically compulsive violence: Violent acts that are committed by a drug abuser to secure money to buy drugs.

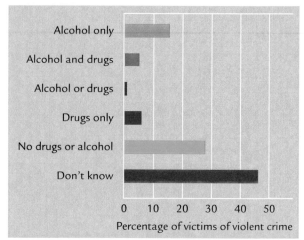

FIGURE 2.7

Victim's perception of the use of alcohol and drugs by the violent offender.

Source: Bureau of Justice Statistics (2008, August). *Criminal victimization in the United States,* 2006 statistical tables. Washington DC: U.S. Department of Justice, Table 32.

social risk factors can be identified that lead toward deviant behavior, as defined by societal norms, and that deviant behavior includes both drug abuse and criminal behavior. One aspect of that deviant behavior cannot be considered the cause of the other. Frequently, individuals with the greatest chance of abusing drugs have socioeconomic backgrounds that also produce the greatest chance of criminal behavior: a low level of education, a broken family, little or no social supervision, and low social status.[35] As one researcher has put it,

> *Teenagers who begin illegal drug use are also likely to have committed other criminal acts beforehand, whether or not they have been caught. It is likely that this relationship may be sufficient to explain the higher crime rate of marijuana users. It is not so much that marijuana use causes crime (except, of course, the crime of using the drug), but that those who use marijuana are also the type of people more likely to commit criminal acts.*[36]

Economically Compulsive Violence

Economic explanations of the relationship between drug use and crime suggest that illicit drug users feel compelled to commit crimes to obtain money to buy drugs and continue a pattern of drug abuse. We can speak of the possibility of **economically compulsive violence,** if the violent act stems from the costliness of the drug-taking behavior.

Several studies show economic considerations to be a major component of the link between drugs and crime. A 1990 study of crack users in the Miami area showed that 59 percent participated in 6,669 robberies over a twelve-month period, averaging thirty-one robberies per individual, or roughly one every twelve days. Yet, while the majority of these robberies were carried out to buy drugs, we cannot assume that they all involved the classic picture of break-ins and holdups. A large percentage involved the theft of drugs from drug dealers or other users, or themselves being victims of a drug robbery.[37] Nonetheless, a large proportion of the crimes committed to obtain drug money involved violent acts directed toward individuals within the community. Particular targets included storekeepers, children, and the elderly.

When robbery is the means for financing drug abuse, the extent of this crime has been shown to be closely related to market conditions at the time. When heroin prices are high, for example, the level of property crime goes up; when heroin prices are low, the crime level goes down. In other words, heroin abusers steal more to maintain a stable consumption of heroin if the drug becomes more expensive to obtain. Therefore, deliberate elevation of drug prices when accomplished by reducing the supply not only fails to reduce the incidence of abuse but also tends to increase the incidence of criminal behavior among drug abusers.[38]

The type of crime a drug user commits under these circumstances is typically related to gender. Males are more likely to commit crimes against persons and property, whereas females are more likely to commit crimes against the public order, such as prostitution. One study, for example, found that 64 percent of female crack users exchanged sex for money to buy drugs and that 24 percent reported trading sex for money. Among women who bartered sex for crack cocaine, many of them would remain in the "crack houses" for extended periods of time, providing sexual favors to multiple customers to secure a continuous supply of the drug.[39]

Systemic Violence

A third important source of social violence and criminal behavior is inherent within the drug world itself. A substantial number of drug users, as their drug use becomes more intense, involve themselves in drug distribution and a criminal subculture that uses violence as a means for maintaining control over its "business."

Researchers use the term **systemic violence** to refer to the violence that arises from characteristic features of

Pharmacological violence

Ingestion of drug causing individuals to become excitable, irrational, or inclined to exhibit violent behavior

Economically compulsive violence

Need for money to buy drugs as the primary motivation for violence

The Drug–Violence Connection

Systemic violence

- Disputes over territory between rival drug dealers
- Violent acts committed to enforce discipline
- Elimination of police informants
- Punishment for selling adulterated drugs
- Punishment for defrauding the drug dealer

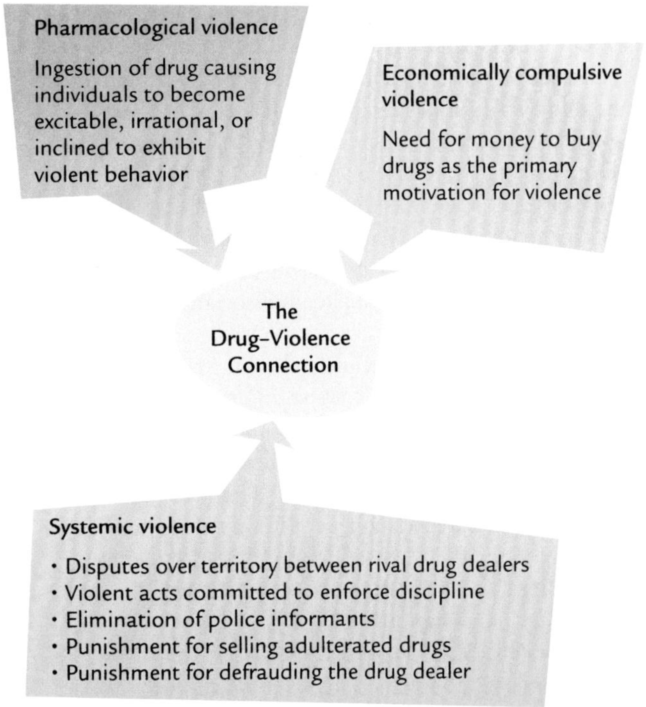

FIGURE 2.8

The tripartite framework: three aspects of drugs and violence.

Source: Goldstein, Paul (1985, Fall). The drug-violence nexus: A tripartite framework. *Journal of Drug Issues*, 493–506.

drug dealing (Figure 2.8). Systemic violence can result from such situations as territorial disputes, the consequences of selling inferior grades of the illicit drug, or fraudulent handling of funds from drug sales (referred to as "messing up the money"). The prominence of systemic violence in crack cocaine abuse since the mid-1980s is particularly striking. Studies show that as the involvement of a youth in crack distribution increases, the more likely that person will become a criminal offender. The probability also increases that major felonies will be committed. The linkage between systemic violence and illicit drug involvement can be phrased in the opposite manner as well. A young person, aged twelve to seventeen, who has a history of serious fighting at school or work, group-against-group fighting, or attacking others with the intent to seriously hurt them has three times the likelihood of having used an illicit drug.[40]

systemic violence: Violence that arises from the traditionally aggressive patterns of behavior within a network of illicit drug trafficking and distribution.

The question of which factor causes the other cannot be easily answered. It is quite possible that a combination of self-selection and modeling behavior is occurring here. Inherently violent individuals may be useful in maintaining tight discipline in groups that focus upon drug taking and drug selling; they may be useful as combatants in territorial disputes in general. As a result, the participation of highly violent individuals in the selling and distribution of crack adds an extremely dangerous dimension to the violence and social upheaval already associated with illicit drugs.[41]

In addition, the most violent drug users may be the most respected role models for young people. Sociologists have observed that in many communities, adolescents feel the need to prove that they can be brutal to avoid being harassed by their peers. The pressure to be an accepted member of such a community may be more responsible for a drug abuser's committing frequent violent acts than the effects of the drugs themselves, or even the need for money to buy drugs.

Given the link between the distribution of crack cocaine and systemic violence, it should not be surprising that a decline in the prevalence of crack abuse, first observed in the latter part of the 1990s, was accompanied by a decline in homicide rates and violent crime in the areas where crack abuse had been dominant. Community-based policing procedures focused on breaking up drug gangs and large street-level drug markets, thereby changing the pattern of drug buying and selling. An expert in the area of criminal justice has put it this way:

> The reconfiguration of drug markets in the mid-1990s appreciably reduced the level of neighborhood violence. As distribution retired indoors, turf battles were eliminated, and because organizers of drug businesses hired a few trusted friends rather than easily replaceable workers, there was less conflict between them. Distributors were robbed by users less frequently because they were more protected selling indoors to known customers.[42]

In addressing the connections between drug-taking behavior and crime, it is important to include patterns of criminal behavior that are associated with affluent populations as well as impoverished ones. The spread of illicit drug dependence to higher socioeconomic levels of society, since the 1970s, has led to an increase in white-collar

laissez-faire (LAY-say FAIR) (Fr.): The philosophy of exerting as little governmental control and regulation as possible.

crimes of fraud and embezzlement that are motivated by the need for drug money. In such cases, we are speaking of economically compulsive acts. While generally nonviolent in nature, these criminal acts involve substantially greater amounts of lost revenue than the burglaries and robberies common to poorer neighborhoods.

Governmental Policy, Regulation, and Laws

How should we as a society respond to the social problems of drug-taking behavior? We are faced with an overwhelming flood of illicit drugs entering the United States from around the world, only a small fraction of which is ever identified, much less confiscated, despite the well-publicized drug seizures.[43]

We can express our moral outrage that the situation has become so bad, that drug abuse is costing society such an enormous amount of money and wasting so many lives. Social despair is so well entrenched in some portions of society that solutions seem to be nonexistent. The official responses U.S. society has made through its history, in terms of regulatory controls over drugs, can be understood more clearly in terms of its attitudes toward drug-taking behavior and drug users than in terms of the drugs themselves.

Efforts to Regulate Drugs, 1900–1970

Until about 1900 in the United States, the governmental attitude toward addictive behavior was one of **laissez-faire,** roughly translated as "allow [people] to do as they please," which meant there was little regulation or control. It was a well-ingrained philosophy, going back to our early days as a nation, that government should stay out of the lives of its citizens. Nonmedical use of opiates was not considered respectable and in some circles was seen as immoral, but it was no more disreputable than heavy drinking.

> Employees were not fired for addiction. Wives did not divorce their addicted husbands, or husbands their addicted wives. Children were not taken from their homes and lodged in foster homes or institutions because one or both parents were addicted. Addicts continued to participate fully in the life of the community. Addicted children and young people continued to go to school, Sunday school, and college.[44]

Prior to the twentieth century, there were movements to ban alcoholic consumption but none to ban the wholesale use of opium, morphine, heroin, or cocaine.

The only exception was the strong opposition to the smoking of opium, an attitude directed principally toward Chinese immigrants in the western states, as noted in Chapter 1.

By the turn of the century, however, a wave of reform sentiment began to sweep the country. In 1905, the popular magazine *Collier's* criticized the fraudulent claims and improper labeling of patent medicines that contained large amounts of alcohol, opiates, and cocaine. Large-scale abuses in the meatpacking industry, publicized in 1906 in Upton Sinclair's novel *The Jungle*, turned the stomach of the American public and quickly pressured President Theodore Roosevelt and Congress to take action.

The result was the enactment of the Pure Food and Drug Act. The 1906 law required that food and drug manufacturers list the amounts of alcohol or "habit-forming" drugs, specified as any opiate or cocaine, on the label of the product, but the sale or use of any of these substances was left unrestricted. The law was the first of a series of legislative controls over food, drinks, drugs, and eventually cosmetics. As Chapter 14 will describe, this legislation eventually evolved into the establishment of the present-day U.S. Food and Drug Administration.

The second major piece of legislation of the early part of the century was the Harrison Act of 1914. This new law concerned itself with opiate drugs (defined as narcotics) and cocaine. The law was designed to regulate drug abuse essentially through a process of governmental taxation. The act required anyone importing, manufacturing, selling, or dispensing opiate drugs or cocaine to register with the Treasury Department, pay a special tax, and keep records of all transactions. From a constitutional perspective, the Harrison Act was a tax law, similar to laws regulating the sale of alcohol. As you can imagine, however, the difficulties in abiding by the law would soon become virtually insurmountable. In effect, the opiate drugs and cocaine were outlawed. Drug-taking behavior that involved these drugs was now driven, from a societal point of view, underground.

Under the Harrison Act, opiate drugs were defined as "narcotics," but cocaine was not. Nonetheless, cocaine became lumped together with opiate drugs in the public mind and was often referred to as a narcotic as well. Although the application of the term to cocaine was incorrect (narcotic literally means "stupor-inducing" and cocaine is anything but that), the association has unfortunately stuck. In the years after the enactment of the Harrison Act, several restricted drugs, including marijuana and the hallucinogenic peyote, were also referred to as narcotics without regard to their pharmacological characteristics. Today, many people still think of any illegal drug as a narcotic, and for many years the bureau at the Treasury Department charged with drug-enforcement responsibilities was called the Federal Bureau of Narcotics (FBN) and their agents known on the street as "narks."

By 1933, as the Prohibition Era ended, the attention of drug-enforcement policymakers, led by Harry Anslinger, the newly installed FBN director, turned from the control of alcohol consumption to the publicizing of marijuana as a major public menace (Portrait). Congressional committees heard testimony from police claiming that marijuana, now called the "killer weed," aroused sexual excitement and led to violent crimes. Movies produced and released in the 1930s, such as *Reefer Madness* (now a cult classic on many university campuses) and *Marihuana: Weed with Roots in Hell*, depicted the moral slide of supposedly innocent young people when introduced to marijuana. The result was the Marijuana Tax Act of 1937, after which growers, sellers, and buyers of marijuana were subject to tax. State laws made possession of marijuana illegal (see Chapter 7).

The 1960s saw a number of amendments to the enforcement laws then in effect, as new drugs of abuse came onto the scene. The Federal Bureau of Narcotics became the Federal Bureau of Narcotics and Dangerous Drugs, and Anslinger, whose tenure as director rivaled that of FBI Director J. Edgar Hoover in longevity and power, retired in 1962.

Rethinking the Approach toward Drug Regulation, 1970–Present

The Comprehensive Drug Abuse Prevention and Control Act of 1970 organized the control of drugs under five classifications called *schedules of controlled substances*, based on their potential for abuse (see Table 2.3, page 52). Since 1970, these categories have defined the extent to which various drugs are authorized to be available to the general public in the United States. Schedules I and II refer to drugs presenting the highest level of abuse potential, and Schedule V refers to drugs presenting the least. All drugs, except those included under Schedule I, are legally available on either a prescription or nonprescription basis.

Under the system establishing schedules of controlled substances, drugs that are considered more dangerous and more easily abused are subject to progressively more stringent restrictions on their possession, the number of prescriptions that can be made, or the manner in which they can be dispensed. In the case of Schedule I drugs (heroin, LSD, mescaline, marijuana, for example), no acceptable medical use has been authorized by the U.S. government and availability of these drugs is limited to research purposes only. The federal penalties for

TABLE 2.3

The five schedules of controlled substances in the Comprehensive Drug Abuse Prevention and Control Act

SCHEDULE I

High potential for abuse. No accepted medical use. Research use only; separate records must be maintained, and the drugs must be stored in secure vaults.

Examples: heroin, LSD, mescaline, marijuana, PCP

SCHEDULE II

High potential for abuse. Some accepted medical use, though use may lead to severe physical or psychological dependence. Prescriptions must be written in ink, or typewritten, and signed by a medical practitioner. Verbal prescriptions must be confirmed in writing within 72 hours and may be given only in a genuine emergency. No prescription renewals are permitted. Separate records must be maintained, and the drugs must be stored in secure vaults.

Examples: codeine, morphine, cocaine, methadone, amphetamines, short-acting barbiturates

SCHEDULE III

Some potential for abuse. Accepted medical use, though use may lead to low-to-moderate physical dependence or high psychological dependence. Prescriptions may be oral or written. Up to five prescription renewals are permitted within 6 months.

Examples: long-acting barbiturates, narcotic solutions (for example, paregoric or tincture of opium in alcohol) or mixtures (for example, 1.8% codeine)

SCHEDULE IV

Low potential for abuse. Accepted medical use. Prescriptions may be oral or written. Up to five prescription renewals are permitted within 6 months.

Examples: antianxiety drugs and sedative-hypnotics (for example, Valium and Klonopin)

SCHEDULE V

Minimal abuse potential. Widespread medical use. Minimal controls for selling and dispensing.

Examples: prescription cough medicines not containing codeine, laxatives

Source: Drug Enforcement Administration, U.S. Department of Justice, Washington DC.

possession and sale of Schedule I drugs, as well as those for violating the restrictions set for other controlled substances, will be examined in Chapter 17.

The 1970 law shifted the responsibility of drug enforcement from the Treasury Department to the Justice Department, ending the long era of attempts to regulate drug-taking behavior through taxation. As prevention and treatment programs for drug abuse were set up and funds were allocated for educational material, the emphasis started to shift from penalties on the drug user to penalties on drug dealing. In 1988 the Anti-Drug Abuse Act imposed penalties for money laundering when associated with drug smuggling and sales. Under this act, a new cabinet-level position, a "drug czar," was established to coordinate the efforts of the many federal agencies and departments that were by now involved in drug regulation and drug-law enforcement. Overall strategic planning and implementation of drug policy in the United States now originates from the White House Office of National Drug Control Policy.

Enforcement of Drug Laws on a Global Scale

The enforcement picture today is far more complex than it was fifty years ago, when the consideration was chiefly the "supply" side (the availability of drugs) of the problem, without much consideration of the "demand" side (the dependence of individuals on drugs capable of being abused). Treatment and prevention programs in the 1980s represented only 30 percent of the federal budget allocated to control drug abuse. More recently, the amount allotted to treatment and prevention programs has increased somewhat, but about 65 percent of funds in the $14.1 billion drug-control budget are still directed toward efforts to reduce the supply of illicit drugs.[45]

A large proportion of the drug-control budget, approximately $5.4 billion annually, is expended specifically to hold back the continuing influx of illicit drugs entering the country. The primary federal agencies involved in this effort include the Drug Enforcement Administration (DEA), the U.S. Customs and Border Patrol Agency, the U.S. Coast Guard and other branches of the U.S. military, and the Immigration and Naturalization Service (INS). In addition, government agents are stationed in more than forty foreign countries, working with the Departments of Defense and State, to limit the exportation of illicit drugs at the source.

Our attempts to stem the flood of illicit drugs into the United States, however, are complicated by a number

PORTRAIT

Harry J. Anslinger—America's First Drug Czar

By the time Harry J. Anslinger became the first commissioner of the Federal Bureau of Narcotics (FBN) in 1930, the nation's drug-law-enforcement policy had been established. Anslinger had been a rising young star in the Prohibition Unit at the Treasury Department during the 1920s. He was convinced that drug addiction was absolutely immoral and that its cure was a matter of preventing the addict from getting hold of the drug.

The end of Prohibition, however, had placed pressure on Congress to reduce the Treasury's enforcement budget, and the Great Depression put strains on federal expenditures in general. Anslinger and the FBN faced hard times. The savior, ironically enough, was marijuana. Beginning in the early 1930s, rumors of "degenerate Spanish-speaking residents" in the Southwest going on criminal rampages while smoking marijuana were being spread in newspapers and popular magazines. Anslinger seized upon these unsubstantiated reports, calling marijuana the "assassin of youth." In his view, a new menace at our shores deserved new legislation, not to men-

tion continued financial support for the agency dedicated to fighting it. The Marijuana Tax Act of 1937 was Anslinger's creation.

Anslinger's thirty-two-year tenure at the FBN and his stature as the defender of the purity of American youth, or at least the purity of their circulatory systems, could not have been possible without strong support from several important conservative U.S. legislators in the House and Senate. During the late 1940s and into the 1950s, Anslinger began to emphasize the link between drug addiction in the United States and the threat of international Communism from abroad.

The target was the People's Republic of China, which Anslinger repeatedly claimed was the primary source of heroin in the United States, despite the available evidence pointing to politically friendlier nations of Southeast Asia as the real culprits. According to Anslinger's testimony, China was not only the source of heroin but was specifically selling opium and heroin to finance the expansion of Communism around the world. Drug abuse now became un-American. Only after Anslinger's resignation in 1962, follow-

ing considerable pressure from President Kennedy, would the focus of attention be turned to the problem of heroin trafficking in Burma, Laos, and Thailand.

Given the anti-Communist stance of the FBN, it is not surprising that one of Anslinger's staunchest supporters during the late 1940s and early 1950s was Senator Joseph R. McCarthy, whose congressional subcommittee was then engaged in a ruthless crusade against "known Communists" inside the government. What was not known at the time, however, was that Anslinger during this period was secretly allowing McCarthy, a morphine addict as well as an alcoholic, to buy unrestricted supplies of morphine without FBN interference. When McCarthy died in 1957 of "acute hepatitis, cause unknown," Anslinger wrote in a memoir, "I thanked God for relieving me of my burden."

Source: McWilliams, John C. (1990). *The protectors: Harry J. Anslinger and the Federal Bureau of Narcotics, 1930–1962.* Cranbury, NJ: Associated University Press.

---

of economic and political factors on a global scale. Since the 1990s, Colombia has established itself as the world's leading producer and distributor of cocaine and a significant supplier of heroin to the United States. In 2000, approximately 59 percent of the heroin seized by U.S. federal authorities was of Colombian origin. In 2001, the U.S.-sponsored Plan Colombia program was authorized to reduce the amount of coca harvested in Colombia and to assist military forces in that nation in reducing drug trafficking operations within specific guerrilla organizations, referred to by the DEA as "narco-terrorists." While nearly $5 billion has been spent in this effort, current analyses indicate that as much coca is cultivated in Colombia as was grown in 2000. The availability of cocaine in the United States, as well as its price and quality, remain unchanged.

Despite its status as a principal U.S. trading partner, the country of Mexico, immediately to our south, remains a major drug trafficking route not only for cocaine from South America (Figure 2.9) and heroin originating from Mexico itself, but also as a source of marijuana, methamphetamine, and illegal prescription medications. A heightened level of security for terrorists and weapons at checkpoints along the Mexican border has produced higher levels of drug seizures following the September 11, 2001, terrorist attacks, but long-range effects on drug trafficking remain unknown.[46]

In 2000, the Taliban governing Afghanistan at the time managed to reduce Afghani opium cultivation by 97 percent. With the U.S.-backed military overthrow of the Taliban regime in late 2001, however, opium production rebounded sharply. Today, Afghanistan

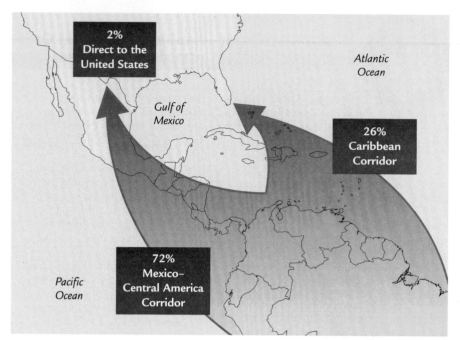

FIGURE 2.9

Nearly three-fourths of the flow of cocaine into the United States is through Mexico. Several Central American countries function as the "trans-shipment corridor" from Colombia to Mexico. Mexico also serves as the main foreign source of marijuana consumed in the United States.

Sources: Office of National Drug Control Policy (2002, March). *Annual assessment of cocaine movement.* Washington DC: Office of National Drug Control Policy. Bureau of International Narcotics and Law Enforcement Affairs (2007, March). *2007 International narcotics control strategy report. Volume 1: Drug and chemical control.* Washington DC: U.S. Department of State, pp. 147–149, 154–166, 173–179.

alone is responsible for approximately 92 percent of the world's supply of heroin.[47]

At this point, where has nearly a century of drug regulation taken us? We are decades into the U.S. "war on drugs," declared officially by President Nixon in 1971; the price tag for this war has exceeded $250 billion. Each year more money is requested to carry on the fight, but the struggle continues to be frustrating in the extreme and the nation grows increasingly battle-weary (see Point/Counterpoint, pages 88–89). While the expenditures are up by more than 1,400 percent since 1981, there is no clear-cut correlation between budget allocations from year to year and the availability of illicit drugs. As a federal drug-law-enforcement official once commented, "It reminds me of that cartoon. This king is slamming his fist on the table, saying 'If all my horses and all my men can't put Humpty Dumpty together again, then what I need is *more* horses and *more* men!'"[48]

Many experts in the field of drug abuse view the solution not to be in foreign countries, at U.S. borders, or in U.S. prisons, but in the communities of the United States. One political scientist has put it this way: "If the 'war' is to be won, it will be won in the hearts and minds of people who might be inclined to consume drugs."

Members of the U.S. Coast Guard law enforcement team gather in Miami around more than 5,000 pounds of cocaine seized from a Honduran fishing boat off the coast of Colombia. The drugs were discovered hidden in compartments within the fuel tank, and eight Colombians were arrested. The 110-foot boat was later towed to Miami and confiscated.

Health Line

Harm Reduction as a National Drug-Abuse Policy

To say that we are waging a "war on drugs" is, in effect, communicating how serious we are in dealing with the problems of drug abuse in the United States. Using the metaphor of warfare, we recognize that there is an acknowledged enemy (drug misuse and abuse), there are victims or casualties (us), there are resources at our disposal to fight the necessary battles (federal and state governments, communities, parents, etc.), and there is a high price to pay (billions of dollars of federal funds each year).

The implications of this real-life struggle, such as our overall strategy and ultimate goals, are also drawn in metaphorical terms. Do we want total victory and complete annihilation of the enemy? Or do we want some kind of negotiated settlement, some type of compromise that gives us some semblance of peace and tranquility? If it is the former, then we require a total elimination, often expressed as "zero tolerance" of abusive drug-taking behavior in America. If it is the latter, then we require a good deal less. We desire, in that case, only a reduction of the harmful consequences of abusive drug-taking behavior, knowing fully well that a total elimination is unrealistic and perhaps unattainable. The second alternative is referred to as the Harm Reduction approach. Whether we choose a harm-reduction approach or an approach based on zero tolerance is the essence of our deliberation on a national drug-abuse policy.

The harm-reduction approach in drug policy has its historical roots in the libertarian philosophy of the nineteenth-century philosopher John Stuart Mill, who argued that the state did not have the duty to protect individual citizens from harming themselves. As Mill expressed it,

> The only purpose for which power can be rightfully executed over any member of a civilized community, against his will, is to prevent harm to others. His own good, either physical or moral, is not a sufficient warrant. . . . Over himself, over his own body and mind, the individual is sovereign.

It is readily evident, however, that drug-taking behavior does indeed harm other people. The question, according to those advocating a harm-reduction strategy, is to look for policies that reduce the harm that drugs do, both directly to the drug user and indirectly to others.

Examples of the Harm Reduction approach include needle-exchange programs to lower the incidence of HIV infection among intravenous drug abusers (see Chapter 2), methadone maintenance programs for the treatment of heroin abusers (see Chapter 5), efforts to reduce the incidence of driving while under the influence of alcohol (see Chapter 10), and the use of nicotine patches to avoid the effects of cigarette smoking such as emphysema and lung cancer (see Chapter 12). A more controversial application of the Harm Reduction approach is the suggestion that we should attempt to reduce the level of heavy drug use down to a level of occasional use, rather than no use at all.

With regard to cigarette smoking and marijuana use, there is an indication that some teenagers may already be "harm reducing." In the University of Michigan survey, high school seniors engaging in occasional marijuana smoking and occasional cigarette smoking indicated a higher perceived risk of "regular substance use" than did high school seniors engaging in heavy use, even though there was no difference in the perceived risk of "occasional substance use." In other words, occasional users may have been moderating their behavior to minimize the harmful effects they associated with heavy drug-taking behavior. Whether a prevention program that emphasizes the risks of heavy drug use, as opposed to emphasizing the risks of any level of use, is the more successful strategy in reducing significant levels of drug-taking behavior is a question that advocates of the Harm Reduction approach will be investigating in the future with great interest.

Sources: Denning, Patt (2003). *Over the influence: The harm reduction guide for managing drugs and alcohol.* New York: Gullford Press. Des Jarlais, Don C. (2000). Prospects for a public health perspective on psychoactive drug use. *American Journal of Public Health, 90,* 335–337. How did we get here? History has a habit of repeating itself (2001, July 28–August 3). *Economist,* pp. 4–5. Quotation of John Stuart Mill on page 5. Levinthal, Charles F. (2003). Question: Should harm reduction be our overall goal in fighting drug abuse? *Point/Counterpoint: Opposing perspectives on issues of drug policy.* Boston: Allyn and Bacon, pp. 70–73. Marlatt, G. Alan (Ed.) (2002). *Harm reduction: Pragmatic strategies for managing high-risk behaviors.* New York: Gullford Press. Resnicow, Ken; Smith, Matt; Harrison, Lana; and Drucker, Ernest (1999). Correlates of occasional cigarette and marijuana use. Are teens harm reducing? *Addictive Behaviors, 24,* 251–266.

A recommendation gaining increasing support would shift the emphasis from "use reduction" to "harm reduction," acknowledging that drugs may never be absent from our society (Health Line).[49]

The public policy issues surrounding the "demand" side of the drug abuse equation, particularly as it pertains to drug-abuse treatment and prevention, will be considered in greater detail in Chapters 17 and 18.

Summary

Drug Toxicity

- A drug's harmful effects are referred to as its toxicity. Acute toxicity can be measured in terms of a drug's therapeutic index or its margin of safety, each of which can be computed from its effective and lethal dose-response curves.

The DAWN Reports

- Drug Abuse Warning Network (DAWN) statistics, which reflect drug-related lethal and nonlethal emergencies in major metropolitan hospitals in the United States, offer another measure of acute drug toxicity. In general, DAWN statistics show that cocaine and narcotic drugs are both highly toxic and that many emergencies involve drugs being taken in combination with alcohol. There are also recent concerns for the increasing number of emergencies associated with club drugs and opiate-based pain-relief medications.

Behavioral Tolerance and Drug Overdose

- A tolerance effect is the capacity of a drug to have a gradually diminished effect over repeated administrations; in effect, a greater dose has to be taken to maintain the original effect of the drug. Tolerance effects can be quite dangerous, since experienced drug users often end up taking potentially lethal dose levels.
- The setting within which drug-taking behavior occurs is an important factor in behavioral tolerance. Behavioral tolerance effects are based on the principles of Pavlovian conditioning.

Physical and Psychological Dependence

- Drugs can be viewed in terms of a physical dependence model, in which the compulsive drug-taking behavior is tied to an avoidance of withdrawal symptoms, or a psychological dependence model, in which the drug-taking behavior is tied to a genuine craving for the drug and highly reinforcing effects of the drug on the user's body and mind.

Psychiatric Definitions

- The American Psychiatric Association currently recognizes two major conditions associated with drug-taking behavior: substance dependence and substance abuse. The broader term "substance" is used instead of "drug," because there is often confusion in the public mind in deciding what is defined as a drug and what is not.

Special Problems in Drug Abuse

- Increasing attention has been directed toward the harmful effects that drug abuse has on pregnant women, in terms of problems with the pregnancy itself and with the neural development of the fetus.
- There is also concern with the increased risk of HIV infection (and the spread of AIDS) among intravenous drug users when needles are shared.

Drugs, Violence, and Crime

- While there is an overall association between the taking of illicit drugs and crime, a careful analysis indicates that the drug with the closest connection to social violence is alcohol, and that heroin and marijuana cause the user to be less inclined toward violent behavior rather than more so.
- It is clear that drug abuse forces many drug users to commit criminal acts (generally property theft) to support the drug habit. It is also clear that there is a high level of social violence and criminal behavior inherent in the trafficking and distribution of illicit drugs.

Governmental Policy, Regulation, and Laws

- Since the beginning of the twentieth century, U.S. society's philosophy toward drug-taking behavior has been that we should restrict it by reducing the availability of illicit drugs and making it as difficult as possible for the potential drug user to engage in drug-taking behavior.
- The Harrison Act of 1914 was the first of several legislative efforts to impose criminal penalties on the use of opiates and cocaine and later marijuana, hallucinogens, and several other types of drugs.
- The Comprehensive Drug Act of 1970 organized the federal control of drugs under five classifications called schedules. Overall planning and implementation of drug policy in the United States now originates from the White House Office of Drug Control Policy.

Enforcement of Drug Laws on a Global Scale

- Today's drug-law-enforcement program in the United States places considerable emphasis upon the interdiction of drugs entering the country, with less emphasis upon treatment and prevention of drug abuse.
- Attempts to reduce the influx of illicit drugs into the United States are complicated by a series of economic and political factors on a global scale. For

example, a major trade route for heroin, cocaine, and marijuana continues to exist through Mexico, despite that nation's status as a principal trading partner for a range of legitimate products and services. An international strategy with respect to nations involved in illicit drug production and/or trafficking that is consistent with U.S. national security concerns has been difficult to achieve.

Key Terms

acute toxicity, p. 32
Arrestee Drug Abuse Monitoring (ADAM) Program, p. 46
behavioral tolerance, p. 39
catheter, p. 42
chronic toxicity, p. 38
dose, p. 32

dose-response curve, p. 32
Drug Abuse Warning Network (DAWN), p. 35
drug-related ED visit, p. 35
economically compulsive violence, p. 48
effective dose (ED), p. 32
laissez-faire, p. 50

lethal dose (LD), p. 32
margin of safety, p. 32
pharmacological violence, p. 47
physical dependence, p. 41
psychological dependence, p. 41
substance abuse, p. 43

substance dependence, p. 43
systemic violence, p. 49
therapeutic index, p. 32
tolerance, p. 39
toxicity, p. 32

Endnotes

1. Inciardi, James A. (1990). The crack–violence connection within a population of hard-core adolescent offenders. In Mario De La Rosa, Elizabeth Y. Lambert, and Bernard Gropper (Eds.), *Drugs and violence: Causes, correlates, and consequences* (NIDA Research Monograph 103). Rockville, MD: National Institute on Drug Abuse, pp. 92–111. Quotation on pp. 98–99.

2. The Gallup Organization (2005, April 5). Drug use still among Americans' top worries. Gallup Organization, Princeton NJ. Gross, Jane (2008, March 6). New generation gap emerges as older addicts seek help. *New York Times*, pp. A1, A24. Martin, S. (2001, June). Substance abuse is nation's number one health problem, but there is hope. *Monitor on Psychology*, p. 10.

3. Cummings, Nicholas A. (1979). Turning bread into stone: Our modern antimiracle. *American Psychologist*, 34, 1119–1129.

4. Treaster, Joseph B., and Holloway, Lynette (1994, September 4). Potent new blend of heroin ends eight very different lives. *New York Times*, pp. 1, 37.

5. Substance Abuse and Mental Health Services Administration (2008). *Drug Abuse Warning Network, 2006. National estimates of drug-related emergency department visits*. Rockville, MD: Office of Applied Studies, Substance Abuse and Mental Health Services Administration. Substance Abuse and Mental Health Services Administration (2008). *Drug Abuse Warning Network, 2004: Area profiles of drug related mortality*. Rockville, MD: Office of Applied Studies, Substance Abuse and Mental Health Services Administration.

6. Substance Abuse, *National estimates of drug-related emergency department visits*, Table 1.

7. Ibid, Table 6 and page 8.

8. Ibid, Table 2.

9. Substance Abuse, *Area profiles of drug-related mortality*, pp. 48–49, 68–69, 78–79, 96–97, and 102–103.

10. Substance Abuse and Mental Health Administration (2004, July). Club drugs, 2002 update. *DAWN Report*, p. 3. Substance Abuse and Mental Health Administration (2004, July). Oxycodone, hydrocodone, and polydrug use, 2002. *DAWN Report*, p. 1.

11. Lankester, E. Ray (1889). Mithridatism. *Nature*, 40, 149.

12. Siegel, Shepard (1990). Drug anticipation and the treatment of dependence. In Barbara A. Ray (Ed.), *Learning factors in substance abuse* (NIDA Research Monograph 84). Rockville, MD: National Institute on Drug Abuse, pp. 1–24.

13. Gerevich, József; Bácskai, Erika; Farkas, Lajos; and Danics, Zoltán (2005). A case report: Pavlovian conditioning as a risk factor of heroin "overdose" death. *Harm Reduction Journal*, 2. Siegel, Shepard (1975). Evidence from rats that morphine tolerance is a learned response. *Journal of Comparative and Physiological Psychology*, 89, 489–506.

14. Brecher, Edward M., and the editors of *Consumer Reports*. (1972). *Licit and illicit drugs*. Mount Vernon, NY: Consumers Union.

15. Siegel, Shepard (1999). Drug anticipation and drug addiction. The 1998 H. David Archibald Lecture. *Addiction*, 94, 1113–1124.

16. Jaffe, Jerome H. (1985). Drug addiction and drug abuse. In Alfred G. Gilman, Louis S. Goodman, Theodore W. Rall, and Ferid Murad (Eds.), *The pharmacological basis of therapeutics*. New York: Macmillan, pp. 532–581.

17. Blum, Kenneth. (1991). *Alcohol and the addictive brain*. New York, Free Press, p. 17.

18. Pinel, John P. J. (2003). *Biopsychology* (5th ed.). Boston: Allyn and Bacon, p. 398.

19. Simpson, D. Dwayne, and Marsh, Kerry L. (1986). Relapse and recovery among opioid addicts 12 years after treatment. In Frank M. Tims and Carl G. Leukefeld (Eds.), *Relapse and recovery in drug abuse* (NIDA Research Monograph 72). Rockville, MD: National Institute on Drug Abuse, pp. 86–103. Simpson, D. Dwayne, and Sells, Saul B. (1982). Effectiveness of treatment for drug abuse: An overview of the DARP research program. *Advances in Alcohol and Substance Abuse, 2*, 7–29.

20. Halikas, James A. (1997). Craving. In Joyce H. Lowinson, Pedro Ruiz, Robert B. Millman, and John G. Langrod (Eds.), *Substance abuse: A comprehensive textbook* (3rd ed.). Baltimore: Williams & Wilkins, pp. 85–90. Pickens, Roy, and Thompson, Travis (1968). Cocaine-reinforced behavior in rats: Effects of reinforcement magnitude and fixed-ratio size. *Journal of Pharmacology and Experimental Therapeutics, 161*, 122–129.

21. Hoffmeister, F. H., and Wuttke, W. (1975). Psychotropic drugs as negative reinforcers. *Pharmacological Reviews, 27*, 419–428. Yokel, R. A. (1987). Intravenous self-administration: Response rates, the effect of pharmacological challenges and drug preferences. In Michael A. Bozarth (Ed.), *Methods of assessing the reinforcing properties of abused drugs.* New York: Springer-Verlag, pp. 1–34.

22. Johanson, Chris E. (1984). Assessment of the abuse potential of cocaine in animals. In John Grabowski (Ed.), *Cocaine: Pharmacology, effects, and treatment of abuse.* Rockville, MD: National Institute on Drug Abuse, pp. 54–71.

23. Quotation from Goode, Erich. (1999). *Drugs in American society* (5th ed.). New York: McGraw-Hill, p. 47. Data from Bozarth, Michael A., and Wise, Roy A. (1985). Toxicity associated with long-term intravenous heroin and cocaine self-administration in the rat. *Journal of the American Medical Association, 254*, 81–83.

24. American Psychiatric Association (2000). *Diagnostic and statistical manual, Text Revision* (4th ed.). Washington DC: American Psychiatric Association, pp. 191, 197, and 199.

25. Substance Abuse and Mental Health Services Administration (2008). *Results from the 2007 National Survey on Drug Use and Health: National findings.* Rockville, MD: Office of Applied Studies, Substance Abuse and Mental Health Services Administration, pp. 24, 33, and 45.

26. Cook, Paddy S., Petersen, Robert C., and Moore, Dorothy T. (1990). *Alcohol, tobacco, and other drugs may harm the unborn.* Washington DC: Office of Substance Abuse Prevention.

27. Riehman, Kara S. (1996, October). Injecting drug use and AIDS in developing countries: Determinants and issues for policy consideration. Background paper for the Policy Research Report *Confronting AIDS.* World Bank, Policy Research Department. Stimson, Gerry V. (1991, May). The prevention of HIV infection in injecting drug users: Recent advances and remaining obstacles. *Newsletter of the International Working Group on AIDS and Drug Use, 5*, 14–19.

28. Department of Health and Human Services (1999). *Drug abuse and addiction research: 25 years of discovery to advance the health of the public. The sixth triennial report to Congress from the Secretary of Health and Human Services.* Washington DC: Department of Health and Human Services.

29. Department of Health and Human Services (1998, April 20). Research shows needle exchange programs reduce HIV infections without increasing drug use. Public announcement. Garrett, Laurie (1997, February 19). Needle exchange debate. *Newsday*, p. A19. National Institute on Drug Abuse (1995). *Cooperative agreement for AIDS community-based outreach/intervention research program, 1990–present.* Rockville MD: National Institute on Drug Abuse.

30. National Institute of Justice (2005). 2003 annual report on drug and alcohol use and related matters among arrestees. Washington DC: Arrestee Drug Abuse Monitoring Program, Department of Justice, Tables 3, 6, 7, and 8.

31. De La Rosa, Mario, Lambert, Elizabeth Y., and Gropper, Bernard (1990). Introduction: Exploring the substance abuse-violence connection. In *Drugs and violence: Causes, correlates, and consequences* (NIDA Research Monograph 103). Rockville, MD: National Institute on Drug Abuse, pp. 1–7.

32. Roth, Jeffrey A. (1994, February). Psychoactive substances and violence: Research brief. Washington DC: National Institute of Justice.

33. Gold, Mark S. (1991). *The good news about drugs and alcohol: Curing, treating and preventing substance abuse in the new age of biopsychiatry.* New York: Villard Books.

34. Koss, Mary P. (1988). Hidden rape: Sexual aggression and victimization in a national sample of students in higher education. In A. W. Burgess (Ed.), *Rape and sexual assault II.* New York: Garland, pp. 3–25. Mohler-Kuo, Meichun; Dowdall, George W.; Koss, Mary P.; and Wechsler, Henry (2004). Correlates of rape while intoxicated in a national sample of college women. *Journal of Studies on Alcohol, 65*, 37–45. Goode, *Drugs* (5th ed.), pp. 153–158. Roth, *Psychoactive substances.* White, Helene Raskin, and Cehn, Ping-Hsen (2002). Problem drinking and intimate partner violence. *Journal of Studies on Alcohol, 63*, 205–214.

35. Harris, Jonathan (1991). *Drugged America.* New York: Four Winds Press, p. 112.

36. White, Jason M. (1991). *Drug dependence.* Englewood Cliffs, NJ: Prentice-Hall, p. 200.

37. Inciardi, The crack–violence connection.

38. Silverman, Lester P., and Spruill, Nancy L. (1977). Urban crime and the price of heroin. *Journal of Urban Economics, 4*, 80–103.

39. Inciardi, James A. (1995). Crack, crack house sex, and HIV risk. *Archives of Sexual Behavior, 24*, 249–269.

McCoy, Virginia H.; Inciardi, James A.; Metsch, Lisa R.; Pottieger, Anne; and Saum, Christine A. (1995). Women, crack, and crime: Gender comparisons of criminal activity among crack cocaine users. *Contemporary Drug Problems, 22* (3), 435–452.

40. Inciardi, The crack–violence connection. Substance Abuse and Mental Health Services Administration (2001, November 9). Youth violence linked to substance use. *The NHSDA Report,* p. 3. Surrat, Hilary L.; Inciardi, James A.; Kurtz, Stephen, P.; and Kiley, Marion C. (2004). Sex work and drug use in a subculture of violence. *Crime and Delinquency, 50,* 43–59.

41. Fagan, Jeffry, and Chin, Ko-lin (1990). Violence as regulation and social control in the distribution of crack. In Mario De La Rosa, Elizabeth Y. Lambert, and Bernard Gropper (Eds.), *Drugs and violence: Causes, correlates, and consequences* (NIDA Research Monograph 103). Rockville, MD: National Institute on Drug Abuse, pp. 8–43. Office of Juvenile Justice and Delinquency Prevention (1999, July). *1996 national youth gang survey. Summary.* Washington DC: U.S. Department of Justice, pp. 38–39.

42. Blumstein, Alfred, and Rosenfeld, Richard (1998, October). Assessing the recent ups and downs in U.S. homicide rates. *National Institute of Justice Journal,* 9–11. Curtis, Richard (1998, October). The improbable transformation of inner-city neighborhoods: Crime, violence, drugs, and youths in the 1990s. *National Institute of Justice Journal,* 16–17. Quotation on p. 17. Harris, *Drugged America,* p. 117.

43. Bugliosi, Vincent T. (1991). *Drugs in America: A citizen's call to action.* New York: Knightsbridge Publishing, p. 25.

44. Brecher. *Licit and illicit drugs,* pp. 6–7.

45. Office of National Drug Control Policy (2008, February). Executive summary. *National Drug Control Strategy: FY 2009 Budget Summary.* Washington DC: White House Office of National Drug Control Policy, Table 1.

46. Forero, Juan (2006, August 19). Colombia's coca survives U.S. plan to uproot it. *New York Times,* pp. A1, A8. Janofsky, Michael (2002, March 6). Border agents on lookout for terrorists are finding drugs. *New York Times,* p. A14. Johnson, Kevin (2003, August 7). Drugs invade via Indian land: Lightly patrolled reservations make inviting entry points for smugglers. *USA Today,* pp. 1A–2A. Office of National Drug Control Policy (2008, February). *The President's National Drug Control Strategy.* Washington DC: White House Office of National Drug Control Policy, Table 1.

47. Moreau, Ron, and Yousafkai, Sami (2006, January 9). A harvest of treachery. *Newsweek,* pp. 32–35. Rohde, David (2002, October 28). Afghans lead world again in poppy crop. *New York Times,* p. A8.

48. Herbert Kleber, quoted in Joseph B. Treaster. (1992, June 14). Twenty years of war on drugs, and no victory yet. *New York Times,* p. E7.

49. Alter, Jonathan (1999, September 9). The buzz on drugs. *Newsweek,* pp. 24–28. Gray, James P. (2001). *Why our drug laws have failed and what we can do about it: A judicial indictment on the war on drugs.* Philadelphia: Temple University Press. Goldstein, Avram (2001). *Addiction: From biology to drug policy* (2nd ed.). New York: Oxford University Press, pp. 307–328. F. LaMond Tullis, quoted in Treaster, Joseph B. (1992, June 14). Twenty years of war on drugs. *New York Times,* p. E7. Marlatt, G. Alan (1996). Harm reduction: Come as you are. *Addictive Behaviors, 21,* 779–788.

chapter 3

How Drugs Work in the Body and on the Mind

After you have completed this chapter, you will understand

- The ways drugs enter and exit the body
- Factors determining the physiological impact of drugs
- The sympathetic and parasympathetic branches of the autonomic nervous system
- The basic organization of the brain
- How neurons work and how they communicate with each other
- The functions of seven major neurotransmitters in the brain
- Explanations of drug actions on neurotransmitters
- Tolerance effects and psychological dependence
- The placebo effect in drug-taking behavior

His brain can be held in one hand, easily in two. It looks like a grayish-colored wrinkled blob, about three pounds in weight. It doesn't pulsate with life like his heart.

Not terribly impressive, you might say—now that he is no longer alive. Yet here was this man's entire life, all the years of memories, his talents and aspirations, his virtues and his shortcomings. And here, at one time, were all the chemicals and billions of neurons that made it work.

If you believe that this man had a soul and the soul had a place, this is where it was.

—*A neurosurgeon reflecting on a human brain and a human mind*

Some of you might have heard of the classic public-service announcement, which aired frequently on television in the late 1980s:

This is your brain (view of egg held in hand).

This is drugs (view of sizzling frying pan).

This is your brain on drugs (view of egg frying in pan).

Any questions?[1]

Giving the viewer considerable "food for thought," this message had an immediate impact: Don't do drugs because they fry your brain. The creators of this message were speaking metaphorically, of course. In effect, they were saying that there are certain classes of drugs that have a devastating impact on the human brain. Therefore, stay away from them.

It was a good message to convey. At the same time, an equally important message is that there are other classes of drugs that have enormously beneficial effects on the brain. Drugs are used to treat major mental illnesses such as schizophrenia and depression (see Chapter 16) and play a major role in reducing pain and relieving feelings of anxiety (see Chapters 5 and 15). Whether drugs in general have a positive or negative effect on us depends, at least in part, upon how they interact with physiological processes in the body.

As noted in Chapter 1, psychoactive drugs affect our behavior and experience through their effects on the functioning of the brain. Therefore, our knowledge about drugs and their effects is closely connected with the progress we have made in our understanding of the ways drugs work in the brain. This chapter will describe the basic functions of the nervous system and the ways in which drugs alter these functions. It will serve as a foundation for understanding specific classes of drugs covered in the chapters that follow.

A reasonable place to start is to address the question: How do drugs get into the body in the first place?

How Drugs Enter the Body

There are four principal routes through which drugs can be delivered into the body: *oral administration, injection, inhalation,* and *absorption through the skin or membranes.* In all four delivery methods, the goal is for the drug to be absorbed into the bloodstream. In the case of psychoactive drugs, a drug effect depends not only on reaching the bloodstream but on reaching the brain as well.

Oral Administration

Ingesting a drug by mouth, digesting it, and absorbing it into the bloodstream through the gastrointestinal tract is the oldest and easiest way of taking a drug. On the one hand, oral administration and reliance upon the digestive process for delivering a drug into the bloodstream provides a degree of safety. Many naturally growing poisons taste so vile that we normally spit them out before swallowing; others will cause us to be nauseous and the drug will be expelled through vomiting.

---

by the numbers . . .

100 billion	Estimated number of neurons in the human brain
10 trillion	Estimated number of synapses in the human brain
250,000	Neurons created each minute, on average, during nine months of pre-natal development
20–25	Approximate wattage of a lightbulb that is equivalent to the total electrical power generated by the brain

---

Sources: Kalat, James W. (2004). *Biological Psychology* (8th ed.). Belmont, CA: Wadsworth/ Thomson Learning, p. 89. Kety, Seymour (1961). Energy metabolism of the brain during sleep. In G.E.W. Wolstenhome and M.O'Connor (Eds.). *CIBA Foundation Symposium on the nature of sleep.* Boston: Little, Brown, pp. 375–381. Thompson, Richard F. (1993). *The brain: A neuroscience primer* (2nd ed.). New York: Freeman, pp. 75, 299.

Alcohol is easily absorbed into the bloodstream and the brain. For other orally consumed drugs, however, absorption is relatively slow, because they must first be processed by the digestive system.

In the case of hazardous substances that are not spontaneously rejected, we can benefit from a relatively long absorption time for orally administered drugs. Most of the absorption process is accomplished between five and thirty minutes after ingestion, but absorption is not usually complete for as long as six to eight hours. Therefore, there is at least a little time after accidental overdoses or suicide attempts to induce vomiting or pump the stomach.

On the other hand, the gastrointestinal tract contains a number of natural barriers that prevent certain drugs that we *want* absorbed into the bloodstream from doing so. We first have to consider the degree of alkalinity or acidity in a drug, defined as its pH value. The interior of the stomach is highly acidic and the fate of a particular drug depends upon how it reacts with that environment. Weakly acidic drugs such as aspirin are absorbed better in the stomach than highly alkaline drugs such as morphine, heroin, or cocaine. Insulin is destroyed by stomach acid so it cannot be administered orally, whereas a neutral substance like alcohol is readily absorbed at all points in the gastrointestinal tract.

If it survives the stomach, the drug needs to proceed from the small intestine into the bloodstream. The membrane separating the intestinal wall from blood capillaries is made up of two layers of fat molecules, making it necessary for substances to be *lipid-soluble*, or soluble in fats, to pass through. Even after successful absorption into blood capillaries, however, substances must still pass through the liver for a "screening process" before being released into the general circulation. Enzymes in the liver are capable of breaking down (metabolizing) the molecular structure of certain drugs, thus reducing the amount that eventually enters the bloodstream. This function of the liver, referred to as *first-pass metabolism*, plays an essential role in protecting us from potentially toxic substances that might have been ingested by mouth.[2] A further barrier, which separates the circulatory system from brain tissue itself, will be discussed in a later section.

As a result of all these natural barriers, orally administered drugs must be ingested at deliberately elevated dose levels, to allow for the fact that some proportion of the drug will not make it through to the bloodstream. We can try to compensate for the loss of the drug during digestion, but even then we are often only making a good guess. The internal state of the gastrointestinal tract changes constantly over time, making it more or less likely that a drug will reach the circulatory system. The presence or absence of undigested food, whether the undigested food interacts with the chemical nature of the drug, and the activity level of specific liver enzymes that control the absorption of the drug into the bloodstream are examples of factors that make it difficult to make exact predictions about the strength of the drug when it finally enters the bloodstream.

Injection

A solution to the problems of oral administration is to bypass the digestive process entirely and deliver the drug more directly into the bloodstream. One option is to inject the drug through a hypodermic syringe and needle.

The fastest means of injection is an **intravenous (i.v.)** injection, since the drug is delivered into a vein without any intermediary tissue. An intravenous injection of heroin in the forearm, for example, arrives at the brain in less than fifteen seconds. The effects of abused drugs delivered in this way, often called *mainlining*, are not only rapid but extremely intense. In a medical setting, intravenous injections provide an extreme amount of control over dosage and the opportunity to administer multiple drugs at the same time. The principal disadvantage, however, is that the effects of intravenous drugs are irreversible. In the event of a mistake or unexpected reaction, there is no turning back unless some other drug is available that can counteract the first one. In addition, repeated injections through a particular vein may cause the vein to collapse or develop a blood clot.

With **intramuscular (i.m.)** injections, the drug is delivered into a large muscle (usually in the upper arm, thigh, or buttock) and is absorbed into the bloodstream through the capillaries serving the muscle. Intramuscular injections have slower absorption times than intravenous injections, but they can be administered more rapidly in emergency situations. Our exposure to intramuscular injections comes early in our lives when we receive the standard schedule of inoculations against diseases such as measles, diphtheria, and typhoid fever. Tetanus and flu shots are also administered in this way.

A third injection technique is the **subcutaneous (s.c. or sub-Q)** delivery, in which a needle is inserted into the tissue just underneath the skin. Because the skin has a less abundant blood supply relative to a muscle, a subcutaneous injection has the slowest absorption time of all the injection techniques. It is best suited for situations in

intravenous (i.v.): Into a vein.

intramuscular (i.m.): Into a muscle.

subcutaneous (s.c. or sub-Q): Underneath the skin.

which it is desirable to have a precise control over the dosage and a steady absorption into the bloodstream. The skin, however, may be easily irritated by this procedure. As a result, only relatively small amounts of a drug can be injected under the skin, compared to the quantity that can be injected into a muscle or vein. When involved in drug abuse, subcutaneous injections are often referred to as *skin-popping*.

All injections require a needle to pierce the skin, so there is an inherent risk of bacterial or viral infection if the needle is not sterile. The practice of injecting heroin or cocaine with shared needles, for example, promotes the spread of infectious hepatitis and AIDS (see Chapter 2). If administered orally, drugs do not have to be any more sterile than the foods we eat or the water we drink.

Inhalation

Next to ingesting a drug by mouth, the simplest way of receiving its effects is to inhale it in some form of gaseous or vaporous state. The alveoli within the lungs can be imagined as a huge surface area with blood vessels lying immediately behind it. Our bodies are so dependent upon the oxygen in the air we breathe that we have evolved an extremely efficient system for getting oxygen to its destinations. As a consequence of this highly developed system, the psychoactive effect of an inhaled drug is even faster than a drug delivered through intravenous injection. Traveling from the lungs to the brain takes only five to eight seconds.

One way of delivering a drug through inhalation is to burn it and breathe in the smoke-borne particles in the air. Drugs administered through smoking include nicotine from cigarettes, opium, tetrahydrocannabinol (THC) from marijuana, free-base cocaine, crack cocaine, and crystallized forms of methamphetamine. Drugs such as paint thinners, gasoline, and glues can also be inhaled because they evaporate easily and the vapors travel freely through the air. In medical settings, general anesthetics are administered through inhalation, since the concentration of the drug can be precisely controlled.

The principal disadvantage of inhaling smoked drugs, as you probably expect, arises from the long-term hazards of breathing particles in the air that contain not only the active drug but also tars and other substances produced by the burning process. Emphysema, asthma, and lung cancer can result from smoking in general (see Chapter 11). There is also the possibility in any form of drug inhalation that the linings leading from the throat to the lungs will be severely irritated over time.

Drugs consumed by inhalation are absorbed extremely quickly, aided by a very efficient delivery system from the alveoli in the lungs to the bloodstream and from the bloodstream to the brain.

Absorption through the Skin or Membranes

Drug users over the ages have been quite creative in finding other routes through which drugs can be administered. One way is to sniff or snort a drug in dust or powder form into the nose. Once inside the nose, it adheres to thin mucous membranes and dissolves through the membranes into the bloodstream. This technique, referred to as an **intranasal** administration, is commonly used in taking snuff tobacco or cocaine. Prescription medications are becoming increasingly available in nasal-spray formulations, avoiding the need for needle injections or difficult-to-swallow pills.

Snuff tobacco, chewing tobacco, and cocaine-containing coca leaves can also be chewed without swallowing over a period of time or simply placed in the inner surface of the cheek and slowly absorbed through the membranes of the mouth. Nicotine chewing gums, available for those individuals who wish to quit tobacco smoking, work in a similar way. Nitroglycerin tablets for heart disease patients are typically administered

intranasal: Applied to the mucous membranes of the nose.

sublingually, with the drug placed underneath the tongue and absorbed into the bloodstream.

At the opposite end of the body, medicines can be placed as a suppository into the rectum, where the suppository gradually melts and the medicine is absorbed through thin rectal membranes. This method is less reliable than an oral administration, but it may be necessary if the individual is vomiting or unconscious.

Another absorption technique involves a **transdermal patch,** which allows a drug to slowly diffuse through the skin without breaking the skin surface. Transdermal patches have been used for long-term administration of nitroglycerin, estrogen, nicotine, and medications for motion sickness, Parkinson's disease, and Alzheimer's disease. Newly developed procedures to enhance the process of skin penetration include the promising technique of administering low-frequency ultrasound, which allows large molecules such as insulin to pass through the skin. Insulin administration is an especially interesting application because, until now, the only effective way of getting it into the bloodstream has been through needle injection. Alternative methods under development include small silicon chip patches containing a grid of microscopic needles that painlessly pierce the skin and allow the passage of large molecules into the bloodstream. Other techniques involve a mild electric current that propels the medication through the skin or the application of medication with special compounds that help the medication slip through skin pores.[3]

Drugs . . . in Focus summarizes the various ways drugs can be administered into the body.

How Drugs Exit the Body

Having reviewed how a drug is absorbed into the bloodstream and, in the case of a psychoactive drug, into the brain, we now will consider the ways in which the body eliminates it. The most common means of elimination is through excretion in the urine after a series of actions in the liver and kidneys. Additionally, elimination occurs through excretion in exhaled breath, feces, sweat, saliva, or (in the case of nursing mothers) breast milk.

The sequence of metabolic events leading to urinary excretion begins with a process called **biotransformation,** chiefly through the action of specific enzymes in the liver. The products of biotransformation, referred to as **metabolites,** are structurally modified forms of the original drug. Generally speaking, if these metabolites are water-soluble, they are passed along to the kidneys and eventually excreted in the urine. If they are less water-soluble, then they are reabsorbed into the intestines and excreted through defecation. On rare occasions, a drug may pass through the liver without any biotransformation at all and be excreted intact. The hallucinogenic drug *Amanita muscaria* is an example of this kind of drug (see Chapter 6).

A number of factors influence the process of biotransformation and urinary excretion and, in turn, the rate of elimination from the body. For most drugs, biotransformation rates will increase as a function of the drug's concentration in the bloodstream. In effect, the larger the quantity of a drug, the faster the body tries to get rid of it. An exception, however, is alcohol, for which the rate of biotransformation is constant no matter how much alcohol has been ingested (see Chapter 9).

The activity of enzymes required for biotransformation may be increased or decreased by the presence of other drugs in the body. As a result, the effect of one drug may interact with the effect of another, creating a potentially dangerous combination. An individual's age can also be a factor. Because enzyme activity in the liver declines after the age of forty, older people eliminate drugs at a slower pace than do younger people. We will look at the consequences of drug interactions and individual differences in the next section of this chapter.

Finally, it is important to point out that drugs are gradually eliminated from the body at different rates simply on the basis of their chemical properties. In general, if a drug is fat-soluble, the rate will be slower than if a drug is water-soluble. On average, we can look at the rate of elimination of a particular drug through an index called its **elimination half-life,** the amount of time it takes for the drug in the bloodstream to decline to 50 percent of its original equilibrium level. Many drugs such as cocaine and nicotine have half-lives of only a few hours; marijuana and some prescription medications are examples of drugs with much longer half-lives.[4] Understanding the variation in the elimination rates of drugs and their metabolites is extremely important in the development of drug-testing procedures to detect drug-taking behavior, a topic to be examined in Chapter 8.

sublingual: Applied under the tongue.

transdermal patch: A device attached to the skin that slowly delivers the drug through skin absorption.

biotransformation: The process of changing the molecular structure of a drug into forms that make it easier to be excreted from the body.

metabolite (me-TAB-oh-lite): A by-product resulting from the biotransformation process.

elimination half-life: The length of time it takes for a drug to be reduced to 50 percent of its equilibrium level in the bloodstream.

Drugs...in Focus

Ways to Take Drugs: Routes of Administration

Oral Administration (by Mouth)

- Method: By swallowing or consuming in eating or drinking
- Advantages: Slow absorption time; possibility of rejecting poisons and overdoses
- Disadvantages: Slow absorption time; no immediate effect
- Examples: Medications in pill form, marijuana (baked in food), amphetamine and methamphetamine, barbiturates, LSD (swallowed or licked off paper), PCP, opium, methadone, codeine, caffeine, alcohol

Injection (by Hypodermic Syringe)

Intravenous Injection

- Method: By needle positioned into a vein
- Advantages: Very fast absorption time; immediate effects
- Disadvantages: Cannot be undone; risks of allergic reactions
- Examples: PCP, methamphetamine, heroin, methadone, morphine

Intramuscular Injection

- Method: By needle positioned into a large muscle
- Advantages: Quicker to administer than an intravenous injection
- Disadvantages: Somewhat slower absorption time than an intravenous injection; risk of piercing a vein by accident
- Examples: Vaccine inoculations

Subcutaneous Injection

- Method: By needle positioned underneath the skin
- Advantages: Easiest administration of all injection techniques

- Disadvantages: Slower absorption time than an intramuscular injection; risk of skin irritation and deterioration
- Examples: Heroin and other narcotics

Inhalation (by Breathing)

Smoking

- Method: By burning drug and breathing smoke-borne particles into the lungs
- Advantages: Extremely fast absorption time
- Disadvantages: Effect limited to time during which drug is being inhaled; risk of emphysema, asthma, and lung cancer from inhaling tars and hydrocarbons in the smoke; lung and throat irritation over chronic use
- Examples: Nicotine (from tobacco), marijuana, hashish, methamphetamine, ice, free-base cocaine, crack cocaine, PCP, heroin, and opium

Vaporous Inhalation

- Method: By breathing in vapors from drug
- Advantages: Extremely fast absorption time
- Disadvantages: Effect limited to time during which drug is being inhaled; lung and throat irritation over chronic use
- Examples: Surgical and dental anesthetics, paint thinners, gasoline, cleaning fluid

Absorption (through Skin or Membranes)

- Method: By positioning drug against skin, inserting it against rectal membrane, snorting it against mucous membranes of the nose, or placing it under the tongue or against the cheek so it diffuses across into bloodstream
- Advantages: Quick absorption time
- Disadvantages: Irritation of skin or membranes
- Examples: Cocaine, amphetamine, methamphetamine, nicotine patches and gums, snuff tobacco, coca leaves

Factors Determining the Physiological Impact of Drugs

The type of delivery route into the bloodstream, as has been discussed, places specific constraints upon the effect a drug may produce. Some drug effects are optimized, for example, by an oral administration, whereas others require more direct access to the bloodstream. Other factors must be considered as well. If a drug is administered repeatedly, the timing of the administrations plays an important role in determining the final result. If two drugs are administered close together in time, we must also consider how these drugs might interact with each other in terms of their acute effects. The chronic effects of two drugs might interact as well. Finally, it is possible that two identical drugs taken by two individuals might have different effects by virtue of the characteristics of the drug user at the time of administration. These four factors will now be considered.

Timing

All drugs, no matter how they are delivered, share some common features when we consider their effects over time. There is initially an interval (the **latency period**) during which the concentration of the drug is increasing in the blood but is not yet high enough for a drug effect to be detected. How long this latency period will last is related generally to the absorption time of the drug. As the concentration of the drug continues to rise, the effect will become stronger. A stage will be eventually reached when the effect attains a maximum strength, even though the concentration in the blood continues to rise. This point is unfortunately the point at which the drug may produce undesirable side effects. One solution to this problem is to administer the drug in a time-release form (designated as controlled-release, extended-release, or sustained-release formulations). In this approach, a large dose is given initially to enable the drug effect to be felt; then smaller doses are programmed to be released at specific intervals afterward to

latency period: An interval of time during which the blood levels of a drug are not yet sufficient for a drug effect to be observed.

synergism (SIN-er-jih-zum): The property of a drug interaction in which the combination effect of two drugs exceeds the effect of either drug administered alone.

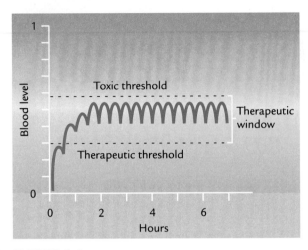

FIGURE 3.1

The therapeutic window. Time-release drugs are formulated to administer the drug in small amounts over time to stay above the threshold for a therapeutic effect but below the threshold for toxicity.

postpone, up to twelve hours or so, the decline in the drug's concentration in the blood. The intention is to keep the concentration of the drug in the blood within a "therapeutic window," high enough for the drug to be effective while low enough to avoid any toxic effects. When drugs are administered repeatedly, there is a risk that the second dose will boost the concentration of the drug in the blood too high before the effect of the first dose has a chance to decline (Figure 3.1).

Drug Interactions

Two basic types of interactions may occur when two drugs are mixed together. In the first type, two drugs in combination may produce an acute effect that is greater than the effect of either drug administered separately. In some cases, the combination effect is purely *additive*. For example, if the effect of one drug alone is equivalent to a 4 and the effect of another drug is a 6, then the combined additive effect is equivalent to a value of 10.

In other cases, however, the acute combination effect is *hyperadditive*, with the combined effect exceeding the sum of the individual drugs administered alone, as in the two drugs in the first example combining to a value of 13 or more. Any hyperadditive effect produced by a combination of two or more drugs is referred to as **synergism.** In some synergistic combinations, one drug may even double or triple the effect of another. It is also possible that one drug might have no effect at all unless it is taken simultaneously with another. This special form of synergism is called **potentiation;** it is as though a drug with no effect at all by itself, when combined with a drug having an effect of 6, produces a result equivalent to a 10. The danger of such interactions is that the combined effect of the drugs is so powerful as to become toxic. In extreme cases, the toxicity can be lethal.

In the second type of interaction, two drugs can be *antagonistic* if the acute effect of one drug is diminished to some degree when administered with another, a situation comparable to a drug with the effect of 6 and a drug with the effect of 4 combining to produce an effect of 3. Later chapters discuss drugs that are totally antagonistic to each other, in that the second exactly cancels out, or neutralizes, the effect of the first. Health Alert (page 68) warns that dangerous interactions can result not only from drug–drug combinations but from food–drug combinations as well. Another Health Alert in Chapter 16 will review the potentially dangerous

consequences of combining drugs with herb-derived dietary supplements.

Cross-Tolerance and Cross-Dependence

If you were taking a barbiturate (a sedation-producing drug that acts to depress bodily functioning) for an extended length of time and you developed a tolerance for its effect, you might also have developed a tolerance for another depressant drug even though you have never taken the second one. In other words, it is possible that a tolerance effect for one drug might automatically induce a tolerance for another. This phenomenon, referred to as **cross-tolerance,** is commonly observed in the physiological and psychological effects of alcohol, barbiturates, and a class of antianxiety medications called benzodiazepines (Chapter 15). As a result of cross-tolerance, an alcoholic will have already developed a tolerance for a barbiturate, or a barbiturate abuser will need a greater amount of an anesthetic when undergoing surgery.

We can view the interconnectedness of depressant drugs in another way as well. If we can relieve the withdrawal symptoms of one drug by administering another drug, then the two drugs show **cross-dependence.** In effect, one drug can substitute for whatever physiological effects have been produced by a second drug that has been discontinued. Unfortunately, cross-dependence provides a means for continuing an abused drug in the guise of a new one:

> When drug abuse becomes obvious and embarrassing or when the preferred drug becomes unavailable, the user can switch to a cross-dependent drug to avoid the withdrawal illness. A woman who wants to conceal her drinking from the family might substitute some diazepam [a benzodiazepine-type antianxiety medication] for her morning eye opener.[5]

Later in this chapter, we will examine the physiological mechanism that underlies the phenomena of cross-tolerance and cross-dependence.

potentiation: The property of a synergistic drug interaction in which one drug combined with another drug produces an enhanced effect when one of the drugs alone would have had no effect.

cross-tolerance: A phenomenon in which the tolerance that results from the chronic use of one drug induces a tolerance effect with regard to a second drug that has not been used before.

cross-dependence: A phenomenon in which one drug can be used to reduce the withdrawal symptoms following the discontinuance of another drug.

HEALTH ALERT!

Adverse Effects of Drug–Drug and Food–Drug Combinations

It would be impossible to list every known drug–drug interaction or food–drug interaction. Nonetheless, here are some examples. Any adverse reaction to a combination of drugs or a combination of a drug with something eaten should be reported to your physician immediately. An awareness of adverse interactions is particularly important for elderly patients, who tend to be treated with multiple medications. The best advice is to ask your physician whether alcohol, specific foods, or other medications might alter the effect of your medication.

Hyperadditive Effects

Alcohol with barbiturate-related sleep medications, cardiovascular medications, insulin, anti-inflammatory medications, antihistamines, painkillers, antianxiety medications

Septra, Bactrim, or related types of antibiotics with Coumadin (an anticoagulant)

Tagamet (a heartburn and ulcer treatment medication) with Coumadin

Aspirin, Aleve, Advil, Tylenol, or related painkillers with Coumadin

Plendil (a blood pressure medication) and Procardia (an angina treatment), as well as Zocor, Lipitor, and Mevacor (all cholesterol-lowering medications), with grapefruit juice

Lanoxin (a medication for heart problems) with licorice

Lanoxin with bran, oatmeal, or other high-fiber foods

Antagonistic Effects

Morphine/heroin with naloxone or naltrexone

Norpramin or related antidepressants with bran, oatmeal, or other high-fiber foods

Soy products and certain vitamin K–rich vegetables such as broccoli, cabbage, and asparagus with Coumadin

Possible Toxic Reactions

Internal bleeding by a combination of Parnate and Anafranil (two types of antidepressants)

Elevated body temperature by a combination of Nardil (an antidepressant) with Demerol (a painkiller)

Excessive blood pressure or stroke by a combination of Parnate, Nardil, or other monoamine-oxidase inhibitors (MAOIs) used to treat depression with cheddar cheese, pickled herring, or other foods high in tyramine

Agitation or elevated body temperature by a combination of Paxil, Prozac, Zoloft, or related antidepressants with Parnate, Nardil, or other monoamine-oxidase inhibitors (MAOIs) used to treat depression

Irregular heartbeat, cardiac arrest, and sudden death by a combination of Hismanal or Seldane (two antihistamines) with Nizoral (an antifungal drug)

Note: The hyperadditive effects of grapefruit on certain medications can be dangerous or useful, depending on the circumstances. If grapefruit enhances the effect of the cholesterol-reducing medication Lipitor, for example, it is possible that drinking grapefruit juice might allow the patient to take less Lipitor (reducing costs and possible side effects) and still receive the same level of benefit. Combinations of this kind, however, should be administered only under the close supervision of one's physician.

> **Where to go for assistance:**
> www.medscape/druginfo/druginterchecker
> Register free and check out any combination of prescription or OTC drugs for potential adverse interactions.

Sources: Graedon, Joe, and Graedon, Teresa (2000, October 16). Say "aaah": The people's pharmacy; drugs and foods can interact adversely. *Los Angeles Times*, p. 2. Graedon, Joe, and Graedon, Teresa (1997). *Deadly drug interactions.* New York: St. Martin's Press. *PDR: Guide to drug interactions, side effects, and indications* (2007). Montvale, NJ: Thomson. Sorensen, Janina M. (2002). Herb–drug, food–drug, nutrient–drug, and drug–drug interactions: Mechanisms involved and their medical implications. *Journal of Alternative and Complementary Medicine, 8,* 293–308.

Individual Differences

Some variations in drug effects may be related to an interaction between the drug itself and specific characteristics of the person taking the drug. One characteristic is an individual's weight. In general, a heavier person will require a greater amount of a drug than a lighter person to receive an equivalent drug effect, all other things being equal. It is for this reason that drug dosages are expressed as a ratio of drug amount to body weight. This ratio is typically expressed in metric terms, as milligrams-per-kilogram (mg/kg).

Another characteristic is gender. Even if a man and a woman are exactly the same weight, differences in drug effects can still result on the basis of gender differences in body composition and sex hormones. Women have, on average, a higher proportion of fat, due to a greater fat-to-muscle ratio, and a lower proportion of water than men. When we look at the effects of alcohol consumption in terms of gender, we find that the lower water content (a factor that tends to dilute the alcohol in the body) in women makes them feel more intoxicated than men, even if the same amount of alcohol is consumed.

Relative to men, women also have reduced levels of enzymes that break down alcohol in the liver, resulting in higher alcohol levels in the blood and a higher level of intoxication.[6] We suspect that the lower level of alcohol biotransformation may be related to an increased level of estrogen and progesterone in women. Whether gender differences exist with regard to drugs other than alcohol is presently unknown.

Still another individual characteristic that influences the ways certain drugs affect the body is ethnic background. About 50 percent of all people of Asian descent, for example, show low levels of one of the enzymes that normally breaks down alcohol in the liver shortly before it is excreted. With this particular deficiency, alcohol metabolites tend to build up in the blood, producing a faster heart rate, facial flushing, and nausea.[7] As a result, many Asians find drinking to be quite unpleasant.

Ethnic variability can be seen in terms of other drug effects as well. It has been found that Caucasians have a faster rate of biotransformation of antipsychotic and antianxiety medications than Asians and, as a result, end up with relatively lower concentrations of drugs in the blood. One consequence of this difference is in the area of psychiatric treatment. Asian schizophrenic patients require significantly lower doses of antipsychotic medication for their symptoms to improve, and they experience medication side effects at much lower doses than do Caucasian patients. Since other possible factors such as diet, life-style, and environment do not account for these differences, we can speculate that these differences have a genetic basis.[8]

In some cases, differences in the physiological response to a particular drug can explain differential patterns of drug-taking behavior. For example, researchers have recently found that African Americans have a slower rate of nicotine metabolism following the smoking of cigarettes, relative to whites. This finding might be the reason why African Americans, on average, report smoking fewer cigarettes per day than whites. If we assume that an equivalent level of nicotine needs to be maintained in both populations, fewer cigarettes smoked but a higher level of nicotine absorbed per cigarette will produce the same effect as a greater number of cigarettes smoked but a lower nicotine level absorbed per cigarette. Consequently, African American smokers may be taking in and retaining relatively more nicotine per cigarette, and as a result not having to smoke as many cigarettes per day.[9] The concerns regarding nicotine intake among African Americans will be examined further in Chapter 11.

Introducing the Nervous System

Before we can begin to deal with the specific impact of drugs on the brain, we need first to understand some basic facts about the overall organization of the *nervous system*, of which the brain is a part.

In simplest terms, the nervous system is designed to do two basic things: to take in information from the environment around us and to control our bodily responses so that we can live effectively in that environment. But, of course, we do a lot more than that. We interpret the information coming in, try to make sense of it, remember some of it for a later time, and more than occasionally generate some information on our own in a process called thinking.

We can understand these different functions in terms of divisions within the nervous system. In general, the nervous system is divided into the **central nervous system (CNS)**, consisting of the brain and the spinal cord, and the **peripheral nervous system,** consisting of all the nerves and nerve fibers that connect the CNS to the environment and to our muscles and glands (Figure 3.2, page 70).

The Peripheral Nervous System

The peripheral nervous system is essentially the system that brings information in and later, after processing in the CNS, executes our behavioral response. On the input side, it includes the visual pathway, the auditory pathway, and other channels of sensory information

central nervous system (CNS): The portion of the nervous system that consists of the spinal cord and the brain.

peripheral nervous system: The portion of the nervous system that consists of nerves and nerve fibers that carry information to the central nervous system and outward to muscles and glands.

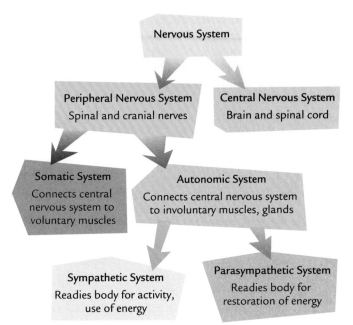

FIGURE 3.2

Organizational chart of the nervous system.

personal experience, blushing often occurs when we do not necessarily want it to, and it is difficult to make it go away. And yet it is a reaction to a situation that has been processed through our sensory pathways and interpreted within the brain; in this case, some emotional content has triggered this autonomic response.

If we were to take the time to execute deliberate commands to breathe regularly, to have our hearts beat at an appropriate rate, or to carry out the thousands of changes that our internal organs make, we certainly would not last very long. The autonomic control that has evolved is a product of the interplay of two subsystems, each delivered to smooth and cardiac muscles and to glands through its own set of nerve fibers. These subsystems are referred to as the **sympathetic** and **parasympathetic branches of the autonomic nervous system.**

Sympathetic and Parasympathetic Responses

Autonomic responses are divided into two general categories (Figure 3.3). The first is oriented toward dealing with some kind of emergency or stress. If we are in a situation that is perceived as a threat to our internal well-being or to our survival, the sympathetic system is in charge. During times of *sympathetic activation*, the heart rate goes up, blood pressure goes up, the bronchi in the lungs dilate to accommodate a greater amount of oxygen, the pupil dilates to allow more light into the eye, and other bodily systems alter their level of functioning, so we are in a better position to fight, to flee, or simply to feel frightened. At the same time, the gastrointestinal tract is inhibited. It makes sense that we should not be digesting our lunch when we are battling for our lives.

The second category of response is totally opposite to the first. We cannot be "on alert" all our lives; we need some time to regroup our forces, to orient ourselves toward a state of calm and rest necessary for nurturance and internal maintenance. Heart rate and blood pressure now go down, bronchi and pupils constrict, and the gastrointestinal tract is now excited rather than inhibited. These and other changes constitute *parasympathetic activation* and are an important counterpoint to the activation of the sympathetic system.

Some psychoactive drugs produce autonomic changes, in addition to their direct effects on the brain. They may produce a swing toward sympathetic activation

about the world around us. On the output side, motor pathways in the peripheral nervous system that control our reactions to that world generate two basic acts.

The first type, called a *somatic* response, is a voluntary reaction, executed by skeletal muscles that are attached to bone. When you lift your arm, for example, you have executed a series of motor commands that ultimately results in contractions of flexor and extensor muscles. In this case, the movement is deliberate, conscious, and controlled.

A second type of reaction, called an *autonomic* response, is usually involuntary and executed by smooth muscles that form the walls of arteries, veins, capillaries, and internal organs as well as cardiac muscles that form the walls of the heart. When you blush, for example, the capillaries are dilating, or enlarging, underneath the surface of your skin, an effect that produces a reddening color and a feeling of warmth. As some of us know from

sympathetic branch of the autonomic nervous system: The portion of the autonomic nervous system that controls bodily changes that deal with stressful or emergency situations.

parasympathetic branch of the autonomic nervous system: The portion of the autonomic nervous system that controls the bodily changes that lead to increased nurturance, rest, and maintenance.

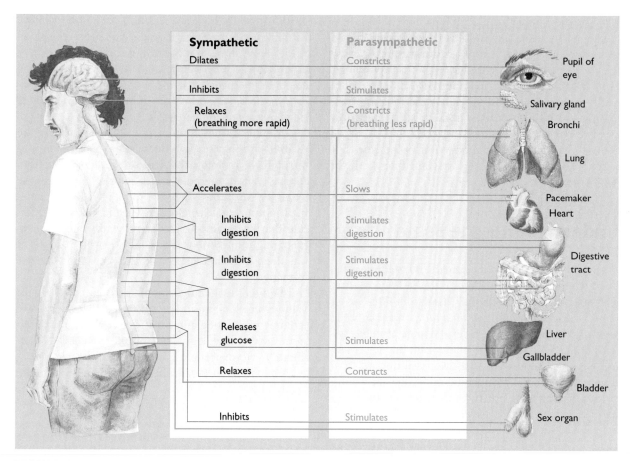

Sympathetic	Parasympathetic	
Dilates	Constricts	Pupil of eye
Inhibits	Stimulates	Salivary gland
Relaxes (breathing more rapid)	Constricts (breathing less rapid)	Bronchi
		Lung
Accelerates	Slows	Pacemaker Heart
Inhibits digestion	Stimulates digestion	
Inhibits digestion	Stimulates digestion	Digestive tract
Releases glucose	Stimulates	Liver Gallbladder
Relaxes	Contracts	Bladder
Inhibits	Stimulates	Sex organ

FIGURE 3.3

Functions of the sympathetic and parasympathetic branches of the autonomic nervous system.

Source: Robert A. Baron, *Psychology: From Science to Practice,* page 73 (reused from 5/e), 2008. Reproduced by permission of Pearson Education, Inc.

During emergency situations, specific bodily changes are produced through stimulation of the sympathetic branch of the autonomic nervous system.

(as with stimulants) or a swing toward parasympathetic activation (as with depressants).

The Central Nervous System

The central nervous system, located along the central axis of the body, consists of the spinal cord and the brain. It is here that interpretations of our sensory input occur and the intricate processing of information is accomplished. Some of our sensory nerves, such as those originating at locations from the neck down, enter the CNS at the level of the spinal cord; others, such as those nerves coming from our eyes and ears, enter at the level of the brain. Complex information entering at the spinal cord is carried by neural pathways upward into the brain for further processing; the processing of simpler information may not involve the brain at all, resulting instead in merely reflexive responses.

The most important part of the CNS, of course, is the brain. It is nearly impossible to overestimate its role in our everyday lives. Every gesture we make, every feeling, every experience we have of our surroundings, every insight or memory, is a result of a complex, beautifully modulated pattern of activity among approximately 100 billion specialized cells called **neurons.** We owe our entire cognitive universe, all of what we are or think we are, to the functioning of these cells. It is here that psychoactive drugs are doing their work, for good or for bad.

Understanding the Brain

Proceeding upward from the spinal cord, starting at the point where the CNS enlarges into the brain, neuroanatomists have classified brain tissue into three major sections: the *hindbrain,* the *midbrain,* and finally the *forebrain* (Figure 3.4). The older and more primitive systems of the brain tend to be underneath the newer and more sophisticated ones, so as we travel upward from hindbrain to midbrain to forebrain on our quick tour, we are dealing with structures that have evolved ever more recently and have greater involvement in complex behaviors. You can think of this arrangement in brain anatomy as similar to an archaeological dig, where the strata of previous civilizations extend downward into greater and greater antiquity. Understanding the brain in terms of the orderliness of its development over the span of evolutionary history helps to make sense of its complexity.

The Hindbrain

At the top of the spinal cord, neural tissue suddenly widens and enlarges into the hindbrain. The *medulla* lies at the point of the hindbrain where this enlargement has just begun. It is essentially the coordinator of the basic life-support systems in our body. Blood pressure is controlled here, as are the rhythms of breathing, heart rate, digestion, and even vomiting. Death would be seconds away, were it not for the normal functioning of the medulla. Unfortunately, it is highly sensitive to opiates, alcohol, barbiturates, and other depressants. When levels of any of these drugs are excessive in overdose cases, the respiratory controls in the medulla are inhibited and

neuron: The specialized cell in the nervous system designed to receive and transmit information.

death can result from asphyxiation (lack of breathing). Even if a person survives, the lack of oxygen in the blood while he or she is not breathing can result in severe brain damage. On a more positive note, the vomiting center in the medulla is sensitive to the presence of poisons in the blood and is able to initiate vomiting to get rid of unwanted and potentially harmful substances.

Another hindbrain structure, situated just above the medulla, is the *pons.* We can view the pons in terms of our ability to maintain the necessary level of alertness to survive. Within the pons are structures that determine when we sleep and when we wake up, as well as the main portion of a structure called the *reticular formation* that energizes the rest of the brain to be alert to incoming information. Drugs affecting the patterns of our sleep influence centers in the pons and reticular formation.

Behind the medulla and the pons in the hindbrain is the *cerebellum,* an important structure for the maintenance of balance and for the execution of smooth movements of the body. The dizziness and lack of coordination we experience after consuming alcohol is related in large part to alcohol's depressive effect on the cerebellum.

The Midbrain

The midbrain, located just above the hindbrain, is a center for the control of important sensory and motor reflexes as well as the processing of pain information.

Without a specific region of the midbrain called the *substantia nigra,* we would not be able to control the movements of our bodies effectively. Parkinson's disease, a disorder characterized by muscular tremors and other motor difficulties, is a result of degeneration of the substantia nigra. Unfortunately, symptoms that resemble Parkinson's disease have been frequently observed in patients taking antipsychotic medications for the treatment of schizophrenia. Efforts to develop antipsychotic medications without this adverse side effect will be explored in Chapter 16.

The Forebrain

In the uppermost section of the brain are two important areas to consider. The first area, lying immediately above the midbrain, includes the *hypothalamus* and the *limbic system.* It is through these structures that we are able to carry out the appropriate motivational and emotional acts that ensure our survival as a species. Feeding behavior, drinking behavior, and sexual behavior are controlled by the hypothalamus.

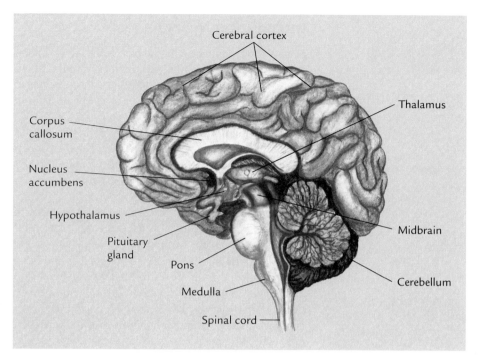

FIGURE 3.4

Basic structures of the human brain, viewed from the side.

Source: Modified from KALAT, *Biological Psychology* w/CD + INFOTRAC, 9th edition. © 2007. Wadsworth, a part of Cengage Learning, Inc. Reproduced by permission. www.cengage.com/permissions.

The limbic system surrounds the hypothalamus and plays a central role in organizing emotional behavior during times of stress. Experimental lesions in points within the limbic system can turn a tame animal into a raging monster or a wild animal into a docile one. Not surprisingly, theories about the basis for psychological dependence have focused on the limbic system. Some of these ideas will be explored later in the chapter. Drugs that deal with symptoms of anxiety, depression, and schizophrenia affect regions within the limbic system.

The second forebrain area of concern, and the most important from the standpoint of understanding human behavior, is a two-sided, wrinkled sheet of neural tissue, with a thickness approximately equivalent to the height of a capital letter on this page and overhanging almost all of the brain: the hemispheres of the **cerebral cortex.** Its appearance resembles that of a giant walnut, an association that prompted early physicians in the Middle Ages to prescribe walnuts as medicine for diseases of the brain (obviously, a nutty idea).

When we arrive at the cerebral cortex (or cortex, for short), we have arrived at the pinnacle of the brain both functionally and spatially. Specific regions of the cerebral cortex are concerned with processing visual, auditory, and somatosensory (touch) information, while other regions control the organization of complex and precise movements.

A large percentage of cortical tissue is devoted to the task of associating one piece of information with another. In the human brain, more than 80 percent of the cortex, called the association cortex, concerns itself with the integration of information. Of all the areas within the association cortex, the most recently evolved is a region closest to the front of the brain called the *prefrontal cortex.* Our higher-order, intellectual abilities (often referred to as executive functioning) as well as our personality characteristics emerge from activity in this region. It has been speculated that a dysfunction in the prefrontal cortex may be associated with a loss of personal control with respect to the abuse of alcohol and other drugs.[10]

cerebral cortex: The portion of the forebrain devoted to a high level of information processing.

Understanding the Biochemistry of Psychoactive Drugs

Gaining some perspective about brain anatomy lays the foundation for our understanding of *where* certain psychoactive drugs are active, but it does not help us to understand *how* they work. To answer this second question, we need to know something about neurons themselves, the specialized cells designed to communicate information within the nervous system.

synapse (SIN-apse): The juncture between neurons. It consists of a synaptic knob, the intervening gap, and receptor sites on a receiving neuron.

Introducing Neurons

Here is a scary thought. There are an estimated 100 billion neurons in the brain, and the number of possible interconnections that exist among them all has been estimated to be greater than the total number of atomic particles in the known universe.[11] Therefore, you might call it an understatement to say that the brain is the most complex organ of the body. How can we possibly begin to understand the brain amidst such complexity? Or rather, are our own brains sophisticated enough to understand how our brains work?

Fortunately, the task is not as insurmountable as it appears. The neuron itself, as the basic unit of the nervous system, can be understood in relatively simple terms. Imagine the neuron at any moment in time as a tiny device that is either on or off, like a light switch. There is no intermediate state. In this respect, the nervous system is digital like a computer, since a computer consists simply of electrical circuits that are permitted only two states, open or closed. In terms of the neuron, the "on" state is accomplished by the generation of an electrical change in its membrane, referred to as a *nerve impulse.* Just as the neuron is the basic unit that forms the structure of the nervous system, the nerve impulse is the basic unit that forms the language of the nervous system.

The role of the neuron is to receive information and to transmit information, carrying out this mission through its three principal components: the *cell body,* the *dendrites,* and the *axon* (Figure 3.5). The cell body comprises the bulk of the neuron and contains the nucleus and other elements that relate it to other types of cells in the body, such as muscle cells, skin cells, and blood cells. The feature that makes the neuron unique is the appendages that extend from the cell body, some of them rather short and one quite long. The short ones are called dendrites and represent the part of the neuron that receives information from the outside. The long appendage, called the axon, is the part that transmits information outward. The axon is essentially the carrier of the messages of the neuron.

When a nerve impulse is generated, the impulse travels down the length of the axon at speeds up to 120 meters per second (roughly 270 miles per hour) until it reaches the axon's end point. If we followed the axon along its length, starting from the cell body (and sometimes that distance may be as long as a meter in length), we would see that toward its end the axon diverges like the branches of a tree. At the terminal point of each of these branches are small button-like structures called *synaptic knobs.* We have arrived at the crucial point of the story: the gap between neurons known as the **synapse.**

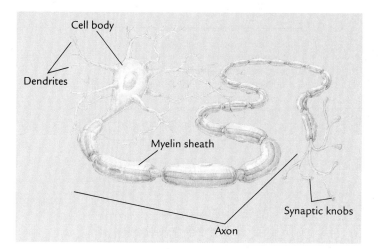

FIGURE 3.5

Basic structure of a neuron. The axon is shown surrounded by the myelin sheath, which increases the transmission speed of nerve impulses.

Synaptic Communication

The neuronal changes that result from the ingestion of psychoactive drugs can be understood in terms of three basic stages of synaptic communication: *neurotransmitter release, receptor binding,* and *reuptake.*

- Located inside the synaptic knobs are *synaptic vesicles* that store millions of chemical molecules called **neurotransmitters.** Without the action of neurotransmitters, the nerve impulse, upon arriving at the terminal points of the axon, would sputter out like a wet fuse.

- The nerve impulse causes the release of neurotransmitter molecules out of the vesicles and into special receptor sites on the surface of a neuron, lying on the other ("receiving") side of the synapse. Drugs can either increase or decrease the number of neurotransmitter molecules that are released.

- Receptors can be imagined as having an internal shape that is designed to match the external shape of the neuron. When neurotransmitter and receptor shapes "fit together," the neurotransmitter binds to the receptor like a key successfully fitting into a lock (Figure 3.6). As a result of receptor binding, an electrical change (technically, a change in the electric potential) occurs in the membrane of the receiving neuron. Neuron A has now communicated with neuron B.

- Synaptic communication takes one of two forms: excitation or inhibition. An excitatory message causes an increase in the rate of nerve impulses; an inhibitory message causes a decrease. Whether receptor binding produces an excitatory or an inhibitory effect depends on the nature of the receptor at the synapse. Neurotransmitters are

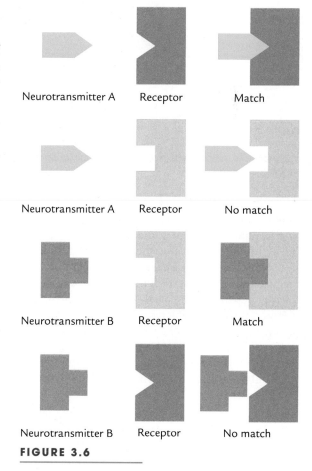

Neurotransmitter A	Receptor	Match
Neurotransmitter A	Receptor	No match
Neurotransmitter B	Receptor	Match
Neurotransmitter B	Receptor	No match

FIGURE 3.6

Communication between neurons depends on a match between neurotransmitter and receptor. The "key and lock" concept is a simplified way of understanding the general process of receptor binding.

neurotransmitter: A chemical substance that a neuron uses to communicate information at the synapse.

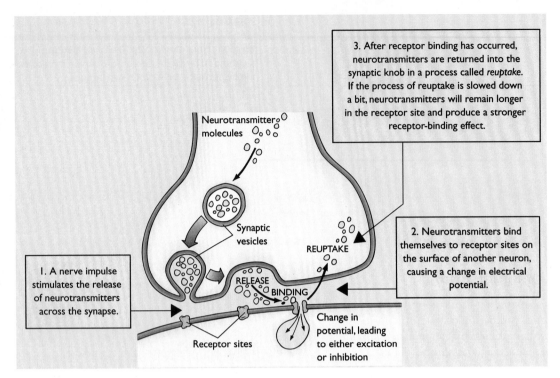

3. After receptor binding has occurred, neurotransmitters are returned into the synaptic knob in a process called *reuptake*. If the process of reuptake is slowed down a bit, neurotransmitters will remain longer in the receptor site and produce a stronger receptor-binding effect.

2. Neurotransmitters bind themselves to receptor sites on the surface of another neuron, causing a change in electrical potential.

1. A nerve impulse stimulates the release of neurotransmitters across the synapse.

Neurotransmitter molecules

Synaptic vesicles

REUPTAKE

RELEASE

BINDING

Change in potential, leading to either excitation or inhibition

Receptor sites

FIGURE 3.7

The sequence of major events in synaptic communication: (1) neurotransmitter release, (2) receptor binding, (3) reuptake.

referred to as excitatory because they bind to excitatory receptors; other neurotransmitters are referred to as inhibitory because they bind to inhibitory receptors. In some cases, such as dopamine and acetylcholine (see next section), either effect can occur, depending on what receptor is involved. Drugs can either enhance receptor binding by mimicking the neurotransmitter at the receptor site (as is the case with amphetamines; see Chapter 4) or diminish receptor binding by blocking the neurotransmitter (as is the case with antipsychotic drugs; see Chapter 16).

■ Because neurons fire in very rapid succession, neurotransmitters cannot remain in the receptor sites for more than a millisecond or two. Therefore, in most cases, once the neurotransmitter binds to the receptor, it is expelled and transported back to the synaptic knob. This process of returning, called **reuptake,** is

reuptake: The process by which a neurotransmitter returns from the receptor site back to the synaptic knob.

essentially a way of getting the neurotransmitter back to the synaptic vesicle where it can be released again (Figure 3.7).

■ The speed of reuptake can be modified by a specific drug, with an important consequence on synaptic communication. If reuptake is slowed down slightly, the neurotransmitter will remain in the receptor site longer, and the effect of receptor binding will be enhanced. Conversely, if reuptake is accelerated, the neurotransmitter will remain a shorter period of time, and the effect of receptor binding will be diminished. Cocaine and some antidepressant drugs work by slowing down or even blocking the reuptake process (see Chapters 4 and 16).

Although the principle of synaptic communication rests on the possibility of conveying only two types of messages, either excitation or inhibition, it turns out that not just two neurotransmitters do all the work. In fact, more than fifty have been studied. In the next section, we will focus on the seven most prominent neurotransmitters and their relationship to the effects of specific psychoactive drugs.

The Major Neurotransmitters in Brief: The Big Seven

Acetylcholine was the first molecule to have been firmly established as a neurotransmitter. There are two types of receptor sites that are sensitive to acetylcholine.

The first type, *muscarinic receptors,* so named because they are responsive to the drug muscarine, are located in the parasympathetic autonomic nervous system. If a drug is antimuscarinic, that means that it interferes with the role of acetylcholine in stimulating parasympathetic reactions of the body. Examples are atropine and scopolamine (see Chapter 6). Atropine, when applied to the eyes, for example, causes the pupils to dilate by inhibiting the parasympathetic tendency for the pupils to constrict. This is useful in eye examinations where the retina needs to be inspected for possible problems.

The second type, *nicotinic receptors,* so named because they are responsive to nicotine (see Chapter 11), are found near the end points of motor neurons, where skeletal muscles are innervated, as well as throughout the cerebral cortex. Some antinicotinic drugs, such as the poison *curare,* affect these motor neurons so dramatically that the body can become paralyzed within seconds. Deficiencies in acetylcholine or in nicotinic receptors have been tied to Alzheimer's disease, a condition resulting in memory loss and mental confusion.

Norepinephrine, the second major neurotransmitter, is concentrated in the hypothalamus and limbic system but also found throughout the brain. In the peripheral nervous system, it is the principal neurotransmitter for sympathetic autonomic activation, but its role here is independent of its effects in the brain. Norepinephrine helps to regulate our mood states; Chapter 16 will discuss how drugs that boost the levels of norepinephrine also help relieve symptoms of depression.

The role of **dopamine,** the third major neurotransmitter, affects three important aspects of our behavior. The first aspect is motor control: the ability to start a movement when we want to, to stop it when we want to, and to execute the movement in a smooth, precisely determined manner. A deficiency in motor control, as mentioned earlier, is dramatically seen in symptoms of Parkinson's disease, a disorder arising from a degeneration of dopamine-releasing neurons in the substantia nigra of the midbrain. The second aspect is emotionality. Problems in dopamine-releasing neurons in the cortex and limbic system are strongly suspected to be at the root of schizophrenia. The role of dopamine in schizophrenia and efforts to develop drugs that relieve schizophrenic symptoms will be discussed in Chapter 16.

Third, as we will see shortly, dopamine in the brain plays a major role in producing the craving feelings that encourage a continuing pattern of compulsive drug-taking behavior.

Serotonin, the fourth neurotransmitter, is concentrated in the pons and medulla, in the limbic system, and in the cortex. At the level of the hindbrain, serotonin plays an important role in regulating patterns of sleep. At the level of the limbic system, it shares with norepinephrine responsibility for establishing appropriate mood levels, avoiding wild swings upward that result in mania or downward that result in depression. As you can predict, many drugs that relieve mania and depression act upon serotonin-releasing neurons. Several hallucinogenic drugs, such as LSD, stimulate serotonin-releasing neurons in the cortex, a topic that will be explored further in Chapter 6.

It should be noted that the technical name for serotonin is 5-hydroxytryptamine (abbreviated 5-HT), and receptors sensitive to serotonin are frequently called 5-HT receptors. Being aware of this terminology is helpful when reviewing the research literature on serotonin in synaptic communication (see earlier section), but it will not be employed here. Any future references to this neurotransmitter will be expressed using the name, serotonin, rather than its biochemical equivalent.

Gamma aminobutyric acid (GABA), the fifth neurotransmitter, is an important inhibitory neurotransmitter throughout the brain. Antianxiety medications, often referred to as tranquilizers, stimulate GABA-releasing neurons, providing a reduction in feelings of stress and fear, as will be discussed in Chapter 15. Since this neurotransmitter is a major source of inhibitory control, it should not be surprising that GABA deficiencies are associated with an increased tendency to suffer epileptic seizures.

acetylcholine (a-SEE-til-KOH-leen): A neurotransmitter active in the parasympathetic autonomic nervous system, cerebral cortex, and peripheral somatic nerves.

norepinephrine (NOR-ep-ih-NEH-frin): A neurotransmitter active in the sympathetic autonomic nervous system and in many regions of the brain.

dopamine (DOPE-ah-meen): A neurotransmitter in the brain whose activity is related to emotionality and motor control.

serotonin (SER-ah-TOH-nin): A neurotransmitter in the brain whose activity is related to emotionality and sleep patterns.

gamma aminobutyric acid (GABA) (GAM-ma a-MEEN-o-byoo-TEER-ik ASS-id): An inhibitory neurotransmitter in the brain. Antianxiety drugs tend to facilitate the activity level of GABA in the brain.

Drugs...in Focus

Endorphins in Our Lives: A Psychosocial Perspective

From the discovery of endorphins in the 1970s, there emerged a new understanding not only of how pain is controlled in the brain but also of the role that opiate-like chemicals play in our daily lives. Here is a sampling of findings from research on the psychosocial aspects of brain endorphins:

- *Pain and Stress.* Under stressful circumstances, people can become temporarily analgesic (relatively insensitive to pain) without any external drugs. There are well-documented cases of soldiers who have ignored their injuries during the heat of battle, of athletes who are unaware of their pain until the game is over, and of individuals in primitive societies who endure painful religious rituals without complaint. Increased levels of endorphins are considered to contribute to these phenomena.

- *Acupuncture.* The effects of the Chinese technique of analgesic acupuncture (the inserting of needles into the skin at precisely defined points in the body to relieve pain) are completely reversible by naloxone (a specific antagonist with respect to receptors sensitive to endorphins; see Chapter 5). It is reasonable, therefore, to conclude that acupuncture effects result from increased levels of endorphins.

- *Labor and Childbirth Pain.* Endorphin levels measured in the placental bloodstream of pregnant women near to the time of childbirth are greatly elevated from levels normally present in nonpregnant women, and they reach a peak during labor itself. It is believed that as a result, women in labor are enduring less pain than they would experience if these endorphin levels were

unchanged. Endorphins may protect them against an even greater amount of discomfort.

- *The "Runner's High."* Some studies have shown increased levels of endorphins among long-distance runners and other athletes, leading to speculation that endorphin activity accounts for the euphoria—and in some instances analgesia—felt during strenuous physical exercise. A 2008 study confirmed that endorphins are specifically involved in the feelings of euphoria ("runner's high") and well-being that many runners report.

- *Anorexia.* Emaciated anorexic women have been found to have higher endorphin levels than control patients without anorexic symptoms. When body weight returns to normal, endorphin levels decline. Anorexic women often report feeling euphoric, particularly while engaging in physical exercise.

- *Chocolate Cravings.* Laboratory rats like chocolate, seemingly as much as humans do. In tasks in which they are trained to work for chocolate rewards, injections of naloxone make them less eager to perform the tasks. It is possible that at least part of the pleasure of eating chocolate is linked to the release of endorphins.

Sources: Boecker, Henning; Sprenger, Till; Spilker, Mary E.; Gjermund, Henriksen; et al. (2008). The runner's high: Opioidergic mechanisms in the human brain. *Cerebral Cortex*, Advance Access published February 21, 2008. Dum, J., and Herz, A. (1984). Endorphinergic modulation of neural reward systems indicated by behavioral changes. *Pharmacology, Biochemistry, and Behavior, 21*, 259–266. Levinthal, Charles F. (1988). *Messengers of paradise: Opiates and the brain. The struggle over pain, rage, uncertainty, and addiction.* New York: Anchor Press/ Doubleday.

Glutamate, the sixth major neurotransmitter, is also widely distributed throughout the brain and functions as an excitatory neurotransmitter in the brain, causing neurons to be more active. There is increasing evidence of a close connection between glutamate activity and

glutamate (GLU-ta-mate): An excitatory neurotransmitter in the brain. Glutamate receptors are associated with actions of PCP and ketamine as well as feelings of drug craving.

the abuse potential of several psychoactive drugs. The exact relationship, however, appears to depend upon the specific subtype of glutamate receptor. On the one hand, the action of two dissociative anesthetics with hallucinogenic properties, phencyclidine (PCP, also known as angel dust) and ketamine, are associated with the blocking of one subgroup of glutamate receptors (see Chapter 6). On the other hand, recent pharmacological research has pointed to the activation of another subgroup of glutamate receptors as a critical element in drug craving and drug-abuse relapse with respect to

TABLE 3.1

Drug Effects and Synaptic Communication in the Nervous System

DRUG	RESULT	MECHANISM
amphetamines	CNS stimulation	Mimicking of norepinephrine at its receptor sites
antianxiety drugs in general	Reduction in anxiety and stress	Stimulation of GABA receptors in the brain
antidepressant drugs, MAO-inhibitor type	Reduction in depressive symptoms	Inhibition of enzymes that metabolize norepinephrine and serotonin
antidepressant drugs, tricyclic type	Reduction in depressive symptoms	Slowing down of reuptake of norepinephrine and serotonin at their receptor sites
antipsychotic drugs, typical type	Reduction in schizophrenic symptoms	Dopamine blocked from entering receptor sites in the brain
caffeine	CNS stimulation	Adenosine (an inhibitory neurotransmitter) blocked from entering its receptor sites
cocaine	CNS stimulation and local anesthesia	Blocking the reuptake of norepinephrine and dopamine at their receptor sites
LSD	Visual hallucinations and disordered thinking	Stimulation of receptor sites sensitive to serotonin
morphine, heroin, and codeine	Pain relief and euphoria	Stimulation of endorphins at their receptors in the spinal cord and brain

Source: Grilly, David M. (2006). *Drugs and human behavior* (5th ed.) Boston: Allyn and Bacon.

cocaine, nicotine, alcohol, and heroin. As a result, the current development of new drugs that block glutamate receptors of the latter type shows great promise in drug abuse treatment.[12]

The seventh major neurotransmitter is actually a grouping of neurotransmitters collectively known as **endorphins.** They are natural painkillers produced by the brain and bear a remarkable resemblance to morphine. Endorphins play an important role in the emotional aspects of our lives (Drugs . . . in Focus). Chapter 5 will discuss how the discovery of endorphins has helped us understand more clearly the nature of opiate dependence.

Table 3.1 shows the ways that various psychoactive drugs work in the brain, in terms of how they alter the activity of a specific neurotransmitter. Some drugs, such as amphetamines, work at the synapse in multiple ways.

Physiological Aspects of Drug-Taking Behavior

There are three important concepts related to drug-taking behavior that arise from the physiology of the nervous system. The first is the blood-brain barrier; the second is the physiological basis for drug tolerance; and the third is

the current hypothesis that psychological dependence is directly related to activity in a specific area of the brain.

The Blood-Brain Barrier

Mentioned earlier in the chapter was a barrier that restricts the passage of drugs and other molecules from the bloodstream to the brain. This exclusionary system is called the **blood-brain barrier.** Because it is important to maintain a level of stability in the brain, we are quite fortunate that this "gatekeeper" keeps the environment of the brain free from the biochemical ups and downs that are a fact of life in the bloodstream. The key factor in determining whether a drug passes through the blood-brain barrier is the degree to which that drug is *fat-soluble*.

Despite the obstacles, many types of drugs easily pass into the brain: nicotine, alcohol, cocaine, barbiturates, and caffeine, to name a few. Among the opiates, heroin,

endorphins (en-DOR-fins): A class of chemical substances, produced in the brain and elsewhere in the body, that mimic the effects of morphine and other opiate drugs.

blood-brain barrier: A system whereby some substances in the bloodstream are excluded from entering the nervous system.

which is highly fat-soluble, crosses the blood-brain barrier faster and more completely than morphine. Penicillin, by contrast, hardly enters the brain at all.[13]

The presence of a blood-brain barrier is an issue not only for the study of psychoactive drugs but for certain medical treatments as well. For example, one of the effective treatments for Parkinson's disease is the administration of the drug L-Dopa, a shortened name for levodopa. The reason for using this drug stems from the root cause of Parkinson's disease: a dopamine deficiency in the substantia nigra. Taking dopamine itself is of no help, since its lack of fat-solubility excludes it from ever getting into the brain. Fortunately, L-Dopa, a metabolic precursor to dopamine, is fat-soluble. Therefore, L-Dopa can enter the brain and then change into dopamine. As a result, dopamine levels in the brain rise, and the symptoms of Parkinson's disease are relieved. Unfortunately, as dopamine receptors continue to degenerate over a period of years, L-Dopa treatment becomes increasingly ineffective.[14]

It has recently become possible to create fat-soluble molecules in the laboratory rather than finding them in nature. Pharmacologists have succeeded in combining protein-based drugs that are presently excluded by the blood-brain barrier with a fatty acid, enabling the drugs to slip through into the brain. It may be possible in the future to design special proteins that not only ferry drugs across the barrier but also regulate the release of the drugs once they are in the brain.[15]

Biochemical Processes Underlying Drug Tolerance

The last chapter considered the phenomenon of drug tolerance as a behavioral effect, accomplished through Pavlovian conditioning. Tolerance can also be examined in terms of two types of physiological processes, one occurring in the liver and the other in the neuron itself.

In the first type, called *metabolic (dispositional) tolerance*, a drug may facilitate over repeated administrations the processes that produce the drug's biotransformation in the liver. The rate of alcohol elimination, for example, increases over time if alcohol is ingested repeatedly over an extended period. When the liver breaks down the drug faster than it had initially, a smaller amount is left available for absorption into the blood. In the case of alcohol, the habitual drinker feels less of an alcoholic effect and compensates by increasing the amount consumed.

In the second type, called *cellular (pharmacodynamic) tolerance*, changes occur in the synapses of neurons themselves. Receptors that have been stimulated by the

drug over time may become less sensitive, and the effect on the receiving neuron at a synapse may be diminished. Repeated blocking of receptor sites by a drug over time may cause a compensatory reaction through an increase in the number of receptor sites or an increased amount of neurotransmitter that is released.[16]

Instances of cross-tolerance and cross-dependence effects can be explained by the fact that we are dealing with multiple drugs that bind to the same receptors in the brain. Imagine that two or more drugs activated different sites on the same receptor; the receptor itself would then not be able to "tell them apart." As far as the receptor was concerned, the effect would be the same. The neuronal

Quick Concept Check 3.3

Understanding Cross-Tolerance and Cross-Dependence

Check your understanding of cross-tolerance and cross-dependence by answering the following questions. Suppose you have two receptors in the brain, as shown here.

Notice that Receptor X has three binding sites, one for drug A, one for drug B, and one for neurotransmitter K. Receptor Y also has three binding sites, one for drug C, one for drug D, and one for neurotransmitter L.

Based on this information, indicate whether the following pairs of drugs show cross-tolerance and cross-dependence with each other.

1.	drug A and drug B	☐ yes	☐ no
2.	drug A and drug C	☐ yes	☐ no
3.	drug B and drug C	☐ yes	☐ no
4.	drug C and drug D	☐ yes	☐ no
5.	drug B and drug D	☐ yes	☐ no
6.	drug A and drug D	☐ yes	☐ no

Answers: 1. yes   2. no   3. no   4. yes   5. no   6. no

effects of the drugs over an extended period of time would be equivalent and interchangeable, producing the effects of cross-tolerance and cross-dependence. In general, drugs that have similar psychoactive effects share common receptor sites.

Physiological Factors in Psychological Dependence

Amphetamines, cocaine, heroin, alcohol, and nicotine may be very different from a pharmacological standpoint, but they are remarkably similar in the way people and animals react to them. There is a tremendous feeling of satisfaction as these drugs enter the bloodstream and the brain, and an intense craving for repeating the experience. The parallels are numerous enough to entertain the idea that there might exist a common physiological process in the brain that links them all together. It may not be a coincidence that there is a system of neurons near the hypothalamus and limbic system that animals will work hard to stimulate electrically. We cannot say how they are feeling at the time, but their behavior indicates that they want to "turn on" this region of their brains. Could there be a connection to the craving and intense "rush" of heroin, cocaine, or amphetamine?

Two of the key elements in the rewarding effect of these psychoactive drugs are dopamine and a grouping of neurons lying in a region of the limbic system called the **nucleus accumbens.** When laboratory animals are injected with amphetamines, heroin, cocaine, alcohol, or nicotine, for example, there is a release of dopamine in the nucleus accumbens, and since dopamine acts as an inhibitory neurotransmitter, the activity level of neurons in the nucleus accumbens goes down.

Administration of any substance that interferes with the action of dopamine in this region eliminates the desire of animals to work for the self-administration of these abused drugs. While we cannot say, of course, that these animals no longer experience feelings of craving as a result, you will recall that self-administration behavior in animals closely parallels the pattern of human behavior that characterizes psychological dependence. Therefore, these studies can be used to understand the neural changes caused by drug abuse. Considering the evidence now in hand, a persuasive argument can be made that dopamine-related processes in the nucleus accumbens underlie the reinforcing effects of many abused drugs. There is also research showing an involvement of the nucleus accumbens with compulsive gambling and compulsive eating disorders.[17]

It is not hard to see the applications to the real-world treatment of drug dependence. Drugs that affect

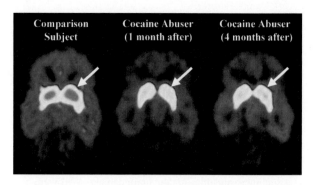

This is literally "your brain on drugs." PET scans from a drug-free subject (left), a detoxified cocaine abuser one month after (middle), and a detoxified cocaine abuser four months after (right). The absence of orange-colored areas in the PET scans in the middle and on the right indicates lower levels of dopamine activity.

activity in the nucleus accumbens are currently being developed to reduce the feelings of craving that cause drug-dependent individuals to relapse.[18]

Continued research on the influence of dopamine in drug dependence has the potential to allow us to understand why some individuals may be more susceptible than others toward drug-taking behavior. As an example, in one study, twenty-three drug-free men with no history of drug abuse were given doses of methylphenidate (brand name: Ritalin), a psychoactive stimulant when ingested by adults. Twelve of the men experienced a pleasant feeling, nine felt annoyed or distrustful, and two felt nothing at all. Measurements of a subclass of dopamine receptors in the brains of these subjects showed a consistent pattern. The men with the least concentration of dopamine receptors were the ones experiencing pleasant effects. It is reasonable to hypothesize that those individuals with the fewest dopamine receptors might be the most vulnerable to drug abuse. Their drug-taking behavior might, in part, be compensation for an inadequate number of dopamine receptors necessary to experience pleasurable feelings without drugs (see Portrait, page 84).[19]

Recent research indicates that individual differences observed in dopamine receptor concentrations are, in part, genetically based. In the case of nicotine, it is estimated that genetics account for about 75 percent of the inclination to begin smoking, for about 60 percent of the tendency to become dependent on nicotine, and for about 54 percent of the ability to quit. In a rapidly

nucleus accumbens (NEW-clee-us ac-CUM-buns): A region in the limbic system of the brain considered to be responsible for the rewarding effects of several drugs of abuse.

advancing area of research, analyses of genes within the human genome are showing specific gene sites that increase the risk of alcohol abuse and the risk of abuse of a variety of illicit substances, including marijuana. On the other hand, it is clear that there is an interplay between genetic and environmental influences in this area, and the total picture is bound to be complex. A recent study, for example, found that the genetic influences in substance abuse in general were more prominent among people in early to middle adulthood and less prominent among adolescents, for whom social environmental factors were dominant.[20]

Psychological Factors in Drug-Taking Behavior

This chapter has considered the physiological effects of psychoactive drugs, down to the level of a single neuron in the brain. It has also pointed out that certain physiological factors such as weight and gender must be taken into account to predict particular drug effects. Yet, even if we controlled these factors completely, we would still frequently find a drug effect in an individual person to be different from time to time, place to place, and situation to situation. Predictions about how a person might react would be far from perfectly accurate.

Therefore, a good way of thinking about an individual's response to a particular drug is to consider the drug effect to be a three-way interaction of the drug's pharmacological properties (the biochemical nature of the substance), the individual taking the drug (set), and the immediate environment within which drug-taking behavior is occurring (setting) (Figure 3.8). Whether one or more of these factors dominate in the final analysis seems to depend upon the dosage level. Generally speaking, the higher the drug dose, the greater the contribution made by the pharmacology of the drug itself; the lower the dose, the greater the contribution of individual characteristics of the drug-taker or environmental conditions.[21]

Expectation Effects

One of the most uncontrollable factors in drug-taking behavior is the set of expectations a person may have

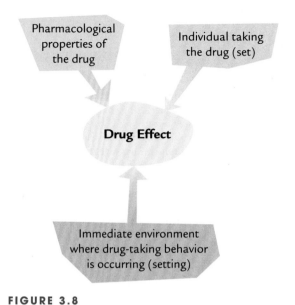

FIGURE 3.8

Viewing a drug effect as a three-way interaction.

about what the drug will do. If you believe that a drug will make you drunk or feel sexy, the chances are increased that it will do so; if you believe that a marijuana cigarette will make you high, the chances are increased that it will. You can consider the impact of negative expectations in the same way; when the feelings are strong that a drug will have no effect on you, the chances are lessened that you will react to it. In the most extreme case, you might experience a drug effect even when the substance you ingested was completely inert—that is, pharmacologically ineffective. Any inert (inactive) substance is referred to as a **placebo** (from the Latin, "I will please"), and the physical reaction to it is referred to as the *placebo effect*.

The concept of a placebo goes back to the earliest days of pharmacology. The bizarre ingredients prescribed in the Ebers Papyrus (see Chapter 1) were effective to the extent that people *believed* that they were effective, not from any known factor in these ingredients. No doubt, the placebo effect was strong enough for medical symptoms to diminish. During the Middle Ages, in one of the more extreme cases of the placebo effect, Pope Boniface VIII reportedly was cured of kidney pains when his personal physician hung a gold seal bearing the image of a lion around the pope's thigh.[22]

It would be a mistake to think of the placebo effect as involving totally imaginary symptoms or totally imaginary reactions. Physical symptoms, involving specific bodily changes, can occur on the basis of placebo effects alone. How likely is it that a person will react to a

placebo? The probability will vary from drug to drug, but in the case of morphine, the data are very clear. In 1959 a review of studies in which morphine or a placebo was administered in clinical studies of pain concluded that a placebo-induced reduction in pain occurred 35 percent of the time. Considering that morphine itself had a positive result in only 75 percent of the cases, the placebo effect was a very strong one.

In a more recent placebo study reported in 2008, volunteer subjects were asked to judge the intensity of electric shocks before and after ingesting a pill that contained no active ingredients. Half of the subjects were told the pill was a drug selling for $2.50 each, and the other half were told the pill cost a "discounted" ten cents. The percentage of subjects reporting a reduction in pain was greater with expensive pill (85 percent) than with the cheaper pill (62 percent). In both cases, a placebo effect was observed. Evidently, higher-priced pills were considered more effective than cheaper pills, even though in both cases they were physiologically inert.[23]

Unfortunately, it is not clear how we can predict whether a person will react strongly or weakly to a

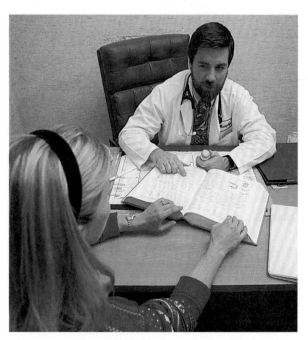

The likelihood of a placebo effect is maximized when the patient highly regards the expertise of the physician prescribing a drug.

placebo (pla-SEE-bo): Latin term translated "I will please." Any inert substance that produces a psychological or physiological reaction.

PORTRAIT

Nora D. Volkow—Imaging the Face of Addiction in the Brain

It is one thing to speculate about the effects of drug abuse on the brain, to assert that the transition from initially being a voluntary drug user to becoming a compulsive drug user is a matter of subtle but significant brain changes. It is quite another thing to show the physical effects themselves. But that is precisely what Nora D. Volkow and her associates at the Brookhaven National Laboratory in New York have done.

Using a brain scanning technique called positron emission tomography (PET), neural activity in the human brain can be captured in graphic detail (see photo on page 81). Volkow and her colleagues have shown that chronic cocaine abuse leads to the loss of about 20 percent of the dopamine receptors in the nucleus accumbens. This effect appears to be long-lasting, enduring for up to four months after the last cocaine exposure, even though the cocaine abuser no longer has cocaine in his or her system. Volkow estimates that a comparable decline in dopamine receptors would take at least 40 years to accomplish in a drug-free brain.

It is not surprising that the nucleus accumbens, with its rich concentration of dopamine receptors, would be the site of this dramatic change. Dopamine and the nucleus accumbens have been associated with feelings of reward and pleasure in a wide range of behavioral activities, from drug use to compulsive exercising to gambling. As Volkow says, "It is through activation of these circuits that we are motivated to do the things we perceive as pleasurable. If you have a decrease in dopamine receptors that transmit pleasurable feelings, you become less responsive to the stimuli, such as food or sex, that normally activate them."

The irony is that it may be precisely those individuals who have fewer dopamine receptors who may be inclined to engage in drug-taking behavior in the first place; the drug exposure evidently makes the deficit worse. As one drug researcher has put it, "In the end, [these people] could be much worse off biologically than when they started."

Following Volkow's pioneering work on brain imaging, other mysteries about drug abuse are being unlocked. For example, what creates the intense craving for specific drugs once an individual has been first exposed to them? The answer lies in the research of Anna R. Childress and her associates at the University of Pennsylvania. When chronic drug abusers were shown video segments of drug-associated paraphernalia (a picture of a syringe or a mound of white powder), PET scans of their brain revealed increased activity in an area of the limbic system. The connection between the limbic system and one's emotional behavior in times of stress makes it reasonable to hypothesize that this area of the brain, in this instance, would be involved in feelings of drug craving.

In 2003, Nora D. Volkow was appointed director of the National Institute of Drug Abuse (NIDA), the first woman to lead this federal agency in its history.

Sources: Childress, Anna Rose; Mozley, David; McElgin, William; Fitzgerald, Josh; Reivich, Martin; and O'Brian, Charles P. (1999). Limbic activation during cue-induced cocaine craving. *American Journal of Psychiatry, 156,* 11–18. National Institute on Drug Abuse (2003, January 23). Press release: Dr. Nora D. Volkow named new director of NIDA. Bethesda, MD: National Institute on Drug Abuse. Volkow, Nora D.; Wang, Gene-Jack; Fowler, Joanna S.; Logan, Jean; Gatley, Samuel J.; Hitzemann, Richard; Chen, A. D.; and Pappas, Naomi (1997). Decrease in striatal dopaminergic responsiveness in detoxified cocaine-dependent subjects. *Nature, 386,* 830–833.

placebo. We do know, however, that the enthusiasm or lack of enthusiasm of the prescribing physician can play a major role. In one study that varied the attitude of the physician toward a particular medication, negative attitudes toward the medication resulted in the least benefits, whereas positive attitudes resulted in the most.[24]

It is not at all clear how the placebo effect is accomplished. In the case of pain relief, there is evidence that we have the natural ability to increase the levels of endorphins in the bloodstream and the brain from one moment to the next, but the nature of our ability to alter other important substances in our bodies is virtually unknown. Recent studies have documented a 33 percent increase in lung capacity among asthmatic children who inhaled a bronchodilator containing a placebo instead of medication and the development of skin rashes in people who have been exposed to fake poison ivy, to name a few examples of placebo-induced physiological reactions. Placebo research forces us to acknowledge the potential for psychological control over physiological processes in our bodies.[25]

Drug Research Procedures

Given the power of the placebo effect in drug-taking behavior, it is necessary to be very careful when carrying out drug research. For a drug to be deemed truly effective, it must be proved to be better not only in comparison to a no-treatment condition (a difference that could conceivably be due to a placebo effect) but also in comparison to an identical-looking drug that lacks the active ingredients of the drug being evaluated. For example, if the drug under study is in the shape of a round red pill, another round red pill without the active ingredients of the drug (called the *active placebo*) must also be administered for comparison.

The procedures of these studies also have to be carefully executed. Neither the individual administering the drug or placebo nor the individual receiving the drug or placebo should know which substance is which. Such precautions, referred to as a **double-blind** procedure, represent the minimal standards for separating the pharmacological effects of a drug from the effects that arise from one's expectations and beliefs.[26] We will return to the issue of interactions between drug effects and expectations when we consider alcohol intoxication in Chapter 9.

> **double-blind:** A procedure in drug research in which neither the individual administering nor the individual receiving a chemical substance knows whether the substance is the drug being evaluated or an active placebo.

Summary

How Drugs Enter the Body

- There are four basic ways to administer drugs into the body: oral administration, injection, inhalation, and absorption through the skin or membranes. Each of these presents constraints on which kinds of drugs will be effectively delivered into the bloodstream.

How Drugs Exit the Body

- Most drugs are eliminated from the body through urinary excretion. Drugs are broken down for elimination by the action of enzymes in the liver. An index of how long this process takes is called the elimination half-life.

Factors Determining the Physiological Impact of Drugs

- The physiological effect of a drug can vary as a factor of the time elapsed since its administration, the possible combination of its administration with other drugs, and finally the personal characteristics of the individual consuming the drug.
- Some characteristics that can play a definite role in the effect of a drug include the individual's weight, gender, and ethnic background.

Introducing the Nervous System

- Understanding the organization of the nervous system helps us to understand where psychoactive drugs are working in our bodies.
- The nervous system consists of the peripheral nervous system and the central nervous system, with the latter divided into the brain and the spinal cord. Autonomic nerves control our cardiac and smooth muscles to respond either to stress (sympathetic activation) or to demands for nurturance and renewal (parasympathetic activation).

Understanding the Brain

- Within the brain are three major divisions: the hindbrain, midbrain, and forebrain. The forebrain is the most recently evolved region of the brain and controls the most complex behaviors and processes the most complex information.
- Many drugs affect all levels of the brain, in one way or another.

Understanding the Biochemistry of Psychoactive Drugs

- Understanding the functioning of neurons and their interaction through synaptic communication helps us to understand how psychoactive drugs work in our bodies.
- In general, drugs work at the neuronal level by altering neurotransmitter release, receptor binding, or reuptake at the synapse.

Physiological Aspects of Drug-Taking Behavior

- Three important issues need to be understood in looking at the physiological effect of drugs: the extent to which drugs pass from the bloodstream to the brain, the extent to which tolerance effects occur, and the extent to which a drug influences neuronal activity in the region of the nucleus accumbens in the brain.

Psychological Factors in Drug-Taking Behavior

- Although the physiological actions of psychoactive drugs are becoming increasingly well understood, great variability in the effect of these drugs remains, largely because of psychological factors.

- The most prominent psychological factor is the influence of personal expectations on the part of the individual consuming the drug. The impact of expectations on one's reaction to a drug, a phenomenon called the placebo effect, is an important consideration in drug evaluation and research.

Key Terms

acetylcholine, p. 77
biotransformation, p. 64
blood-brain barrier, p. 79
central nervous system (CNS), p. 69
cerebral cortex, p. 73
cross-dependence, p. 67
cross-tolerance, p. 67
dopamine, p. 77
double-blind, p. 85
elimination half-life, p. 64

endorphins, p. 79
gamma aminobutyric acid (GABA), p. 77
glutamate, p. 78
intramuscular (i.m.), p. 62
intranasal, p. 63
intravenous (i.v.), p. 62
latency period, p. 66
metabolite, p. 64
neuron, p. 72
neurotransmitter, p. 75

norepinephrine, p. 77
nucleus accumbens, p. 81
parasympathetic branch of the autonomic nervous system, p. 70
peripheral nervous system, p. 69
placebo, p. 83
potentiation, p. 67
reuptake, p. 76
serotonin, p. 77

subcutaneous (s.c. or sub-Q), p. 62
sublingual, p. 64
sympathetic branch of the autonomic nervous system, p. 70
synapse, p. 74
synergism, p. 66
transdermal patch, p. 64

Endnotes

1. Public-service message, "Frying Pan." Partners for a Drug-free America, New York, 1987.
2. Grilly, David M. (2006). *Drugs and human behavior* (5th ed.). Boston: Allyn and Bacon, p. 50.
3. Bhattacharjee, Yudhijit (2002, July 2). More than a patch: New ways to take medicine via skin. *New York Times*, p. F5. Drugmakers trying to retire the needle (2002, September 24). *New York Times*, p. F7. Mitragotri, Samir; Blankschtein, Daniel; and Langer, Robert (1995). Ultrasound-mediated transdermal protein delivery. *Science*, 269, 850–853.
4. Julien, Robert M. (2001). *A primer of drug action* (9th ed.). New York: Worth, pp. 27–31. McKim, William A. (2000). *Drugs and behavior: An introduction to behavioral pharmacology* (4th ed.). Upper Saddle River, NJ: Prentice-Hall, pp. 1–25.
5. Lickey, Marvin E., and Gordon, Barbara (1991). *Medicine and mental illness.* New York: Freeman, p. 323.
6. Frezza, Mario; DiPadova, Carlo; Pozzato, Gabrielle; Terpin, Maddalena; Baraona, Enrique; and Lieber, Charles S. (1990). High blood alcohol levels in women: The role of decreased gastric alcohol dehydrogenase activity and first-pass metabolism. *New England Journal of Medicine*, 322, 95–99.
7. Nakawatase, Tomoko V.; Yamamoto, Joe; and Sasao, Toshiaki (1993). The association between fast-flushing response and alcohol use among Japanese Americans. *Journal of Studies on Alcohol*, 54, 48–53.
8. Goodman, Deborah (1992, January–February). NIMH grantee finds drug responses differ among ethnic groups. *ADAMHA News*, pp. 5, 15.
9. Perez-Stable, Eliseo J.; Herrera, Brenda; Jacob III, Peyton; and Benowita, Neal L. (1998). Nicotine metabolism and intake in black and white smokers. *Journal of the American Medical Association*, 280, 152–156.
10. Levinthal, Charles F. (1990). *Introduction to physiological psychology* (3rd ed.). Englewood Cliffs, NJ: Prentice-Hall, p. 63. Lyvers, Michael (2000). "Loss of control" in alcoholism and drug addiction: A neuroscientific interpretation. *Experimental and Clinical Psychopharmacology, 8,* 225–249. Weinstein, Cheryl S., and Shaffer, Howard J. (1993). Neurocognitive aspects of substance abuse treatment: A psychotherapist's primer. *Psychotherapy, 30,* 317–333.
11. Thompson, Richard F. (1993). *The brain: A neuroscience primer* (2nd ed.). New York: Freeman, p. 3.
12. Carlezon, William A., and Wise, Robert A. (1996). Rewarding reactions of phencyclide and related drugs in nucleus accumbens shell and frontal cortex. *Journal of Neuroscience, 16,* 3112–3122. Heidbreder, Christian A., and Hagan, Jim J. (2005). Novel pharmacotherapeutic approaches to the treatment of drug addiction and

craving. *Current Opinion in Pharmacology, 5,* 107–118. Weiss, Friedbert (2005). Neurobiology of craving, conditioned reward and relapse. *Current Opinion in Pharmacology, 5,* 9–19.

13. Julien, *A primer of drug action,* pp. 18–19.

14. Pinel, John P. J. (2003). *Biopsychology* (5th ed.). Boston: Allyn and Bacon, p. 250.

15. Goldstein, Gary W., and Betz, A. Lorris (1986). The blood-brain barrier. *Scientific American, 255* (3), 74–83. Kumar, Priti; Wu, Haoquan; McBride, Jodi L.; et al. (2007). Transvascular delivery of small interfering RNA to the central nervous system. *Nature, 448,* 39–43. Pardridge, W. H. (1998). CNS drug design based on principles of blood-brain barrier transport. *Journal of Neurochemistry, 70,* 1781–1792.

16. Martin, William R. (1987). Tolerance and physical dependence. In George Adelman (Ed.), *Encyclopedia of neuroscience.* Boston: Birkhauser, pp. 1223–1225.

17. Blakeslee, Sandra (2002, February 19). Hijacking the brain circuits with a nickel slot machine. *New York Times,* pp. F1, F5. Nestler, Eric J., and Malenka, Robert C. (2004, March). The addicted brain. *Scientific American,* pp. 78–85. Phillips, Paul E. M.; Stuber, Garret D.; Helen, Michael, L. A. V.; Wightman, R. Mark; and Carelli, Regina, M. (2003). Subsecond dopamine release promotes cocaine seeking. *Nature, 422,* 614–618.

18. Vestag, Brian (2002, December 25). Addiction treatment strives for legitimacy. *Journal of the American Medical Association,* 3096–3099. Volkow, Nora D.; Fowler, Joanna S.; Wang, Gene-Jack; and Swanson J. M. (2004). Dopamine in drug abuse and addiction: Results from imaging studies and treatment implications. *Molecular Psychiatry, 9,* 557–569.

19. Volkow, Nora D.; Wang, Gene-Jack; Fowler, Joanna S.; Logan, Jean; Gatley, Samuel J.; et al. (1999). Prediction of reinforcing responses to psychostimulants in humans by brain dopamine D_2 receptor levels. *American Journal of Psychiatry, 156,* 1440–1443.

20. Agrawal, Arpana, and Lynskey, Michael T. (2008). Are there genetic influences on addiction: Evidence from family, adoption and twin studies. *Addiction, 103,* 1069–1081. Agrawal, Arpana; Pergadia, Michele L.; Saccone, Scott F.; Lynskey, Michel T.; Wang, Jen C.; et al. (2008). An autosomal linkage scan for cannabis use disorders in the Nicotine Addiction Genetics Project.

Archives of General Psychiatry, 65, 713–722. Kendler, Kenneth S.; Schmitt, Eric; Aggen, Steven H.; and Prescott, Carol A. (2008). Genetic and environmental influences on alcohol, caffeine, cannabis, and nicotine use from early adolescence to middle adulthood. *Archives of General Psychiatry, 65,* 674–682. Price, Michael (2008, June). Genes matter in addiction. *Monitor on Psychology,* p. 16. Uhl, George R.; Qing-Rong, Liu; Drgon, Tomas; Johnson, Catherine; et al. (2008). Molecular genetics of successful smoking cessation. *Archives of General Psychiatry, 65,* 683–693.

21. Goode, Erich (1999). *Drugs in American society* (5th ed.). New York: McGraw-Hill College, p. 9.

22. Kornetsky, Conan (1976). *Pharmacology: Drugs affecting behavior.* New York, Wiley, p. 23. Morris, David B. (1999). Placebo, pain, and belief: A biocultural model. In Anne Harrington (Ed.), *The placebo effect: An interdisciplinary exploration.* Cambridge, MA: Harvard University Press, pp. 187–207. Shapiro, Arthur K., and Shapiro, Elaine (1997). *The powerful placebo: From ancient priest to modern physician.* Baltimore: Johns Hopkins University Press.

23. Beecher, H. K. (1959). *Measurement of subjective responses: Quantitative effects of drugs.* New York: Oxford University Press. Waber, Rebecca L.; Shiv, Baba; Carmon, Ziv; and Ariely, Dan (2008). Commercial features of placebo and therapeutic efficacy. *Journal of the American Medical Association, 299,* 1016–1017.

24. Benedetti, F. (2002). How the doctor's words affect the patient's brain. *Evaluation and the Health Professions, 25,* 369–386. Schindel, L. E. (1962). Placebo in theory and practice. *Antibiotica et Chemotherapia, Advances, 10,* 398–430. Cited in Kornetsky, *Pharmacology,* p. 36.

25. De la Fuente-Fernández, R., and Stoessl, A. J. (2002). The biochemical bases for reward: Implications for the placebo effect. *Evaluation and the Health Professions, 25,* 387–398. Levinthal, Charles F. (1988). *Messengers of paradise: Opiates and the brain.* New York: Anchor Press/Doubleday. Talbot, Margaret (2000, January 9). The placebo prescription. *New York Times Magazine,* pp. 34–39, 44, 58–60. Wager, Tor D. (2005). The neural bases of placebo effects in pain. *Current Directions in Psychological Science, 14,* 175–179.

26. Quitkin, Frederic M. (1999). Placebos, drug effects, and study design: A clinician's guide. *American Journal of Psychiatry, 156,* 829–836.

POINT/COUNTERPOINT

Should We Legalize Drugs?

The following discussion of viewpoints represents the opinions of people on both sides of the controversial issue of the legalization of drugs. Read them with an open mind. Don't think you have to come up with the final answer, nor should you necessarily agree with the argument you heard last. Many of the ideas in this discussion come from the sources listed.

POINT

Legalization would get the problem under some degree of control. The "war on drugs" does nothing but increase the price of illicit drugs to what the market will bear, and it subsidizes the drug dealers and drug barons around the world. If we legalize drugs, we can take the profit out of the drug business because legalization would bring the price down dramatically. We could regulate drug sales, as we do now with nicotine and alcohol, by setting up centers that would be licensed to sell cocaine and heroin, as well as sterile syringes, while any drug sales to minors would remain a criminal offense. Regulations would also ensure that drugs maintained standards of purity; the health risks of drug contamination would be avoided.

COUNTERPOINT

Legalization is fundamentally immoral. How can we allow people to run to the nearest store and destroy their lives? Don't we as a society have a responsibility for the health and welfare of people in general? If the drugs (pure or impure) were available, the only effect would be to increase the number of drug abusers. When Britain allowed physicians to prescribe heroin to "registered" addicts, the number of heroin addicts rose five-fold (or more according to some informal estimates), and there were then cases of medical abuse as well as drug abuse. A few unscrupulous doctors were prescribing heroin in enormous amounts, and a new drug culture was created.

POINT

How moral is the situation now? We have whole communities living at the mercy of drug dealers. Any increase in drug users would be more than compensated for by the gains of freedom from such people. Even if the sale of crack were kept illegal, conceding that this drug is highly dangerous to society, we would have an 80 percent reduction in the black market for drugs, a substantial gain for the welfare of society. We can't guarantee that our inner cities would no longer be places of hopelessness and despair, but at least we would not have the systemic violence associated with the drug world. Besides, with all the money saved from programs set up to prevent people from getting hold of illicit drugs, we could increase the funding for drug treatment programs for all the drug abusers who want them and for research into ways of understanding the nature of drug dependence.

COUNTERPOINT

No doubt, many drug abusers seek out treatment and want to break their drug dependence. Perhaps there may be some individuals who seek treatment under legalization because there would no longer be a social stigma associated with drug abuse, but many drug abusers have little or no long-term commitment toward drug treatment. In the present situation, the illegality of their behavior allows us to compel them to seek and stay in treatment, as well as monitor their abstinence by periodic drug testing. How could we do this when the drug was legal? Besides, how would we approach the education of young people if drugs were legal? We could not tell them that cocaine would give them cancer or emphysema, as we warn them of the dangers of nicotine, only that it would prevent them from being a productive member of society and would have long-term effects on their brains. If the adults around them were allowed to take cocaine, what would be the message to the young? Simply wait until you're twenty-one?

POINT

We already have educational programs about alcohol abuse; the message for heroin and cocaine abuse would be similar. The loss of productivity due to any increased availability of drugs would not be as significant as the present loss of productivity we have with alcohol and cigarettes. With the tax revenues obtained from selling drugs legally, we could have money for more extensive anti-drug advertising. We could send a comprehensive message to our youth that there are alternatives to their lives that do not include psychoactive substances. In the meantime, we would be removing the "forbidden fruit" factor in drug-taking behavior. Drugs wouldn't be a big deal.

COUNTERPOINT

Arguing that people take drugs because they are forbidden or hard to get ignores the basic psychological allure of drugs. If you lowered the price of a very expensive sports car, would you have fewer people wanting to buy one? Of course not. People would want a fast car because they like fast cars, just as people will still want to get high on drugs. Legalizing present drugs would only encourage the development of more dangerous drugs in the future. Look at what happened with crack. Cocaine was bad enough but crack appeared on the scene, making the situation far worse.

POINT

It can be argued that crack was marketed because standard cocaine powder was too expensive for people in the inner cities. If cocaine had been legally available, crack might not ever have been created because the market would not have been there. Even with crack remaining illegal under a legalization plan, there is at least the possibility that the appeal of crack would decline. The trend has been lately that illegal drugs are getting stronger, while legal drugs (alcoholic beverages and cigarettes) are getting weaker as people become more health—conscious. Legalization might make presently illicit drugs weaker in strength, as public opinion turns against them. The main problem we face is that spending 60 percent of a multibillion-dollar drug-law-enforcement program on the "supply" side of the question, and only 40 percent on reducing the demand for drugs is not working. If one source of drugs is controlled, another source takes its place. The link between drugs and crime is a direct result of the illegality of drugs. It's not the drug addicts that are destroying the country; it's the drug dealers. Right now, the criminals are in charge. We have to change that. Only legalization would take away their profits and refocus our law-enforcement efforts on other crimes that continue to undermine our society.

COUNTERPOINT

The frustration is understandable, but let's not jump into something merely because we're frustrated. We can allocate more funds for treatment without making drugs legal. We can increase funds for scientific research without making drugs legal. We need a more balanced program, not an entirely new one. Polls do not indicate general support for drug legalization. Between 60 percent and 80 percent of the U.S. public supports continued prohibition of drugs. Most citizens appear to recognize that legalization would make a bad situation worse, not better.

Critical Thinking Questions for Further Debate

1. Suppose you were a legislator considering new regulatory laws with respect to psychoactive drugs. What would be your argument in favor of making a distinction between "hard drugs" such as heroin, cocaine, and methamphetamine, and "soft drugs" such as marijuana and hallucinogens? On what basis would you make such a distinction?

2. Suppose that social regulations based on a Harm Reduction approach were implemented and the consequence was that drug abuse became more prevalent. Would you revert to a Zero Tolerance approach or reexamine the assumptions of the Harm Reduction approach and alter it to produce more positive societal effects?

Sources: Dennis, Richard J. (1990, November). The economics of legalizing drugs. *The Atlantic,* 126–132. Goldstein, Avram (2001). *Addiction: From biology to drug policy* (2nd ed.). New York: Oxford University Press. Goode, Erich (1997). *Between politics and reason: The drug legalization debate.* New York: St. Martin's Press. Gray, James P. (2001). *Why our drug laws have failed and what we can do about it.* Philadelphia: Temple University Press. Levinthal, Charles F. (2003). *Point/Counterpoint: Opposing perspectives on issues of drug policy.* Boston: Allyn and Bacon, Chapter 1. Wilson, James Q. (1990, February). Against the legalization of drugs. *Commentary,* 21–28.

chapter 4

The Major Stimulants: Cocaine and Amphetamines

S. F. is a brilliant young physician attending a case conference at a metropolitan medical center where he is a resident. He has been on call for thirty-six hours and cannot concentrate on the presentation. S. F. is lonely, depressed, and overworked. All he can think about is his fiancée, Martha, who is several hundred miles away. He knows that her father will not permit her to marry until he is able to support her, and with his loans and meager salary, that could take years.

He excuses himself from the conference, takes a needle syringe from the nurses' station, and locks himself in a bathroom stall. He fills the syringe with cocaine and plunges the needle into his arm. Within seconds, the young doctor feels a rush of euphoria. His tears dry up; he regains his composure and quickly rejoins the conference.

—The date is 1884, the place is Vienna, and the doctor is Sigmund Freud.

The time, place, and identity of S. F. in this fictionalized clinical vignette, based on the facts of Freud's life, may have surprised you, but unfortunately the overall picture of cocaine abuse is all too familiar.[1] The year could have been 1984 (or any other year in the past quarter-century) instead of 1884, and the individual involved could have been anyone twenty-eight years old, as Freud was at the time, or some other age. Freud was extremely lucky; he never became dependent upon cocaine, though a close friend did and millions of people have since Freud's time.

The story of cocaine is both ancient and modern. While its origins stretch back more than four thousand years, cocaine abuse continues to represent a major portion of the present-day drug crisis. For this reason, it is important to understand its history, the properties of the drug itself, and the ways in which it has the ability to control and ultimately, in many cases, destroy a person's life.

This chapter will focus not only on cocaine but also on another group of stimulant drugs, referred to collectively as amphetamines. Although cocaine and amphetamines are distinct in terms of their pharmacology (their characteristics as biochemical substances), there are enough similarities in their behavioral and physiological effects and patterns of abuse to warrant their being discussed together. In general, cocaine and amphetamines represent the two major classes of psychoactive stimulants, drugs that energize the body and create feelings of euphoria. Other, less powerful stimulants, such as nicotine, caffeine, and clinical antidepressants, will be discussed in later chapters.

The History of Cocaine

Cocaine is derived from small leaves of the coca shrub (*Erythroxylon coca*), grown in the high-altitude rain forests and fields that run along the slopes of the Peruvian and Bolivian Andes in South America. Like many other psychoactive drugs, cocaine use has a long history. We can trace the practice of chewing coca leaves, which contain about 2 percent cocaine, back to the Inca civilization, which flourished from the thirteenth century until its conquest by the Spaniards in 1532, as well as to other Andean cultures dating back five thousand years. Coca was considered a gift from the god Inti to the Incas, allowing them to endure life in the Andes without suffering.[2]

To this day, coca chewing is part of the culture of this region. It is estimated that about 2 million Peruvian

by the numbers . . .

5.7 million	Americans, aged 12 or older, who reported in 2007 having used cocaine during the past year
1.5 million	Americans, aged 12 or older, who reported in 2007 having used crack cocaine during the past year
92	Percentage of 50 one-dollar bills randomly sampled from five U.S. cities that have been found to be contaminated with detectable levels of cocaine. Drug contamination begins with contact during drug deals and snorting, then transfers from bill to bill in money-counting machines in banks

Sources: Substance Abuse and Mental Health Administration (2008). *Results from the 2007 National Survey on Drug Use and Health: Detailed tables.* Rockville, MD: Office of Applied Studies, Substance Abuse and Mental Health Administration, Table 1.1A. Jenkins, Amanda J. (2001). Drug contamination of U.S. paper currency. *Forensic Science International, 121,* 189–193.

men who live in the Andean highlands, representing 90 percent of the male population in that area, chew coca leaves.[3] These people, called *acullicadores*, mix their own blend of coca, chalk, lime, and ash to achieve the desired effects, whether it is to fight fatigue or socialize with friends.[4]

This form of cocaine use among these people produces few instances of toxicity or abuse. The reason lies in the very low doses of cocaine that chewed coca leaves provide; in this form, absorption from the digestive system is slow, and relatively little cocaine enters the bloodstream and is distributed to the brain (Chapter 3). A much more serious problem is the availability of a coca paste containing a much higher percentage of cocaine mixed with tobacco. It is called a *bazuco* and smoked as a cigarette. Making matters worse, dangerously high levels of kerosene, gasoline, and ether are involved in the coca-refining process and end up as adulterants in the cigarettes themselves.[5]

cocaine: An extremely potent and dependence-producing stimulant drug, derived from the coca leaf.

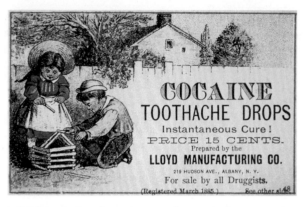

In the late nineteenth century, cocaine products were used by children as well as adults.

Cocaine in Nineteenth-Century Life

Coca leaves were brought back to Europe from the Spanish colonies soon after the conquest of the Incas in 1533, but their potency was nearly gone after the long sea voyage. Perhaps, it was said at the time, the legendary effects of coca were merely exaggerations after all. Coca leaves were ignored for three hundred years. By the late 1850s, however, the active ingredient of the coca plant had been chemically isolated. In 1859, Alfred Niemann, a German chemist, observed its anesthetic effect on his tongue and its bitter taste and named it "cocaine." Interest in the drug was renewed, and by the 1860s the patent medicine industry in the United States and Europe (see Chapter 1) had lost no time in taking advantage of cocaine's appeal.

Commercial Uses of Cocaine

By far the most successful commercial use of cocaine in the nineteenth century was a mixture of coca and wine invented in 1863 by a Corsican chemist and businessman, Angelo Mariani. We know now that the combination of alcohol and cocaine produces a metabolite with an elimination half-life several times longer than cocaine alone, so the mixture tends to be quite intoxicating (see Health Alert on page 96).

No wonder "Vin Mariani" became an instant sensation. A long list of endorsements by celebrities accumulated over the next few decades from satisfied customers such as U.S. President William McKinley, Thomas Edison, the surgeon general of the U.S. Army, General Ulysses S. Grant, Sarah Bernhardt, Jules Verne, the Prince of Wales, the czar of Russia, and Popes Pius X and Leo XII. In a letter to Mariani, Frederic Bartholdi, the sculptor of the Statue of Liberty, wrote that if he had been drinking Vin Mariani while designing the statue, it

would have been more than three times taller.[6] We can only assume that this comment was intended to be complimentary.

Meanwhile in the United States, Atlanta pharmacist John Pemberton promoted an imitation form of Vin Mariani that he called French Wine Cola. Shortly after, in 1885, he took out the alcohol as a concession to the American temperance movement (see Chapter 9), added soda water, and reformulated the basic mixture to combine coca with the syrup of the African kola nut containing about 2 percent caffeine. Coca-Cola was born. Early advertisements for Coca-Cola emphasized the drink as a stimulating brain tonic that made you feel more productive and as a remedy for such assorted nervous ailments as sick headaches and melancholia (a word used at the time to mean depression).[7] The medicinal slant to the early promotion of Coca-Cola is probably the reason why soda fountains began to appear in drugstores.[8]

In the late nineteenth century, the Coca-Cola Company advertised its beverage in medicinal terms. A company letterhead of this period spoke of Coca-Cola as containing "the tonic properties of the wonderful coca plant."

A number of competing brands with similar formulations sprang up with names such as Care-Cola, Dope Cola, Kola Ade, and Wiseola.[9] Eventually, public pressure brought about official restrictions on the patent medicine industry, which, by the beginning of the twentieth century, was marketing more than fifty thousand unregulated products.[10] The Pure Food and Drug Act of 1906 specified that all active ingredients had to be listed on patent medicine labels. In Canada, the Proprietary and Patent Medicine Act of 1908 banned cocaine from patent medicines entirely, but in the United States no further restrictions on cocaine sales or use were imposed until the Harrison Act of 1914 (see Chapter 2).

The Coca-Cola Company, aware of the growing tide of sentiment against cocaine, changed the formula in 1903 from regular coca leaves to decocainized coca leaves, which eliminated the cocaine but retained the coca flavoring that remains to this day (Drugs . . . in Focus). The "pause that refreshed" America would henceforth be due only to the presence of sugar and caffeine.

The use of cocaine also was becoming a major factor in the practice of medicine. In the United States, William Halsted, one of the most distinguished surgeons of the time and one of the founders of Johns Hopkins Medical School, studied the effect of cocaine on anesthetizing nerves and whole limbs. In the process, he acquired a cocaine habit of his own (which was replaced several years later by a dependence on morphine). It was in Europe, however, that the psychological implications of cocaine were explored most extensively, ironically through the triumphs and tribulations of Sigmund Freud.

Freud and Cocaine

In 1884 Freud was a struggling young neurologist, given to bouts of depression and self-doubt but nonetheless determined to make his mark in the medical world. He had read a report by a German army physician that supplies of pure cocaine could help soldiers endure fatigue and feel better in general. Freud secured some cocaine for himself and found the experience exhilarating; his depression lifted, and he felt a new sense of boundless energy. His friend and colleague Dr. Ernst von Fleischl-Marxow, taking morphine and enduring a painful illness, borrowed some cocaine from Freud and found favorable results as well. Freud immediately saw the prospects of fame and fortune. In a letter to his

Drugs...in Focus

What Happened to the Coca in Coca-Cola?

Every day, in a drab factory building in a New Jersey suburb of Maywood, a select team of employees of the Stepan Company carries out a chemical procedure that has been one of the primary responsibilities of the company since 1903. They remove cocaine from high-grade coca leaves. The remainder, technically called "decocainized flavor essence" is then sent to the Coca-Cola Company as part of the secret recipe for the world's favorite soft drink.

Each year, the Stepan Company is legally sanctioned by the U.S. government (and carefully monitored by the DEA) to receive shipments of about 175,000 kilograms of coca leaves from Peruvian coca farms, separate the cocaine chemically, and produce about 1,750 kilograms of high-quality cocaine. Its annual output is equivalent to approximately 20 million hits of crack, worth about $200 million if it were to make it to the illicit drug market.

Fortunately, the Stepan Company has an impeccable security record.

In case you are wondering what happens to the cocaine after it is removed from the coca leaves, it turns out that Stepan finds a legitimate market in the world of medicine. Tincture of cocaine is used regularly as a local anesthetic to numb the skin prior to minor surgical procedures such as stitching up a wound. Surgeons frequently use cocaine as a topical ointment when working on the nose or throat.

As a result, the Stepan Company essentially has it both ways. It is the exclusive U.S. supplier of cocaine for use in medical settings as well as decocainized coca for your next can of Coke. As an article in the *Wall Street Journal* has put it, "The two markets end up sending Stepan's products into virtually every bloodstream in America."

Sources: Inciardi, James A. (2002). *The war on drugs III.* Boston: Allyn and Bacon, p. 21. Miller, Michael W. (1994, October 17). Quality stuff: Firm is peddling cocaine, and deals are legit. *Wall Street Journal*, pp. A1, A14.

fiancée, Martha Bernays, he wrote: "If it goes well I will write an essay on it and I expect it will win its place in therapeutics by the side of morphium [morphine] and superior to it."[11]

Before long, Freud was distributing cocaine to his friends and his sisters and even sent a supply to Martha. In the words of Freud's biographer Ernest Jones, "From the vantage point of our present knowledge, he was rapidly becoming a public menace."[12] We can gain some perspective on the effect cocaine was having on Freud's behavior at this time through an excerpt from a personal letter to Martha:

> *Woe to you, my Princess, when I come. I will kiss you quite red and feed you till you are plump. And if you are forward you shall see who is the stronger, a gentle little girl who doesn't eat enough or a big wild man who has cocaine in his body [underlined in the original]. In my last severe depression I took coca again and a small dose lifted me to the heights in a wonderful fashion. I am just now busy collecting the literature for a song of praise to this magical substance.*[13]

Within four months, his "song of praise" essay, "Über Coca" (Concerning Coca), was written and published.

Unfortunately, the sweetness of Freud's romance with cocaine soon turned sour. Freud himself escaped becoming dependent upon cocaine, though later in his life he clearly became dependent on nicotine (see Chapter 11). His friend, Fleischl, however, was not so lucky. Within a year, Fleischl had increased his cocaine dose to twenty times the amount Freud had taken and had developed a severe cocaine-induced psychosis in which he experienced hallucinations that snakes were crawling over his skin (an example of a phenomenon now referred to as **formication**). Fleischl suffered six years of agony and anguish until his death. By 1887, Freud had retracted his earlier stance on the drug.

The story of Freud's infatuation with cocaine and his later disillusionment with it can be seen as a miniature version of the modern history of cocaine itself.[14] Between 1880 and 1910, the public reaction to cocaine went from wild enthusiasm to widespread disapproval. As this chapter will later describe, a similar cycle of attitudes swept the United States and the world between 1970 and 1985.

Quick Concept Check 4.1

Understanding the History of Cocaine

Check your understanding of the history of cocaine by matching the names on the left with the identifications on the right. Be careful; some identifications may not match up with any of the names.

1. Angelo Mariani
2. John Pemberton
3. William Halsted
4. Sigmund Freud
5. Ernst von Fleischl-Marxow

a. Friend of Sigmund Freud; first documented case of cocaine psychosis

b. Developer of Coca-Cola, originally containing cocaine

c. Early advocate of restricting cocaine use in the United States

d. Cofounder of Johns Hopkins Medical School; early developer of cocaine to anesthetize nerves and whole limbs

e. A popular figure in present-day Peru

f. Early advocate of cocaine use; originator of psycho-analysis

g. Promoter of a popular coca-laced wine

Answers: 1. g 2. b 3. d 4. f 5. a

formication: Hallucinatory behavior produced by chronic cocaine or amphetamine abuse, in which the individual feels insects or snakes crawling either over or under the skin.

Acute Effects of Cocaine

Although the effects of cocaine on the user vary in degree with the route of administration, the purity of the dose, and the user's expectations about the experience, certain features remain the same. The most characteristic reaction is a powerful burst of energy. If the cocaine is injected intravenously, the extremely intense effect (often referred to as a "rush") is felt within a matter of seconds, peaking in three to five minutes and wearing off in thirty to forty minutes. If snorted through the nose, the effect

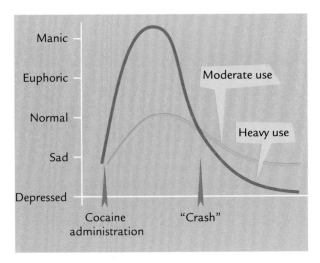

Manic —	
Euphoric —	Moderate use
Normal —	Heavy use
Sad —	
Depressed —	

Cocaine administration   "Crash"

FIGURE 4.1

Ups and downs of a typical dose of cocaine.

begins in about three minutes, peaking after fifteen to twenty minutes, and wearing off in sixty to ninety minutes.

Users also experience a general sense of well-being, although in some instances cocaine may precipitate a panic attack.[15] When cocaine levels diminish, the mood changes dramatically. The user becomes irritable, despondent, and depressed (Figure 4.1). These after-effects are uncomfortable enough to produce a powerful craving for another dose.

The depression induced in the aftermath of a cocaine high can lead to suicide. In 1985, during one of the peak years of cocaine abuse in the United States, as many as one out of five suicide victims in New York City showed evidence of cocaine in their blood at autopsy. The prevalence of cocaine use was greatest among victims who were in their twenties and thirties, and for African Americans and Latinos.[16] In a 1989 survey of teenage callers to the 800-COCAINE hotline, one out of seven reported a previous suicide attempt.[17] On the basis of these studies, cocaine use has become recognized as a significant risk factor for suicide attempts.

Cocaine's effect on sexual arousal is often cited as having been the basis for calling it "the aphrodisiac of the 1980s." On the one hand, interviews of cocaine users frequently include reports of spontaneous and prolonged erections in males and multiple orgasms in females during initial doses of the drug. On the other hand, cocaine's reputation for increasing sexual performance (recall Freud's reference in his letter to Martha) may bias users toward a strong expectation that there will be a sexually stimulating reaction, when in reality the effect is a much weaker one. As one cocaine abuser

expressed it, "Everybody says that it's an aphrodisiac. Again, I think some people say it because it's supposed to be. I think that it's just peer group identification.... I never felt that way. I was more content to sit there and enjoy it."[18] The fact is that chronic cocaine use results in decreased sexual performance and a loss of sexual desire, as the drug essentially takes the place of sex.

Cocaine produces a sudden elevation in the sympathetic branch of the autonomic nervous system. Heart rate and respiration are increased, while appetite is diminished. Blood vessels constrict, pupils in the eyes dilate, and blood pressure rises. The cocaine user may start to sweat and appear suddenly pale. The powerful sympathetic changes can lead to a cerebral hemorrhage or heart failure. Cardiac arrhythmia results from cocaine's tendency to bind to heart tissue itself. As you may recall from Chapter 2, cocaine is one of the drugs mentioned most frequently by medical examiners in hospital emergency departments.[19]

The extreme effects of cocaine on bodily organs, particularly the heart, stem from its ability not only to

A *Time* magazine cover story (July 6, 1981) depicted cocaine in a manner that was long on "status" and short on "menace." It described the social phenomenon in this way: "In part precisely because it is such an emblem of wealth and status, coke is the drug of choice for perhaps millions of solid, conventional and often upwardly mobile citizens—lawyers, businessmen, students, government bureaucrats, politicians, policemen, secretaries, bankers, mechanics, real estate brokers, and waitresses."

Cocaine after Alcohol: The Risk of Cocaethylene Toxicity

The risks of dying from cocaine arise from the drug's powerful excitatory effects on the body, such as abnormal heart rhythms, labored breathing, and increased blood pressure. The toxicity potential for any of these toxic reactions is, unfortunately, increased when alcohol is already in the bloodstream. The biotransformation of cocaine and alcohol (ethanol), when ingested in combination, produces a metabolite called *cocaethylene*. One effect of cocaethylene is a three- to five-fold increase in the elimination half-life of cocaine. As a result, cocaine remains in the bloodstream for a much longer time. More important, cocaethylene has a specific excitatory effect on blood pressure and heart rate that is greater than that produced by cocaine alone.

While the combination of alcohol and cocaine is associated with a prolonged and enhanced euphoria, it also brings an eighteen- to twenty-five-fold increased risk of immediate death. The fact that 62–90 percent of cocaine abusers are also abusers of alcohol makes the dangers of cocaethylene toxicity a significant health concern.

> **Where to go for assistance:**
> www.nida.nih.gov/MedAdv/00/NR6-26.html
>
> This web site is sponsored by the National Institute of Drug Abuse and contains a comprehensive examination of cocaine risks, including the combination of cocaine with alcohol.

Sources: Andrews, Paul (1997). Cocaethylene toxicity. *Journal of Addictive Diseases, 16,* 75–84. Harris, Debra S.; Everhart, E. Thomas; Mendelson, John; and Jones, Reese T. (2003). The pharmacology of cocaethylene in humans following cocaine and ethanol administration. *Drug and Alcohol Dependence, 72,* 169–182.

excite the sympathetic system but to inhibit the parasympathetic system as well (Health Alert). Given the high level of sympathetic arousal, it is not surprising that behavioral skills will be adversely affected. In a study of drivers showing reckless behavior on the road, those found to have been under the influence of cocaine were wildly overconfident in their abilities, taking turns too fast or weaving through traffic. One highway patrol officer called this behavior "diagonal driving. They were just as involved in changing lanes as in going forward." Yet they passed the standard sobriety tests designed to detect alcohol intoxication.[20]

Chronic Effects of Cocaine

Repeated and continued use of cocaine produces undesirable mood changes that can only be alleviated when the person is under the acute effects of the drug. Chronic cocaine abusers are often irritable, depressed, and paranoid. As was true in Fleischl's experience with cocaine, long-term abuse can produce the disturbing hallucinatory experience of formication. The sensation of "cocaine bugs" crawling on or under the skin can become so severe that abusers may scratch the skin into open sores or even pierce themselves with a knife to cut out the imaginary creatures. These hallucinations, together with feelings of anxiety and paranoia, make up a serious mental disorder referred to as **cocaine psychosis.**

When snorted, cocaine causes bronchial muscles to relax and nasal blood vessels to constrict; the opposite effects occur when the drug wears off. As the bronchial muscles contract and nasal blood vessels relax, chronic abusers endure continuously stuffy or runny noses and bleeding of nasal membranes. In advanced cases of this problem, the septum of the nose can develop lesions or become perforated with small holes, both of which present serious problems for breathing.

Medical Uses of Cocaine

When applied topically on the skin, cocaine has the ability to block the transmission of nerve impulses, deadening all sensations from the area. This local anesthetic effect of cocaine remains its only legitimate medical application. In procedures in which tubes are passed through the nose or throat, cocaine is applied on the membranes to ease the discomfort.

cocaine psychosis: A set of symptoms, including hallucinations, paranoia, and disordered thinking, produced from chronic use of cocaine.

There are, however, potential problems in the use of cocaine even for these specific, beneficial circumstances. One danger is that cocaine may be inadvertently absorbed into the bloodstream, leading to possible cocaine abuse. Finally, the local anesthetic effects are brief because cocaine breaks down so rapidly. Synthetic drugs such as lidocaine (brand name: Xylocaine) have the advantage of acting as local anesthetics over a longer period of time, and because they do not have the euphoriant effects of cocaine, the abuse potential is reduced. Consequently, lidocaine and other similar drugs, by injection into the gums, are used widely as local anesthetics during dental procedures.

How Cocaine Works in the Brain

Cocaine greatly enhances the activity of dopamine, and, to a lesser extent, norepinephrine in the brain. In the case of both neurotransmitters, the actual effect is to block the reuptake process at the synapse, so the neurotransmitters stimulate the postsynaptic receptors longer and to a greater degree. Unlike the amphetamines (discussed later in this chapter), the structure of cocaine does not appear to resemble the structure of either norepinephrine or dopamine, so why cocaine should block their reuptake so effectively is not at all clear. Nonetheless, what has been determined is that the acute effect of euphoria experienced through cocaine is directly related to an increase in dopamine in the region of the brain that controls pleasure and reinforcement in general: the nucleus accumbens (see Chapter 3).

Chronic cocaine abuse, however, leads to the loss of about 20 percent of the dopamine receptors in this region of the brain over time. The depletion of dopamine receptors among long-term cocaine abusers has been observed up to four months after the last cocaine exposure, even though the cocaine abuser no longer has cocaine in his or her system. As a result, there is a tendency toward a decline in the experience of pleasure from any source. In fact, cocaine abusers frequently report that their craving for cocaine no longer stems from the pleasure they felt when taking it initially. Their lives may be in shambles and the acute effects of euphoria from cocaine may no longer be strong, but they still crave the drug more than ever. In other words, there is now a dissociation between "liking" and "wanting."[21]

One feature of cocaine is quite unlike that of other psychoactive drugs. While cocaine abusers over repeated cocaine exposures develop a pattern of drug

tolerance to its euphoric effect, they develop a pattern of sensitization (a heightened responsiveness) with respect to motor behavior and brain excitation. This phenomenon, referred to as the **kindling effect,** makes cocaine particularly dangerous because cocaine has the potential for setting off brain seizures. Repeated exposure to cocaine can lower the threshold for seizures, through a sensitization of neurons in the limbic system over time. As a result of the kindling effect, deaths from cocaine overdose may occur from relatively low dose levels (Health Alert).[22]

Present-Day Cocaine Abuse

The difficult problems of cocaine abuse in the United States and around the world mushroomed during the early 1970s and continue to the present day, though the incidence of abuse is down from peak levels reached

kindling effect: A phenomenon in the brain that produces a heightened sensitivity to repeated administrations of some drugs, such as cocaine. This heightened sensitivity is the opposite of the phenomenon of tolerance.

around 1986. In ways that resembled the brief period of enthusiasm for cocaine in 1884, attitudes during the early period of this "second epidemic" were incredibly naive. Fueled by media reports of use among the rich and famous, touted as the "champagne of drugs," cocaine became synonymous with the glamorous life.

The medical profession at this time was equally nonchalant about cocaine. The widely respected *Comprehensive Textbook of Psychiatry* (1980) stated the following: "If it is used no more than two or three times a week, cocaine creates no serious problem.... At present chronic cocaine use does not usually present a medical problem."[23]

These attitudes began to change as the 1980s unfolded. The death of actor-comedian John Belushi in 1982, followed by the drug-related deaths of other entertainers and sport figures (see Drugs ... in Focus, page 34) produced a reversal of opinion about the safety and desirability of cocaine. The greatest influence, however, was the arrival of crack cocaine on the drug scene in 1985, which will be examined in the next sections.

From Coca to Cocaine

To understand the full picture of present-day cocaine abuse, it is necessary to examine the various forms that cocaine can take, beginning with the extraction of cocaine from the coca plant itself (Figure 4.2). During the initial extraction process, coca leaves are soaked in various chemical solvents so that cocaine can be drawn out of the plant material itself. Leaves are then crushed, and alcohol is percolated through them to remove extraneous matter. After sequential washings and a treatment with kerosene, the yield is cocaine that is approximately 60 percent pure. This is the coca paste, which, as mentioned earlier, is combined with tobacco and smoked in many South American countries.

Cocaine in this form, however, is not water-soluble and therefore cannot be injected into the bloodstream. An additional step of treatment with oxidizing agents and acids is required to produce a water-soluble drug. The result is a white crystalline powder called **cocaine hydrochloride,** about 99 percent pure cocaine and classified chemically as a salt. When in the form of cocaine

cocaine hydrochloride: The form of cocaine that is inhaled (snorted) or injected into the bloodstream.

free-base cocaine: A smokable form of cocaine.

crack cocaine or crack: A smokable form of cocaine.

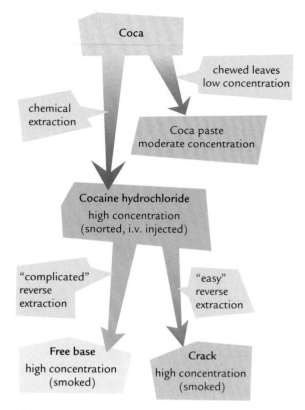

FIGURE 4.2

Steps in producing various forms of cocaine from raw coca.

hydrochloride, the drug can be injected intravenously or snorted. The amount injected at one time is about 16 mg. Intravenous cocaine also can be combined with heroin in a highly dangerous mixture called a *speedball*.

If cocaine is snorted, the user generally has the option of two methods. In one method, a tiny spoonful of cocaine is carried to one nostril while the other nostril is shut, and the drug is taken with a rapid inhalation. In the other method, cocaine is spread out on a highly polished surface (often a mirror) and arranged with a razor blade in several lines, each containing from 20 to 30 mg. The cocaine is then inhaled into one nostril by means of a straw or rolled piece of paper. During the early 1980s, a $100 bill was a fashionable alternative, emphasizing the level of income necessary to be using cocaine in the first place.[24]

From Cocaine to Crack

Options beyond the intake of cocaine hydrochloride widened with the development of **free-base cocaine** during the 1970s and **crack cocaine** (or simply **crack**) during

A message of prevention is a community's response to the desolation and misery resulting from crack cocaine abuse.

TABLE 4.1

Street names for cocaine

TYPE OF COCAINE	STREET NAME
Cocaine, hydrochloride (powder)	blow, C, coke, big C, lady, nose candy, snowbirds, snow, stardust, toot, white girl, happydust, cola, flake, pearl, Peruvian lady, freeze, geeze, doing the line
Free-base cocaine	freebase, base
Crack cocaine	crack, rock, kibbles and bits, crell
Crack cocaine combined with PCP (see Chapter 6)	beam me up Scottie, space cadet, tragic magic
Cocaine combined with heroin	speedball, snowball
Cocaine combined with heroin and LSD	Frisco special, Frisco speedball

Source: Bureau of Justice Statistics Clearinghouse (1992). *Drugs, behavior and crime.* Washington DC: U.S. Department of Justice, pp. 24–25.

the mid-1980s. In free-base cocaine, the hydrochloride is removed from the salt form of cocaine, thus liberating it as a free base. The aim is to obtain a smokable form of cocaine, which, by entering the brain more quickly, produces a more intense effect. The technique for producing free-base cocaine, however, is extremely hazardous, since it is necessary to treat cocaine powder with highly flammable agents such as ether. If the free base still contains some ether residue, igniting the drug will cause it to explode into flames.

Crack cocaine is the result of a cheaper and safer chemical method, but the result is essentially the same: a smokable form of cocaine. Treatment with baking soda yields small rocks, which can then be smoked in a small pipe.[25] When they are smoked, a cracking noise accompanies the burning, hence the origin of the name "crack."

How dangerous is crack? There is no question that the effect of cocaine when smoked exceeds the effect of cocaine when snorted; for some users, it even exceeds the effect of cocaine when injected. Inhaling high-potency cocaine (the purity of cocaine in crack averages about 75 percent) into the lungs, and almost immediately into the brain, sets the stage for a pattern of psychological dependence. And at a price of $3 to $20 per dose, cocaine is no longer out of financial reach (Table 4.1). The answer is that crack is very dangerous indeed.

Beyond its effect on the user, however, is the effect on the society where crack is prevalent. Women who are crack abusers find that their drug cravings overwhelm their maternal instincts, resulting in the neglect of the basic needs of their children, either in postnatal or prenatal stages of life. In New York, for example, the number of reported cases of child abuse and neglect increased from 36,000 in 1985 to 59,000 in 1989, a change largely attributed to the introduction of crack. As discussed in Chapter 2, the enormous monetary profits from the selling of crack caused inner-city crime and violence to skyrocket (Figure 4.3, page 100).[26]

While crack abuse remains a problem, the number of new crack abusers has declined substantially, particularly in the inner-city communities of the United States. While 36 percent of all males over thirty-six years old who were arrested in New York in 1998 had used crack, little more than 4 percent of those fifteen to twenty years old had done so. A principal reason for this change in prevalence rates has been the present-day stigmatized image of the "crack head," considered by one's peers to be a social loser in his or her community.[27]

Patterns of Cocaine Abuse

In 2007, the National Survey on Drug Use and Health estimated that approximately 36 million Americans aged 12 or older had used cocaine at some time in their lives, 5.7 million had used it during the past year, and 2.1 million had used it during the past month. Approximately 8.6 million Americans had used crack at some time in their lives, 1.5 million had used it during the past year, and 610,000 had used it during the past month.[28]

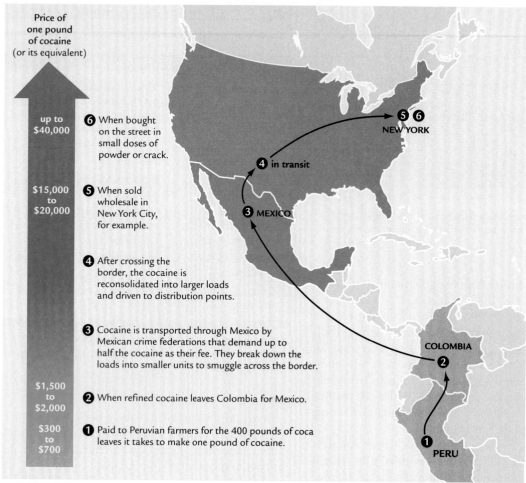

Price of one pound of cocaine (or its equivalent)

⑥ up to $40,000 — When bought on the street in small doses of powder or crack.

⑤ $15,000 to $20,000 — When sold wholesale in New York City, for example.

④ After crossing the border, the cocaine is reconsolidated into larger loads and driven to distribution points.

③ Cocaine is transported through Mexico by Mexican crime federations that demand up to half the cocaine as their fee. They break down the loads into smaller units to smuggle across the border.

② $1,500 to $2,000 — When refined cocaine leaves Colombia for Mexico.

① $300 to $700 — Paid to Peruvian farmers for the 400 pounds of coca leaves it takes to make one pound of cocaine.

④ in transit

⑤ ⑥ NEW YORK

③ MEXICO

② COLOMBIA

① PERU

FIGURE 4.3

From farm prices in Peru to current street prices as crack, the estimated value of cocaine escalates from as little as $300 for the 400 pounds of coca necessary to produce one pound of cocaine to $40,000 for the crack doses made from that pound of cocaine.

Source: New York Times, March 4, 1997, p. A20. Copyright © 1997 by The New York Times Company. Reprinted by permission. Information updated courtesy of the Drug Enforcement Administration, Washington DC.

Although the incidence of cocaine abuse in the United States is presently lower than it was during the 1980s, medical emergencies associated with cocaine use, as measured through the DAWN statistics, have increased dramatically. In 2006, there were approximately 548,600 cocaine-related ED visits reported by metropolitan hospitals. Equally serious are recent signs of a shift in attitudes toward cocaine among young adults, particularly in the clubs and bars in major American cities. A prominent researcher in substance abuse remarked in 2007 that "there seems to be less of a stigma about (cocaine)... people don't feel nearly as much need to hide it. They feel that they can use it in a more open fashion." This new blasé feeling with regard to cocaine use is an example of what public health officials refer to as generational forgetting (see Chapter 1). Whether the hard lessons learned in the 1980s and 1990s will be totally ignored remains to be seen. In the meantime, a new form of cheap cocaine has emerged as a significant social problem in Argentina and threatens to expand into neighboring countries in South America (Drugs . . . in Focus).[29]

Drugs...in Focus

Paco: A New Cheap Form of Cocaine Floods Argentine Slums and Beyond

Paco is a shortened name for "pasta de cocaine" (cocaine paste), but it is actually just a chemical by-product that is left over (and usually discarded) when coca is converted to coca paste along the way to being transformed into high-grade cocaine hydrochloride. It is essentially lab trash, but unfortunately it has become the center of a major public health and social problem in the impoverished neighborhoods of Buenos Aires and other metropolitan ghettos in Argentina—a problem comparable, according to public health officials, to the epidemic of crack cocaine in American cities during the 1980s.

Like crack, paco is smoked so that psychoactive effects are felt within seconds (Chapter 3). In addition, even by the standards of the Argentine poor, paco is extraordinarily cheap. A dose costing about 30 cents produces a powerful high that lasts for two minutes or so. Abusers frequently smoke 20 to 50 paco cigarettes, or as many as they can afford, during an average day. Its toxicity is augmented by paco contaminants such as solvents and chemicals like kerosene. Paco dependence is rampant.

Paco abusers are referred to as *muertos vivientes* ("the undead"). They will sell anything they have or can get their hands on to buy paco. Attempts to control the flow of cocaine paste and the availability of paco from neighboring Bolivia, where coca is grown, have largely failed. Recently, Brazil has had to contend with the spill-over of paco abuse from Argentina, while becoming a prime customer for cocaine itself. Presently, Brazil is the second largest consumer of cocaine in the world after the United States.

Sources: Barrionuevo, Alexei (2008, February 23). Cheap cocaine floods a slum in Argentina, devouring lives. *New York Times,* pp. A1, A6. Hearn, Kathy (2006, April 5). Abuse of the highly addictive cocaine by-product "paco" is causing officials to revamp drug laws. *Christian Science Monitor,* p. 4.

Treatment Programs for Cocaine Abuse

One way of grasping the extent of the cocaine-abuse problem is to look at the number of people who have wanted to get help. In 1983 a nationwide toll-free hotline, 1-800-COCAINE, was established as a twenty-four-hour service for emergency and treatment information. From 1983 to 1990, more than 3 million callers responded, averaging more than 1,000 per day.[30] From 1983 to 1988, the percentage of individuals reporting an abuse of a free-base form of cocaine had more than doubled to 56 percent. In 1986 alone, one year after the introduction of crack, half of all calls to the hotline referred to problems of crack abuse.[31]

Treating cocaine abuse presents difficulties that are peculiar to the power of cocaine itself. This is the way one treatment expert has put it:

> Coming off cocaine is one of the most anguished, depressing experiences. I've watched people talk about coming off freebase and one of the things I noticed was the nonverbal maneuvers they use to describe it. It looks like they're describing a heart attack. They have fists clenched to the chest. You can see that it hurts. They can re-create that hurt for you because it's a devastating event. They'll do almost anything to keep from crashing on cocaine. And on top of that they'll do just about anything to keep their supply coming. Postcocaine anguish is a strong inducement to use again—to keep the pain away.[32]

The varieties of treatment for cocaine abuse all have certain features in common. The initial phase is detoxification and total abstinence: The cocaine abuser aims to achieve total withdrawal with the least possibility of physical injury and minimal psychological discomfort. During the first twenty-four to forty-eight hours, the chances are high that there will be profound depression, severe headaches, irritability, and disturbances in sleep.[33]

In severe cases involving a pattern of compulsive use that cannot be easily broken, the cocaine abuser needs to be admitted for inpatient treatment in a hospital facility. The most intensive interventions, medical supervision with psychological counseling, can be made in this kind of environment. The early stages of withdrawal are clearly the most difficult, and the recovering abuser can benefit from around-the-clock attention that only a hospital staff can give.

The alternative approach is an outpatient program, under which the individual remains at home but travels regularly to a facility for treatment. An outpatient program is clearly a less expensive route to take, but it works only for those who recognize the destructive impact of cocaine dependence on their lives and enter treatment with a sincere desire to do whatever is needed to stop.[34]

For cocaine abusers who have failed in previous attempts in outpatient treatment or for those who are in denial of their cocaine dependence, an inpatient approach may be the only answer (Health Line). For most abusers, it is important to stay away from an environment where cocaine and other drugs are prevalent and peer pressure to resume drug-taking behavior is intense. This factor is particularly crucial among adolescents:

Peer acceptance is of utmost importance to adolescents. In order to interrupt the addiction cycle, youth are cautioned to avoid drug-using friends. Since many addicted adolescents are alienated from the mainstream and what few friends they have are users, this challenge can appear overwhelming. Recovering adolescents often comment that they can't find friends who don't at least drink.[35]

A third alternative is a combined approach in which a shortened inpatient program, seven to fourteen days in length, is followed by an intensive outpatient program that continues for several months (Portrait).

Whether on an inpatient or outpatient basis, there are several approaches for treatment. One alternative is the self-help support group Cocaine Anonymous, modeled after the famous twelve-step Alcoholics Anonymous program (see Chapter 10). In this program, recovering cocaine abusers meet in group sessions, learn from the life experiences of other members, and gain a sense of accomplishment from remaining drug-free in an atmosphere of fellowship and mutual support. In another drug-treatment option, cocaine abusers meet with cognitive-behavioral therapists, who teach them new ways of acting and thinking in response to their environment. During the course of cognitive-behavioral therapy, cocaine abusers are urged to avoid situations that lead to drug use, recognize and change irrational thoughts, manage negative moods, and

---

Health Line
Seven Rules for Cocaine Abusers Who Want to Quit

- **The time to stop using cocaine is now.** If you say, "I'll quit tomorrow," then you are saying, "I have no intention of quitting."

- **Stop all at once, not gradually.** Each time you use cocaine, you are fueling the desire for more and postponing the process of recovery.

- **Stop using all other drugs of abuse, including alcohol and marijuana.** Cocaine abusers often think that the problem is with cocaine alone. Use of alcohol and marijuana can be the initial step to a relapse back to cocaine.

- **Change your life-style.** If you encounter conditions that are associated with cocaine, your craving will increase. This problem is particularly difficult in the early stages of cocaine withdrawal.

- **Whenever possible, avoid situations, people, and places that cause drug urges.** Yesterday's abstinence doesn't guarantee the same result today. It's a matter of "one day at a time." Trying to test yourself by

approaching drug situations and monitoring your reaction is a big mistake, according to drug-treatment experts.

- **Find other rewards.** Learn to enjoy life without cocaine. Learn how to reconnect with a drug-free world. You may have even forgotten how to talk about anything except cocaine.

- **Take good care of your body. Eat right and exercise.** Normal eating habits are wrecked while you are abusing cocaine. Chances are good that your physical condition has deteriorated, and you may be suffering from significant vitamin deficiencies. A healthy diet and a program of regular exercise are two major factors in your long-term recovery prospects.

Source: Platt, Jerome J. (1997). *Cocaine addiction: Theory, research, and treatment.* Cambridge, MA: Harvard University Press. Weiss, Roger D., and Mirin, Steven, M. (1987). *Cocaine.* Washington DC: American Psychiatric Press, pp. 136–139.

Robert Downey, Jr.—Cleaning Up His Life after Cocaine

The parade of celebrities who have struggled against cocaine abuse is seemingly endless. Over the years, we have witnessed their personal triumphs and failures and have seen some lives lost (see Chapter 2), some careers lost, and occasionally careers regained. In 1986, the nation was galvanized by the untimely deaths of college basketball player Len Bias and professional football player Dan Rogers, within months of each other, as well as the death of comedian and actor John Belushi four years earlier. The deaths of River Phoenix in 1993, Chris Farley in 1998, and Mitch Hedberg in 2005, all of them due to a lethal combination of cocaine and heroin, have underscored the ever-present dangers of drug-taking behavior.

The story of Robert Downey, Jr., an Academy Award nominee for his portrayal of the title role in the movie *Chaplin* in 1992, has been an emotional roller-coaster, and for a time, fans held their breath as events unfolded. But by January 2003, Downey, at the age of thirty-seven, could remark, "I'm a little older. I'm mildly wiser. My frequent appearances on Court TV have brought me to another level than just always 'the acting guy.' . . . I think I've become very, I don't want to say real, but I'm

very tangible to people." He made these comments while at the premiere of a new film, his first since completing a year-long court-ordered drug rehabilitation program in 2002. At the time, he was about one year into a three-year probation period, after pleading no-contest to cocaine possession and being under the influence during a November 2000 arrest in a Palm Springs hotel.

In 1999, Downey had spent a year in prison after being convicted on charges of cocaine possession. Upon his release, he was featured on the successful *Aly McBeal* TV show, only to be fired in 2000. His drug-abuse problems had first begun making headlines in 1996 when he was found with cocaine, heroin, and a pistol in his car.

In earlier editions of the text, this Portrait feature portrayed the story of Robert Downey, Jr., in considerably less positive terms. However, today there is reason for optimism. His self-destructive life-style appears to be over. As he has said, "I think part of my destiny has to be realizing that I'm not the poster boy for drug abuse."

In 2008, Downey achieved a major comeback in his starring role in the successful movie *Ironman*. There are indications that his career now has an upward trajectory and his personal life has regained a stability that bodes well

for the future. Downey sees his life in a new perspective, acknowledging the fragility of his present state of recovery:

If I see somebody who is throwing their life away with both hands and is raging around and destroying their family, I can't understand that person. I'm not in that sphere of activity anymore, and I don't understand it any more than I understood 10 or 20 years ago that somehow everything was going to turn out O.K. from this lousy, exotic, and dark triple chapter of my life. . . . I don't think I will ever go that fast again, but that is based on my behavior moment to moment, whether I'm able to maintain this nice groove I'm on or whether it will all go away in a second for something that I could justify or rationalize [as] was none of my own doing."

Sources: Carr, David (2008, April 20). Been up, been down. Now? Super. *New York Times*, pp. 1, 13. Third quotation, p. 13. Robert Downey Jr. cleans up (2005, October 26). CNN.com. Second quotation. Downey's back, older and "mildly wiser" (2003, January 21). First quotation. *Newsday*, p. A12. Lemonick, Michael D. (2000, December 11). Downey's downfall. *Time*, p. 97.

---

practice drug-refusal skills. While the success rates of both approaches are approximately the same for patients in cocaine-abuse treatment overall, some evidence suggests that a cocaine abuser's personal characteristics may affect the kind of treatment that will work best (Figure 4.4, page 104). Whatever the approach taken, however, it is clear that an intensive relearning process has to go on, because cocaine abusers often cannot remember a life without cocaine.[36]

Currently pharmacological approaches in cocaine-abuse treatment, as well as the combination of pharmacological and behavioral approaches, are being vigorously pursued. An extremely promising example of a purely pharmacological strategy is the development of the

compound gamma vinyl-GABA (GVG), currently available as an antiepileptic drug called Vigabatrin. Essentially, it has been established that GVG "short-circuits" the reinforcing effect of cocaine by preventing the sudden surge of dopamine in the brain when cocaine is administered. Animals that have become cocaine-dependent no longer self-administer the drug after taking GVG and are no longer attracted to locations that have been associated with cocaine in the past. In other words, GVG allows animals to resist the conditioned cues for chronic cocaine use. In 2007, clinical trials of Vigabatrin in a sample of long-time cocaine abusers showed that 28 percent of abusers treated with Vigabatrin showed negative urine tests for cocaine lasting for three weeks, while only 7.6

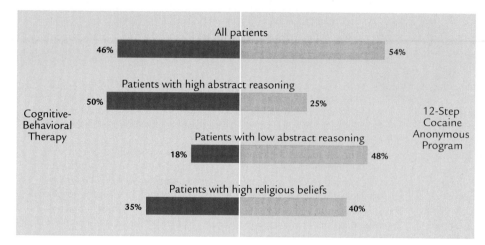

FIGURE 4.4

Percentage of patients achieving four consecutive weeks of cocaine abstinence, comparing two types of treatment.

Source: Adapted from Shine, Barbara (2000, March). Some cocaine abusers fare better with cognitive-behavioral therapy, others with 12-step programs. *NIDA Notes, 15* (1), 9.

percent treated with a placebo did so. Even though this medication helped only about one in four abusers, that was almost four times the success rate of using nothing.[37]

The potential for relapse is a particularly challenging element among recovering cocaine abusers, primarily as a result of powerful conditioned cues that have been associated with the drug. A specialist in cocaine abuse rehabilitation tells this story: "A woman was doing well in treatment. Then one day she was changing her baby's diaper. She used baby powder and the sight of the white powder induced a tremendous craving for cocaine."[38] The development of any drug that reduces craving would be a great advance in the treatment of cocaine dependence and in the prevention of problems associated with cocaine dependence (Drugs . . . in Focus).

The continuing investigation of treatment and prevention approaches to cocaine abuse reflects a general orientation toward reducing the negative impact of drug-taking behavior on the individual and society (the "demand" side), as opposed to reducing the availability of the drugs themselves (the "supply" side).

Amphetamines

One of humanity's fondest dreams is to have the power of unlimited endurance, to be able to banish fatigue from our lives, to be capable of endless energy as if we had discovered some internal perpetual-motion machine. We all have wanted, at some time in our lives, to be a super-hero. Cocaine, as we know, gives us that illusion. The remainder of this chapter will examine

amphetamine (am-FEH-ta-meen): A family of ephedrine-based stimulant drugs.

another powerful drug source for these feelings of invincibility: amphetamines. As we will see, the attractions and problems of abuse associated with cocaine and amphetamines are quite similar.

The History of Amphetamines

The origin of modern amphetamines dates back almost five thousand years to a Chinese medicinal herb called *ma huang* (*Ephedra vulgaris*) that was used to clear bronchial passageways during bouts of asthma and other forms of respiratory distress. According to Chinese legend, this herb was first identified by the Emperor Shen Nung, who also is credited with the discovery of tea and marijuana.

German chemists isolated the active ingredient of *ma huang* in 1887, naming it ephedrine. It was soon obvious that ephedrine mimicked the stimulation of the sympathetic nervous system in general (see Portrait in Chapter 1). The pharmaceutical company Smith, Kline and French Laboratories marketed a synthetic form of ephedrine called **amphetamine** under the brand name Benzedrine in 1932 as a nonprescription CNS stimulant appetite suppressant and bronchial dilator.

During World War II, both U.S. and German troops were being given amphetamine to keep them awake and alert. Japanese kamikaze pilots were on amphetamine during their suicide missions. The advantages over cocaine, the other stimulant drug available at the time, were two-fold: Amphetamine was easily absorbed into the nervous system from the gastrointestinal tract, so it could be taken orally, and its effects were much longer lasting.

After the war, amphetamine use was adapted for peacetime purposes. Amphetamine, often referred to as *bennies*, was a way for college students to stay awake to

Drugs...in Focus

Crack Babies Revisited: Is There an Adverse Effect?

In the late 1980s, at the height of the crack abuse explosion, one particularly alarming possibility concerned the children of women who had been crack abusers during their pregnancies (frequently referred to as "crack babies"). Might these innocents incur long-term mental and physical deficits later in life as a result of *in utero* exposure to cocaine? The early signs were not promising. These newborns had lower birth weights and smaller head circumferences, and they displayed tremors, excessive crying, disturbed sleep patterns, and diminished responsiveness, all of which were abnormalities typical of cocaine exposure. The question remained, however, whether there would be deficits in social skills and mental ability when these infants grew older.

One of the difficulties in arriving at an answer is the fact that the mothers who are cocaine abusers during their pregnancies are more accurately polydrug abusers, in that they typically abuse alcohol, marijuana, and tobacco as well as cocaine. Studies comparing cocaine-exposed and non-cocaine-exposed children, therefore, must control for prenatal exposure to other drugs, gestational age and size at birth, ethnicity, and gender, as well as the socioeconomic status of the mother. When these factors are taken into account, few if any differences in cognitive functioning are found.

The consensus among health professionals, therefore, is that developmental difficulties of children can be the result of many risk factors (see Chapter 1), including inadequate prenatal care, poor nutrition, and exposure to licit drugs such as alcohol and nicotine; cocaine exposure itself prior to their birth, however, does not play a unique role.

Ongoing studies continue to investigate whether subtle differences might be observed as a delayed influence when children advance into adolescence.

Why the intense interest in the effects of *in utero* exposure to cocaine, when the evidence is so much stronger with respect to the much more widely available licit drugs of alcohol (Chapter 10) and nicotine (Chapter 11)? As expressed in a recent editorial in the *Journal of the American Medical Association*, the answer might lie beyond the concerns of public health:

> The "crack baby" has become a convenient symbol for an aggressive war on drug users because of the implication that anyone who is selfish enough to irreparably damage an innocent child for the sake of a quick high deserves retribution. This image, promoted by the mass media, makes it easier to advocate a simplistic punitive response than to address the complex causes of drug use.

Sources: Chavkin, Wendy (2001, March 28). Cocaine and pregnancy—time to look at the evidence. *Journal of the American Medical Association, 285,* 1626–1628. Quotation on p. 1627. Lumeng, Julie C.; Cabral, Howard J.; Cannon, Katherine; Heeren, Timothy; and Frank, Deborah A. (2007). Prenatal exposures to cocaine and alcohol and physical growth patterns to age 8 years. *Neurotoxicology and Teratology, 29,* 446–457. Singer, Lynn T.; Minnes, Sonia; Short, Elizabeth; Arendt, Robert; et al. (2004). Cognitive outcomes of preschool children with prenatal cocaine exposure. *Journal of the American Medical Association, 291,* 2448–2456. Zuckerman, Barry, Frank, Deborah A., and Mayes, Linda (2002). Cocaine-exposed infants and developmental outcomes. *Journal of the American Medical Association, 287,* 1990–1991.

study for exams and for long-distance truck drivers to fight fatigue on the road. Truckers would take a "St. Louis" if they had to go from New York to Missouri and back or a "Pacific turnabout" if they needed to travel completely across country and back, without stopping to sleep.[39]

In the meantime, the word got around that amphetamine produced euphoria as well, and soon amphetamine began to be sought for recreational purposes. People found ways of opening up the nonprescription amphetamine inhalers, withdrawing the contents, and getting high by drinking it or injecting it intravenously. Since each inhaler contained 250 mg of amphetamine, there was enough for several powerful doses. During the early 1960s, injectable amphetamines could be bought with forged prescriptions or even by telephoning a pharmacy and posing as a physician. By 1965, amendments to federal drug laws tightened the supply of prescription amphetamines, requiring manufacturers, wholesalers, and pharmacies to keep careful records of amphetamine transactions, but amphetamines soon became available from illegal laboratories.[40]

Amphetamine abuse in the United States reached a peak about 1967, declining slowly over the 1970s as other drugs of abuse, notably cocaine, grew in popularity. By 1970, 10 percent of the U.S. population over fourteen years of age had used amphetamine, and more than

8 percent of all drug prescriptions were for amphetamine in some form.[41] For about two decades afterward, amphetamine abuse steadily faded from prominence in the drug scene. Cocaine and later crack cocaine became the dominant illicit stimulant of abuse. Only since the mid-1990s has amphetamine abuse resurfaced as a significant social concern.

The Different Forms of Amphetamines

To understand amphetamine abuse, both past and present, it is necessary to know something about the molecular structure of amphetamines themselves. Amphetamine can be represented chiefly as a specific arrangement of carbon (C), hydrogen (H), and nitrogen (N) atoms (Figure 4.5), either in a "right-handed" version or a "left-handed" version (mirror image). The more potent version is the right-handed form, called dextroamphetamine or **d-amphetamine** (brand name: Dexedrine). It is stronger than the left-handed form, called levoamphetamine or l-amphetamine, which is not commonly available by itself. It is, however, combined with d-amphetamine in the medication Adderall.

A modified form of d-amphetamine, formulated by substituting CH_3 (called a methyl group) instead of H at one end, is called **methamphetamine.** This slight change in the formula allows for a quicker passage across the blood-brain barrier. It is methamphetamine, often called *meth*, *speed*, or *crank*, that has been the primary form of amphetamine abuse in recent years.

How Amphetamines Work in the Brain

We can get a good idea of how amphetamines work in the brain by looking carefully at the molecular structures of dopamine and norepinephrine alongside d-amphetamine and methamphetamine in Figure 4.5. Note that there are only slight differences among them. Because of the close resemblance to dopamine and norepinephrine, it is not hard to imagine amphetamines increasing the activity level of these two neurotrans-

d-amphetamine: Shortened name for dextroamphetamine, a potent form of amphetamine, marketed under the brand name Dexedrine.

methamphetamine: A type of amphetamine, once marketed under the brand name Methedrine. Methamphetamine abusers refer to it as meth, speed, or crank.

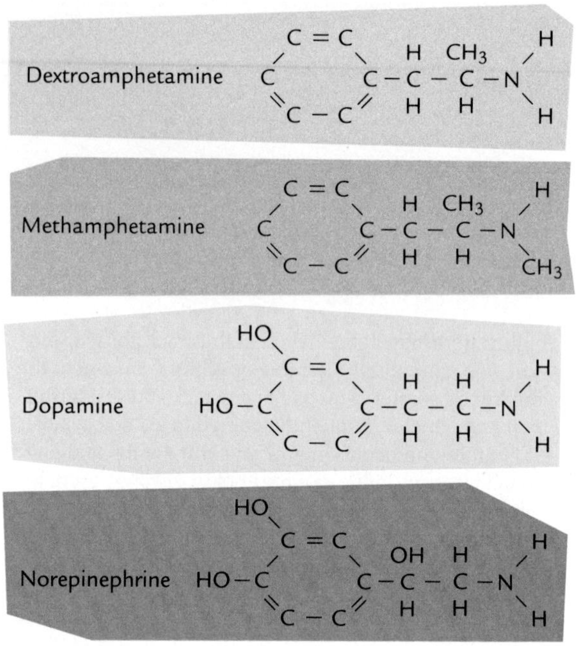

FIGURE 4.5

The molecular structure of dextroamphetamine, methamphetamine, dopamine, and norepinephrine.

mitters. Specifically, amphetamines cause increased amounts of dopamine and norepinephrine to be released from synaptic knobs and also slow down their reuptake from receptor sites. As described in Chapter 3, dopamine figures prominently in regions of the brain (notably the nucleus accumbens) associated with positive reinforcement. The euphoric effects of amphetamines, and the craving for them during abstinence, are considered to result from changes in dopamine activity.

Acute and Chronic Effects of Amphetamines

The acute effects of amphetamine, in either d-amphetamine or methamphetamine form, closely resemble those of cocaine. However, amphetamine effects extend over a longer period of time. For intervals of eight to twenty-four hours, there are signs of increased sympathetic autonomic activity, such as faster breathing and heart rate as well as hyperthermia (increased body temperature) and elevated blood pressure. Users experience feelings of euphoria and invincibility, decreased appetite, and an extraordinary boost in alertness and energy. Adverse and potentially lethal bodily changes include convulsions, chest pains, and stroke. In 2006, approximately 80,000 of all drug-related ED visits in the United States were attributable specifically to methamphetamine abuse, accounting for about three-fourths of visits related to stimulant abuse in general.[42]

Chronic effects of amphetamine abuse are both bizarre and unpleasant, particularly in the case of methamphetamine. Heavy methamphetamine abusers may experience formication hallucinations similar to those endured by cocaine abusers. They may become obsessed with the delusion that parasites or insects have lodged in their skin and so attempt to scratch, cut, or burn their skin in an effort to remove them. It is also likely that they will engage in compulsive or repetitive behaviors that are fixated upon ordinarily trivial aspects of life; an entire night might be spent, for example, counting the corn flakes in a cereal box.[43]

The most serious societal consequence of methamphetamine abuse is the appearance of paranoia, wildly bizarre delusions, hallucinations, tendencies toward violence, and intense mood swings. In the words of one health professional, "It's about the ugliest drug there is."[44] Because the symptoms have been observed with the chronic abuse of amphetamines of any type, they are referred to collectively as **amphetamine psychosis.** The possibility that methamphetamine abusers may not have slept for three to five days increases their tendency toward extremely irritable, paranoid, and potentially violent behavior. These symptoms, referred to as "tweaking" by the drug-abuse community, are displayed by up to 50 percent of methamphetamine abusers and present particular challenges to law-enforcement officers who have to deal with them under these circumstances. The close resemblance to paranoid schizophrenia has led to speculation that the two conditions may have a common underlying neurochemical basis: an overstimulation of dopamine-releasing neurons in those regions in the brain that control emotional reactivity.[45]

A study of heavy methamphetamine abusers has shown changes in chemical metabolites in those regions of the brain that are associated with Parkinson's disease, suggesting that this group may be predisposed to acquiring Parkinson symptoms later in life, due to their methamphetamine exposure. Fortunately, however, recent evidence indicates that chemical changes in the brain in chronic methamphetamine abusers can be at least partially reversed by abstaining from the drug for a year or more.[46]

Methamphetamine Abuse

In the United States, the emergence of widespread methamphetamine abuse was intermingled with the marijuana and LSD scene during San Francisco's "Summer of Love and Peace" in 1967. Almost from the beginning, however, speed freaks—as methamphetamine abusers were called—whose behaviors were anything but loving or peaceful, became the outcasts of that society:

> These wild-eyed, manic burnout cases would blither on endlessly, rip off anything not welded in place, then go into fits of erratic and violent behavior.... They were shunned by other sorts of drug users, and ended up congregating with the only segment of the population who could stomach their company— other speed freaks.[47]

In the meantime, prescription amphetamines, widely administered during the 1960s for weight control and as a way to combat drowsiness, resulted in large numbers of abusers from practically every segment of society. Even though d-amphetamine was classified as a Schedule II drug in 1970 and the number of d-amphetamine prescriptions decreased by 90 percent from 1971 and 1986, the pills were still out there, and people found ways to continue an abusive pattern of drug-taking behavior.

Present-Day Patterns of Methamphetamine Abuse

As crack cocaine became increasingly associated with the urban poor and powder cocaine with upscale affluence in the 1980s, amphetamine abuse declined dramatically. In the 1990s, however, as crack cocaine and powder cocaine abuse began to diminish, methamphetamine abuse reemerged on the drug scene. Once identified with the countercultural 1960s, methamphetamine has become a major stimulant of abuse in the United States, with its popularity now concentrated among working-class people rather than among the poor or the affluent (Table 4.2, page 108).

> Methamphetamine... made inroads among many blue-collar people because it did not carry the stigma of being a hard drug.... It's what people used to get them through a shift at the factory or keep up on a construction site.[48]

Administered by snorting, injecting, or smoking, methamphetamine has become one of the few drugs reported as equally or more prevalent than other illicit

amphetamine psychosis: A set of symptoms, including hallucinations, paranoia, and disordered thinking, resulting from high doses of amphetamines.

TABLE 4.2

Street names for amphetamines

TYPE OF AMPHETAMINE	STREET NAME
amphetamine in general	bennies, uppers, ups, A, pep pills, white crowns, whites
dextroamphetamine	dexies, cadillacs, black beauties
methamphetamine*	meth, speed, Tina, crank, little whites, white cross-tops, crystal meth, quill, yellow bam, zip, go fast, chalk, shabu, spoosh, get go
smokable methamphetamine*	ice, crystal, crystal meth, L.A., L.A. glass, quartz, cristy, hanyak, Christina, Tina
methcathinone (a synthetic analog of methamphetamine)	khat, cat, goob

* Slang terms often confuse smokable and nonsmokable forms of methamphetamine, so some street names may overlap the two categories.

Sources: Drug Enforcement Administration and the Office of National Drug Control Policy, Washington DC.

In a makeshift but sophisticated "meth factory," a combination of ephedrine, hydrochloric acid, and red phosphorus (shown as red liquid in the picture) is heated in a flask placed in an electric pot. Rubber tubes attached to each side of the glass condenser circulate cold water to reduce the escape of toxic fumes.

drugs in areas outside America's inner cities. In the early 1990s, distribution of methamphetamine was dominated by organized groups operating out of southern California and Mexico, with trafficking routes extending through several U.S. states, including Arizona, Colorado, Iowa, Missouri, Nebraska, North Dakota, and Texas.

In the late 1990s, thousands of "homegrown" methamphetamine laboratories proliferated in small towns and rural areas throughout the nation. They were typically situated in mobile homes, campers, vans, and easily hidden farm sheds, making their detection by law enforcement agencies extremely difficult. Since 2006, retail outlets have been required by federal law to limit the sales of numerous cold remedies (Sudafed, Tylenol Cold, among others) that contain pseudoepinephrine—an essential ingredient in the making of methamphetamine.

A number of products that have formerly been "over-the-counter" (see Chapter 14) are now "behind-the-counter." Customers cannot buy more than the equivalent of approximately seventy 60 mg pseudo-epinephrine tablets per day and must provide photo identification upon purchase and sign a logbook recording the transaction. Because liquid anhydrous ammonia, commonly used as a farm fertilizer, is another ingredient in the making of methamphetamine, fertilizer dealers have installed security systems to protect their supplies from theft. Toxic residue from methamphetamine manufacture, approximately five pounds of waste for every one pound of methamphetamine produced, has seeped into the soil and contaminated rivers and streams. Increasing attention has been directed to children who have suffered from inhaling the toxic fumes emitted during the process of methamphetamine manufacture, from the risks of fire and explosions, and from abuse and neglect by methamphetamine-dependent parents (Drugs . . . in Focus).[49]

Methamphetamine has become a major club drug in New York, Los Angeles, and other cities (see Chapter 1). A smokable form of methamphetamine hydrochloride called **ice** (also referred to as *crystal meth*)

ice: A smokable form of methamphetamine hydrochloride. It is often referred to as crystal meth, due to its quartz-like appearance.

Drugs...in Focus

Methamphetamine across America

The methamphetamine abuse epidemic in Watauga County, North Carolina, had gotten so bad that it has nicknamed itself "the county that never sleeps." Dozens of methamphetamine laboratories in the region were raided. Every fire emergency was treated as if it were a meth-lab fire.

Watauga County was not alone. A survey of more than 500 county sheriffs in the United States, conducted by the National Association of Counties in 2005, documented the alarming proportions of meth abuse across the country since 2000. Fifty-eight percent of sheriffs in the survey regarded methamphetamine abuse as the biggest drug problem they faced, ahead of concerns about heroin, cocaine, or marijuana.

The law enforcement and criminal justice challenges have been immense. In half of the counties surveyed, one in five current prison inmates had been incarcerated due to meth-related crimes. In 17 percent of the counties, more than half of the inmate population had been incarcerated for such crimes. A majority of sheriffs reported that meth use was the major contributing factor for increases in robberies or burglaries, domestic violence, and simple assaults. At the same time, only one in six counties reported that they had the financial resources to support a meth rehabilitation center or program.

The adverse impact on children has been of particular concern. There have been significant increases in cases in which children need to be placed out of the home as a result of neglect and abuse by parents who are meth abusers or a child's proximity to the hazards of meth labs. Nearly three-fourths of county child welfare officials in California and Colorado, for example, have reported increases in such cases since 2000. More than 69 percent of counties in Minnesota have reported an increase in meth-related child placements between 2004 and 2005.

Two exacerbating factors have made it particularly difficult for children who are affected by the meth epidemic.

First, meth abuse has been concentrated in mostly rural areas, where social service networks are ill-prepared to handle the increased numbers of foster children. Second, the chances of reunifying families torn apart by meth abuse has been considerably lower than in cases involving other forms of drug abuse, due to the high rate of relapse among meth abusers in treatment.

In recent years, the picture of meth abuse in America has changed. Federal reports indicate a decline in the number of meth lab seizures, particularly in western U.S. states most dramatically affected by meth abuse, from 10,000 in 2004 to about 2,000 in 2007. This decline is due to the restrictions on acquiring basic ingredients for meth production. The influx of illegal methamphetamine from Mexico, however, has increased. This new drug-trafficking pattern indicates that meth abusers in the United States will have simply shifted their reliance from domestic sources to foreign sources.

Meanwhile, a new concern has arisen over the sudden rise in meth lab seizures in the Czech Republic and a dozen or so other nations in Europe, an indication that Europeans may be soon experiencing a meth-abuse crisis similar to that experienced by Americans over the last few years.

Sources: Doyle, Rodger (2006, August). The crystal crisis: Meth abuse moves eastward. *Scientific American*, p. 28. Kulish, Nicholas (2007, November 23). Europe fears meth foothold is expanding. *New York Times*, pp. A1, A14. National Association of Counties (2005, July 5). The meth epidemic in America. Two surveys of U.S. counties: The criminal effect of meth on communities and the impact of meth on children. Washington DC: National Association of Counties. Reports suggest gain in fight on meth labs (2006, June 20). *New York Times*, p. A15. Substance Abuse and Mental Health Services Administration (2007, January 26). Methamphetamine use. *The NSDUH Report*. Washington DC: Office of Applied Studies, Substance Abuse and Mental Health Services Administration. Zernike, Kate (2005, July 11). A drug scourge creates its own form of orphan. *New York Times*, pp. A1, A15.

is particularly dangerous. Its name originates from its quartz-like, chunky crystallized appearance. Ice appeared on the drug scene in Hawaii in the late 1980s, but its abuse did not expand to the mainland to a significant degree until the latter 1990s. The combination of a purity of 98 to 100 percent and a highly efficient delivery route through the lungs produces a high level of potential for dependence and a significant social problem. An association between methamphetamine abuse and increased

high-risk sexual behavior among HIV-positive gay or bisexual men has raised public health concerns.[50]

While both methamphetamine and cocaine are similar in their stimulant effects and both trigger a major elevation in dopamine levels in the brain, the pattern of drug-taking behavior for each type of drug has its own distinctive character. Methamphetamine abusers typically use the drug throughout their waking day, at two- to four-hour intervals, in a pattern that resembles taking medication. Cocaine abusers typically use the drug in the evening and nighttime rather than during the day, taking it in a continuous (binge-like) fashion until all the cocaine on hand has been exhausted. This latter pattern of drug-taking behavior fits the typical picture of the recreational user.

The duration of effect in the two drugs may help to explain the differences in usage. Methamphetamine effects generally last more than ten hours, and its elimination half-life is about twelve hours. Cocaine effects last about twenty to thirty minutes, and its elimination half-life is about one hour.

On tests that evaluate different forms of cognitive functioning, methamphetamine and cocaine abusers show significant differences in terms of the type of cognitive impairment that is produced. Methamphetamine abusers are impaired on tests of perceptual speed or manipulation of information, effects observed to a lesser extent among cocaine abusers. The greatest difference between the two groups is observed when tests require both speed and the manipulation of information.[51]

The course of methamphetamine withdrawal—and amphetamine withdrawal in general—is very similar to the course of events described earlier for cocaine. First there is the "crash" when the abuser feels intense depression, hunger, agitation, and anxiety within one to four hours after the drug-taking behavior has stopped. Withdrawal from amphetamines, during total abstinence from the drug, takes between six and eighteen weeks, during which the intense craving for amphetamine slowly subsides.

As in cocaine-abuse treatment, there are inpatient and outpatient programs, depending on the circumstances and motivation of the abuser. Self-help groups such as Cocaine Anonymous can be useful as well, since the symptoms of amphetamine withdrawal and cocaine withdrawal are nearly identical. Unfortunately, relatively few methamphetamine abusers attempt treatment because they perceive themselves as in control over their drug use. One research report expressed it this way:

> This perception is particularly dangerous because the crossover from initial use to loss of control is rapid for meth users, and generally they have lost control long before they can acknowledge it. . . . This attitude of denial makes it difficult to convince meth abusers to enter and stay in treatment.[52]

attention deficit/hyperactivity disorder (ADHD): A behavioral disorder characterized by increased motor activity and reduced attention span.

Quick Concept Check 4.2

Understanding Patterns of Stimulant Abuse

Check your understanding of the changing patterns of stimulant drug abuse from 1975 to the present by identifying the following statements with (a) an event prior to 1986 or (b) an event subsequent to 1986.

1. Cocaine use is very expensive and restricted primarily to the wealthy. _____

2. Crack cocaine presents serious societal problems in the inner cities. _____

3. Methamphetamine abuse affects small towns and rural areas in the United States. _____

4. The nationwide toll-free hotline 1-800-COCAINE is established. _____

5. A smokable form of methamphetamine called ice (crystal meth) becomes a major drug of abuse. _____

6. The number of d-amphetamine prescriptions declines by 90 percent. _____

Answers: 1. prior   2. subsequent   3. subsequent
4. prior   5. subsequent   6. prior

Overall, methamphetamine abusers find it extremely difficult to become drug-free, and their relapse rate is one of the highest for any category of illicit or licit drug abuse.

Medical Uses for Amphetamines and Similar Stimulant Drugs

While amphetamines in general continue to present potential problems of abuse, there are approved medical applications for amphetamines and amphetamine-like stimulant drugs in specific circumstances. Stimulant drugs are prescribed widely for elementary-school-age children diagnosed as unable to maintain sufficient attention levels and impulse control in school or as behaviorally hyperactive. These symptoms are collectively referred to as **attention deficit/hyperactivity disorder (ADHD).** When there is no evidence of hyperactivity, the designation is shortened to *attention deficit disorder* (ADD).

ADHD is the most common psychological disorder among children. It is estimated that 3 to 5 percent of all school-age children meet the criteria for ADHD. The prevalence rate is three times greater and the symptoms are generally more severe for boys than for girls. These children have average to above-average intelligence but typically underperform academically. As many as two-thirds of school-age children with ADHD have at least one other psychiatric disorder, including anxiety and depression.[53]

Despite the public image of ADHD as an exclusively childhood phenomenon, about 40 to 60 percent of ADHD children show symptoms that persist into adulthood. As adults, these individuals are ten times more likely to be diagnosed with an antisocial personality disorder, twenty-five times more likely to have been institutionalized for delinquency, and nine times more likely to serve a prison sentence.[54]

Stimulant Drug Treatment for ADHD

Commonly prescribed stimulant medications for the treatment of ADHD include oral administrations of dextroamphetamine (brand name: Dexedrine), a combination of dextroamphetamine and levoamphetamine (brand name: Adderall), and an amphetamine-like drug, methylphenidate (brand name: Ritalin).

Ritalin dominates the market in prescriptions written for ADHD. In this drug's original formulation, the rapid onset and short duration of Ritalin requires two administrations during a school day: one at breakfast and another at lunchtime, supervised by a school nurse. In the evening, blood levels of Ritalin decline to levels that permit normal sleep. Adderall has a longer duration of action, making it possible to administer a single dose and avoiding school involvement in treatment. In comparative studies, Ritalin and Adderall have been found to be equivalent in effectiveness.[55]

Recently, new drug treatments for ADHD have become available that are essentially variations of the traditional methylphenidate medication. They include a sustained-release formulation (Concerta), a formulation that produces an initial rapid dose of methylphenidate followed by a second sustained-release phase (Metadate), and a chemical variation of methylphenidate that allows for a longer duration of action (Attenade, Focalin). A methylphenidate patch, designed to release the drug through the skin slowly over a period of nine hours, was approved in 2006.

About 70 percent of the approximately 1 million children in the United States who take stimulants for ADHD each year respond successfully to the treatment. In 1999, a major study examining the effects of medication over a fourteen-month period found that medication was more effective in reducing ADHD symptoms than behavioral treatment and nearly as effective as a combined approach of medication and behavioral treatment. The major side effect of stimulant medications, however, is a suppression of height and weight gains during these formative years, reducing growth to about 80 to 90 percent normal levels. Fortunately, growth spurts during the summer, when children are typically no longer taking medication (referred to as "drug holidays"), usually compensate for this problem. Discontinuance, however, has to be carefully monitored. Symptoms such as lethargy, lack of motivation, and, in some cases, depression can occur during this time. In 2007, the FDA mandated a "black box" warning on ADHD medications, as a guide for patients and physicians.

Recent studies indicate that stimulant treatment for ADHD in childhood does not increase the risk for substance abuse later in life. In fact, the risks for future problems with alcohol and other drugs appear to be reduced.[56]

Until recently, the phenomenon of *reducing* hyperactivity with methylphenidate and related stimulant drugs, rather than increasing it, had been quite puzzling to professionals in this field. It is now known that orally administered methylphenidate and related stimulant drugs produce a relatively slow but steady increase in dopamine activity in the brain. This change in brain chemistry is hypothesized to have two effects that are beneficial to an individual with ADHD. First, increased dopamine may amplify the effects of environmental stimulation, while reducing the background firing rates of neurons. Thus, there would be a greater "signal-to-noise" ratio in the brain, analogous to having now a stronger radio signal received by a radio that no longer emits a large amount of background static. The behavioral effect would be an improvement in attention and decreased distractibility. Symptoms of ADHD may be a result of not having a sufficient "signal-to-noise" ratio in the processing of information for tasks that require concentration and focus. Second, increased dopamine may heighten one's motivation with regard to a particular task, enhancing the salience and interest in that task and improving performance. An individual might perform better on a task simply because he or she likes doing it. The slow rate of absorption achieved through oral administration (Chapter 3) avoids the emotional high that is experienced when stimulants are smoked, snorted, or injected.[57]

The theory that increased dopamine activity accounts for the reduction in ADHD symptoms, however, may be incomplete. In 2003, a selective norepinephrine reuptake inhibitor, atomoxetine (brand name: Strattera) was approved by the Food and Drug Administration (FDA) for the treatment of ADHD in both children and adults. Since Strattera produces an increase in norepinephrine activity in the brain, it is possible that lowered norepinephrine levels may play a role in ADHD as well. Strattera has been marketed as a once-a-day nonstimulant medication that reduces ADHD symptoms by increasing norepinephrine levels—not dopamine levels—in the brain. The full story may be either that both norepinephrine and dopamine are jointly involved in ADHD or that ADHD itself may be two separable disorders, one related to dopamine activity and the other related to norepinephrine activity. According to this hypothesis, the symptoms may overlap to such a degree that it is difficult to distinguish the two disorders on a strictly behavioral basis.

Ritalin and Adderall Abuse

In 1996, the Swiss pharmaceutical company Ciba-Geigy sent letters to hundreds of thousands of pharmacies and physicians in the United States, warning them to exert greater control over Ritalin tablets and prescriptions to obtain them. The alert came in response to reports that Ritalin was becoming a drug of abuse among young people, who were crushing the tablets and snorting the powder as a new way of getting a stimulant high. Many high school and college students are obtaining Ritalin and Adderall from classmates who have been prescribed these medications or through drug thefts of unsecured school offices. The drugs are crushed and snorted either for recreational use or to enhance school performance by being able to study late into the night (Health Line).[58]

Other Medical Applications

Narcolepsy (an unpredictable and uncontrollable urge to fall asleep during the day) is another condition for which stimulant drugs have been applied in treatment. In 1999, modafinil (brand name: Provigil) was approved for treating narcolepsy. The advantage of Provigil over traditional stimulant treatments such as dextroamphetamine is that it does not present problems of abuse and produces fewer adverse side effects. Alternative medications for narcolepsy that do not work by stimulating the CNS are presently under development.[59]

There are also several amphetamine-like drugs available to the public, some of them on a nonprescription basis, for use as nasal decongestants. In most cases, their effectiveness stems from their primary action on

---

Health Line
Stimulant Medications as "Smart Pills"

When twenty-four-year-old Jeff Ewing was first prescribed Adderall to help him maintain his focus after a major automobile accident cost him a year at a midwestern university, he was surprised to find so many healthy students who were taking the same drug to help them study. Some of them were putting all of their study time into two nights, when it would have ordinarily required a week.

The misuse of stimulant medications such as Ritalin, Adderall, and Provigil is clearly on the rise in this population. An estimated 2.3 million adolescents in middle or high school are taking stimulant medications, sometimes called "smart pills" or "academic steroids," without a prescription. Approximately 9 percent of students in a New England liberal arts college reported in 2006 taking stimulants for nonmedical purposes. This pattern of drug-taking has not received much notice from law enforcement agencies or the FDA. As Richard Restak of the American Neuropsychiatric Association has put it, these drugs users are "an entirely different population of people—from the unmotivated to the supermotivated. . . .

[They] may be at the top of the class, instead of the ones hanging around the corners."

The role of prescription drug use to enhance athletic performance will be discussed in Chapter 8. The Point/Counterpoint Debate at the end of Part Two (pp. 214–215) will examine the controversy over cognitive performance-enhancing drugs among healthy adults.

Sources: Carey, Benedict (2008, March 9). Brain enhancement is wrong, right? New York Times, pp. 1–2. Carroll, Bronwen C., McLaughlin, Thomas J., and Blake, Diane R. (2006). Patterns and knowledge of nonmedical use of stimulants among college students. Archives of Pediatric and Adolescent Medicine, 160, 481–485. Cohen, Randy (2007, September 30). Test prep or perp? New York Times Magazine, p. 48. Machniak, Christofer, and Garreau, Joel (2006, June 19). "Smart pills" drug use on rise in classroom. Schermer, M. (2008). On the argument that enhancement is "cheating." Journal of Medical Ethics, 34, 85–88. The Flint Journal, www.cmarchiak@flintjournal.com. Students tapping pills for academic boost (2006, June 20). Newsday, p. B13, quotation.

---

the peripheral nervous system rather than on the CNS. Even so, the potential for misuse exists: Some continue to take these drugs over a long period of time because stopping their use results in unpleasant rebound effects such as nasal stuffiness. This reaction, by the way, is similar to the stuffy nose that is experienced in the chronic administration of cocaine.[60]

Summary

The History of Cocaine

- Cocaine, one of the two major psychoactive stimulants, is derived from coca leaves grown in the mountainous regions of South America. Coca chewing is still prevalent among certain groups of South American Indians.

- During the last half of the nineteenth century, several patent medicines and beverages were sold that contained cocaine, including the original (pre-1903) formulation for Coca-Cola.

- Sigmund Freud was an early enthusiast of cocaine as an important medicinal drug, promoting cocaine as a cure for morphine dependence and depression. Soon afterward, Freud realized the strong dependence that cocaine could bring about.

Acute Effects of Cocaine

- Cocaine produces a powerful burst of energy and sense of well-being. In general, cocaine causes an elevation in the sympathetic autonomic nervous system.

Chronic Effects of Cocaine

- Long-term cocaine use can produce hallucinations and deep depression, as well as physical deterioration of the nasal membranes if cocaine is administered intranasally.

Medical Uses of Cocaine

- The only accepted medical application for cocaine is its use as a local anesthetic.

How Cocaine Works in the Brain

- Within the CNS, cocaine blocks the reuptake of receptors sensitive to dopamine and norepinephrine. As a result, the activity level of these two neurotransmitters in the brain is enhanced.

Present-Day Cocaine Abuse

- Compared with the permissive attitude toward cocaine use seen during the 1970s and early 1980s, attitudes toward cocaine use since the second half of the 1980s have changed dramatically.

- The emergence in 1986 of relatively inexpensive, smokable crack cocaine expanded the cocaine-abuse problem to new segments of the U.S. population and made cocaine abuse one of the major social issues of our time.

Treatment Programs for Cocaine Abuse

- Cocaine abusers can receive treatment through inpatient programs, outpatient programs, or a combination of the two. Relapse is a continual concern for recovering cocaine abusers.

Amphetamines

- Amphetamines, the second of the two major psychoactive stimulants, have their origin in a Chinese medicinal herb, used for thousands of years as a bronchial dilator; its active ingredient, ephedrine, was isolated in 1887.

- The drug amphetamine (brand name: Benzedrine) was developed in 1927 as a synthetic form of ephedrine. By the 1930s, various forms of amphetamines, specifically d-amphetamine and methamphetamine, became available around the world.

Acute and Chronic Effects of Amphetamines

- Amphetamine is effective as a general arousing agent, as an antidepressant, and as an appetite suppressant, in addition to its ability to keep people awake for long periods of time.

- While the acute effects of amphetamines resemble those of cocaine, amphetamines have the particular feature of producing (when taken in large doses) symptoms of paranoia, delusions, hallucinations, and violent behaviors, referred to as amphetamine psychosis. The bizarre behaviors of the "speed freak," the name given to a chronic abuser of methamphetamine, illustrate the dangers of amphetamine abuse.

Patterns of Methamphetamine Abuse and Treatment

- With the emphasis on cocaine abuse during the 1980s, amphetamine abuse was less prominent in the public mind. Recently, however, there has been a resurgence of amphetamine-abuse cases involving methamphetamine, particularly in nonurban regions of the United States.

- Treatment for methamphetamine abuse generally follows along the same lines as treatment for cocaine abuse.

Medical Uses for Amphetamines and Similar Stimulant Drugs

- Amphetamine-like stimulant drugs have been developed for approved medical purposes.

- Methylphenidate (brand name: Ritalin), atomoxetine (brand name: Strattera), and dextroamphetamine (brand name: Adderall) are three examples of drugs prescribed for children diagnosed with attention deficit/hyperactivity disorder (ADHD). Recently, there has been growing concern over the recreational use of these medications.

- Other medical applications for amphetamine-like drugs include their use as a treatment for narcolepsy and as a means for the temporary relief of nasal congestion.

Key Terms

amphetamine, p. 104
amphetamine psychosis, p. 107
attention deficit/ hyperactivity disorder (ADHD), p. 110

cocaine, p. 91
cocaine hydrochloride, p. 98
cocaine psychosis, p. 96
crack cocaine or crack, p. 98

d-amphetamine, p. 106
formication, p. 94
free-base cocaine, p. 98
ice, p. 108

kindling effect, p. 97
methamphetamine, p. 106

Endnotes

1. Rosencan, Jeffrey S., and Spitz, Henry I. (1987). Cocaine reconceptualized: Historical overview. In Henry I. Spitz and Jeffrey S. Rosencan (Eds.), *Cocaine abuse: New directions in treatment and research.* New York: Brunner/Mazel, p. 5.

2. Inciardi, James A. (2002). *The war on drugs III.* Boston: Allyn and Bacon, p. 129. Inglis, Brian (1975). *The forbidden game: A social history of drugs.* New York: Scribner, pp. 49–50. Montoya, Ivan D., and Chilcoat, Howard D. (1996). Epidemiology of coca derivatives use in the Andean region: A tale of five countries. *Substance Use and Misuse, 31,* 1227–1240.

3. Jaffe, Jerome (1985). Drug addiction and drug abuse. In Louis S. Goodman and Alfred Gilman (Eds.), *The pharmacological basis of therapeutics* (7th ed.). New York: Macmillan, p. 552.

4. Nahas, Gabriel G. (1989). *Cocaine: The great white plague.* Middlebury, VT: Paul S. Eriksson, pp. 154–162.

5. Kusinitz, Marc (1988). *Drug use around the world.* New York: Chelsea House Publishers, pp. 91–95.

6. Karch, Steven B. (1996). *The pathology of drug abuse* (2nd ed.). Boca Raton, FL: CRC Press, pp. 2–3. Nuckols, Caldwell C. (1989). *Cocaine: From dependency to recovery* (2nd ed.). Blue Ridge Summit, PA: Tab Books, p. x.

7. Brecher, Edward M., and the editors of *Consumer Reports* (1972). *Licit and illicit drugs.* Boston: Little, Brown, p. 270. Weiss, Roger D., and Mirin, Steven M. (1987). *Cocaine.* Washington DC: American Psychiatric Press, p. 6.

8. McKim, William A. (2000). *Drugs and behavior* (4th ed.). Upper Saddle River, NJ: Prentice-Hall, p. 203.

9. Erickson, Patricia G.; Adlaf, Edward M.; Murray, Glenn F.; and Smart, Reginald G. (1987). *The steel drug: Cocaine in perspective.* Lexington, MA: D.C. Heath, p. 9.

10. Musto, David (1973). *The American disease: Origins of narcotic control.* New Haven, CT: Yale University Press.

11. Cole, John R. (1998). Freud's dream of the botanical monograph and cocaine the wonder drug. *Dreaming, 8,* 187–204. Quotation from Jones, Ernest (1953). *The life and work of Sigmund Freud.* Vol. 1. New York: Basic Books, p. 81.

12. Jones, *The life and work of Sigmund Freud,* p. 81. White, William L. (1998). *Slaying the dragon: The history of addiction treatment and recovery in America.* Bloomington, IL: Chestnut Health Systems, pp. 108–119.

13. Ibid., Jones, p. 84.

14. Brecher, *Licit and illicit drugs,* pp. 272–280.

15. Aronson, T. A., and Craig, T. J. (1986). Cocaine precipitation of panic disorder. *American Journal of Psychiatry, 143,* 643–645.

16. Marsuk, Peter M.; Tardiff, Kenneth; Leon, Andrew C.; Stajic, Marina; Morgan, Edward B.; et al (1992). Prevalence of cocaine use among residents of New York City who commited suicide during a one-year period. *American Journal of Psychiatry, 149,* 371–375.

17. Office of Substance Abuse Prevention (1989). *What you can do about drug use in America* (DHHS publication No. ADM 88–1572). Rockville, MD: National Clearinghouse for Alcohol and Drug Information.

18. Philips, J. L., and Wynne, R. D. (1974). *A cocaine bibliography—nonannotated.* Rockville, MD: National

Institute on Drug Abuse, 1974. Cited in Ernest L. Abel. (1985). *Psychoactive drugs and sex.* New York: Plenum Press, p. 100.

19. Kaufman, Marc J.; Levin, Jonathan M.; Ross, Marjorie H.; Lange, Nicholas; Rose, Stephanie L.; et al. (1998). Cocaine-induced cerebral vasoconstriction detected in humans with magnetic resonance angiography. *Journal of the American Medical Association, 279,* 376–380.

20. Experiment in Memphis suggests many drive after using drugs (1994, August 28). *New York Times,* p. 30.

21. Robinson, Terry E., and Berridge, Kent C. (2000). The psychology and neurobiology of addiction: An incentive-sensitization view. *Addiction, 95* (supplement), S91–S117. Volkow, Nora D.; Wang, Gene-Jack; Fowler, Joanna S.; Logan, Jean; Gatley, Samuel J.; et al. (1997). Decrease in striatal dopaminergic responsiveness in detoxified cocaine-dependent subjects. *Nature, 386,* 830–833.

22. Robinson, Terry E. (1993). Persistent sensitizing effects of drugs on brain dopamine systems and behavior: Implications for addiction and relapse. In Stanley G. Korenman and Jack D. Barchas (Eds.), *The biological basis of substance abuse.* New York: Oxford University Press, pp. 373–402. Weiss and Mirin, *Cocaine,* pp. 48–49.

23. Kaplan, Harold I., Freedman, Arnold M., and Sadock, Benjamin J. (1980). *Comprehensive textbook of psychiatry.* Vol. 3. Baltimore, MD: Williams & Wilkins, p. 1621.

24. Flynn, John C. (1991). *Cocaine: An in-depth look at the facts, science, history, and future of the world's most addictive drug.* New York: Birch Lane/Carol Publishing, pp. 38–46.

25. Ibid., p. 44.

26. Humphries, Drew (1998). Crack mothers at 6: Prime-time news, crack/cocaine, and women. *Violence against Women, 4,* 45–61. Massing, Michael (1998). *The fix.* New York: Simon and Schuster, p. 41. Singer, Lynn T.; Minnes, Sonia; Short, Elizabeth; Arendt, Robert; Farkas, Kathleen; et al. (2004). Cognitive outcomes of preschool children with prenatal cocaine exposure. *Journal of the American Medical Association, 291,* 2448–2456.

27. Egan, Timothy (1999, September 19). A drug ran its course, then hid with its users. *New York Times,* pp. 1, 46. Furst, R. Terry; Johnson, Bruce D.; Dunlap, Eloise; and Curtis, Richard (1999). The stigmatized image of the "crack head": A sociocultural exploration of a barrier to cocaine smoking among a cohort of youth in New York City. *Deviant Behavior, 20,* 153–181.

28. Substance Abuse and Mental Health Services Administration (2008). *Results from the 2007 National Survey on Drug Use and Health: Detailed tables.* Rockville, MD: Office of Applied Studies, Substance Abuse and Mental Health Services Administration, Table 1.1A.

29. Barrionuevo, Alexei (2008, February 23). Cheap cocaine floods a slum in Argentina, devouring lives. *New York Times,* pp. A1, A6. Hearn, Kathy (2006, April 5). Abuse of the highly addictive cocaine by-product "paco" is causing officials to revamp drug laws. *Christian Science Monitor,*

p. 4. Ryzik, Melena (2007, June 10). Cocaine: Hidden in plain sight. *New York Times,* Section 9, pp. 1, 9. Quotation on pp. 1 and 9. Substance Abuse and Mental Health Administration (2008). *Drug Abuse Warning Network, 2006: National estimates of drug-related emergency department visits.* Rockville, MD: Office of Applied Studies, Substance Abuse and Mental Health Administration, Table 2.

30. Gold, Mark S. (1990). *800–COCAINE.* New York: Bantam Books.

31. Nuckols, *Cocaine,* pp. 144–146. Lee, Felicia R. (1994, September 10). A drug dealer's rapid rise and ugly fall. *New York Times,* pp. 1, 22.

32. Nuckols, *Cocaine,* p. 42.

33. Ibid., pp. 71–72.

34. Weiss and Mirin, *Cocaine,* p. 125.

35. Fox, C. Lynn, and Forbing, Shirley E. (1992). *Creating drug-free schools and communities: A comprehensive approach.* New York: HarperCollins, p. 165.

36. Shine, Barbara (2000, March). Some cocaine abusers fare better with cognitive-behavioral therapy, others with 12-step programs. *NIDA Notes, 15* (1), 9–11.

37. Brodie, Jonathan D.; Figueroa, Emilia; Laska, Eugene M., and Dewey, Stephen L. (2005). Safety and efficacy of gamma-vinyl GABA (GVG) for the treatment of methamphetamine and/or cocaine addiction. *Synapse, 55,* 122–125. Brookhaven National Laboratories (2007, December 7). Catalyst Pharmaceutical Partners announces positive Phase II trial results for vigabatrin in the treatment of cocaine addiction. *Laboratory News.* Upton, NY: Brookhaven National Laboratories. Interlandi, Janeen (2008, March 3). What addicts need. *Newsweek,* pp. 36–42. Sergo, Peter (2008, April/May). New weapons against cocaine addiction. *Scientific American Mind,* pp. 54–57. Schiffer, Wynne K., Marsteller, Douglas, and Dewey, Stephen L. (2003). Sub-chronic low dose gamma-vinyl GABA (vigabatrin) inhibits cocaine-induced increases in nucleus accumbens dopamine. *Psychopharmacology, 168,* 339–343. Talan, Jamie (2004, November 23). Anti-seizure drug helps meth, cocaine addicts. *Newsday,* p. A26.

38. Barnes, Deborah M. (1988). Breaking the cycle of addiction. *Science, 241,* p. 1029. Whitten, Lori (2005, August). Cocaine-related environmental cues elicit physiological stress responses. *NIDA Notes, 20*(1), pp. 1, 6–7.

39. McKim, *Drugs and behavior,* p. 205. Rasmussen, Nicolas (2008). *On speed: The many lives of amphetamine.* New York: New York University Press.

40. Brecher, *Licit and illicit drugs,* pp. 282–283.

41. Greaves, George B. (1980). Psychosocial aspects of amphetamine and related substance abuse. In John Caldwell (Ed.), *Amphetamines and related stimulants: Chemical, biological, clinical, and sociological aspects.* Boca Raton, FL: CRC Press, pp. 175–192. Peluso, Emanuel, and Peluso, Lucy S. (1988). *Women and drugs.* Minneapolis: CompCare Publishing.

42. Substance Abuse and Mental Health Services Administration (2008). *Drug Abuse Warning Network, 2006*, Table 2.

43. Goode, Erich (2005). *Drugs in American society* (6th ed.). New York: McGraw-Hill College, p. 276.

44. Bai, Matt (1997, March 31). White storm warning: In Fargo and the prairie states, speed kills. *Newsweek*, pp. 66–67. Quotation by Mark A. R. Kleiman, p. 67.

45. Goode, *Drugs in American society*, p. 276. Sheff, David (2008). *Beautiful boy: A father's journey through his son's addiction*. New York: Houghton Mifflin. Sheff, Nic (2008), pp. 113–115. *Tweak: Growing up with methamphetamine*. New York: Ginee See Books/ Atheneum Books for Young Readers.

46. Ernst, Thomas; Chang, Linda; Leonido-Yee, Maria; and Speck, Oliver (2000). Evidence for long-term neurotoxicity associated with methamphetamine abuse: A 1H MRS study. *Neurology, 54*, 1344–1349. London, E. D.; Simon, S. L.; Berman, S. M.; Mandelhern, M. A. et al. (2004). Mood disturbances and regional cerebral metabolic abnormalities in recently abstinent methamphetamine abusers. *Archives of General Psychiatry, 61*, 73–84.

47. Young, Stanley (1989, July). Zing! Speed: The choice of a new generation. *Spin magazine*, pp. 83, 124–125. Reprinted in Erich Goode (Ed.) (1992), *Drugs, society, and behavior 92/93*. Guilford, CT: Dushkin Publishing, p. 116.

48. Johnson, Dirk (1996, February 22). Good people go bad in Iowa, and a drug is being blamed. *New York Times*, pp. A1, A19. Quotation on p. A19.

49. Butterfield, Fox (2004, January 4). Across rural America, drug casts a grim shadow. *New York Times*, p. 10. Harris, Gardiner (2005, December 15). Fighting methamphetamine, lawmakers reach accord to curb sales of cold medicines. *New York Times*, p. A33. Jefferson, David J. (2005, August 5). America's most dangerous drug. *Newsweek*, pp. 41–48. Johnson, Dirk (2004, March 8). Policing a rural plague: Meth is ravaging the Midwest. *Newsweek*, p. 41. National Association of Counties (2006, January). *The meth epidemic in America*. Washington DC: National Association of Counties.

50. Jacobs, Andrew J. (2004, January 12). The beast in the bathhouse: Crystal meth use by gay men threatens to reignite an epidemic. *New York Times*, pp. B1, B5. Shernoff, Michael (2005, July-August). Crystal's sexual persuasion. *The Gay & Lesbian Review*, pp. 24–26.

51. Zickler, Patrick (2001). Methamphetamine, cocaine abusers have different patterns of drug use, suffer different cognitive impairments. *NIDA Notes, 16* (5), 11–12.

52. Drug and Alcohol Services Information System (2008, February 7). Primary methamphetamine/amphetamine admissions to substance abuse treatment: 2005. *The DASIS Report*. Washington DC: Office of Applied Studies,

Substance Abuse and Mental Health Services Administration. Gawin, Frank H., and Ellinwood, Everett H. (1988). Cocaine and other stimulants: Action, abuse, and treatment. *New England Journal of Medicine, 318*, 1173–1182. National Drug Intelligence Center (2007, December). *National methamphetamine threat assessment 2008*. Washington DC: National Drug Intelligence Center, U.S. Department of Justice. National Institute of Justice (1999, May). *Meth matters: Report on methamphetamine users in five western cities*. Washington DC: National Institute of Justice, U.S. Department of Justice. Quotation on p. xii.

53. Julien, Robert M. (2001). *A primer of drug action* (9th ed.). New York: Worth, pp. 207–213.

54. Julien, *A primer of drug action*, p. 208. Wilens, Timothy E. (2003). Drug therapy for adults with attention-deficit hyperactivity disorder. *Drugs, 63*, 2385–2411. Wilens, Timothy E.; Biederman, Joseph; Spencer, Thomas J.; and Prince, Jefferson (1995). Pharmacotherapy of adult attention deficit/hyperactivity disorder: A review. *Journal of Clinical Psychopharmacology, 15*, 270–279.

55. Julien, *A primer of drug action*, pp. 211–212.

56. Meyers, Laurie (2007, March). Empty bottles: Easing clients off meds. *Monitor on Psychology*, pp. 20–21. The MTA Cooperative Group (1999). A 14-month randomized clinical trial of treatment strategies for attention-deficit/hyperactivity disorder. *Archives of General Psychiatry, 56*, 1073–1086. Wilens, Timothy E.; Faraone, Stephen V.; Biederman, Joseph; and Gunawardene, Samantha (2003). Does stimulant therapy of attention deficit/hyperactivity disorder beget later substance abuse? A meta-analytic review of the literature. *Pediatrics, 111*, 179–185.

57. Julien, *A primer of drug action*, p. 211. Volkow, Nora D.; Wang, Gene.-Jack; Fowler, Joanna S.; Logan, Jean; Gerasimov, Madina; et al. (2001). Therapeutic doses of oral methylphenidate significantly increase extracellular dopamine in the human being. *Journal of Neuroscience, 21* (121RC), 1–5.

58. Marks, Alexandria (2000, October 31). Schoolyard hustler's new drug: Ritalin. *Christian Science Monitor*, p. 1. Thomas, Karen (2000, November 27). Stealing, dealing and Ritalin: Adults and students are involved in abuse of drug. *USA Today*, p. D1.

59. Green, P. M. and Stillman, M. J. (1998). Narcolepsy: Signs, symptoms, differential diagnosis, and management. *Archives of Family Medicine, 7*, 472–478. Ricks, Delthia (2005, August 4). Work nights? So does a pill, study says. *Newsday*, p. A2. Tuller, David (2002, January 8). A quiet revolution for those prone to nodding off. *New York Times*, p. F7.

60. Julien, Robert M. (1998). *A primer of drug action* (8th ed.). New York: Freeman, pp. 141–143.

chapter 5

Narcotics: Opium, Heroin, and Synthetic Opiates

Mary, age sixteen, is a self-described "garbage head"—she will ingest anything she thinks will give her a high. Recently, her drug of choice has been OxyContin. She downs a few pills with a shot of vodka, calling the combination "the sorority girl's diet cocktail" because it allows for a stronger state of intoxication and has fewer calories.

After Mary had a tonsillectomy, her surgeon wrote a prescription for eighty tablets of OxyContin for postoperative pain. Mary took sixty of them over the next two weeks, averaging five a day.

Presently, Mary is in substance abuse treatment, focusing on the problem of prescription medication abuse. When asked whether he had read Mary's medical chart detailing her history of substance abuse before prescribing OxyContin, instead of alternatives such as acetaminophen, Mary's surgeon replied, sheepishly, "Well, I guess I wasn't thinking."[1]

There is no escaping the love-hate relationship we have with opium and the opiates that are derived from it. Here is a family of drugs that has the astonishing power to banish pain from our lives and at the same time the power to enslave our minds.

This chapter will concern itself with the medical uses and recreational abuses of opiate-derived and opiate-related drugs. Together, these drugs are referred to as **narcotics** (from the Greek word for "stupor"), in that they produce a dreamlike effect on the user and at higher doses induce a state of sleep. The most important characteristic of narcotic drugs, however, is that they have powerful analgesic properties; they greatly reduce feelings of pain.

As noted in Chapter 2, the term "narcotic" often has been used inappropriately to mean *any* illicit psychoactive drug or at least any drug that causes some degree of dependence, including such unlikely examples as cocaine and amphetamine. Even today, the term can be misleading, because other drugs having no relationship to opium are far more effective in inducing sleep (see Chapter 15). Nonetheless, we are stuck with this inexact terminology; it is not likely to disappear anytime soon.

Narcotic drugs, in general, are divided into three main categories. The first includes **opium** and three natural components that can be extracted from it: morphine, codeine, and thebaine (Figure 5.1). The second category includes opium derivatives that are created by making slight changes in the chemical composition of morphine. The best example of this type is heroin. Although technically an opiate derivative, heroin is commonly included with morphine, codeine, and thebaine, and collectively all four chemicals, along with opium itself, are referred to simply as **opiates**. The third category includes synthetic drugs that are not chemically related to morphine or any of its derivatives but nonetheless produce opiate-like effects that are behaviorally indistinguishable from the effects of opiates themselves. Drugs of this type are commonly referred to as **synthetic opiates** or *synthetic opiate-like drugs*. This

---

narcotics: A general term technically referring to opiate-related or opiate-derived drugs. It is often mistakenly used to include several other illicit drug categories as well.

opium: An analgesic and euphoriant drug acquired from the dried juice of the opium poppy.

opiates: Any Ingredients of opium or chemical derivatives of these ingredients. Opiates generally refer to opium, morphine, codeine, thebaine, and heroin.

synthetic opiates: Synthetic drugs unrelated to morphine that produce opiate-like effects.

---

last category is a result of a continuing effort to discover a drug that achieves the same degree of analgesia as the opiates but without the potential for abuse.

Opium in History

Like cocaine, the origins of heroin and other opiates go back to the fields of faraway times and places. This particular story begins with the harvesting of raw opium in remote villages of Myanmar (formerly Burma), Laos, Thailand, Afghanistan, Mexico, Colombia, Peru, and other countries where the weather is hot and labor is cheap. The source is the opium poppy, known by its botanical name as *Papaver somniferum* (literally "the poppy that brings sleep"), an annual plant growing three to four feet high. Its large flowers are typically about four or five inches in diameter and can be white, pink, red, or purple. This variety is the only type of poppy that produces opium; common garden plants such as the red Oriental poppy or the yellow California poppy look similar but do not produce psychoactive effects.

The present-day method of opium harvesting has not essentially changed for more than three thousand years. When the petals of the opium poppy have fallen but the seed capsule of the plant underneath the petals is not yet completely ripe, laborers make small, shallow incisions in the capsules, allowing a milky white juice to ooze out. The next day, this substance will have oxidized and hardened by contact with the air. At this point, now reddish brown and having a consistency of heavy syrup, it is collected, plant by plant, onto large poppy leaves.[2]

Opium was first described in specific detail in the early third century B.C., but we can be fairly sure that it

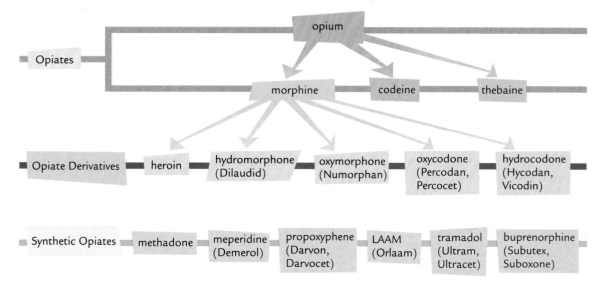

FIGURE 5.1

Major opiates, opiate derivatives, and synthetic opiates. (Note: Brand names are shown in parentheses.)

Sources: Physicians' desk reference (62nd ed.) (2008). Montvale, NJ: Medical Economics Data. Raj, P. Prithvi (1996). *Pain medicine: A comprehensive review.* St. Louis: Mosby, pp. 126–153.

was used for at least a thousand years before that. A ceramic opium pipe has been excavated in Cyprus, dating from the Late Bronze Age, about 1200 B.C. Cypriot vases from that era depict incised poppy capsules. From evidence contained in the Ebers Papyrus writings (see Chapter 1), Egyptians were knowledgeable about the medicinal value of opium.[3]

In the second century A.D., Claudius Galen, the famous Greek physician and surgeon to Roman gladiators, recommended opium for practically everything. He wrote that it

> . . . *resists poison and venomous bites, cures chronic headache, vertigo, deafness, apoplexy, dimness of sight, loss of voice, asthma, coughs of all kinds, spitting of blood, tightness of breath, colic, . . . jaundice, hardness of the spleen, . . . urinary complaints, fever, . . . leprosies, the troubles to which women are subject, melancholy, and all pestilences.*[4]

Galen's enthusiasm for the instrumental use of opium is an early example of "over-prescribing." Interestingly, however, there are no records in ancient times that refer to the recreational use of opium, nor with any problems of opium dependence.[5]

Western Europe was introduced to opium in the eleventh and twelfth centuries by returning crusaders who had learned of it from the Arabs. During the first stirrings of modern medicine in Europe, opium began to be regarded as a therapeutic drug. In 1520, a physician named Paracelsus, promoting himself as the foremost medical authority of his day, introduced a medicinal drink combining opium, wine, and an assortment of spices. He called the mixture *laudanum* (derived from the Latin phrase meaning "something to be praised"), and before long the formula of Paracelsus was being called the stone of immortality. Even though Paracelsus himself denounced many of the doctrines of earlier physicians in history, he continued the time-honored tradition of recommending opium for practically every known disease.

A young harvester tends to his crop of opium poppies in the rugged mountains of Colombia.

In 1680, the English physician Thomas Sydenham, considered the father of clinical medicine, introduced a highly popular version of opium drink similar to that of Paracelsus, called Sydenham's Laudanum. For the next two hundred years or so, the acceptable form of taking opium among Europeans and later Americans would be in the form of a drink, either Sydenham's recipe or a host of variations. Sydenham's enthusiasm for the drug was no less than that of his predecessors. "Among the remedies," he wrote, "which it has pleased Almighty God to give man to relieve his sufferings, none is so universal and so efficacious as opium."[6] The popularity of opium drinking eventually would lead to the emergence of opium as a recreational drug in Europe and the United States.

The Opium War

Sometime in the eighteenth century, China invented a novel form of opium use, opium smoking, which eventually became synonymous in the Western mind with China itself. However, for at least eight hundred years before that, the Chinese used opium only in a very limited way. They took it almost exclusively on a medicinal basis, consuming it orally in its raw state as a painkiller and treatment for diarrhea.

The picture changed dramatically in the eighteenth century for the basic reason that the British people had fallen in love with Chinese tea. British merchants wanted to buy tea and send it home, but what could they sell to China in exchange? The problem was that there were few, if any, commodities that China really wanted from the outside. In their eyes, the rest of the world was populated by "barbarians" with inferior cultures, offering little or nothing the Chinese people needed.

The answer was opium. In 1773, British forces had conquered Bengal Province in India and suddenly had a monopoly on raw opium. It was now easy to introduce opium to China as a major item of trade. Opium was successfully smuggled into China through local British and Portuguese merchants, allowing the British government and its official trade representative, the East India Company, to present a public image of not being directly involved in the opium trade. Huge quantities of opium, flooding into China from its southern port of Canton, found a ready market as a recreational drug in the form of opium smoking, and not surprisingly opium dependence soon became a major social problem. Despite repeated edicts by the Chinese emperor to reduce the use of opium within China or cut the supply line from India, the monster flourished.[7]

In 1839, tensions had reached a peak. In a historic act of defiance against the European powers, including Britain, an imperial commissioner appointed by the Chinese emperor to deal with the opium problem once and for all confiscated a shipment of opium and burned it publicly in Canton. Events escalated shortly after until open fighting between Chinese and British soldiers broke out. The Opium War had begun.

By 1842, British artillery and warships had overwhelmed a nation unprepared to deal with European firepower. In a humiliating treaty, China was forced to sign over to Britain the island of Hong Kong and its harbor (until the distant year of 1997), grant to British merchants exclusive trading rights in major Chinese ports, and pay a large amount of money to reimburse Britain for losses during the war. Despite these agreements, fighting broke out again between 1858 and 1860; this time the British soldiers and sailors were joined by French and American forces. Finally, in a treaty signed in 1860, China was required to legalize opium within its borders. The Opium War opened up the gates of China, much against its will, to the rest of the world.[8]

Opium in Britain

To the average Briton in the mid-1800s, the Opium War in China was purely a trade issue, with little or no direct impact upon his or her daily life. Nonetheless, opium itself was everywhere. The important difference between China and Britain with respect to opium was not in the *extent* of its consumption but in the *way* it was consumed. The acceptable form of opium use in Victorian England was opium drinking in the form of laudanum, whereas the Asian practice of opium smoking was linked to a perceived life-style of vice and degradation and associated with the very lowest fringes of society. The contrast was strikingly ironic. Opium dens, with all the evil connotations that the phrase has carried into modern times, were the places where opium was *smoked*; the respectable parlors of middle-class British families were the places where opium was *drunk*.

Supplies of opium were unlimited and cheaper than gin or beer; medical opinion was at most divided on the question of any potential harm; there was no negative public opinion and seldom any trouble with the police. As long as there were no signs of opium smoking, a chronic opium abuser was considered no worse than a drunkard. Nearly all infants and young children in Britain during this period were given opium, often from the day they were born. Dozens of laudanum-based patent medicines, with appealing names like Godfrey's Cordial, A Pennysworth of Peace, and Mrs. Winslow's

Soothing Syrup, were used to dull teething pain or colic, or merely to keep the children quiet. The administration of opium to babies was particularly attractive in the new, industrial-age life-style of female workers, who had to leave their infants in the care of elderly women or young children when they went off to work in the factories.[9]

Out of this climate of acceptance sprang a new cultural phenomenon: the opium-addict writer. Just as LSD and other hallucinogens were to be promoted in the 1960s as an avenue toward a greatly expanded level of creativity and imagination (see Chapter 6), a similar belief was spreading during this period with respect to opium. The leader of the movement was Thomas DeQuincey, and his book *Confessions of an English Opium Eater*, published in 1821, became the movement's bible. It is impossible to say how many people started to use opium recreationally as a direct result of reading DeQuincey's *Confessions*, but there is no doubt that the book made the practice fashionable.

Opium in the United States

In many ways, opium consumption in the United States paralleled its widespread use in Britain. In one survey of thirty-five Boston drugstores in 1888, 78 percent of the prescriptions that had been refilled three or more times contained opium. Until 1942, opium poppies were cultivated in Vermont and New Hampshire, in Florida and Louisiana, and later in California and Arizona. Women outnumbered men in opium use during the nineteenth century by as much as three to one. As one researcher has expressed it, "husbands drank alcohol in the saloon; wives took opium at home."[10]

Throughout the 1800s, opium coexisted alongside alcohol, nicotine (in tobacco products), and cocaine as dominant recreational drugs. As late as 1897, the Sears,

A nineteenth-century advertising card for Mrs. Winslow's Soothing Syrup, a popular opium remedy, was directed toward young mothers and their children.

Roebuck mail-order catalog was advertising laudanum for sale for about six cents an ounce, while other opium products were addressed specifically to the alcoholic. For example, Sears's "White Star Secret Liquor Cure" was advertised as designed to be added to the gentleman's after-dinner coffee so that he would be less inclined to join his friends at the local saloon. In effect, he would probably nearly fall asleep at the table, since the "cure" was opium. If customers became dependent on opium, perhaps as a result of the "liquor cure," fortunately they could order "A Cure for the Opium Habit," promoted on another page of the same catalog. Chances were good that the ingredients in this one included alcohol.[11] Opium habits often were replaced by cocaine habits (see Chapter 4) and vice versa.

Given the openness of opium drinking in the nineteenth-century United States, we can only surmise that the fanatical reaction against opium smoking was based on anti-Chinese prejudice. It is clear that intense hostility existed toward the thousands of Chinese men and boys brought to the West in the 1850s and 1860s to build the railroads. Since most of the Chinese workers were recruited from the Canton area, where opium trafficking was particularly intense, the practice of opium smoking was well known to them and it served as a safety valve for an obviously oppressed society of men. In 1875 San Francisco outlawed opium smoking for fear, to quote a newspaper of the time, that "many women and young girls, as well as young men of respectable family, were being induced to visit the dens, where they were ruined morally and otherwise."[12] No mention was ever made of any moral ruin coming out of drinking opium at home.

A federal law forbidding opium smoking soon followed, whereas the regulation of opium use by any other means failed to receive legislative attention at that time. By the beginning of the twentieth century, however, the desire for social control of opium dens became overshadowed by the emergence of opium-related drugs that presented a substantially greater threat than smoked opium.[13]

Morphine and the Advent of Heroin

In 1803, a German drug clerk named Friedrich Wilhelm Adam Sertürner first isolated a yellowish-white substance in raw opium that turned out to be its primary active ingredient. He called it **morphine,** in honor of

morphine: The major active ingredient in opium.

This late-nineteenth-century illustration of young working girls in a New York City opium den was part of a widespread media campaign at the time to outlaw the smoking of opium.

Morpheus, the Greek god of dreams. For the first time, more than three-fourths of the total weight of opium (containing inactive resins, oils, and sugars) could be separated out and discarded. Morphine represented roughly 10 percent of the total weight of opium, but it was found to be roughly ten times stronger than raw opium. All the twenty-five or so opiate products that were eventually isolated from opium were found to be weaker than morphine and formed a far smaller proportion of opium. Besides morphine, other major opiate products were **codeine** (0.5 percent of raw opium) and **thebaine** (0.2 percent of raw opium), both of which were found to have a considerably weaker opiate effect.

With the invention of the hypodermic syringe in 1856, morphine could be injected into the bloodstream rather than administered orally, bypassing the gastrointestinal tract and thus speeding the delivery of effects. The new potential of a morphine

injection coincided with the traumas of the Civil War in the United States (1861–1865) and later the Franco-Prussian War in Europe (1870–1871). It is not surprising that large numbers of soldiers became dependent on opiates and maintained the condition in the years that followed. After the Civil War, opiate dependence in general was so widespread among returning veterans that the condition was often called the "soldier's disease."[14]

Against the backdrop of increasing worry about opiate dependence, a new painkilling morphine derivative called **heroin** was introduced into the market in 1898 by the Bayer Company in Germany, the same company that had been highly successful in developing acetylsalicylic acid as an analgesic drug and marketing it as "Bayer's Aspirin" (see Chapter 14). About three times stronger than morphine, and strangely enough believed initially to be free of morphine's dependence-producing properties, heroin (from the German *heroisch*, meaning "powerful") was hailed as an entirely safe cough suppressant (preferable to codeine) and as a medication to relieve the chest discomfort associated with pneumonia and tuberculosis. In retrospect, it is incredible that from 1895 to 1905, no fewer than forty medical studies concerning injections of heroin failed to pick up on its potential for dependence! The abuse potential of heroin, which we now know exceeds that of morphine, was not fully recognized until as late as 1910.[15]

Why is heroin more potent than morphine? The answer lies in its chemical composition. Heroin consists of two acetyl groups joined to a basic morphine molecule. These attachments make heroin more fat-soluble and hence more rapidly absorbed into the brain. Once inside the brain, the two acetyl groups break off, making the effects of heroin chemically identical to that of morphine. One way of understanding the relationship between the two drugs is to imagine morphine as the contents inside a plain cardboard box and the heroin as the box with gift wrapping. The contents remain the same, but the wrapping increases the chances the box will be opened.

Opiates and Heroin in American Society

The end of the nineteenth century marked a turning point in the history of opium and its derivatives. Opiate dependence would never again be treated casually. By 1900, there were, by one conservative estimate, 250,000 opiate-dependent people in the United States, and the actual

---

codeine (COH-deen): One of the three active ingredients in opium, used primarily to treat coughing.

thebaine (THEE-bayn): One of three active ingredients in opium.

heroin: A chemical derivative of morphine. It is approximately three times as potent as morphine and a major drug of abuse.

number could have been closer to 750,000 or more. If we rely upon the upper estimate, then we would be speaking of roughly one out of every hundred Americans, young or old, living at that time. Compare this figure with the 2007 estimate of 366,000 Americans (aged twelve or older) who have used heroin within the past year out of a current population four times the population in 1900, and you can appreciate the impact opiate abuse was having on society in the early twentieth century.[16]

The size of the opiate-abusing population alone at that time probably would have been sufficient grounds for social reformers to seek some way of controlling these drugs, but there was also the growing fear that the problems of opiate abuse were becoming closely associated with criminal elements or the underworld. There was a gnawing anxiety that opiates were creating a significant disruption in American society. A movement began to build toward instituting some system of governmental regulation.

Opiate Use and Abuse after 1914

The Harrison Act of 1914 (see Chapter 2) radically changed the face of opiate use and abuse in the United States. It ushered in an era in which the abuser was

> . . . no longer seen as a victim of drugs, an unfortunate with no place to turn and deserving of society's sympathy and help. He became instead a base, vile, degenerate who was weak and self-indulgent, who contaminated all he came in contact with and who deserved nothing short of condemnation and society's moral outrage and legal sanction.[17]

The situation, however, did not change overnight. Most important, the 1914 legislation did not actually ban opiate use. It simply required that doctors register with the Internal Revenue Service the opiate drugs (as well as cocaine and other coca products) that were being prescribed to their patients and pay a small fee for the right to prescribe such drugs. The real impact of the new law came later, in the early 1920s, as a result of several landmark decisions sent down from the U.S. Supreme Court. In effect, the decisions interpreted the Harrison Act more broadly. Under the Court's interpretation of the Harrison Act, no physician was permitted to prescribe opiate drugs for "nonmedical" use. In other words, it was now illegal for addicted individuals to obtain drugs merely to maintain their habit, even from a physician. Without a legal source for their drugs, opiate abusers were forced to abandon opiates altogether or to turn to illegal means, and the drug dealer suddenly provided the only place where opiate drugs could be obtained.

Heroin became the perfect black market drug. It was easier and more profitable to refine it from raw opium overseas and ship it into the country in small bags of odorless heroin powder than it was to transport raw opium with its characteristic odor. In addition, because it had to be obtained illegally, heroin's price tag skyrocketed to thirty to fifty times what it had cost when it was available from legitimate sources.[18]

With the emergence of restrictive legislation, the demographic picture also changed dramatically. No longer were the typical takers of narcotic drugs characterized as female, predominantly white, middle-aged, and middle-class, as likely to be living on a Nebraskan farm as in a Chicago townhouse. In their place were young, predominantly white, urban adult males, whose opiate drug of choice was intravenous heroin and whose drug supply was controlled by increasingly sophisticated crime organizations. In the minds of most Americans, heroin could be comfortably relegated to the fringes of society.[19]

Heroin Abuse in the 1960s and 1970s

Three major social developments in the 1960s brought the heroin story back into the mainstream of the United States. The first began in late 1961, when a crackdown on heroin smuggling resulted in a significant shortage of heroin on the street. The price of heroin suddenly increased, and heroin dosages became more adulterated than ever before. Predictably, the high costs of maintaining heroin dependence encouraged new levels of criminal behavior, particularly in urban ghettos. Heroin abuse soon imposed a cultural stranglehold on many African American and Latino communities in major U.S. cities.

A second development, beginning in the 1960s, affected the white majority more directly. Fanned by extensive media attention, a youthful counterculture of hippies, flower children, and the sexually liberated swept the country.

> It was a time of unconventional fashions and anti-establishment attitudes. In unprecedented numbers, middle- and upper-class people experimented with illegal drugs to get high. They smoked marijuana; tried the new synthetic properties of amphetamines and barbiturates; rediscovered the almost forgotten product of the coca plant, cocaine; and, for the first time, people from the mainstream of American life began to experiment with derivatives of the opium poppy. Thus, heroin addiction made its insidious way back to the forefront of national concern.[20]

Finally, disturbing news about heroin abuse began to appear that focused not only on Americans at home but also on American armed forces personnel stationed in Southeast Asia in connection with the Vietnam War. Reports beginning in the late 1960s indicated an increasingly widespread recreational abuse of heroin, along with alcohol, marijuana, and other drugs, among U.S. soldiers. One returning Vietnam veteran related the atmosphere of polydrug abuse at the time:

> The last few months over there were unbelievable. My first tour there in '67, a few of our guys smoked grass, you know. Now the guys walk right in the hootch with a jar of heroin or cocaine. Almost pure stuff. Getting smack [heroin] is like getting a bottle of beer. Everybody sells it. Half my company is on the stuff.[21]

With respect to heroin, the problem was exacerbated by the fact that Vietnamese heroin was 90 to 98 percent pure, compared to 2 to 10 percent pure in the United States at the time, and incredibly cheap to buy. A 250-mg dose of heroin, for example, could be purchased for $10, whereas the standard intravenous dose on the streets of a major U.S. city would amount to only 10 mg. A comparable 250 mg of highly diluted U.S. heroin would have cost about $500. With the purity of heroin supplies so high, most U.S. soldiers smoked or sniffed it to get an effect; some drank it mixed with alcohol, even though most of the drug was lost as it was filtered through the liver en route to the bloodstream.[22]

Beyond the concern about the soldiers overseas, there was also the worry that up to 100,000 Vietnam veterans would be returning home hopelessly dependent on heroin. It has been estimated from survey data that about 11 percent of Army returnees in 1971 were regular users of heroin and about 22 percent had tried it at least once. Urine tests (appropriately named Operation Golden Flow), conducted near the end of a soldier's tour of duty, revealed a percentage of about one-half of that level, but there were strong indications that users in uniform had voluntarily given up heroin prior to their being shipped home.

Fortunately, the worst fears were not borne out. A comprehensive investigation in 1974 showed that only 1 to 2 percent of Vietnam veterans were regular heroin abusers one year following their return from overseas, approximately the same percentage as those entering the military from the general population.[23] Why were we so lucky? Evidently, the use of heroin was situationally specific to involvement in Vietnam. Once home in the states, in the vast majority of cases, the environmental cues and motivational factors for drug abuse were no

Military involvement in Vietnam brought U.S. soldiers in contact with unusually potent doses of heroin and other psychoactive drugs.

longer present. Does that mean that it is possible to abuse heroin without becoming dependent upon it? This question will be addressed later in the chapter.

Heroin and Synthetic Opiates since the 1980s

At one time, the major source of white powder heroin smuggled into the United States was Turkey, where the opium was grown, and the center of heroin manufacture and distribution was Marseilles in southern France (the infamous French Connection, as popularized in the 1970 movie of the same name). International control over the growing of Turkish opium in 1973 brought this route of heroin distribution to an end, but it succeeded only in encouraging other parts of the world to fill the vacuum. The "Golden Triangle" region of Laos, Myanmar (formerly Burma), and Thailand became the principal players in providing the United States with heroin. Joining southeast Asian heroin suppliers were southwest Asian nations such as Afghanistan, Pakistan, and Iran (in the "Golden Crescent"), as well as the central Asian nations of Kazakhstan, Kyrgystan, Tajikistan, Turkmenistan, and Uzbekistan that had been, until 1991, regions of the Soviet Union. As a consequence of these new sources, the purity of imported heroin increased from around 5 percent to over 18 percent.[24]

Although the growth of crack cocaine abuse in the 1980s pushed the issue of heroin abuse temporarily off the front page, heroin abuse itself continued in new forms and variations. One significant development was the appearance around 1985 of a relatively pure and inexpensive form of Mexican heroin called **black tar.** In addition, new synthetic forms of heroin were appearing on the street, created in illegal drug laboratories within the United States. One such synthetic drug was derived from **fentanyl,** a prescription narcotic drug. Chemical modifications of fentanyl, anywhere from ten to a thousand times stronger than heroin, were sold under the common name "China White." The risks of overdose death increased dramatically.

From a technical point of view, fentanyl derivatives and other similar "designer drugs" were legal, owing to a loophole in the drug laws; because they were not chemically identical to heroin, no specific law applied to them. In 1986 the Controlled Substance Analogue Act closed this unfortunate loophole. The laws now state that any drug with a chemical structure or pharmacological effect similar to that of a controlled substance is as illegal as the genuine article. Nonetheless, such look-alike opiates are still available as illicit drugs of abuse.

The mid-1990s witnessed still another shift in the pattern of heroin trafficking. The dominant supply of white powder heroin in the United States, judged from the analysis of drug seizures, no longer originated in Asia but rather South America, principally Colombia (see Drugs . . . in Focus).

Street heroin from South American sources was now both cheaper and purer. Heroin purities exceeded 60 percent, at least ten times more powerful than the typical street heroin in the 1970s. In 1994, a 90-percent-pure brand of heroin circulating in New York City took heroin abusers by surprise; several overdose deaths occurred within a period of five days. Street prices for a milligram of heroin in New York fell from $1.81 in 1988 to as little as 37 cents in 1994. By government estimates, heroin consumption nationwide in 1996 had doubled from a decade earlier. As one writer put it, "If the U.S. auto industry cut the price of its sedans by half and redesigned them to go 180 mph, no one would wonder why sales hit the roof."[25]

In the mid-1990s, there was also a shift in the perception of heroin abuse itself. As the popularity of cocaine abuse declined and the incidence of crack abuse began to ebb, the spotlight once more turned toward the allure of heroin. For a brief time, popular movies (*Pulp Fiction* in 1994, *Trainspotting* in 1995) and fashion photography (Calvin Klein fragrance advertisements in 1996) provided provocative images that glamorized heroin abuse, referred to in the media as "heroin chic."

The increased potency of present-day heroin has produced a long-lasting effect on the way heroin is abused. Due to the availability of increasingly pure heroin, the drug no longer needs to be injected. Instead, it can be snorted (inhaled through the nose) or smoked. New heroin abusers are frequently smoking mixtures of heroin and crack cocaine or heating heroin and inhaling its vapors. These methods of heroin abuse may avoid potential HIV infections or hepatitis through contaminated needles, but they do not prevent the dependence that heroin can produce or the risk of heroin overdose.

Unfortunately, heroin snorting or smoking also has opened the door to new populations of potential heroin abusers who had previously stayed away from the drug because of their aversion to hypodermic needles. University of Michigan surveys from 1991 to 2008 have indicated that one to two percent of all high school seniors

---

black tar: A potent form of heroin, generally brownish in color, originating in Mexico.

fentanyl (FEN-teh-nil): A chemical derivative of thebaine, used as a prescription painkiller. The street name for fentanyl and related compounds is China White.

The New Face of Heroin Trafficking in the United States

In 1990, all but 4 percent of the heroin seized by U.S. federal agents came from Asian sources and none from Colombia or any other region in South America. As recently as 1994, Asian suppliers accounted for more than 60 percent of the total entering the United States. A dramatic reversal in less than a year's time, however, made Colombia the main supplier, generating nearly two-thirds of the heroin market.

In a post–September 11 world, heroin traffickers have tended to operate less like multinational corporations or shadowy cartels centered in Colombia and more like highly compartmentalized terrorist cells. Currently, immigrants are the dominant importers and distributors of heroin in the United States, loosely organized in relatively small smuggling networks, and dealing chiefly with individuals from countries of common origin and mistrusting outsiders.

The American market for heroin, worth about $10 billion annually, is thus roughly divided into ethnic spheres of influence. Los Angeles–based Mexican groups control wholesale markets west of the Mississippi. Nigerians operating out of Chicago have the northern parts of the Midwest. And New York–based Dominican syndicates fronting for Colombians dominate the East Coast. Smaller Chinese gangs operate on the fringes, moving mostly in areas of San Francisco or New York that have larger Asian communities.

Of course, the character of heroin trafficking is in constant flux, subject to shifting market demands and the continuing challenges posed by law-enforcement agencies.

Sources: Brzezinski, Matthew (2002, June 23). Heroin: The sleek new business model for the ultimate global product. *New York Times Magazine*, pp. 24–29, 46, 54, 56. Quotation on p. 54. Quirk, Matthew (2005, March). The new opium war. *Atlantic Monthly*, pp. 52–54. Wren, Christopher (1996, February 11). Colombians taking over heroin trade. *New York Times*, p. 51.

report heroin use at some time in their lives, with a majority of them smoking heroin rather than injecting it. However, the prevalence rate is not uniform across the United States in demographic or geographic terms. The incidence of heroin smoking among young people is generally higher than the national average and is currently rising in suburban communities, particularly in the Northeast.[26]

Effects on the Mind and the Body

While recreational narcotic use in the United States involves a range of drugs other than heroin itself, we will concentrate on the effects of narcotic drugs from the perspective of the heroin abuser. We have to be careful, however, to recognize that the specific effects are quite variable. The intensity of a response to heroin changes as a factor of (1) the quantity and purity of the heroin taken, (2) the route through which heroin is administered, (3) the interval since the previous dose of heroin, and (4) the degree of tolerance of the user to heroin itself. In addition, there are psychological factors related to the setting, circumstances, and expectations of the user that make an important difference in what an individual feels after taking heroin.[27] Nonetheless, there are several major effects that occur often enough to qualify as typical of the experience.

If heroin is injected intravenously, there is an almost immediate tingling sensation and sudden feeling of warmth in the lower abdomen, resembling a sexual orgasm, for the first minute or two. There is a feeling of intense euphoria, variously described as a "rush" or a "flash," followed later by a state of tranquil drowsiness that heroin abusers often call being "on the nod." During this period, lasting from three to four hours, any interest in sex is greatly diminished. In the case of male heroin abusers, the decline in sexual desire is due, at least in part, to the fact that narcotics reduce the levels of testosterone, the major male sex hormone.[28]

An individual's first-time experience with heroin may be considerably unpleasant. Opiates in general cause nausea and vomiting, as the reflex centers in the medulla are suddenly stimulated. Some first-time abusers find the vomiting so aversive that they never try the drug again; others consider the discomfort largely irrelevant because the euphoria is so powerful.

There are a number of additional physiological changes in the body. A sudden release of histamine in the bloodstream produces an often intense itching over the entire body and a reddening of the eyes. Heroin also will cause pupillary constriction, resulting in the characteristic "pinpoint pupils" that are used as an important diagnostic sign for narcotic abuse in general. As with sedative-hypnotic drugs (see Chapter 15), heroin also reduces the sensitivity of respiratory centers in the medulla to levels of carbon dioxide, resulting in a depression in breathing. At high doses, respiratory depression is a major risk factor that can result in death. Blood pressure is also depressed from heroin intake. Finally, a distressing, though nonlethal, effect of heroin is the slowing down of the gastrointestinal tract, causing a labored defecation and long-term constipation.[29]

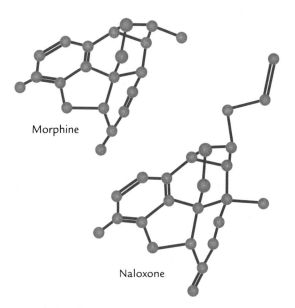

Morphine

Naloxone

FIGURE 5.2

Only minor differences exist between a morphine molecule and a naloxone molecule. Yet naloxone is a complete antagonist to morphine.

How Opiates Work in the Brain

It is useful to view the neurochemical basis for a number of psychoactive drugs in terms of their influence upon specific neurotransmitters in the brain. For example, the stimulant effects of cocaine and amphetamine are related to changes in norepinephrine and dopamine (see Chapter 4). In the case of opiate drugs, however, as a result of major discoveries in the 1970s, it is clear that we are dealing with a more direct effect: the activation of receptors in the brain that are specifically sensitive to morphine.

During the 1960s, suspicions grew that a morphine-sensitive receptor, or a family of them, exists in the brain. One major clue came from the discovery that small chemical alterations in the morphine molecule would result in a group of new drugs with strange and intriguing properties. Not only would these drugs produce little or no *agonistic* effects—that is, they would not act like morphine—but they would instead act as *opiate antagonists*—that is, they would reverse or block the effects of morphine (Figure 5.2).

The most complete opiate antagonist to be identified, **naloxone** (brand name: Narcan), has turned out to have enormous therapeutic benefits in the emergency treatment of narcotic-overdose patients. In such cases, intramuscular or intravenous injections of naloxone reverse the depressed breathing and blood pressure in a matter of a minute or so, an effect so fast that emergency-department specialists view the reaction as "miraculous." The effect lasts for one to four hours. Higher doses of naloxone bring on symptoms that are similar to those observed following an abrupt withdrawal of narcotic drugs. Interestingly, in normal undrugged people, nalox-

one produces only negligible changes, either on a physiological or a psychological level. Only if morphine or other narcotic drugs are already in the body does naloxone have an effect.[30]

Beyond its practical application, the discovery of naloxone had theoretical implications as well. The argument went as follows: If such small molecular changes could so dramatically transform an agonist into an antagonist, then some receptor in the brain must exist in such a way that it can be easily excited or inhibited. The concept of a special morphine-sensitive receptor fulfilled these requirements.

The actual receptors themselves were discovered in 1973, precisely where you would have expected them to be: in the spinal cord and brain, where pain signals are known to be processed, and in the limbic system of the brain, where emotional behaviors are coordinated. In other words, it was clear that the analgesic and euphoric properties of morphine were due to the stimulation of these receptors.

Why would these receptors exist in the first place? No one seriously considers the possibility that receptors in the brain have been patiently waiting millions of years in evolutionary history for the day that the juice of the

naloxone (nah-LOX-ohn): A pure antagonist for morphine and other opiate drugs. Brand name is Narcan.

opium poppy could finally slip inside them! The only logical answer is that we must be producing our own morphine-like chemicals that activate these receptors.

As a result of a series of important discoveries from 1975 to the early 1980s, three groups of natural morphine-like molecules have been identified: enkephalins, beta-endorphin, and dynorphins. Together, they are known as **endogenous opioid peptides,** inasmuch as they are (1) all peptide molecules (amino acids strung together like a necklace), (2) opiate-like in function, and (3) produced within the central nervous system. Unfortunately, this is such an unwieldy name that more frequently they are simply referred to as *endorphins*.

What can we then conclude about the effect of opiates on the brain? The answer, as we now understand it, is that the brain has the ability to produce its own "opiate-like" substances, called endorphins, and contains a special set of receptor sites to receive them. By an amazing quirk of fate, the opium poppy yields a similarly shaped chemical that fits into these receptor sites, thus producing equivalent psychological and physiological effects. Naloxone acts as an opiate antagonist because its structural features enable it to fit into these receptor sites, replacing the opiate molecules that have gotten in. The receptors themselves, however, are *inactivated* by naloxone. This is why naloxone can "undo" the acute effects of an opiate drug like heroin.

A long-acting form of naloxone, **naltrexone** (brand name: ReVia, previously marketed as Trexan), administered orally three times per week, has since been found to be a useful medication in the treatment of heroin abuse, mainly for patients who are highly motivated to stop their drug-taking behavior. Such patients include doctors, nurses, and other health professionals who must end a pattern of heroin abuse to retain their licenses and former heroin abusers on parole who are at risk of returning to prison if they suffer a relapse. Injectable slow-release formulations that extend the effects of naltrexone over thirty days or more are presently being investigated, in an effort to free patients from having to rely on a more frequent oral administration schedule. A once-per-month slow-release form of naltrexone (brand name: Vivitrol) has been available for alcohol dependence since 2006 (see Chapter 10).[31]

---

endogenous opioid peptides (en-DODGE-eh-nus OH-pee-oid PEP-tides): also known as *endorphins*: A class of chemicals produced inside the body that mimic the effects of opiate drugs.

naltrexone (nal-TREX-ohn): A long-lasting form of naloxone. Brand name prior to 1994 was Trexan; brand name has since been changed to ReVia.

Patterns of Heroin Abuse

The dominant route of administration in heroin abuse is intravenous injection, usually referred to as either *mainlining* or *shooting*. Heroin also can be administered by a variety of other routes. Heroin smoking is popular in Middle Eastern countries and in Asia, but until very recently it has seldom been observed in the United States. Newcomers to heroin may begin their abuse either by snorting the drug through the nose or injecting it subcutaneously (skin-popping). Experienced heroin abusers may snort heroin to avoid using a needle or choose the subcutaneous route when they can no longer find veins in good enough condition to handle an intravenous injection. As mentioned earlier, an oral administration of heroin is usually worthless because absorption is extremely poor. American soldiers in Vietnam who were abusing heroin often took the drug orally, but because of the extremely high purity of the heroin they were consuming, their effective dose levels merely equaled or only slightly exceeded levels found on American streets at the time.

Tolerance and Withdrawal Symptoms

A prime feature of chronic heroin abuse is the tolerance that develops, but the tolerance effects themselves do not occur in every system. Gastrointestinal effects of constipation and spasms do not show much tolerance at all, whereas distinctive pupillary responses (the pinpoint feature of the eyes) eventually subside with chronic use. The greatest signs of tolerance are seen in the degree of analgesia, euphoria, and respiratory depression. The intense thrill of the intravenous injection will be noticeably lessened. The overall decline in heroin reactions, however, is dose-dependent. If the continuing dose level is high, then tolerance effects will be more dramatic than if the dose level is low.

The first sign of heroin withdrawal, a marked craving for another fix, generally begins about four to six hours after the previous dose and intensifies gradually to a peak over the next thirty-six to seventy-two hours, with other symptoms beginning from a few hours later (Table 5.1). The abuser is essentially over the withdrawal period in five to ten days, though mild physiological disturbances, chiefly elevations in blood pressure and heart rate, are observed as long as six months later. Generally, these long-term effects are associated with a gradual withdrawal from heroin rather than an abrupt one.

TABLE 5.1

Symptoms of administering heroin and of withdrawing heroin

ADMINISTERING	WITHDRAWING
Lowered body temperature	Elevated body temperature
Decreased blood pressure	Increased blood pressure
Skin flushed and warm	Piloerection (gooseflesh)
Pupillary constriction	Tearing, runny nose
Constipation	Diarrhea
Respiratory depression	Yawning, panting, sneezing
Decreased sex drive	Spontaneous ejaculations and orgasms
Muscular relaxation	Restlessness, involuntary twitching and kicking movements*
Nodding, stupor	Insomnia
Analgesia	Pain and irritability
Euphoria and calm	Depression and anxiety

* Probably the source of the expression "kicking the habit."

Source: Adapted from Grilly, David M. (2006). *Drugs and human behavior* (5th ed.). Boston: Allyn and Bacon, p. 229.

The overall severity of heroin-withdrawal symptoms is a function of the dosage levels of heroin that have been sustained. When dosage levels are less than 10 percent, the withdrawal symptoms are comparable to a moderate to intense case of the flu. In more severe cases, the withdrawal process can result in a significant loss of weight and body fluids. With recent increases in the purities of street heroin in the 1990s, the symptoms of withdrawal are greater. Only rarely, however, is the process of heroin withdrawal life threatening, unlike the withdrawal from barbiturate drugs (see Chapter 15).

It should not be surprising that withdrawal symptoms are essentially the mirror image of symptoms observed when a person is under the influence of heroin. If we are dealing with a group of endorphin-sensitive receptors that are, in the case of the heroin abuser, being stimulated by the opiates coming in from the outside, then it is reasonable to assume that over time, the production of endorphins would decline. Why produce stuff on your own when you are getting it from an external source? By that argument, withdrawal from heroin would then be a matter of cutting off those receptors from that external source, resulting in a reaction opposite to the one that would have occurred had the receptors been satisfied in

the first place. Over a period of time, coinciding with the withdrawal period for a heroin abuser, we would expect that the normal production of endorphins would reestablish itself and there would be little or no need for the external supply of heroin.

The receptor explanation for heroin dependence sounds reasonable and does account for the presence of withdrawal symptoms, but unfortunately it is an oversimplification for heroin abuse in general. We would expect that once the endorphin-sensitive receptors regain their natural supply of endorphins, heroin abuse should end, but we know that it does not.

In the case of heroin abusers, their tendency to continue taking heroin is propelled by a number of factors. There is, first of all, the combination of fear and distress associated with the prospect of experiencing withdrawal symptoms, along with a genuine craving for the effects themselves, reflecting the physical and psychological dependence that heroin brings.

In addition, long-term heroin abuse frequently produces such a powerful conditioned-learning effect that the social setting in which the drug-taking behavior has occurred takes on reinforcing properties of its own (see Chapter 2). Even the act of inserting a needle can become pleasurable. Some heroin abusers (called *needle freaks*) continue to insert needles into their skin and experience heroin-like effects even when there is no heroin in the syringe. In effect, the heroin abuser is responding to a placebo. Any long-term treatment for heroin abuse, as will be discussed in a later section, must address itself to a range of physical, psychological, and social factors to be successful.

The Lethality of Heroin Abuse

Considering the statistics of deaths and hospital emergencies associated with heroin abuse (see Chapter 2), you might be surprised that one would question the toxicity of heroin itself. To understand the toxicity of heroin, we first need to separate the effects of chronic heroin abuse from the drug's acute effects. From a long-term perspective with regard to one's physical health, heroin is considered relatively nontoxic, particularly when compared to several other drugs of abuse. As one expert has put it:

Unlike alcohol, the amphetamines, and the barbiturates, which are toxic to the body over the long run with relatively heavy use, the narcotics are relatively safe. The organs are not damaged, destroyed, or even threatened by even a lifetime of narcotic addiction. There are no major malformations of the body, no tissue damage, no physical deterioration directly trace-able to the use of any narcotic, including heroin.[32]

A notable exception, however, is found in the case of heroin administered through inhalation. Smoked heroin has been linked to leukoencephalopathy, an incurable neurological disease in which a progressive loss of muscle coordination can lead to paralysis and death, as well as kidney degeneration.[33]

On the other hand, it is abundantly clear that the practice of heroin abuse is highly dangerous and potentially lethal. The reasons have to do with situations resulting from the acute effects of the drug.

- Heroin has a relatively small ratio of LD (lethal dose) to ED (effective dose). Increase a dose that produces a high in a heroin abuser by ten or fifteen times and you will be in the dosage range that is potentially fatal. As a result, death by overdose is an ever-present risk. If we take into account the virtually unknown potency of street heroin in any given fix, we can appreciate the hazards of a drug overdose. The "bag" sold to a heroin abuser may look like the same amount each time, but the actual heroin content may be anywhere from none at all to 90 percent. Therefore, it is easy to under-estimate the amount of heroin being taken in.

- The user risks possible adverse effects from any toxic substance that has been "cut" with the heroin. Adding to the complexity, deaths from heroin over-dose are frequently consequences of synergistic com-binations of heroin with other abused drugs such as stimulants like cocaine or depressants like alcohol, Valium, or barbiturates. In some cases, individuals have smoked crack as their primary drug of abuse and snorted heroin to ease the agitation associated with crack. In other cases, lines of cocaine and heroin are alternately inhaled in a single session, a practice referred to as "criss-crossing." In the DAWN reports (see Chapter 2), the combinations of heroin with cocaine or heroin with alcohol are frequently observed causes of heroin-related deaths. Relatively few heroin-related fatalities are due to the abuse of heroin alone. A listing of street names for heroin and heroin combinations is given in Table 5.2.

- It is also possible that some heroin abusers develop unstable levels of tolerance that are tied to the envi-ronmental setting in which the heroin is adminis-tered. As a result of conditioned tolerance, a heroin dose experienced in an environment that has not been previously associated with drug taking may have a significantly greater effect on the abuser than the same dose taken in more familiar surroundings. Con-

---

Quick Concept Check 5.2

Understanding the Effects of Administering and Withdrawing Heroin

Without peeking at Table 5.1, check your understanding of the effects of heroin, relative to withdrawal symptoms, by noting whether the following symptoms are associ-ated with administering heroin or withdrawing it.

SYMPTOM	ADMINISTERING	WITHDRAWING
1. twitching and sneezing		
2. skin flushed and warm		
3. decreased sex drive		
4. yawning and panting		
5. pain and irritability		
6. pupillary constriction		
7. increased blood pressure		
8. diarrhea		
9. analgesia		

Answers: 1. withdrawing   2. administering
3. administering   4. withdrawing   5. withdrawing
6. administering   7. withdrawing   8. withdrawing
9. administering

---

sequently, the specific effect on the abuser is highly unpredictable (see Chapter 2).

- While the overriding danger of excessive amounts of heroin is the potentially lethal effects of respiratory depression, abusers can die from other physiological reactions. In some instances, death can come so quickly that the victims are found with a needle still in their veins, due to a massive release of histamine or an allergic reaction to some filler in the heroin to which the abuser was hypersensitive. Intravenous injections of heroin increase the risks of hepatitis or HIV infections, while unsterile water used in the mixing of heroin for these injections can be contami-nated with bacteria.

- An extra risk began to appear during the mid-1980s. In some forms of synthetic heroin illicitly produced in clandestine laboratories in the United States, manufacturers failed to remove an impurity called MPTP that destroys dopamine-sensitive neurons in the substantia nigra of the midbrain. As a result, young people exposed to this type of heroin can acquire full-blown symptoms of Parkinson's disease (see Chapter 3) that are virtually identical in character to the symptoms observed in elderly patients suffering from a progressive loss of dopamine-sensitive neurons in their brains.

Heroin Abuse and Society

While society over the years has had to deal with the reality of drug abuse in many forms, many people still look upon heroin abuse as the ultimate drug addiction and the heroin abuser as the ultimate "dope addict." It is true that many heroin abusers fit this image: people driven to stay high on a four- to eight-hour schedule, committing a continuing series of predatory crimes. Yet the actual picture of the present-day heroin abuser is more complex. A major study has shown that while robbery, burglary, and shoplifting accounted for 44 percent of an abuser's income and nearly two-thirds of that abuser's criminal income, a substantial amount of income came from either victimless crimes (such as pimping or prostitution) or noncriminal activity. Often a heroin abuser would work in some capacity in the underground drug industry and be paid in heroin instead of dollars.[34]

A related question with regard to our image of the heroin abuser is whether controlled heroin abuse is possible. Is heroin abuse a situation that is, by definition, out of control? For most heroin abusers, the answer is yes. Yet for some individuals, heroin may not be a compulsion. The practice of controlled or paced heroin intake is referred to as **chipping,** and the occasional heroin abuser is known as a *chipper* (Drugs in Focus, page 132).

An important study conducted by Norman E. Zinberg in 1984 analyzed a group of people who had been using heroin on a controlled basis for more than four years.[35] Over the course of one year, 23 percent reported taking heroin less than once a month, 36 percent reported taking it one to three times a month, and 41 percent reported taking it twice a week. Four years of exposure to heroin would seem to have been sufficient time to develop a compulsive dependence, but that did not happen. The observation that most compulsive heroin-dependent individuals never had any period of controlled use implies that controlled heroin abuse

TABLE 5.2

Street names for narcotic drugs

TYPE OF NARCOTIC	STREET NAME
morphine	Big M, Miss Emma, white stuff, M, dope, hocus, unkie, stuff, morpho
white heroin	junk, smack, horse, scag, H, stuff, hard stuff, dope, boy, boot, blow, jolt, spike, slam
Mexican heroin	black tar, tootsie roll, chapapote (Spanish for "tar"), Mexican mud, peanut butter, poison, gummy balls, black jack
heroin combined with amphetamines	bombitas
heroin combined with cocaine	dynamite, speedball, whizbang, goofball
heroin combined with marijuana	atom bomb, A-bomb
heroin combined with cocaine and marijuana	Frisco special, Frisco speedball
heroin combined with cocaine and morphine	cotton brothers
codeine combined with Doriden (a nonbarbiturate sedative-hypnotic)	loads, four doors, hits

Sources: U.S. Department of Justice, Drug Enforcement Administration. (1986). *Special report: Black tar heroin in the United States,* p. 4. U.S. Department of Justice, Bureau of Justice Statistics Clearinghouse. (1992). *Drugs, crime, and the justice system,* pp. 24–25.

might not be merely an early transitional stage that eventually turns into uncontrolled heroin dependence.

While the Zinberg findings have provided support for the possibility of long-term heroin abuse on a controlled basis, newer evidence from studies of heroin abusers over more than three decades—a period of time much longer than that studied by Zinberg—indicates a somewhat darker scenario. A series of follow-up investigations during the 1970s, 1980s, and 1990s were carried out of nearly six hundred male heroin abusers who had been admitted to a compulsory drug-treatment program for heroin-dependent criminal offenders from 1962 to 1964. By 1996–1997, only 42 percent of the original sample, on average about fifty-eight years old at the time, were available for interview. About 9 percent were of unknown status and 49 percent had died. The most common cause of

chipping: The taking of heroin on an occasional basis.

The Secret and Dangerous Life of a (Heroin) Chipper

The man lives in a condo on the fashionable Upper East Side of Manhattan, drives an expensive car, takes vacations with his wife to Europe and the Caribbean, pulls down a six-figure salary as a company executive, and has been taking heroin for the last twenty years. Outwardly, he seems to have his life in firm control, and upon casual inspection he appears to be the model of the successful chipper. A closer look, however, reveals the elements of a struggle with forces he has yet to subdue.

His life has been an alternating cycle in which he would take heroin for a week or two, then stop for three weeks, and begin again. "For the first two weeks after I've stopped," he has said, "it does not occupy my thoughts in an overwhelming sense. But by the third week it is creeping in there and it just gets to the point when I want it. I say:

'It's time. I've been good enough. I want my reward.' . . . The drug is an enhancement of my life. I see it as similar to a guy coming home and having a drink of alcohol."

Despite the façade of security, his life as a chipper is full of dangers. After an overdose eleven years ago, he no longer injects his heroin, preferring to snort it from the corner of a credit card or the clip of a ballpoint pen. He buys his heroin from a friend who has been his supplier for years, but he runs the continual risk of being detected and losing his job. Sampling as potentially dependence-inducing a drug as heroin has to be an extremely risky business. One drug abuse expert has commented that it is a little like playing Russian roulette: "Not everyone will become addicted, but you can't predict who will and who won't."

Source: Treaster, Joseph B. (1992, July 22). Executive's secret struggle with heroin's powerful grip. *New York Times*, pp. A1, B4.

---

death (22 percent) was accidental poisoning from heroin adulterants or heroin overdose. Homicide, suicide, or accident accounted for 20 percent of the deaths, with the remainder being related to liver disease, cardiovascular disease, or cancer. Regarding the drug-taking behavior of the survivors, the researchers concluded that heroin dependence had been very difficult for them to avoid. As the principal investigator of the study has expressed it:

> *Although many of the survivors reported that they had been able to stop using heroin for extensive periods, fewer than half reported abstinence for periods of more than five years. Abstinence for five years significantly reduced the likelihood of relapse, but even among those who achieved fifteen years of abstinence, a quarter still relapsed.*[36]

Moreover, large proportions of these men were engaged in alcohol, cocaine, or amphetamine abuse as well.

---

detoxification: The process of drug withdrawal in which the body is allowed to rid itself of the chemical effects of the drug in the bloodstream.

propoxyphene (pro-POX-ee-feen): A synthetic opiate useful in treating heroin abuse. Brand name is Darvon.

methadone: A synthetic opiate useful in treating heroin abuse.

Treatment for Heroin Abuse

For the heroin abuser seeking treatment for heroin dependence, the two primary difficulties are the short-term effects of heroin withdrawal and the long-term effects of heroin craving. Any successful treatment, therefore, must combine a short-term and long-term solution.

Opiate Detoxification

Traditionally, it has been possible to make the process of withdrawal from heroin, called **detoxification** ("detox"), less distressing to the abuser by reducing the level of heroin in a gradual fashion under medical supervision rather than by stopping "cold turkey" (a term inspired by the gooseflesh appearance of the abuser's skin during abrupt withdrawal). In medical settings, synthetic opiates such as **propoxyphene** (brand name: Darvon) or **methadone** have been administered to replace the heroin initially; then doses of these so-called transitional drugs are decreased over a period of two weeks or so.[37]

Methadone Maintenance

For the heroin abuser seeking out medical treatment for heroin dependence, the most immediate problem is getting the drug out of the abuser's system during detoxification with a minimum of discomfort and distress. As mentioned earlier, the naloxone and clonidine combination has been particularly important in speeding up withdrawal and reducing the severity of physiological symptoms.

After detoxification, however, the long-term problem of drug dependence remains. The craving for heroin persists, and the abuser most often has little choice but to return to a drug-oriented environment where the temptations to satisfy the craving still exist. Since the mid-1960s, one strategy has been to have a detoxified heroin abuser participate in a program in which oral administrations of the synthetic opiate methadone are essentially substituted for the injected heroin. This treatment approach, called **methadone maintenance,** was initiated in New York City through the joint efforts of Vincent Dole, a specialist in metabolic disorders, and Marie Nyswander, a psychiatrist whose interest had focused on narcotic dependence. Their idea was that if a legally and carefully controlled narcotic drug was available to heroin abusers on a regular basis, the craving for heroin would be eliminated, their drug-taking life-style would no longer be needed, and they could now turn to more appropriate social behaviors such as steady employment and a more stable family life.

For the Dole–Nyswander treatment program, now serving more than 100,000 former heroin abusers in the United States, methadone has definite advantages. First of all, since it is a legal, inexpensive narcotic drug (when dispensed through authorized drug-treatment centers), criminal activity involved in the purchase of heroin on the street can be avoided. Methadone is slower acting and more slowly metabolized, so that, unlike heroin, its effects last approximately twenty-four hours and can be easily absorbed through an oral administration. Since it is a narcotic drug, methadone binds to the endorphin-sensitive receptors in the brain and prevents feelings of heroin craving, yet its slow action avoids the rush of a heroin high.

Typically, clients in the program come to the treatment center daily for an oral dose of methadone, dispensed in orange juice, and the dose is gradually increased to a maintenance level over a period of four to six weeks. The chances of an abuser turning away from illicit drug use are increased if the higher doses of methadone are made conditional upon a "clean" (drug-free) urinanalysis.[38]

The general philosophy behind maintenance programs is that heroin abuse is a metabolic disorder requiring a maintenance drug for the body, just as a diabetic patient needs a maintenance supply of insulin. In other words, the maintenance drug "normalizes" the drug abuser.

As a social experiment, methadone-maintenance programs have met with a mixture of success and failure.

On the one hand, evaluations of this program have found that 71 percent of former heroin abusers who have stayed in methadone maintenance for a year or more have stopped intravenous drug taking, thus lessening the risk of AIDS. In a major study, drug-associated problems declined from about 80 percent to between 17 and 28 percent, criminal behavior was reduced from more than 20 percent to less than 10 percent, and there was a slight increase in permanent employment.[39] While attracting only a fraction of the heroin-dependent community, methadone maintenance does attract those who perceive themselves as having a negligible chance of becoming abstinent on their own. It is reasonable to assume that we are looking at the potential rehabilitation of a hard-core subpopulation within heroin abusers.[40]

On the other hand, maintenance programs are not without problems. The first has to do with the moral question of opiate maintenance itself. Some critics have seen these treatments as a cop-out that perpetuates rather than discourages the sense of low self-esteem among heroin abusers, a system that serves the needs of society over the needs of the individual. Methadone programs, they argue, simply substitute one type of dependence with another, and the goal should eventually be abstinence from all drugs.[41]

Although maintenance programs do help many heroin abusers, particularly those who stay in the program over an extended period of time, there are strong indications that the programs do not reduce the overall vulnerability to drug abuse in general. In other words, methadone blocks the yearning for heroin but it is less effective in blocking the simple craving to get high. Alcohol abuse among methadone-maintenance clients, for example, ranges from 10 percent to 40 percent, suggesting that alcohol may be substituting for narcotics during the course of treatment, and one study found that as many as 43 percent of those who had successfully given up heroin had become dependent on alcohol.[42] Furthermore, methadone is sometimes diverted away from the clinics and onto the streets for illicit use. The availability of street methadone remains a matter of great concern.[43]

Alternative Maintenance Programs

Two alternative orally administered maintenance drugs for heroin abusers have been recently developed that avoid the problems associated with the daily dosage approach of methadone programs. The first is the

methadone maintenance: A treatment program for heroin abusers in which heroin is replaced by the long-term intake of methadone.

synthetic opiate **LAAM** (levo-alpha-acetylmethadol), marketed under the brand name Orlaam. The advantage of LAAM is a substantially longer duration, relative to methadone, so that treatment clients need to receive the drug only three times a week instead of every day.[44]

The second drug is the synthetic opiate **buprenorphine** (brand name: Subutex), also available as a three-times-a-week medication. Both medications have been shown to be useful in heroin abuse treatment. To reduce the potential for buprenorphine tablets to be made into an injectable form and abused, buprenorphine is also available in combination with naloxone (brand name: Suboxone). If the tablets are crushed and dissolved into an injectable solution, the combined formulation triggers undesirable withdrawal symptoms.

The advantage of buprenorphine as a heroin-abuse treatment is that it can be prescribed by office-based physicians rather than being required to be dispensed through maintenance centers, as is the case with methadone or LAAM. When combined with naloxone, the abuse potential of buprenorphine is minimized and, while long-term blockage of opiate receptors occurs, there is less of an opiate "high." Buprenorphine treatment substantially reduces the cost to public health clinics because it can be administered more widely in less heavily secured medical locations, such as primary care clinics and physicians' offices. It also reduces the inconvenience and stigmatization faced by treatment clients, particularly for teenage heroin abusers who would be disinclined to seek treatment at facilities that are associated with older people (Health Alert).[45]

Behavioral and Social-Community Programs

To help deal with the tremendous social stresses that reinforce a continuation of heroin abuse, programs called **therapeutic communities** (Daytop Village, Samaritan Village, and Phoenix House are examples) have been developed, in which the abuser establishes temporary residence in a drug-free group setting and receives intensive counseling. Typically, counselors are former heroin abusers or former abusers of other drugs who have successfully given up drugs.

Other approaches have been developed that combine detoxification, treatment with naltrexone, psychotherapy, and vocational rehabilitation, under one comprehensive plan of action. These programs, called **multimodality programs,** are designed to focus simultaneously on the multitude of needs facing the heroin abuser, with the goal being a successful reintegration into society. As a continuing effort to help the recovering heroin abuser, there are also twelve-step group support programs such as Narcotics Anonymous, modeled after similar programs for those recovering from alcohol or cocaine dependence.[46]

Medical Uses of Narcotic Drugs

We have focused upon the acute effects of narcotic drugs in the context of heroin abuse, but it is also important to look at the beneficial effects that narcotic drugs can have in a medical setting (Table 5.3, page 136).

Beneficial Effects

Excluding heroin, which is a Schedule I drug in the United States and therefore unavailable even for medical use, narcotic drugs are administered with three primary therapeutic goals in mind: the relief of pain, the treatment of acute diarrhea, and the suppression of coughing. These applications are not at all new; they have been employed throughout the long history of opiate drugs.

The first and foremost medical use of narcotic drugs today is for the treatment of pain. For a patient suffering severe pain following surgical procedures or from burns or cancer, the traditional drug of choice has been morphine. Recently, pain treatment with fentanyl through a transdermal patch administration has been found to be more effective as an analgesic than morphine in an oral time-release administration and is preferred by patients with chronic pain because the pain relief is achieved with less constipation and an enhanced quality of life.[47]

The second application capitalizes on the effect of opiates in slowing down peristaltic contractions in the intestines that occur as part of the digestive process. As noted earlier, one problem associated with the chronic

LAAM: A synthetic narcotic drug levo-alpha-acetylmethadol used in the treatment of heroin abuse. Brand name is Orlaam.

buprenorphine (BYOO-preh-NOR-feen): A synthetic opiate used in the treatment of heroin abuse. Brand names are Subutex and (in combination with naloxone) Suboxone.

therapeutic communities: Living environment for individuals in treatment for heroin and other drug abuse, where they learn social and psychological skills needed to lead a drug-free life.

multimodality programs: Treatment programs in which a combination of detoxification, psychotherapy, and group support is implemented.

HEALTH ALERT!

Sustained-Release Buprenorphine: Ushering in a New Era

When buprenorphine (brand name: Subutex) and its combination with naloxone (brand name: Suboxone) received FDA approval in 2002, a new era of heroin-abuse treatment began. Because buprenorphine is only a partial activator of opiate-sensitive receptors in the brain, as opposed to full activators such as heroin and methadone, clients in treatment are more likely to discontinue their heroin intake without experiencing withdrawal symptoms, and the symptoms that do occur are considerably milder. At the same time, buprenorphine administration avoids the typical heroin effects of euphoria and respiratory depression. There is also no evidence of significant impairment of cognitive or motor performance in the course of long-term buprenorphine maintenance.

In recent years, two significant developments have expanded the social benefits of buprenorphine as a heroin-abuse treatment. First, a sustained-release version of buprenorphine, administered by injection at a treatment facility on a once-per-month basis, is now available. As a result, heroin abusers in treatment need visit the physician's office only on a monthly basis. Second, federal legislation enacted in 2007 allows a certified physician to treat a caseload of up to one hundred patients. Previous regulations had limited caseloads to no more than thirty patients.

> **Where to go for assistance:**
>
> www.buprenorphine.samhsa.gov/about.html
>
> This web site, sponsored by the Substance Abuse and Mental Health Services Administration of the U.S. Department of Health and Human Services, provides extensive information on treatment options and a list of available buprenorphine treatment locations. There are more than eight hundred physicians certified for buprenorphine treatment in New York State alone.

Sources: Martin, Kimberly R. (2004, September). Once-a-month medication for heroin addiction? *NIDA Notes*, p. 9. Mitka, Mike (2003). Office-based primary care physicians called on to treat the "new" addict. *Journal of the American Medical Association, 290*, 735–738. Opioid detox study shows buprenorphine improves retention rate for teens (2005, October 10). *Alcoholism and Drug Abuse Weekly*, pp. 1–2. Substance Abuse and Mental Health Services Administration (2007, January/ February). Buprenorphine: Patient limits increase. *SAMHSA Report*, p. 7.

---

abuse of heroin, as well as of other opiates, is constipation. However, for individuals with dysentery, a bacterial infection of the lower intestinal tract causing pain and severe diarrhea, this negative side effect becomes desirable. Therefore, the control of diarrhea by an opiate is literally life-saving, since acute dehydration (loss of water from the body) can be fatal. Fortunately, the opioid medication loperamide (brand name: Imodium), which is available on an over-the-counter basis, effectively controls diarrhea symptoms by its action on the gastrointestinal system. Because it cannot cross the blood-brain barrier, loperamide does not produce any psychoactive effects.

The third application focuses on the effect of narcotic drugs to suppress the cough reflex center in the medulla. In cases in which an **antitussive** (cough-suppressing) drug is necessary, codeine is frequently prescribed, either by itself or combined with other medications such as aspirin or acetaminophen (brand names: Tylenol, among others). As an alternative treatment for coughing, a nonopiate drug, **dextromethorphan,** is available in over-the-counter syrups and lozenges as well as in combination with antihistamines. Unfortunately, widespread abuse of dextromethorphan among young people, who are consuming it on a recreational basis, has become a new public health concern (see Chapter 1).

Potential Adverse Effects

Given the many simultaneous effects of opiates on the body, it is natural that some concerns should be attached to their medical use, even though the overall effect is beneficial. For example, respiration will be depressed for four to five hours even following a therapeutic dose of morphine, so caution is advised when the patient suffers from asthma, emphysema, or pulmonary heart disease. In addition, opiate medications decrease the secretion of hydrochloric acid in the stomach and reduce the pushing of food through the intestines, a condition that can lead to intestinal spasms. Finally, although opiates will have a

---

antitussive: Having an effect that controls coughing.

dextromethorphan (DEX-troh-meh-THOR-fan): A popular non-narcotic ingredient used in over-the-counter cough remedies. The "DM" designation on these preparations refers to dextromethorphan.

TABLE 5.3

Major narcotic drugs in medical use

GENERIC NAME	BRAND NAME*	RECOMMENDED DOSE FOR ADULTS	GENERIC NAME	BRAND NAME*	RECOMMENDED DOSE FOR ADULTS
morphine	Avinza	30–120 mg (oral, combined immediate release, and extended-release)	hydrocodone	Hycodan Vicodin	5 mg (oral) 5 mg (oral) with acetaminophen
	Duramorph	5–10 mg (i.v.)	methadone	Dolorphine	5–10 mg (oral, i.v., or s.c.)
	Kadian	10–200 mg (oral, extended-release)	meperidine	Demerol	50–100 mg (oral, i.m., i.v.)
	MS Contin	15–200 mg (oral, controlled-release)	propoxyphene	Darvocet-N	50 mg (oral) with acetaminophen
	Oramorph SR	15–100 mg (oral, sustained-release)		Darvon	65 mg (oral)
codeine		30–60 mg (oral, i.m., or s.c.)	fentanyl	Duragesic	12.5–100 mcg/hour (extended-release transdermal patch)
hydromorphone	Dilaudid	1–8 mg (oral, i.m., i.v., or s.c.)		Actiq	200–1,600 mcg ("lollipop" form)
oxycodone	OxyContin	10–80 mg (oral, controlled-release)	tramadol	Ultram ER	100–300 mg (oral, extended-release)
	Percocet	2.5–10 mg (oral) with acetaminophen			
	Percodan	4.5 mg (oral) with aspirin			

* Only a few of the brands are listed here. Some narcotic drugs are available only under their generic names, some under either their generic or brand names.

Note: i.v. = intravenous; i.m. = intramuscular; s.c. = subcutaneous.

Source: Physicians' desk reference (62nd ed.) (2008). Montvale, NJ: Thomson HealthCare.

sleep-inducing effect in high doses, it is not recommended that they be used as a general sedative-hypnotic treatment, unless sleep is being prevented by pain or coughing.[48]

Current Use and Abuse of OxyContin

Since the late 1990s, there has been a dramatic increase in cases in which prescription narcotic medications, developed with the intention to be used for the relief of pain, have been subject to abuse. While a variety of narcotic analgesics such as Vicodin, Darvon, Percodan, and Demerol have abuse potential, the most dramatic example has been the time-release form of oxycodone (brand name: **OxyContin**).

Since the drug was introduced in 1995, the availabil-

OxyContin: A time-release form of oxycodone, used in the treatment of chronic pain.

ity of OxyContin has increased rapidly. This powerful analgesic drug for debilitating pain was promoted initially as being relatively safe from potential abuse and more acceptable to the general public because it lacked the social stigma associated with morphine. Its FDA-approved formulation permits OxyContin to be taken orally and absorbed slowly over a period of twelve hours, killing the pain without inducing a sudden feeling of euphoria. However, when OxyContin tablets are crushed and then either swallowed or inhaled as a powder, or are injected after diluting the powder into a solution, the effect can be similar to that of heroin. Even with the prescribed formulation, some patients have suffered severe withdrawal symptoms, similar to those experienced during heroin withdrawal, when they abruptly stopped taking high-dosage levels of the medication. Since the mid-1990s, a dramatic increase in drug-related ED visits associated with narcotic analgesics (see Chapter 2) has been attributed largely to physical problems deriving from OxyContin abuse.[49]

PORTRAIT

By 2000, Barry Tuttle's pain had become so excruciating that he was on the verge of suicide. A former salesman of plumbing supplies in North Plainfield, New Jersey, Tuttle (above left photo) had endured pulsating back pain for six years. Seven surgeries, endless doctor's appointments, thousands of pills, acupuncture, and other alternative treatments had all proved unsuccessful. When Tuttle began taking OxyContin, however, a relatively normal life-style returned. His perceived pain level (on a scale of 1 to 10, with 10 being the most horrible pain imaginable) was an acceptable 2 or 3—a dramatic improvement from his continual ratings of 8 or 9 before the advent of OxyContin. The drug had literally saved his life.

For every Barry Tuttle, however, there is a Russell Fitch (above right photo). Prescribed OxyContin following hip-replacement surgery, Fitch found that the drug was difficult to give up even after his recovery was complete. In 1999, this resident of rural Maine was convicted of selling guns to finance the purchase of a steady supply of OxyContin. In May 2001, while on parole for the firearms theft conviction, Fitch was charged with walking into a pharmacy with a gun and pushing a note across the counter that read: "Give me all your OxyContin or I will shoot you."

Fitch is not alone in his descent into criminal activity as a result of compulsive OxyContin abuse. Arrests have been made in all parts of the United States (the drug has been called the "rural heroin") for crimes ranging from simple theft to murder and drug trafficking, all related to the illicit abuse of this drug. At the same time, demands to remove OxyContin from the market until an abuse-reducing formulation is developed would return people like Barry Tuttle to a life of abject misery. From Tuttle's perspective, some individuals simply cannot handle any form of a powerful drug. Perhaps, in the absence of OxyContin, Fitch would have become dependent on something else. In Tuttle's words, "Drugs don't addict people. People addict people."

The problem is that it is difficult to predict which path a patient will follow. As a neurologist and pain-management specialist has expressed it, "A practicing physician has to be mindful that someone, even if they don't come with 'addict' written all over them, may be one. . . . The physician has to establish a relationship with the patient they're taking care of on a long-term basis."

Sources: Adler, Jerry (2003, October 20). In the grip of a deeper pain. *Newsweek,* pp. 48–49. Meier, Barry (2003). *Pain killer: A "wonder" drug's trail of addiction and death.* New York: Rodale Press. Susman, Tina (2001, July 29). Good drug, bad drug: OxyContin eases pain, lures addicts. *Newsday,* pp. A6, A36. Quotations on p. A36.

OxyContin abusers vary widely across age groups, socioeconomic status levels, geographic locations, and gender. Particularly striking have been the outbreaks in the United States of OxyContin abuse and the criminal activity that is associated with obtaining it (when legitimate prescription access fails) in rural towns and small cities, places where traditional opiate-related abuse cases have been relatively rare (Portrait).

Recent efforts have been made to reduce OxyContin abuse in a number of ways. An FDA-mandated warning label now states that the drug is as potentially addictive as morphine and that chewing, snorting, or injecting it could be lethal. Additionally, physicians are receiving special training in spotting potential abusers of narcotic analgesics in general. A reformulation, combining Oxy-Contin and naloxone, is in development. In the future, if the tablet is crushed instead of taken orally as an intact tablet, naloxone will be released and will counteract the opiate-related effects. You may recall that a similar approach has been taken in the case of one form of buprenorphine (Suboxone) to reduce its abuse potential.[50]

Misuse or Abuse of Prescription Pain Medication

The misuse or abuse of prescription pain relievers is an increasingly significant public health problem. It is estimated that in 2007, more than 12 million Americans older than age twelve (about 5 percent) had used a prescription pain reliever for nonmedical reasons in the past year. Here "nonmedical use" is defined as circumstances in which the drug has not been specifically prescribed for the individual by a physician or that the drug has been used only for the experience or feeling that it imparts. The percentage rose to 13 percent among young adults aged eighteen to twenty. Nearly half of total cases (46 percent) reported that the prescription pain reliever had been obtained free from a friend or relative, and in four out of five cases that friend or relative had obtained the drug through a legitimate medical prescription. Incidentally, similar percentages have been observed in the pattern of obtaining a prescription stimulant for nonmedical use (Chapter 4).

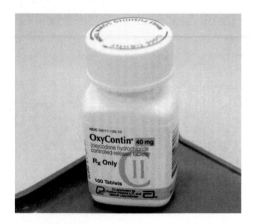

In May 2007, three top executives of Purdue Pharma, the company that makes OxyContin, pleaded guilty to criminal charges that from 1995 to 2001 they had misled federal regulators, physicians, and patients about the potential for OxyContin to be an abused drug. The company agreed to $600 million in fines and other payments; the executives themselves were fined $34 million for their wrongdoing.

Judging from information obtained in other surveys that have identified specific prescription pain relievers, the dominant abused medication in this category is hydrocodone (brand name: Vicodin). According to the University of Michigan survey (see Chapter 1), 10 percent of high school seniors in 2008 reported nonmedical use of Vicodin during the previous year, and 5 percent reported nonmedical use of OxyContin. In a survey of four-year colleges in 2001, the annual prevalence of nonmedical use of a prescription pain reliever was 7 percent. About one in four colleges among the 117-college sample reported an annual prevalence of 10 percent or higher. In any given year since 2002, the number of people using pain relievers nonmedically for the first time has exceeded the number of new marijuana users.[51]

Summary

Opium in History

- A drug with a very long history, opium's medicinal and recreational uses stretch back approximately 5,000 years.
- During the nineteenth century, opium even figured in global politics as the instigating factor for the Opium War fought between China and Britain. At the time, opium use was widespread in Britain and the United States at all levels of society.

Morphine and the Advent of Heroin

- The discovery of morphine in 1803 as the principal active ingredient in opium revolutionized medical treatment of pain and chronic diseases.
- At the end of the nineteenth century, heroin was introduced by the Bayer Company in Germany. Initially, it was believed that heroin lacked the dependence-producing properties of morphine.

Opiates and Heroin in American Society

- The abuse potential of morphine and especially heroin was not fully realized until the beginning of the twentieth century. Social and political developments in the United States after the passage of the Harrison Act in 1914 drove heroin underground, where it acquired a growing association with criminal life.
- Heroin abuse became associated with African American and other minority communities in urban ghettos after World War II; later, the drug revolution and the military involvement in Vietnam during the 1960s and 1970s brought the issues of heroin abuse to a wider population.

Effects on the Mind and the Body

- The effects of narcotic drugs such as heroin include euphoria, analgesia, gastrointestinal slowing, and respiratory depression.
- Respiratory depression is the major risk factor for heroin intake.

How Opiates Work in the Brain

- Since the 1970s, we have known that the effects of morphine and similar drugs are the result of the activation of morphine-sensitive receptors in the brain.
- Three families of chemical substances produced by the brain bind to these receptors. These chemicals are collectively known as endorphins.

Patterns of Heroin Abuse

- Chronic heroin abuse is subject to tolerance effects over time. Withdrawal effects include intense craving for heroin and physical symptoms such as diarrhea and dehydration.
- One of the major problems surrounding heroin abuse is the unpredictability in the content of a heroin dose.

Treatment for Heroin Abuse

- Treatment for heroin abuse includes short-term detoxification and long-term interventions addressing

- the continuing craving for the drug and physical dependence factors in the body.
- Methadone-maintenance programs focus primarily on the physiological needs of the heroin abuser, whereas therapeutic communities and support groups focus on a long-term reintegration into society.

Narcotic Drug Use, Misuse, and Abuse

- In medical settings, narcotic drugs have been extremely helpful in the treatment of pain, in the treatment of dysentery, and in the suppression of coughing.

- Side effects of narcotic medication include respiratory depression, intestinal spasms, and sedation.
- There has been great concern since the late 1990s that narcotic analgesic medications have been diverted to nonmedical purposes and are subject to abuse. The most frequently misused or abused drug of this type has been a time-release formulation of oxycodone (brand name: OxyContin).
- Hydrocodone (brand name: Vicodin) is currently the analgesic medication most likely to be misused or abused.

Key Terms

antitussive, p. 135
black tar, p. 125
buprenorphine, p. 134
chipping, p. 131
codeine, p. 122
detoxification, p. 132
dextromethorphan, p. 135
endogenous opioid peptides, p. 128

fentanyl, p. 125
heroin, p. 122
LAAM, p. 134
methadone, p. 132
methadone maintenance, p. 133
morphine, p. 121
multimodality programs, p. 134

naloxone, p. 127
naltrexone, p. 128
narcotics, p. 118
opiates, p. 118
opium, p. 118
OxyContin, p. 136
propoxyphene, p. 132
synthetic opiates, p. 118

thebaine, p. 122
therapeutic communities, p. 134

Endnotes

1. Modified from Markel, Howard (2005, December 27). When teenagers abuse prescription drugs, the fault may be the doctor's. *New York Times*, p. F5.
2. Levinthal, Charles F. (1988). *Messengers of paradise: Opiates and the brain.* New York: Anchor Press/ Doubleday, p. 4.
3. Courtwright, David T. (2001). *Forces of habit: Drugs and the making of the modern world.* Cambridge, MA: Harvard University Press, pp. 31–39. Merlin, M. D. (1984). *On the trail of the ancient opium poppy.* Cranbury, NJ: Associated University Press.
4. Scott, James M. (1969). *The white poppy: A history of opium.* New York: Funk and Wagnalls, p. 111.
5. Nencini, Paolo (1997). The rules of drug-taking: Wine and poppy derivatives in the ancient world. VIII. Lack of evidence of opium addiction. *Substance Use and Misuse,* 32, 1581–1586.
6. Levinthal, *Messengers of paradise,* pp. 3–25. Snyder, Solomon H. (1977). Opiate receptors and internal opiates. *Scientific American,* 236 (3), 44.
7. Beeching, Jack (1975). *The Chinese opium wars.* New York: Harcourt Brace Jovanovich, p. 23. Hanes, W. Travis III, and Sanello, Frank (2002). *The opium wars.* Naperville, IL: Sourcebooks.
8. Owen, David E. (1934). *British opium policy in China and India.* New Haven, CT: Yale University Press. Waley, Arthur (1958). *The opium war through Chinese eyes.* London: Allen and Unwin.
9. Fay, Peter W. (1975). *The opium war 1840–1842.* Chapel Hill: University of North Carolina Press, p. 11.
10. Brecher, Edward M., and the editors of *Consumer Reports* (1972). *Licit and illicit drugs.* Boston: Little, Brown, p. 17.
11. Kaplan, Eugene H., and Wieder, Herbert. (1974). *Drugs don't take people; people take drugs.* Secaucus, NJ: Lyle Stuart.
12. Brecher, *Licit and illicit drugs,* pp. 42–43.
13. Levinthal, *Messengers of paradise,* pp. 16–17.
14. Courtwright, David T. (1982). *Dark paradise: Opiate addiction in America before 1940.* Cambridge, MA: Harvard University Press, p. 47.
15. Inciardi, James A. (2002). *The war on drugs III.* Boston: Allyn and Bacon, p. 24. Terry, Charles E., and Pellens, Mildred. (1928/1970). *The opium problem.* Montclair, NJ: Patterson Smith.
16. Substance Abuse and Mental Health Services Administration (2008). *Results from the 2007 National Survey on Drug Use and Health: Detailed tables.* Rockville, MD: Office of Applied Studies, Substance Abuse and Mental Health Services Administration, Table 1.1A.
17. Smith, Roger (1966). Status politics and the image of the addict. *Issues in Criminology,* 2 (2), 172–173.
18. Zackon, Fred (1986). *Heroin: The street narcotic.* New York: Chelsea House Publishers, p. 44.
19. McCoy, Alfred W., with Read, Cathleen B., and Adams, Leonard P. (1972). *The politics of heroin in southeast Asia.* New York: Harper & Row, pp. 5–6.

20. Zackon, *Heroin*, p. 45.
21. Bentel, David J., Crim, D., and Smith, David E. (1972). Drug abuse in combat: The crisis of drugs and addiction among American troops in Vietnam. In David E. Smith and George R. Gay (Eds.), *It's so good, don't even try it once: Heroin in perspective.* Englewood Cliffs, NJ: Prentice-Hall, p. 58.
22. Karch, Steven B. (1996). *The pathology of drug abuse* (2nd ed.). Boca Raton, FL: CRC Press, p. 288. McCoy, *The politics of heroin*, pp. 220–221.
23. Robins, Lee N., David, Darlene H., and Goodwin, Donald W. (1974). Drug use by U.S. Army enlisted men in Vietnam: A follow-up on their return home. *American Journal of Epidemiology*, 99 (4), 235–249.
24. Greenhouse, Steven (1995, February 12). Heroin from Burmese surges as U.S. debates strategy. *New York Times*, p. 3.
25. Holloway, Lynette (1994, August 31). 13 heroin deaths spark wide police investigation. *New York Times*, pp. A1, B2. Leland, John (1996, August 26). The fear of heroin is shooting up. *Newsweek*, pp. 55–56. Quotation on p. 56.
26. Hernandez, Daisy (2003, May 23). Heroin's new generation: Young, white, and middle class. *New York Times*, p. 34. Johnston, Lloyd D.; O'Malley, Patrick M.; Bachman, Jerald G.; and Schulenberg, John E. (2008, December 11). Various stimulant drugs show continuing gradual declines among teens in 2008, most illicit drugs hold steady, Table 2. Jones, Richard G. (2008, January 13). Heroin's hold on the young. *New York Times*, Long Island section, pp. 1, 8. Warrem (1996, October 26). Boycott groups: Klein ads carry scent of "heroin chic." *Christian Science Monitor*, p. 3. Thomson, Stephanie (2005, September 26). Heroin chic OK, cocaine use not. *Advertising Age*, pp. 3–4.
27. Winger, Gail, Hofmann, Frederick G., and Woods, James H. (1992). *A handbook on drug and alcohol abuse: The biomedical aspects.* New York: Oxford University Press, 1992, pp. 44–46.
28. Abel, Ernest L. (1985). *Psychoactive drugs and sex.* New York: Plenum Press, pp. 175–204.
29. Winger, Hofmann, and Woods, *Handbook on drug and alcohol abuse*, pp. 46–50.
30. Jaffe, Jerome H., and Martin, William M. (1985). Opioid analgesics and antagonists. In Alfred C. Gilman, Louis S. Goodman, Theodore W. Rall, and Ferid Murad (Eds.), *The pharmacological basis of therapeutics* (7th ed.). New York: Macmillan, pp. 491–531.
31. Levinthal, *Messengers of paradise*. Mathias, Robert (2003, March). New approaches seek to expand naltrexone use in heroin treatment. *NIDA Notes*, 17 (6), p. 8. Self, David W. (1998). Neural substrates of drug craving and relapse in drug addiction. *Annals of Medicine*, 30, 379–389. Teagle, Sarah (2007, April). Depot naltrexone appears safe and effective for heroin addiction. *NIDA Notes*, p. 7.
32. Goode, Erich (1999). *Drugs in American society* (5th ed.). New York: McGraw-Hill, p. 328. Strang, J., Griffiths, P., and Gossop, M. (1997). Heroin smoking by "chasing the dragon": Origins and history. *Addiction*, 92, 673–684.
33. Karch, Steven B. (2002). *Pathology of drug abuse* (3rd ed.). Boca Raton, FL: CRC Press, p. 323.
34. Johnson, Bruce D.; Goldstein, Paul J.; Preble, Edward; Schmeidler, James; Lipton, Douglas S.; et al. (1985). *Taking care of business: The economics of crime by heroin abusers.* Lexington, MA: Lexington Books.
35. Zinberg, Norman E. (1984). *Drug, set, and setting: The basis for controlled intoxicant use.* New Haven, CT: Yale University Press, pp. 46–81.
36. Hser, Yih-Ing; Hoffman, Valerie; Grella, Christine; and Anglin, M. Douglas (2001). A 33-year follow-up of narcotics addicts. *Archives of General Psychiatry*, 58, 503–508. Goode, Erica (2001, May 22). For users of heroin, decades of despair. *New York Times*, p. F5. National Institute on Drug Abuse (2001). 33-year study finds lifelong, lethal consequences of heroin addiction. *NIDA Notes*, 16 (4), 1, 5, 7. Quotation on p. 5.
37. Schuckit, Marc A. (1995). *Drug and alcohol abuse: A clinical guide to diagnosis and treatment* (4th ed.). New York: Plenum Press, pp. 155–162.
38. Stitzer, Maxine L.; Bickel, Warren K.; Bigelow, George E.; and Liebson, Ira A. (1986). Effect of methadone dose contingencies on urinalysis test results of polydrug-abusing methadone-maintenance patients. *Drug and Alcohol Dependence*, 18, 341–348.
39. Ball, John C.; Lange, W. Robert; Myers, C. Patrick; and Friedman, Samuel R. (1988). Reducing the risk of AIDS through methadone maintenance treatment. *Journal of Health and Social Behavior*, 29, 214–226. Maddux, James F., and Desmond, David P. (1997). Outcomes of methadone maintenance 1 year after admission. *Journal of Drug Issues*, 27, 225–238. Rhoades, Howard M.; Creson, Dan; Elk, Ronith; Schmitz, Joy; and Grabowski, John (1998). Retention, HIV risk, and illicit drug use during treatment: Methadone dose and visit frequency. *American Journal of Public Health*, 88, 34–39. Sees, Karen L.; Delucchi, Kevin L.; Masson, Carmen; Rosen, Amy; Clark, H. Westley; et al. (2000). Methadone maintenance vs 180-day psychosocially enriched detoxification for treatment of opioid dependence. *Journal of the American Medical Association*, 283, 1303–1310.
40. Kreek, Mary Jeanne (1991). Using methadone effectively: Achieving goals by application of laboratory, clinical, and evaluation research and by development of innovative programs. In Roy W. Pickens, Carl G. Leukefeld, and Charles R. Schuster (Eds.), *Improving drug abuse treatment* (NIDA Research Monograph 106), pp. 245–266.
41. Myerson, D.J. (1969). Methadone treatment of addicts. *New England Journal of Medicine*, 281, 380. Prendergast, Michael L., and Podus, Deborah (1999, May 10). Methadone debate reflects deep-rooted conflicts in field. *Alcoholism and Drug Abuse Weekly*, p. 5.
42. Kosten, Thomas R., Rounsaville, Bruce J., and Kleber, Herbert D. (1986). A 2.5 year follow-up of treatment retention and reentry among opioid addicts. *Journal of*

Substance Abuse Treatment, 3, 181–189. Wasserman, David A.; Korcha, Rachel; Havassy, Barbara E.; and Hall, Sharon M. (1999). Detection of illicit opioid and cocaine use in methadone maintenance treatment. *American Journal of Drug and Alcohol Abuse*, 25, 561–571.

43. Faupel, Charles E. (1991). *Shooting dope: Career patterns of hard-core heroin users*. Gainesville: University of Florida Press, pp. 170–173. Gollnisch, Gernot (1997). Multiple predictors of illicit drug use in methadone maintenance clients. *Addictive Behaviors*, 22, 353–366. Substance Abuse and Mental Health Services Administration (2003, January). Narcotic analgesics. *The DAWN report*. Rockville, MD: Office of Applied Studies, Substance Abuse and Mental Health Services Administration, Figure 2.

44. Eissenberg, Thomas; Bigelow, George F.; Strain, Eric C.; Walsh, Sharon L.; Brooner, Robert K.; et al. (1997). Dose-related efficacy of levomethadyl acetate for treatment of opioid dependence: A randomized clinical trial. *Journal of the American Medical Association*, 277, 1945–1951.

45. Martin, Kimberly R. (2004, September). Once-a-month medication for heroin addiction? *NIDA Notes*, 19 (3), 9. Mitka, Mike (2003). Office-based primary care physicians called on to treat the "new" addict. *Journal of the American Medical Association*, 290, 735–736. O'Connor, Amahad (2004, August 4). New ways to loosen addiction's grip. *New York Times*, pp. F1, F6. Substance Abuse and Mental Health Services Administration (2007, January/February). Buprenorphine: Patient limits increase. *SAMHSA Report*, p. 7.

46. Greenstein, Robert A., Fudala, Paul J., and O'Brien, Charles P. (1997). Alternative pharmacotherapies for opiate addiction. In Joyce H. Lowinson, Pedro Ruiz, Robert B. Millman, and John G. Langrod (Eds.), *Substance abuse: A comprehensive textbook* (3rd ed.). Baltimore, MD: Williams & Wilkins, pp. 415–425. Ward, Adrian; Kasinski, Kajetan; Pooley, Jane; and Worthington, Alan (Eds.) (2003). *Therapeutic communities for children and young people*. London: Kingsley Publishers.

47. Allan, Laurie; Hays, Helen; Jensen, Niels-Henrik; Le Polain de Waroux, Bernard; Bolt, Michiel; et al. (2001). Randomised crossover trial of transdermal fentanyl and sustained release oral morphine for treating chronic non-cancer pain. *British Medical Journal*, 322, 1154–1158.

48. Jaffe and Martin, Opioid analgesics and antagonists.

49. Kalb, Claudia (2001, April 9). Playing with pain killers. *Newsweek*, pp. 45–48. Meier, Barry, and Petersen, Melody (2001, March 5). Sales of painkiller grew rapidly but success brought a high cost. *New York Times*, pp. A1, A15. Rosenberg, Debra (2001, April 9). How one town got hooked. *Newsweek*, pp. 49–50. Tough, Paul (2001, July 29). The alchemy of OxyContin. *New York Times Magazine*, pp. 31–37, 52, 62–64.

50. Ammann, Melinda (2003, April). The agony and the ecstasy. *Reason*, pp. 28–34. Meier, Barry (2003, November 23). The delicate balance between pain and addiction. *New York Times*, pp. F1, F6. Basbaum, Allan I., and Julius, David (2006, June). Toward better pain control. *Scientific American*, pp. 60–67. Meier, Barry (2007, May 11). Narcotic maker guilty of deceit over marketing. *New York Times*, pp. A1, C4.

51. Johnston, O'Malley, Bachman, and Schulenberg (2008). Various stimulant drugs show continuing gradual declines, Table 2. McCabe, Sean E.; Teter, Christian J.; Boyd, Carol J.; Knight, John R.; and Wechsler, Henry (2005). Nonmedical use of prescription opioids among U.S. college students: Prevalence and correlates from a national survey. *Addictive Behaviors*, 30, 789–805. Substance Abuse and Mental Health Services Administration (2008, June 19). Nonmedical use of pain relievers in substate regions: 2004 to 2006. *The NSDUH Report*. Rockville, MD: Substance Abuse and Mental Health Services Administration, p.1. Substance Abuse and Mental Health Services Administration (2008). *Results from the 2007 Detailed tables*. Tables 1.1A, 1.1B, 1.5B, 7.43B, 7.45B, 7.46B, 7.49B, and 7.50B.

chapter **6**

LSD and Other Hallucinogens

I was forced to interrupt my work in the laboratory in the middle of the afternoon and proceed home, being affected by a remarkable restlessness combined with a slight dizziness. At home I lay down and sank into a not unpleasant intoxicated-like condition, characterized by an extremely stimulated imagination. In a dreamlike state with eyes closed . . . I perceived an uninterrupted stream of fantastic pictures, extraordinary shapes with intense, kaleidoscopic play of colors.

—Albert Hofmann, the discoverer of LSD,
reflecting on the day he took a sample of the drug
LSD: My Problem Child *(1980)*

After you have completed this chapter, you will understand

- The classification of hallucinogenic drugs
- The history of LSD
- Facts and fiction about LSD effects
- Prominent hallucinogens other than LSD
- The special dangers of MDMA (Ecstasy), phencyclidine (PCP), and ketamine

On an April afternoon in 1943, Albert Hofmann, a research chemist at Sandoz Pharmaceuticals in Basel, Switzerland, went home early from work, unaware that his fingertips had made contact with an extremely minute trace of a new synthetic chemical he had been testing that day. The chemical was **lysergic acid diethylamide (LSD)**, and as the opening passage indicates, Hofmann unknowingly experienced history's first "acid trip."

Three days later, having pieced together the origin of his strange experience, he decided to try a more deliberate experiment. He chose a dose of 0.25 mg, a concentration that could not, so he thought, possibly be effective. His plan was to start with this dose and gradually increase it to see what would happen.

The dose Hofmann had considered inadequate was actually about five times greater than an average dose for LSD. As he later recalled his experience,

> My condition began to assume threatening forms. Everything in my field of vision wavered and was distorted as if seen in a curved mirror. I also had the sensation of being unable to move from the spot.[1]

A little while later, his experience worsened:

> The dizziness and sensation of fainting became so strong at times that I could no longer hold myself erect, and had to lie down on a sofa. My surroundings had now transformed themselves in more terrifying ways. Everything in the room spun around, and the familiar objects and pieces of furniture assumed grotesque, threatening forms.... I was seized by the dreadful fear of going insane. I was taken to another place, another time.[2]

His experience then became pleasant:

> Kaleidoscopic, fantastic images surged in on me, alternating, variegated, opening and then closing themselves in circles and spirals.... It was particularly remarkable how every acoustic perception, such as the sound of a door handle or a passing automobile, became transformed into optical perceptions. Every sound generated a vividly changing image, with its own consistent form and color.[3]

Hofmann's vivid remembrances are presented here at length because they succinctly convey some of the major facets of a hallucinogenic drug experience: the distortions of visual images and body sense, the frightening reaction that often occurs when everyday reality is so dramatically changed, and the strange intermingling of visual and auditory sensations. These effects will be considered later in more detail as this chapter explores the bizarre world of hallucinogenic drugs.

by the numbers . . .

566,990	Approximate number of LSD doses in one ounce of pure LSD, based on 50 micrograms as a typical LSD dosage level
1	The number of documented cases of deaths due to LSD ingestion alone, since 1960

Source: Fysh, R. R.; Oon, M. C. H.; Robinson, K. N.; Smith, R. N.; White, P. C.; and Whitehouse, M. J. (1985). A fatal poisoning with LSD. *Forensic Science International, 28,* 109–113.

Like many of the drugs that have been examined in the preceding chapters, hallucinogenic drugs such as LSD and several others have a story that belongs both in our contemporary culture and in the distant past. Hofmann worked in the modern facilities of an international pharmaceutical company, but the basic material on his laboratory bench was a fungus that has been around for millions of years. It has been estimated that as many as six thousand plant species around the world have some psychoactive properties.[4] This chapter will focus on a collection of special chemicals called *hallucinogenic drugs* or simply **hallucinogens,** often pharmacologically dissimilar to one another but with the common ability to distort perceptions and alter the user's sense of reality.

A Matter of Definition

Definitions are frequently reflections of the definer's attitude toward the thing that is being defined, and the terminology used to describe hallucinogens is no exception. For those viewing these drugs with a "positive spin," particularly for those who took LSD in the 1960s, hallucinogens have been described as *psychedelic,* meaning "mind-expanding" or "making the mind manifest." For others viewing these drugs with more alarm than acceptance, the popular descriptive adjectives have been *psychotomimetic,* meaning "having the appearance of a

lysergic acid diethylamide (LSD) (lye-SER-jik ASS-id di-ETH-il-la-mide): A synthetic, serotonin-related hallucinogenic drug.

hallucinogens (ha-LOO-sin-oh-jens): A class of drugs producing distortions in perception and body image at moderate doses.

psychosis," *psychodysleptic*, meaning "mind-disrupting," or even worse, *psycholytic*, meaning "mind-dissolving." You can see that the description one chooses to use conveys a strong attitude, pro or con, with regard to the drug's effects.

As a result of all this emotional baggage, the description of these drugs as hallucinogenic, meaning "hallucination-producing," is probably the most even-handed way of defining their effects; that is the way they will be referred to in this chapter. Some problems, however, still need to be considered. Technically, a hallucination is the reported perception of something that does not physically exist. For example, a schizophrenic might hear voices that no one else hears, and therefore we must conclude (at least the nonschizophrenic world must conclude) that such voices are not real. In the case of hallucinogens, the effect is more complicated because we are dealing with a perceived alteration in the existing physical environment. Some researchers have used the term *illusionogenic*, as a more accurate way of describing drugs that produce these kinds of experiences.

We also should be aware of another qualification when we use the term "hallucinogen." Many drugs that produce distinctive effects when taken at low to moderate dose levels turn out to produce hallucinations when the dose levels are extremely high. Examples of this phenomenon appeared in Chapter 4 with cocaine and amphetamines and will appear in Chapter 13 with inhalants. Here the category of hallucinogens will be limited to only those drugs that produce marked changes in perceived reality at relatively low dosages.

Classifying Hallucinogens

Most hallucinogens can be classified in terms of the particular neurotransmitter in the brain that bears a close resemblance to the molecular features of the drug. As shown in Table 6.1, hallucinogens fall into three principal categories: (1) those that are chemically similar to serotonin (LSD, psilocybin, morning glory seeds, DMT, and

TABLE 6.1

Major categories of hallucinogens

CATEGORY	SOURCE
Hallucinogens related to serotonin	
lysergic acid diethylamide (LSD)	a synthetic derivative of lysergic acid, which is, in turn, a component of ergot
psilocybin	various species of North American mushrooms
lysergic acid amide or morning glory seeds	morning glory seeds
dimethyltryptamine (DMT)	the bark resin of several varieties of trees and some nuts native to Central and South America
harmine	the bark of a South American vine
Hallucinogens related to norepinephrine	
mescaline	the peyote cactus in Mexico and the U.S. Southwest
2,5,-dimethoxy-4-methylamphetamine (DOM or more commonly STP)	a synthetic mescaline-like hallucinogen
MDMA (Ecstasy) and MDA	two synthetic hallucinogens
Hallucinogens related to acetylcholine	
atropine	*Atropa belladonna* plant, known as deadly nightshade, and the datura plant
scopolamine (hyoscine)	roots of the mandrake plant, henbane herb, and the datura plant
hyoscyamine	roots of the mandrake plant, henbane herb, and the datura plant
ibotenic acid	*Amanita muscaria* mushrooms
Miscellaneous hallucinogens	
phencyclidine (PCP)	a synthetic preparation, developed in 1963, referred to as angel dust
ketamine	a PCP-like hallucinogen

Source: Schultes, Richard E., and Hofmann, Albert (1979). *Plants of the gods: Origins of hallucinogenic use.* New York: McGraw-Hill.

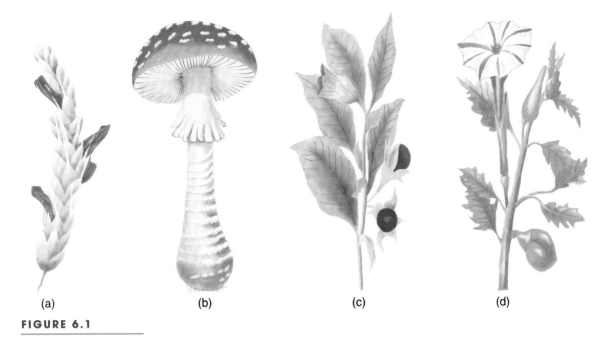

FIGURE 6.1

Botanical sources for four hallucinogenic drugs: (a) *Claviceps tulasne* (ergot), (b) *Amanita muscaria* (ibotenic acid), (c) *Atropa belladonna* (atropine), (d) *Datura stramonium,* called jimsonweed (atropine, scopolamine, and hyoscyamine). These sources are not shown to the same scale; actually, they differ in size.

harmine), (2) those that are chemically similar to norepinephrine (mescaline, DOM, MDMA, and MDA), and (3) those that are chemically similar to acetylcholine (atropine, scopolamine, hyoscyamine, and ibotenic acid). In addition, a fourth category comprises a few hallucinogens (PCP and ketamine are examples) that are chemically unlike any known neurotransmitter; these drugs will be called miscellaneous hallucinogens. As Figure 6.1 indicates, several of these drugs have natural botanical origins.

Lysergic Acid Diethylamide (LSD)

The most widely known hallucinogen is LSD, which does not exist in nature but is synthetically derived from **ergot,** a fungus present in moldy rye and other grains. One of the compounds in ergot, lysergic acid, is highly toxic, inducing a condition called **ergotism.** Historians have surmised that widespread epidemics of ergotism (called St. Anthony's fire) occurred periodically in Europe during the Middle Ages, when extreme famine forced people to bake bread from infected grain (Drugs . . . in Focus on page 146).

In one particularly deadly episode in 944, an outbreak of ergotism claimed as many as forty thousand lives. The features of this calamity were two-fold. One form of ergotism produced a reduction in blood flow toward the extremities, leading to gangrene, burning pain, and the eventual loss of limbs. The other form produced a tingling sensation on the skin, convulsions, disordered thinking, and hallucinations.[5]

Even though the link between this strange affliction and ergot in moldy grain has been known since the 1700s, outbreaks of ergotism have continued to occur in recent times. A major one took place in a small French community in 1951. Hundreds of townspeople went totally mad on a single night:

> *Many of the most highly regarded citizens leaped from windows or jumped into the Rhône, screaming that their heads were made of copper, their bodies wrapped in snakes, their limbs swollen to gigantic size or shrunken to tiny appendages. . . . Animals went berserk. Dogs ripped bark from trees until their teeth fell out.*[6]

ergot (ER-got): A fungus infecting rye and other grains.

ergotism: A physical and/or psychological disorder acquired by ingesting ergot-infected grains. One form of ergotism involves gangrene and eventual loss of limbs; the other form is associated with convulsions, disordered thinking, and hallucinations.

Drugs...in Focus

Strange Days in Salem: Witchcraft or Hallucinogens?

In the early months of 1692, in Salem, Massachusetts, eight young girls suddenly developed a combination of bizarre symptoms: disordered speech, odd body postures, and convulsive fits. They also began to accuse various townspeople of witchcraft. During the summer, in a series of trials, more than 150 people were convicted of being witches and 20 were executed. Accusations were also made in neighboring villages in the county and in Connecticut. Nothing approaching the magnitude of the Salem witch trials has since occurred in American history.

Over the years, a number of theories have attempted to account for these strange events: a case of adolescent pranks, general hysteria, or some kind of political scapegoating. An interesting and controversial speculation has been advanced that these girls were showing the hallucinogenic and convulsive symptoms of ergotism, acquired from fungus-infected rye grain. Arguments that support this theory include the following:

- Rye grain, once harvested, was stored in barns for months, and the unusually moist weather in the area that year could have promoted the growth of ergot fungus during storage. Of twenty-two Salem households with some afflicted member, sixteen were located close to riverbanks or swamps.

- Children and teenagers would have been particularly vulnerable to ergotism because they ingest more food, and hence more poison, per body weight than do adults.

- The Salem girls as well as the accused "witches" frequently displayed hallucinatory behavior and physical symptoms common to convulsive ergotism.

The role of ergotism in the Salem witch trials of 1692 has been vigorously debated by both historians and pharmacologists. The readings listed below provide more information on this intriguing possibility.

Sources: In favor: Caporael, Linnda R. (1976). Ergotism: The Satan loosed in Salem? *Science, 192,* 21–26. Matossian, Mary K. (1982). Ergot and the Salem witchcraft affair. *American Scientist, 70,* 355–357. Matossian, Mary K. (1989). *Poisons of the past: Molds, epidemics, and history.* New Haven, CT: Yale University Press, pp. 113–122. Against: Spanos, Nicholas P., and Gottlieb, Jack (1976). Ergotism and the Salem village witch trials. *Science, 194,* 1390–1394.

Albert Hofmann's professional interest in lysergic acid centered on its ability to reduce bleeding and increase contractions in smooth muscle, particularly the uterus. He was trying to find a nontoxic chemical version that would be useful in treating problems associated with childbirth. The LSD molecule was number twenty-five in a series of variations that Hofmann studied in 1938, and his creation was officially named LSD-25 for that reason. He thought at the time that the compound had possibilities for medical use but went on to other pursuits, returning to it five years later in 1943, the year of his famous LSD experience.

The Beginning of the Psychedelic Era

Sandoz Pharmaceuticals applied for Food and Drug Administration (FDA) approval of LSD in 1953, and as was a common practice at the time, the company sent out samples of LSD to laboratories around the world for scientific study. The idea was that LSD might be helpful in the treatment of schizophrenia by allowing psychiatrists to gain insight into subconscious processes, which this drug supposedly unlocked. One of the researchers intrigued by the potential psychotherapeutic applications of LSD was the psychiatrist Humphrey Osmond of the University of Saskatchewan in Canada, who coined the word "psychedelic" to describe its effects and whose interest also extended to other hallucinogens such as mescaline.

In 1953, Osmond introduced the British writer Aldous Huxley to mescaline, and Huxley later reported his experiences, under Osmond's supervision, in his essay *The Doors of Experience.* Prior to 1960, LSD was being administered to humans under fairly limited circumstances, chiefly as part of research studies in psychiatric hospitals and psychotherapy sessions on the West Coast. As would be revealed later in court testimony in the 1970s, there were also top-secret experiments conducted by the Central Intelligence Agency (CIA), which was interested in LSD for possible application in espionage work. Word of its extraordinary effects, however, gradually spread to regions outside laboratories or hospitals. One of those who picked up on these events was a young clinical psychologist and lecturer at Harvard University named Timothy Leary.

Leary's first hallucinatory experience (in fact his first psychoactive drug experience of any kind, other than alcoholic intoxication) was in Mexico in 1960, when he ate some mushrooms containing the hallucinogen psilocybin. This is his recollection of his response:

> *During the next five hours, I was whirled through an experience which could be described in many extravagant metaphors but which was above all and without question the deepest religious experience of my life.*[7]

Back at Harvard, his revelations sparked the interest of a colleague, Richard Alpert (later to be known as Baba Ram Dass). The two men were soon holding psilocybin sessions with university students and whoever else was interested, on and off campus. At first these studies retained some semblance of scientific control. For example, a physician was on hand, and objective observers of behavior reported the reactions of the subjects. Later, these procedures were altered. Physicians were no longer invited to the sessions, and Leary himself began taking the drug at the same time. His argument was that he could communicate better with the subject during the drug experience, but his participation seriously undermined the scientific nature of the studies.

In 1961, Leary, Alpert, and other associates turned to LSD as the focus of their investigations, in their homes and other locations off the Harvard campus. Though these experiments were technically separate from the university itself, public relations concerns on the part of the academic community were mounting. Leary further aggravated the situation through his writings. In a 1962 article published in the *Bulletin of the Atomic Scientists*, he suggested that the Soviets could conceivably dump LSD into the water supply and, to prepare for such an attack, Americans should dump LSD into their own water supply so that citizens would then know what to expect. The U.S. government was not amused.

In 1963, after a Harvard investigation, Leary and Alpert were dismissed from their academic positions, making it the first time in the twentieth century that a Harvard faculty member had been fired. As you can imagine, such events brought enormous media exposure. Leary was now "Mr. LSD" (see Portrait), and suddenly the public became acquainted with a class of drugs that had been previously unknown to them.[8]

For the rest of the 1960s, LSD became not only a drug but also one of the symbols for the cultural revolt of a generation of youth against the perceived inadequacies of the established, older generation. Leary himself told his followers that they were "the wisest and holiest generation that the human race has ever seen" and advised them to "turn on to the scene, tune in to what's happening; and drop out—of high school, college, grad school . . . and follow me, the hard way."[9] The era has been described in this way:

> *There were psychedelic churches, ashrams, rock festivals, light shows, posters, comic books and newspapers, psychedelic jargon and slang. Every middle-sized city had its enclaves, and there was a drug culture touring circuit.... Everyone had his own idea of what was meant by turning on, tuning in, and dropping out— his own set and setting—and the drug culture provided almost as many variations in doctrine, attitude, and way of life, from rational and sedate to lewd and violent, as the rest of society.*[10]

It was not long before LSD became a battleground unto itself. In congressional hearings on LSD use by the nation's youth, scientists, health officials, and law-enforcement experts testified to a growing panic over the drug. Newspaper stories emphasized the dangers with alarmist headlines: "A monster in our midst—a drug called LSD" and "Thrill drug warps mind, kills," among them. Sandoz quietly allowed its LSD patent to lapse in 1966 and did everything it could to distance itself from the controversy. Hofmann himself called LSD his "problem child."

In 1966, LSD was made illegal, later becoming a

The multicolored images, inspired by the LSD experience, epitomized the psychedelic era of the 1960s.

PORTRAIT

Timothy Leary—Whatever Happened to Him?

For the average college student, the question regarding Timothy Leary might be not "Whatever happened to him?" but rather "Who was this guy anyway?" For those of you who ask the latter question, here is a capsule rendition of Leary's impact on the drug scene in the 1960s, along with an update.

Until 1960, Leary's career was a world apart from what would follow. It had none of the unconventionality that would later characterize his life. As a clinical psychologist, he had written a widely acclaimed textbook and devised a respected personality test (called the Leary). An experience with psilocybin in Mexico in 1960, however, turned his life around. The more extensive his exposure to hallucinogenic drugs became, the more he took on the self-appointed role of Pied Piper for what was referred to then as the "acid generation."

By the middle of the 1970s, Leary had been sentenced to twenty years for marijuana possession (the longest sentence ever imposed for such an offense), gone to federal prison, escaped, evaded the authorities in Algeria and Switzerland for a few years, been recaptured, and finally been released. LSD advocacy was no longer on his agenda by this time, and in fact LSD had lost its mystique years earlier. Leary hit the college lecture circuit, talking about space migration and life extension and calling himself a "stand-up philosopher."

In the late 1980s, Leary discovered computers. He formed a software company, marketed a number of successful video games, and viewed interactive computer programming and virtual reality in particular as the consciousness expansion of the 1990s, the newest route to cerebral stimulation.

Leary never stopped being a social activist. In 1994 he was detained by the police in an Austin, Texas, airport for smoking—a cigarette, this time. Leary said that he wanted to draw attention to people being "demonized" by no-smoking restrictions on their lives.

A year after his death in 1996, Leary's friends arranged to have his cremated remains delivered by rocket into space. It is estimated that he orbited Earth every ninety minutes for approximately two years, perhaps as many as ten, before burning up during reentry. You might say it was his ultimate trip.

Sources: Brozan, Nadine (1994, May 12). Chronicle: Timothy Leary lights up. *New York Times*, p. D26. Greenfield, Robert (2006). *Timothy Leary: A biography.* New York: Harcourt. Lee, Martin A., and Shlain, Bruce (1985). *Acid dreams: The complete social history of LSD.* New York: Grove Weidenfeld. Simons, Marlise (1997, April 22). A final turn-on lifts Timothy Leary off. *New York Times*, pp. A1, A4. Stone, Judith (1991, June). Turn on, tune in, boot up. *Discover*, pp. 32–35.

Schedule I drug, with possession originally set as a misdemeanor and later upgraded to a felony. By the 1970s, LSD had become entrenched as a street drug, and taking LSD had become a component of the already dangerous world of illicit drugs. The story of LSD will be updated in a later section, but first it is important to understand the range of effects LSD typically produces.

Acute Effects of LSD

LSD is considered one of the most, if not *the* most, powerful psychoactive drugs known. Its potency is so great that effective dose levels have to be expressed in terms of micrograms, one-millionths of a gram, often called *mikes*. The typical street dose ranges from 50 to 150 micrograms, though sellers often claim that their product contains more. The effective dose can be as small as 10 micrograms, with only one-hundredth of a percent being absorbed into the brain. Compare these figures to the fact that a single regular-strength aspirin tablet contains 325,000 micrograms of aspirin, and you can appreciate the enormous potency of LSD.[11]

Taken orally, LSD is rapidly absorbed into the bloodstream and the brain, with effects beginning within thirty to sixty minutes. Once its concentration has peaked (in about ninety minutes), the elimination half-life, or the time it takes for 50 percent of the drug to diminish in the bloodstream (see Chapter 3), is approximately three hours. Within five to twelve hours, LSD effects are over.[12]

Surprisingly, given its extreme potency, the toxicity of LSD is relatively low. Generalizing from studies of animals given varying doses of LSD, we can estimate that a lethal dose of LSD for humans would have to be roughly three hundred to six hundred times the effective dose, a fairly comfortable margin of safety. In 2005, the DAWN statistics showed that the ingestion of LSD represented about 0.1 percent of drug-related ED visits. To this day, there has been only one definitive case in which a death has been attributed solely to an LSD overdose.[13]

Street forms of LSD may contain color additives or adulterants with specific flavors, but the drug itself is odorless, tasteless, and colorless. LSD is sold on the street in single-dose "hits." It is typically swallowed in the form of powder pellets (microdots) or gelatin chips (windowpanes) or else licked off small squares of absorbent paper that have been soaked in liquid LSD (blotters). In the past, blotters soaked with LSD have been decorated with pictures of mystical symbols and signs, rocket ships, or representations of Mickey Mouse, Snoopy, Bart Simpson, or other popular cartoon characters.

LSD initially produces an excitation of the sympathetic autonomic activity: increased heart rate, elevated blood pressure, dilated pupils, and a slightly raised body temperature. There is an accompanying feeling of restlessness, euphoria, and a sensation that inner tension has been released. There may be laughing or crying, depending on one's expectations and the setting.[14]

Between thirty minutes and two hours later, a "psychedelic trip" begins, characterized by four distinctive features. The best way to describe these effects is in the words of individuals who have experienced them:[15]

- Images seen with the eyes closed.

  Closing my eyes, I saw millions of color droplets, like rain, like a shower of stars, all different colors.

- An intermingling of senses called **synesthesia,** which usually involves sounds appearing as hallucinatory visions.

  I clapped my hands and saw sound waves passing before my eyes.

- Perception of a multilevel reality.

  I was sitting on a chair and I could see the molecules. I could see right through things to the molecules.

- Strange and exaggerated configurations of common objects or experiences.

  A towel falling off the edge of my tub looked like a giant lizard crawling down.

  When my girlfriend was peeling an orange for me, it was like she was ripping a small animal apart.

During the third and final phase, approximately three to five hours after first taking LSD, the following features begin to appear:

- Great swings in emotions or feelings of panic.

  It started off beautifully. I looked into a garden . . . and suddenly, it got terrible . . . and I started to cry. . . . And then, my attention wandered, and something else was happening, beautiful music was turned on. . . . Then suddenly I felt happy.

- A feeling of timelessness.

  Has an hour gone by since I last looked at the clock? Maybe it was a lifetime. Maybe it was no time at all.

- A feeling of ego disintegration, or a separation of one's mind from one's body.

  Boundaries between self and nonself evaporate, giving rise to a serene sense of being at one with the universe. I recall muttering to myself again and again, "All is one, all is one."

Whether these strong reactions result in a "good trip" or a "bad trip" depends heavily on the set of expectations for the drug, the setting or environment in which the LSD is experienced, and the overall psychological health of the individual.

Effects of LSD on the Brain

LSD closely resembles the molecular structure of serotonin. Therefore, it is not surprising that LSD should have effects on receptors in the brain that are sensitive to serotonin (see Chapter 3). As a result of research in the 1980s, it turns out that the critical factor behind LSD's hallucinogenic effects lies in its ability to stimulate a special subtype of serotonin-sensitive receptors called serotonin-2A receptors. In fact, all hallucinogens, even those drugs whose structures do not resemble serotonin, are linked together by the common ability to excite these

A microdot tablet of LSD positioned against a British postage stamp (to the left of the queen) underscores the minute amount necessary for a single dose.

synesthesia: A subjective sensation in a modality other than the one being stimulated. An example is a visual experience when a sound is heard.

receptor sites. Drugs that specifically block serotonin-2A receptors, leaving all other subtypes unchanged, will block the behavioral effects of hallucinogens. In addition, the ability of a particular drug to produce hallucinogenic effects is directly proportional to its ability to bind to serotonin-2A receptors.[16]

Patterns of LSD Use

The enormous publicity surrounding Timothy Leary and his followers in the 1960s made LSD a household word. As many as fifty popular articles about LSD were published in major U.S. newspapers and magazines between March 1966 and February 1967 alone. By 1970, however, the media had lost interest, and hardly anything was appearing about LSD. Even so, while media attention was diminishing, the incidence of LSD abuse was steadily rising. In four Gallup Poll surveys conducted between 1967 and 1971, the percentage of college students reported to have taken LSD at least once in their lives rose dramatically from 1 to 18 percent.[17]

From the middle 1970s to the early 1990s, the numbers showed a steady decline. By 1986, the University of Michigan survey indicated that the lifetime incidence of LSD taking among high school seniors was 7 percent, down from 11 percent in 1975. By the end of the 1990s, prevalence rates were once again on the rise, reaching and later exceeding the levels of a quarter-century earlier. Since 1997, however, LSD use has declined substantially. Four percent of high school seniors in 2008 reported taking LSD at some time in their lives. A parallel trend has been observed in college students as well.

It should be noted that today's LSD users are different from those of a previous generation in a number of ways. Typical LSD users now take the drug less frequently and, because the dosage of street LSD is presently about one-fourth the level common to the 1960s and 1970s, they remain high for a briefer period of time. They also report using LSD simply to get high, rather than to explore alternative states of consciousness or gain a greater insight into life. For current users, LSD no longer has the symbolic significance that it had in an earlier time.[18]

Facts and Fiction about LSD

Given the history of LSD use and the publicity about it, it is all the more important to look carefully at the facts about LSD and to unmask the myths. Six basic questions that are often asked about this drug are examined in the following sections.

Will LSD Produce a Dependence?

There are three major reasons why LSD is not likely to result in a drug dependence, despite the fact that the experience at times is quite pleasant.[19] First, LSD and other hallucinogens cause the body to build up a tolerance to their effects faster than any other drug category. As a result, one cannot remain on an LSD-induced high day after day, for an extended period of time. Second, LSD is not the drug for someone seeking an easy way to get high. As one drug expert has put it,

> The LSD experience requires a monumental effort. To go through eight hours of an LSD high—sensory bombardment, psychic turmoil, emotional insecurity, alternations of despair and bliss, one exploding insight upon the heels of another, images hurtling through the mind as fast as the spinning fruit of a slot machine—is draining and exhausting in the extreme.[20]

Third, the LSD experience seems to control the user rather than the other way around. It is virtually impossible to "come down" from LSD at will. Besides, the unpredictability of the LSD experience is an unpopular feature for those who would want a specific and reliable drug effect every time the drug is taken.

Will LSD Produce a Panic or a Psychosis?

One of the most notorious features of LSD is the possibility of a bad trip. Personal accounts abound of sweet, dreamlike states rapidly turning into nightmares. Perhaps the greatest risks are taken when a person is slipped a dose of LSD and begins to experience its effect without knowing that he or she has taken a drug. Panic reactions do occur, however, even when a person is fully aware of having taken LSD. Although the probability of having a bad trip is difficult to estimate, there are very few regular LSD abusers who have not experienced a bad trip or had a disturbing experience as part of an LSD trip. The best treatment for adverse effects is the companionship and reassurance of others throughout the period when LSD is active. Health Alert includes some specific procedures for dealing with LSD panic episodes.

Despite the possibility of an LSD panic, there is no strong evidence that the panic will lead to a permanent psychiatric breakdown. Long-term psychiatric problems are relatively uncommon, with one study conducted in 1960 showing that there was no greater probability of a person's attempting suicide or developing a psychosis after taking LSD than when undergoing ordinary forms of psychotherapy.[21] The incidents that do occur typi-

HEALTH ALERT!

Emergency Guidelines for a Bad Trip on LSD

- Stay calm with the individual. Do not move around quickly, shout, cry, or become hysterical. Any sense of panic on your part will make an LSD panic worse. Speak in a relaxed, controlled manner.

- Reassure the individual that the situation is temporary and that you will not leave until he or she returns to a normal state. Encourage the individual to breathe deeply and calmly. Advise him or her to view the trip as though watching a movie or TV program.

- Reduce any loud noises or bright lights but do not let the individual be in the dark. Darkness tends to encourage hallucinations in a person under LSD.

- Allow the individual to move around without undue restrictions. He or she can sit, stand, walk, or lie down if this helps the situation. You can divert attention from the panic by encouraging the individual to beat time to music or by dancing.

- If your assistance does not produce a reduction in the panic, seek out medical attention immediately. Under medical supervision, LSD-induced panics can be treated with benzodiazepines such as chlordiazepoxide (Librium) or diazepam (Valium), or if the symptoms are severe, by antipsychotic medication such as haloperidol (Haldol).

> **Where to go for assistance:**
> www.brown.edu/Student_Services/Health_Education/atod/od_lsd.htm
> Brown University sponsors a series of web sites related to drug use and abuse.

Sources: Palfai, Tibor, and Jankiewicz, Henry (1991). *Drugs and human behavior.* Dubuque, IA: W. C. Brown, p. 445. Robbins, Paul R. (1996). *Hallucinogens.* Springfield, NJ: Enslow Publishers, pp. 83–85. Trulson, Michael E. (1985). *LSD: Visions or nightmares.* New York: Chelsea House, p. 101.

---

cally involve people who were unaware that they were taking LSD, showed unstable personality characteristics prior to taking LSD, or were experiencing LSD under hostile or threatening circumstances.

The possible link between the character of LSD effects and symptoms of schizophrenia also has been examined closely. It is true that on a superficial level, the two behaviors show some similarities, but there are important differences. LSD hallucinations are primarily visual, best seen in the dark, and, as mentioned earlier, more accurately characterized as illusions or pseudohallucinations; schizophrenic hallucinations are primarily auditory, seen with open eyes, and qualify as true hallucinations. Individuals taking LSD are highly susceptible to suggestion and usually will try to communicate the experience to others; the schizophrenic individual is typically resistant to suggestion and withdrawn from his or her surroundings. Therefore, it is unlikely that LSD is mimicking the experience of schizophrenia (see Chapter 16).

Will LSD Increase Creativity?

The unusual visual effects of an LSD experience may lead you to assume that your creativity is enhanced, but the evidence indicates otherwise. Professional artists and musicians creating new works of art or songs while under the influence of LSD typically think that their creations are better than anything they have yet produced, but when the LSD has worn off, they are far less impressed. Controlled studies generally show that individuals under LSD *feel* that they are creative, but objective ratings do not show a significant difference from levels prior to the LSD.[22]

Will LSD Damage Chromosomes?

In March 1967, a study published in the prestigious scientific journal *Science* described a marked increase in chromosomal abnormalities in human white blood cells that had been treated with LSD in vitro (that is, the cells were outside the body at the time).[23] Shortly after, three other studies were reported in which chromosomal abnormalities in the white blood cells of LSD abusers were higher than those of people who did not use drugs, whereas three additional studies reported no chromosomal effect at all.

By the end of that year, a second study was published by the people whose report had started the controversy in the first place. They wrote that eighteen LSD abusers had two to four times the number of chromosomal abnormalities in their white blood cells, when compared with fourteen control subjects. Interestingly, the subjects in this study were not exactly model citizens. Every one of them had taken either one or more of amphetamines, barbiturates, cocaine, hallucinogens, opiates, or antipsychotic medication.

The picture was confused, to say the least. Not only were many of these studies unreplicable, but many were methodologically flawed as well. Most important, when studies actually looked at the chromosomes of *reproductive cells themselves* for signs of breakage from exposure to LSD, the results were either ambiguous or entirely negative. By 1971, after nearly a hundred studies had been carried out, the conclusion was that LSD did not cause chromosomal damage in human beings at normal doses, and that there was no evidence of a high rate of birth defects in the children of LSD users.[24] Yet, in the highly politicized climate of the late 1960s, the media tended to emphasize the negative findings without any scrutiny into their validity or relevance. The public image of LSD causing genetic damage still persists, despite the lack of scientific evidence. This is not to say, however, that there is no basis for exercising some degree of caution. Women should avoid LSD, as well as other psychoactive drugs, during pregnancy, especially in the first three months.[25]

Will LSD Have Residual (Flashback) Effects?

One of the most disturbing aspects of taking LSD is the possibility of reexperiencing the effects of the drug long after the drug has worn off, sometimes as long as several years later. These experiences are referred to as *hallucinogen persisting perception disorder,* or simply "flashbacks." The likelihood of LSD flashbacks is not precisely known. Some studies estimate its rate of incidence as only 5 percent, whereas others estimate it as high as 33 percent. It is reasonable to assume that the range of estimates is related to differences in the dosage levels ingested.

Flashback effects sometimes can be frightening and other times be quite pleasant; they can occur among LSD novices or "once-only" drug takers as well as among experienced LSD abusers. While they appear without warning, there is a higher probability that they will occur when the individual is beginning to go to sleep or has just entered a dark environment.[26]

Because they are not common to any other psychoac-tive drug, the reason why LSD flashbacks might occur is not well understood. It is possible that LSD has a peculiar ability to produce some biochemical changes that remain dormant for a period of time and then suddenly reappear or that some remnant of the drug has the ability to persist over extended periods of time. It is also possible that individuals who ingest LSD are highly suggestible to social reminders about the original exposure to LSD.

Whether LSD produces major long-term deficits in the behavior of the user remains largely unknown. Memory problems and visuospatial impairments have been reported in some studies but not confirmed in others. Unfortunately, several problems persist in research studies examining long-term effects of LSD. Often, they have included either individuals with a history of psychiatric disorders prior to LSD ingestion or regular users of other illicit drugs and alcohol. As a result, it has been impos-sible to tease apart the long-term effects of LSD alone.[27]

Will LSD Increase Criminal or Violent Behavior?

As noted in Chapter 2, it is very difficult to establish a clear cause-and-effect relationship between a drug and criminal or violent behavior. In the highly charged era of the 1960s, stories related to this question were publicized and conclusions were drawn without any careful examination of the actual facts. Take, for example, the 1964 case of a woman undergoing LSD therapy treatment who murdered her lover three days after her last LSD session.[28] The details of the case, overlooked by most subsequent media reports, reveal that the woman had been physically abused by the man, he had caused her to have an abortion, and the woman already had a serious mental disorder before going into treatment. The fact that the homicide took place well after the LSD had left her body indicates that the murder was not pharmacologically based (see Chapter 2). Other cases in which violent behavior appeared to be associated with an LSD experience turned out in fact to be associated with the use of other hallucinogenic drugs.

It is possible, however, for an individual to "freak out" on LSD. The effects of a euphoriant drug such as LSD can lead to a feeling of invulnerability. This feeling, in turn, can lead to dangerous and possibly life-threatening behavior. While we cannot reliably estimate the likelihood of these effects or pinpoint the circumstances under which they might occur, we should recognize that psychological reactions to LSD are inherently unpredictable, and caution is advised.

Psilocybin and Other Hallucinogens Related to Serotonin

Psilocybe mexicana mushrooms, the source of psilocybin.

The source of the drug **psilocybin** is a family of mushrooms native to southern Mexico and Central America. Spanish chroniclers in the sixteenth century wrote of "sacred mushrooms" revered by the Aztecs as *teo-nanacatl* (roughly translated as "God's flesh") and capable of providing extraordinary visions when eaten. Their psychoactive properties had been known for a long time, judging from stone-carved representations of these mushrooms discovered in El Salvador and dating back to as early as 500 B.C. Today, shamans in remote villages in Mexico and Central America (see Chapter 1) continue the use of psilocybin mushrooms, among other hallucinogenic plants, to provide healing on both physical and spiritual levels.[29]

Native use of these mushrooms disappeared from historical accounts until the late 1930s, when several varieties were identified. In 1955, a group of Western observers documented the hallucinogenic effects of the *Psilocybe mexicana* in a native community living in a remote mountainous region of southern Mexico. Three years later, samples worked their way to Switzerland, where Albert Hofmann, already known for his work on LSD, identified the active ingredient and named it psilocybin. As was his habit, Hofmann sampled some of the mushrooms himself and wrote later of his reactions:

> Thirty minutes after my taking the mushrooms, the exterior world began to undergo a Mexican character. . . . I saw only Mexican motifs and colors. When the doctor supervising the experiment bent over me to check my blood pressure, he was transformed into an Aztec priest.[30]

We can never know whether the Aztec character of these hallucinogenic effects was a result of suggestion or that Aztec designs may have been inspired over the centuries by the effects of psilocybin.

Once ingested, psilocybin loses a portion of its molecule, making it more fat-soluble and more easily absorbed into the brain. This new version, called **psilocin,** is the actual agent that works on the brain. Since LSD and psilocin are chemically similar, the biochemical effects are also similar. Cross-tolerance will occur (see Chapter 3). If you develop a tolerance to LSD, you have become tolerant to psilocybin effects, and vice versa.[31]

Far less potent than LSD, psilocybin is effective at dose levels measured in the more traditional units of milligrams rather than micrograms. At doses of 4 to 5 mg, psilocybin causes a pleasant, relaxing feeling; at doses of 15 mg and more, hallucinations, time distortions, and changes in body perception appear. A psilocybin trip generally lasts from two to five hours, considerably shorter than an LSD trip.

Individuals who have experienced both kinds of hallucinogens report that, relative to LSD, psilocybin produces effects that are more strongly visual, less emotionally intense, and more euphoric, with fewer panic reactions and less chance of paranoia. On the other hand, experimental studies of volunteers taking high doses of psilocybin have established that the drug produces drastic enough changes in mood, sensory perception, and thought processes to qualify as a psychotic experience.

As with LSD, psilocybin (often called simply "shrooms") has become increasingly available as a drug of abuse. In 2008, about 43 percent of high school seniors reported that non-LSD hallucinogens (including "shrooms") were "fairly easy" or "very easy" to get, whereas about 29 percent felt the same way about LSD itself.[32]

Lysergic Acid Amide (LAA)

In addition to their reverence for psilocybin mushrooms, the Aztecs ingested locally grown morning glory seeds, calling them *ololiuqui*, and used their hallucinogenic effects in religious rites and healing. Like many Native

psilocybin (SIL-oh-SIGH-bin): A serotonin-related hallucinogenic drug originating from a species of mushrooms.

psilocin (SIL-oh-sin): A brain chemical related to serotonin, resulting from the ingestion of psilocybin.

American practices, the recreational use of morning glory seeds has survived in remote areas of southern Mexico. In 1961, Albert Hofmann (once again) identified the active ingredient in these seeds as **lysergic acid amide (LAA),** after having sampled its hallucinogenic properties. As the chemical name suggests, this drug is a close relative to LSD.

The LAA experience, judging from Hofmann's report, is similar to that of LSD, though LAA is only one-tenth to one-thirtieth as potent and the hallucinations tend to be dominated by auditory rather than visual images. Commercial varieties of morning glory seeds are available to the public, but suppliers have taken the precaution of coating them with an additive that causes nausea and vomiting, if eaten, to minimize their abuse.[33]

Dimethyltryptamine (DMT)

The drug **dimethyltryptamine (DMT)** is obtained chiefly from the resin of the bark of trees and nuts native to the West Indies as well as to Central and South America, where it is generally inhaled as a snuff. An oral administration does not produce psychoactive effects. The similarity of this drug's effects to those of LSD and its very short duration gave DMT the reputation, during the psychedelic years of the 1960s, of being "the businessman's LSD." Presumably, someone could take a DMT trip during lunch and be back at the office in time for work in the afternoon.

An inhaled 30-mg dose of DMT produces physiological changes within ten seconds, with hallucinogenic effects peaking around ten to fifteen minutes later. Paranoia, anxiety, and panic also can result at this time, but most symptoms are over in about an hour.[34] A chemical found in *Bufo* toads is similar to DMT (Health Line).

lysergic acid amide (LAA) (lye-SER-jik ASS-id A-mide): A hallucinogenic drug found in morning glory seeds, producing effects similar to those of LSD.

dimethyltryptamine (DMT) (dye-METH-il-TRIP-ta-meen): A short-acting hallucinogenic drug.

harmine (HAR-meen): A serotonin-related hallucinogenic drug frequently used by South American shamans in healing rituals.

mescaline (MES-kul-leen): A norepinephrine-related hallucinogenic drug. Its source is the peyote cactus.

peyote (pay-YO-tay): A species of cactus and the source for the hallucinogenic drug mescaline.

Harmine

Among native tribes in the western Amazon region of South America, the bark of the *Banisteriopsis* vine yields the powerful drug **harmine.** A drink containing harmine, called *ayahuasca,* is frequently used by local shamans for healing rites. It is chemically similar to serotonin, like LSD and the other hallucinogens examined so far. Its psychological effects, however, are somewhat different. Unlike LSD, harmine makes the individual withdraw into a trance, and the hallucinatory images (often visions of animals and supernatural beings) are experienced within the context of a dreamlike state. Reports among shamans refer to a sense of suspension in space or flying, falling into one's body, or experiencing one's own death.[35]

Hallucinogens Related to Norepinephrine

Several types of hallucinogens have a chemical composition similar to norepinephrine. As you may recall from Chapter 4, amphetamines are also chemically similar to norepinephrine. Consequently, sometimes norepinephrine-related hallucinogens produce amphetamine-like stimulant effects. As we will see, this is the case with MDMA but not with mescaline or DOM.

Mescaline

The hallucinogen **mescaline** is derived from the **peyote** plant, a spineless cactus with a small, greenish crown that grows above ground and a long carrot-like root. This cactus is found over a wide area, from the southwestern United States to northern regions of South America, and many communities in these regions have discovered its psychoactive properties. Given the large distances between these groups, it is remarkable that they prepare and ingest mescaline in a highly similar manner. The crowns of the cactus are cut off, sliced in small disks called buttons, dried in the sun, and then consumed. An effective dose of mescaline from peyote is 200 mg, equivalent to about five buttons. Peak response to the drug takes place thirty minutes to two hours after consumption. Mescaline is still used today as part of religious worship among many Native Americans in the United States and Canada (Drugs . . . in Focus, page 156).

The psychological and physiological effects of mescaline are highly similar to those of LSD, though some have reported that mescaline hallucinations are

Bufotenine is a drug with a strange past. Found in a family of beans native to Central and South America, bufotenine is better known as a chemical that can be isolated from the skin and glands of the *Bufo* toad, from which it gets its name. As noted in Chapter 1, *Bufo* toads figured prominently in the magical potions of European witches. Evidence also exists that *Bufo* toads were incorporated into the ceremonial rituals of ancient Aztec and Mayan cultures. Largely as a result of these historical references, it has been widely assumed that bufotenine was the primary contributor to the psychoactive effects of these concoctions and that bufotenine itself is a powerful hallucinogen.

It turns out that these conclusions are wrong. The few studies in which human volunteers were administered bufotenine indicate that the substance induces strong excitatory effects on blood pressure and heart rate but no hallucinatory experiences. Some subjects report distorted images with high dosages of the drug, but this might well occur as oxygen is cut off from parts of the body, particularly the optic nerve carrying visual information to the brain. It is likely that whatever hallucinogenic effects *Bufo* toads may produce are brought on by another chemical also found in these toads that functions similarly to the hallucinogen DMT.

Despite the confusion as to which substance is responsible for its psychoactive properties, *Bufo* toads continue to fascinate the public. Wildly exaggerated and frequently unsubstantiated accounts of "toad licking" and "toad smoking" periodically circulate in the media. Reportedly, a small group calling themselves Amphibians Anonymous was formed in the late 1980s; the group's motto was "Never has it been so easy to just say no."

The bottom line, however, is that the dangers of consuming toad tissue are substantial. Besides the extreme cardiovascular reactions, toxic effects include a skin condition called **cyanosis** (literally, "turning blue"). Actually, the description may be an understatement. Skin color has been observed to be closer to an eggplant purple.

Sources: Horgan, J. (1990, August). Bufo abuse. *Scientific American*, pp. 26–27. Inciardi, James A. (2002). *The war on drugs III.* Boston: Allyn and Bacon, pp. 4–5. Lyttle, Thomas, Goldstein, David, and Gartz, Jochen (1996). Bufo toads and bufotenine: Fact and fiction surrounding an alleged psychedelic. *Journal of Psychoactive Drugs, 28,* 267–290.

---

more sensual, with fewer changes in mood and the sense of self. Nonetheless, double-blind studies comparing the reactions to LSD and mescaline show that subjects cannot distinguish between the two when dose levels are equivalent. While the reactions may be the same, the mescaline trip comes at a greater price, as far as physiological reactions are concerned. Peyote buttons taste extremely bitter and can cause vomiting, headaches,

and, unless the stomach is empty, distressing levels of nausea.[36]

Today mescaline can be synthesized as well as obtained from the peyote cactus. The mescaline molecule resembles the chemical structure of norepinephrine but stimulates the same serotonin-2A receptors as LSD and other hallucinogens that resemble serotonin. As a result, mescaline and LSD share a common brain mechanism.[37]

DOM

A group of synthetic hallucinogens has been developed that shares mescaline's resemblance to amphetamine but does not produce the strong stimulant effects of amphetamine. One example of these synthetic drugs,

The peyote cactus, source of mescaline.

bufotenine (byoo-FOT-eh-neen): A serotonin-related drug obtained either from a bean plant in Central and South America or the skin of a particular type of toad.

cyanosis (SIGH-ah-NOH-sis): A tendency for the skin to turn bluish purple. It can be a side effect of the drug bufotenine.

Drugs...in Focus

Present-Day Peyotism and the Native American Church

Among Native Americans within the United States, the ritual use of peyote buttons, called *peyotism*, can be traced to the eighteenth century when the Mescalero Apaches (from whom the word *mescaline* was derived) adopted the custom from Mexican Indians who had been using peyote for more than three thousand years. By the late 1800s, peyotism had become widely popular among tribes from Wisconsin and Minnesota to the West Coast. It was not until the early twentieth century, however, that peyote use became incorporated into an official religious organization, the Native American Church of North America, chartered in 1918.

The beliefs of the Native American Church membership, estimated to include anywhere from 50,000 to 250,000 Native Americans in the United States and Canada, combine traditional tribal customs and practices with Christian morality. To them, life is a choice between two roads that meet at a junction. The Profane Road is paved and wide, surrounded by worldly passions and temptations. The Peyote Road is a narrow and winding path, surrounded by natural, unspoiled beauty; it is also a path of sobriety (since alcohol poisons the goodness of the body), hard work, caring for one's family, and brotherly love. Only the Peyote Road leads to salvation. In their weekly ceremonies, lasting from Saturday night until Sunday afternoon, church members swallow small peyote buttons as a sacrament, similar to the ritual of taking Holy Communion, or drink peyote tea. It is considered sacrilegious to take peyote outside the ceremonies in the church.

The Religious Freedom Restoration Act of 1993 established an exemption from federal and state controlled substance laws when peyote is used for religious purposes in traditional Native American ceremonies. In 2005, a study found that peyote use among church members does not result in impairments on tests of memory, attention, and other aspects of cognitive functioning.

Today, a handful of people are licensed by state and federal authorities to harvest peyote for religious purposes, in the brushland of south Texas near Laredo. This locale is the only place in the United States where peyote grows in the wild. As one of the harvesters has put it, "This is sacred ground to a lot of Native American tribes. To some, the land here is very holy because it is the home to the sacred peyote."

Sources: Calabrese, Joseph D. (1997). Spiritual healing and human development in the Native American Church: Toward a cultural psychiatry of peyote. *Psychoanalytic Review, 84,* 237–255. Halpern, John H.; Sherwod, Andrea, R., Hudson, James I., Yurgelum-Tod, Deborah; and Pope, Harrison G., Jr. (2005). Psychological and cognitive effects of long-term peyote use among Native Americans. *Biological Psychiatry, 58,* 624–631. Milloy, Ross E. (2002, May 7). A forbidding landscape that's Eden for peyote. *New York Times,* p. A20. Quotation on p. A20. Morgan, George (1983). Recollections of the peyote road. In Lester Grinspoon and James B. Bakalar (Eds.), *Psychedelic reflections.* New York: Human Sciences Press, pp. 91–99.

DOM, appeared in the 1960s and 1970s, when it was frequently combined with LSD and carried the street name of STP. The nickname supposedly was a reference to the well-known engine oil additive, but others took it to mean "super terrific psychedelic." It is roughly eighty times more potent than mescaline, though still far weaker than LSD. At low doses of about 3 to 5 mg, DOM produces euphoria; with higher doses of 10 mg or more, severe hallucinations result, often lasting from sixteen to twenty-five hours. Though similar to LSD in many respects, DOM has the reputation of producing a far higher incidence of panic attacks, psychotic episodes, and other symptoms of a very bad trip. Cases have been reported of STP being added as an adulterant to marijuana.[38]

DOM: A synthetic norepinephrine-related hallucinogenic drug, derived from amphetamine. DOM or a combination of DOM and LSD is often referred to by the street name STP.

MDMA (Ecstasy): A synthetic norepinephrine-related hallucinogenic drug. Once considered useful for psychotherapeutic purposes, this drug is now known to produce significant adverse side effects, including neuronal hyperthermia, dehydration, and neurochemical changes.

MDMA (Ecstasy)

Another synthetic amphetamine-related hallucinogen, abbreviated **MDMA,** first appeared on the scene in the 1980s. While subject to abuse as a new designer drug, it also became known to a number of psychiatrists who used the drug as part of their therapy, believing that MDMA had a special ability to enhance empathy among their patients. In fact, some therapists at the time suggested the name *empathogens* (meaning "generating a state of empathy") to describe MDMA and related drugs. Eventually, after several years of hesitations and reversals, the Drug Enforcement Administration put MDMA permanently on the Schedule I list of controlled substances, meaning that there was no accepted medical application for the drug.[39]

Since the early 1990s, MDMA has become prominent among the new club drugs (see Chapter 1), especially popular at dance clubs and all-night "rave" parties. Widely available under names such as Ecstasy (not to be confused with the stimulant Herbal Ecstasy), E, XTC, X, Essence, Clarity, and Adam, MDMA has the reputation of having the stimulant qualities of amphetamines and the hallucinogenic qualities of mescaline.

The physical health concerns with respect to Ecstasy center on its short-term and long-term toxicity. The principal acute effect is severe hyperthermia (and heatstroke), which can be potentially lethal when Ecstasy is ingested while engaged in the physical exertion of dancing in an already overheated club environment. The dehydration associated with hyperthermia causes an elevation in blood pressure and heart rate and places a strain on kidney functioning. These problems are compounded by the highly risky practice of "Ecstasy stacking," in which multiple Ecstasy tablets are taken at once or Ecstasy is combined with LSD, alcohol, marijuana, or other drugs. Chronic effects of Ecstasy in animal studies have included significant degeneration of serotonin-using neurons in areas of the brain associated with attention, learning, and memory. In human studies, brain imaging has shown a depletion of serotonin in the brain among long-term Ecstasy users, possibly as a response to the overstimulation of serotonin-using neurons while under the effects of the drug.

Ecstasy use also has been linked to long-term cognitive impairments and emotional difficulties. Heavy and prolonged Ecstasy use can produce confusion, anxiety, sleep problems, reductions in impulse control, and declines in memory and attention. In general, women show greater behavioral effects from chronic Ecstasy use than do men.[40] The Health Alert feature summarizes the major areas of MDMA toxicity.

In 2008, according to the University of Michigan survey, about 6 percent of high school seniors and about 2 percent of eighth graders reported having taken Ecstasy at some point in their lives. There is evidence that after a sharp rise in prevalence rates observed between 1998 and 2001, Ecstasy use among adolescents has been on the decline. This development is likely to be related to increased recognition of its adverse

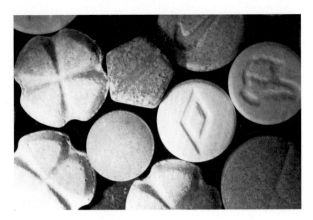
Assorted Ecstasy tablets.

health effects. Beginning in 2001, increasing numbers of high school seniors reported that they viewed Ecstasy use as representing a great risk of harm and disapproved of its use.[41]

Another factor played a role in the decline of Ecstasy use after 2001. Increased scrutiny of passengers and baggage at airports in New York City and Newark, New Jersey, as a response to the September 11 attacks in 2001 resulted in record seizures of Ecstasy pills. As a consequence, the flow of Ecstasy from abroad slowed dramatically, reducing its availability and increasing its expense. Drug Enforcement Administration (DEA) officials theorized that the popularity of narcotic analgesics (prescription painkillers) such as OxyContin and Vicodin (see Chapters 1 and 5) outstripped that of Ecstasy, in part because of their greater availability and lower cost.[42]

Nonetheless, as is the case with so many abused substances, there remains a concern that the lower current prevalence rate for Ecstasy among secondary school students, relative to its peak around 2001, may not sustain itself in the near future or—worse—that high levels of Ecstasy use might return. As Lloyd D. Johnston, chief researcher for the University of Michigan surveys, warned in 2007,

> *The fact that eighth graders are showing the sharpest erosion in perceived risk and disapproval suggests that there may be what [we] call a "generational forgetting" of the hazards of this drug as new cohorts of students enter adolescence and replace those who knew more about the consequences of use.*[43]

Furthermore, post-2001 interference in Ecstasy trafficking through increased surveillance at U.S. airports may become less effective in reducing the overall availability of Ecstasy as alternative trafficking routes are established.

HEALTH ALERT!

MDMA Toxicity: The Other Side of Ecstasy

- **Possible Physical Effects**
  Hyperthermia and heatstroke
  Dehydration and electrolyte depletion
  Irregular heartbeat or increased heart rate
  Kidney and liver failure
  Jaw-clenching and other forms of muscle spasms
  Long-term neurochemical changes
- **Possible Psychological Effects**
  Agitation and confusion
  Depression and anxiety
  Long-term impairments in memory recall

Note: As with other illicit drugs, adulterated versions raise significant concerns. In the case of MDMA, adulterants include dextromethorphan (a common cough suppressant) at approximately thirteen times the dose found in over-the-counter cough medications. At this dosage, dextromethorphan itself functions as a hallucinogen and inhibits sweating, further risking hyperthermia and heatstroke. More powerful hallucinogens and hyperthermic drugs have also been identified as adulterants in MDMA batches.

In 2003, the federal RAVE (Reducing Americans' Vulnerability to Ecstasy) Act was signed into law, making it unlawful to "knowingly open, lease, rent, use, or maintain any place, whether permanently or temporarily" for the purpose of manufacturing, distributing, or using any controlled substance." Supporters of the law view it as helping to reduce illicit drug use in dance clubs; opponents view it more as reflection of prejudice against youth culture.

> **Where to go for assistance:**
>   www.nida.nih.gov/infofacts/ecstasy.html
> This web site is sponsored by the National Institute on Drug Abuse and includes an extensive treatment on the hazards of Ecstasy (MDMA).

Sources: Boils, Karen I. (1999). Memory impairment in abstinent MDMA ("Ecstasy") users. *Journal of the American Medical Association, 281,* 494. Chonin, Neva (2003, April 27). Congress acts out against club culture. *San Francisco Chronicle,* p. 35. Leshner, Alan I. (2002). Ecstasy abuse and control: Hearing before the Senate Subcommittee on Governmental Affairs—July 30, 2001. Statement for the record. *Journal of Psychoactive Drugs, 34,* 133–135. Schwartz, Richard H., and Miller, Norman S. (1997). MDMA (Ecstasy) and the rave: A review. *Pediatrics, 100,* 705–708. Stryker, Jeff (2001, September 25). For partygoers who can't say no, experts try to reduce the risks. *New York Times,* p. F5.

Hallucinogens Related to Acetylcholine

Of the acetylcholine-related hallucinogens, some enhance the neurotransmitter and some inhibit it. Some examples include *Amanita muscaria* mushrooms, atropine, scopolamine, and hyoscyamine.

Amanita muscaria

The **Amanita muscaria** mushroom, also called the fly agaric mushroom because of its ability to lure and sedate flies and other insects, grows in the upper latitudes of the Northern Hemisphere, usually among the roots of birch trees. The mushroom has a bright red cap speckled with white dots; the dancing mushrooms in Walt Disney's film

Amanita muscaria (a-ma-NEE-ta mus-CAR-ee-ah): A species of mushroom containing the hallucinogenic drug ibotenic acid.

Fantasia were inspired by the appearance (if not the hallucinogenic effects) of this fungus (see Figure 6.1b).

Amanita mushrooms are one of the world's oldest intoxicants. Many historians hypothesize that this mushroom was the basis for the mysterious and divine substance called soma that is celebrated in the *Rig-Veda,* one of Hinduism's oldest holy books, dating from 1000 B.C. It is strongly suspected that amanita mushrooms were used in Greek mystery cults and were probably the basis for the legendary "nectar of the gods" on Mount Olympus.[44]

The effects of amanita mushrooms can be lethal if dose levels are not watched very carefully. They produce muscular twitching and spasms, vivid hallucinations, dizziness, and heightened aggressive behavior. It was briefly mentioned in Chapter 1 that Viking warriors were reputed to have ingested amanita mushrooms before sailing off to battle. The drug-induced strength and savagery of these "berserk" invaders were so widely feared that a medieval prayer was written especially for protection from their attacks: "From the intolerable fury of the Norseman, O Lord, deliver us." The principal psychoactive agent in these mushrooms that accomplishes this effect is actually a chemical called *ibotenic acid.*[45]

The Hexing Drugs and Witchcraft

A number of natural plants contain chemicals that share a common feature: the ability to block the parasympathetic effects of acetylcholine in the body. The drugs with this ability, called *anticholinergic drugs*, produce specific physiological effects (Health Line). The production of mucus in the nose and throat, as well as saliva in the mouth, is reduced. Body temperature is elevated, sometimes to very high fever levels. Heart rate and blood pressure go up, and the pupils dilate considerably. Psychological effects include a feeling of delirium, confusion, and generally a loss of memory for events occurring during the drugged state.[46] The amnesic property is one of the primary reasons for the minimal street appeal of these drugs.

The principal anticholinergic drugs are **atropine, scopolamine** (also called hyoscine), and **hyoscyamine.** They are found in various combinations and relative amounts in a large number of psychoactive plants. Four of the better known ones are examined here.

- Atropine is principally derived from the *Atropa belladonna* plant, also called deadly nightshade. Its lethal reputation is quite justified, since it is estimated that ingesting only a dozen or so berries is sufficient for

death to occur. Many recipes for poisons through history have been based on this plant. At lower, more benign dose levels, plant extracts can be applied to the eyes, causing the pupils to dilate. Egyptian and Roman women used this technique to enhance their beauty or at least improve their appearance. The term "belladonna" ("beautiful lady") originates from this application. The psychological effects of atropine are generally associated with the anticholinergic effects of heart-rate acceleration and general arousal.

- The **mandrake** plant is an oddly shaped, potato-like plant with a long forked root that has traditionally been imagined to resemble a human body. In ancient times, mandrake was considered to have aphrodisiac

atropine (AT-tro-peen): An anticholinergic hallucinogenic drug derived from the *Atropa belladonna* plant.

scopolamine (scoh-POL-ah-meen): An anticholinergic hallucinogenic drug. Also called hyoscine.

hyoscyamine (HEYE-oh-SEYE-eh-meen): An anticholinergic hallucinogenic drug found in mandrake, henbane, and various species of the datura plant.

***Atropa belladonna* (a-TROH-pah BEL-ah-DON-ah):** A plant species, also called deadly nightshade, whose berries can be highly toxic. It is the principal source of atropine.

mandrake: A potato-like plant containing anticholinergic hallucinogenic drugs.

Health Line
Defining Drugs: Nutmeg as a Spice and a Hallucinogen

As we noted in Chapter 1, the distinction between drug and nondrug can be sometimes blurry, with the final judgment based on whether the substance in question was intended to be used primarily as a way of inducing a bodily or psychological change. In the case of the common spice nutmeg, the intention issue typically comes down to a matter of dosage.

Oral ingestions of between two teaspoons and two tablespoons of nutmeg (which obviously exceeds the quantity used as a flavoring) cause visual and tactile hallucinations, accelerated heart rate, tremors, dryness of the mouth, thirst, palpitations, and feelings of impending doom. This unpleasant combination of effects, in addition to the nausea associated with taking such amounts, make nutmeg abuse quite rare. However, among prison inmates, soldiers and seamen, and struggling musicians, nutmeg has been substituted for various psychoactive drugs, such as marijuana, when they have been either unavailable or unaffordable. Occasionally,

acute toxicity has resulted from intentional or accidental use. Nutmeg contains from 5 to 15 percent myristicin, an oil that acts as an anticholinergic agent, inhibiting parasympathetic autonomic changes (see Chapter 3).

Like other natural substances, nutmeg has specific therapeutic effects as well, by virtue of its myristicin content. On the basis of research showing its protective properties in preventing liver damage in mice, myristicin might be useful as a future treatment for liver disease.

Sources: Forrester, Mathias B. (2005). Nutmeg intoxication in Texas, 1998–2004. *Human and Experimental Toxicology, 24,* 563–566. Julien, Robert M. (2005). *A primer of drug action* (10th ed.). New York: Worth, pp. 599, 602. Moirta, Tatsuya, Jinno, Keiko, et al. (2003). Hepatoprotective effect of myristicin from nutmeg (*Myristica fragrans*) on lipopolysaccharide/D-galactosamine-induced liver injury. *Journal of Agrricultural and Food Chemistry, 81,* 1560–1565.

properties. According to medieval folklore, mandrake plants supposedly shrieked when they were uprooted, understandably driving people mad.

Mandrake contains a combination of atropine, scopolamine, and hyoscyamine. Because low doses act as a depressant, mandrake has been used as a sedative-hypnotic drug to relieve anxiety and induce sleep. At higher doses, it produces bizarre hallucinations and muscular paralysis.

henbane: An herb containing anticholinergic hallucinogenic drugs.

Datura stramonium (duh-TOOR-ah strah-MOH-nee-um): A species of the datura family of plants with hallucinogenic properties. In the United States, the plant is called jimsonweed.

phencyclidine (PCP) (fen-SIGH-klih-deen): A dissociative anesthetic hallucinogen that produces disorientation, agitation, aggressive behavior, analgesia, and amnesia. It has various street names, including angel dust.

- **Henbane** is a strong-smelling herb, native to widespread areas of the Northern Hemisphere, with purple-veined, yellowish flowers and hairy leaves. Its English name, meaning "harmful to hens," originates from the observation that henbane seeds were toxic to chickens and other birds. The lethal possibilities for henbane potions have been described by writers since the days of the Roman Empire. Hamlet's father in Shakespeare's play was supposedly murdered with henbane poison. Lower doses of henbane, however, have been used in a more benign way, as an anesthetic and painkiller. We now know that the predominant drugs in henbane are scopolamine and hyoscyamine.

- Various species of the datura plant, containing a combination of atropine, scopolamine, and hyoscyamine, grow wild in locations throughout the world. In the United States, one particular species, **Datura stramonium,** is called "jimsonweed," a contraction of "Jamestown weed" (the name given to it by early American colonists). Consumption of the seeds or berries of jimsonweed produces hypnotic and hallucinogenic effects, together with disorientation, confusion, and amnesia. At high doses, jimsonweed is quite toxic. In recent years, there have been occasional reports of hospitalizations and even deaths among teenagers who have eaten jimsonweed seeds as an inexpensive way to get high.[47]

During medieval times, mixtures of deadly nightshade, mandrake, and henbane were responsible for the psychoactive effects of witches' potions, producing a disastrous combination of physiological and psychological effects. Satanic celebrations of the Black Mass centered on the ingestion of such brews. The atropine, in particular, produced a substantial elevation in arousal, probably leading to the feeling that the person was flying (or at least capable of it), while the hallucinogenic effects enabled the person to imagine communing with the Devil.[48] Witches were reputed to have prepared these mixtures as ointments and rubbed them on their bodies and on broomsticks, which they straddled. The chemicals would have been easily absorbed through the skin and the membranes of the vagina. The Halloween image of a witch flying on a broomstick has been with us ever since.

Phencyclidine (PCP)

Perhaps the most notorious of all the hallucinogens is **phencyclidine (PCP),** commonly known as *angel dust.* The appearance of this drug from the miscellaneous group as an illicit drug in the late 1960s brought special problems to the already dangerous drug scene.

The weird combination of stimulant, depressant, and hallucinogenic effects makes PCP difficult to classify. Some textbooks treat the discussion of PCP in a chapter on hallucinogens, as is done here, whereas others include it in a chapter on stimulants because some features of PCP intoxication resemble the effect of cocaine, though ironically its medical use was originally as a depressant. A growing consensus of opinion has it that PCP, because it produces a feeling of being dissociated or cut off from one's environment, should be described as a *dissociative anesthetic hallucinogen.*[49]

History and Abuse of PCP

Technically PCP is a synthetic depressant, and it was originally introduced in 1963 as a depressant drug by the Parke-Davis pharmaceutical company, under the brand name of Sernyl. It was marketed as a promising new surgical anesthetic that had the advantage of not depressing respiration or blood pressure or causing heartbeat irregularities like other anesthetics. In addition, PCP had a higher therapeutic ratio than many other anesthetics available at that time. By 1965, however, it was withdrawn from human applications after reports that nearly half of all patients receiving PCP showed signs of delirium, disorientation, hallucinations, intense anxiety, or agitation. For a time, PCP was used for animal anesthesia, but this application ended by the late 1970s. In 1979, PCP was classified as a Schedule I drug.

PCP can be taken orally, intravenously, or by inhalation, but commonly it is smoked either alone or in combination with other drugs. Whatever its mode of administration, the results are extremely dangerous, with an unpredictability that far exceeds that of LSD or other hallucinogens. The symptoms may include manic excitement, depression, severe anxiety, sudden mood changes, disordered and confused thought, paranoid thoughts, and unpredictable aggression. Because PCP has analgesic properties as well, individuals taking the drug often feel invulnerable to threats against them and may be willing and able to withstand considerable pain. The mechanism behind PCP effects appears to be the blocking of a specific subtype of glutamate receptors in the brain (see Chapter 3).

Hallucinations also occur, but they are quite different from the hallucinations experienced under the influence of LSD. There are no colorful images, no intermingling of sight and sound, no mystical sense of being "one with the world." Instead, a prominent feature of PCP-induced hallucinations is the change in one's body image. As one PCP abuser has expressed it:

The most frequent hallucination is that parts of your body are extremely large or extremely small. You can imagine yourself small enough to walk through a key hole, or you can be lying there and all of a sudden you just hallucinate that your arm is twice the length of your body.[50]

Individuals under the influence of PCP also may stagger, speak in a slurred way, and feel depersonalized or detached from people around them. A prominent feature is a prolonged visual stare, often called "doll's eyes."

The effects of PCP last from as little as a few hours to as long as two weeks, and they are followed by partial or total amnesia and dissociation from the entire experience. Considering these bizarre reactions, it is not surprising that PCP deaths occur more frequently from the behavioral consequences of the PCP experience than from its physiological effects. Suicides, accidental or intentional mutilations, drownings (sometimes in very small amounts of water), falls, and threatening behavior leading to the individual's being shot are only some of the possible consequences.[51]

Patterns of PCP Abuse

It is strange that a drug with so many adverse effects would be subject to deliberate abuse, but such is the case with PCP. Reports of PCP abuse began surfacing in 1967 among the hippie community in San Francisco, where it became known as the PeaCe Pill. Word quickly spread that PCP did not live up to its name. Inexperienced PCP abusers were suffering the same bizarre effects as had the clinical patients earlier in the decade. By 1969, PCP had been written off as a garbage drug, and it dropped out of sight as a drug of abuse.

In the early 1970s, PCP returned under new street names and in new forms (Table 6.2, page 162). No longer a pill to be taken orally, PCP was now in powdered or liquid form. Powdered PCP could be added to parsley, mint, oregano, tobacco, or marijuana, rolled as a cigarette, and smoked.[52] Liquid PCP could be used to soak leaf mixtures of all types, including manufactured cigarettes, which could then be dried and smoked. Many new users have turned to PCP as a way to boost the effects of marijuana.

Making matters worse, as many as 120 different designer-drug variations of PCP have been developed in illicit laboratories around the country and the world. The dangers of PCP abuse, therefore, are complicated by the difficulty in knowing whether a street drug has been adulterated with PCP and what version of PCP may be present. Unfortunately, the common practice of

TABLE 6.2

Street names for phencyclidine (PCP) and PCP-like drugs

PCP	jet fuel
angel dust	sherms (derived from the reaction that it hits you like a Sherman tank)
monkey dust	
peep	superkools
supergrass	cyclones
killer weed	zombie dust
ozone	ketamine
embalming fluid	special K
rocket fuel	

Note: In the illicit drug market, PCP and ketamine are frequently misrepresented and sold as mescaline, LSD, marijuana, amphetamine, or cocaine.

Source: Milburn, H. Thomas (1991). Diagnosis and management of phencyclidine intoxication. *American Family Physician, 43,* 1293.

mixing PCP with alcohol or marijuana adds to the unpredictability of the final result.[53]

Ketamine

Ketamine, a drug chemically similar to PCP, is also classified as a dissociative anesthetic hallucinogen. Like PCP, ketamine has a mixture of stimulant and depressive properties, though its depressive effect is more extreme and does not last as long as that of PCP. Ketamine was used as an emergency surgical anesthetic on the battlefield in Vietnam as well as in standard hospital-based operations in which gaseous anesthetics could not be employed. It has also been used occasionally in short surgical procedures involving the head and neck or in the treatment of facial burns where it is not possible to use an anesthetic mask. Adverse side effects, however, have limited its therapeutic use. These problems include unpredictable and sometimes violent jerking and twitching of the body, as well as vivid and unpleasant dreams during and after surgery. During recovery, patients may experience hal-

lucinations and feelings of disorientation. Delayed effects of ketamine, such as nightmares, have been reported to occur for weeks or longer after surgery.[54]

Ketamine abuse began to be reported in the 1980s. More recently, under the names "Special K" and "Vitamin K," it has been included among current club drugs on the scene (see Chapter 1). Its popularity has increased among college students and patrons of dance clubs and all-night "rave" parties. Like PCP, ketamine produces a dream-like intoxication, accompanied by an inability to move or feel pain. There are also experiences of dizziness, confusion, and slurred speech. As is the case with dissociative hallucinogens, ketamine produces amnesia, in that abusers frequently cannot later remember what has happened while under its influence. The primary hazard of acute ketamine ingestion is the depression of breathing. Little is known, however, of the chronic effects of extended ketamine abuse over time, except that experiences of "flashbacks" have been reported.[55] As with PCP, the effects of ketamine are associated with the blocking of specific glutamate receptors.

As with other club drugs that produce depressive effects on the central nervous system, there is the dangerous potential for ketamine to be abused as a "date-rape" drug. Women who may unwittingly take the drug can be rendered incapacitated, without the ability to recall the experience. In 1999, ketamine became classified as a Schedule III controlled substance.[56]

ketamine (KET-ah-meen): A dissociative anesthetic hallucinogen related to phencyclidine (PCP).

Summary

A Matter of Definition

- Hallucinogens are, by definition, drugs that produce distortions of perception and of one's sense of reality. These drugs have also been called psychedelic ("mind-expanding") drugs. In some cases, users of hallucinogens feel that they have been transported to a new reality.

- Other classes of drugs may produce hallucinations at high dose levels, but hallucinogens produce these effects at low or moderate dose levels.

Classifying Hallucinogens

- Hallucinogens can be classified in four basic groups. The first three relate to the chemical similarity between the particular drug and one of three major neurotransmitters: serotonin, norepinephrine, or acetylcholine.

- The fourth, miscellaneous group includes synthetic hallucinogens, such as phencyclidine (PCP) and ketamine, which bear little resemblance to any known neurotransmitter.

Lysergic Acid Diethylamide (LSD)

- Lysergic acid diethylamide (LSD), the best-known hallucinogenic drug, belongs to the serotonin group. It is synthetically derived from ergot, a toxic rye fungus that has been documented as being responsible for thousands of deaths over the centuries.

- Albert Hofmann synthesized LSD in 1943, and Timothy Leary led the psychedelic movement in the 1960s that popularized LSD use.

- Though the LSD experience is often unpredictable, certain features are commonly observed: colorful hallucinations, synesthesia in which sounds often appear as visions, a distortion of perceptual reality, emotional swings, a feeling of timelessness, and an illusory separation of mind from body.

- It is now known that LSD affects a subtype of brain receptors sensitive to serotonin, referred to as serotonin-2 receptors.

- In the early 1990s, there was a resurgence in LSD abuse, particularly among young individuals, a trend that began to reverse in 1997.

Facts and Fiction about LSD

- LSD does not produce psychological or physical dependence and has only a slight chance of inducing a panic or psychotic state (providing that there is a supportive setting for the taking of LSD).

- LSD does not elevate one's level of creativity. It does not damage chromosomes (though there remains a chance of birth defects if LSD is ingested when pregnant), and a relationship between LSD abuse and violent behavior has not been established. Flashback experiences, however, are potential hazards.

Psilocybin and Other Hallucinogens Related to Serotonin

- Other hallucinogens related to serotonin are psilocybin, lysergic acid amide (LAA), dimethyltryptamine (DMT), and harmine.

Hallucinogens Related to Norepinephrine

- Mescaline is chemically related to norepinephrine, even though serotonin-2 receptors are responsible for its hallucinogenic effects.

- Two synthetic hallucinogens, DOM and MDMA, are variations of the amphetamine molecule. MDMA (Ecstasy) is currently a popular club drug, but research studies indicate that it poses serious health risks to the user.

Hallucinogens Related to Acetylcholine

- A number of anticholinergic hallucinogens, so named because they diminish the effects of acetylcholine in the parasympathetic nervous system, have been involved in sorcery and witchcraft since the Middle Ages.

- These so-called hexing drugs contain a combination of atropine, scopolamine, and/or hyoscyamine. Sources for such drugs include the deadly nightshade plant, mandrake roots, henbane seeds, and the datura plant family.

Phencyclidine (PCP) and Ketamine

- A dangerous form of hallucinogen abuse involves phencyclidine (PCP). Originally a psychedelic street drug in the 1960s, PCP quickly developed a reputation for producing a number of adverse reactions.

- PCP reappeared in the early 1970s, in smokable forms either alone or in combination with marijuana. Extremely aggressive tendencies, as well as behaviors resembling acute schizophrenia, have been associated with PCP intoxication.

- Ketamine is popular as a club drug and produces a dream-like intoxication, accompanied by an inability to move or feel pain. Like PCP, ketamine also produces amnesia and potentially a depression in breathing.

Key Terms

Amanita muscaria, p. 158
Atropa belladonna, p. 159
atropine, p. 159
bufotenine, p. 155
cyanosis, p. 155
Datura stramonium, p. 160
dimethyltryptamine (DMT), p. 154

DOM, p. 156
ergot, p. 145
ergotism, p. 145
hallucinogens, p. 143
harmine, p. 154
henbane, p. 160
hyoscyamine, p. 159

ketamine, p. 162
lysergic acid amide (LAA), p. 154
lysergic acid diethylamide (LSD), p. 143
mandrake, p. 159
MDMA (Ecstasy), p. 156

mescaline, p. 154
peyote, p. 154
phencyclidine (PCP), p. 160
psilocin, p. 153
psilocybin, p. 153
scopolamine, p. 159
synesthesia, p. 149

Endnotes

1. Hofmann, Albert (1980). *LSD: My problem child.* New York: McGraw-Hill, p. 17.
2. Ibid., pp. 17–18.
3. Ibid., p. 19.
4. Brophy, James J. (1985). Psychiatric disorders. In Marcus A. Krupp, Milton J. Chatton, and David Werdegar (Eds.), *Current medical diagnosis and treatment.* Los Altos, CA: Lange Medical Publication, p. 674.
5. Mann, John (1992). *Murder, magic, and medicine.* New York: Oxford University Press, pp. 41–51.
6. Fuller, John G. (1968). *The day of St. Anthony's fire.* New York: Macmillan, preface.
7. Leary, Timothy (1973). The religious experience: Its production and interpretation. In Gunther Weil, Ralph Metzner, and Timothy Leary (Eds.), *The psychedelic reader.* Secaucus, NJ: Citadel Press, p. 191.
8. Lee, Martin A., and Shlain, Bruce (1985). *Acid dreams: The complete social history of LSD.* New York: Grove Weidenfeld, pp. 71–118.
9. Leary, Timothy (1968). *High priest.* New York: New American Library, p. 46. Manchester, William R. (1974). *The glory and the dream: A narrative history of America, 1932–1972.* Boston: Little, Brown, p. 1362.
10. Grinspoon, Lester, and Bakalar, James B. (1979). *Psychedelic drugs reconsidered.* New York: Basic Books, p. 68.
11. Brown, F. Christine (1972). *Hallucinogenic drugs.* Springfield, IL: Charles C Thomas, pp. 46–49. Goode, Erich (2005). *Drugs and American society* (6th ed.). New York: McGraw-Hill College, p. 255.
12. Schuckit, Marc A. (1995). *Drug and alcohol abuse: A clinical guide to diagnosis and treatment* (4th ed.). New York: Plenum, pp. 189–190.
13. Jacobs, Michael R., and Fehr, Kevin O'B. (1987). *Drugs and drug abuse: A reference text* (2nd ed.). Toronto: Addiction Research Foundation, p. 345. Substance Abuse and Mental Health Services Administration (2008). Drug Abuse Warning Network, 2006: National estimates of drug-related emergency department visits. Rockville, MD: Office of Applied Studies, Substance Abuse and Mental Health Services Administration, Table 2.
14. Brophy, Psychiatric disorders. Jacobs and Fehr, *Drugs and drug abuse,* pp. 337–347.
15. Goode, *Drugs and American society,* pp. 245–249. Snyder, Solomon H. (1986). *Drugs and the brain.* New York: Freeman, pp. 180–181.
16. Aghajanian, G. K., and Marek, G. J. (1999). Serotonin and hallucinogens. *Neuropsychopharmacology, 21 (Suppl. 2),* 16S–23S. Gresch, Paul J.; Smith, Randy, L.; Barrett, Robert J.; and Sanders-Bush, Elaine (2005). Behavioral tolerance to lysergic acid diethylamide is associated with reduced serotonin-2A receptor signaling in rat cortex. *Neuropsychopharmacology, 30,* 1693–1702. Julien, Robert M. (2005). *A primer of drug action* (10th ed.). New York: Worth, p. 602.
17. Goode, *Drugs and American society,* pp. 255–258.
18. Brands, Bruna, Sproule, Beth, and Marshman, Joan (1998). *Drugs and drug abuse: A reference text.* Toronto, Canada: Addiction Research Foundation, p. 328. Henderson, Leigh A., and Glass, William J. (Eds.) (1994). *LSD: Still with us after all these years.* New York: Lexington Books. Johnston, Lloyd D.; O'Malley, Patrick M.; Bachman, Jerald G.; and Schulenberg, John E. (2007a, December 11). Various stimulant drugs show continuing gradual declines among teens in 2008, most illicit drugs hold steady. University of Michigan News Service, Ann Arbor, Table 1. Johnston, Lloyd D.; O'Malley, Patrick M.; Bachman, Jerald G.; and Schulenberg, John E. (2008b). *Monitoring the future: National survey results on drug use, 1975–2007. Vol. II: College students and adults ages 19–45.* Bethesda, MD: National Institute on Drug Abuse, Table 2-1. Karch, Steven B. (1996). *The pathology of drug abuse* (2nd ed.). Boca Raton, FL: CRC Press, p. 269.
19. Goode, *Drugs and American society,* p. 257.
20. Ibid., p. 256.
21. Cohen, Sidney (1960). Lysergic acid diethylamide: Side effects and complications. *Journal of Nervous and Mental Diseases, 130,* 30–40. Levine, Jerome, and Ludwig, Arnold M. (1964). The LSD controversy. *Comprehensive Psychiatry, 5* (5), 314–321.

22. Wells, Brian (1974). *Psychedelic drugs: Psychological, medical, and social issues.* New York: Jason Aronson, pp. 170–188.

23. Cohen, M. M., and Marmillo, M. J. (1967). Chromosomal damage in human leukocytes induced by lysergic acid diethylamide. *Science, 155,* 1417–1419.

24. Dishotsky, Norman I.; Loughman, William D.; Mogar, Robert E.; and Lipscomb, Wendell R. (1971). LSD and genetic damage. *Science, 172,* 431–440. Grinspoon and Bakalar, *Psychedelic drugs reconsidered,* pp. 188–191.

25. Brown, *Hallucinogenic drugs,* pp. 61–64. Wells, *Psychedelic drugs,* pp. 104–109.

26. Abraham, Henry D. (1983). Visual phenomenology of the LSD flashback. *Archives of General Psychiatry, 40,* 884–889. Schlaadt, Richard G., and Shannon, Peter T. (1994). *Drugs: Use, misuse, and abuse.* Englewood Cliffs, NJ: Prentice-Hall, p. 273.

27. Halpern, John H., and Pope, Harrison G. (1999). Do hallucinogens cause residual neuropsychological toxicity? *Drugs and Alcohol Dependence, 53,* 247–256.

28. Knudsen, Knud (1964). Homicide after treatment with lysergic acid diethylamide. *Acta Psychiatrica Scandinavica, 40* (Supplement 180), 389–395.

29. Metzner, Ralph (1998). Hallucinogenic drugs and plants in psychotherapy and shamanism. *Journal of Psychoactive Drugs, 30,* 333–341.

30. Hofmann, *LSD,* p. 112.

31. Brown, *Hallucinogenic drugs,* pp. 81–88.

32. Johnston, O'Malley, Bachman, and Schulenberg (2008a), Various stimulant drugs show continuing gradual declines, Table 13. Vollenweider, Franz X.; Vollenweider-Scherpenhuyzen, Margaret F. I.; Babler, Andreas; Vogel, Helen; and Hell, Daniel (1998). Psilocybin induces schizophrenia-like psychosis in humans via a serotonin-2 agonist action. *Neuroreport, 9,* 3897–3902.

33. Hofmann, *LSD,* pp. 119–127. Schultes, Richard E., and Hofmann, Albert (1979). *Plants of the gods: Origins of hallucinogenic use.* New York: McGraw-Hill, pp. 158–163.

34. Brands, Sproule, and Marshman, *Drugs and drug abuse,* pp. 512–513.

35. Frecska, Ede, White, Keith, D., and Luna, Luis E. (2003). Effects of Amazonian psychoactive beverage *ayuhuasca* on binocular rivalry: Interhemispheric switching or interhemispheric fusion? *Journal of Psychoactive Drugs, 35,* 367–374. Grinspoon and Bakalar, *Psychedelic drugs reconsidered,* pp. 14–15.

36. Ibid., pp. 20–21. Hollister, Leo E., and Sjoberg, Bernard M. (1964). Clinical syndromes and biochemical alterations following mescaline, lysergic acid diethylamide, psilocybin, and a combination of the three psychotomimetic drugs. *Comprehensive Psychiatry, 5,* 170–178.

37. Jacobs, *How hallucinogenic drugs work,* pp. 386–392.

38. Brecher, Edward, and the editors of *Consumer Reports* (1972). *Licit and illicit drugs.* Boston: Little, Brown, pp. 376–377.

39. Metzner, Hallucinogenic drugs and plants. Schmidt, C. J. (1987). Psychedelic amphetamine, methylendioxymethamphetamine. *Journal of Pharmacology and Experimental Therapeutics, 240,* 1–7.

40. Boils, Karen I. (1999). Memory impairment in abstinent MDMA ("Ecstasy") users. *Journal of the American Medical Association, 281,* 494. Leshner, Alan I. (2002). Ecstasy abuse and control: Hearing before the Senate Subcommittee on Governmental Affairs—July 30, 2001. Statement for the record. *Journal of Psychoactive Drugs, 34,* 133–135. Vollenweider, Franz X.; Liechti, Matthias E.; Gamma, Alex; Greer, George; and Geyer, Mark (2002). Acute psychological and neurophysiological effects of MDMA in humans. *Journal of Psychoactive Drugs, 34,* 171–184.

41. Cloud, John (2000, June 5). The lure of ecstasy. *Time,* pp. 62–68. Feuer, Alan (2000, August 6). Distilling the truth in the ecstasy buzz. *New York Times,* pp. 25, 28. Johnston, O'Malley, Bachman, and Schulenberg (2008a), Various stimulant drugs show continuing gradual declines, Tables 1, 7, and 10. Martins, Silvia, S., Mazzotti, Guido, and Chilcoat, Howard D. (2005). Trends in ecstasy use in the United States from 1995 to 2001: Comparison with marijuana users and association with other drug use. *Experimental and Clinical Psychopharmacology, 13,* 244–252.

42. Leinwand, Donna (2005, April 22–24). Post-9/11 security cuts into Ecstasy: Youths turning to prescription drugs. *USA Today,* p. 1A. Leinward, Donna (2005, April 22–24). Ecstasy's lost "its panache" among teens. *USA Today,* p. 3A.

43. Johnston, Lloyd D.; O'Malley, Patrick M.; Bachman, Jerald G.; and Schulenberg, John E. (2007, December 11). Overall, illicit drug use by American teens continues gradual decline in 2007. University of Michigan News Service, Ann Arbor. Quotation on p. 4.

44. Wasson, R. Gordon (1968). *Soma: Divine mushroom of immortality.* New York: Harcourt, Brace and World.

45. Cohen, Sidney (1964). *The beyond within: The LSD story.* New York: Atheneum, p. 17. Popik, Piotr, and Glick, Stanley D. (1996). Ibogaine: A putatively anti-addictive alkaloid. *Drugs of the Future, 21,* 1109–1115.

46. Levinthal, Charles F. (1990). *Introduction to physiological psychology* (3rd ed.). Englewood Cliffs, NJ: Prentice-Hall, pp. 157–158. Ramachandran, Vilayanur S., and Hubbard, Edward M. (2003, May). Hearing colors, tasting shapes. *Scientific American,* pp. 52–59.

47. Freedman, Mitchell (1994, October 15). One teen's tale of jimsonweed. *Newsday,* p. A14. Schultes and Hofmann, *Plants of the gods,* pp. 106–111.

48. Schultes and Hofmann, *Plants of the gods,* pp. 86–91.

49. Julien, Robert M. (2001). *A primer of drug action* (9th ed.). New York: Worth, pp. 353–359.

50. James, Jennifer, and Andresen, Elena (1979). Sea-Tac and PCP. In Harvey V. Feldman, Michael H. Agar, and George M. Beschner (Eds.), *Angel dust: An ethnographic study of PCP users.* Lexington, MA: Lexington Books, p. 133.

51. Grinspoon and Bakalar, *Psychedelic drugs reconsidered*, pp. 32–33. Petersen, Robert C., and Stillman, Richard C. (1978). Phencyclidine: An overview. In Robert C. Petersen and Richard C. Stillman (Eds.), *Phencyclidine (PCP) abuse: An appraisal* (NIDA Research Monograph 21). Rockville, MD: National Institute on Drug Abuse, pp. 1–17. Robbins, *Hallucinogens*, pp. 12–14. Seeman, P., Ko, F., and Tallerico, T. (2005). Dopamine receptor contribution to the action of PCP, LSD and ketamine psychotomimetics. *Molecular Psychiatry, 10*, 877–883.

52. Zukin, Stephen, Sloboda, Zili, and Javitt, Daniel C. (1997). Phencyclidine (PCP). In Joyce H. Lowinson, Pedro Ruiz, Robert B. Millman, and John G. Langrod (Eds.), *Substance abuse: A comprehensive textbook* (3rd ed.). Baltimore, MD: Williams & Wilkins, pp. 238–246.

53. Trends in PCP-related emergency department visits (2004, January). *The DAWN Report*, pp. 1–4.

54. Brands, Sproule, and Marshman, *Drugs and drug abuse*, pp. 523–525.

55. Ibid.

56. Feds classify ketamine as controlled substance (1999, August 2). *Alcoholism and Drug Abuse Weekly*, p. 7.

chapter 7

Marijuana

"Hunters and fishermen have snared the most ferocious creatures, from the tiger to the shark, in its Herculean weave. . . . Hangmen have snapped the necks of thieves and murderers with its fiber. Obstetricians have eased the pain of childbirth with its leaves. Farmers have crushed its seeds and used the oil within to light their lamps. Mourners have thrown its seeds into blazing fires and have had their sorrows transformed into blissful ecstacy by the fumes that filled the air. . . .

(Cannabis) is as vigorous as a weed. It is ubiquitous. It flourishes under nearly every possible climatic condition. It sprouts from the earth not meekly, not cautiously in suspense of where it is and what it may find, but defiantly, arrogantly, confident that whatever the conditions it has the stamina to survive."

—Ernest L. Abel, referring to the cannabis plant
(hemp and marijuana), its diverse uses over history,
and its amazing hardiness as a botanical entity
Marihuana, the First Twelve Thousand Years *(1980)*

After you have completed this chapter, you will understand

- The history of marijuana and other cannabis products
- Acute effects of marijuana
- The neural basis for the effects of marijuana
- Long-term effects of marijuana
- The amotivational syndrome and the gateway theory
- Patterns of marijuana smoking
- The medical marijuana controversy
- The question of marijuana decriminalization

It might be fair to characterize *Cannabis sativa*, the botanical source of marijuana, as a scrawny weed with an attitude. Whether it is hot or cold, wet or dry, cannabis will grow abundantly from seeds that are unbelievably hardy and prolific. A handful of cannabis seeds, tossed on the ground and pressed in with one's foot, will usually anchor and become plants. Its roots devour whatever nutrients there are in the soil, like a vampire sucking the life blood from the earth.[1]

It is not surprising that, as a result, marijuana has managed to grow in some unorthodox places. It can be found in median strips of interstate highways or in ditches alongside country roads. The top prize for most unusual location, if the story is true and not simply an urban legend, has to go to a variety known as Manhattan Silver. Reportedly, it originated from cannabis seeds flushed down a New York sewer during a sudden police raid in the 1960s. Once the seeds hit the sewer, they produced a plant that, in the absence of light, grew silverish white leaves instead of green, hence its name.[2]

Considering its botanical origin, it is fitting that the pharmacological effects of marijuana should show something of an independent nature as well. It is not easy to place marijuana within a classification of psychoactive drugs. When we consider a category for marijuana, we are faced with an odd assortment of unconnected properties. Marijuana produces some excitatory effects, but it is not generally regarded as a stimulant. It produces some sedative effects, but a person faces no risk of slipping into a coma or dying. It produces mild analgesic effects, but it

A Mexican harvester gathers his crop of *Cannabis sativa,* later to be processed into marijuana or hashish.

is not related chemically to opiates or opiate-like drugs. It produces hallucinations at high doses, but its structure does not resemble LSD or any other drug formally categorized as a hallucinogen. Marijuana is clearly a hybrid drug, in a league of its own.

Few other drugs have been so politicized in recent history as marijuana. It is frequently praised by one side or condemned by the other, on the basis of emotionally charged issues rather than an objective view of research data. The pro-marijuana faction tends to dismiss or downplay reports of potential dangers and emphasize the benefits; the antimarijuana faction tends to do the opposite, pointing out that marijuana continues to be classified as a Schedule I controlled substance, along with heroin and LSD. Marijuana often has been regarded, over the last forty years or so, not only as a drug with psychoactive properties but also as a symbol of an individual's attitude toward the establishment. This makes it even more critical that we look at the effects of marijuana as dispassionately as possible.

A Matter of Terminology

Although *marijuana* (sometimes spelled *marihuana*) is frequently referred to as a synonym for cannabis, the two terms need to be differentiated. Cannabis is the botanical

by the numbers . . .

586,000	On an average day in 2006, the number of adolescents in the United States, aged twelve to seventeen, who smoked marijuana
3,600	On an average day in 2006, the number who smoked marijuana for the first time
11	Number of U.S. states in 2008 that have authorized marijuana smoking for the relief of pain and discomfort or for the control of nausea and weight loss, when prescribed by a physician

Sources: Substance Abuse and Mental Health Services Administration (2007). *A day in the life of American adolescents: Substance use facts.* Rockville, MD: Office of Applied Studies, Substance Abuse and Mental Health Services Administration. Media Sources.

term for the hemp plant *Cannabis sativa.* With a potential height of about eighteen feet, cannabis has sturdy stalks, four-cornered in cross-section, that have been commercially valuable for thousands of years in the manufacture of rope, twine, shoes, sailcloth, and containers of all kinds. Pots made of hemp fiber discovered at archaeological sites in China date the origins of cannabis cultivation as far back as the Stone Age. It is arguably the oldest cultivated plant not used for food.[3]

Spaniards brought cannabis to the New World in 1545, and English settlers brought it to Jamestown, Virginia, in 1611, where it became a major commercial crop, along with tobacco. Like other eighteenth-century farmers in the region, George Washington grew cannabis in the fields of his estate at Mount Vernon. Entries in his diary indicate that he maintained a keen interest in cultivating better strains of cannabis, but there is no reason to believe he was interested in anything more than a better-quality rope.

Marijuana is obtained not from the stalks of the cannabis plant but from its serrated leaves. The key psychoactive factor is contained in a sticky substance, or resin, that accumulates on these leaves. Depending on the growing conditions, cannabis will produce either a greater amount of resin or a greater amount of fiber. In a hot, dry climate—such as North Africa, for example—the fiber content is weak, but so much resin is produced that the plant looks as if it is covered with dew. In a cooler, more humid climate, such as North America, less resin is produced, but the fiber is stronger and more durable.[4]

As many as eighty separate chemical compounds, called **cannabinoids,** have been identified from cannabis resin. Among these, the chief psychoactive compound and the active ingredient that produces the intoxicating effects is **delta-9-tetrahydrocannabinol (THC).** The isolation and identification of THC in 1964 was a major step toward understanding the effects on the brain of marijuana and similar preparations obtained from *Cannabis sativa.*

Knowing these facts, we are now in a position to categorize various forms of cannabis products in terms of the origin within the cannabis plant and the relative THC concentration. The first and best known of these products, **marijuana,** consists of leaves and occasionally flowers of the cannabis plant that are first dried and then shredded. During the 1960s and 1970s, the typical THC concentration of street marijuana imported from Mexico was about 1 to 2 percent. More recently, higher-potency marijuana grown in remote areas of Canada has been found to contain a THC concentration of 6 to 8 percent and sometimes greater. Marijuana, smoked as a cigarette, is the form of cannabis most familiar to North Americans.

A more potent form of marijuana is obtained by cultivating only the unpollinated, or seedless, portion of the cannabis plant. Without pollination, the cannabis plant grows bushier, the resin content is increased, and a greater THC concentration, 8 to 15 percent, is achieved. This form is called **sinsemilla,** from the Spanish meaning "without seed."

Another cannabis product is achieved when the resin itself is scraped from cannabis leaves and then dried. It is either smoked by itself or in combination with tobacco. This form of cannabis, called **hashish,** has a THC concentration of 8 to 14 percent and is commonly available in Europe, Asia, and the Middle East. The most potent forms of cannabis are **hashish oil** and **hashish oil crystals,** produced by boiling hashish in alcohol or some other solvent, filtering out the alcohol, and leaving a residue with a THC concentration ranging from 15 to 60 percent.[5]

The History of Marijuana and Hashish

The first direct reference to a cannabis product as a psychoactive agent dates from 2737 B.C., in the writings of the mythical Chinese emperor Shen Nung. The focus was on its powers as a medication for rheumatism, gout, malaria, and, strangely enough, absent-mindedness.

Cannabis sativa (CAN-uh-bus sah-TEE-vah): A plant species, commonly called hemp, from which marijuana and hashish are obtained.

cannabinoids (can-NAB-ih-noids): Any of several dozen active substances in marijuana and other cannabis products.

delta-9-tetrahydrocannabinol (THC) (DEL-tah-9-TEH-trah-HIGH-dro-CAN-a-bih-nol): The active psychoactive ingredient in marijuana and hashish.

marijuana: The most commonly available psychoactive drug originating from the cannabis plant. The THC concentration ranges from approximately 1 to 6 percent. Also spelled marihuana.

sinsemilla (SIN-sih-MEE-yah): A form of marijuana obtained from the unpollinated or seedless portion of the cannabis plant. It has a higher THC concentration than regular marijuana, as high as 15 percent.

hashish (hah-SHEESH): A drug containing the resin of cannabis flowers. The THC concentration ranges from approximately 8 to 14 percent.

hashish oil: A drug produced by boiling hashish, leaving a potent psychoactive residue. The THC concentration ranges from approximately 15 to 60 percent.

hashish oil crystals: A solid form of hashish oil.

A merchant sits outside his bhang shop in North India. *Bhang ki thandai* is a popular cold drink prepared with bhang combined with almonds, spices, milk, and sugar. *Bhang lassi,* a mixture of bhang and iced yogurt, is another popular drink. It is traditional for many Hindus to drink bhang during religious festivals, particularly in Bengal during the Kali Puja (Festival of Kali, the Mother Goddess).

Mention was made of its intoxicating properties, but the medicinal possibilities evidently were considered more important. In India, however, its use was clearly recreational. The most popular form, in ancient times as well as in the present day, can be found in a syrupy liquid made from cannabis leaves called **bhang,** with a THC potency usually equal to that of a marijuana cigarette in the United States.[6]

The Muslim world also grew to appreciate the psychoactive potential of cannabis, encouraged by the fact that, in contrast to its stern prohibition of alcohol consumption, the Koran did not specifically ban its use. It was here in a hot, dry climate conducive to maximizing the resin content of cannabis that hashish was born, and its popularity spread quickly during the twelfth cen-

bhang: A liquid form of marijuana popular in India.

tury from Persia (Iran) in the east to North Africa in the west.

Hashish in the Nineteenth Century

In Western Europe knowledge about hashish or any other cannabis product was limited until the beginning of the nineteenth century. Judging from the decree made by Pope Innocent VIII in 1484 condemning witchcraft and the use of hemp in the Black Mass, we can assume that the psychoactive properties of cannabis were known by some portions of the population. Nonetheless, there is no evidence of widespread use.

By about 1800, however, cannabis had become more widely known and the subject of a popular craze. One reason was that French soldiers who had served in Napoleon's military campaigns in Egypt brought hashish back with them to their homes in France. Another reason was a wave of romanticism that swept Europe, including an increased interest in exotic stories of the East, notably the *Arabian Nights* and the tales of Marco Polo, which contained references to hashish.

In Paris during the 1840s, a small group of prominent French artists, writers, and intellectuals formed the Club des Hachichins ("Club of the Hashish-Eaters"), where they would gather, in the words of their leader, "to talk of literature, art, and love" while consuming large quantities of hashish. The mixture consisted of a concentrated hemp paste, mixed with butter, sweeteners, and flavorings such as vanilla and cinnamon. Members included Victor Hugo, Alexandre Dumas, Charles Baudelaire, and Honoré de Balzac.

Marijuana and Hashish in the Twentieth Century

Chances are that anyone living in the United States at the beginning of the twentieth century would not have heard of marijuana, much less hashish. By 1890, cotton had replaced hemp as a major cash crop in southern states, although cannabis plants continued to grow wild along roadsides and in the fields. Some patent medicines during this era contained marijuana, but it was a small percentage compared with the number containing opium or cocaine.[7]

It was not until the 1920s that marijuana began to be a noticeable phenomenon. Some historians have related the appearance of marijuana as a recreational drug to social changes brought on by Prohibition, when it was suddenly difficult to obtain good-quality liquor at affordable prices. Its recreational use was largely restricted to jazz musicians and people in show business. "Reefer songs" became the rage of the jazz world; even the mainstream clarinetist and bandleader Benny Goodman had his popular hit "Sweet Marihuana Brown." Marijuana clubs, called tea pads, sprang up in the major cities; more than five hundred were estimated in Harlem alone, outnumbering the speakeasies where illegal alcohol was dispensed. These marijuana establishments were largely tolerated by the authorities because at that time marijuana was not illegal and patrons showed no evidence of making a nuisance of themselves or disturbing the community. Marijuana was not considered a social threat at all.[8]

The Antimarijuana Crusade

This picture started to change by the end of the 1920s and early 1930s. Even though millions of people had never heard of the plant, much less smoked it, marijuana suddenly became widely publicized as a "killer weed." The antimarijuana campaign, orchestrated by the Federal Bureau of Narcotics (FBN), was so intense that the American public quickly became persuaded that marijuana was a pestilence singlehandedly destroying a generation of American youth (see Portrait in Chapter 2).

How did this transformation occur? To understand the way in which marijuana smoking went from relative obscurity to a national social issue, we have to look at some important changes in American society that were taking place at the time.

The practice of smoking marijuana and the cultivation of cannabis plants for that purpose had been filtering slowly into the United States since 1900 as a result of the migration of Mexican immigrants. They entered the country through towns along the Mexican border and along the Gulf Coast. In Mexican communities, marijuana was, in the words of one historian, "a casual adjunct to life ... —a relaxant, a folk remedy for headaches, a mild euphoriant cheaply obtained for two cigarettes for the dollar."[9]

These immigrant communities were met with hostility and prejudice, and the smoking of an alien and foreign-sounding substance did not smooth their reception. In effect, it was a social rerun of the Chinese-opium panic of the 1870s (see Chapter 5) but with the Mexicans on the receiving end. Unsubstantiated rumors about the violent behavioral consequences of marijuana smoking among Mexicans began to spread. In addition, economic upheavals during the Depression made it particularly convenient to vent frustrations on an immigrant group perceived as competing for a dwindling number of American jobs and straining an already weak economy. Anti-marijuana-themed movies with provocative titles such as *Reefer Madness* and *Marihuana: Weed with Roots in Hell* were produced and distributed during the late 1930s and early 1940s with the encouragement of the FBN.

Considering the mounting hysteria against marijuana smoking and cannabis use in general during this period, it is not surprising that the Marijuana Tax Act of 1937 had little difficulty in gaining support in Congress. As with the Harrison Act of 1914, the regulation of marijuana was accomplished indirectly. The act did not ban marijuana; it merely required everyone connected with marijuana, from growers to buyers, to pay a tax. It was a deceptively simple procedure that, in effect, made it virtually impossible to comply with the law. In the absence of compliance, a person was in violation of the act and therefore subject to arrest. It was the state's responsibility to make possession of marijuana or any other product of *Cannabis sativa* illegal. Shortly after the tax act of 1937 was imposed, all of the states adopted a uniform law that did just that.

The official stance of the federal government continued to be that marijuana smoking was tied to antisocial behavior. Harry Anslinger, FBN director, wrote in 1953:

> Those who are accustomed to habitual use of the drug are said eventually to develop a delirious rage after its administration during which they are temporarily, at least, irresponsible and prone to commit violent crimes.... Much of the most irrational juvenile violence and killing that has written a new chapter of shame and tragedy is traceable directly to this hemp intoxication.[10]

Over time, the "pharmacological violence" theory faded into oblivion, in the absence of any evidence to support it. In its place, however, a new concept regarding marijuana smoking was introduced by the FBN: the gateway theory. According to this idea, marijuana was purported to be dangerous because its abuse would lead to the abuse of heroin, cocaine, or other illicit drugs. This gateway hypothesis will be closely examined later in the chapter.

While marijuana research declined, penalties for involvement with it steadily increased. In certain states, the penalties were severe. Judges frequently had the option of sentencing a marijuana seller or user to life imprisonment. In Georgia, a second offense of selling marijuana to a minor could be punishable by death.

Ironically, in 1969, more than three decades after its passage, the U.S. Supreme Court ruled the 1937 Marijuana Tax Act to be unconstitutional precisely because marijuana possession was illegal. The argument was made that requiring a person to pay a tax (and that was all that the 1937 act concerned) so as to possess an illegal substance amounted to a form of self-incrimination, which would violate that person's rights under the Fifth Amendment to the Constitution. The case in question here was brought to the high court by none other than

This promotional poster for the 1942 film *Devil's Harvest* depicted the supposed evils of smoking marijuana.

Timothy Leary (see Portrait in Chapter 6), and the court's decision succeeded in overturning a marijuana conviction judged against him.[11]

Challenging Old Ideas about Marijuana

Prior to 1960, arrests and seizures for possession of marijuana were relatively rare and attracted little or no public attention. The social consensus was that marijuana was a drug that could be comfortably associated with, and isolated to, ethnic and racial minorities. It was relatively easy for most Americans to avoid the drug entirely. In any event, until 1960, involvement with marijuana was a

reefer: A marijuana cigarette.
joint: A marijuana cigarette.

deviant act, during an era when there was little tolerance for personal deviance.

By the mid-1960s, this consensus began to dissolve. Marijuana smoking suddenly was an attraction on the campuses of U.S. colleges and universities, affecting a wide cross-section of the nation. At the same time, the experimental use of drugs, particularly marijuana, by young people set the stage for a wholesale questioning of what it meant to respect authority, on an individual as well as a governmental level. The more recent issues of medical marijuana and marijuana decriminalization will be addressed later in the chapter.

Acute Effects of Marijuana

In the United States, THC is usually ingested by smoking a hand-rolled marijuana cigarette referred to as a **reefer** or, more commonly, a **joint.** Exactly how much THC is administered depends on the specific THC concentration level in the marijuana (often referred to as its quality), how deeply the smoke is inhaled into the lungs, and how long it is held in the lungs before being exhaled. In general, an experienced smoker will ingest more THC than a novice smoker by virtue of being able to inhale more deeply and hold the marijuana smoke in his or her lungs longer, for twenty-five seconds or longer, thus maximizing THC absorption into the bloodstream.

The inhalation of any drug into the lungs produces extremely rapid absorption, as noted in earlier chapters, and marijuana is no exception. In the case of THC, effects are felt within seconds. Peak levels are reached in the blood within ten minutes and start to decline shortly afterward. Behavioral and psychological effects generally last from two to four hours. At this point, low levels of THC linger for several days because they are absorbed into fatty tissue and excretion from fatty tissue is notoriously slow.[12]

One implication arising from a slow elimination rate is that the residual THC, left over from a previous administration, can intensify the effect of marijuana on a subsequent occasion. In this way, regular marijuana smokers often report a quicker and more easily obtained high, achieved with a smaller quantity of drug, than more intermittent smokers.[13]

It is also important to see the implication of slow marijuana elimination with regard to drug testing. Urine tests for possible marijuana abuse typically measure levels of THC metabolites (broken down remnants of THC); because of the slow biotransformation of marijuana, these metabolites are detectable in the urine even when the smoker no longer feels high or shows any behavioral effects. Metabolites can remain in the body several days after smoking a single joint and several weeks later if there has been chronic marijuana smoking. Some tests are so sensitive that a positive level for marijuana can result from passive inhalation of marijuana smoke-filled air in a closed environment, even though the THC levels in these cases are substantially below levels that result from active smoking. The bottom line is that marijuana testing procedures generally are unable to indicate *when* marijuana has been smoked (if it has been smoked at all), only that exposure to marijuana has occurred (see Chapter 8).[14]

Acute Physiological Effects

Immediate physiological effects after smoking marijuana are relatively minor. It has been estimated that a human would need to ingest a dose of marijuana that was from twenty thousand to forty thousand times the effective dose before death would occur.[15] Nonetheless, there is a dose-related increase in heart rate during early stages of marijuana ingestion, up to 160 beats per minute when dose levels are high. Blood pressure either increases, decreases, or remains the same, depending primarily on whether the individual is standing, sitting, or lying down.[16] A dilation of blood vessels on the cornea resulting in bloodshot eyes peaks about an hour after smoking a joint. Frequently there is a drying of the mouth and an urge to drink.

Other physiological reactions are inconsistent, and at least part of the inconsistency can be attributed to cultural and interpersonal influences. For example, the observation that marijuana smoking makes you feel extremely hungry and crave especially sweet things to eat (often referred to as "having the munchies") generally holds true in studies of North Americans but not for Jamaicans, who consider marijuana an appetite suppressant.

Likewise, North Americans often report enhanced sexual responses following marijuana use, whereas in India marijuana is considered a sexual depressant. These reactions, being subjective in nature, can very well be slanted in one direction or the other by the mind-set (expectations) of the marijuana smoker going into the experience. A good example is the effect on sexual responses. If you believe that marijuana turns you on sexually, the chances are that it will.

Although expectations undoubtedly play a prominent role here, we should be aware of the possibility that varying effects also may be due to differences in the THC concentration of the marijuana being smoked. In the case of sexual reactivity, studies of male marijuana smokers have shown that low-dose marijuana tends to enhance sexual desire, while high-dose marijuana tends to depress it, even to the point of impotence. It is quite possible that the enhancement is a result of a brief rise in the male sex hormone, testosterone, and the depression a result of a rebound effect that lowers testosterone below normal levels. Typically, the THC concentration in India is higher than that in North America. As a result, we would expect different effects on sexual reactivity. The same argument could be made with respect to the differences in marijuana's effect on appetite.[17]

In 2006, approximately 291,000 drug-related emergency department (ED) visits in the DAWN statistics (see Chapter 2) involved marijuana, making it the second highest category behind cocaine. In only a small percentage of these cases, however, was marijuana the sole drug present in the patient's system at the time. In general, marijuana-related emergency department incidents have risen since the 1990s. Whether this increase is the result of more people smoking marijuana, higher THC concentration in the available marijuana, or the greater incidence of marijuana being combined with alcohol or some other drug remains uncertain.[18]

Acute Psychological and Behavioral Effects

Chapter 5 noted that a first-time heroin abuser frequently finds the experience more aversive than pleasurable. With marijuana, it is likely that a first-time smoker will feel no discernible effects at all. It takes some practice to be able to inhale deeply and keep the smoke in the lungs long enough (up to forty seconds) for a minimal level of THC, particularly in low-quality marijuana, to take effect. Novices often have to be instructed to focus on some aspect of the intoxicated state to start to feel intoxicated, but the psychological reactions, once they do occur, are fairly predictable.

The marijuana high, as the name implies, is a feeling of euphoria and well-being. Marijuana smokers typically report an increased awareness of their surroundings, as well as a sharpened sense of sight and sound. Frequently they feel that everything is suddenly very funny, and even the most innocent comments or events can set off uproarious laughter. Usually mundane ideas can seem filled with profound implications, and the individual may feel that creativity has been increased. As with LSD, however, no objective evidence shows that creativity is enhanced by marijuana. Commonly, time seems to pass more slowly while a person is under the influence of marijuana, and events appear to be elongated in duration. Finally, marijuana smokers frequently report that they feel sleepy and sometimes dreamy. The usual THC concentrations of

Health Line

Can You Control a Marijuana High?

Experienced marijuana smokers often report that they can turn off their high, if the motivation is sufficiently strong, and behave as if in a normal (undrugged) state. Is this really true?

Controlled laboratory studies, in which specific behaviors can be carefully measured, provide the only source for a scientific answer. In one such study, a group of marijuana smokers were instructed to minimize, as much as they could, the subjective effects of marijuana. When given a time estimation task, these subjects performed more accurately than subjects who were not given the instructions. When given a recall task, however, the two groups were not different in their performance. All the marijuana smokers showed an impairment, regardless of efforts by some of them to resist the drug's effects.

So it appears that only some behaviors are subject to manipulation. Marijuana smokers may *feel* normal, but other aspects of their behavior remain impaired.

Source: Cappell, Howard, and Pliner, Patricia (1974). Cannabis intoxication: The role of pharmacological and psychological variables. In Loren L. Miller (Ed.), *Marijuana: Effects of human behavior.* Orlando, FL: Academic Press, pp. 233–264.

---

a marijuana joint are not sufficient to be particularly sleep-inducing, though stronger cannabis preparations with higher THC can have strong sleep-inducing effects, particularly when combined with alcohol.[19]

At the same time, marijuana produces significant deficits in behavior. The major deficit is a decline in the ability to carry out tasks that involve attention and memory. Speech will be increasingly fragmented and disjointed; individuals often will forget what they, or others, have just said. The problem is that marijuana typically causes such a rush of distracting ideas to come to mind that it is difficult to concentrate on new information coming in. By virtue of a diminished focus of concentration, the performance of both short-term and long-term memory tasks is impaired. In general, these difficulties increase in magnitude as a direct function of the level of THC in the marijuana (Health Line).[20]

It should not be surprising that complex motor tasks, such as driving a car, are also more poorly performed while a person is under the influence of marijuana. It is not necessarily a matter of reaction time; studies of marijuana smokers in automobile simulators indicate that they are as quick to respond as control subjects. The problem arises from a difficulty in attending to peripheral information and making an appropriate response while driving.[21] One researcher has put it this way:

> Marijuana-intoxicated drivers might be able to stop a car as fast as they normally could, but they may not be as quick to notice things that they should stop for. This is probably because they are attending to internal events rather than what is happening on the road.[22]

Given these observations in the laboratory and on the road, it should not be surprising that marijuana use would increase the risk of having an automobile accident. Surveys that have examined accident rates among drivers testing positive for THC in their bloodstreams have shown them to be about three to seven times more likely to be involved in an accident than drivers testing negative for THC or alcohol.[23]

The decline in sensory–motor performance will persist well after the point at which the marijuana smoker no longer feels high, when there has been chronic heavy marijuana use. Significant impairments in attention and memory tasks have been demonstrated among heavy marijuana users (daily smokers) twenty-four hours after they had last used the drug. Therefore, we have to recognize the possibility that some important aspects of behavior can be impaired following marijuana smoking, even when an individual is not aware of it. This effect may be due to the very slow rate with which marijuana is eliminated from the body.[24]

Acute emotional problems as a result of smoking marijuana are rare among Americans, who typically are exposed to relatively low THC concentrations, though some distortion of body image, paranoia, and anxiety may occur. It is possible that marijuana smoking among individuals predisposed toward or recovering from a psychosis may trigger psychotic behavior. Nonetheless, there is little or no support for the idea that low doses of marijuana will provoke such reactions in otherwise normal individuals.

In contrast, a substantially higher incidence of psychiatric problems arising from THC exposure has been reported in India and North Africa. In such cases, however, the THC concentrations being ingested, the frequency with which THC is ingested, and the duration of THC exposure over a lifetime are all generally greater than would be encountered in the United States.[25]

Effects of Marijuana on the Brain

When THC was isolated in 1964 as the primary agent for the intoxicating properties of marijuana, the next step was to find out specifically how THC affected the brain to produce these effects. In 1990, the mechanism was discovered. Just as with morphine, special receptors in the brain are stimulated specifically by THC. They are concentrated in areas of the brain that are important for short-term memory and motor control. Unlike morphine-sensitive receptors, however, the THC-sensitive receptors are not found in the lower portions of the brain that control breathing. As a result, no matter how high the THC

concentration in the brain, there is no danger of an accidental death by asphyxiation.

Once we have identified a specific receptor for a drug, the question inevitably becomes, Why is it there? As noted in Chapter 5, when the morphine-sensitive receptor was discovered, it made sense to speculate about a natural morphine-like substance that would fit into that receptor. The same speculation surrounded the discovery of the THC-sensitive receptor until 1992, when researchers isolated a natural substance, dubbed **anandamide,** that activates this receptor and appears to produce the same effects as THC in the brain.

The functions of anandamide and THC-sensitive receptors remain largely a mystery. One study has found that THC stimulates neurons in the nucleus accumbens in rats, the same area that is affected by a host of other psychoactive drugs, including heroin, cocaine, and nicotine. The effect, however, is much weaker than with drugs that produce strong signs of dependence. Animals will self-administer marijuana in laboratory studies and, in fact, are able to discriminate high-potency from low-potency marijuana, but their behavior is not as compulsive as that observed with heroin, cocaine, or nicotine.[26]

Chronic Effects of Marijuana

Is chronic marijuana smoking harmful over a period of time? What is the extent of tolerance and dependence? Are there long-term consequences for organ systems in the body? Will marijuana lessen one's potential as a productive human being in society? Will marijuana abuse lead to the abuse of other drugs? These are questions to be considered next.

Tolerance

It is frequently reported that experienced marijuana smokers become intoxicated more quickly and to a greater extent than nonexperienced smokers, when exposed to marijuana joints with equivalent THC concentrations. For many years, this observation suggested that repeated administrations of marijuana produced sensitization, or reverse tolerance (a greater sensitivity), rather than tolerance (a lesser sensitivity). If this were true, then we would have been faced with the troubling

---

anandamide (a-NAN-duh-mide): A naturally occurring chemical in the brain that fits into THC-sensitive receptor sites, producing many of the same effects as marijuana.

conclusion that marijuana operates in a totally opposite way to any other psychoactive drug considered so far. As it turns out, when animals or humans are studied in the laboratory, marijuana smoking shows tolerance effects that are consistent and clear-cut.

Why, then, the difference with the experience of humans outside the laboratory? One factor involves the way in which we measure the quantity of THC consumed. Reaching an effective high from marijuana requires some degree of practice. For example, novice marijuana smokers may not have mastered the breathing technique necessary to allow the minimal level of THC to enter the lungs. They may have to smoke a relatively large number of marijuana joints initially before they achieve a high. Later, when they have acquired the technique, they may need fewer joints to accomplish the same effect. In these circumstances, a calculation of the number of joints consumed does not reflect the amount of THC ingested. If you were to control the THC content entering the body, as is done in laboratory studies, you would find the predictable results of tolerance over repeated administrations.

Another factor complicating tolerance studies involves the slow elimination rate of marijuana. Regular marijuana smokers are likely to have a residual amount of THC still in the system. This buildup of THC would elevate the total quantity of THC consumed with every joint and induce a quicker high. Once again, the impression of sensitization is false; it is a matter of enhanced effects being a result of an accumulation of THC in the body. When dosage levels are controlled, the results indicate a consistent pattern of tolerance rather than sensitization. In general, tolerance effects following repeated administrations of THC are greater as the dosage level of THC increases.[27]

Withdrawal and Dependence

On the basis of early studies conducted in the 1970s, it appeared that evidence of physical dependence (that is, the observation of withdrawal symptoms) following chronic administration of marijuana was limited to circumstances in which the level of THC ingestion was extreme. In one study, human volunteers were administered large doses of THC every four hours for ten to twenty days. Within twelve hours after the last administration, subjects reported physical symptoms that included hot flashes, irritability, restlessness, and insomnia. In contrast, in another study in which subjects smoked one marijuana cigarette daily for twenty-eight days, a condition closer to the typical exposure to marijuana, no withdrawal symptoms were observed.[28]

More recent studies, however, have shown that withdrawal effects can occur even with more moderate levels of THC consumed over shorter periods of time. Abstinence from smoking marijuana cigarettes with approximately 2 to 3 percent THC levels or equivalent oral doses of THC, administered four times a day over a four-day period, resulted in feelings of irritability, stomach pain, anxiety, and loss of appetite. These symptoms began within forty-eight hours and lasted at least two days.[29] Therefore, it is quite possible that daily marijuana use among chronic marijuana smokers is maintained, at least in part, because of its alleviation of withdrawal symptoms. Nonetheless, the symptoms involved here are substantially milder than those associated with the chronic use of heroin (Chapter 5) or alcohol (Chapter 10).

There is also evidence of marijuana craving, indicating a level of psychological dependence in some marijuana smokers, but it is difficult to measure the extent of these feelings or to determine whether these effects are due to circumstances in which marijuana is used in conjunction with other drugs. With marijuana smoking at the THC levels commonly encountered in the United States, there is nowhere near the degree of obsessive drug seeking and compulsive drug-taking behavior associated with alcohol, opiates, or stimulant drugs.[30]

Cardiovascular Effects

THC produces significant increases in heart rate, but there is no conclusive evidence of adverse effects in the cardiovascular functioning in young, healthy people. The reason why the emphasis is on a specific age group is that most of the studies looking at possible long-term cardiovascular effects have involved marijuana smokers under the age of thirty-five; little or no information has been compiled about older populations. For those people with preexisting disorders such as heart disease, high blood pressure, or arteriosclerosis (hardening of the arteries), it is known that the acute effects of marijuana on heart rate and blood pressure can worsen their condition.

Respiratory Effects and the Risk of Cancer

The technique of marijuana smoking involves the deep and maintained inhalation into the lungs of unfiltered smoke on a repetitive basis, probably the worst scenario for incurring chronic pulmonary problems. In addition, a marijuana joint (when compared with a tobacco cigarette) typically contains about the same levels of tars, 50 percent more hydrocarbons, and an unknown amount of possible contaminants (Table 7.1). Joints are often smoked more completely because the smoker tries to waste as little marijuana as possible.

TABLE 7.1

A comparison of the components of marijuana and tobacco smoke

COMPONENT	MARIJUANA	TOBACCO
Carbon monoxide (mg)	17.6	20.2
Carbon dioxide (mg)	57.3	65.0
Ammonia (micrograms)	228.0	178.0
Acetaldehyde (micrograms)	1,200.0	980.0
Acetone (micrograms)*	443.0	578.0
Benzene (micrograms)*	76.0	67.0
Toluene (micrograms)*	112.0	108.0
THC (tetrahydrocannabinol) (micrograms)	820.0	—
Nicotine (micrograms)	—	2,850.0
Napthalene (nanograms)	3,000.0	1,200.0

*See Chapter 13 for information about the health risks of inhaling some of these chemicals.

Source: Julien, Robert M. (2001). *A primer of drug action* (9th ed.). New York: Worth, p. 317.

Given all these factors, marijuana smoking presents several risks. One of the immediate consequences affects the process of breathing. When marijuana is inhaled initially, the passageways for air entering and leaving the lungs widen, but after chronic exposure, an opposite reaction occurs. As a result, symptoms of asthma and other breathing difficulties are increased. Overall, while the effects of a single inhalation of marijuana smoke present greater problems than a single inhalation of tobacco smoke, we need to remember that the patterns of consumption are far from comparable. All things considered, on a statistical basis, you can think of one joint as being equivalent to five cigarettes in terms of the amount of carbon monoxide intake and to four cigarettes in terms of tar intake. The use of a water pipe reduces the harm somewhat, but the risks are still present.

Molecular abnormalities in the respiratory tracts of heavy marijuana smokers have been identified that resemble the changes in the respiratory tracts of cigarette smokers. A recent study has shown that long-term marijuana smoking causes an obstruction of air flow in the lungs, resulting in asthma and bronchitis. The effect of a single marijuana joint is equivalent to up to five tobacco cigarettes in this regard. However, marijuana smoking does not increase the risk of developing emphysema, a chronic lung disease associated with tobacco smoking (see Chapter 11).

Given these risks, does smoking marijuana produce a higher incidence of cancer? There is no evidence of definitive increases in lung cancer rates among marijuana smokers, after controlling for tobacco use. In fact, no increases in risk for many types of cancer have been found as a result of marijuana use, once alcohol and cigarette use has been excluded from the analysis. But it may still be too soon to answer the question of cancer risk definitively. The marijuana smokers who were twenty years old in the late 1960s have just approached the peak ages when cancers appear. Those individuals more recently exposed to higher-potency marijuana, such as those whose marijuana experience began in the 1990s, are substantially younger. Therefore, the extent to which marijuana smoking is a risk factor for cancer remains a question for the future. Fortunately, there is the possibility, as is the case with cigarette smoking (see Chapter 11), that the risk of cancer will decline after a person has stopped smoking marijuana.[31]

Effects on the Immune System

When THC is administered to animals, the immune system is suppressed, resulting in a reduction in the body's defense reactions to infection and disease. In humans, the evidence is inconclusive. Some studies indicate that THC has a suppressive effect; others indicate that no immunological changes occur at all. Because marijuana smoking has not been found to be associated with a higher incidence of any major chronic disease, we can tentatively conclude that marijuana smoking does not have a major impact on the immune system. Yet long-term epidemiological studies, in which marijuana-exposed and control populations are compared with regard to the frequency of various diseases, have not been conducted on a large-scale basis.[32]

Effects on Sexual Functioning and Reproduction

The reproductive systems of both men and women are adversely affected by marijuana smoking. In men, marijuana reduces the level of testosterone, reduces sperm count in the semen, and increases the percentage of abnormally formed sperm. In women, marijuana use results in a reduction in the level of luteinizing hormone (LH), a hormone necessary for the fertilized egg to be implanted in the uterus. As little as one marijuana joint smoked immediately following ovulation is evidently sufficient for this LH suppression to occur. Despite these hormonal changes in both males and females, however, little or no effect on fertility has been observed.[33]

The research is sparse on the question, but there does not appear to be evidence of birth defects in the offspring of women who have smoked marijuana during their pregnancy. Studies indicate, however, a lower birth weight and shorter length among newborns, as well as a reduction in the mother's milk. It may be unfair to associate these effects specifically with marijuana smoking because other drugs including alcohol and nicotine are often being consumed during the same period. Even so, the best advice remains that women should avoid marijuana during pregnancy.[34]

Long-Term Cognitive Effects and the Amotivational Syndrome

In 1968, William McGlothin, a psychologist, and Louis West, a psychiatrist, proposed that chronic marijuana smoking among young people was responsible for a generalized sense of apathy in their lives and an indifference to any long-term plans or conventional goals. These changes were called the **amotivational syndrome**. In their words,

> Regular marijuana use may contribute to the development of more passive, inward-turning personality characteristics. For numerous middle-class students, the subtly progressive change from conforming, achievement-oriented behavior to a state of relaxed and careless drifting has followed their use of significant amounts of marijuana. . . . Such individuals exhibit greater introversion, become totally involved with the present at the expense of future goals, and demonstrate a strong tendency toward regressive, childlike magical thinking.[35]

In effect, McGothlin and West, and probably a large number of other people in the late 1960s, were saying, "These people don't seem to care anymore and marijuana's to blame for it."

The issue of the amotivational syndrome revolves around two basic questions that need to be examined separately. The first question deals with whether such a syndrome exists in the first place, and the second deals with whether chronic abuse of marijuana is a causal factor. As to the existence of the syndrome, the evidence does suggest that students who smoke marijuana are at a disadvantage academically. Studies of high school stu-

amotivational syndrome: A state of listlessness and personality change involving a generalized apathy and indifference to long-range plans.

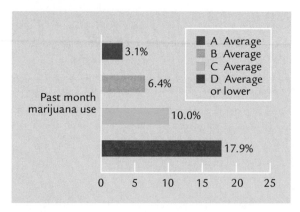

FIGURE 7.1

Percentages of past month marijuana and blunt use among students aged 12 to 17 and semester grade average.

Note: Blunts are hollowed-out cigars refilled with marijuana.

Source: Substance Abuse and Mental Health Services Administration (2007). Use of marijuana and blunts among adolescents: 2005. *The NSDUH Report,* p. 3.

dents indicate that those who smoke marijuana on a regular basis (weekly or more frequently) earn lower grades in school (Figure 7.1), are less likely to continue on to college, are more likely to drop out, and miss more classes than those who do not smoke it.[36] In a survey of high school students graduating in the early 1980s, those who smoked marijuana on a daily basis reported several problems in their lives that are related to motivation: a loss of energy (43 percent), negative effects on relationships (39 percent), interference with work and the ability to think clearly (37 percent), less interest in other activities (37 percent), and inferior performance in school or on the job (34 percent).[37] It is likely that these percentages would be roughly the same today.

These changes are genuine, but we cannot easily establish a direct *causal* link between marijuana and such global problems, other than to acknowledge that the presence of THC in a student's system during school hours would be reflected in relatively low levels of overall academic performance. More broadly speaking, we cannot exclude the possibility that marijuana smoking may be, in the words of one expert in the field, "just one behavior in a constellation of related problem behaviors and personality and familial factors" that hamper an adolescent's ability to do well in school and in life.[38] We also cannot exclude the possibility that an involvement with marijuana may closely correlate with involvement in a deviant subculture, a group of friends and associates who feel alienated from traditional values such as school achievement and a promising future (see Chapter 1). Either of these factors, in combination with the regular ingestion of marijuana, can account for the motivational changes that are observed. The point is that we cannot conclude that such life-style changes are purely pharmacological.

While it is clear that acute marijuana intoxication produces significant cognitive deficits, as evidenced by reduced scores on tasks of attentiveness and memory, the question remains whether these problems are increased or perhaps may become irreversible as a result of long-term marijuana use. Large and well-controlled studies have shown that cognitive deficits in heavy marijuana smokers, relative to nonusers, are observed after twelve to seventy-two hours of abstinence. In other words, the specific signs of cognitive impairment among long-term marijuana smokers may linger for as long as three days after active marijuana smoking. In one study, however, testing after twenty-eight days of abstinence revealed *equivalent* performance scores between nonusers and users of marijuana, even though the latter group had smoked on average about fifteen thousand times over a period ranging from ten to thirty-three years. No correlation was seen between the test scores after twenty-eight days of abstinence and the number of episodes of marijuana use over an individual's lifetime. Therefore, it appears that behavioral problems related to attention and memory among heavy marijuana smokers can be reversed by stopping marijuana use.[39] On the other hand, recent studies indicate that specific brain abnormalities associated with long-term heavy marijuana use have a negative impact on successful information-processing abilities. These neuroanatomical changes may not be reversible.[40]

The Gateway Hypothesis

A widely publicized concern with respect to marijuana smoking deals with the relationship between marijuana use and the subsequent abuse of illicit drugs such as amphetamines, cocaine, or heroin. The contention that marijuana leads to a greater incidence of drug abuse in general is referred to as the **gateway hypothesis.** As in the consideration of the amotivational syndrome, the evidence for this hypothesis must be studied very carefully.

With respect to the gateway hypothesis, we should address three separate issues: (1) whether a fixed sequential relationship exists between the initiation of marijuana use and other forms of drug-taking behavior, (2) whether marijuana use represents a significant risk factor for future drug-taking behavior, specifically increasing the likelihood of using other illicit drugs, and (3) whether marijuana actually causes the use of other illicit drugs.

The Sequencing Question

One of the best-replicated findings in the long-term study of drug use is a developmental sequence of involvement (stages of progression) in drug-taking behavior. In the United States as well as other Western societies, use of alcohol and cigarettes precedes marijuana use, and marijuana use precedes use of other illicit drugs. As public health researcher Denise Kandel has expressed it:

> Very few individuals who have tried cocaine and heroin have not already used marijuana; the majority have previously used alcohol or tobacco.[41]

Nonetheless, it is important to point out that an overwhelming proportion of young marijuana smokers do *not* go on to use other illicit drugs. As expressed in a 1999 newspaper editorial on this point, "millions of baby boomers . . . once did, indeed, inhale. They later went into business, not cocaine or heroin."[42]

The Association Question

From a statistical perspective, the association between marijuana use and subsequent use of other illicit drugs is not controversial. Generally speaking, marijuana smokers are several times more likely to consume illicit drugs such as cocaine and heroin during their lifetimes than are nonmarijuana smokers. Not surprisingly, the greater the frequency of marijuana smoking and the earlier an individual first engages in marijuana smoking, the greater the likelihood of his or her becoming involved with other illicit drugs in the future.

A precise determination of the magnitude of risk involved in marijuana use requires studies that take into account a range of genetic and environmental variables that might act as risk or protective factors for drug-taking behavior (see Chapter 1). A recent study set out to control for these variables by investigating a specific subpopulation of twins, one of whom reported marijuana use by the age of seventeen and the other who reported no marijuana use at all. Examining twins permitted the researchers to calculate the increased risk of future drug-taking behavior when environmental factors (in the case of fraternal twins) and both environmental and genetic factors (in the case of identical twins) were controlled. Results showed that early marijuana users were about two and one-half times more likely to use heroin later in life, four times more likely to use cocaine or other stimulants, and five times more likely

gateway hypothesis: The idea that the abuse of a specific drug will inherently lead to the abuse of other, more harmful drugs.

to use hallucinogens. In general, they were twice as likely to become alcoholic and twice as likely to develop any form of illicit drug abuse or dependence.

The question of whether future twin studies using this approach will find the increased risk from marijuana use to be *higher than the increased risk from alcohol or tobacco use* remains unanswered. In any case, the fact that marijuana use is one of the risk factors for illicit drug use in other forms reinforces the need to develop intervention programs for marijuana users that might serve to prevent subsequent drug use, as well as prevention programs for youths to reduce the incidence of marijuana use in the first place.[43]

In the final analysis, however, the statistical relationship between marijuana smoking and other forms of drug-taking behavior merely reflects the sequential pattern of drug use among multiple-drug (polydrug) users. Essentially, they initiate the use of high-prevalence drugs (such as alcohol, tobacco, and/or marijuana) earlier than they initiate the use of low-prevalence drugs (such as cocaine or heroin). This effect can be viewed as not due to the drugs themselves but rather to the relative differences in prevalence rates. Numerous statistical relationships exist between other types of common and uncommon behaviors in our lives:

> *For example, most people who ride a motorcycle (a fairly rare activity) have ridden a bicycle (a fairly common activity). Indeed, the prevalence of motorcycle riding among people who have never ridden a bicycle is probably extremely low. However, bicycle riding does not cause motorcycle riding, and increases in the former will not lead automatically to increases in the latter.[44]*

The Causation Question

The strongest form of the gateway hypothesis relates to the possibility of a causal link between marijuana smoking and the use of other illicit drugs. With respect to the causation issue, Erich Goode, a sociologist and drug-abuse researcher, has distinguished between two schools of thought, which he calls the intrinsic argument and the sociocultural argument.

The *intrinsic argument* asserts that some inherent property of marijuana exposure itself leads to physical or psychological dependence on other illicit drugs. According to this viewpoint, the pleasurable sensations of marijuana create a biological urge to consume more potent substances, through a combination of drug tolerance and drug dependence.

In contrast, the *sociocultural argument* holds that the relationship exists not because of the pharmacological effects of marijuana but because of the activities, friends, and acquaintances that are associated with marijuana smoking. In other words, the sociocultural explanation asserts that those who smoke marijuana tend to have friends who not only smoke marijuana themselves but also abuse other drugs. These friends are likely to have positive attitudes toward substance abuse in general and to provide opportunities for drug experimentation.

Professionals in the drug-abuse field have concluded that if any such causal link exists, the result would be

---

Quick Concept Check 7.2

Understanding the Adverse Effects of Chronic Marijuana Abuse

Check your understanding of the possible adverse effects of either acute or chronic exposure to marijuana by checking off true or false next to each of the assertions.

ASSERTION	TRUE	FALSE
1. The immune system will be impaired.		
2. The chances of getting cancer will be unaffected.		
3. Driving ability will be significantly impaired.		
4. Birth defects will be more frequent.		
5. It is likely that academic performance will decline when a person smokes marijuana regularly.		
6. Marijuana smoking will cause the smoker to experiment with cocaine or heroin in the future.		
7. Marijuana smoking in adolescence will generally be preceded by experimentation with tobacco or alcohol.		

Answers: 1. false   2. false   3. true   4. false   5. true
6. false   7. true

---

socioculturally based rather than related to the pharmacological properties of marijuana itself. The consensus is that any early exposure to psychoactive substances in general, and illicit drugs such as marijuana in particular, represents a "deviance-prone pattern of behavior" that will be reflected in a higher incidence of exposure to psychoactive drugs of many types later in life. It is interesting to note that early adolescent marijuana use among males also increases the risk in late adolescence of delinquency, having multiple sexual partners, not always using condoms during sex, perceiving drugs as not harmful, and having problems with cigarettes and alcohol. Generally speaking, marijuana smokers show a greater inclination toward risk-taking behavior and are more unconventional with regard to social norms.[45]

Patterns of Marijuana Smoking

From as early as their days in elementary school, most young Americans have had to come to terms with marijuana as a pervasive element in their lives. Just as nearly all adolescents have had to make the decision whether to drink or not to drink, and whether to smoke cigarettes or not to smoke them, they also have had to decide whether to smoke or not smoke marijuana.

Marijuana is undoubtedly the dominant illicit drug in U.S. society, used by 73 percent of current illicit drug users (Figure 7.2). For about half of illicit drug users, marijuana is the *only* illicit drug being used. From the National Survey on Drug Use and Health conducted in 2007, it is estimated that an astounding 101 million Americans, about 40 percent of the U.S. population over the age of twelve, have smoked marijuana at least once during their lives. About 14 million Americans, about one out of sixteen, are estimated to have smoked marijuana within the last thirty days. Among forty-five-year-old Americans who have attained at least a high school education, approximately 75 percent have tried marijuana at least once in their lives.

Domestic marijuana growing represents the number one cash crop in the United States, with revenues of more than $30 billion per year. Large-scale marijuana farms, financed by Mexican drug cartels, have been discovered recently in the steep Sierra Nevada foothills of Sequoia National Park in California. Almost 60 percent of the marijuana plants eradicated in California in 2002 were found on state or federal land. In addition, Canadian growers in British Columbia have developed a hydroponic technique of marijuana cultivation, in which plants are grown indoors in nutrient-rich water rather than soil. This form of cultivation allows plants to grow faster and produce

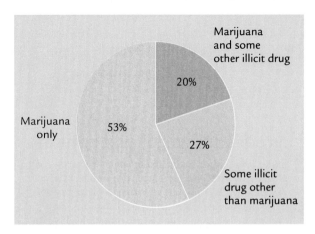

FIGURE 7.2

Types of drugs used by illicit drug users aged twelve or older in the past month in 2007.

Source: Substance Abuse and Mental Health Services Administration (2008). *Results from the 2007 National Survey on Drug Use and Health: National findings.* Rockville, MD: Office of Applied Studies, Substance Abuse and Mental Health Services Administration, p. 16.

larger leaves, flowers, and buds. As a result, a higher-potency marijuana, with THC levels as high as 15 to 25 percent, can be marketed.[46]

Through the University of Michigan survey we can get an idea of the prevalence rates among young people, particularly since 1992. Among high school seniors surveyed in 2008, approximately 32 percent reported having smoked marijuana in the past year, 19 percent reported having done so in the past month, and 5 percent smoked on a daily basis. Granted, these numbers are still below the peak levels reached in the late 1970s. However, they continue to be substantially higher than levels observed in 1990 and 1991. Among eighth graders, 11 percent reported smoking marijuana in the past year and 6 percent in the past month, also up substantially from the early 1990s. The current status of prevention programs, understandably under considerable pressure to reduce rates of marijuana smoking as well as involvement in other drugs among young people, will be examined in Chapter 18.[47]

Current Trends as Causes for Concern

We noted in Chapter 1 that until 1991, the trend in the percentage of students who thought that marijuana smoking and drug abuse in general carried significant

Street Language for Marijuana

In the 1960s, when marijuana smoking first became widely popular, the street language was fairly simple. Marijuana was either grass or pot, and a marijuana cigarette was a joint. Here is an updated sampling of the street language, though the names (and prices) are constantly changing.

- marijuana: grass, weed, 420, skunk, boom, doobie, bud, herb, BC bud (Over the years, more than 600 slang names have been given to marijuana.)
- marijuana and alcohol: Herb and Al
- getting high on marijuana: getting lifted, booted, red, smoked out or choked out, hit the hay, poke, toke up, blast a stick, burn one, fly Mexican Airlines, mow the grass, boot the gong
- $3 bag of marijuana: a tray
- $5 "nickel" bag: a nick (usually just enough for one joint)
- $40 bag: a sandwich bag
- kinds of marijuana: chronic, chocolate tide, indigo, Hawaiian, Tropicana, Acapulco gold, Panama red

- water pipe similar to a bong: a shotgun
- joints: "blunts" (after the Phillies Blunt cigars that marijuana smokers cut open, hollow out, and fill with marijuana; other brands used, White Owls and Dutch Masters)
- hydro: hydroponic marijuana, grown in water

According to the National Survey on Drug Use and Health, more than 50 percent of marijuana users in 2005 between the age of twelve and seventeen employed blunts in marijuana smoking. The popularity of blunts increased with age. Males reported more often than females having smoked marijuana in a blunt during the past month.

Sources: Bureau of Justice Statistics Clearinghouse (1992). *Drugs, crime, and the justice system,* Washington, DC: Department of Justice, pp. 24–25. Henneberger, Melinda (1994, February 6). "Pot" surges back, but it's, like, a whole new world. *New York Times,* Sect. 4, p. 18. Inciardi, James A. (2002). *The war on drugs III.* Boston: Allyn and Bacon, pp. 56–57. Substance Abuse and Mental Health Services Administration (2007, March 9). Use of marijuana and blunts among adolescents: 2005. *The NSDUH Report,* p. 1.

personal risks had been steadily upward. Survey results showed a reversal after 1991. Although roughly half of high school seniors (52 percent) in 2008 considered "regular marijuana smoking" harmful, this figure was down substantially from 79 percent in 1991.[48]

A second concern with regard to present-day marijuana use has to do with an increased potency in the cannabis products that are available. A typical marijuana joint in the psychedelic era contained approximately 1 to 2 percent THC; the average concentration now is around 6 percent. The higher-potency form, sinsemilla, is more widely available than ever before, as is hashish. It is reasonable to assume that the adverse effects of chronic marijuana smoking, with THC concentrations approaching 15 percent in some strains of sinsemilla, will be more intense than the relatively mild symptoms associated with marijuana use in the past (Drugs. . . in Focus).

A third concern applies to any illicit street drug: the possibility for adulteration. As emphasized in earlier chapters, what you buy is not always what you get. Each year brings with it a new group of ingredients, some of them newly introduced drugs and others merely inventive creations from already available materials, ready to be combined with marijuana either to weaken its effects (and increase the profits of the seller) or to change the overall psychoactive result by some synergistic or other interactive effect.

Medical Uses for Marijuana

Even though the medicinal benefits of marijuana have been noted for thousands of years, strong antimarijuana sentiment in the United States made it difficult until the 1970s to conduct an objective appraisal of its clinical applications. Early research in the effectiveness of marijuana to reduce intraocular (within the eye) pressure and dilate bronchioles in the lungs suggested uses as a possible therapy for glaucoma and asthma, respectively. However, new prescription medications have been shown to be as effective as marijuana in the treatment of these disorders. Today the focus has turned toward the treatment of nausea and weight loss, conditions for which medications have been unsuccessful in offering significant relief.

Nausea and Weight Loss

Chemotherapy in the course of cancer treatment produces an extreme and debilitating nausea, lack of appetite, and loss of body weight, symptoms that are clearly counterproductive in helping an individual contend with an ongoing fight against cancer. AIDS patients suffer from similar symptoms, as do those diagnosed with the gastrointestinal ailment Crohn's disease. During these circumstances, standard antiemetic (antivomiting) drugs are frequently ineffective. The beneficial effect of marijuana, specifically THC, as an antiemetic drug is an important application of marijuana as a medical treatment.[49] This chapter's Portrait examines the present-day dilemma of turning to an illegal drug for medicinal purposes.

At the same time, the use of marijuana per se as a therapeutic agent has distinct disadvantages. First, the typical administration through smoking presents, as described earlier, a significant health risk to the lungs. Second, because marijuana is insoluble in water, suspensions in an injectable form cannot be prepared. Since 1985, however, two legal prescription drugs containing THC or a variation of it have been made available in capsule form. **Dronabinol** (brand name: Marinol) is essentially THC in a sesame oil suspension; **nabilone** (brand name: Cesamet) is a synthetic variation of THC. Both drugs have been shown to be clinically effective as anti-nausea treatments, although the personal reactions of patients taking these drugs vary considerably.[50]

The Medical Marijuana Controversy

While Marinol and Cesamet are presently in use, U.S. federal authorities have resisted the reclassification of marijuana itself or any other cannabis product from the Schedule I category of controlled substances (drugs that have no medical application) to the Schedule II category (which includes morphine and cocaine). Only a handful of "compassionate use" applications have been approved, and the entire program for reviewing new applications was curtailed in 1992 (see Portrait).

Despite opposition from federal authorities, advocacy for the medical application of marijuana has grown considerably. Unfortunately, the facts about medical marijuana sometimes have been lost in a thicket of politics and opposing ideologies. A case in point is the interpretation of a major report on the possibility of marijuana as a medical treatment, issued by the Institute of Medicine, a branch of

the National Academy of Sciences, in 1999. In its preface, the report began by acknowledging the problems involved:

> *Although marijuana smoke delivers THC and other cannabinoids to the body, it also delivers harmful substances, including most of those found in tobacco smoke. In addition, plants contain a variable mixture of biologically-active compounds and cannot be expected to provide a precisely defined drug effect. For these reasons, this report concludes that the future of cannabinoid drugs lies not in smoked marijuana, but in chemically-defined drugs that act on the cannabinoid systems that are a natural component of human physiology.*[51]

In focusing on the report's preface, the federal Office of National Drug Control Strategy has emphasized the potential health risks of marijuana smoking and the imprecision of its administration as its justification for the continued prohibition of marijuana for medical purposes. Largely ignored has been one of the report's main statements:

> *Until a nonsmoked, rapid-onset cannabinoid drug delivery system becomes available, we acknowledge that there is no clear alternative for people suffering from chronic conditions that might be relieved by smoking marijuana, such as pain or AIDS wasting.*[52]

In effect, the report concluded that, while not recommending smoked marijuana for long-term use, short-term use appeared to be suitable for treating specific conditions, when patients failed to respond well to traditional medications.

By 2005, eleven U.S. States (Alaska, California, Colorado, Hawaii, Maine, Maryland, Montana, Nevada, Oregon, Vermont, and Washington) had authorized marijuana smoking for the relief of pain and discomfort or the control of nausea and weight loss, when prescribed by a physician. Nonetheless, the U.S. Supreme Court in 2005 ruled that legalization of medical marijuana at the state level could not supersede federal regulations on the matter. The majority opinion upheld the power of the federal government to prohibit the possession and use of marijuana for medical purposes, even in those states that permit it.

Interestingly, the decision was based not on arguments related to the possible merits of medical marijuana as a treatment, but rather on the issue of interstate commerce. In effect, the court asserted that it was well

---

dronabinol (droh-NAB-ih-nol): A prescription drug containing delta-9-tetrahydrocannabinol (THC). Brand name is Marinol.

nabilone (NAB-ih-lone): A prescription drug containing a synthetic variation of delta-9-tetrahydrocannabinol (THC). Brand name is Cesamet.

PORTRAIT

Angel McClary Raich—The Woman Behind the *Raich v. Ashcroft* Decision

In the 2005 U.S. Supreme Court case *Raich v. Ashcroft*, the legal status of medical marijuana within the state of California was overturned in favor of arguments that federal regulations prohibiting marijuana use under any circumstances were paramount. It was a landmark decision, and the consequences with respect to marijuana as a medical treatment remain uncertain. But who was behind *Raich v. Ashcroft* in this case? Who was Raich?

Angel McClary Raich was permanently disabled in 1995. Her medical condition included an inoperable brain tumor, life-threatening wasting syndrome, chronic pain disorders, seizure disorder, nausea, and scoliosis (a painful back condition). Her physician recommended cannabis use as a medication for her symptoms. In a legal deposition submitted at the time, she described her life:

I suffer greatly from severe chronic pain every single day. The prolonged pain and suffering from my medical condition significantly interferes with my quality of life. My treatment is complicated by the fact that I am violently allergic and have severe multiple sensitivities to almost all pharmaceutical medicines.... This makes it extremely difficult for doctors to effectively help me combat my diseases. Without cannabis my life would be a death sentence.

Raich's primary care physician, Dr. Frank Lucido, was the one who made the recommendation of medical marijuana. He recognized that Raich was at significant risk of malnutrition and starvation as well as suffering intolerable pain. He wrote,

Angel has no reasonable legal alternative to cannabis for the effective treatment or alleviation of her medical conditions or symptoms associated with medical conditions because she has tried essentially all other legal alternatives to cannabis and the alternatives have been ineffective or [cause] intolerable side effects. Angel will suffer imminent harm without access to cannabis.... It would be malpractice to subject the patient to further unnecessary harm.... Cannabis works well for Angel in a way that no other medicine has or can be expected to in order to alleviate Angel's medical conditions or symptoms associated with them.

Raich became one of the fourteen "medical necessity" patients at the Oakland Cannabis Buyers' Cooperative who were represented in the court cases that led up to the Supreme Court. In 1996, California voters passed the Compassionate Use Act, legalizing marijuana for medical use within the state. After the Drug Enforcement Administration (DEA)

seized doctor-prescribed marijuana from the home of a patient, advocates of medical marijuana sued the DEA and then–U.S. Attorney General John Ashcroft in federal district court and won. Their case was upheld until the Supreme Court decision in 2005.

In November 2005, Raich filed legal papers in a federal appeals court, arguing that federal efforts and the Supreme Court decision to restrict medical marijuana violated her constitutionally guaranteed rights to take the only medication allowing her to avoid intolerable pain and death. The brief marks a new legal strategy, claiming that the concern for federal control of interstate commerce (see text) does not apply to her use of locally grown marijuana. As Raich puts it, "I just want the opportunity to be a mother to my children without having to live in constant fear that the federal government will raid my home and throw me in jail."

Sources: Who is Angel McClary Raich? Angel Wings Patient Outreach, Inc. web site, angeljustice.org. Declaration of Frank Henry Lucido, M.D., in support of the plaintiff Angel McClary Raich, October 20, 2002, U.S. District Court for the Northern District of California. Ashley, Guy (2005, November 24). Woman pursues new legal strategy in medical marijuana fight. Knight-Ridder/Tribune News Service.

within federal jurisdiction to "regulate purely local activities that are part of an economic 'class of activities' that have a substantial effect on interstate commerce." A restriction of medical marijuana to intrastate (within a state) commerce could not be guaranteed, and therefore federal jurisdiction took over.

While not the last word on the question, the 2005 court decision has nevertheless been a blow to advocates of medical marijuana and the movement toward its legalization at the state level. Technically, federal prosecutions can be carried out in those states where medical marijuana is legal. Whether large numbers of prosecutions will occur in the future, however,

is unclear. Presently, the federal government conducts only 1 percent of marijuana prosecutions in the United States.[53]

In contrast to the policy in the United States, Canada has officially approved the medicinal use of marijuana since 2001. It is legal for Canadian patients to grow and smoke marijuana if their symptoms have been certified by a physician as warranting this treatment. It is also permitted, under these circumstances, to request marijuana, free of charge, from government-operated cannabis farms in Manitoba. In 2005, the FDA-equivalent agency in Canada approved the prescription use of Sativex, a liquid spray derived from the cannabis plant. In 2006, the FDA approved clinical testing of Sativex for potential sale in the United States. By providing a nonsmoking means of administration, this formulation circumvents arguments that medical marijuana smoking presents increased risks of smoking-related diseases (see Chapter 11).[54]

The Issue of Decriminalization

What, then, should public policy be toward marijuana smoking in the United States today? To deal with this question, we need first to review how public policy with respect to marijuana regulation has evolved since the 1970s. As described earlier, the dramatic emergence during the 1960s of marijuana as a major psychoactive drug initiated a slow but steady reassessment of myths that had been attached to it for decades. By 1972, the American Medical Association and the American Bar Association had proposed a liberalization of laws regarding the possession of marijuana. In 1972, the National Commission on Marijuana and Drug Abuse, authorized by the Comprehensive Drug Abuse Prevention and Control Act of 1970, encouraged state legislators around the country to consider changes in their particular regulatory statutes related to marijuana.[55] Since

that time, several states, including California, New York, Colorado, Minnesota, and North Carolina, have adopted some form of decriminalization laws with respect to the possession of marijuana in small amounts (usually less than one ounce or so). Essentially, **decriminalization** has meant that possession under these circumstances is considered a civil (noncriminal) offense, punishable by a fine, rather than imprisonment.

The trend toward marijuana decriminalization on a state-by-state basis has largely stalled in recent years. No U.S. state has voted for decriminalization since the 1980s, and two states (Alaska and Oregon) that had previously decriminalized marijuana possession have since voted to recriminalize it. As discussed earlier, the focus of changes in legislation regarding marijuana use has been directed toward the question of its limited use as a medical application rather than decriminalization per se.

In 2002, a national survey indicated that 72 percent of Americans favored decriminalization of marijuana, even though a majority still opposed outright legalization. As the sociologist Erich Goode has expressed it,

decriminalization: The policy of making the possession of small amounts of a drug subject to a small fine but not criminal prosecution.

Drugs...in Focus

Hemp in America—Coming Full Circle

Faced with depressed corn and soybean prices, farmers in North Dakota and other states in the region have recently considered an interesting alternative crop: high-fiber, high-protein hemp. There is only one drawback. The U.S. government views hemp in the same category as marijuana. Since the Comprehensive Drug Abuse Prevention and Control Act of 1970, hemp has remained a Schedule I controlled substance. Hence, growing "industrial" hemp in the United States is illegal.

Pro-hemp advocates argue that the government permits manufacturers of cosmetics, clothing, paper, and foods (hemp bread being a popular example) to import hemp fiber, seed, and oil from Canada and Europe for use in their products. It is hypocritical, from their point of view, to ban its domestic cultivation. Representing the opposite side of the issue, the DEA sees hemp fields turning into marijuana fields. According to a federal official, "The pro-dope people have been pushing hemp for twenty years because they know that if they can have hemp fields, then they can have

marijuana fields. It's . . . stoner logic." The retort is that industrial hemp is high in fiber, protein, vitamin E, and essential fatty acids, and because it has very low concentrations of THC, you don't get high from it.

The economic aspect of the issue weighs heavily on North Dakota farmers. There has been a rapidly emerging global market for hemp over the last decade or so, and they simply do not want to be left out. They would like to return to the days when it was legal to grow hemp in the United States. Indeed, during World War II, the government encouraged farmers to grow hemp for wartime rope and textiles. Today, the United States is the only developed nation in the world that has not established hemp as an agricultural commodity. If the current policy changes, we would be returning full circle to the colonial period of U.S. history, when hemp growers (notably George Washington himself) were dominant figures in the agricultural life of the nation.

Sources: Leinwand, Donna (2005, November 22). "Industrial" hemp support takes root. *USA Today,* p. 3A. Brown, Patricia Leigh (2006, August 28). California seeks to clear hemp of a bad name. *New York Times,* pp. A1, A13.

For all practical purposes, the possession of [small amounts of] marijuana has become decriminalized in the United States. Since present trends are moving toward de facto legal acceptance of small-quantity marijuana possession, it will not make a great deal of difference whether this attitude is recognized by law or not. Consequently, the debate over marijuana criminalization borders on being obsolete.[56]

Nonetheless, present-day law enforcement related to low-level marijuana possession remains at high levels and is disproportionately applied on the basis of gender, race, and ethnicity. In a study of arrests made in New York City from 1998 to 2007, 90 percent of arrests of this type involved males, despite national surveys indicating that equal numbers of men and women use marijuana. Moreover, 83 percent of arrests involved African Americans or Latinos, and 52 percent involved African Americans alone (twice their share of the city's population). Whites,

A DEA officer confiscates and destroys a domestic crop of *Cannabis sativa* in Kentucky. Presumably, people living downwind of this operation had been evacuated.

representing about 35 percent of the population, accounted for 15 percent of those charged.[57]

You may find it surprising or not surprising (depending on your personal views) that official decriminalization has not been demonstrated to result in an upturn in the incidence of marijuana smoking. Statistics drawn from states that either have or have not decriminalized show little or no difference.[58] In addition, attitude surveys conducted in California before and after the enactment of such statutes indicate that the acceptance of marijuana among college students actually declined following decriminalization.[59]

Whether or not some form of marijuana ingestion becomes officially sanctioned in the United States recently has been intertwined with the question of whether agricultural cultivation of the cannabis plant itself should be permitted for purposes other than the harvesting of marijuana. As pointed out earlier in the chapter, *Cannabis sativa* has been harvested for thousands of years for the manufacture of hemp products rather than for its leaves. The potential economic benefit for a struggling agricultural industry in the United States has framed the argument for a reexamination of the current policy (Drugs . . . in Focus).

Summary

A Matter of Terminology

- Marijuana is one of several products of the *Cannabis sativa*, or common hemp plant, grown abundantly throughout the world.
- Various cannabis products are distinguished in terms of the content of cannabis resin and, in turn, the concentration of THC, the active psychoactive agent.

The History of Marijuana and Hashish

- The earliest records of marijuana come from Chinese writings nearly five thousand years ago; hashish has its origins in North Africa and Persia in the ninth or tenth century A.D.
- In the United States, marijuana was available in patent medicines during the late 1800s, but its popularity did not become extensive until the 1920s.
- Federal and state regulation of marijuana began in the 1930s; penalties for possessing and selling marijuana escalated during the 1940s and 1950s.
- The emergence of marijuana on American college campuses and among American youth in general during the late 1960s, however, forced a reexamination of public policy regarding this drug, leading to a more lenient approach in the 1970s.

Acute Effects of Marijuana

- Because marijuana is almost always consumed through smoking, the acute effects are rapid, but because it is absorbed into fatty tissue, its elimination is slow. It may require days or weeks in the case of extensive exposure to marijuana for THC to leave the body completely.
- Acute physiological effects include cardiac acceleration and a reddening of the eyes. Acute psychological effects, with typical dosages, include euphoria, giddiness, a perception of time elongation, and an increased hunger and sexual desire. There are impairments in attention and memory, which interfere with complex visual–motor skills such as driving an automobile.
- The acute effects of marijuana are now known to be due to the binding of THC at special receptors in the brain.

Chronic Effects of Marijuana

- Chronic marijuana use produces tolerance effects; there is no physical dependence when doses are moderate and only a mild psychological dependence.
- Carcinogenic effects are suspected because marijuana smoke contains many of the same harmful components that tobacco smoke does, and in the case of marijuana smoking inhalation is deeper and more prolonged.

The Amotivational Syndrome and the Gateway Hypothesis

- The idea that there exists an amotivational syndrome, characterized by general apathy and an indifference to long-range planning, as a result of the pharmacological effects of chronic marijuana use has been largely discredited. An alternative explanation for the behavioral changes is that chronic marijuana users are involved in a deviant subculture that is directed away from traditional values of school achievement and long-term aspirations.
- Another idea that has been related to chronic marijuana use is the gateway hypothesis, which refers to the possibility that marijuana inherently sets the stage for future patterns of drug abuse. Research studies have

indicated that the use of alcohol and cigarettes precedes marijuana use, and marijuana use precedes the use of other illicit drugs. In addition, marijuana use and subsequent use of other illicit drugs are statistically correlated. However, there is little evidence that some inherent property of marijuana exposure itself leads to physical or psychological dependence on other drugs.

Patterns of Marijuana Smoking

● The current incidence of marijuana smoking among adolescents and young adults is lower than in the late 1970s, but clearly a resurgence has occurred since 1991.

● Other areas of concern are the greater potency of marijuana that is now available and the continuing potential risk of marijuana adulteration.

Medical Marijuana and Marijuana Decriminalization

● While marijuana has been useful in the treatment of glaucoma and asthma, its most effective application to date has been in the treatment of symptoms of nausea and weight loss. In 2005, the U.S. Supreme Court upheld the power of the federal government to prohibit the possession and use of marijuana for medical purposes, even in U.S. states that permit it. As a result of this decision, federal prosecutions can be carried out in these states. Whether large numbers of prosecutions will occur in the future, however, is unclear.

● Present public policy toward marijuana smoking has evolved to the point of essentially decriminalizing the possession of marijuana in small amounts.

Key Terms

amotivational syndrome, p. 178
anandamide, p. 175
bhang, p. 170
cannabinoids, p. 169

Cannabis sativa, p. 169
decriminalization, p. 185
delta-9-tetrahydrocannabinol (THC), p. 169
dronabinol (Marinol), p. 183

gateway hypothesis, p. 179
hashish, p. 169
hashish oil, p. 169
hashish oil crystals, p. 169
joint, p. 172

marijuana, p. 169
nabilone (Cesamet), p. 183
reefer, p. 172
sinsemilla, p. 169

Endnotes

1. Abel, Ernest L. (1980). *Marihuana, the first twelve thousand years*. New York: Plenum Press, p. ix.
2. Bloomquist, Edward R. (1968). *Marijuana*. Beverly Hills, CA: Glencoe Press, pp. 4–5.
3. Abel, *Marihuana*, p. 4. Palfai, Tibor, and Jankiewicz, Henry (1991). *Drugs and human behavior*. Dubuque, IA: W. C. Brown, p. 452.
4. Abel, *Marihuana*, pp. x–xi.
5. Goode, Erich (2008). *Drugs in American society* (7th ed.). New York: McGraw-Hill Higher Education, p. 239. Office of Drug Control Policy (2002, November). National Drug Intelligence Center (2007). *National Drug Threat Assessment: 2008*. Washington DC: U.S. Department of Justice, p. 14. *Pulse check: Marijuana report*. Washington DC: White House Office of Drug Control Policy.
6. Abel, *Marihuana*, p. 12.
7. Bonnie, Richard J., and Whitebread, Charles H. (1974). *The marihuana conviction: A history of marihuana prohibition in the United States*. Charlottesville, VA: University Press of Virginia, p. 3.
8. Abel, *Marihuana*, pp. 218–222.
9. Bonnie and Whitebread, *The marihuana conviction*, p. 33.
10. Anslinger, Harry J., and Tompkins, William F. (1953). *The traffic in narcotics*. New York: Funk & Wagnalls, pp. 37–38. Cited in Inciardi, James A. (2002). *The war on drugs III*. Boston: Allyn and Bacon, p. 46.
11. Lee, Martin A., and Shlain, Bruce (1985). *Acid dreams: The complete social history of LSD*. New York: Grove Weidenfeld.
12. Julien, Robert M. (1998). *A primer of drug action* (8th ed.). New York: Freeman, pp. 327–331.
13. Ibid., pp. 330–331.
14. *Allen and Hanbury's athletic drug reference* (1992). Research Triangle Park, NC: Clean Data, p. 33. Wadler, Gary I., and Hainline, Brian (1989). *Drugs and the athlete*. Philadelphia: F. A. Davis, pp. 208–209.
15. Grinspoon, Lester, and Bakalar, James B. (1997). Marihuana. In Joyce H. Lowinson, Pedro Ruiz, Robert B. Millman, and John G. Langrod (Eds.), *Substance abuse: A comprehensive textbook* (3rd ed.). Baltimore, MD: Williams and Wilkins, pp. 199–206.
16. Jones, Reese T. (1980). Human effects: An overview. In Robert C. Petersen (Ed.), *Marijuana research findings: 1980* (NIDA Research Monograph 31). Rockville, MD: National Institute on Drug Abuse, p. 65.
17. Grilly, David M. (2006). *Drugs and human behavior* (5th ed.). Boston: Allyn and Bacon, p. 268.
18. Substance Abuse and Mental Health Services Administration (2008). *Drug Abuse Warning Network, 2006: National estimates of drug-related emergency department visits*. Rockville, MD: Office of Applied Studies, Substance Abuse and Mental Health Services Administration, Table 2.

19. Winger, Gail; Hofmann, Frederick G.; and Woods, James H. (1992). *A handbook on drug and alcohol abuse* (3rd ed.). New York: Oxford University Press, pp. 123–125.

20. Hooker, William D., and Jones, Reese T. (1987). Increased susceptibility to memory intrusions and the Stroop interference effect during acute marijuana intoxication. *Psychopharmacology, 91,* 20–24. Ilan, Aaron B.; Gevins, A.; Coleman, M.; ElSohly, M. A.; and de Wit, H. (2005). Neurophysiological and subjective profile of marijuana with varying concentrations of cannabinoids. *Behavioural Pharmacology, 16,* 487–496.

21. Delong, Fonya L., and Levy, Bernard I. (1974). A model of attention describing the cognitive effects of marijuana. In Loren L. Miller (Ed.), *Marijuana: Effects on human behavior.* New York: Academic Press, pp. 103–117. Gieringer, Dale H. (1988). Marijuana, driving, and accident safety. *Journal of Psychoactive Drugs, 20,* 93–101.

22. McKim, William A. (2000). *Drugs and behavior* (4th ed.). Englewood Cliffs, NJ: Prentice-Hall, p. 309.

23. Ramaekers, J. G.; Berghaus, G.; van Laar, M.; and Drummer, O. H. (2004). Dose related risk of motor vehicle crashes after cannabis use. *Drugs and Alcohol Dependence, 73,* 109–119.

24. Block, Robert I. (1997). Editorial: Does heavy marijuana use impair human cognition and brain function? *Journal of the American Medical Association, 275,* 560–561. Pope, Harrison G., Jr., and Yurgelun-Todd, Deborah (1996). The residual cognitive effects of heavy marijuana use in college students. *Journal of the American Medical Association, 275,* 521–527.

25. Winger, Hofmann, and Woods, *A handbook on drug and alcohol abuse,* pp. 118, 127–129.

26. Ameri, Angela (1999). The effects of cannabinoids on the brain. *Progress in Neurobiology, 58,* 315–348. Chait, L. D., and Burke, K. A. (1994). Preference for high- versus low-potency marijuana. *Pharmacology, Biochemistry, and Behavior, 49,* 643–647. Tanda, Gianluigi, Pontieri, Francesco E., and Di Chiara, Gaetano (1997). Cannabinoid and heroin activation of mesolimbic dopamine transmission by a common μ_1 opioid receptor mechanism. *Science, 276,* 2048–2049. Wickelgren, Ingrid (1997). Research news: Marijuana: Harder than thought? *Science, 276,* 1967–1968.

27. Abood, M., and Martin, B. (1992). Neurobiology of marijuana abuse. *Trends in Pharmacological Sciences, 13,* 201–206.

28. Frank, Ira M.; Lessin, Phyllis J.; Tyrrell, Eleanore D.; Hahn, Pierre M.; and Szara, Stephen. (1976). Acute and cumulative effects of marijuana smoking on hospitalized subjects: A 36-day study. In Monique C. Braude and Stephen Szara (Eds.), *Pharmacology of marijuana.* Vol. 2. Orlando, FL: Academic Press, pp. 673–680. Jones, Reese T., and Benowitz, Neal (1976). The 30-day trip: Clinical studies of cannabis tolerance and dependence. In Monique C. Braude and Stephen Szara (Eds.), *Pharmacology of marijuana.* Vol. 2. Orlando, FL: Academic Press, pp. 627–642.

29. Haney, Margaret; Ward, Amie S.; Comer, Sandra D.; Foltin, Richard W; and Fischman, Marian W. (1999a). Abstinence symptoms following oral THC administration in humans. *Psychopharmacology, 141,* 385–394. Haney, Margaret; Ward, Amie S.; Comer, Sandra D.; Foltin, Richard W; and Fischman, Marian W. (1999b). Abstinence symptoms following smoked marijuana in humans. *Psychopharmacology, 141,* 395–404.

30. Duffy, Anne, and Milin, Robert (1996). Case study: Withdrawal syndrome in adolescent chronic cannabis users. *Journal of the American Academy of Child and Adolescent Psychiatry, 35,* 1618–1621. Julien, Robert M. (2001). *A primer of drug action* (9th ed.). New York: Worth, pp. 320–322.

31. Earlywine, Mitch (2002). *Understanding marijuana: A new look at the scientific evidence.* New York: Oxford University Press, pp. 156–157. Julien (2001), *A primer of drug action,* pp. 316–319. Marijuana as medicine: How strong is the science? (1997, May). *Consumer Reports,* pp. 62–63. Study: Marijuana, cocaine have harmful effects on lungs (1998, September 7). *Alcoholism and Drug Abuse Weekly, 10,* p. 8. Sussman, Steve; Stacy, Alan W.; Dent, Clyde W.; Simon, Thomas R.; and Johnson, C. Anderson (1995). Marijuana use: Current issues and new research directions. *Journal of Drug Issues, 26,* 695–733.

32. Committee on Substance Abuse, American Academy of Pediatrics (1999). Marijuana: A continuing concern for pediatricians. *Pediatrics, 104,* 982–985. Hollister, Leo E. (1988). Marijuana and immunity. *Journal of Psychoactive Drugs, 20,* 3–7. Petersen, Robert C. (1984). Marijuana overview. In Meyer D. Glantz (Ed.), *Correlates and consequences of marijuana use* (Research Issues 34). Rockville, MD: National Institute on Drug Abuse, p. 10.

33. Brands, Bruna, Sproule, Beth, and Marshman, Joan (Eds.) (1998). *Drugs and drug abuse: A reference text* (3rd ed.). Toronto: Addiction Research Foundation. Committee on Substance Abuse, Marijuana. Grinspoon and Bakalar, Marihuana, pp. 203–204. Male infertility: Sperm from marijuana smokers move too fast, too early (2003, November 3). *Health and Medicine Week,* pp. 459–460.

34. Grinspoon and Bakalar, Marihuana, p. 203.

35. McGothlin, William H., and West, Louis J. (1968). The marijuana problem: An overview. *American Journal of Psychiatry, 125,* 372.

36. Goode, Erich (1999). *Drugs in American Society* (5th ed.). New York: McGraw-Hill College, pp. 232–233.

37. Fox, C. Lynn, and Forbing, Shirley E. (1992). *Creating drug-free schools and communities: A comprehensive approach.* New York: HarperCollins, p. 60. Roebuck, M. Christopher, French, Michael T., and Dennis, Michael L. (2004). Adolescent marijuana use and school attendance. *Economics of Education Review, 23,* 133–141.

38. Goode (1999), *Drugs in American society,* p. 233.

39. Fried, P. A., Wilkinson, B., and Gray, R. (2005). Neurocognitive consequences of marihuana—A comparison with pre-drug performance. *Neurotoxicology and Teratology, 27,*

231–239. Hollister, Leo E. (1986). Health aspects of cannabis. *Pharmacological Reviews*, 38, 1–20. Pope, Harrison (2002). Cannabis, cognition, and residual confounding. *Journal of the American Medical Association*, 287, 1172–1174. Solowij, Nadia; Stephens, Robert S.; Roffman, Roger A.; Babor, Thomas; Kadden, Ronald; et al. (2002). Cognitive functioning of long-term heavy cannabis users seeking treatment. *Journal of the American Medical Association*, 287, 1123–1131.

40. Yücel, Murat; Solowij, Nadia; Respondek, Colleen; Whittle, Sarah; Fornito, Alex; et al. (2008, June). Regional brain abnormalities associated with long-term heavy cannabis use. *Archives of General Psychiatry*, 65, 694–701.

41. Kandel, Denise B. (2003). Does marijuana use cause the use of other drugs? *Journal of the American Medical Association*, 289, 482–483. Quotation on p. 482. Kandel, Denise B. (Ed.) (2002). *Stages and pathways of drug involvement: Examining the gateway hypothesis.* Cambridge: Cambridge University Press.

42. Cited in Medical marijuana: Editorials debate "gateway" effect (1999, April 12). *American Health Line*, URL: http://www.ahl.com.

43. Kandel, Does marijuana use cause the use of other drugs? Lynskey, Michael T.; Hath, Andrew C.; Bucholz, Kathleen K.; Slutske, Wendy S.; Madden, Pamela A. F.; et al. (2003). The escalation of drug use in early-onset cannabis users vs co-twin controls. *Journal of the American Medical Association*, 289, 427–433. Martin, Kimberly R. (2001). Adolescent treatment programs reduce drug abuse, produce other improvements. *NIDA Notes*, 16 (1), 11–12. Martin, Kimberly R. (2001). Television public service announcements decrease marijuana use in targeted teens. *NIDA Notes*, 16 (1), 14.

44. Zimmer, Lynn, and Morgan, John P. (1997). *Marijuana myths, marijuana facts: A review of the scientific evidence.* New York: Lindesmith Center, p. 37.

45. Goode (2008), *Drugs in American society*, pp. 250–251.

46. Cart, Julie (2003, May 25). A national park going to pot: Marijuana farms boom in Sequoia. *Newsday*, p. A65. Johnston, Lloyd D.; O'Malley, Patrick M.; Bachman, Jerald G.; and Schulenberg, John E. (2008). *Monitoring the Future: National survey results on drug use, 1975–2007. Volume II: College students and adults ages 19–45.* Bethesda, MD: National Institute on Drug Abuse, p. 30. Pollan, M. (1995, February 13). How pot is grown. *New York Times Magazine*, p. 31. Substance Abuse and Mental Health Services Administration (2008). *Results from the 2007 National Survey on Drug Use and Health: Detailed tables.* Rockville, MD: Office of Applied Studies, Substance Abuse and Mental Health Services Administration, Tables 1.1A and 1.1B.

47. Johnston, Lloyd D.; O'Malley, Patrick M.; Bachman, Jerald G.; and Schulenberg, John E. (2008, December 11). Various stimulant drugs show continuing gradual declines among teens in 2008, most illicit drugs hold steady. University of Michigan News Service, Ann Arbor, Tables 2, 3, and 4.

48. Johnston, O'Malley, Bachman, and Schulenberg (2008), Table 7.

49. Cohen, Sidney (1980). Therapeutic aspects. In Robert C. Petersen (Ed.), *Marijuana research findings: 1980* (NIDA Research Monograph 31). Rockville, MD: National Institute on Drug Abuse, pp. 199–221. Julien, *A primer of drug action* (9th ed.), pp. 322–324. Vestag, Brian (2003). Medical marijuana center opens its doors. *Journal of the American Medical Association*, 290, 877–879.

50. Plasse, Terry F.; Gorter, Robert W.; Krasnow, Steven H.; Lane, Montague; Shepard, Kirk V.; et al. (1991). Recent clinical experience with dronabinol. International conference on cannabis and cannabinoids, Chania, Greece. *Pharmacology, Biochemistry, and Behavior*, 40, 695–700.

51. Institute of Medicine (1999). *Marijuana as medicine: Assessing the science base.* Washington DC: National Academy Press, p. vii.

52. Inciardi, *The war on drugs III*, pp. 300–301. Institute of Medicine, *Marijuana as medicine*, p. 8.

53. Greenhouse, Linda (2005, June 7). Justices say U.S. may prohibit the use of medical marijuana. *New York Times*, pp. A1, A21. McKinley, Jesse (2008, June 9). Marijuana hotbed retreats on medicinal use. *New York Times*, pp. A1, A17. Murphy, Dean E. (2005, June 7). Drug's users say ruling won't end their efforts. *New York Times*, p. A21.

54. Bailey, Eric (2005, April 21). Canada OKs pot medicine. *Newsday*, p. A32. Rock announces medical marijuana regulation and progress report on research and domestic supply (2001, July 4). Health Canada news release.

55. National Commission on Marihuana and Drug Abuse (1972). *Marihuana: A signal of misunderstanding.* Washington DC: Government Printing Office, pp. 151–167.

56. Goode (1999). *Drugs in American Society*, p. 401. CNN/Time Poll conducted by Harris Interactive, October 23–24, 2002.

57. Dwyer, Jim (2008, April 30). On arrests, demographics, and marijuana. *New York Times*, pp. B1, B2.

58. Johnston, Lloyd D. (1980, January 16). Marijuana use and the effects of marijuana decriminalization. Unpublished testimony delivered at the hearings on the effects of marijuana held by the Subcommittee on Criminal Justice, Judiciary Committee, U.S. Senate, Washington DC, p. 5.

59. Dreyfuss, Robert (2005, August 11). Bush's war on pot. *Rolling Stone*, pp. 46–48. Canada ponders drug liberalization (2005, November 10). *Economist*, p. xx. Melamede, Robert J. (2005). Harm reduction—The cannabis paradox. *Harm Reduction Journal*, 2:17. O'Driscoll, Patrick (2005, November 13). Denver votes to legalize marijuana possession. *USA Today*, p. 3A. Sommer, Robert (1988). Two decades of marijuana attitudes: The more it changes, the more it is the same. *Journal of Psychoactive Drugs*, 20, 67–70.

chapter **8**

Performance-Enhancing Drugs and Drug Testing in Sports

The public needs to be informed about the reality of steroids and how they have affected the lives of many star baseball players, including me. Have I used steroids? You bet I did. Did steroids make me a better baseball player? Of course they did. If I had it all to do over again, would I live a steroid-enriched life? Yes, I would. Do I have any regrets or qualms about relying on chemicals to help me hit a baseball so far? To be honest, no, I don't.

—*José Canseco*, Juiced *(2005)*

After you have completed this chapter, you will understand

- The history of performance-enhancing drugs in sports
- How anabolic steroids work
- The health risks of steroid abuse
- Patterns of steroid abuse
- Performance-enhancing nonsteroid hormones
- Dietary supplements marketed as performance-enhancing aids
- Nonmedical use of stimulant medications in baseball
- Present-day drug testing in amateur and professional sports

In a world where running a hundredth of a second faster can mean the difference between a gold medal or a silver, where throwing a javelin a centimeter farther, lifting a kilogram more, or hitting a baseball twenty feet farther can make you either the champion or an also-ran, temptations abound. In this high-pressure world, athletes are continually on the lookout for a winning edge. The advantage formula may involve an unusual technique in training, a new attitude toward winning, or a special diet. Or it could involve the use of drugs. This chapter focuses on the abuse of performance-enhancing drugs in the world of sports, with particular attention to the abuse of anabolic steroids.

The use of anabolic steroids and other performance-enhancing drugs to achieve that winning edge is a problem not only among athletes who are in the public eye but also among a growing number of young people who simply want to look better by developing the musculature of their bodies. The serious dangers in such drug-taking behavior, whether the motivation lies in competitive drive or in personal vanity, are major problems that need to be examined closely. It is instructive to look first at how performance-enhancing drugs have affected competitive sports over the centuries.

Drug-Taking Behavior in Sports

The first recorded athletic competition, the ancient Olympic Games in Greece, is also the place where we find the first recorded use of psychoactive drugs in sports. As early as 300 B.C., Greek athletes ate hallucinogenic mushrooms either to improve their performance in the competition or to achieve some kind of mystical connection to the gods. Later, Roman gladiators and charioteers used stimulants to sustain themselves longer in competition, even when injured by their opponents.

In the modern era, drugs have continued to be a factor in athletic competitions. By the end of the nineteenth century, world-class athletes were experimenting with a variety of stimulant and depressant drugs, including cocaine, caffeine, alcohol, nitroglycerine, opiates, strychnine, and amphetamines. In 1886, while competing in a cross-country race, a Welsh cyclist died of a combination of opiates and cocaine (now referred to as a speedball), the first drug-related death ever recorded in sports. During the 1904 Olympics, U.S. marathoner Tom Hicks collapsed after winning the race and lost

ergogenic (ER-go-JEN-ik): Performance-enhancing.

consciousness. When he was revived, doctors were told that he had taken a potentially lethal mixture of strychnine (a CNS stimulant when administered in low doses) and brandy.[1]

With the introduction in the 1930s of anabolic steroid drugs specifically patterned after the male sex hormone testosterone, a new element entered the arena of competitive sports. Here was a class of performance-enhancing drugs that did more than alter the behavior or experience of the athlete; these particular drugs actually altered the structure of the athlete's body.

Anabolic steroid drugs had been studied since the 1930s as a treatment for anemia (low red blood cell count) and conditions that caused muscles to waste away. Following the end of World War II, steroid drugs were administered to people who were near death from starvation and weight loss. It quickly became apparent, however, that steroids could be useful when given to otherwise healthy individuals as well. As pharmaceutical companies began to introduce dozens of new body-building drugs based on the testosterone molecule, it was natural that information about anabolic steroids would come to the attention of athletes, as well as their coaches and trainers.[2]

What Are Anabolic Steroids?

To understand how testosterone-based steroids produce **ergogenic** (performance-enhancing) changes, we first have to recognize that testosterone itself has two primary effects on the human body. The first and most obvious effect is **androgenic** (literally, "man-producing"), in that the hormone promotes the development of male sex characteristics. As testosterone levels rise during puberty, boys acquire an enlarged larynx (resulting in a deeper voice), body hair, and an increase in body size, as well as genital changes that make them sexually mature adults. The second effect is **anabolic** (upward-changing), in that it promotes the development of protein and, as a result, an increase in muscle tissue. Muscles in men are inherently larger than muscles in women because of the anabolic action of testosterone in the male body.

Steroid drugs based on alterations in the testosterone molecule are therefore called **anabolic-androgenic steroids.** The goal, however, has been to develop drugs that emphasize the anabolic function while retaining as little of the androgenic function as possible. For that reason, they are most often called simply **anabolic steroids.** Unfortunately, as we will see, it has not been possible to develop a testosterone-derived drug without at least some androgenic effects (Table 8.1).

It is important that anabolic steroids not be confused with **adrenocortical steroids,** drugs that are patterned after glucocorticoid hormones secreted by the adrenal glands. The major drug of this latter type is *cortisone* (brand name, among others: Hydrocortone injection or tablets). The molecular structure of these drugs qualifies them to belong to the steroid family, but there is no relationship to testosterone or any testosterone-like effects. Adrenocortical steroids are useful in the medical treatment of tissue inflammation; in sports, they reduce the inflammation associated with muscular injuries. Their effect on muscular development can be viewed as *catabolic* (downward-changing), in that muscles tend to weaken as a result, so their long-term use is unlikely to be a desirable option for athletes.[3]

Anabolic Steroids at the Modern Olympic Games

By the time of the 1952 Olympic Games in Helsinki, athletes were well acquainted with ergogenic drugs. Legally available amphetamines (see Chapter 4), in particular, were commonplace, particularly in events that

TABLE 8.1
Anabolic steroids currently available in the United States

TYPE OF STEROID	GENERIC NAME	BRAND NAME
Oral	danazol	Danocrine
	drostanolone	Masteron
	methandrostenolone	Dianabol
	methyltestosterone	Android, Testred, Virilon
	oxyandrolone	Oxandrin, Anavar
	oxymetholone	Anadrol
	stanozolol	Winstrol V
	boldanone undecylenate	Equipoise, Equi-Gan, Equidren
Intramuscular injection	nandrolone decanoate	Deca-Durabolin IM
	nandrolone phenprionate	Durabolin IM
	testosterone cyprionate	Virilon IM
	testosterone enantrate	Delatestryl IM
Transdermal patch	testosterone	Androderm transdermal system, Testoderm transdermal system

Note: Anabolic steroids are Schedule III controlled substances. As such, they are considered illicit drugs under federal guidelines when not obtained with a medical prescription and restricted to medical use along with other Schedule III controlled substances. Several "brand names" marketed for performance-enhancing purposes are combinations of various forms of steroids.

Sources: National Institute on Drug Abuse (2000, April). Anabolic steroids. *Community drug alert bulletin.* Bethesda, MD: National Institute on Drug Abuse. *Physicians' desk reference* (62nd ed.) (2008). Montvale, NJ: Thomson HealthCare. Shipley, Amy (2003, March 23). Drug testers have designs on new steroid. *Washington Post,* p. D1.

androgenic (AN-droh-JEN-ik): Acting to promote masculinizing changes in the body.

anabolic (AN-ah-BALL-ik): Acting to promote protein growth and muscular development.

anabolic-androgenic steroids: Drugs that promote masculinizing changes in the body and increased muscular development.

anabolic steroids: Drugs patterned after the testosterone molecule that promote masculine changes in the body and increased muscular development. The full name is anabolic-androgenic steroids.

adrenocortical steroids: A group of hormones secreted by the adrenal glands. Their anti-inflammatory action makes them useful for treating arthritis and muscular injuries.

emphasized speed and endurance. Among events requiring strength and size, anabolic steroids were seen to be perfectly suited for gaining a competitive advantage.

Steroid use was clearly out in the open during the 1968 Olympic Games in Mexico City. An estimated one-third of the entire U.S. track and field team, not merely the strength-event and field-event competitors but the sprinters and middle-distance runners as well, were using anabolic steroids. The controversy did not concern the appropriateness or morality of taking steroids, only which particular steroids worked best. Strength-event athletes were taking at least two to five times the therapeutic recommendations (based on the original intent of replacing body protein). The following year, an editor of *Track and Field News* dubbed anabolic steroids "the breakfast of champions." In 1971, one U.S. weight lifter commented in reference to his Soviet rival,

> Last year the only difference between me and him was I couldn't afford his drug bill. Now I can. When I hit Munich [in 1972] I'll weigh in at about 340, or maybe 350. Then we'll see which is better, his steroids or mine.[4]

In the meantime, the masculine features of many female athletes from eastern European countries in the 1960s and 1970s, not to mention the number of Olympic records that were suddenly broken, made it reasonable to ask whether they were either men disguised as women or genetic "mistakes." Questions about the unusually deep

Russian pentathlon champion Nadezhda Tkachenko was one of several world-class female athletes in the 1970s who later tested positive for anabolic steroids.

voices of East German women swimmers prompted their coach, at one point, to respond: "We came here to swim, not to sing."

From information that has come to light since then, we now know that the effects were chiefly due to large doses of steroids. Until the late 1980s, the East German government was conducting a scientific program specifically to develop new steroid formulations that would benefit their national athletes and, at the same time, be undetectable by standard screening procedures. In 2000, the principal physician in the East German Swimming Federation at the time when these steroids were being administered was convicted on charges that from 1975 to 1985 the program caused bodily harm to more than four dozen young female swimmers.[5]

The 2000 Olympic Games in Sydney, Australia, instituted the strictest drug-testing procedures to date for all competing athletes, including a new screening for EPO, a drug that enhances endurance by increasing red blood cells. For the first time, a specific phrase was inserted into the Olympic Oath, recited by all athletes at the beginning of the games: ". . . committing ourselves to a sport without doping and without drugs."

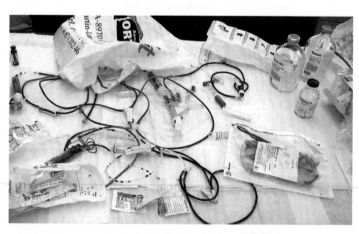

In 2002, cleanup workers found blood-transfusion equipment in a house that had been rented by the Austrian Nordic cross-country ski team at the Salt Lake City Olympics. The Austrian federation claimed the equipment had been used for ultraviolet radiation treatment of athletes' blood to prevent colds and flu. The International Olympic Committee rejected this claim and ruled two nonmedalist Austrian skiers disqualified and their performance scores stricken from the official record.

In 2004, the World Anti-Doping Code was created as an agreed-upon list of prohibited performance-enhancing drugs and performance-enhancing methods in international sports competitions, testing procedures for their use, and specific penalties for violations. Under the auspices of the World Anti-Doping Agency (WADA), rules and regulations have been formally accepted by more than 200 National Olympic Committees as well as by professional leagues (such as the National Basketball Association and the National Hockey League) representing the United States in the Olympic Games and other international competitions. The Code has been updated over the years as the development and availability of new drugs of this kind have changed; the latest revision went into effect in January 2009. Despite these steps toward controlling the impact of performance-enhancing drugs in international competitions, however, drug-related controversies continue (Drugs . . . in Focus).[6]

Anabolic Steroids in Professional and Collegiate Sports

The wholesale use of anabolic steroids in international athletics in the 1950s soon filtered down to sports closer to home. Beginning in the early 1960s, trainers in the National Football League began to administer anabolic steroids to their players. By the 1970s and 1980s, virtually all the NFL teams were familiar with these drugs. Estimates of how many players were on anabolic steroids varied from 50 to 90 percent. We will never know precisely the full extent of the practice, except to say that it was certainly substantial.

Several professional football players remarked at the time that their steroid use had begun while they were playing on collegiate teams, and indeed, football players in several colleges and universities during the 1980s were implicated in steroid use. Football players were not alone

---

Drugs . . . in Focus

Gene Doping: Disqualified by DNA?

Since the 1964 Winter Olympic Games in Innsbruck, Finland's gold-medalist cross-country skier Eero Mantyranta had been rumored to be using performance-enhancing drugs in competition, though he never failed a drug test. Decades later, DNA technology has made it possible for Mantyranta to be exonerated of any wrongdoing. It turns out that Mantyranta had a naturally occurring genetic mutation that produced increased levels of erythropoietin (EPO), a hormone that regulates red blood cells in the body. Since 2000, synthetic forms of EPO have been among the many steroid and nonsteroid drugs screened in the Olympic Games. In the drug testing administered in today's competitions, Mantyranta would have failed the test and would have been required to submit his DNA to prove himself innocent of "blood doping."

As gene therapy techniques are perfected, it is conceivable that we will be able to alter the EPO gene so as to increase the number of red blood cells carrying oxygen to muscles, the vascular endothelial growth factor (VEGF) gene so as to increase the number of blood vessels, or the short form of the angiotensin-converting enzyme (ACE) gene so as to increase the performance of "fast-twitch" muscles necessary for sudden bursts of speed. On the one hand, increasing EPO levels might help people who are anemic, increasing VEGF levels might help people with

clogged arteries and other circulatory diseases, and increasing ACE levels might help people suffering from chronic fatigue, or quicken the rate of recovery from sports-related injuries. On the other hand, for healthy athletes, the procedure would be, in effect, "gene doping."

As investigations of the human genome continue, it will be possible to specify sets of naturally occurring gene mutations that result in unusually high levels of athletic prowess. Would the identification of these mutations in future world champions justify a potential disqualification by virtue of their DNA? Today, the burden of proof is on officials to establish that an athlete is guilty of using a banned ergogenic substance. In the future, the burden of proof might be on the athlete to establish his or her innocence. How would athletes prove that their DNA had not been intentionally modified? Some interesting questions to ponder.

Sources: Pincock, Stephen (2005). Gene doping. Lancet, 366, 518–519. Schneider, Angela J., and Friedman, Theodore (2006). Gene doping in sports: The science and ethics of genetically modified athletes. New York: Academic Press. Sokolove, Michael (2004, January 18). The lab animal: Elite athletes always have and always will pursue every competitive advantage—health and the law be damned. Is genetic manipulation next? New York Times Magazine, pp. 28–33. Sweeney, H. Lee (2004, July). Gene doping. Scientific American, pp. 37–43. Trent, R. J., and Alexander, I. E. (2006). Gene therapy in sport. British Journal of Sports Medicine, 40, 4–5.

in this regard. Use of anabolic steroids had found its way into other collegiate and even high school sports of all kinds, including track and field, baseball, basketball, gymnastics, lacrosse, swimming, volleyball, wrestling, and tennis. It is fair to say that until the late 1980s, when screening procedures became commonplace, there was no sport, professional or amateur, for which the use of anabolic steroids was not an accepted element in athletic training.[7]

A Watershed Year in the History of Anabolic Steroids

Two events in 1988 made that year a turning point in the history of anabolic steroids in sports. Magazine articles and news accounts had been exposing their widespread use. In September 1988 at the Seoul Olympic Games, the Canadian sprinter Ben Johnson won the gold medal in the men's 100-meter dash in the world-record-breaking time of 9.79 seconds, only to be denied his achievement shortly afterward when it was determined that he had tested positive for anabolic steroids. Stunned, the world suddenly had to confront the pervasiveness of the practice as well as its consequences once and for all.

At about the same time, a major study published in the *Journal of the American Medical Association* reported the outcome of the first nationwide survey on use of anabolic steroids among adolescent boys in the United States. The survey found that approximately 7 percent of all high school seniors were using or had used anabolic steroids. More than 77 percent of the users were white and middle class; more than 52 percent had parents who were college graduates; nearly 50 percent had started using steroids before they were fifteen years old. More than 47 percent said that their motivation was to improve their athletic performance, but almost 27 percent said that the motivation was completely outside the realm of organized sports: They simply wanted to look better.[8]

Steroid Abuse and Baseball

Record-breaking home-run performances in the late 1990s and early 2000s raised suspicions that these achievements in baseball may not have been solely due to athletic prowess but rather to some pharmacological assistance. Yet, until recently, major league baseball stood apart from other professional sports in the United States and sports organizations around the world that had set up regulatory policies regarding steroid abuse and the use of other performance-enhancing drugs.

In 2004, a prominent track coach, two executives of BALCO, a nutritional supplements laboratory in California, and Barry Bonds's personal trainer were indicted on charges of illegally distributing steroids and other performance-enhancing drugs to dozens of professional athletes in baseball and other sports. In late 2007, Barry Bonds was indicted on four counts of perjury and obstruction of justice in connection with the BALCO case, on the basis of his testimony that he had never used anabolic steroids or human growth hormone.

With intense pressure from public opinion as well as governmental officials, major league baseball (MLB) players agreed in early 2005 to a policy of steroid testing that was more in line with those of the National Football League and the National Basketball Association. In late 2005, MLB penalties for steroid use were stiffened (Drugs...in Focus, page 197). Testing for amphetamine use, previously omitted from consideration in the earlier agreement, was added with its own set of penalties for violation.

Recent revelations indicate that drug testing in MLB has failed to eliminate the use of performance-enhancing drugs. In 2007, a major investigation, under the direction of former U.S. senator and federal prosecutor George J. Mitchell, concluded that MLB policies had reduced the use of steroids but that other nonsteroid performance-enhancing drugs, particularly human growth hormone, had increased in popularity and have continued to be widely used. At present, human growth hormone cannot be detected by the standard urine tests that have been approved by the MLB players union. The issue of drug testing in sports will be taken up in a later section of this chapter.[9]

The Hazards of Anabolic Steroids

One of the problems that complicates any look at the adverse effects of steroid abuse is that the dosage levels vary over an enormous range. Further, since nonmedical steroid use is illegal, it is virtually impossible to know the exact dosage levels or even the exact combinations of steroids a particular individual may be taking. It is estimated that a "typical" body builder on anabolic steroids may be taking in a minimum of five to twenty-nine times the therapeutic doses recommended for the medical use of these drugs, but in some cases, the estimates have gone much higher.[10]

Effects on Hormonal Systems

At these huge dosages, anabolic steroids are literally flooding into the body, upsetting the delicate balance of

Drugs...in Focus

Suspension Penalties for Steroid Use in Sports

The 2005 agreement on regulations against steroid use in major league baseball (MLB) included a ban on "all substances regarded now, or in the future, by the federal government as steroids" as well as human growth hormone and steroid precursor hormones such as androstenedione. Suspension penalties for positive-test infractions under these new regulations are shown in comparison to previous MLB regulations and those of other U.S. and international athletic organizations.

| | POSITIVE TEST | | | | |
	First	Second	Third	Fourth	Fifth
Major League Baseball					
Pre-2005	counseling	15 days	25 days	50 days	1 year
Late 2005	50 games	100 games	lifetime suspension, with right of reinstatement after two years		
Minor League Baseball	15 days	30 days	60 days	1 year	lifetime
National Football League	4 games	6 games	1 year	1 year	1 year
National Basketball Association	5 games	10 games	25 games	25 games	25 games
National Hockey League			—no testing for steroids—		
World Anti-Doping Association (Olympic sports)	2 years	lifetime			

Source: Curry, Jack (2006, November 16). Baseball lacks stiffer penalties for steroid use. *New York Times*, pp. A1, D2. NFL will ban amphetamines as enhancers (2006, June 28). *Newsday*, p. A53.

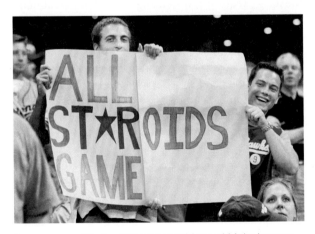

Fans expressed their opinion on steroid use at Major League Baseball's All-Star Game in 2002. Between 5 and 7 percent of MLB players tested positive for anabolic steroids as a result of randomized screening conducted during spring training in 2003. Players involved in steroid use have been dubbed "the syringe generation."

hormones and other chemicals that are normally controlled by testosterone. The primary effect in men is for the testes gland to react to the newly increased testosterone levels in the blood by producing *less* testosterone on its own. In other words, the gland is getting the incorrect message that its services are no longer needed. As a result, the testicles shrink, and a lower sperm count leads to sterility, reversible for most men but irreversible in a small number of cases. Paradoxically, the male breasts enlarge (a condition called **gynecomastia**) because steroids break down eventually into estradiol, the female sex hormone. Other related consequences include frequent, sustained, and often painful penile erections (a condition called **priapism**)

gynecomastia (GUY-neh-coh-MAST-ee-ah): An enlargement of the breasts.

priapism (PRY-ah-pih-zem): A condition marked by persistent and frequently painful penile erections.

Anabolic steroids produce massive development of muscula-ture, a prized asset in competitive body building.

EFFECT	NUMBER REPORTING THE EFFECT	REVERSIBLE AFTER END OF USE
Lower voice	10	no
Increased facial hair	9	no
Enlarged clitoris	8	no
Increased aggressiveness	8	yes
Increased appetite	8	unknown
Decreased body fat	8	unknown
Diminished or stopped menstruation	7	yes
Increased sexual drive	6	yes
Increased acne	6	yes
Decreased breast size	5	unknown
Increased body hair	5	no
Increased loss of scalp hair	2	no

TABLE 8.2

Reported side effects of anabolic steroids in ten women

Note: The ten women were all weight-trained athletes.

Sources: Strauss, Richard H., and Yesalis, Charles E. (1993). Additional effects of anabolic steroids in women. In Charles E. Yesalis (Ed.), *Anabolic steroids in sport and exercise.* Champaign, IL: Human Kinetics Publishers, pp. 151–160. Strauss, Richard H., Ligget, M. T., and Lanese R. R. (1985). Anabolic steroid use and perceived effects in ten weight-trained women athletes. *Journal of the American Medical Association, 253,* 2871–2873.

and an enlargement of the prostate gland. Severe acne, particularly on the shoulders and back, results from an increase in the secretions of the sebaceous glands in the skin. Other testosterone-related effects include two changes in hair growth patterns: increased facial hair growth and accelerated balding on the top of the head.

Some athletes attempt to counter these undesirable hormonal effects by combining anabolic steroids with human chorionic gonadotropin (HCG), a hormone that ordinarily stimulates the testes to secrete testosterone. In theory, this strategy can work, but the dosages have to be carefully controlled, something that self-medicating athletes are unlikely to do. Repeated HCG treatments actually can have the opposite effect from the one that is intended, making matters worse rather than better. In addition, HCG itself has its own adverse effects, including headaches, mood swings, depression, and retention of fluids.[11]

Among women taking anabolic steroids, the dramatically increased levels of testosterone in bodies that normally have only trace amounts produce major physiological changes, only some of which return to normal when steroids are withdrawn. Table 8.2 lists the major reversible and irreversible effects among women.

Effects on Other Systems of the Body

Given the fact that the liver is the primary means for clearing drugs from the body (see Chapter 3), it is not surprising that large doses of anabolic steroids should take their toll on this particular organ. The principal result is a greatly increased risk of developing liver tumors. The type of liver tumors frequently seen in these circumstances are benign (noncancerous) blood-filled cysts, with the potential for causing liver failure. In addition, a rupture in these cysts can produce abdominal bleeding, requiring life-saving emergency treatment. Fortunately, these liver abnormalities are reversible when steroids are withdrawn from use.[12]

There is evidence from animal studies that increased steroid levels in the body can produce high blood pressure and high cholesterol levels, as well as heart abnormalities. In human studies, chronic steroid abuse has been associated with an increased risk of cardiovascular disease. There are documented cases of heart-related sudden death among athletes who have been steroid users, even though there was no history of illness or any family history that would predispose them to heart trouble. Cardiac abnormalities such as enlargement of the left ventricle are not reversible when steroid use is discontinued.[13]

Psychological Problems

Stories abound of mood swings and increased aggressiveness, often referred to by athletes as 'roid rage, when taking anabolic steroids. Numerous anecdotal reports force us to consider the possibility that real psychological changes are going on.[14] As an example, this is how one sportswriter recalled the unusual behavior of the professional football player Lyle Alzado during the 1980s:

> I was covering the Los Angeles Raiders when Alzado, who had played previously with the Denver Broncos and Cleveland Browns, joined [the team] in 1982. In 1984, I was talking to one of his teammates across the Raiders' dressing room, when Alzado, with no provocation, picked up his gray metal stool and threw it in my direction, shouting something about "reporters in the locker room." Shaken, I asked several players who knew him best what was bugging him. They said Alzado probably just had a steroid injection and to stay out of his way. Good advice.[15]

Beyond the well-publicized anecdotal reports, however, more rigorous laboratory investigations into the relationship between anabolic steroid use and psychological problems are required to provide a better understanding of the phenomenon. In a major study addressing this issue, a group of male volunteers were randomly administered intramuscular injections of testosterone cyprionate or a placebo over a period of twenty-five weeks. All of them were screened for current or prior psychological problems. One subgroup was engaged in weight training but had no prior history of steroid use. A second subgroup had no training experience and had not used steroids. A third group reported a history of steroid use but had refrained from any use for a minimum of three months prior to the beginning of the study.

The results showed that, on average, testosterone significantly increased manic behavior and feelings of aggressiveness, but the individual reactions were quite variable. Only eight of the fifty men in the study showed any mood changes at all. Two of them showed marked symptoms. One of these men experienced an aggressive outburst at work and, on one occasion, reacted to being cut off in traffic by following the person in his car for several miles. The other man developed extreme euphoria and reported a decreased need for sleep. Six other study participants showed more moderate changes. One man in this category found himself wanting to beat up his opponent in a college sports competition, even though he had never had such aggressive feelings before in the course of a game. All of the other participants in the study showed minimal or no effects, and in no case was there an incident of actual violent behavior. Neither previous steroid use nor regular weight training was associated with the symptoms observed in the men responding to testosterone.

Quick Concept Check 8.1

Understanding the Effects of Anabolic Steroids

Check your understanding of the effects of anabolic steroids by indicating whether the following conditions can be attributed to steroid use.

1. severe acne on the lower extremities of the body
2. increased aggressiveness and mood swings
3. premature balding in men
4. increased development of the testicles
5. enlarged breasts (gynecomastia) among women
6. accelerated growth in adolescents around the time of puberty

Answers: 1. no 2. yes 3. yes 4. no 5. no 6. no

Because the study used a double-blind design, neither the experimenters nor the men being studied knew whether they were being injected with testosterone or a placebo (see Chapter 3); half the men started with the active drug condition, and half started with the placebo condition. Therefore, we can eliminate the possible influences of expectations and preconceptions about what different behaviors and experiences might result from anabolic steroids to explain the study findings.

On the basis of this information, mood changes and aggressiveness as a result of an elevation in testosterone levels appears to be a genuine effect, though the reactions of people taking anabolic steroids are far from uniform. It has been estimated, by extrapolating from the available research literature, that somewhere between 2 and 20 percent of men will develop mood-related psychological problems from anabolic steroid use.

However, it is important to realize that experimental studies of this type underestimate the extent of the phenomenon in the real world. In the study reported here, the maximum dosage of testosterone was 600 mg per week. In actual practice, steroid abusers often take drugs that boost testosterone to as much as 1,000 to 1,500 mg per week, levels that far exceed those that can be safely studied in the laboratory. As a consequence, the percentage of individuals developing significant mood changes and behavioral problems is likely to be much higher, and the changes and problems themselves can be expected to be substantially greater.[16]

Steve T. isn't his real name. But his story is not only real but undoubtedly a recognizable one to young men in nearly every American community where the importance of personal appearance has managed to outweigh physical risks and criminal prosecution.

Steve was not an aspiring athlete or competitive body builder. The drug-testing program at his school would not have affected him in any way. He was simply a sixteen-year-old sub-urban teenager, short of stature and self-confidence and convinced that muscles would make the difference. "I wanted people to notice me," he said. In particular, he wanted the girls to notice him.

It began with hours pumping weights at home and poring over muscle web sites on the Internet. One day, he asked for a "shortcut"

at a gym he had joined. Soon, he was injecting $150 doses of testosterone on a regular basis. In the meantime, Steve packed on twenty pounds of muscle and finally got all the attention he had always craved from his friends and from girls. He could now bench-press 180 pounds with ease and curl 100 pounds "For a little guy, I was really putting it up," he said. He ignored the acne that spread across his back.

Steve was also getting careless. Afraid to keep his steroids at home, he would take them to school. When they were discovered, school officials notified the police, and Steve was arrested for possession of a controlled substance. Charges were reduced to a misdemeanor offense, but the real punishment came later when a family physician noted a low sperm count.

His mother was convinced that Steve's growth had been stunted. "I was scared," he said. "I kept saying to myself: 'I don't belong here [in this predicament]. I'm not a bad kid.'"

Steve canceled his gym member-ship and set his sights on turning his life around. Working out was no longer so important to him. Currently, he has a girlfriend and claims that he is off steroids. His parents still worry.

Source: Bruchey, Samuel (2004, December 19). Steroids in the suburbs. *Newsday*, pp. A3, A48–A49. Kaplan, Thomas (2007, September 27). Teenagers can buy steroids by just browsing the web, Connecticut officials say. *New York Times*, p. B3. Kilgannon, Corey (2007, September 26). Long Island steroid labs found to be big busi-ness. *New York Times*, p. B1.

Special Problems for Adolescents

During puberty, a particularly crucial process among boys is growth of the long bones of the body, which results in an increase in height. Anabolic steroids suppress growth hor-mones; as a result, muscular development is enhanced but overall body growth is stunted. Among girls, testosterone-related drugs delay the onset of puberty, making the body shorter, lighter, and more "girl-like" while enhancing the user's overall strength. On a psychological level, feelings of euphoria and aggression that adolescents experience while using anabolic steroids can be replaced by lethargy, loss of confidence, and depression when these drugs are discon-tinued (Portrait).[17]

Patterns of Anabolic Steroid Abuse

In 1990, as a response to the increasing awareness of the abuse of anabolic steroids both in and out of competi-tive sports, Congress passed the Anabolic Steroid Control Act, reclassifying anabolic steroids as Schedule III con-trolled substances, on a par with codeine preparations and

barbiturates. Jurisdiction was transferred from the Food and Drug Administration (FDA) to the Drug Enforce-ment Administration (DEA). As a result of this legislation, pharmacies are permitted to fill anabolic-steroid prescrip-tions up to a maximum of five times, but penalties for violating the law can result in a five-year prison term and a $250,000 fine for illegal nonmedical sales and a one-year term and a $1,000 fine for nonmedical possession. Penal-ties are doubled for repeated offenses or for selling these drugs to minors (see Chapter 17). States are permitted to draft their own laws regarding the definition of anabolic steroids and set sentencing guidelines for steroid offend-ers. While most states follow the federally mandated Schedule III classification, New York lists steroids in Schedule II, and Alaska does not schedule them at all. In some states, possession of small quantities of steroids is regarded as a misdemeanor; other states regard it as a felony. In most but not all states, first-time offenses do not result in imprisonment, unless there are aggravating cir-cumstances such as possession of large quantities or evi-dence of intent to sell or distribute the drugs.[18]

Despite the regulations now in effect, steroid abuse today remains a major problem. Steroid distribution has become an enormous black-market enterprise. With their use commonly referred to as being "on the juice," these drugs are channeled principally through people associated with body-building gyms and through Internet web sites that frequently change the identity of a company's location in an effort to stay one step ahead of the law. Some Internet-based suppliers include a warning on their web sites, "Due to their profound effects and potencies, it is recommended to seek the guidance of a physician prior to use," to protect themselves from liability, though no customer would voluntarily divulge his or her steroid abuse, much less seek medical guidance.

It is estimated that the illicit anabolic steroid market is valued at between $300 million to $400 million each year, with the drugs smuggled into the United States from Europe, Canada, and Mexico. In 2008, the University of Michigan survey reported that between 1 and 2 percent of eighth graders, tenth graders, and high school seniors had used anabolic steroids in their lifetime.[19]

The Potential for Steroid Dependence

While some anabolic steroids can be taken orally and others through intramuscular injections, abusers often administer a combination of both types in a practice called *stacking*. Hard-core abusers may take a combination of three to five different pills and injectables simultaneously, or they may consume any steroid that is available ("shotgunning"), with the total exceeding a dozen. In addition to the complications that result from so many different types of steroids being taken at the same time, multiple injections into the buttocks or thighs, with 1.5-inch needles (called "darts" or "points"), are painful and inevitably leave scars. If these needles are shared, as they frequently are, the risk of hepatitis or HIV contamination is significant.

Steroid abusers often follow a pattern called *cycling*, in which steroids are taken for periods lasting from four to eighteen weeks, each separated by an "off" period of abstention. Unfortunately, when the drugs are withdrawn, the newly developed muscles tend to "shrink up," throwing the abuser into a panic that his or her body is losing the gains that have been achieved. In addition, abstention from steroids can lead to signs of depression, such as problems sleeping, lack of appetite, and general moodiness. All these effects encourage a return to steroids, frequently in even larger doses, and a craving for the euphoria that the person felt while on them.

A variation of the cycling pattern is the practice of *pyramiding*. An individual starts with low doses of steroids, gradually increases the doses over several weeks prior to an athletic competition, then tapers off entirely before the competition itself in an attempt to escape detection during drug testing. However, pyramiding leads to the same problems during withdrawal and abstention as cycling, except that the symptoms occur during the competition itself.

A major problem associated with steroid abuse is the potential for an individual to believe that his or her physique will forever be imperfect. In a kind of "reverse anorexia" that has been called **muscle dysmorphia**, some body builders continue to see their bodies as weak and small when they look at themselves in the mirror despite their greatly enhanced physical development. Peer pressure at the gyms and clubs is a factor in never being satisfied with the size of one's muscles, but it is becoming apparent that societal pressures play a role as well. In the case of males, it is interesting to examine the evolution of the design of G.I. Joe action figures over the years, from the original toy introduced in 1964 to the most recent incarnation introduced in 1998 (Figure 8.1, page 202). Just as the Barbie doll has been criticized as setting an impossible ideal for the female body among girls, male-oriented action figures can be criticized on the same basis for boys.[20]

Traditional estimates of substance dependence among steroid users range between 13 and 18 percent, but more recent studies indicate that the prevalence rate may be somewhat higher. In an Internet survey, about one in four weight lifters and body builders using steroids have reported that they were taking larger amounts of steroids over a longer period of time than originally intended, that they needed increased amounts of steroids to achieve the desired effect, or that they experienced physical or emotional problems when steroids were discontinued. One in eight admitted that they had resumed steroid use to relieve a problem that occurred when they stopped (Health Alert). About one-third of them met the criteria for substance dependence, according to DSM-IV guidelines (see Chapter 2).[21]

In light of the potential for steroid dependence and the adverse effects of acute steroid use, prevention programs have been instituted to address the problems of steroid abuse, particularly among male adolescents involved in sports. The most prominent example, developed by Linn Goldberg at Oregon Health and Science University at Portland, is called the Adolescents Training and Learning to Avoid Steroids (ATLAS) program. Young

---

muscle dysmorphia (dis-MORF-ee-ah): The perception of one's own body as small and weak and one's musculature as inadequately developed, despite evidence to the contrary. Also known as megorexia, the condition of muscle dysmorphia is a form of body dysmorphic disorder.

FIGURE 8.1

The muscular development of the G.I. Joe action figure has increased dramatically since its introduction in 1964. The estimated bicep circumference for a six-foot man, based on dimensions of the action figure, more than doubled from 1964 to 1998.

Source: As G.I. Joe bulks up, concern for the 98-pound weakling (1999, May 30). *New York Times*, p. D2.

athletes, team coaches, and team captains receive instruction on both sides of the issue—the desirable effects as well as the adverse effects of steroid use. This approach is taken because a failure to acknowledge potential benefits reduces the credibility of the intervention.

Evaluations of the ATLAS program have shown that program participants, relative to a control group, were better informed about proper exercise, had a better understanding of the harmful effects of steroids, developed a more negative attitude toward others who used

---

HEALTH ALERT!

The Symptoms of Steroid Abuse

For Both Sexes

1. Rapid increases in strength and/or size beyond what you would expect in a relatively short time. Putting on ten to twenty pounds of solid muscle within a period of a few weeks or so should be a major warning.

2. Involvement in activities in which steroid abuse is known to be condoned or encouraged

3. Sudden increases in appetite and preoccupation with changes in one's physical condition

4. Recent appearance of acne, particularly on the upper back, shoulders, and arms

5. Premature male-pattern baldness, including a rapidly receding hairline or loss of hair from the top rear of the head

6. A puffy appearance in the face as if the individual is retaining water

7. An increase in moodiness or unusual shifts in mood

8. A reddening of the face, neck, and upper chest, appearing as if one is constantly flushed

9. A yellowing of the skin or the whites of the eyes, stemming from a disturbance in liver function

For Men

1. An enlargement of the breasts, often accompanied by protruding nipples

2. An increase in sexual interest and a tendency to display that interest more aggressively

For Women

1. A lowering of the vocal range

2. Smaller or flatter breasts (see Table 8.2)

Where to go for assistance:
www.nida.nih.gov/Infofacts/Steroids.html
www.steroidabuse.gov

The National Institute on Drug Abuse sponsors a vast array of web sites related to drug use and abuse. The first web site on steroid abuse includes a comprehensive list of potential adverse effects of anabolic steroids; the second web site emphasizes issues of prevention and education.

Source: Wright, James E., and Cowart, Virginia S. (1990). *Anabolic steroids: Altered states.* Carmel, IN: Benchmark Press, pp. 71–91.

steroids, and were more likely to engage in healthier eating habits. They also showed a 53 percent reduction in new use of anabolic steroids after one year as well as a 63 percent reduction in the intention to use these drugs in the future.[22]

Another prevention and education program originating at the Oregon Health and Science University at Portland, called Athletes Targeting Healthy Exercise and Nutrition (ATHENA), is specifically oriented toward female athletes, addressing issues such as the connection between disordered eating behaviors and use of body-shaping and performance-enhancing drugs. The program promotes healthy sports nutrition and strength-training alternatives, as well as the training needed to make healthy choices in sports and throughout their lives.[23]

Counterfeit Steroids and the Placebo Effect

As with many illicit drugs, some products marketed to look like anabolic steroids are not the real thing. The problem here is that athletes are notoriously superstitious and easily leave themselves open to placebo effects. On the one hand, in the case of anabolic steroids, the effects on muscle development are usually so dramatic that it is difficult to mistake the response as simply a result of a placebo effect. On the other hand, several other forms of performance-enhancing drugs have far more subtle effects, and psychological factors can end up playing a greater role. Consider the clever strategy a baseball trainer claims to have used for the St. Louis Cardinals in the 1960s:

> In 1964, I devised a yellow RBI pill, a red shutout pill, and a potent green hitting pill. Virtually every player on the team took them, and some wouldn't go out on the field until they took my pills. They worked so well that we won the pennant. We used them again in 1967 and 1968 and also won the pennant. They worked because I never told them that the pills were placebos.[24]

Frequently, a bogus drug can achieve enormous popularity simply by word of mouth. A former steroid "customer" relates the following story:

> Bolasterone. It swept the country. They made millions. Millions, those California guys. All it was, was vegetable oil, a little bit of testosterone, and liquid aspirin. And they called it Bolasterone. And they hyped it up so much. It was selling for $250 to $275 a bottle. You would do anything to get this stuff. [They said] "Mr. Olympia used it! Secretly." I tell you, Madison Avenue could not have come up with a better campaign to sell this stuff.... If you had a bottle of

> it, I mean you could sell it for anything.... [It was hyped] through the grapevine. Underground. The network was incredible. From gym to gym to gym.... They'll say, "Did you see M.? He put on 15 pounds in a week." "What the hell is he using?" "Don't say anything. He's using Bolasterone!" "Wow. What the hell is it? Can you get it?" "Yeah, I can."[25]

Nonsteroid Hormones and Performance-Enhancing Supplements

Certainly anabolic steroids have dominated the performance-enhancing drug scene, but other products have been promoted as having performance-enhancing properties. They include human growth hormone, androstenedione, and creatine.

Human Growth Hormone

One illicit alternative, **human growth hormone (hGH),** has become increasingly popular, according to experts in this field, because it is more widely available and cheaper than in previous years, in contrast to the ever more costly illicit steroids. Those who take this pituitary hormone, however, face the increased risk of developing a significant side effect called **acromegaly,** a condition resulting in a coarse and misshapen head, enlarged hands and feet, and damage to various internal organs.

Prior to 1985, hGH was obtained from the pituitary glands of human cadavers, but now genetically engineered hGH (brand names: Protropin and Humatrope) is available, approved by the FDA for the treatment of rare cases of stunted growth. Although the distribution of these drugs is controlled by their manufacturers as carefully as possible, supplies manage to get diverted for illicit use.

Testimony in 2008 that prominent major league baseball players had used hGH for performance-enhancing purposes revealed the abuse potential of this hormone in professional sports. It is doubtful, however, that its reputation for performance enhancement is justified, according to a major review of more than forty studies of hGH in

human growth hormone (hGH): A naturally occurring hormone promoting growth, particularly in the long bones of the body.

acromegaly (A-kroh-MEG-ah-lee): A condition resulting in structural abnormalities of the head, hands, and feet, as well as damage to internal organs.

healthy athletes, conducted between 1966 to 2007. The conclusion is that hGH use increases lean body mass, but the increased bulk does not raise levels of strength or endurance. Indeed, hGH produces higher levels of lactate in muscle tissue, leading to fatigue; hGH users are more likely than non-users to develop joint pain and carpal tunnel syndrome. In the absence of scientific evidence of any performance-enhancing effects, it has been suggested that reports by athletes that hGH helped to increase their athletic performance are probably due to a placebo effect. Nonetheless, despite hGH's dubious value, hGH screening, capable of differentiating naturally produced hGH from synthetic hGH, became a fixture of drug testing at the 2008 Summer Olympics Games in Beijing. Because hGH has a relatively short half-life, athletes tested positive only if the drug had been injected in the previous twelve to twenty-four hours.[26]

Dietary Supplements as Performance-Enhancing Aids

As recently as ten to twenty years ago, fitness-oriented young people might have taken only basic vitamins and minerals to help them build muscle mass or improve cardiovascular performance. Today, the fitness market is inundated with a growing number of dietary supplement products with presumed ergogenic properties, with sales of more than $2 billion each year in the United States. They are sold under short, appealing names like Adenergy and Lean Stack alongside impressive before-and-after photographs or under long, pseudoscientific names like Vaso XP Xtreme Vasodilator and Xenadrine-NRG that are accompanied by complex molecular diagrams.

> A product called Aftermath, for example, boasts that it can help "swell your muscles to grotesque size" and eliminate the chance of "dooming yourself to girly-man status." Xpand Nitric Oxide Reactor, a drink mix that comes in tropical berry and piña colada flavors, offers bodybuilders "the most unbelievable muscular and vascular pumps you have ever experienced."[27]

Because dietary supplements are not classified by the FDA as drugs (see Chapter 1), they can be marketed and sold without a prescription. Moreover, except in rare instances, there is no regulatory authority over their safety or effectiveness.

A prominent example of a dietary supplement used for performance-enhancing purposes is **androstenedione.** Technically speaking, androstenedione is not an anabolic steroid because it is not based on the specific structure of testosterone itself. Nonetheless, it is testosterone-related because it is a naturally occurring metabolic precursor to testosterone. In other words, the body converts androstenedione to testosterone due to the action of specific enzymes in the liver. At the recommended daily dose of 300 mg, androstenedione has been found to increase testosterone levels by an average of 34 percent above normal. Despite the increase in testosterone, however, no change in body composition or strength is observed when compared to placebo controls. There is no evidence that androstenedione promotes muscle protein synthesis at these dosage levels.[28]

Androstenedione rose to prominence in the late 1990s when it became public that St. Louis Cardinals baseball player Mark McGwire had been taking the supplement during his phenomenal 1998 hitting season (seventy home runs, far eclipsing the previous record). A storm of controversy ensued, with some commentators suggesting that McGwire's record be disallowed because of his androstenedione use. While banned by the National Football League and other professional and amateur sports organizations, androstenedione is not banned in major league baseball, so McGwire's use was not illegal.

In 1999, McGwire discontinued taking the supplement, basing his decision largely on his concern about his effect as a role model on young people. Interestingly, his 1999 hitting record diminished only slightly, still reaching the third-highest total home runs in professional baseball history at that time. However, the publicity surrounding McGwire's use of androstenedione and its easy availability were blamed for a 30 percent increase among eighth-grade boys and a 75 percent increase among tenth-grade boys in the use of anabolic steroids from 1998 to 2000. In 2005, the FDA banned the over-the-counter sale of androstenedione (Andro) and other testosterone precursors. By this time, the Anabolic Steroid Control Act of 2004 had expanded the Schedule III classification (see Chapter 2) to include androstenedione and other testosterone precursors, along with anabolic steroids themselves.[29]

Another dietary supplement marketed as a performance-enhancing agent is **creatine** (brand names Creatine Fuel, Muscle Power, and many others), a non-protein amino acid synthesized in the kidney, liver, and pancreas from L-arginine, glycine, and L-methionine.

androstenedione (AN-dro-steen-DYE-own): A dietary supplement, acting as a metabolic precursor to testosterone and used as an ergogenic agent.

creatine (CREE-ah-teen): A dietary supplement available for ergogenic uses.

Ingestion of creatine has been found to enhance the retention of water by muscle cells, causing them to expand in size. One hypothesis is that water retention might stimulate protein synthesis and increase muscle mass as a result, but there is no evidence from controlled studies that this is the case. Although creatine appears to enhance performance in repetitive bouts of high-intensity cycling and sprints, the weight gain experienced by creatine users makes it undesirable for runners or swimmers.

Short-term use of creatine has been found to produce muscle cramping, and its long-term adverse effects have not been fully explored. In 2007, one out of six twelfth-grade boys in the United States had used creatine in the previous twelve months, a very high prevalence rate given the marginal ergogenic advantage that creatine appears to yield and the present uncertainty about possible adverse health consequences.[30]

Nonmedical Use of Stimulant Medication in Baseball

Earlier in the chapter, nineteenth-century examples were cited of world-class athletes experimenting with stimulants in attempts to achieve some level of performance enhancement in their sport. More than a century later, stimulants have continued to be an attractive option. Amphetamines were officially banned in major league baseball in 2005, but before that time, amphetamine use may have been a mainstay for players to stay focused and ward off fatigue in a grueling and lengthy competitive season. According to a professional baseball team psychiatrist, testifying in congressional hearings in 2008, "Amphetamines are the real performance-enhancing drugs that people should always have been worried about."

It is therefore not surprising that since 2005, some players have attempted to circumvent the amphetamine ban by taking stimulant medications intended for the treatment of attention deficit/hyperactivity disorder (ADHD). In 2007, 103 therapeutic-use exemptions for ADHD were approved for MLB players—a suspiciously high number considering that only 28 players had received such approval in 2006. Whether these exemptions reflected a fourfold increase in the incidence of ADHD symptoms over a single year or an effort to benefit from the performance-enhancing effects of stimulant drugs, without violating the amphetamine ban, is a matter of concern to MLB management as well as baseball fans (see Health Line, Chapter 4, page 112).[31]

Current Drug-Testing Procedures and Policies

Since the mid-1960s, organizers of major athletic competitions have attempted to develop effective screening procedures to prevent the use of performance-enhancing drugs from resulting in one competitor having an unfair advantage over another. Needless to say, these procedures have neither proved perfect nor served as an effective deterrent for drug use among athletes. We are used to hearing about championship events accompanied by reports of an athlete disqualified from competing or denied the honor of winning because he or she tested positive for a particular banned substance. Ironically, the present status of drug testing as a fact of life in modern sports has brought with it a new form of contest, pitting the skill and ingenuity of the laboratory scientist whose job it is to detect the presence of performance-enhancing drugs against the skill and ingenuity of the athlete in devising ways to use them without detection (Drugs . . . in Focus, page 206).[32]

This section looks at drug-testing techniques designed to detect not only performance-enhancing drugs that are relevant to sports but also a wider range of illicit drugs, such as heroin, cocaine, and marijuana. Within some sports organizations, such as the National Collegiate Athletic Association (NCAA), drug tests are conducted not only for the presence of performance-enhancing drugs but also for the presence of drugs that have no particular performance-enhancing benefits. In the case of marijuana, for example, the proper description for its effects with regard to athletic competitions might be *ergolytic* ("performance-reducing"). The policy is defended on the premise that athletes have the potential for exposure to illicit substances, and no collegiate athlete should be permitted to compete while engaging in illegal activity. Related issues surrounding drug testing in the general population, particularly in the workplace, will be examined in Chapter 17.

Techniques for Drug Testing

Present-day drug-testing procedures begin with a urine sample from the individual in question. The advantages lie in the ease and noninvasiveness of collecting urine, the ease with which urine can be analyzed for specific factors, and the fact that drugs or their metabolites (by-products) are usually very stable in frozen urine. Therefore, it is possible to provide long-term storage of positive samples, in the event that the results are disputed. The disadvantages are that many perceive urine collection to be a humiliating experience, a dehydrated athlete immediately after

Drugs...in Focus

THG and the War on Performance-Enhancing Drugs

In June 2003, Donald H. Catlin, director of the Olympic drug-testing laboratory at the University of California at Los Angeles, received an unexpected package. According to an attached note written by a track coach who wished to remain anonymous, the test tube inside the package contained the residue of an undetectable anabolic steroid from a used syringe. Catlin had suspected for several years that designer-type steroids were being used by both amateur and professional athletes, but these drugs had remained undetected by standard testing procedures. Within three months, the drug in question had been identified as tetrahydrogestrinone (THG), which has a chemical structure resembling steroids such as gestrinole, used as a therapy for gynecological problems, and trenbolone, used by ranchers to increase the beef content of cattle.

THG had been undetectable because the substance would ordinarily disintegrate during standard drug screening. When Catlin's laboratory succeeded in stabilizing THG, its "chemical fingerprint" became obvious. By September, a test for THG was developed and ready to be used to screen 550 refrigerated urine samples obtained from athletes at the U.S. track and field championships held three months earlier, as well as samples forwarded from international track and field competitions. As a result, two U.S. track and field champions, 1,500-meter runner Regina Jacobs and shotputter Kevin Troth, tested positive for THG, as did other athletes in the United States and the United Kingdom.

Indictments were issued in 2004 to two executives of the nutritional supplement laboratory in California where THG was made, as well as to the personal trainer of San Francisco Giants star Barry Bonds and a prominent track-and-field coach. They were charged with illegally distribut-ing steroids and other performance-enhancing drugs to dozens of professional athletes in football, baseball, and track and field. Whether athletes testing positive for THG eventually will be disqualified remains to be determined, as is the question of how widely used THG might be in the present-day sports world. The scope of THG use is expected to become clearer in the future as international sports federations undertake retrospective tests from frozen urine samples collected during championship events that occurred in the past few years.

Despite the negative publicity of the THG scandal, some view these developments in a positive light. According to Gary I. Wadler, an expert on the subject of drug testing in sports, "There is no question that this is a real blow to the integrity of sport, but there's a silver lining to the black cloud." Wadler has noted that the United States Anti-Doping Association quickly shared the THG data with the World Anti-Doping Agency (WADA), which then distributed the findings to sports organizations throughout the world.

To some, increased public attention to the problems of performance-enhancing drugs might help to make doping in sports as socially unacceptable as drinking and driving. Others, however, view the THG scandal from a darker perspective—as simply a small victory in an unending game of pharmacological cat and mouse.

Sources: Ashley, Steven (2004, February). Doping by design. *Scientific American*, pp. 22–23. Curry, Jack (2004, February 13). Four indicted in a steroid scheme that involves top pro athletes. *New York Times*, pp. A1, D3. Kondro, Wayne (2003). Athletes' "designer steroid" leads to widening scandal. *The Lancet, 362*, 1466. Longman, Jere, and Drape, Joe (2003, November 2). Decoding a steroid: Hunches, sweat, and vindication. *New York Times*, pp. 1, 26. Schnirring, Lisa (2003). Experts see silver lining in THG scandal. *Physician and Sportsmedicine, 31*, 16–17. Quotation on page 16.

---

competing may find it difficult to urinate, and there may be ways to tamper with the urine sample prior to testing.

The two major urinanalysis methods are the **enzyme** **immunoassay (EIA)** technique and a procedure combining **gas chromatography and mass spectrometry (GC/MS).** In both methods, the collected urine is divided into two samples prior to being sent off to the laboratory so that if the analysis of one sample yields a positive outcome, the analysis can be repeated on the other sample. This reanalysis procedure is often required if an individual appeals the original test result.[33]

With the EIA method, a separate test must be run on each particular drug that is being screened. First, at an earlier time, the substance to be tested for (THC or

enzyme immunoassay (EIA): One of the two major drug-testing techniques for detecting banned substances or drugs.

gas chromatography/mass spectrometry (GC/MS): A drug-testing technique based on the combination of gas chromatography and mass spectrometry.

cocaine, for example) has been injected into an animal, eliciting specific immunological antibodies to that substance. The antibodies are then purified into a testing substrate. The combination of the collected urine and the testing substrate will yield a specific reaction if the urine contains the banned substance. A popular commercial testing kit for screening major controlled substances (opiates, amphetamines, cocaine, benzodiazepines, and marijuana), called **EMIT (enzyme multiplied immunoassay technique),** has been marketed by Syva Laboratories, a subsidiary of Syntex Corporation in Palo Alto, California, since the early 1970s. This kit is relatively inexpensive and can be used to screen large numbers of urine samples. It is so widely available that its trademark name, EMIT, is often used to mean any form of EIA method.

With the GC/MS method, the urine is first vaporized and combined with an inert gas and then passed over a number of chemically treated columns. Through the process of gas chromatography, technicians are able to identify the presence of a banned substance by the different colorations that are left on the columns. After this has been done, the gas is then ionized (converted into an electrically active form) and sent through an electric current and magnetic field that separates out each of the different ions (electrically charged particles) in the gas. Through the process of mass spectrometry, a particular "fingerprint," or "signature," of each chemical substance can be detected and measured. The GC/MS technique is considered more definitive than the EIA technique, but it is considerably more expensive and time-consuming. It is also the only testing procedure adequate to screen for anabolic steroids.[34]

Until recently, the predominant means for drug testing has been through urinanalysis. Since the late 1990s, however, increasing interest has been directed toward oral fluid testing. In this procedure, a collection pad is placed between the lower cheek and gum for two to five minutes. The collection pad is then sealed and later analyzed by EIA. Sensitivity and specificity of the results (see the next section) are comparable with those obtained through urinanalysis. As with positive urinanalysis tests, confirmation of positive oral fluid results is made by GC/MS.

Currently available FDA-approved drug-testing systems using oral fluid samples can now provide test results in approximately fifteen minutes. The advantages over traditional urinanalysis are obvious. Analyses of samples are accomplished on-site rather than having to send samples to laboratories for analysis. Specimen collection can be performed face-to-face (literally) with the donor, with little risk of sample substitution, dilution, or adulteration. Embarrassment on the part of the donor is eliminated as well as privacy concerns.[35]

National concern about drug abuse in all its forms has caused us to consider an increased level of drug testing in our society. Here is an editorial cartoonist's commentary on the extent to which this policy might be applied.

Sensitivity and Specificity

As you might imagine, the two principal questions surrounding drug-testing methods are (1) how much of the banned substance needs to be in the body fluid before it is picked up as a positive test (the sensitivity of the test) and (2) whether it is possible to yield a false-positive result in which the test comes out positive but the body fluid is in actuality "clean" (the specificity of the test). In this regard, the GC/MS test is more sensitive and specific than the EIA test.

Frequently, the GC/MS analysis is performed as a confirmation of a positive EIA test. Nonetheless, false positives can occur even with the GC/MS test. Eating a poppy seed roll prior to drug testing or taking quinolone antibiotic medications such as ofloxacin (brand name: Floxin) and ciprofloxacin (brand name: Cipro), for example, has resulted in false-positive indications of opiate use. Therapeutic levels of ibuprofen (brand names: Advil, Motrin, and Nuprin, among others) have resulted in false-positive indications of marijuana smoking. In addition, the passive inhalation of marijuana smoke can leave sufficient levels of THC metabolites to result in false-positive indications of marijuana smoking, though the density of smoke that needs to be present for this to happen makes it unlikely that individuals would be completely unaware that they were being exposed to marijuana.[36]

EMIT (enzyme multiplied immunoassay technique): A commercial testing kit for screening major controlled substances, based on enzyme immunoassay analysis.

Masking Drugs and Chemical Manipulations

Two specific tactics have been employed to disguise the prior use of anabolic steroids so that the outcome of a drug test becomes, in effect, a false negative; both are now relatively obsolete. The first strategy was to take the antigout drug probenecid (brand name: Benemid). Available since 1987, it does mask the presence of anabolic steroids, but it is now on the list of banned substances for competitive athletes and is easily detected by GC/MS techniques. The second strategy was to increase the level of epitestosterone in the body. The standard procedure for determining the present or prior use of anabolic steroids is to calculate the ratio of testosterone against the level of epitestosterone, a naturally occurring hormone that is usually stable at relatively low levels in the body. International athletic organizations now use a ratio of 4:1 (formerly 6:1) or higher as the standard for indicating steroid use. If epitestosterone is artificially elevated, the ratio can be manipulated downward so as to indicate a false-negative result in drug testing. However, suspiciously high levels of epitestosterone can now be detected by GC/MS techniques, so this form of manipulation is no longer successful.[37]

Pinpointing the Time of Drug Use

It is important to remember that a positive result in a drug test indicates merely that the test has detected a minimal level of a drug or its metabolite. It is difficult to determine when that drug was introduced into the body or how long the drug-taking behavior continued. In the case of urinalysis testing, the time it takes for the body to get rid of the metabolites of a particular drug varies considerably, from a few hours to a few weeks (Table 8.3). In the case of oral-fluid drug testing, the window of detection may be different, depending on the drug being screened. Opiates and cocaine are detected within two to three days of ingestion; THC in marijuana is detected within a period ranging from one hour after ingestion to fourteen hours later. Because THC metabolites are excreted into the urine for several days or in some cases for several weeks, oral-fluid testing for marijuana is better suited for determining when marijuana has been last used. In effect, the "window of detection" is more narrow. If the interval between use and testing has been longer than fourteen hours or so but shorter than a few days, urinalysis would pick up a positive result, while oral-fluid testing would not.[38]

Owing to the expense of randomized drug-testing programs, not every institution can afford the costs.

TABLE 8.3

Detection periods for various drugs in urinanalysis tests

DRUG	DETECTION PERIOD	DRUG	DETECTION PERIOD
alcohol	1/2 to 1 day	opiates and opiate-like drugs	
amphetamines and derivatives	1–7 days	Dilaudid	2–4 days
barbiturates		Darvon	6–48 hours
amobarbital, pentobarbital	2–4 days	heroin or morphine	2–4 days
phenobarbital	up to 30 days	methadone	2–3 days
secobarbital	2–4 days	phencyclidine (PCP)	
benzodiazepines	up to 30 days	casual use	2–7 days
cocaine		chronic, heavy use	several months
occasional use	6–12 hours	Quaalude	2–4 days
repeated use	up to 48 hours	anabolic steroids	
marijuana (THC)		fat-soluble injectables	6–8 months
casual use up to 4 joints per week	5–7 days	water-soluble oral types	3–6 weeks
daily use	10–15 days	over-the-counter cold medications containing ephedrine derivatives as decongestants	48–72 hours
chronic, heavy use	1–2 months		

Sources: *Allen and Hanbury's athletic drug reference* (1994). Durham, NC: Clean Data, p. 19. Inaba, Darryl S., and Cohen, William E. (1989). *Uppers, downers, all arounders.* Ashland, OR: Cinemed, p. 206.

The Social Context of Performance-Enhancing Drugs

Anabolic steroids and other performance-enhancing agents are quite different from many of the abused drugs covered in previous chapters in that they affect the way we look and how we compare to others rather than the way we feel. Charles E. Yesalis, one of the leading experts in steroid abuse, has put it this way:

> *If you were stranded on a desert island, you might use cocaine if it were available, but nobody would use steroids. On a desert island, nobody cares what you look like and there is nothing to win. We are the ones who have made the determination that appearance and winning are all important. We're telling kids in our society that sports is more than a game. Until we change those signals, for the most part, we might as well tell people to get used to drug use.*[40]

The future of the fight against anabolic steroid abuse and the abuse of performance-enhancing drugs in general depends, in part, on whether we can change the winner-take-all mentality of our culture. Unfortunately, there seems to be little cause for optimism. Numerous

The pressure to be number one exists in all areas of athletic competition. The intensity of competition in our culture, however, extends beyond the world of sports. Temptations to secure a competitive edge in the corporate world have led to a growing and disturbing acceptance of stimulant abuse as a means of keeping pace with increasingly rapid technologies for communication and business transactions.

Large corporations may be able to budget for potentially thousands of tests for preemployment screening purposes, but relatively few colleges and considerably fewer high schools may be able to establish the level of funding needed to test their respective student populations. Even if the costs were lower, the question still remains as to whether illicit drug-taking behavior would be reduced in the long run as a result. Interestingly, recent evidence indicates that the prospect of randomized drug testing in schools fails to act as a deterrent among students. University of Michigan researchers in 2003 found virtually identical rates of illicit drug use in schools that had drug-testing programs and schools that did not. This general finding was replicated in a study reported in 2008. The deterrent effect of drug testing on illicit drug use in schools clearly has not been demonstrated.[39]

It is also worth considering the following fact regarding abusers of steroids and related performance-enhancing drugs: Individuals who are no longer students in a public institution or participants in an organized athletic program do not need to fear a positive drug test because they will never be required to undergo *any* form of drug testing, random or otherwise.

surveys taken among young athletes and nonathletes alike indicate that the social signals are crystal clear and they are more than willing to take up the challenge, despite the risks. They have typically been asked variations on the following question: "If you had a magic drug that was so fantastic that if you took it once you would win every competition you would enter, from the Olympic decathlon to Mr. Universe, for the next five years, but it had one minor drawback—it would kill you five years after you took it—would you still take the drug?" More than half of those polled have answered "yes" to this question.[41]

In the context of steroid abuse, it is important to recognize that a sense of competition goes beyond dreams of athletic performance. It is apparent that an idealized body image is part of today's standard for a sense of sexuality and social acceptance. This standard might not be news at all to women, but it is a fairly recent development in men. The temptations of steroids as a way of accelerating the effects of weight training are increasing

in our culture. One high school senior has said, "The majority now are guys that don't do it for sports. They do it for girls. For the look." Another senior has remarked on a different kind of lifter in weight rooms and gyms: the vanity body builder (see Portrait, page 200). As he expressed it, "We notice a lot of kids now; they just want this certain type of body—with the abs and the ripped chest—and they want it quick."[42] Exercise physiologist David Pearson has remarked on the social pressures involved:

The teenage years are the skinniest and most awkward, and the idea of being the skinniest kid in the locker room is absolutely terrifying to a teenage boy.[43]

Internet web sites deliver mixed messages, promoting anabolic steroids as well as steroid precursors such as androstenedione with the promise "You'll get huge!" while saying on the labels of their products that people younger than age eighteen should not take them or that they should consult a physician first.

Summary

Drug-Taking Behavior in Sports

- The use of ergogenic (performance-enhancing) drugs in athletic competition has a long history, dating from the original Olympic Games in ancient Greece.
- In the modern era, the principal type of performance-enhancing drugs has been anabolic steroids. These synthetic drugs are all based on variations of the testosterone molecule.
- Since the late 1980s, anabolic steroids have been popular with body builders as well as competitive athletes. This latter group typically takes steroids in enormous quantities and administers them in a largely unsupervised fashion.
- Recently, great concerns have been raised with regard to the use of anabolic steroids, as well as other performance-enhancing drugs, in major league baseball.

The Hazards of Anabolic Steroids

- The hazards of steroid use include liver tumors, mood swings, and increased aggressiveness.
- For men, the effects include lower sperm count, enlargement of the breasts, atrophy of the testicles, baldness, and severe acne. For women, masculinizing changes occur, only some of which are reversible if steroids are withdrawn.

Patterns of Anabolic Steroid Abuse

- Since 1990, possession and sales of anabolic steroids have been illegal without specific medical prescriptions. These drugs are now distributed through illicit black-market channels.
- About 13 to 18 percent of individuals taking large doses of steroids develop both physical and psychological dependence.

Nonsteroid Hormones and Performance-Enhancing Supplements

- Human growth hormone (hGH) is a nonsteroid hormone that has been used for performance-enhancing purposes.
- Two dietary supplements, androstenedione and creatine, have been prominent recently as performance-enhancing aids.

Nonmedical Use of Stimulant Medication in Baseball

- Although amphetamines were officially banned in major league baseball (MLB) in 2005, for a long time players had been taking amphetamines to stay focused and ward off fatigue.
- In 2007, an unusually large number of MLB players reported taking stimulant medications for ADHD

treatment, raising suspicions that this was an effort to circumvent prohibitions against nonmedical stimulant use.

Current Drug-Testing Procedures and Policies

- Drug-testing procedures, chiefly for those in organized athletics, have become increasingly sophisticated in their ability to detect the presence of banned substances.

- Two major techniques, based either on urine or on oral-fluid samples, are enzyme immunoassay (EIA) and a combination of gas chromatography and mass spectrometry (GC/MS).

- The ultimate goal of drug-testing procedures is to make it impossible to yield either a false-negative or false-positive result.

Key Terms

acromegaly, p. 203
adrenocortical steroids, p. 193
anabolic, p. 193
anabolic-androgenic steroids, p. 193
anabolic steroids, p. 193

androgenic, p. 193
androstenedione, p. 204
creatine, p. 204
EMIT (enzyme multiplied immunoassay technique), p. 207

enzyme immunoassay (EIA), p. 206
ergogenic, p. 192
gas chromatography/mass spectrometry (GC/MS), p. 206

gynecomastia, p. 197
human growth hormone (hGH), p. 203
muscle dysmorphia, p. 201
priapism, p. 197

Endnotes

1. Dolan, Edward F. (1986). *Drugs in sports* (rev. ed.). New York: Franklin Watts, pp. 17–18. Meer, Jeff (1987). *Drugs and sports.* New York: Chelsea House, p. 21. Wadler, Gary I., and Hainline, Brian (1989). *Drugs and the athlete.* Philadelphia: F. A. Davis, pp. 3–17.

2. Meer, *Drugs and sports*, pp. 61–75. Taylor, William N. (1991). *Macho medicine: The history of the anabolic steroid epidemic.* Jefferson, NC: McFarland and Co., pp. 3–16.

3. Bhasin, Shalender; Storer, Thomas W.; Berman, Nancy; Callegari, Carlos; Clevenger, Brenda; et al. (1996). The effects of supraphysiologic doses of testosterone on muscle size and strength in normal men. *New England Journal of Medicine, 335,* 1–7. Lombardo, John (1993). The efficacy and mechanisms of action of anabolic steroids. In Charles E. Yesalis (Ed.), *Anabolic steroids in sport and exercise.* Champaign, IL: Human Kinetics Publishers, p. 100.

4. Scott, Jack (1971, October 17). It's not how you play the game, but what pill you take. *New York Times Magazine,* p. 41.

5. Catlin, Don H., and Murray, Thomas H. (1996). Performance-enhancing drugs, fair competition, and Olympic sport. *Journal of the American Medical Association, 276,* 231–237. Maimon, Alan (2000, February 6). Doping's sad toll: One athlete's tale from East Germany. *New York Times,* pp. A1, A6. Yesalis, Charles E., Courson, Stephen P., and Wright, James (1993). History of anabolic steroid use in sport and exercise. In Charles E. Yesalis (Ed.), *Anabolic steroids in sport and exercise.* Champaign, IL: Human Kinetics Publishers, pp. 1–33.

6. Dobie, Michael (2004, August 30). Good job, Athens, and good night. *Newsday,* p. A61. Litsky, Frank (2003,

March 6). International drug code is adopted. *New York Times,* p. D5. Longman, Jere (2003, October 24). Steroid is reportedly found in top runner's urine test. *New York Times,* p. D2. Starr, Mark (2003, November 3). Blowing the whistle on drugs: A raid on a California laboratory threatens to blemish America's athletes—again. *Newsweek,* pp. 60–61. Vecsey, George (2002, March 1). More curious material in skiing's closet. *New York Times,* pp. D1, D4. World Anti-Doping Association, Montreal.

7. W.W.F.'s McMahon indicted (1993, November 19). *New York Times,* p. B12. Yesalis, Courson, and Wright, History of anabolic steroid use, pp. 40–42.

8. Buckley, William E.; Yesalis, Charles E.; Friedl, Karl E.; Anderson, William A.; Streit, Andrea L.; et al. (1988). Estimated prevalence of anabolic steroid use among male high school seniors. *Journal of the American Medical Association, 260,* 3441–3445. Dolphin, Ric (1989, March 13). The steroid scandal. *Maclean's,* pp. 36–39.

9. Curry, Jack (2006, June 8). A new front in baseball's drug war. Player's testimony points to holes in testing policy. *New York Times,* pp. D1, D5. Curry, Jack (2005, November 16). Baseball backs stiffer penalties for steroid use. *New York Times,* pp. A1, D2. Fainaru-Wada, Mark and Williams, Lance (2006). *Game of shadows: Barry Bonds, Balco and the steroids scandal that rocked professional sports.* New York: Gotham Books. Longman, Jere (2005, May 18). Steroid-assisted fastballs? Pitchers face new spotlight. *New York Times,* pp. A1, D3. Schwarz, Alan (2007, December 14). Head of players' union says tests are working. *New York Times,* p. D5. Veesey, George (2008, January 16). Spring training and the

syringe generation. *New York Times*, pp. D1, D3. Wilson, Duff, and Schmidt, Michael S. (2007, November 17). Bonds charged with perjury in steroids case. *New York Times*, pp. A1, D3.

10. Council on Scientific Affairs (1990). Medical and non-medical uses of anabolic-androgenic steroids. *Journal of the American Medical Association*, 264, 2923–2927. Hartgens, Fred, and Kuipers, Harm (2004). Effects of androgenic-anabolic steroids in athletes. *Sports Medicine*, 34, 513–554. Perry, Paul J.; Lund, Brian C.; Deninger, Michael J.; Kutscher, Eric C.; and Schneider, Justin (2005). Anabolic steroid use in weightlifters and body-builders: An Internet survey of drug utilization. *Clinical Journal of Sport Medicine*, 15, 326–330.

11. Friedl, Karl E. (1993). Effects of anabolic steroids on physical health. In Charles E. Yesalis (Ed.), *Anabolic steroids in sport and exercise*. Champaign, IL: Human Kinetics Publishers, pp. 107–150. Galloway, Gantt P. (1997). Anabolic-androgenic steroids. In Joyce H. Lowinson; Pedro Ruiz; Robert B. Millman; and John G. Langrod (Eds.). *Substance abuse: A comprehensive textbook* (3rd ed.). Baltimore: Williams & Wilkins, pp. 308–318.

12. Friedl, *Effects of anabolic steroids*, pp. 121–131.

13. Ibid., pp. 116–121. DiPaolo, Marco; Agozzino, Manuela; Toni, Chiara; Luciani, Allesandro Bassi; et al. (2005). Sudden anabolic steroid abuse–related death in athletes. *International Journal of Cardiology*, 114, 114–117. Hartgens and Kuipers, Effects of androgenic-anabolic steroids in athletes, pp. 536–540. Maravelias, C.; Dona, A.; Stefanidou, M.; and Spiliopoulou, C. (2005). Adverse effects of anabolic steroids in athletes: A constant threat. *Toxicology Letters*, 158, 167–175. Urhausen, A., Albers, T., and Kindermann, W. (2004). Are the cardiac effects of anabolic steroid abuse in strength athletes reversible? *Heart*, 90, 496–501.

14. Su, Tung-Ping; Pagliaro, Michael; Schmidt, Peter J.; Pickar, David; Wolkowitz, Owen; et al. (1993). Neuropsychiatric effects of anabolic steroids in male normal volunteers. *Journal of the American Medical Association*, 269, 2760–2764.

15. Greenberg, Alan (1991, June 29). Alzado has a serious message to kids about steroids—Don't use them. *Hartford (CT) Courant*, cited in Jim Ferstle (1993), Evolution and politics of drug testing. In Charles E. Yesalis (Ed.), *Anabolic steroids*, p. 276.

16. Pope, Harrison G., Jr., Kouri, Elena M., and Hudson, James I. (2000). Effects of supraphysiologic doses of testosterone on mood and aggressiveness in normal men: A randomized controlled trial. *Archives of General Psychiatry*, 57, 133–140. Stocker, Steven (2000). Study provides additional evidence that high steroid doses elicit psychiatric symptoms in some men. *NIDA Notes*, 15 (4), pp. 8–9. Trenton, Adam J., and Currier, Glenn W. (2005). Behavioural manifestations of anabolic steroid use. *CNS Drugs*, 19, 571–595.

17. Adler, Jerry (2004, December 20). Toxic strength. *Newsweek*, pp. 45–52. Bahrke, Michael S. (1993). Psychological effects of endogenous testosterone and anabolic-androgenic steroids. In Charles E. Yesalis (Ed.), *Anabolic steroids in sport and exercise*. Champaign, IL: Human Kinetics Publishers, pp. 161–192. Doff, Wilson (2005, March 10). After a young athlete's suicide, steroids called the culprit. *New York Times*, pp. A1, D8. Estrada, Manuel, Varshney, Anurag, and Ehrlich, Barbara E. (2006). Elevated testosterone induces apoptosis in neuronal cells. *Journal of Biological Chemistry*, 281, 25492–25501. Longman, Jere (2003, November 26). An athlete's dangerous experiment: Using steroids enhanced his physique, but he died trying to stop. *New York Times*, pp. D1, D4.

18. National Institute on Drug Abuse (2000, April). Anabolic steroids. *Research report series*. Bethesda, MD: National Institute on Drug Abuse. Collins, Rick (2003, January 5). Federal and state steroid laws. Posted on the web site of Collins, McDonald, and Gann, P. C., Attorneys-at-law, Nassau County and New York, NY, www.steroidlaw.com.

19. DEA leads largest steroid bust in history (2005, December 15). Drug Enforcement Administration, U.S. Department of Justice. Johnston, Lloyd D.; O'Malley, Patrick M.; Bachman, Jerald G.; and Schulenberg, John E. (2008, December 11). Various stimulant drugs show continuing gradual declines among teens in 2008, most illicit drugs hold steady. University of Michigan News Service, Ann Arbor, Table 1.

20. Pope, Harrison G.; Gruber, Amanda J.; Choi, Priscilla; Olivardia, Roberto; and Phillips, Katherine A. (1997). Muscle dysmorphia: An underrecognized form of body dysmorphic disorder. *Psychosomatics*, 38, 548–557. Wroblewska, Anna-M. (1997). Androgenic-anabolic steroids and body dysmorphia in young men. *Journal of Psychosomatic Research*, 42, 225–234.

21. Bahrke, Michael S., Yesalis, Charles E., and Brower, Kirk J. (1998). Anabolic-androgenic steroid abuse and performance-enhancing drugs among adolescents. *Sport Psychiatry*, 7, 821–838. Beel, Andrea, Maycock, Bruce, and McLean, Neil (1998). Current perspectives on anabolic steroids. *Drug and Alcohol Review*, 17, 87–103. Karch, *The pathology of drug abuse*. Kashkin, Kenneth B., and Kleber, Herbert D. (1989). Hooked on hormones? An anabolic steroid addiction hypothesis. *Journal of the American Medical Association*, 262, 3166–3169. Monaghan, Lee F. (2000). *Bodybuilding, drugs, and risk*. New York: Routledge. Perry, Lund, Deninger, Kutscher, and Schneider, Anabolic steroid use. Schrof, Joanne M. (1992, June 1). Pumped up. *U.S. News and World Report*, pp. 55–63.

22. Goldberg, Linn; Mackinnon, David P.; Elliot, Diane L.; Moe, Esther L.; Clarke, Greg; and Cheong, JeeWon (2000). The Adolescents Training and Learning to Avoid Steroids program. *Archives of Pediatrics and Adolescent Medicine*, 154, 332–338. Moe, Esther L.; Goldberg, Linn D.; MacKinnon, David P.; and Cheong, JeeWon (1999). Reducing drug use and promoting healthy

behaviors among athletes: The ATLAS program. *Medical Science Sports Exercise, 31* (5), S122.

23. Information courtesy of the Oregon Health and Science University, Portland, 2008.

24. Quotation by Bob Bauman (1992). In Bob Goldman and Ronald Klatz, *Death in the locker room II: Drugs and sports.* Chicago: Elite Sports Medicine Publications, pp. 10–11.

25. Goldstein, Paul J. (1990). Anabolic steroids: An ethnographic approach. In Geraline C. Lin and Lynda Erinoff (Eds.), *Anabolic steroid abuse* (NIDA Research Monograph 102). Rockville, MD: National Institute on Drug Abuse, p. 84.

26. Interlandi, Jeneen (2008, February 25). Myth meets science. *Newsweek*, p. 48. Juhn, Mark S. (2003). Popular sports supplements and ergogenic aids. *Sports Medicine, 33*, 921–939. Liu, Hau; Bravata, Dena M.; Olkin, Ingram; Friedlander, Anne; et al. (2008). Systematic review: The effects of growth hormone on athletic performance. *Annals of Internal Medicine, 148*, 747–748. Macur, Juliet (2008, June). Who has the horse tranquilizers? *Play*, p. 18. Macur, Janet (2008, October 9). Olympic blood samples to be retested. *New York Times*, p. B17.

27. Tuller, David (2005, January 18). For sale: "muscles" in a bottle. *New York Times*, pp. F5, F10. Quotation on p. F5.

28. Androstenedione (2001). *PDR for nutritional supplements* (1st ed.). Montvale, NJ: Medical Economics, pp. 26–28. Juhn, Popular sports supplements. Leder, Benjamin Z.; Longcope, Christopher; Catlin, Don H.; Ahrens, Brian; and Schoenfeld, Joel S. (2000). Oral androstenedione administration and serum testosterone concentrations in young men. *Journal of the American Medical Association, 283*, 779–782.

29. Denham, Bryan E. (2006). The Anabolic Steroid Control Act of 2004: A study in the political economy of drug policy. *Journal of Health and Social Policy, 22*, 51–78. FDA bans andro sales (2004, March 12). *Newsday*, p. A38. Johnston, O'Malley, Bachman, and Schulenberg (2006), Table 1. Mravic, Mark (2000, February 21). Ban it, bud. *Sports Illustrated*, pp. 24, 26.

30. Buford, Thomas W.; Kreider, Richard B.; Stout, Jeffrey R.; et al. (2007). International Society of Sports Nutrition position stand: Creatine supplementation and exercise. *Journal of the International Society of Sports Nutrition, 4,* 6. Creatine (2001). *PDR for nutritional supplements* (1st ed.). Montvale, NJ: Medical Economics, pp. 114–117. Freeman, Mike (2003, October 21). Scientist fears athletes are using unsafe drugs: Discovery of an undetected steroid confirms suspicions. *New York Times*, p. D2. Gregory, Andrew J. M., and Fitch, Robert W. (2007). Sports medicine: Performance-enhancing drugs. *Pediatric Clinics of North America, 54*, 797–806. Johnston, Lloyd D.; O'Malley, Patrick M.; Bachman, Jerald G.; and Schulenberg, John E. (2008). *Monitoring the Future national survey results on drug use, 1975–2007, Volume I: Secondary school students 2007.* Bethesda, MD: National Institute on Drug Abuse, Table 10-5c. Juhn, Popular sports supplements.

31. Jeansonne, John (2008, January 17). Still sidestepping problem. *Newsday*, p. A57. Schmidt, Michael S. (2008, January 16). Baseball is challenged on rise in stimulant use. *New York Times*, pp. A1, A16. Quotation on page A16.

32. Hamilton, Martha McNeil (2003, February 23). Beating drug screening builds cottage industry. Evaders change faster than testing technology. *Houston Chronicle*, p. 2.

33. Wadler and Hainline, *Drugs and the athlete*, pp. 201–202.

34. Hatton, Caroline K. (2007). Beyond sports-doping headlines: The science of laboratory tests for performance-enhancing drugs. *Pediatric Clinics of North America, 54*, 713–733. Meer, *Drugs and sports*, pp. 92–95.

35. Alternate specimen testing policies may be set soon (2005, September). *Occupational Health and Safety*, p. 26. Cone, Edward J.; Presley, Lance; Lehrer, Michael; Seiter, William; Smith, Melissa; et al. (2002). Oral fluid testing for drugs of abuse: Positive prevalence rates by Intercept immunoassay screening and GC-MS-MS confirmation and suggested cutoff concentrations. *Journal of Analytical Toxicology, 26*, 540–546.

36. *Allen and Hanbury's athletic drug reference* (1994). Durham NC: Clean Data, pp. 65–66. Baden, Lindsey R.; Horowitz, Gary; Jacoby, Helen; and Eliopoulos, George M. (2001). Quinolones and false-positive urine screening for opiates by immunoassay technology. *Journal of the American Medical Association, 286*, 3115–3119. Struempler, Richard E. (1987, May/June). Excretion of codeine and morphine following ingestion of poppy seeds. *Journal of Analytical Toxicology, 11*, 97–99. Wadler and Hainline, *Drugs and the athlete*, pp. 208–209.

37. Catlin, Wright, Pope, and Liggett, Assessing the threat, p. 39.

38. Rosenberg, Ronald (2000, October 12). Citgo to use Avitar drug tests, job applicants to undergo new saliva-based exam. *Boston Globe*, p. C3.

39. Brookman, Richard R. (2008). Unintended consequences of drug and alcohol testing in student athletes. *AAP (American Academy of Pediatrics) Grand Rounds, 19*, 15–16. Yamaguchi, Ryoko, Johnston, Lloyd D., and O'Malley, Patrick M. (2003). Relationship between student illicit drug use and school drug-testing policies. *Journal of School Health, 73*, 159–164.

40. Quotation of Charles E. Yesalis. In Wright and Cowart, *Anabolic steriods*, p. 196. Schwerin, Michael J.; Corcoran, Kevin J.; Fisher, Leslee; Patterson, David; Askew, Waide; et al. (1996). Social physique anxiety, body esteem, and social anxiety in bodybuilders and self-reported anabolic steroid users. *Addictive Behaviors, 21*, 1–8.

41. Goldman, Bob, and Klatz, Ronald (1992). *Death in the locker room II: Drugs and sports.* Chicago: Elite Sports Medicine Publications, pp. 23–24. McHenry, Christopher R. (2007, December). Presidential address to the American Association of Endocrine Surgeons: The illicit use of hormones for enhancement of athletic performance: A major

threat to the integrity of organized athletic competition. *Surgery*, 785-792. Shermer, Michael (2008, April). The doping dilemma. *Scientific American*, pp. 82–89.

42. Egan, Timothy (2002, November 22). Body-conscious boys adopt athlete's taste for steroids. *New York Times*, pp. A1, A24. Quotations on p. A24. Kolata, Gina; Longman, Jere; Weiner, Tim; and Egan, Timothy (2002, December 2). With no answers on risks, steroid users still say "yes." *New York Times*, pp. A1, A19. Pope, Harrison G., Jr., Phillips, Katherine A., and Olivardia, Roberto (2002).

The Adonis complex: How to identify, treat, and prevent body obsession in men and boys. New York: Simon and Schuster.

43. Kilgannon, Corey (2001, May 27). Strong Island: More youngsters seek great physiques, and risky ways to get them. *New York Times*, Section 14 (Long Island), pp. 1, 9. Quotation on p. 9. Kolata, Gina (2002, December 2). With no answers on risks, steroid users still say "yes." *New York Times*, pp. A1, A10. Morgan, Richard (2002). The men in the mirror. *Chronicle of Higher Education*, 49, A53–A54.

PART TWO
Legally Restricted Drugs in Our Society

POINT/COUNTERPOINT

Should Cognitive Performance-Enhancing Drugs Be Used by Healthy People?

The following discussion of viewpoints presents the opinions of people on both sides of the controversial issue of whether cognitive performance-enhancing drugs, originally intended for the treatment of ADHD and other behavioral disorders, should be used by healthy people to enhance their behavior on the job or in an academic or research environment. Read them with an open mind. Don't think you have to come up with the final answer, nor should you necessarily agree with the argument presented last. Many of the ideas in this feature come from the sources listed.

POINT

In a surprising survey report published in 2008 in *Nature*, one of the world's leading scientific journals, 62 percent of respondents said that they took Ritalin, an FDA-approved medication for the treatment of attention deficit/hyperactivity disorder (ADHD), to enhance their mental performance. Fourteen hundred presumably healthy people in sixty different countries participated in the survey. This is a ghastly example

of scientists and scholars engaging in uncontrolled pharmacological experimentation. Here was evidence of psychostimulant drugs, intended for therapeutic use for a specific disorder, being used by healthy adults to improve their productivity. Isn't anything sacred anymore? Say it ain't so, Mr. Wizard.

COUNTERPOINT

How is this different from dosing yourself with caffeine with a couple of strong cups of coffee to get through that boring afternoon meeting or that all-nighter to finish a term paper? You are taking a psychoactive drug (caffeine) to enhance your cognitive performance, just as others have been doing for centuries.

POINT

Granted that we already engage in a form of cognitive performance enhancement with the consumption of caffeine. But let's talk about a level playing field. Caffeine can be gotten anywhere; it's ubiquitous. In contrast, Ritalin is a prescription drug. Were the pills obtained

through prescriptions written for them, and if so, were the prescriptions obtained under false pretenses? This is dishonest at best, illegal at worst. The *Nature* survey reported that a third of the respondents had obtained their drugs through the Internet, where the industry is largely unregulated. They ran the risk of great harm to themselves. They may have ingested all sorts of contaminants. They may have risked dying.

COUNTERPOINT

Health risks from contaminated drugs ordered through the Internet don't seem to be higher in these cases than health risks among people who are ordering their prescriptions online to save money. I don't buy the argument that obtaining cognitive performance-enhancing drugs through the Internet suddenly plunges you into the dark world of illicit drug abuse. Besides, the side effects of Ritalin are relatively mild—moderate increases in heart rate and blood pressure. When these drugs went through the FDA approval process, clinical trials (see Chapter 14) revealed no serious cardiac problems in healthy adults. There was a problem in older adults and in those with preexisting cardiovascular problems, but generally these drugs were deemed safe and effective if you're healthy.

POINT

You're missing a bigger point here. Where is your basic sense of fair play? Not everyone has equivalent access. It's morally wrong to put one person at an advantage over other people who might be without access to these enhancements.

COUNTERPOINT

There isn't equivalent access to SAT preparation courses either. Yet people don't discount a high SAT score just because someone else couldn't afford the expense of such preparation.

POINT

That may be true, but there is an effort to provide SAT preparation courses and instruction to as wide a population as possible, through a number of community programs. To make the same argument here, you would have to ensure that as many people as possible have access to Ritalin. Isn't this getting absurd?

Until that day comes (and hopefully it will not), how do we make an ultimate judgment about a per-son's achievements in life? Do we need an asterisk next to someone's Nobel or Pulitzer Prize if it was determined that cognitive performance-enhancing drugs were used. Such a move is being considered for sports records achieved by athletes who were taking anabolic steroids and other performance-enhancing drugs when they set these records. Why not in the case of cognitive performance-enhancing drugs? Conversely, would a disclaimer (perhaps a negative urinanalysis) be required on a professor's tenure candidacy file to indicate that the record of productivity was achieved without the aid of cognitive performance-enhancing drugs?

COUNTERPOINT

The current phenomenon of cognitive performance-enhancing drugs such as Ritalin is only the most recent instance in a long history of human enhancement. People have always taken steps to improve the human condition or the circumstances under which they work and serve society. Isn't it an obligation to use one's full potential and resources to the greatest benefit of humanity? If cognitive performance-enhancing drugs advance that process, the drugs are serving humankind.

Consider it a mental form of cosmetic surgery. Besides, it hasn't been scientifically determined that cognitive performance-enhancing drugs actually make you smarter. Probably, at most, they allow you to stay alert longer than you would have under ordinary circumstances. But if their effects turn out to be more profound than that, we need to consider ccarefully the issues of *responsible use*.

Critical Thinking Questions for Further Debate

1. Suppose you are a new employee in a high-pressure corporation where your coworkers are ingesting a cognitive performance-enhancing drug such as Ritalin to increase their work productivity, but you have a preexisting cardiovascular disorder that would make taking this drug unwise. There is no overt coercion to join in with your coworkers, but you know that you will be at a disadvantage in terms of promotion and salary incentives if you don't. Is this a form of discrimination in the workplace?

2. Suppose you are taking a chemistry exam and you know that a person next to you took Ritalin in order to study 50 percent longer than you were able to without taking a cognitive performance-enhancing drug. That other person outscores you by a full letter grade. Do you have any recourse in appealing your grade?

Sources: Austin, Anastacia Mott (2008, April 24). Academia's use of "scientist's little helper" drugs. Buzzle.com. Carey, Benedict (2008, March 9). Brain enhancement is wrong, right? *New York Times, Week in Review*, pp. 1–2. Greely, Henry; Sahakian, Barbara; Harris, John; Kessler, Ronald C.; Gazzaniga, Michael; et al. (2008). Toward responsible use of cognitive-enhancing drugs by the healthy. *Nature, 456* 702–705. Harris, John, and Quigley, Mulreann (2008). Commentary on "Professor's little helper": Humans have always tried to improve their condition. *Nature, 451*, 521. Monatersky, Richard (2008, April 25). Some professors pop pills for an intellectual edge. *The Chronicle of Higher Education*, pp. A1, A10. Sahakian, Barbara, and Morein-Zamir, Sharon (2007). Professor's little helper. *Nature, 450*, 1157–1159.

chapter **9**

Alcohol: Social Beverage/Social Drug

I was invited to address a convention of high school teachers on the topic of drug abuse. When I arrived at the convention center to give my talk, I was escorted to a special suite, where I was encouraged to join the executive committee in a round of drug taking—the drug was a special high-proof single-malt whiskey. Later, the irony of the situation had its full impact. As I stepped to the podium under the influence of a psychoactive drug (the whiskey), I looked out through the haze of cigarette smoke at an audience of educators who had invited me to speak to them because they were concerned about the unhealthy impact of drugs on their students. The welcoming applause gradually gave way to the melodic tinkling of ice cubes in liquor glasses, and I began. They did not like what I had to say.

—*John P.J. Pinel,* Biopsychology *(2003)*

After you have completed this chapter, you will understand

- How alcoholic beverages are produced
- Alcohol use through history
- Patterns of alcohol consumption
- The pharmacology of alcohol
- Acute physiological and behavioral effects of alcohol
- Alcohol and health benefits
- Strategies for responsible alcohol consumption

Pinel's experience in this opening vignette sums up the central problem facing American society in its dealings with alcohol use and abuse: the frequent failure to acknowledge that alcohol is indeed a psychoactive drug.[1] You may have heard someone remark, "He drinks a little too much, but at least he's not doing drugs." To many people, an alcoholic beverage is simply a social beverage; in actuality, it is a social drug.

We can see this problem reflected in a number of ways. College courses that cover drug abuse and its effect on society, perhaps the one you are taking right now, are often entitled "Drugs and Alcohol." Would you personally have expected to cover the effects of alcohol in a course simply entitled "Drugs" in your college catalog? If you answer no, then alcohol had better stay in the course title.

Even the U.S. federal government perpetuates the distinction, with separate agencies for alcohol abuse (the National Institute on Alcohol Abuse and Alcoholism, NIAAA) and the abuse of other drugs (the National Institute on Drug Abuse, NIDA). This bureaucratic partitioning admittedly has historic roots, and there may be valid reasons to continue the division from a management or budgetary point of view, but it has inadvertently reinforced an unfortunate and inaccurate notion that alcohol is somehow a substance that stands apart from other drugs of potential abuse. Fortunately, the phrase "alcohol and other drug abuse," often shortened to "AOD abuse," has become increasingly popular as a way of conveying the idea that problems of substance abuse can come from many sources (see Chapter 17).

To recognize the special status of alcohol as a psychoactive drug in our society, two chapters are devoted to alcohol-related issues. This chapter considers alcohol as a drug, with a unique history and tradition and its own set of acute risks. The next chapter turns to an examination of alcohol's chronic effects, specifically the potential problems of alcohol abuse and alcoholism. We begin by considering the nature of alcohol itself.

What Makes an Alcoholic Beverage?

Creating **ethyl alcohol,** through a process known as **fermentation,** is a remarkably easy thing to do. Almost every culture in the world, at one time or another, has stumbled on the basic procedure. All you need is organic material with a sugar content (honey, grapes, berries, molasses, rye, apples, corn, sugar cane, rice, pumpkins, to name some examples) left undisturbed in a warm container for a time, and nature does the work.

by the numbers . . .

74 Percentage of perpetrators of rape, in a nationally representative college student sample, who report having been drinking alcohol at the time of the rape

30 Percentage of high school seniors who in 2006 reported having been exposed to a drugged or drunk driver in the past two weeks

11.7 Percentage of deaths among American Indians and Alaska Natives in 2001 through 2005 that were attributed to excessive alcohol consumption. The percentage of alcohol-attributed deaths in the United States as a whole was 3.3 percent.

Sources: Alcohol-attributed deaths and years of potential life lost among American Indians and Alaska Natives—United States, 2001-2005 (2008, August 29). *Morbidity and Mortality Weekly Report, 57,* 938–941. Koss, Mary P. (1988). Hidden rape: Sexual aggression and victimization in a national sample of students in higher education. In A. W. Burgess (Ed.), *Rape and sexual assault II.* New York: Garland, pp. 3–25. O'Malley, Patrick M., and Johnston, Lloyd D. (2007). Drugs and driving by American high school seniors, 2001–2006. *Journal of Studies on Alcohol and Drugs, 68,* 834–842.

Microscopic yeast cells, floating through the air, land on this material and literally consume the sugar in it, so that, for every one sugar molecule consumed, two molecules of alcohol and two molecules of carbon dioxide are left behind as waste. The carbon dioxide bubbles out, and what remains is an alcoholic beverage, less sweet than the substance that began it all but with a new, noticeable kick. Basic fermentation results in a beverage with an alcohol content of between 12 and 14 percent, best exemplified by standard grape wine.

The process of fermenting starchy grains such as barley to produce beer, called **brewing,** is somewhat more complicated. The barley first needs to be soaked in water until it sprouts, producing an enzyme that is capable of breaking down the starch into sugar. It is then slowly dried, the sprouts are removed, and the remainder (now called

ethyl alcohol: The product of fermentation of natural sugars. It is generally referred to simply as *alcohol,* though several types of nonethyl alcohol exist.

fermentation: The process of converting natural sugars into ethyl alcohol by the action of yeasts.

brewing: The process of producing beer from barley grain.

barley malt) is crushed into a powder. The barley malt is combined with water, corn, and rice to form a mixture called a **mash.** The water activates the enzyme so that the starches convert into sugars. The addition of yeast to the mash starts the fermentation process and produces an alcohol content of approximately 4.5 percent. The dried blossoms of the hop plant, called *hops*, are then added to the brew for the characteristic pungent flavoring and aroma.

Relying on fermentation alone gives a potentially maximal concentration of alcohol of about 15 to 16 percent. The reason for this limit is that an alcohol content above this level starts to kill the yeast and, in doing so, stops the fermentation process. To obtain a higher alcoholic content, another process, called **distillation,** must occur.

The social chaos of "Gin Lane" in London, as interpreted in this satirical engraving by William Hogarth (1697–1764).

barley malt: Barley after it has been soaked in water, sprouts have grown, sprouts have been removed, and the mixture has been dried and crushed to a powder.

mash: Fermented barley malt, following liquification and combination with yeasts.

distillation: A process by which fermented liquid is boiled and then cooled, so that the condensed product contains a higher alcoholic concentration than before.

distilled spirits: The liquid product of distillation, also known as *liquor.*

aqua vitae (AH-kwa VEYE-tee): A brandy, the first distilled liquor in recorded history.

Distillation involves heating a container of some fermented mixture until it boils. Because alcohol has a lower boiling temperature than water, the vapor produced has a higher alcohol-to-water ratio than the original mixture. This alcohol-laden vapor is then drawn off into a special coiled apparatus (often referred to as a *still*), cooled until it condenses back to a liquid, and poured drop by drop into a second container. This new liquid, referred to as **distilled spirits** or simply *liquor*, has an alcohol content considerably higher than 15 percent, generally in the neighborhood of 40 to 50 percent.

It is possible through further distillations to achieve an alcohol content of up to 95 percent. At this point, however, the alcohol content of distilled spirits is not commonly described by percentage but rather by the designation "proof." Any proof is twice the percentage of alcohol: An 80-proof whiskey contains 40 percent alcohol; a 190-proof vodka contains 95 percent alcohol.

The three basic forms of alcoholic beverages are wine, beer, and distilled spirits. Table 9.1 shows the sources of some well-known examples.

Alcohol Use through History

Historians point out that fermented honey, called *mead*, was probably the original alcoholic beverage, dating from approximately 8000 B.C. Beer, requiring more effort than simple fermentation, came on the scene much later, with the Egyptians establishing the first official brewery about 3700 B.C. At that time, beer was quite different from the watery forms we know today. It was more similar to a bread than a beverage, and the process of producing beer was closer to baking than to brewing.[2]

Evidence of the development of wine comes from references to its sale in the Code of Hammurabi, King of Babylonia, recorded about 1700 B.C. Wine-making itself, however, appears to have begun more than three thousand years before that. Excavations of an ancient village in modern-day Iran have revealed the remains of wine-stained pottery dating back to as early as 5400 B.C.[3]

The first documented distillation of alcohol was the conversion of wine into brandy during the Middle Ages, at a medical school in Salerno, Italy. With an emphasis on its medicinal applications, the new beverage became known in Latin as **aqua vitae** ("the water of life"). People quickly caught on to its inebriating possibilities, and brandy became the primary distilled liquor in Europe until the middle of the seventeenth century. At that time the Dutch perfected the process of distilling liquor and flavoring it with juniper berries. A new alcoholic beverage was born: gin.

TABLE 9.1

Prominent alcoholic beverages and their sources

BEVERAGE	SOURCE	BEVERAGE	SOURCE
Distilled spirits		**Wines**	
Brandy	Distilled from grape wine, cherries, or peaches	Red table wine	Fermented red grapes with skins
Liqueur or cordial	Brandy or gin, flavored with blackberry, cherry, chocolate, peppermint, licorice, etc. Alcohol content ranges from 20% to 55%	White table wine	Fermented skinless grapes
		Champagne	White wine bottled before yeast is gone so that remaining carbon dioxide produces a carbonated effect
Rum	Distilled from the syrup of sugar cane or from molasses	Sparkling wine	Red wine prepared like champagne or with carbonation added
Scotch whiskey	Distilled from fermented corn and barley malt		
Rye whiskey	Distilled from rye and barley malt	**Fortified wines**	Wines whose alcohol content is raised or fortified to 20% by the addition of brandy (see below)—for example, sherry, port, Marsala, and Madeira
Blended whiskey	A mixture of two or more types of whiskey		
Bourbon whiskey	Distilled primarily from fermented corn		
Gin	Distilled from barley, potato, corn, wheat, or rye, and flavored with juniper berries	**Wine-like variations**	
		Hard cider	Fermented apples
		Sake	Fermented rice
Vodka	Approximately 95% pure alcohol, distilled from grains or potatoes and diluted by mixing with water	**Beers**	Types of beer vary depending on brewing procedures.
Tequila	Distilled from the fermented juice of the maguey plant	Draft beer	Contains 3–6% alcohol
		Lager beer	Contains 3–6% alcohol
Grain neutral spirits	Approximately 95% pure alcohol, used either for medicinal purposes or diluted and mixed in less-concentrated distilled spirits	Ale	Contains 3–6% alcohol
		Malt liquor	Contains up to 8% alcohol

Source: Adapted from Becker, Charles E., Roe, Robert L., and Scott, Robert A. (1979). *Alcohol as a drug: A curriculum on pharmacology, neurology, and toxicology.* Huntington, NY: Robert Krieger Publishing, pp. 10–12.

The enormous popularity of gin throughout Europe marked a crucial point in the history of alcohol's effect on European society. Because it was easily produced, cheaper than brandy, and faster-acting than wine, gin became attractive as an alcoholic beverage to all levels of society, particularly the poorer classes of people. By the mid-1700s, alcohol abuse was being condemned as a major societal problem, and concerns about drunkenness had become a public issue.

Although gin affected life in many parts of Europe, it was in English cities that the gin epidemic became a genuine crisis. By 1750, gin consumption in England had grown to twenty-two times the level in 1685, and the social devastation was obvious. In London, infant mortality rose during this period, with only one of four baptized babies between 1730 and 1749 surviving to the age of five, despite the fact that mortality rates were falling in the countryside. In one section of the city, as many as one in five houses was a gin shop.

Consumption of other distilled spirits introduced

during this period, such as rum and whiskey, added to the overall problem, but gin was undoubtedly the prime culprit. The epidemic of gin drinking in England during the first half of the eighteenth century illustrates how destructive the introduction of a potent and easily available psychoactive drug into an urban society already suffering from social dislocation and instability can be. The consequences in many ways mirrored the introduction of crack cocaine into the ghettos of the United States during the 1980s.[4]

Alcohol in Early U.S. History

Judging from the records of Pilgrims aboard the *Mayflower* in 1620, alcohol played a pivotal role in the earliest days of settling the American colonies. William Bradford, historian of the *Mayflower* voyage and later governor of Plymouth Colony in Massachusetts, wrote that in looking for a place to land, they had decided not to "take time for further search or consideration, our victuals [supplies] being much spent, especially our Beere." Evidently, the Pilgrims arrived at Plymouth Rock not only with a passion for freedom but also with a considerable thirst.[5]

To be fair, however, we need to understand that these English settlers, like other travelers at that time, had little choice but to take along alcoholic beverages. Water would have spoiled easily during the sea voyage. Besides, the Pilgrims were not against alcohol per se, merely against the drunken behavior that resulted from its excessive use.

General approval of the moderate use of alcohol was a fact of American life well into the nineteenth century. It is not surprising, therefore, that the social focus for communities in colonial America was the tavern. Not only did taverns serve as public dispensers of alcoholic beverages, but they also served as centers for local business dealings and town politics. Mail was delivered there; travelers could stay the night; elections were held there. As an institution, the tavern was as highly regarded, and as regularly attended, as the local church.[6]

By today's standards, it is difficult to imagine the extent of alcohol consumption during the early decades of American history. In 1830, the average per capita intake was an immoderate five drinks a day, roughly four times the level of consumption today. It was common to take "whiskey breaks" at 11 A.M. and 4 P.M. each day (except Sunday), much as we take coffee breaks today. As far as types of liquor were concerned, rum was the favorite in New England and along the North Atlantic coast, but elsewhere whiskey was king. George Washington himself went into the whiskey business at Mount Vernon in 1797, eventually establishing the largest whiskey distillery of his time.[7]

The Rise of Temperance in the United States

In or about 1830, alcohol consumption in the United States started to decrease. This decline coincided with the growing influence of a **temperance movement** among religious leaders, physicians, and social reformers across the nation. Temperance goals originally focused on the moderation, not necessarily the prohibition, of alcohol consumption in society and drew attention to the long-term consequences of chronic alcohol abuse. The distinction between temperate use and total prohibition, however, began to blur over the years. The shift from temperance to prohibition, from 1830 through the beginning of the twentieth century, will be examined in the next chapter.

Patterns of Alcohol Consumption Today

It has been theorized that the earliest systems of agriculture in human history were born of the desire to secure a dependable supply of beer.[8] If this is so, then alcohol, commercialization, and economics have been linked from the very beginning. Today, of course, alcohol is not merely a big business, but an enormous business. Americans spend more than $140 billion on the purchase of alcoholic beverages each year, and the alcohol industry spends about $1.4 billion advertising its products. More than one-third of this advertising budget is typically devoted to television commercials for beer.[9]

Overall Patterns of Alcohol Consumption

How much do Americans actually drink? Estimates of the current annual per capita consumption of pure alcohol in the United States vary between 1.3 gallons (4.9 liters), according to alcohol industry statistics, and 2.2 gallons (8.5 liters), according to World Health Organization statistics. If we take the lower estimate, the per capita consumption amounts to about one-half of an ounce of alcohol per day; if we take the higher estimate, the daily consumption rises to about three-fourths of an ounce per day. Owing to the difficulty of obtaining this kind of information and the varying standards upon which information is based, it is fair to say that the true value is probably somewhere in the middle.[10]

temperance movement: The social movement in the United States, beginning in the nineteenth century, that advocated the renunciation of alcohol consumption.

The stainless steel tanks of the world's largest wine maker, the Ernest and Julio Gallo Winery, are located in Modesto, California. Nearly 900 million gallons of wine were produced by E. & J. Gallo in 2008.

How many alcoholic drinks do these estimated daily amounts add up to? To answer this question, it is important first to consider the amount of pure alcohol that is contained in each of four basic types of alcoholic beverages. Health Line shows that a single half-ounce of alcohol is approximately equivalent to any of the following:

- One 5-ounce glass of wine
- One 12-ounce bottle or can of beer
- One 12-ounce bottle of wine cooler
- One shot (1.5-ounce size) of 80-proof liquor

All these quantities are approximately equal to about one-half ounce in terms of pure alcohol, and they are often referred to as "standard drinks."

Based on these equivalencies, the average alcohol consumption in the United States can be approximated as between 1 and 1.5 "standard drinks" per day. Bear in mind, however, that a "standard drink" may not be the drink you consume and, therefore, is not necessarily the appropriate unit to use when computing your own personal level of alcohol consumption. Draft beer, for example, is typically dispensed in large glasses that exceed 12 ounces in capacity. A mixed drink in a bar might contain a quantity of liquor that exceeds a standard amount, if the bartender is particularly generous. In either of these circumstances, an individual can be misled into believing that an "average" amount is being consumed (in terms of drinks) when, in fact, the quantity of alcohol being consumed is considerably larger.

Another consideration when looking at statistics based on population averages is the obvious fact that not everyone is "average." There is an enormous disparity in terms of how much alcohol each person actually consumes during a given year. Some people drink no alcohol at all, whereas others drink heavily. *In fact, 80 percent of the total amount of alcohol consumed in the United States each year is consumed by only the 30 percent of Americans who drink and only 20 percent of the population in general.* Drugs . . . in Focus, on page 223, provides a demonstration that illustrates the uneven pattern of alcohol consumption in the United States today.

Looking at the types of alcohol consumed in the United States, beer consumption represents 67 percent of overall alcoholic consumption and a disproportionate share of heavy alcohol drinking. When five or more 12-ounce beers are consumed in a day, there is a stronger association with alcohol-related problems than when there are comparable consumption levels of wine or liquor. We can conclude that beer is the most problematic form of alcohol consumption in the United States today.[11]

Trends in Alcohol Consumption since the Late 1970s

Overall, alcohol consumption levels among Americans steadily declined each year from the late 1970s through the mid-1990s and has remained roughly stable since then. Because a large part of the decline was tied to a growing attention to weight, health, and fitness, the industry responded with the introduction of lighter wines, with fewer calories and a reduced alcohol content, as well as a popular line of wine coolers (wine mixed with sugar and fruit juice), roughly equal in alcoholic content to regular beer (Health Line, page 222).

According to a 2007 national poll, among Americans who drink alcohol there is a slight preference for beer over wine, with the advantage having been narrowed over the years. About 40 percent of drinkers in the

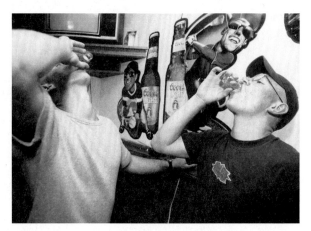

Binge drinking among college students and other young adults is a common social ritual as well as a continuing social concern.

Health Line

What Is a Standard Drink?

A standard drink is any drink that contains about 14 grams of pure alcohol (about 0.5 fluid ounce). These are some standard drink equivalents.

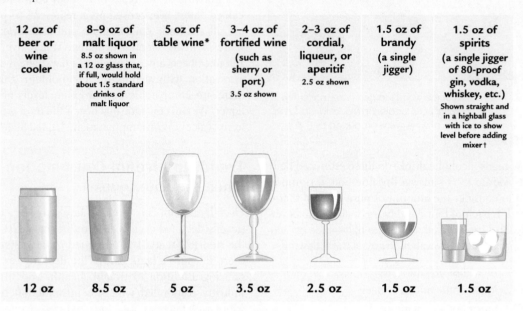

12 oz of beer or wine cooler	8–9 oz of malt liquor 8.5 oz shown in a 12 oz glass that, if full, would hold about 1.5 standard drinks of malt liquor	5 oz of table wine*	3–4 oz of fortified wine (such as sherry or port) 3.5 oz shown	2–3 oz of cordial, liqueur, or aperitif 2.5 oz shown	1.5 oz of brandy (a single jigger)	1.5 oz of spirits (a single jigger of 80-proof gin, vodka, whiskey, etc.) Shown straight and in a highball glass with ice to show level before adding mixer †
12 oz	8.5 oz	5 oz	3.5 oz	2.5 oz	1.5 oz	1.5 oz

Many people do not know what counts as a standard drink, and thus are unaware of how many standard drinks are held in the containers in which these drinks are often sold. Some examples:

- For beer or wine cooler, the approximate number of standard drinks in
  - 12 oz = 1
  - 16 oz = 1.3
  - 22 oz = 2
  - 40 oz = 3.3
- For malt liquor, the approximate number of standard drinks in
  - 12 oz = 1.5
  - 16 oz = 2
  - 22 oz = 2.5
  - 40 oz = 4.5
- For table wine, the approximate number of standard drinks in
  - a standard 750 mL (25 oz) bottle = 5
- For 80-proof spirits, or "hard liquor," the approximate number of standard drinks in
  - a mixed drink = 1 or more†
  - a pint (16 oz) = 11
  - a fifth (25 oz) = 17
  - 1.75 L (59 oz) = 39

*In recent years it has been common for wines to contain an alcohol concentration of 16 percent. In these instances, 5 ounces of wine would be equivalent to 0.80 ounces of alcohol, which is 33 percent higher than when a 12 percent wine is considered. Another way of thinking about this is that for a drink of wine with 16 percent alcohol concentration to be equivalent to a 12-ounce can of beer or a typical shot of liquor, the quantity of wine consumed should be reduced to approximately 4 ounces. In this chapter, however, we will retain the concept of 5 ounces of wine as representing a standard drink, since it is traditional that alcohol equivalencies are calculated on this basis.

†It can be difficult to estimate the number of standard drinks served in a single mixed drink made with hard liquor. Depending on factors such as the type of spirits and the recipe, one mixed drink can contain from one to three or more standard drinks.

Source: National Institute on Alcohol Abuse and Alcoholism (2005). *Helping patients who drink too much: A clinician's guide.* Bethesda, MD: National Institute on Alcohol Abuse and Alcoholism, p. 12.

Drugs...in Focus

Visualizing the Pattern of Alcohol Consumption in the United States

To appreciate the uneven pattern of alcohol consumption in the population, try the following demonstration:

Assemble ten people and ten bottles of beer (preferably empty).

Separate three people who hold nothing. They represent the 30 percent of the population that does not drink alcohol at all.

Separate five people; together they hold two bottles. They represent the 50 percent of the population that drinks 20 percent of the total alcohol supply.

Separate the ninth person; this person holds two bottles. This individual represents the 10 percent of the population that drinks another 20 percent of the total alcohol supply.

Separate the tenth person; this person holds a six-pack of bottles. This individual represents the 10 percent of the population that drinks 60 percent of the total alcohol supply.

The Moral of the Story

Twenty percent of the entire population (the ninth and tenth persons in this demonstration) drink 80 percent of the total alcohol consumed in the United States each year. Of those who drink some alcohol, two-sevenths (roughly 30 percent) of them drink 80 percent of the total alcohol consumed each year, while five-sevenths (roughly 70 percent) of them drink the remaining 20 percent. These figures correspond to those expressed in the text.

Source: Kinney, G. Jean (2006). *Loosening the grip: A handbook of alcohol information,* 8th ed. New York: McGraw-Hill, p. 30.

A Tale of 10 Beers and 10 People

3 drink none

5 share 2 beers

1 drinks 2

1 drinks 6

United States reported that they drank beer most often, whereas about 34 percent reported that they usually drank wine. Beer had been preferred over wine by an almost two-to-one ratio in 1992.[12]

The Demographics of Alcohol Consumption

Preferences for particular types of alcoholic beverages are influenced by a host of factors, including age, gender, education, and income. In general, among individuals in the United States who drink alcoholic beverages, women are twice as likely as men not to prefer beer, three times as likely as men to prefer wine, and somewhat more likely than men to prefer liquor. The preference for wine and liquor over beer increases as people get older.

Increased years of education are also associated with an increased preference for wine over beer and liquor. The same is true with income levels, except that the change in preference for liquor is less clear. Individuals earning more than $50,000 prefer wine and beer to liquor, and those earning less than $20,000 prefer beer to liquor and wine. In general, the relationship between personal income and overall alcohol consumption is a curvilinear one: Abstainers and heavy drinkers both earn less than moderate drinkers.[13]

In general, college students consume a large amount of alcohol, though it appears that the establishment of twenty-one as a mandated legal drinking age in all states has delayed the occurrence of *peak* consumption levels to the junior or senior year. Nonetheless, the prevalence of moderate alcohol consumption in college, assessed by those having a drink in the last thirty days, rises substantially from levels encountered in high school.

Among young adults, *binge drinking*—defined for men as having five or more alcoholic drinks and for women as having four or more alcoholic drinks in a row—rises sharply from age eighteen, peaks at ages twenty-one to twenty-two, then steadily declines over the next ten years. The prevalence of daily drinking also rises from levels encountered in high school but remains relatively stable afterward, through age thirty-two.

Table 9.2 shows the results of a 2001 survey of the drinking habits of nearly 11,000 college students at 119 U.S. campuses, the latest survey in a series that began in 1993. Overall, 44 percent of students reported having engaged in binge drinking during the two weeks prior to the administration of the survey—41 percent of the women and 49 percent of the men. About one in five students abstained from alcohol, whereas one in four was a

TABLE 9.2

Alcohol-related problems and secondary effects among college students, 2001

Alcohol-related problems among college students who drank alcohol

PROBLEM	PERCENTAGE REPORTING AN OCCURRENCE DURING THE PAST 30 DAYS	SIGNIFICANT INCREASE/ DECREASE SINCE 1993
Missed a class	29.5	Increase
Got behind in schoolwork	21.6	Increase
Did something I regretted	35.0	Increase
Forgot where I was or what I did	26.8	Increase
Argued with friends	22.9	Increase
Engaged in unplanned sex	21.3	Increase
Had unprotected sex	21.3	Increase
Had five or more alcohol-related problems	20.3	Increase

Secondary effects of binge drinking on nonbinge drinkers

PROBLEM	PERCENTAGE REPORTING INCIDENT	SIGNIFICANT INCREASE/ DECREASE SINCE 1993
Been insulted or humiliated	29.2	No change
Had a serious argument or quarrel	19.0	No change
Been pushed, hit, or assaulted	8.7	No change
Had to take care of drunken student	15.2	No change
Experienced an unwanted sexual advance	18.9	Increase
Been a victim of sexual assault or date rape (women only)	1.0	Decrease

Note: Drinking alcohol refers to consumption within the past year. Binge drinking is defined as having consumed five or more alcoholic drinks on one occasion (in the case of men) and four or more alcoholic drinks on one occasion (in the case of women).

Source: Wechsler, Henry; Lee, Jae Eun; Kuo, Meichun; Seibring, Mark; Nelson, Toben F.; and Lee, Hang (2002). Trends in college binge drinking during a period of increased prevention efforts: Findings from four Harvard School of Public Health College Alcohol Study Surveys: 1993–2001. *Journal of American College Health, 50,* 203–217. Reprinted with permission of the Helen Dwight Reid Educational Foundation. Published by Heldref Publications, 1319 Eighteenth St., NW, Washington DC 20036-1802. Copyright © 2002.

Quick Concept Check 9.1

Understanding Alcoholic Beverages

Check your understanding of the alcohol content of various types of alcoholic beverages by rank ordering the alcohol content of the following five "bar orders," with 1 being the largest amount and 5 being the smallest. Are there any ties?

_____ A. three 1-shot servings of liquor and one 5-oz glass of wine

_____ B. two 1-shot servings of liquor

_____ C. one 1-shot serving of liquor, one 5-oz glass of wine, and three 12-oz beers

_____ D. three 5-oz glasses of wine

_____ E. one 1-shot serving of liquor, one 5-oz glass of wine, and one 12-oz beer

Answers: 1 = C   2 = A   3 = D and E (tie)   5 = B

frequent binge drinker. Not surprisingly, students who drank alcohol at some time over the past year frequently reported alcohol-related problems while at college. These problems included missing a class, doing something they regretted, forgetting where they were or what they did while intoxicated, arguing with friends, and failing to practice safe sex. While the percentages of binge drinkers in 2001 remained approximately the same as those reported in 1993, the percentage who reported alcohol-related problems increased.

The survey also reported that a large number of *nondrinkers* (defined as either abstainers or non-binge drinkers) were adversely affected by binge drinking patterns of behavior on their campus. These situations, called secondhand effects (because the individuals themselves were not intoxicated but were affected by those who were), are analogous to the problems of secondhand smoking, which will be examined in Chapter 11.

In general, an estimated 500,000 full-time four-year college students (drinkers and nondrinkers) were unintentionally injured and more than 1,400 were killed while under the influence of alcohol, principally due to motor vehicle accidents. In addition, more than 600,000 were unintentionally assaulted by another student who had been drinking, and 400,000 reported having unprotected sex as a result of being intoxicated.[14]

Looking at the early years of teenage drinking, we find that alcohol use has been extensive by the eighth grade. In fact, among young people who report some alcohol consumption between the ages of twelve and twenty, the average age when drinking began is fourteen years. In the 2008 University of Michigan survey, 39 percent of eighth graders reported that they had consumed alcohol and 18 percent reported that they had been drunk sometime in their lives. Fortunately, these figures are down significantly from those found in earlier surveys. However, approximately 8 percent of students at this age reported consuming more than five drinks on a single occasion in the previous two weeks, a pattern of behavior that is only slightly down from that reported in 1991.

The problem of underage alcohol use is exacerbated by two major factors. First, there is the extent of access that underage drinkers have to alcohol itself, despite legal restrictions. Studies suggest that more than 40 percent of the estimated 11 million underage drinkers, defined as persons aged twelve to twenty who drank in the past 30 days, were provided free alcohol by adults twenty-one or older. About 6 percent of underage drinkers were given alcohol by their parents in the past month. Second, there are pressures brought on by the development of attractive alcohol products. In recent years, malt liquor products called Spykes have been introduced; they are sold in sweet flavor varieties (such as chocolate, mango, and melon) and marketed in 2-ounce bottles resembling beauty products. Costing less than a dollar each, Spykes have an approximately 12 percent alcohol content and are advertised as shots to be drunk on their own or added to beer. The option of adding them to beer is particularly troublesome since many young people refrain from drinking excessive amounts of beer because they do not like its taste.[15]

The Pharmacology of Alcohol

Alcohol is a very small molecule, in liquid form, that is moderately soluble in fat and highly soluble in water—all characteristics that make it easily absorbed through the gastrointestinal tract once it is ingested, without needing any digestion. About 20 percent of it is absorbed into the bloodstream directly from the stomach, whereas the remaining 80 percent is absorbed from the upper portion of the small intestine.

On entering the stomach, alcohol acts initially as an irritant, increasing the flow of hydrochloric acid and pepsin, chemicals that aid digestion. Therefore, in small amounts, alcohol can help digest a meal. In large amounts, however, alcohol will irritate the stomach lining. This is a concern for those already having stomach problems; preexisting ulcers are worsened by drinking alcohol, and heavy alcohol drinking can produce ulcers.

The irritating effect on the stomach explains why the alcohol proceeds on to the small intestine more quickly if alcohol concentrations are high. The stomach is simply trying to get rid of its irritant. Over time, the chronic consumption of alcohol can produce an inflammation of the stomach (gastritis) or the pancreas (pancreatitis).

Because the small intestine assumes the lion's share of the responsibilities and acts extremely rapidly (more rapidly than the stomach), the rate of total alcohol absorption is based largely on the condition of the stomach when the alcohol arrives and the time required for the stomach to empty its contents into the small intestine. If the stomach is empty, an intoxicating effect (the "buzz") will be felt very quickly. If the stomach is full, absorption will be delayed as the alcohol is retained by the stomach along with the food being digested, and the passage of alcohol into the small intestine will slow down.

Besides the condition of the stomach, there are other factors related to the alcohol itself and the behavior of the drinker that influence the rate of alcohol absorption. The principal factor is the concentration of alcohol in the beverage being ingested. An ounce of 80-proof (40 percent) alcohol will be felt more quickly than an ounce of wine containing 12 percent alcohol, and of course the level of alcohol in the blood will be higher as well. Also, if the alcoholic beverage is carbonated, as are champagne and other sparkling wines, the stomach will empty its contents faster and effects will be felt sooner. Finally, if the alcohol enters the body at a rapid pace, such as when drinks are consumed in quick succession, the level of alcohol in the blood will be higher because the liver cannot eliminate it at a fast enough pace. All other factors being equal, a bigger person requires a larger quantity of alcohol to have equivalent levels accumulating in the blood, simply because there are more body fluids to absorb the alcohol, thus diluting the overall effect.[16]

The Breakdown and Elimination of Alcohol

Its solubility in water helps alcohol to be distributed to all bodily tissues, with those tissues having greater water content receiving a relatively greater proportion of alcohol. The excretion of alcohol is accomplished in two basic ways. About 5 percent will be eliminated by the lungs through exhalation, causing the characteristic "alcohol breath" of heavy drinkers. Breathalyzers, designed to test for alcohol concentrations in the body and used frequently by law-enforcement officials to test for drunkenness, work on this principle. The remaining 95 percent will be eliminated in the urine, after the alcohol has been biotransformed into carbon dioxide and water.[17]

The solubility of alcohol in fat facilitates its passage across the blood-brain barrier (see Chapter 3). As a result, approximately 90 percent of the alcohol in the blood reaches the brain almost immediately. Unfortunately, alcohol passes the blood-placenta barrier with equal ease, so alcohol intake by women during pregnancy affects the developing fetus. As a result, fetal alcohol levels are essentially identical to those of the mother who is drink-

ing.[18] This important matter will be discussed in the next chapter, when we consider a type of mental and physical retardation called *fetal alcohol syndrome.*

The body recognizes alcohol as a visitor with no real biological purpose. It contains calories but no vitamins, minerals, or other components that have any nutritional value. Therefore, the primary bodily reaction is to break it down for eventual removal, through a process called **oxidation.** This biotransformation process consists of two basic steps. First, an enzyme, **alcohol dehydrogenase,** breaks down alcohol into **acetaldehyde.** This enzyme is present in the stomach, where about 20 percent of alcohol is broken down prior to absorption into the bloodstream, and in the liver, where the remaining 80 percent is broken down from accumulations in the blood. Second, another enzyme, **acetaldehyde dehydrogenase,** breaks down acetaldehyde in the liver into **acetic acid.** From there, further oxidation results in oxygen, carbon dioxide, and calories of energy.

The entire process is determined by the speed with which alcohol dehydrogenase does its work, and for a given individual, it works at a constant rate, no matter how much alcohol needs to be broken down. Imagine a bank at which only one teller window stays open, no matter how long the line of customers grows, and you will understand the limitations under which the body is operating.

The specific rate of oxidation is approximately 100 milligrams of alcohol per hour per kilogram of body weight. To put this in perspective, 8 grams of alcohol will be broken down in an hour if you weigh 176 pounds (80 kilograms), and 5 grams of alcohol will be broken down in an hour if you weigh 110 pounds (50 kilograms). Certain conditions and circumstances, however, can alter this basic biotransformation rate (Health Line).

In terms of alcoholic beverages, the oxidation rate for adults in general is approximately one-third to one-half ounce of pure alcohol an hour. If you sipped (not gulped) slightly less than the contents of one 12-ounce bottle of beer, 5-ounce glass of wine, or any equivalent portion of alcohol (see Health Line, page 222) very slowly over an hour's time, the enzymes in the stomach and liver would keep up, and you would not feel intoxicated. Naturally, if you consume larger amounts of alcohol at faster rates of consumption, all bets are off.[19]

It is no secret that alcohol consumption is conducive to the accumulation of body fat, most noticeably in the form of the notorious beer belly. It turns out that alcohol does not have significant effects on the biotransformation of dietary carbohydrates and proteins, so a drinking individual who consumes a healthy diet does not have to worry about getting enough nutrients. Alcohol does, however, reduce the breakdown of fat, so dietary fat has a

---

oxidation: A chemical process in alcohol metabolism.

alcohol dehydrogenase (AL-co-haul DEE-high-DRAW-juh-nays): An enzyme in the stomach and liver that converts alcohol into acetaldehyde.

acetaldehyde (ASS-ee-TAL-duh-hide): A by-product of alcohol metabolism, produced through the action of alcohol dehydrogenase.

acetaldehyde dehydrogenase (ASS-ee-TAL-duh-hide DEE-high-DRAW-juh-nays): An enzyme in the liver that converts acetaldehyde to acetic acid in alcohol metabolism.

acetic acid (a-SEE-tik ASS-id): A by-product of alcohol metabolism, produced through the action of acetaldehyde dehydrogenase.

Health Line

Gender, Race, and Medication: Factors in Alcohol Metabolism

Since enzymes play such a critical role in alcohol breakdown, it is important to consider factors that alter the levels of these enzymes. As mentioned in Chapter 3, two of the factors involve gender and ethnicity. In general, women have about 60 percent less alcohol dehydrogenase in the stomach than men; thus their oxidation of alcohol is relatively slower, even when different body weights have been taken into account.

In addition, about 50 percent of all people of Asian descent have a genetically imposed lower level of acetaldehyde dehydrogenase in the liver. As a consequence, acetaldehyde builds up, causing nausea, itching, facial flushing, and cardiac acceleration. The combination of these symptoms, often referred to as *fast-flushing*, makes alcohol consumption very unpleasant for many Asians.

It would be reasonable to expect then that those who experienced fast-flushing would drink less alcohol than those who do not. This is true when you look at the population at large. For Japanese American college students who have to contend with peer pressure to drink, however, the relationship between the physiological response and the quantity of alcohol consumed is not nearly as strong. For them, environmental factors encourage alcohol consumption, despite their genetically determined predisposition to get sick. In a similar way, the social life of Japanese businessmen has promoted alcohol consumption, though many get sick as a result. A journalist describes the dilemma in present-day Japan in this way:

> Perhaps in no other nation is drinking so extensively and tightly woven in business. Drinking after work is not only an extension of the company, it is virtually a requirement. Refuse the boss's offer to go out drinking, and your standing in the firm begins to slide.

Medications also can influence alcohol breakdown by altering levels of alcohol dehydrogenase in the stomach. Aspirin, for example, when taken on a full stomach, reduces enzyme levels by one-half, causing more alcohol to accumulate in the blood. Among women, aspirin has a greater inhibiting effect than among men, so it is possible that enzyme levels may be reduced to nearly zero if a woman is taking aspirin prior to drinking alcoholic beverages. Gastric ulcer medications also inhibit alcohol dehydrogenase and thus increase the physiological impact of alcohol. Any combination of these factors appears to produce additive effects. (See Table 9.4 on page 231 for other examples of alcohol–medication interactions.)

Sources: Edenberg, Howard J. (2007, Winter). The genetics of alcohol metabolism: Role of alcohol dehydrogenase and aldehyde dehydrogenase variants. *Alcohol Research and Health,* 5–37. Frezza, Mario; DiPadova, Carlo; Pozzato, Gabrielle; Terpin, Maddalena; Baraona, Enrique; and Lieber, Charles S. (1990). High blood alcohol levels in women: The role of decreased gastric alcohol dehydrogenase activity and first-pass metabolism. *New England Journal of Medicine, 322,* 95–99. Nakawatase, Tomoko V., Joe, and Sasao, Toshiaki (1993). The association between fast-flushing response and alcohol use among Japanese Americans. *Journal of Studies on Alcohol, 54,* 48–53. Roine, Risto; Gentry, Thomas; Hernandez-Muñoz, Rolando; Baraona, Enrique; and Lieber, Charles S. (1990). Aspirin increases blood alcohol concentrations in humans after ingestion of ethanol. *Journal of the American Medical Association, 264,* 2406–2408. Scott, Denise M., and Taylor, Robert E. (2007, Winter). Health-related effects of genetic variations of alcohol-metabolizing enzymes in African Americans. *Alcohol Research and Health,* 18–21.

greater chance of being stored rather than expended. Over time, the accumulation of fat in the liver is particularly serious because it eventually interferes with normal liver function. This condition will be examined in the next chapter as one of the major adverse effects of chronic alcohol consumption on the body.[20]

Measuring Alcohol in the Blood

Alcohol levels in the blood, like levels of any drug, vary considerably not only by virtue of how much is ingested and how long ago but also as a result of differences in an individual's body size and relative proportions of body fat. Consequently, we have to consider a specific ratio referred to as the **blood-alcohol concentration (BAC)** when assessing physiological and psychological effects (an alternative term is blood-alcohol level [BAL]).

The BAC refers to the number of grams of alcohol in the blood relative to 100 milliliters of blood, expressed as a percentage. For example, 0.1 gram (100 mg) of alcohol in 100 milliliters of blood is represented by a BAC of 0.10 percent. Table 9.3 (page 228) shows the BAC levels that can be estimated from one's body weight, number of standard drinks consumed, and hours elapsed since starting the first drink.

blood-alcohol concentration (BAC): The number of grams of alcohol in the blood relative to 100 milliliters of blood, expressed as a percentage.

TABLE 9.3

When are you drunk? Calculating your blood-alcohol concentration (BAC) level

		Standard Drinks									
		1	2	3	4	5	6	7	8	9	10
WEIGHT (LB)	100	.029	.058	.088	.117	.146	.175	.204	.233	.262	.290
	120	.024	.048	.073	.097	.121	.145	.170	.194	.219	.243
	140	.021	.042	.063	.083	.104	.125	.146	.166	.187	.208
	160	.019	.037	.055	.073	.091	.109	.128	.146	.164	.182
	180	.017	.033	.049	.065	.081	.097	.113	.130	.146	.162
	200	.015	.029	.044	.058	.073	.087	.102	.117	.131	.146
	220	.014	.027	.040	.053	.067	.080	.093	.106	.119	.133
	240	.012	.024	.037	.048	.061	.073	.085	.097	.109	.122

CAUTION   DRIVING IMPAIRED   LEGALLY DRUNK

Alcohol is "burned up" by your body at .015% per hour, as follows:

Hours since starting first drink	1	2	3	4	5	6
Percent alcohol burned up	.015	.030	.045	.060	.075	.090

To calculate your BAC level correctly, you must consider the number of standard drinks you have consumed, your body weight, and how much time has passed since the first drink. Note that a BAC level of .10% or higher has been, until recently, the standard for drunk driving in most U.S. states. All U.S. states have now adopted the .08% standard.

Source: Updated from *A primer of drug action,* 8th ed., by Robert M. Julien, M.D. © 2001 Worth Publishers. Used with permission.

From these figures, BAC levels typically are considered in terms of three broad categories of behavior: caution (0.01 to 0.05 percent), driving impaired (0.05 to 0.08 percent), and legally drunk (in all U.S. states, 0.08 percent and higher). In effect, you need to compute the accumulated BAC levels for your body weight after having a specific number of drinks, and then subtract 0.015 percent BAC for each hour since the drinking occurred.[21]

Effects of Alcohol on the Brain

Alcohol is clearly a CNS depressant drug, though it is often misidentified as a stimulant. The reason for this confusion is that alcohol, at low doses, first releases the cerebral cortex from its inhibitory control over subcortical systems in the brain, a kind of double-negative effect. In other words, alcohol is depressing an area of the brain that normally would be an inhibitor, and the result is the illusion of stimulation. The impairment in judgment and thinking (the classic features of being drunk) stems from a loosening of social inhibitions that allow us to be relatively civil and well behaved.

As the BAC level increases, more widespread areas of the brain are affected until an inhibition of the respiratory centers in the medulla becomes a distinct possibility. As with other depressant drugs, acute alcoholic poisoning produces death by asphyxiation. The LD50 level (the lethal dose for 50 percent of the population) for alcohol, at which death is likely to occur, is approximately 0.50 percent. Remember, however, the nature of the LD50 curve (see Chapter 2); deaths can occur at lower concentrations and fail to occur at higher ones.[22]

The effect of alcohol at the neuronal level is less well understood, but the picture is starting to emerge. At present, the leading candidate for a mechanism is the GABA receptor in the brain. This receptor contains three locations: one sensitive specifically to the neurotransmitter GABA, one sensitive to barbiturates, and one sensitive to a type of antianxiety medication (see Chapter 15). The last location is also sensitive to alcohol, and the research suggests that alcohol acts at this site, making it more difficult for the neuron to be stimulated.[23]

More worrisome than alcohol's depressive effects on the brain, however, is its ability to set up a pattern of psychological dependence (see Chapter 3). Since the late 1980s, evidence has accumulated that the reinforcing action of alcohol is a result of its influence on dopamine-releasing neurons in the nucleus accumbens of the brain. The fact that alcohol shares this effect with other abused drugs, including heroin, cocaine, and nicotine, suggests the possibility that treatments for one form of drug abuse might also be useful for others. Chapter 10 will describe the recent research concerning the use of naltrexone, an opiate antagonist, in the treatment of alcohol abuse.[24]

Acute Physiological Effects

Alcohol can produce a number of immediate physiological effects; they will be examined here. The physiological effects resulting from *chronic* alcohol consumption will be covered in the next chapter.

Toxic Reactions

We need to consider potentially life-threatening situations associated with alcohol as seriously as we would those with any other depressant drug. In general, the therapeutic index for alcohol, as measured by the LD50/ED50 ratio (see Chapter 2), is approximately 6. Because this figure is not very high, caution is strongly advised; the risks in being the "big winner" in a drinking contest should be weighed very carefully. On the one hand, to achieve a lethal BAC level of 0.50 percent, a 165-pound man needs to have consumed approximately twenty-three drinks over a four-hour period.[25] On the other hand, consuming ten drinks in one hour, a drinking schedule that achieves a BAC level of 0.35 percent, puts a person in extremely dangerous territory. We need to remember that LD50 is the *average* level for a lethal effect; there is no way to predict where a particular person might be located on the normal curve!

Fortunately, two mechanisms are designed to protect us to a certain degree. First, alcohol acts as a gastric irritant so that frequently the drinker will feel nauseated and vomit. Second, the drinker may simply pass out, and the risk potential from further drinking becomes irrelevant. Nonetheless, there are residual dangers in becoming unconscious; vomiting while in this state can prevent breathing, and so death can occur from asphyxiation (Health Alert).

HEALTH ALERT!

Emergency Signs and Procedures in Acute Alcohol Intoxication

Emergency Signs

- Stupor or unconsciousness
- Cool or damp skin
- Weak, rapid pulse (more than 100 beats per minute)
- Shallow and irregular breathing rate, averaging around one every three or four seconds
- Pale or bluish skin

Note: Among African Americans, color changes will be apparent in the fingernail beds, mucous membranes inside the mouth, or underneath the eyelids.

Emergency Procedures

- Seek medical help immediately.
- Drinker should lie on his or her side, with the head slightly lower than the rest of the body. This will prevent blockage of the airway and possible asphyxiation if the drinker starts to vomit.
- If drinker is put to bed, maintain some system of monitoring until he or she regains consciousness.

Note: There is no evidence that home remedies for "sobering up," such as cold showers, strong coffee, forced activity, or induction of vomiting, have any effect in reducing the level of intoxication. The only factors that help are the passage of time, rest, and perhaps an analgesic if there is a headache.

> **Where to go for assistance:**
> www.postgradmed.com/issues/2002/12_02/yost1.htm.
> This web site is adapted from Yost, David A. (2002). Acute care for alcohol intoxication: Be prepared to consider clinical dilemmas. *Postgraduate Medicine Online.*

Source: Victor, Maurice (1976). Treatment of alcohol intoxication and the withdrawal syndrome: A critical analysis of the use of drugs and other forms of therapy. In Peter G. Bourne (Ed.), *Acute drug abuse emergencies: A treatment manual.* New York: Academic Press, pp. 197–228.

Heat Loss and the Saint Bernard Myth

Alcohol is a peripheral dilator, which means that blood vessels near the skin surface enlarge, leading to overall warmth and redness. This effect is most likely the basis for the myth that alcohol can keep you warm in freezing weather. In actuality, however, alcohol produces a greater heat loss than would occur without it. In studies conducted of exercising men and women following consumption of alcohol, exaggerated heat loss was significantly greater in men than in women.[26] So if you are marooned in the snow and you see an approaching Saint Bernard with a cask of brandy strapped to its neck, politely refuse the offer. It will not help and could very well do you harm. (But feel free to hug the dog!)

Diuretic Effects

As concentration levels rise in the blood, alcohol begins to inhibit **antidiuretic hormone (ADH),** a hormone that normally would act to reabsorb water in the kidneys prior to elimination in the urine. As a result, urine is more diluted and, because large amounts of liquid are typically being consumed at the time, more copious. Once blood alcohol concentrations have peaked, however, the reverse occurs. Water is now retained in a condition called **antidiuresis,** resulting in swollen fingers, hands, and feet. This effect is more pronounced if salty foods (peanuts or pretzels, for example) have been eaten along with the alcohol.

The inhibition of ADH during the drinking of alcoholic beverages can be a serious concern, particularly following vigorous exercise when the body is already suffering from a loss of water and fluid levels are low. Therefore, the advice to the marathoner, whose body may lose more than a gallon of water over the course of a warm three-hour run, is to celebrate the end of the race not with a beer but with nonintoxicating liquids such as Gatorade or similar mineral-rich drinks.[27]

Cardiovascular Effects

Long-term, excessive consumption of alcohol increases the risk of heart disease, elevated blood pressure, and stroke. These chronic effects will be examined more closely in Chapter 10. In addition, when alcohol con-

---

antidiuretic hormone (ADH): A hormone that acts to reabsorb water in the kidneys prior to excretion from the body.

antidiuresis: A condition resulting from excessive reabsorption of water in the kidneys.

---

sumption continues for at least two days in an extended bout of drinking (the more extreme definition of binge drinking), the acute effects can be severe. In these cases, there is an increased likelihood of cardiac arrhythmia, owing to the lowered threshold for ventricular fibrillation and the scarring of heart muscle. Cardiovascular deaths reported by emergency departments in hospitals around the world that peak in frequency on Mondays and during weekends have been attributed, at least in part, to increased cardiovascular risk within this subpopulation of heavy drinkers.[28]

Effects on Sleep

It might seem tempting to induce sleep with a relaxing "nightcap," but in fact the resulting sleep patterns are adversely affected. Alcohol reduces the duration of a phase of sleep called rapid eye movement (REM) sleep (see Chapter 15). Depending on the dose, REM sleep can be either partially or completely suppressed during the night. When alcohol is withdrawn, REM sleep rebounds and represents a higher percentage of total sleep time than before alcohol consumption began. As a result, individuals sleep poorly and experience nightmares.[29]

Effects on Pregnancy

The consumption of alcohol during pregnancy, even in moderation, greatly increases the risk of retardation in the development of the fetus (see Chapter 10), and reducing the incidence of this behavior has been a major public health objective since the mid-1990s. From data averaged over 2006 and 2007, it has been estimated that about 12 percent of pregnant women consume alcohol, exposing approximately one in eight fetuses to alcohol *in utero.* National public health goals for the United States in 2010 (see Chapter 18) have included reducing this percentage to 6 percent. To help attain this objective, brief interventions to help pregnant women achieve abstinence from alcohol have been developed. In one program of this kind, women were five times more likely to have abstained by the third trimester of pregnancy, relative to controls, after a 10–15-minute counseling session in a walk-in center.[30]

Interactions with Other Drugs

A very serious concern is the complex interaction of alcohol with many drugs. As noted in Chapter 2, the DAWN reports of emergency department admissions and deaths show an extremely high incidence of

TABLE 9.4

A partial listing of possible drug-alcohol interactions

GENERIC DRUG (BRAND NAME OR TYPE)	CONDITION BEING TREATED	EFFECT OF INTERACTION
chloral hydrate (Noctec)	Insomnia	Excessive sedation that can be fatal; irregular heartbeat; flushing
glutethimide (Doriden)	Insomnia	Excessive sedation; reduced driving and machine-operating skills
antihypertensives (Apresoline, Diuril)	High blood pressure	Exaggeration of blood pressure–lowering effect; dizziness on rising
diuretics (Aldactone)	High blood pressure	Exaggeration of blood pressure–lowering effect; dizziness on rising
antibiotics (penicillin)	Bacterial infections	Reduced therapeutic effectiveness
nitroglycerin (Nitro-bid)	Angina pain	Severe decrease in blood pressure; intense flushing; headache; dizziness on rising
warfarin (Coumadin)	Blood clot	Decreased anti–blood clotting effect, easy bruising
insulin	Diabetes	Excessive low blood sugar; nausea; flushing
disulfiram (Antabuse)	Alcoholic drinking	Intense flushing; severe headache; vomiting; heart palpitations; could be fatal
methotrexate	Various cancers	Increased risk of liver damage
phenytoin (Dilantin)	Epileptic seizures	Reduced drug effectiveness in preventing seizures; drowsiness
prednisone (Deltasone)	Inflammatory conditions (arthritis, bursitis)	Stomach irritation
various antihistamines	Nasal congestion	Excessive sedation that could be fatal
acetaminophen (Tylenol)	Pain	Increased risk of liver damage

Sources: National Institute on Alcohol Abuse and Alcoholism (1995, January). Alcohol alert: Alcohol-medication interactions. No. 27, PH355. Bethesda, MD: National Institute on Alcohol Abuse and Alcoholism. Office of Substance Abuse Prevention (1988). *The fact is . . . It's dangerous to drink alcohol while taking certain medications.* Rockville, MD: National Institute on Drug Abuse. Parker, Christy (1985). *Simple facts about combinations with other drugs.* Phoenix, AZ: Do It Now Foundation.

medical crises arising from the combination of alcohol not only with prescribed medications but also with virtually all the illicit drugs on the street. Opiates and opiate-like drugs, marijuana, and many prescription medicines interact with alcohol such that the resulting combination produces effects that are either the sum of the parts or greater than the sum of the parts. In other cases, the ingestion of medications with alcohol significantly lessens the medication's benefits. Anticoagulants, anticonvulsants, and monoamine oxidase inhibitors (used as an antidepressant medication) fit into this second category. Table 9.4 shows a partial listing of major therapeutic drugs that interact with alcohol with undesirable, if not dangerous, outcomes. The complete list is so lengthy that it is fair to say that, whenever any medication is taken, the individual should inquire about possible interactions with alcohol.

Hangovers

About four to twelve hours after heavy consumption of alcohol, usually the next day, unpleasant symptoms of headache, nausea, fatigue, and thirst may occur, collectively known as a *hangover*. At least one such experience has been undergone by 40 percent of all men and 27 percent of all women over the age of eighteen.[31] Why these symptoms occur is not at all clear. The probable explanations at present focus on individual aspects of a hangover, though it is likely that several factors contribute to the total phenomenon.

One factor, beyond the simple fact of drinking too much, is the type of alcohol that has been consumed. Among distilled spirits, for example, vodka has a lower probability of inducing hangovers than whiskey. A possible reason is the relatively lower amount of

congeners. These are substances in alcoholic beverages, including trace amounts of nonethyl alcohol, oils, and other organic matter, that are by-products of the fermentation and distillation processes and give the drinks their distinctive smell, taste, and color. A common congener is the tannin found in red wines. Although no harm is caused by congeners in minute concentrations, they are still toxic substances, and they probably contribute to hangover symptoms.[32]

Other possible factors include traces of nonoxidized acetaldehyde in the blood, residual irritation in the stomach, and a low blood sugar level rebounding from the high levels induced by the previous ingestion of alcohol. The feeling of swollenness from the antidiuresis, discussed earlier, may contribute to the headache pain. The thirst may be due to the dehydration that occurred the night before.

Numerous "remedies" for a hangover have been concocted over the centuries, but it appears that the best treatment consists of rest, an analgesic medication for the headache (see Chapter 14), and the passage of time. Since the hangover can be considered basically as a collection of symptoms of withdrawal from alcohol, some people have taken to the remedy of consuming more alcohol, a strategy known as "the hair of the dog that bit you." This approach can relieve the symptoms, but it merely delays the inevitable consequences and leads to further alcohol use. Recently, herbal products have been marketed as hangover remedies or even preventives, but their effectiveness remains untested. As a spokesman for a major alcohol abuse treatment center has put it, "The best advice I can give in regard to 'hangover teas and pills' would be to avoid the need for them."[33]

Acute Behavioral Effects

The consumption of alcoholic beverages is so pervasive in the world that it seems almost unnecessary to comment on how it feels to be intoxicated by alcohol. The behavioral effects of consuming alcohol in more than very moderate quantities range from the relatively harmless effects of exhilaration and excitement, talkativeness, slurred speech, and irritability to behaviors that have the potential for causing great harm: uncoordinated movement, drowsiness, sensorimotor difficulties, and stupor.[34] Some of the prominent behavioral problems associated with acute alcohol intoxication will be examined in this section.

Blackouts

A **blackout** is an inability to remember events that occurred during the period of intoxication, even though the individual was conscious at the time. For example, a drinker having too much to drink at a party drives home, parks the car on a nearby street, and goes to bed. The next morning, he or she has no memory of having driven home and cannot locate the car. Owing to the possibility of blackouts, drinkers can be easily misled into thinking that because they can understand some information given to them during drinking, they will remember it later. The risk of blackouts is greatest when alcohol is consumed very quickly, forcing the BAC to rise rapidly. In a recent e-mail survey of college students to learn more about their experiences with blackouts, approximately half of those who had ever consumed alcohol reported having experienced a blackout at some point in their lives and 40 percent reported having had at least one experience in the twelve months prior to the survey.[35]

Driving Skills

There is no question that alcohol consumption significantly impairs the ability to drive or deal with automobile traffic, particularly among young people. In 2007, of the 41,100 traffic fatalities that occurred in the United States, approximately 13,000 of them (about 32 percent) were alcohol-related. To put this statistic in perspective, there were approximately 36 alcohol-related fatalities every day during that year (one instance every 40 minutes), with a potential loss of an average of 32 years of one's life. About 84 percent resulted from conditions in which drivers had a BAC of 0.08 percent or higher, the minimum standard for legal intoxication in all U.S. states.[36]

It is important to recognize that a BAC level of 0.08 percent does not have to be reached to cause impairment in driving. It has been estimated that the risk of a single-vehicle fatal crash escalates rapidly as alcohol consumption increases. Relative to drivers who have not consumed any alcohol at all, those with BAC levels between 0.02 and 0.04 percent have a 40 percent greater risk. When BAC levels are between 0.05 and 0.09 percent, the risk is 11 times greater; when BAC levels are between 0.10 and 0.14 percent, the risk is 48 times greater; when BAC levels are above 0.15 percent, the risk is 380 times greater. Therefore, it is quite possible for an accident to

---

congeners (KON-jen-ers): Nonethyl alcohols, oils, and other organic substances found in trace amounts in some distilled spirits.

blackout: Amnesia concerning events occurring during the period of alcoholic intoxication, even though consciousness had been maintained at that time.

Every community has its tragic stories of preventable deaths due to drunk driving. Alcohol is also recognized as a major factor in more than 800 boating fatalities in the United States each year.

occur even though the driver is not officially "driving while intoxicated" (DWI).

All these statistics could be viewed as correlational and not necessarily proof of a causal relationship between alcohol and automobile accidents, were it not for the data from laboratory-based experiments showing a clear deterioration of sensorimotor skills following the ingestion of alcohol. Reaction times are significantly prolonged, the coordination necessary to steer a car steadily is hampered, and the ability to stay awake when fatigued is impaired following BAC levels as low as 0.03 percent. More important, however, is a major decline in the ability to be aware of peripheral events and stimuli.[37] One researcher in this area expresses the deficit in this way:

> The overwhelming majority of accidents involving alcohol are not accidents in which tracking is the prime error. Contrary to what most people think, it isn't that people are weaving down the road, which is a sign of very high blood alcohol levels; it's that they have failed to see something. They go through a red light, they fail to see a pedestrian or a motorcyclist, they fail to see that the road is curving. Their perceptual and attentive mechanisms are affected very early, after just one drink. These are the things that are the prime causes of accidents.[38]

Unfortunately, it is the weaving behavior, or other extreme examples of driving impairments, that most often signals the police to stop a car for a possible DWI violation; other impairments frequently go unnoticed until it is too late.

Increasing the minimum age for alcoholic consumption from eighteen to twenty-one, now mandated throughout the United States, has had a major impact on the likelihood of accident fatalities among young people.

During the early 1980s, when changes in the minimum age were taking place state by state, it was possible to anticipate the improvements that could be made. On average, fatal nighttime accidents involving eighteen- and nineteen-year-old drivers decreased 13 percent between 1975 and 1984 in twenty-six states that raised the minimum drinking age during that interval. A decrease of 16 percent in night-time accidents in Michigan following the change in the drinking law was maintained six years later.[39]

With the minimum age now set at twenty-one years and the minimum BAC level for intoxication lowered to 0.08 percent, there is reason to be cautiously optimistic. According to estimates made by the National Highway Traffic Safety Administration, the reduction of the minimum BAC level to 0.08 percent has saved five hundred lives each year on the nation's highways. In 1998, a nationwide minimum level of intoxication for drivers younger than twenty-one years of age was set at a BAC level of 0.02 percent. Prior to 1998, averaging across fourteen years during which thirty U.S. individual states had adopted their own reduced minimum BAC levels for youths, the frequency with which high school seniors reported having driven after drinking any alcohol declined by 19 percent and the frequency with which they reported having driven after drinking five drinks or more declined by 23 percent. In addition, educational programs in schools and communities emphasizing the advantage of "designated drivers" as well as public education and lobbying groups such as Mothers Against Drunk Driving (MADD) and Students Against Drunk Driving (SADD) have had positive effects (see Portrait, page 234).[40]

Despite efforts to enforce a minimum age for alcohol consumption and a minimum BAC level as a definition of DWI, however, the number of deaths in automobile accidents due to a drunken driver in the general U.S. population has been literally "stalled" at approximately 13,000 per year since the early 1990s. Fortunately, new technologies have been developed that attack the problem at the source.

The most widely used technology is known as an ignition interlock device. When activated by the detection of a minimum BAC level in the breath of the driver, the ignition interlock will prevent the car from starting. In 2007, New Mexico became the first state to require ignition interlocks to be installed after a first DWI offense; alcohol-related fatalities decreased 11 percent in the first year. When, in 2004, Maryland mandated that the system be installed after several DWI arrests, fatalities were reduced by 18 percent. Currently, MADD is sponsoring a campaign to mandate that all U.S. states require ignition interlock devices after a single DWI incident.[41]

Much work remains to be done. The United States presently has one of the most lenient standards for

In 1980, Candace Lightner's thirteen-year-old daughter, Cari, was killed by a hit-and-run intoxicated driver in California. The driver had been out of jail on bail for only two days, a consequence of another hit-and-run drunk-driving crash, and he had three previous drunk-driving arrests and two previous convictions. He was allowed to plea bargain to vehicular manslaughter. Although the sentence was to serve two years in prison, the judge allowed him to serve time in a work camp and later a halfway house.

It was appalling to Lightner that drunk drivers, similar to the one who had killed her daughter, were receiving such lenient treatment, with many of them never going to jail for a single day. Lightner quit her job and started an organization that has become a household name: Mothers Against Drunk Driving (MADD).

Since then, MADD has campaigned for stricter laws against drunk driving, and most of the present DWI legislation around the country is a result of its intense efforts. In addition, MADD acts as a voice for victims of drunk-driving injuries and the families of those who have been killed. From a single act of courage, despite enormous grief, Lightner has spawned an organization that boasts more than 3 million members in the United States, with groups in virtually every state and more than four hundred local chapters.

More recently, MADD has set for itself the goal of reducing the number of all traffic fatalities associated with alcohol drinking. These are some of the group's proposals for change:

1. More effective enforcement of the minimum-drinking-age law.
2. A "0.00 percent BAC" criterion for drivers under twenty-one, making it illegal to drive with *any* measurable level of blood alcohol in any state.
3. Driver's license suspensions for underage persons convicted of purchasing or possession of alcoholic beverages.
4. Alcohol-free zones for youth gatherings.
5. Criminal sanctions against adults who provide or allow alcoholic beverages at events for underage participants.
6. Mandatory alcohol and drug testing for all drivers in all traffic crashes resulting in fatalities or serious bodily injury.
7. Sobriety checkpoints to detect and apprehend alcohol-impaired drivers and as a visible deterrent to drinking and driving.

The most recent initiative of MADD has been its campaign to have ignition interlock systems installed in vehicles driven by individuals convicted of drunk driving (see page 233).

Source: Information courtesy of Mothers Against Drunk Driving, Dallas, Texas, 2008. Interview with Candace Lightner.

---

driving while intoxicated among nations in the world (Table 9.5). The number of alcohol-related accidents, particularly among male drivers, whose involvement exceeds that of female drivers by a factor of more than 2:1, is far too high. Meanwhile, the drinking-and-driving phenomenon is widespread throughout the population. In 2007, approximately 31 million people over the age of 12 reported drinking and driving during the past year, with the peak age being between 21 and 25.[42]

Alcohol, Violence, and Aggression

It is difficult to avoid sweeping generalizations when confronted with statistics about alcohol and violent behavior both in the United States and in other countries. In a major study conducted in a community in northwestern Ontario, Canada, reported in 1991, more than 50 percent of the most recent occasions of physical violence were found to be preceded by alcohol use on the part of the assailant and/or the victims themselves.[43] Other studies show from 50 to 60 percent of all murders being committed when the killer had been drinking. About 40 percent of all acts of male sexual aggression against adult women and from 60 to 70 percent of male-instigated domestic violence occur when the offender has been drunk; more than 60 percent of all acts of child molestation involve drunkenness.[44]

Researchers have advanced several theories to account for the linkage between alcohol intoxication and violent behavior. The traditional *disinhibition theory* holds that alcohol on a pharmacological level impairs normal cortical mechanisms responsible for inhibiting the expression of innate or suppressed aggressive inclinations. Another viewpoint, referred to as the *cognitive-expectation theory*, holds that learned beliefs or expectations about alcohol's effects can facilitate aggressive behaviors. This second theory implies that violence is induced by virtue of the act of drinking combined with one's personal view of how a person is "supposed to respond" rather than by the pharmacological effects of alcohol itself (Drugs . . . in Focus).[45]

Expectations about the consequences of drug-

TABLE 9.5

Blood alcohol concentration at which drivers in different nations are legally drunk.

BAC	0.00+	0.02	0.03	0.05	0.08
COUNTRY	Czech Republic, Slovakia, Hungary	Norway, Poland, Sweden	Japan, China	Argentina, Australia, Costa Rica, Denmark, Finland, France, Italy, Germany, Greece, Netherlands, Peru, Russia, South Africa, Spain, Thailand	Brazil, Britain, Canada, Chile, Ecuador, Ireland, Jamaica, New Zealand, Singapore, United States

Sources: Valenti, John (2005, July 13). U.S. lags others in DWI toughness. *Newsday,* p. A15.

taking behavior or of any behavior at all, as noted in Chapter 3, are studied experimentally through the placebo research design. In the case of the cognitive-expectation theory, it is necessary to use a variation of this design, called the **balanced placebo design.**

balanced placebo design: An experimental design that can separate psychological effects (due to subjective expectations) and physiological effects (due to the pharmacology of the drug).

Drugs. . .in Focus

Alcohol, Security, and Spectator Sports

The National Basketball Association (NBA) issued in 2005 a new set of security guidelines for all thirty teams, including a Fan Code of Conduct specifying that "guests will enjoy the basketball experience free from disruptive behavior, including foul or abusive language or obscene gestures." In the words of NBA Commissioner David Stern, "We look at this as an opportunity to remind people that coming to an arena is an opportunity to share an experience of rooting a home team on to victory and booing the opposition, but not doing it in an antisocial way that goes against our civil society."

Acknowledging the connection between disruptive behavior and alcohol, the NBA now bans alcohol sales during the fourth quarter of every game and imposes a 24-ounce limit on the size of alcoholic drinks sold in an arena, with a maximum of two alcoholic drinks per customer. It is presently unclear how the two-drink limit will be enforced.

Increased security measures and restrictions on alcohol sales came about after basketball players and fans brawled in the stands and on the court at the end of a game in November 2004 between the Indiana Pacers and Detroit Pistons. Indiana's Ron Artest went into the seats after being hit by a full cup of beer that had been tossed by a spectator. As a result of the melee, considered to be one of the most violent episodes in NBA history, Artest was suspended for the rest of the 2004–2005 season, and other players were given suspensions of as many as thirty games. All told, ten players and fans were charged with fighting.

Alcohol consumption has also come under scrutiny during college and professional football games, where binge drinking at tailgating parties and after-game celebrations frequently results in property damage and sometimes leads to injuries or deaths. At the University of Virginia, a tradition that began in the 1980s has seniors individually drinking a fifth of liquor by kick off time at the final game of the football season (the so-called "Fourth-Year Fifth"). This practice has been associated with the deaths of eighteen students between 1990 and 2002. Since 1999, a university organization, Fourth-years Acting Responsibly (FAR), has coordinated an annual pledge drive to reduce abusive drinking at the final home game, as part of a campus-wide alcohol-abuse prevention program.

Sources: Eskenazi, Gerald (2005, December 21). For Patriots and Jets, a sobering experience. *New York Times,* p. D3. Football, tailgating parties, and alcohol safety (2005, October 1). *The NCADI Reporter.* Bethesda, MD: National Clearinghouse for Drug Information. NBA issuing sterner security, beer guidelines. *USA Today.com,* accessed May 8, 2005.

Subjects are randomly divided into four groups. Two groups are given an alcoholic drink, with one group being told that they are ingesting alcohol and the other that they are ingesting a nonalcohol substitute that tastes and smells like alcohol. Two other groups are given the nonalcohol substitute, with one group being told that they are ingesting this substitute and the other that they are ingesting alcohol.

Studies using the balanced placebo design have shown clearly that beliefs (mind-sets) concerning the effects of drinking are more influential in determining a subject's behavior than the more direct physiological effects of the alcohol. In other words, *what they are told they are consuming is more important than what they consume* (Health Line). Unfortunately, for a true test of the cognitive-expectation theory, a balanced placebo design cannot be used with BAC levels above 0.035 percent because subjects are no longer fooled by the deception with larger quantities, and most alcohol-associated acts of violence occur with BAC levels at least six times higher.[46]

Sex and Sexual Desire

If they were asked, most people would say that alcohol has an enhancing or aphrodisiac effect on sexual desire and performance. The actual effect of alcohol, however, is more complex than these commonly held beliefs express. In fact, it is because of these beliefs that people are frequently more susceptible to the expectations of what alcohol *should* do for them than they are to the actual physiological effects of alcohol.

To examine the complex relationship between alco-

Quick Concept Check 9.2

Understanding the Data from Balanced Placebo Designs

Check your understanding of the balanced placebo design by identifying whether the following experimental results reflect (a) psychological effects, (b) physiological effects, or (c) a combination of psychological and physiological effects:

- Scenario 1: Subjects felt sexy after receiving low doses of drug X, regardless of whether they knew what they were receiving.
- Scenario 2: Subjects felt sexy if they received low doses of drug X but were told that they did not receive it and also felt sexy if they did not receive low doses of drug X but were told that they did.
- Scenario 3: Subjects felt sexy after being told they would receive low doses of drug X, regardless of whether they actually received it.

Answers: Scenario 1. b   Scenario 2. c   Scenario 3. a

hol and sex, we need to turn again to studies using the balanced placebo design. The general results from such studies are quite different for men and women. Among men, those who expected to be receiving low levels of alcohol had greater penile responses, reported greater subjective arousal, and spent more time watching erotic pictures, *regardless of whether they did indeed receive alcohol.* When alcohol concentrations rise to levels that reflect genuine intoxication, however, the pharmacological actions outweigh the expectations, and the overall effect is definitely inhibitory. Men who are drunk have less sexual desire and a decreased capacity to perform sexually.

In contrast, expectations among women play a lesser role. They are more inclined to react to the pharmacological properties of alcohol itself, but the direction of their response depends on whether we are talking about subjective or physiological measures. For women receiving increasing alcohol concentrations, measures of subjective arousal increase but measures of vaginal arousal decrease. The pattern of their responses mirrors Shakespeare's observation in *Macbeth* that alcohol "provokes the desire, but it takes away from the performance," a comment originally intended to reflect only the male point of view.[47]

Alcohol and Health Benefits

The documented health benefits of moderate levels of alcohol consumption over the last thirty years of research have presented a major dilemma among medical and public health professionals. The crux of the dilemma is that moderate amounts of alcohol can possibly save your life, while immoderate amounts can possibly destroy it. As one writer has expressed it, "Alcohol has become the sharpest double-edged sword in medicine."

It started as an observation that did not seem to make sense. Epidemiological studies of French and other European populations who consumed large amounts of butter, cheese, liver, and other animal fats—a diet associated with elevated cholesterol and an elevated risk for coronary failure—found that these populations had a remarkably low incidence of coronary heart disease. The answer seemed to be that relatively more alcohol was consumed along with their dietary food. The "French paradox" was resolved when later research showed that alcohol increases high-density lipoprotein (HDL) cholesterol (the so-called good cholesterol) levels in the blood, with HDL acting as a protective mechanism against a possible restriction of blood flow through arteries. The greatest benefit was seen in those individuals who had high concentrations of low-density lipoprotein (LDL) cholesterol (the so-called bad cholesterol) and therefore had the

A modern-day medical dilemma: health benefits of moderate alcohol consumption versus the potential for alcohol abuse. (By permission of Mike Luckovich and Creators Syndicate, Inc.)

greatest risk for coronary heart disease. It was estimated that consumption of approximately 8 ounces of wine (a bit less than two standard drinks) per day resulted in a 25 percent reduction in the risk of coronary heart disease.

In recent animal studies, a natural substance in red wine known as *resveratrol* has been identified as a possible factor in explaining the health benefits of drinking red wine. Mice administered resveratrol in very large quantities were higher in endurance levels, relative to controls, and were less susceptible to the elevations in glucose and insulin that normally result from eating a high-fat diet. However, these animals received a daily dosage of resveratrol far larger than a human would ingest from drinking wine, so the question of whether this substance is a key factor remains unsettled. Human intake of resveratrol at comparable dosages would have a significant potential for toxicity (Chapter 2).[48]

Frequently, the focus is on wine consumption, and particularly red wine consumption, but the accumulated research findings indicate that beneficial health effects result from the consumption of *any* type of alcoholic beverage, whether it is beer, wine, or liquor. And the benefits extend beyond coronary heart disease. Moderate alcohol intake reduces the risk of diabetes mellitus, reduces the risk of stroke, and reduces the risk of dementia (possibly by reducing the incidence of mini-strokes or by boosting concentrations of vitamin B_6, which is essential for the formation of essential brain chemicals). A recent study indicates that moderate alcohol consumption can also lower the risk of rheumatoid arthritis by up to 50 percent.[49]

Of course, the key to the health benefits of alcohol consumption lies in its moderation. Moderate drinking has been defined as taking no more than one drink per day for

HEALTH ALERT!

Guidelines for Responsible Drinking

- **Know how much you are drinking.** Measure your drinks. Beer is often premeasured (unless you are drinking draft beer from a keg), but wine and liquor drinks frequently are not. Learn what a 5-ounce quantity of wine or a 1 1/2-ounce shot of liquor looks like, and use these measures to guide your drinking.

- **Choose beer or wine over liquor.** Beer especially will make you feel fuller more quickly, with a smaller intake of alcohol. But be careful. A 12-ounce beer is equivalent in alcohol content to a 5-ounce glass of wine or a 1-shot drink of liquor.

- **Drink slowly.** One drink an hour stays relatively even with your body's metabolism of the alcohol you consume. Sipping your drinks is a good strategy for slowing down your consumption. If you are a man, you'll look cool; if you are a woman, you'll look refined.

- **Don't cluster your drinking.** If you are going to have seven drinks during a week, don't drink them all on the weekend.

- **Eat something substantial while you are drinking.** Protein is an excellent accompaniment to alcohol. Avoid salty foods because they will make you thirstier and more inclined to have another drink.

- **Drink only when you are already relaxed.** Chronic alcohol abuse occurs more easily when alcohol is viewed as a way to relax. If you have a problem, seek some nondrug alternative.

- **When you drink, savor the experience.** If you focus on the quality of what you drink rather than the quantity you are drinking, you will avoid drinking too much.

- **Never drink alone.** Drinking is never an appropriate answer to social isolation. Besides, when there are people around, there is someone to look out for you.

- **Beware of unfamiliar drinks.** Some drinks, such as zombies and other fruit and rum drinks, are deceptively high in kinds of alcohol that are not easily detected by taste.

- **Never drive a car after having had a drink.** Driving impairment begins after very low quantities of alcohol consumption.

- **Be a good host or hostess.** If you are serving alcohol at a party, do not make drinking the focus of activity. Do not refill your guests' glasses. Discourage intoxication and do not condone drunkenness. Provide transportation options for those who drink at your party. Present nonalcoholic beverages as prominently as alcoholic ones. Prior to the end of the party, stop serving alcohol and offer coffee or other warm nonalcoholic beverages and a substantial snack, providing an interval of non-drinking time before people leave.

- **Support organizations that encourage responsible drinking.** If you are on a college campus, get involved with the local chapter of BACCHUS (Boost Alcohol Consciousness Concerning the Health of University Students). If there is no chapter, start one.

> **Where to go for assistance:**
>
> www.indiana.edu/~engs/hints/holiday.html
>
> This web site on sensible, moderate, and responsible alcohol consumption and party hosting is adapted from Engs, R.C. (1987). *Alcohol and other drugs: Self responsibility.* Bloomington, IN: Tichenor Publishing.

Sources: Gross, Leonard (1983). *How much is too much? The effects of social drinking.* New York: Random House, pp. 149–152. Hanson, David J., and Engs, Ruth C. (1994). Drinking behavior: Taking personal responsibility. In Peter J. Venturelli (Ed.), *Drug use in America: Social, cultural, and political perspectives.* Boston: Jones and Bartlett, pp. 175–181. *Managing alcohol in your life.* Mansfield, MA: Steele Publishing and Consulting.

women and no more than two drinks per day for men. The newest (2000) Dietary Guidelines for Americans, released by the U.S. Department of Agriculture and the U.S. Department of Health and Human Services, acknowledge the effect of alcohol on reducing the risk of coronary heart disease but limits the recommendation of moderate drinking to men over age forty-five and women over age fifty-five, a subpopulation that carries an elevated risk for the disease.

Despite the weight of evidence tilting toward the potential health benefits of alcohol, the medical field remains divided on the question of whether to encourage patients who do not drink alcohol to start at a moderate level of consumption. In some cases, moderate intake is not advisable. Even one drink per day slightly increases the risk for breast cancer in women, and in no circumstances should alcohol be consumed during pregnancy. Some public health researchers are concerned that an endorsement of moderate alcohol drinking may open up a range of possible risks, in effect giving alcohol a kind of "halo effect" that might be confusing to the public. In any case, public opinion remains unconvinced that moderate alcohol consumption has health benefits. About three-fourths (73 percent) of American adults believe that it is either bad for one's health or makes no difference one way or another, a perception that has remained unchanged since this survey question was asked in 2001.[50]

Strategies for Responsible Drinking

The various negative acute effects of alcohol on physiological responses and behavior have been considered. Yet it is necessary to remember that there are very large numbers of people who drink alcoholic beverages and avoid the adverse effects that have been detailed here. An overwhelming proportion of the population, for example, drink on occasion and have never engaged in any violent or aggressive acts. They drink in moderate amounts, according to the federal guidelines for diet and nutrition. In addition, they avoid situations (such as driving) in which alcohol consumption would impair their performance and endanger their lives. The issue of responsible drinking is an important one; it may not be easy for us to accomplish but, fortunately, guidelines exist that make it easier.[51] Health Alert features some strategies to reduce the problems associated with alcoholic intake.

At the same time, however, we must remember that, regardless of how it is consumed, alcohol remains a drug with a significant potential for dependence. It is not difficult to get hooked. As it has been said, people may plan to get drunk, but no one plans to be an alcoholic. The problems surrounding chronic alcohol abuse and alcoholism will be examined in the next chapter.

Summary

What Makes an Alcoholic Beverage?

- Drinkable alcohol is obtained from the fermentation of sugar in some natural products such as grapes, apples, honey, or molasses. The result is some form of wine.

- Beer is obtained from barley, after the starch has first been converted into sugar and then fermented along with other grains and hops, and aged.

- To obtain very strong alcoholic beverages, it is necessary to boil the fermented liquid and condense it later by cooling. This process, called distillation, results in alcohol concentrations of up to 95 percent, and the products are known as distilled spirits or liquors.

Alcohol Use through History

- The history of alcohol use dates back many thousands of years; the process of fermentation is very simple and its discovery was probably accidental.

- Distillation techniques were perfected during the Middle Ages, with brandy being the first distilled spirit. In later centuries, gin gained popularity in Europe, as did whiskey in the United States.

Patterns of Alcohol Consumption Today

- The demographics of alcohol consumption reveal a large disparity in the drinking habits of the population.

About a third do not drink at all, and only about 30 percent of those who drink account for 80 percent of all the alcoholic beverages consumed in the United States.

- Peak alcohol consumption occurs at ages twenty-one to twenty-two.

The Pharmacology of Alcohol

- Alcohol is a very small molecule, easily soluble in both water and fat. Its absorption into the bloodstream is extremely rapid. The breakdown of alcohol is handled by two special enzymes in the stomach and liver.

- The rate of alcohol biodegradation is constant, so alcohol can only leave the body at a specific pace, despite the quantity taken in.

- The effective level of alcohol in the body is measured by the blood-alcohol concentration (BAC) level, which adjusts for differences in body weight and the time since ingestion of the last alcoholic beverage.

Effects of Alcohol on the Brain

- Although alcohol affects several neurotransmitters in the brain, it is presently agreed that the principal effect is the stimulation of the GABA receptor.

- Generally, the neural effect of alcohol proceeds downward, beginning with an inhibition of the cerebral cortex, then lower brain regions. Inhibition of respiratory systems in the medulla, usually accomplished at BAC levels in the neighborhood of 0.50 percent, results in asphyxiation and death.

Acute Physiological Effects

- Alcohol at very high levels produces life-threatening consequences and at moderate levels produces a loss of body heat, increased excretion of water, an increase in heart rate and constriction of coronary arteries, disturbed patterns of sleep, and serious interactions with other drugs.

Acute Behavioral Effects

- On a behavioral level, serious adverse effects include blackouts, significant impairment in sensorimotor skills such as driving an automobile, and an increased potential for aggressive or violent acts.
- The relationship between alcohol consumption and sexual desire and performance is a complex one, with differences being observed for men and women.

Alcohol and Health Benefits

- The accumulated evidence of medical research has indicated that there is a reduced risk for coronary heart disease and stroke with moderate consumption levels of alcohol. Possible health benefits include a reduction of risk for diabetes, dementia, and rheumatoid arthritis.
- Moderate alcohol consumption has been defined as no more than one drink per day for women and no more than two drinks per day for men. There should be zero tolerance for alcohol consumption among pregnant women.

Strategies for Responsible Drinking

- Despite the potential for alcohol consumption to produce adverse effects, most people can drink alcohol in a responsible way that avoids these harmful consequences. However, the risk of alcohol dependence is always present.

Key Terms

acetaldehyde, p. 226
acetaldehyde dehydrogenase, p. 226
acetic acid, p. 226
alcohol dehydrogenase, p. 226
antidiuresis, p. 230

antidiuretic hormone (ADH), p. 230
aqua vitae, p. 218
balanced placebo design, p. 235
barley malt, p. 218
blackout, p. 232

blood-alcohol concentration (BAC), p. 227
brewing, p. 217
congeners, p. 232
distillation, p. 218
distilled spirits, p. 218
ethyl alcohol, p. 217

fermentation, p. 217
mash, p. 218
oxidation, p. 226
temperance movement, p. 220

Endnotes

1. Pinel, John P. J. (2003). *Biopsychology* (5th ed.). Boston: Allyn and Bacon, p. 381.
2. Gibbons, Boyd (1992, February). Alcohol: The legal drug. *National Geographic Magazine*, pp. 2–35. Roueché, Berton (1963). Alcohol in human culture. In Salvatore P. Lucia (Ed.), *Alcohol and civilization*. New York: McGraw-Hill, pp. 167–182. Vallee, Bert L. (1998, June). Alcohol in the western world. *Scientific American*, pp. 80–85.
3. McGovern, Patrick E.; Glusker, Donald L.; Exner, Lawrence J.; and Voigt, Mary M. (1996). Neolithic resinated wine. *Nature*, 381, 480–481.
4. Sournia, Jean-Charles (1990). *A history of alcoholism*. Cambridge, MA: Basil Blackwell, pp. 14–50. U.S. Department of Health, Education, and Welfare (1978). *Perspectives on the history of psychoactive substance use*, pp. 67–75.
5. Grimes, William (1993). *Straight up or on the rocks: A cultural history of American drink*. New York: Simon and Schuster, p. 36. Musto, David F. (1996, April). Alcohol in American history. *Scientific American*, pp. 78–83.
6. Lender, Mark E., and Martin, James K. (1982). *Drinking in America: A history*. New York: Free Press, pp. 13–14.
7. First in war, peace—and hooch, by George! (2000, December 7). *Newsday*, p. A86. Grimes, *Straight up*, p. 51.
8. Gibbons, Alcohol, p. 7.
9. Garfield, Craig F., Chung, Paul J., and Rathouz, Paul J. (2003). Alcohol advertising in magazines and adolescent readership. *Journal of the American Medical Association*, 289, 2424–2429. Hanson, Glen R., and Li, Ting-Kai (2003). Public health implications of excessive alcohol consumption. *Journal of the American Medical Associa-*

tion, 289, 1031–1032. National Association of Convenience Stores (2008). That's the spirit—U.S. alcohol sales growing. www.nacsonline.com. US top five beer companies ranked by prime-time network television advertising outlays in dollars with the top three network TV programs ranked by beer ad expenditures. *Adweek* (2003, April 21), p. SR14.

10. Statistics on 1998 consumption from Holleran, Joan (1999, May). Drinking up: U.S. alcoholic beverage consumption in gallons per capita by type (beer, wine, distilled spirits) in 1993 and 1998. *Beverage Industry*, pp. 17–21. Statistics on consumption from World Health Statistical Information System (2004). *Global Status Report on Alcohol 2004*. Geneva: World Health Organization, Table 3.

11. Center for Science in the Public Interest (2003, December 16). Press release: "Alcohol facts" label proposed for beer, wine, and liquor. Center for Science in the Public Interest, Washington DC. Rogers, John D., and Greenfield, Thomas K. (1999). Beer drinking accounts for most of the hazardous alcohol consumption reported in the United States. *Journal of Studies on Alcohol*, 60, 732–739.

12. The Gallup Organization (2007, July 27). Beer again edges out wine as Americans' drink of choice. Gallup Organization, Princeton, NJ.

13. Dawson, Deborah A., Grant, Bridget F., and Chou, Patricia S. (1995). Gender differences in alcohol intake. In Walter A. Hunt and Sam Zakhari (Eds.), *Stress, gender, and alcohol-seeking behavior* (NIAAA Research Monograph 29). Bethesda, MD: National Institute on Alcohol Abuse and Alcoholism, pp. 1–21. Heien, Dale (1996). The relationship between alcohol consumption and earnings. *Journal of Studies on Alcohol*, 57, 536–542.

14. Denizet-Lewis, Benoit (2005, January 5). Band of brothers. *New York Times Magazine*, pp. 32–33, 52, 73–74. Hingson, Ralph W.; Heeren, Timothy; Zakocs, Ronda C.; and Kopstein, Andrea (2002). Age of first intoxication, heavy drinking, driving after drinking and risk of unintentional injury among U.S. college students. *Journal of Studies on Alcohol*, 63, 136–144. Substance Abuse and Mental Health Services Administration (2006, November/ December). Who's drinking? More than half underage college students. *SAMHSA News*, p. 9. Wechsler, Henry; Lee, Jae Eun; Kuo, Meichun; Seibring, Mark; Nelson, Toben F.; et al. (2002). Trends in college binge drinking during a period of increased prevention efforts: Findings from four Harvard School of Public Health College Alcohol Study Surveys: 1993–2001. *Journal of American College Health*, 50, 203–217. Zernike, Kate (2005, March 15). A 21st-birthday drinking game can be a deadly rite of passage. *New York Times*, pp. A1, A13.

15. Foster, Susan E.; Vaughan, Roger D.; Foster, William H.; and Califano, Joseph A. (2003). Alcohol consumption and expenditures for underage drinking and adult excessive drinking. *Journal of the American Medical Association*, 289, 989–995. Johnston, Lloyd D.; O'Malley, Patrick M.; Bachman, Jerald G.; and Schulenberg, John E. (2008, December

11). Various stimulant drugs show continuing gradual declines among teens in 2008, most illicit drugs hold steady. Ann Arbor: University of Michigan News Service, Figures 1 and 4. Radnofsky, Louise (2007, April 6). Outrage flows over Spykes. *Newsday*, p. A17. Substance Abuse and Mental Health Services Administration (2008, March 31). Quantity and frequency of alcohol use among underage drinkers. *SAMHSA News*, pp. 1–4. Substance Abuse and Mental Health Services Administration (2008, June 26). News release: New nationwide report estimates that 40 percent of underage drinkers received free alcohol from adults over 21. Rockville, MD: Substance Abuse and Mental Health Services Administration.

16. U.S. Department of Health and Human Services (1990). *Alcohol and health*. (The Seventh Special Report to the U.S. Congress). Rockville, MD: National Institute on Alcohol Abuse and Alcoholism.

17. Dubowski, Kurt M. (1991). *The technology of breath-alcohol analysis*. Rockville, MD: National Institute on Alcohol Abuse and Alcoholism.

18. Julien, Robert M. (2000). *A primer of drug action* (9th ed.). New York: Worth, p. 95.

19. National Institute on Alcohol Abuse and Alcoholism (1997, January). Alcohol alert: Alcohol metabolism. No. 35, PH371. Bethesda, MD: National Institute on Alcohol Abuse and Alcoholism. Friedman, Nancy (1985, August–September). Anatomy of a drink. *Campus Voice*, pp. 61–63. Julien, *A primer of drug action*, pp. 91–97.

20. Suter, Paolo M.; Schutz, Yves; and Jequier, Eric (1992). The effect of ethanol on fat storage in healthy subjects. *New England Journal of Medicine*, 326, 983–987.

21. Hawks, Richard L., and Chiang, C. Nora (1986). Examples of specific drug assays. In Richard L. Hawks and C. Nora Chiang (Eds.), *Urine testing for drugs of abuse* (NIDA Research Monograph 73). Rockville, MD: National Institute on Drug Abuse, p. 103. Julien, *A primer of drug action*, pp. 91–97.

22. Levinthal, Charles F. (1990). *Introduction to physiological psychology* (3rd ed.). Englewood Cliffs, NJ: Prentice-Hall, pp. 181–184.

23. U.S. Department of Health and Human Services (1994). *Alcohol and health*. (The Eighth Special Report to the U.S. Congress). Bethesda, MD: National Institute on Alcohol Abuse and Alcoholism, pp. 4-6, 4-7.

24. Koob, G. F.; Rassnick, S.; Heinrichs, S.; and Weiss, F. (1994). Alcohol, the reward system and dependence. In B. Jansson, H. Jörnvall, U. Rydberg, L. Terenius, and B. L. Vallee (Eds.), *Toward a molecular basis of alcohol use and abuse*. Basel: Birkhäuser-Verlag, pp. 103–114. Schuckit, Marc A. (1994, August). Naltrexone and the treatment of alcoholism. *Drug Abuse and Alcoholism Newsletter*, San Diego, CA: Vista Hill Foundation.

25. Grilly, David M. (2006). *Drugs and human behavior* (5th ed.). Boston: Allyn and Bacon, p. 144.

26. Luks, Allan, and Barbato, Joseph (1989). *You are what you drink*. New York: Villiard, p. 44.

27. Ibid., pp. 42–43.

28. Chenet, Laurent, and Britton, Annie (2001). Weekend binge drinking may be linked to Monday peaks in cardiovascular deaths. *British Medical Journal, 322,* 998.

29. National Institute on Alcohol Abuse and Alcoholism (1998, July). Alcohol alert: Alcohol and sleep. No. 41. Bethesda, MD: National Institute on Alcohol Abuse and Alcoholism.

30. Centers for Disease Control (2002). Alcohol consumption among pregnant and childbearing-aged women—United States, 1991–1999. *Morbidity and Mortality Weekly Report, 511,* 273–276. O'Connor, Mary J., and Wahley, Shannon E. (2007). Brief intervention for alcohol use by pregnant women. *American Journal of Public Health, 97,* 252–258. Substance Abuse and Mental Health Services Administration (2008). *Results from the 2007 National Survey on Drug Use and Health: National findings.* Rockville, MD: Office of Applied Studies, Substance Abuse and Mental Health Services Administration, p. 33.

31. Schuckit, Marc A. (1989). *Drug and alcohol abuse: A clinical guide to diagnosis and treatment* (3rd ed.). New York: Plenum, p. 62.

32. Wiese, Jeffrey G., Shlipak, Michael G., and Browner, Warren S. (2000). The alcohol hangover. *Annals of Internal Medicine, 232,* 897–902.

33. Wotapka, Dawn (2003, May 20). Effects of hangover remedy still dim. *Newsday,* p. A39. Quotation by Ames Sweet of the National Council on Alcoholism and Drug Dependence, New York.

34. Victor, Maurice (1976). Treatment of alcohol intoxication and the withdrawal syndrome: A critical analysis of the use of drugs and other forms of therapy. In Peter G. Bourne (Ed.), *Acute drug emergencies: A treatment manual.* New York: Academic Press, p. 199.

35. Luks and Barbato, *You are what you drink,* pp. 52–53. White, Aaron M., Jamieson-Drake, David W., and Swartzwelder, H. Scott (2002). Prevalence and correlates of alcohol-induced blackouts among college students: Results of an e-mail survey. *Journal of American College Health, 51,* 117–131.

36. National Highway Traffic Safety Administration (2008, August). 2007 Traffic Safety Annual Assessment—Alcohol-impaired driving fatalities.

37. Hoyer, William J., Semenec, Silvie C., and Buchler, Norbou E. G. (2007). Acute alcohol intoxication impairs controlled search across the visual field. *Journal of Studies on Alcohol and Drugs, 68,* 748–758. National Institute on Alcohol Abuse and Alcoholism (1996, January). Alcohol Alert: Drinking and driving. No. 31, PH362. Bethesda, MD: National Institute on Alcohol Abuse and Alcoholism.

38. Gross, Leonard (1983). *How much is too much: The effects of social drinking.* New York: Random House, p. 29. Quotation of Dr. Herbert Moskowitz.

39. Fortini, Mary-Ellen (1995). Youth, alcohol, and automobiles: Attitudes and behaviors. In Ronald R. Watson (Ed.), *Alcohol, cocaine, and accidents.* Totowa, NJ: Humana Press, pp. 25–39. National Institute on Alcohol Abuse and Alcoholism (2003, April). Alcohol Alert: Underage drinking: A major public health challenge, No. 59. Bethesda, MD: National Institute on Alcohol Abuse and Alcoholism. U.S. Department of Health and Human Services (1990). *Alcohol and health,* pp. 216–217. Wald, Matthew L. (2006, November 20). A new strategy to discourage driving drunk. *New York Times,* pp. A1, A20.

40. National Institute on Alcohol Abuse and Alcoholism (2001, April). Alcohol alert: Alcohol and transportation safety. No. 52. Bethesda, MD: National Institute on Alcohol Abuse and Alcoholism. Wagenaar, Alexander C., O'Malley, Patrick M., and LaFond, Colette (2001). Lowered legal blood alcohol limits for young drivers: Effects on drinking, driving, and driving-after-drinking behaviors in 30 states. *American Journal of Public Health, 91,* 801–803.

41. Wald, A new strategy, pp. A1, A20.

42. Hingson, Ralph; Heeren, Timothy; Zakocs, Ronda; Winter, Michael; and Wechsler, Henry (2003). Age of first intoxication, heavy drinking, driving after drinking and risk of unintentional injury among U.S. college students. *Journal of Studies on Alcohol, 64,* 23–31. Liu, Simin; Siegel, Paul Z.; Brewer, Robert D.; Mokdad, Ali H.; Sleet, David A.; et al. (1997). Prevalence of alcohol-impaired driving: Results from a national self-reported survey of health behaviors. *Journal of the American Medical Association, 277,* 122–125. National Highway Traffic Administration (1999, March). The relationship of alcohol safety laws to drinking drivers in fatal crashes. Washington DC: U.S. Department of Transportation. Substance Abuse and Mental Health Services Administration (2008). *Results from the 2007 National Survey on Drug Use and Health: Detailed tables.* Rockville, MD: Office of Applied Studies, Substance Abuse and Mental Health Services Administration, Tables 7.94A and 7.94B.

43. Abbey, Antonia; Zawacki, Tina; Buck, Philip O.; Clinton, A. Monique; and McAuslan, Pam (2004). Sexual assault and alcohol consumption: What do we know about their relationship and what types of research are still needed? *Aggression and Violent Behavior, 9,* 271–303. Haggård-Grann, Ulrika; Hallqvist, Johan; Långström, Niklas; and Möller, Jette (2006). The role of alcohol and drugs in triggering criminal violence: A case-crossover study. *Addiction, 101,* 100–108. Pernanen, Kai (1991). *Alcohol in human violence.* New York: Guilford Press, pp. 192–193.

44. Collins, James J., and Messerschmidt, Pamela M. (1993). Epidemiology of alcohol-related violence. *Alcohol Health and Research World, 17,* 93–100. Goode, Erich (2005). *Drugs in American society* (6th ed.). New York: McGraw-Hill, pp. 340–343. National Institute on Alcohol Abuse and Alcoholism (1997, October). Alcohol alert: Alcohol, violence, and aggression. No. 38. Bethesda, MD: National Institute on Alcohol Abuse and Alcoholism.

45. Giancola, Peter R. (2000). Executive functioning: A conceptual framework for alcohol-related aggression. *Experimental and Clinical Psychopharmacology, 8,* 576–597. Giancola, Peter R. (2002). Alcohol-related aggression in men and women: The influence of dispositional aggressivity. *Journal of Studies on Alcohol, 63,* 696–708.

Norris, Jeanette; David, Kelly Cue; George, William H.; Martell, Joel; and Heiman, Julia R. (2002). Alcohol's direct and indirect effects on men's self-reported sexual aggression likelihood. *Journal of Studies on Alcohol, 63*, 688–695. Parrott, Dominic, and Zeichner, Amos (2002). Effects of alcohol and trait anger on physical aggression in men. *Journal of Studies on Alcohol, 63*, 196–204.

46. Pernanen, Kai (1993). Research approaches in the study of alcohol-related violence. *Alcohol Health and Research World, 17*, 101–107. Taylor, Stuart P. (1993). Experimental investigation of alcohol-induced aggression in humans. *Alcohol Health and Research World, 17*, 108–112.

47. Abel, Ernest L. (1985). *Psychoactive drugs and sex*. New York: Plenum Press, pp. 19–54. Cooper, M. Lynne (2006). Does drinking promote risky sexual behavior? A complex answer to a simple question. *Current Directions in Psychological Science, 15*, 19–23. George, William H., and Norris, Jeanette (1993). Alcohol, disinhibition, sexual arousal, and deviant sexual behavior. *Alcohol Health and Research World, 17*, 133–138. Testa, Maria, Vanzile-Tamsen, Carol, and Livingston, Jennifer A. (2004). The role of victim and perpetrator intoxication on sexual assault outcomes. *Journal of Studies on Alcohol, 65*, 320–329.

48. Rimm, Eric B. (2000). Moderate alcohol intake and lower risk of coronary heart disease: Meta-analysis of effects on lipids and haemostatic factors. *Journal of the American Medical Association, 283*, 1269. Wade, Nicholas (2006, November 2). Yes, red wine holds answer. Check dosage. *New York Times*, pp. A1, A20. Wade, Nicholas (2006, November 17). Red wine ingredient increases endurance, study shows. *New York Times*, p. A20. Wade, Nicholas (2008, June 4). New hints seen that red wine may slow aging. *New York Times*, pp. A1, A22. Zuger, Abigail (2002, December 31). The case for drinking (all together now: in moderation). *New York Times*, pp. F1, F6. Quotation on p. F1.

49. Howard, Andrea A., Arnsten, Julia H., and Gourevitch, Marc N. (2004). Effect of alcohol consumption on diabetes mellitus: A systematic review. *Annals of Internal Medicine, 140*, 211–219. Källberg, Henrik; Jacobsen, Soren; Bengtsson, Camilla; Pdersen, Merete; Padyukov, Leonid; et al. (online, 2008, June 6). Alcohol consumption is associated with decreased risk of rheumatoid arthritis: Results from two Scandinavian case-control studies. *Annals of the Rheumatic Diseases*. Mukamal, Kenneth J.; Conigrave, Katherine M.; Mittleman, Murray A.; Carmargo, Carlos A., Jr.; Stampfer, Meir J.; et al. (2003). Roles of drinking pattern and type of alcohol consumed in coronary heart disease in men. *New England Journal of Medicine, 348*, 109–118. Mukamal, Kenneth J.; Kuller, Lewis H.; Longstreth, W. T.; Mittleman, Murray A; and Siscovick, David S. (2003). Prospective study of alcohol consumption and risk of dementia in older adults. *Journal of the American Medical Association, 289*, 1405–1413. Reynold, Kristi; Lewis, L. Brian; Nolen, John David L.; Kinney, Gregory L.; Sathya, Bhavani; et al. (2003). Alcohol consumption and risk of stroke: A meta-analysis. *Journal of the American Medical Association, 289*, 579–588.

50. Alcohol Policies Project, Center for Science in the Public Interest (2000). Victory for public health: New U.S. guidelines on alcohol consumption drop positive spin on drinking. Washington DC: Center for Science in the Public Interest. The Gallup Organization (2005, July 22). Fewer young adults drinking to excess. Gallup Organization, Princeton, NJ. Goldberg, Ira (2003). To drink or not to drink. *New England Journal of Medicine, 348*, 163–164. Klatsky, Arthur (2003, February). Drink to your health? *Scientific American*, pp. 75–81.

51. Darby, William, and Heinz, Agnes (1991, January). *The responsible use of alcohol: Defining the parameters of moderation*. New York: American Council on Science and Health, pp. 1–26. Hanson, David J., and Engs, Ruth C. (1994). Drinking behavior: Taking personal responsibility. In Peter J. Venturelli (Ed.), *Drug use in America: Social, cultural, and political perspectives*. Boston: Jones and Bartlett, pp. 175–181.

chapter 10

Chronic Alcohol Abuse and Alcoholism

When you live in an alcoholic family, you sometimes lie in bed and dream. You dream that your parents are going to quit drinking, that you are going to get closer to them. You are going to have a better life. . . . You picture your parents beginning to care for themselves and for you. You imagine it being beautiful. Your home is clean and organized. Instead of abusing you, or being nice to you just to get rid of you, your parents are helping you with your homework.

—*Teens talk about alcohol and alcoholism (1987)*

After you have completed this chapter, you will understand

- Problems surrounding the definition of alcoholism
- The history of attempts to regulate chronic alcohol abuse
- Chronic effects of alcohol
- Patterns of chronic alcohol abuse
- Special problems among the elderly
- Family dynamics in alcoholism
- Genetic and environmental influences in alcoholism
- Approaches to treatment for alcoholism
- Chronic alcohol abuse and alcoholism in the workplace

Chronic abuse of alcohol has been called the hidden addiction. There is no need to get out on the street and find a pusher; for many people, it is remarkably easy to conceal their problem (at least in the beginning) from family and friends. Alcohol consumption is so tightly woven into the fabric of U.S. social life that it may be difficult to catch on that an individual is drinking too much too often. All too frequently, chronic abuse of alcohol has been treated as a genteel affair, rarely with the same degree of concern as that associated with the chronic abuse of other drugs. Yet from a pharmacological point of view, it is the same, and we have to realize that fact. This chapter will deal with the very serious consequences of this condition on almost 20 million Americans and on society at large.

Alcoholism: Stereotypes, Definitions, and Criteria

Close your eyes and try to imagine a picture of an alcoholic. You might form an image of someone, probably male, who is down on his heels, perhaps a dirty, skid-row bum with a bottle of cheap wine in his hands, living from day to day in a state of deteriorating health, with no one caring about him except a social worker or police officer or, inevitably, the medical examiner. You would be imagining less than 5 percent of all alcoholics; more than 95 percent of them look quite different. The demographics of alcoholism include every possible category. Alcoholics can be fourteen years old or eighty-four, male or female, professional or blue-collar, urbanite, suburbanite, or rural resident in any community large or small.

What aspects of their behavior tie them all together, allowing us to describe their condition with a single label? Because of the wide diversity of alcoholics, no one has come up with one encompassing definition of alcoholism. Instead, we are left with a set of criteria, basically a collection of signs, symptoms, and behaviors that help us make the diagnosis. A single individual may not fulfill all of these criteria, but if he or she fulfills enough of them, we decide that the standard has been met.

The criteria adopted here focus on four basic life problems that are tied to the consumption of alcohol: (1) problems associated with a preoccupation with drinking, (2) emotional problems, (3) vocational, social, and family problems, and (4) problems associated with physical health.[1] Notice that these criteria make no mention of the cause or causes of alcoholism, only its behavioral, social, and physical consequences. In short, we are recognizing that **alcoholism** is a complex phenomenon with psychological-behavioral components (criteria 1 and 2), social components (criterion 3), and a physical component (criterion 4).

by the numbers . . .

29 Percentage of persons who reported in 2005 that drinking has been a cause of trouble in their family

18.2 million Number of Americans who met the criteria for alcohol dependence or abuse in the past year, based on averaged data from surveys in 2002, 2003, and 2004

2.1 million Estimated number of Americans who report that they have worked under the influence of alcohol in the past twelve months, from a national sample of employed adults

Sources: Frone, Michael R. (2006). Prevalence and distribution of alcohol use and impairment in the workplace: A U.S. survey. *Journal of Studies on Alcohol and Drugs, 67*, 147–156. Roper Center at the University of Connecticut (2005). Organization conducting the survey: The Gallup Organization. Substance Abuse and Mental Health Services Administration (2006). *The NSDUH Report: Alcohol dependence or abuse: 2002, 2003, and 2004.* Bethesda, MD: Office of Applied Studies, Substance Abuse and Mental Health Services Administration.

Problems Associated with a Preoccupation with Drinking

The dominant characteristic of alcoholics is their preoccupation with the act of drinking and their incorporation of drinking into their everyday lives. An alcoholic may need a drink prior to a social occasion to feel "fortified." With increasing frequency, such a person sees alcohol as a way of dealing with stress and anxiety. Drinking itself becomes a routine, no longer a social, affair. The habit of taking a few drinks on a daily basis on arriving home from work is an example of **symptomatic drinking,** in which alcohol is viewed specifically as a way of relieving tension. Also increasing are incidences of unintentional states of severe intoxication and blackouts of events

alcoholism: A condition in which the consumption of alcohol has produced major psychological, physical, social, or occupational problems.

symptomatic drinking: A pattern of alcohol consumption aimed at reducing stress and anxiety.

The typical alcoholic American

Doctor, age 54

Farmer, age 35

Unemployed, age 40

College student, age 19

Counselor, age 38

Retired editor, age 86

Dancer, age 22

Police officer, age 46

Military officer, age 31

Student, age 14

Executive, age 50

Taxi driver, age 61

Homemaker, age 43

Bricklayer, age 29

Computer programmer, age 25

Lawyer, age 52

There's no such thing as typical. We have all kinds.
10 million Americans are alcoholic.
It's our number one drug problem.

Alcoholism affects such a diverse group of people that it is virtually impossible to make generalizations about the typical profile of an alcoholic. Here are sixteen examples of individuals with whom many people might not have immediately associated the term "alcoholic."

surrounding the time of drinking, a condition quite different from "passing out" from a high BAC level. One such occurrence may not be a particularly critical sign, but recurrences definitely are.[2]

Traditionally, alcoholism is associated with consumption of a large quantity of alcohol. This sounds pretty obvious and it is true of most alcoholics, but we still have to be careful about overgeneralizing. There are significant differences in the way alcoholics consume their alcohol. Not all of them drink alone or begin every day with a drink. Many of them drink on a daily basis, but others are spree or binge alcoholics who might become grossly intoxicated on occasion and totally abstain from drinking the rest of the time.[3]

Another feature often attributed to alcoholics is the loss of control over their drinking. The alcoholic typically craves a drink and frequently engages in compulsive behavior related to alcohol. There may be a stockpiling of liquor, taking a drink or two before going to a party, or feeling uncomfortable unless alcohol is present. The alcoholic may be sneaking drinks or having drinks that others do not know about, such as surreptitiously having an extra drink or two in the kitchen out of the sight of the party guests.[4] Particularly when the alcoholic is trying to abstain from or reduce the quantity of alcohol consumed, his or her thoughts become focused on the possibility of drinking or ways to rationalize it.[5]

Yet professionals disagree whether all alcoholics are necessarily out of control with respect to alcohol. As discussed later in the chapter, this controversy has major implications for choosing the treatment approach in cases of alcohol abuse. If it is true that even a small amount of alcohol will propel a recovering alcoholic back to alcohol abuse, then a primary focus of treatment should be on no drinking at all, better known as absolute **abstinence.** If it is not true, then there is the possibility of controlled drinking without the fear of "falling off the wagon." The well-known alcohol treatment program Alcoholics Anonymous, for example, functions under the premise that an alcoholic must never drink again, even in minute quantities, if recovery is to be long lasting.

Emotional Problems

Given that alcohol is a depressant drug on the central nervous system, it should not be surprising that chronic alcohol intake produces depressive symptoms. Serious depressions and thoughts of suicide frequently occur in the midst of heavy drinking. However, only about 15 percent of individuals who meet the criteria for alcohol dependence (see page 249) have experienced major depression either before the onset of their alcoholic condition or during extended periods of abstinence. Therefore, it is reasonable to conclude that the depressive symptoms are alcohol-induced. Alcoholics are no more likely than others in the general population to have suffered an episode of major depression.[6]

Vocational, Social, and Family Problems

No one questions the potential problems that chronic alcohol abuse can bring to the maintenance of a job or career, social relationships, and a stable family life. These three areas frequently intertwine, and trouble in one usually exacerbates the others. A job loss puts stress on marital and family relationships, just as marital and family difficulties put stress on occupational performance.

Numerous clinical studies support the idea of increased domestic instability in the lives of alcoholics, but the true extent of these problems is difficult to assess. Family violence, for example, is frequently examined through cases seen in treatment or social service programs. As a result, these agencies may interpret the domestic behavior of a father not known to have a drinking problem differently from that of a father with a history of alcoholism. A man who drinks heavily and abuses his children may be more likely to be "counted" as an alcoholic than a nonabusive father who consumes just as much alcohol. It is much easier to assess the likelihood of domestic violence or decline in job performance due to acute intoxication than it is to evaluate the influence of chronic abuse of alcohol. Even so, there is no doubt that the cumulative effects of alcoholism on family dynamics are devastating.[7]

Physical Problems

There is also no question that chronic alcohol consumption has a destructive effect on the body. Not surprisingly, a principal site of damage is the brain. Neuroimaging procedures, such as CT and MRI scans, reveal a consistent link between heavy drinking and physical shrinkage of brain matter, particularly in the cerebral cortex, cerebellum, and regions associated with memory and other cognitive functions. These neurological changes are observed even in the absence of other alcohol-related medical conditions such as chronic liver disease.[8]

abstinence: The avoidance of some consumable item or behavior.

Health Line

A Self-Administered Short Michigan Alcoholism Screening Test (SMAST)

The Michigan Alcoholism Screening Test (MAST), twenty-four questions to be answered in ten to fifteen minutes, is designed as a structured interview instrument to detect alcoholism. A shorter thirteen-question version (SMAST-13), shown here, has approximately the same level of reliability and validity. Score one point for each response that matches the one in parentheses. According to the authors of the test, a total score of 0 or 1 indicates a nonalcoholic, 2 a possible alcoholic, and 3 or more an alcoholic.

1. Do you feel you are a normal drinker? (By normal we mean you drink less than or as much as most other people.) (NO)

2. Does your wife, husband, a parent, or other near relative ever worry or complain about your drinking? (YES)

3. Do you ever feel guilty about your drinking? (YES)

4. Do friends or relatives think you are a normal drinker? (NO)

5. Are you able to stop drinking when you want to? (NO)

6. Have you ever attended a meeting of Alcoholics Anonymous? (YES)

7. Has drinking ever created problems between you and your wife, husband, a parent, or other near relative? (YES)

8. Have you ever gotten into trouble at work because of drinking? (YES)

9. Have you ever neglected your obligations, your family, or your work for two or more days in a row because you were drinking? (YES)

10. Have you ever gone to anyone for help about your drinking? (YES)

11. Have you ever been in a hospital because of drinking? (YES)

12. Have you ever been arrested for drunken driving, driving while intoxicated, or driving under the influence of alcoholic beverages? (YES)

13. Have you ever been arrested, even for a few hours, because of other drunken behavior? (YES)

Sources: Barry, Kristen L., and Fleming, Michael F. (1993). The Alcohol Use Disorders Identification Test (AUDIT) and the SMAST-13: Predictive validity in a rural primary care sample. *Alcohol and Alcoholism, 28,* 33–42. Selzer, Melvin L., Vinokur, Amiram, and van Rooijen, Louis (1975). A self-administered Short Michigan Alcoholism Screening Test (SMAST). *Journal of Studies on Alcohol, 36,* 117–126.

Hiding the Problems: Denial and Enabling

The major life problems that serve as rough criteria for determining the condition of alcoholism are often not recognized by alcoholics themselves because of their tendency to deny that their drinking has any influence on their lives or the lives of people around them. When in denial, the alcoholic can be extremely sensitive to any mention of problems associated with drinking. A hangover the next day, for example, is seldom discussed because it would draw attention to the fact that drinking has occurred.[9]

Denial also can be manifest among the people around the alcoholic. Members of an alcoholic's family, for example, may try to function as if life were normal. Through their excuse making and efforts to undo or cover up the frequent physical and psychological damage the alcoholic causes, they inadvertently prevent the alcoholic from seeking treatment or delay that treatment until the alcoholism is more severe. These people are referred to as **enablers** because they enable the alcoholic to function as an alcoholic as opposed to a sober person. Both processes of denial and enabling present major difficulties not only in establishing problem-oriented criteria for diagnosing alcoholism but also in introducing necessary interventions. Denial and enabling are clearly relevant processes in the area of alcoholism, but it is not difficult to see that they present problems with regard to *any* form of drug abuse (see Chapter 17).

Health Line provides a useful self-survey for determining the signs of potential alcoholism. You may want to try it out on yourself and people that you know.

enablers: Individuals whose behavior consciously or unconsciously encourages another person's continuation in a pattern of alcohol or other drug abuse.

Alcohol Abuse and Alcohol Dependence: The Professional's View

As you can see, the criteria commonly employed in determining the presence of alcoholism are at times quite murky, and often there are nearly as many counterexamples to each of the criteria as there are examples. The American Psychiatric Association, through its *Diagnostic and Statistical Manual, Text Revision,* fourth edition (DSM-IV-TR), has attempted to put together as many common features as possible and has established two basic syndromes. It is important to understand these technical definitions, because professionals in the field of alcoholism commonly use the DSM-IV-TR either in their research or in clinical practice.[10]

The first syndrome, referred to as **alcohol abuse,** is characterized as either (1) the continued use of alcohol for at least one month despite the knowledge of having a persistent or recurring physical problem or some difficulty in social or occupational functioning, or (2) the recurring use of alcohol in situations (such as driving) when alcohol consumption is physically hazardous.

The second syndrome, referred to as **alcohol dependence,** is characterized as alcohol abuse that involves any three of the following seven situations:

- Consuming alcohol in amounts or over a longer period than the person intends
- A persistent desire, or one or more unsuccessful attempts, to cut down or control drinking
- A great deal of time spent drinking or recovering from the effects of drinking
- Alcohol consumption continuing despite knowledge that drinking either causes or exacerbates recurrent physical or psychological problems
- Important social, occupational, or recreational activities given up or reduced because of alcohol
- Marked tolerance or the need to drink more than before to achieve previous levels of intoxication
- Symptoms of alcohol withdrawal or the consumption of alcohol to relieve or avoid withdrawal symptoms

Obviously, individuals fitting the second definition are considered more greatly impaired than those fitting the first. That distinction also was true with regard to the more general criteria for substance abuse and substance dependence (see Chapter 2). Approximately 8.5 percent of U.S. adults, about one in twelve, are either alcohol abusers or alcohol dependent according to the DSM-IV-TR standards.

As you might expect, the highest percentages of "heavy drinkers" are found among people eighteen to twenty-five years old. The "heavy drinker" category is defined as having consumed five or more alcoholic drinks on the same occasion on at least five different days within the previous month. The incidence among those eighteen to twenty-five years old has been estimated to be about 15 percent, with a peak incidence of 20 percent at age twenty-one.[11]

alcohol abuse: A syndrome characterized primarily by the continued use of alcohol despite the drinker's knowledge of having a persistent physical problem or some social or occupational difficulty.

alcohol dependence: A syndrome in which alcohol abuse involves a variety of significant physical, psychological, social, and behavioral problems.

The History of Efforts to Regulate Chronic Alcohol Abuse

In the late 1700s, prominent physicians, writers, and scientists began to consider the long-term adverse effects of alcohol consumption and tried to formulate some kind of social reform to mitigate them. The goal at that time was to reduce the consumption of distilled spirits (liquor) only. It was a temperate attitude toward drinking (hence the phrase "temperance movement") rather than an insistence on the total prohibition of alcohol.

In the United States, where the temperance movement was to be stronger than anywhere else, its most influential spokesman was Benjamin Rush, a physician, Revolutionary War hero, and signer of the Declaration of Independence. In his 1785 pamphlet, *An Inquiry into the Effects of Ardent Spirits on the Human Mind and Body*, Rush vividly described the range of mental and physical dangers associated with alcohol abuse:

> *Strong liquor is more destructive than the sword. The destruction of war is periodic, whereas alcohol exerts its influence upon human life at all times and in all seasons. . . . A nation corrupted by alcohol can never be free.*[12]

Rush's efforts did not have a major impact on the drinking habits of American society during his lifetime. As described in Chapter 9, alcohol consumption in the United States at that time was enormous and continued to rise until about 1830. Rush's words, however, served as an inspiration to political and religious groups around the country who saw alcohol abuse in social and moral terms. In their view, drunkenness led to poverty, a disorderly society, and civil disobedience. In short, it was unpatriotic at best and subversive at worst. When we hear the phrase "demon rum," we have to recognize that many Americans during the nineteenth century took the phrase quite literally. Liquor was demonized as a direct source of evil in the world.

The temperance point of view toward liquor, like any other form of scapegoating, spread like wildfire. In 1831, the American Temperance Society reported that nearly 2 million Americans had renounced strong liquor and that more than eight hundred local societies had been established. With characteristic succinctness, Abraham Lincoln observed, in an 1842 address before a national temperance organization, that prior to the temperance era, the harm done by alcohol was considered to be a result of the "abuse of a very good thing," whereas

Even though this 1874 engraving shows a temperance crusader in full battle regalia, relatively few temperance activists resorted to physical violence.

his contemporaries now viewed the harm as coming "from the use of a bad thing."[13] By the 1850s, twelve U.S. states (about one-third of the nation at the time) and two Canadian provinces had introduced legislation forbidding the sale of "alcoholic" (distilled) drink.

Whether or not they were justified in doing so, temperance groups took credit for a drastic change that was occurring in the levels of alcohol consumption in the United States. From 1830 to 1850, consumption of all types of alcohol plummeted from an annual per capita level of roughly 7 gallons to roughly 2 gallons, approximately today's consumption level (see Chapter 9). It is quite possible that this decline encouraged the temperance movement to formulate its ultimate goal, a prohibition of alcohol consumption in any form.

The Road to National Prohibition

A major development in the temperance movement was the formation in 1873 of a women's organization called the Woman's Christian Temperance Union (WCTU). Almost from the beginning, its primary target was a highly visible fixture of late-nineteenth-century American life: the saloon. These establishments were now vilified as the source of all the troubles alcohol could bring. It is not difficult to imagine how the saloon would have been seen as a significant threat to American women in general.

> *Bars appeared to invite family catastrophe. They introduced children to drunkenness and vice and drove husbands to alcoholism; they also caused squandering of wages, wife beating, and child abuse; and, with the patron's inhibitions lowered through drink, the saloon led many men into the arms of prostitutes (and not incidentally, contributed to the alarming spread of syphilis).*[14]

No wonder the WCTU hated the saloon, and no saloon in the country was safe from their "pray-in" demonstrations, vocal opposition, and in some cases violent interventions. Their influence eventually extended into every aspect of American culture. The WCTU and other anti-alcohol forces, such as the newly formed Anti-Saloon League and National Prohibition Party, were soon electing congressional candidates who pledged to enact national legislation banning alcohol consumption throughout the land.

The Beginning and Ending of a "Noble Experiment"

In December 1917, Congress passed a resolution "prohibiting the manufacture, sale, transportation, or importation of intoxicating liquors," the simple wording that would form the basis for the Eighteenth Amendment to the U.S. Constitution. (Notice that it did not forbid purchase or use of alcohol.) The Volstead Act of 1919 set up the enforcement procedures. By the end of the year, the necessary thirty-six states had ratified the amendment, and Prohibition took effect in January 1920.

Despite its lofty aims, Prohibition was doomed to failure. In the countryside, operators of illegal stills (called "moonshiners" because they worked largely at night) continued their production despite the efforts of an occasional half-hearted raid by Treasury agents (known as "revenooers"). The major cities became centers of open defiance. Liquor, having been smuggled into the country, flowed abundantly as saloons turned into speakeasies and operated in violation of the law.

The early years of Prohibition did, however, show positive effects in the area of public health. Alcohol-related deaths, cirrhosis of the liver, mental disorders, and alcohol-related crime declined in 1920 and 1921, but in a few years, the figures began to creep up again, and the level of criminal activity associated with illegal drinking was clearly intolerable.[15] By the end of the decade, for the vast majority of Americans, it had become obvious that the experiment was not working.

In 1933, President Franklin D. Roosevelt, having run on a platform to repeal the Volstead Act, signed the necessary legislation that became the Twenty-first Amendment; ratification was swift. Alcohol was restored as a legal commodity and its regulation was returned once more to local authorities. Over the years, state prohibition laws were gradually repealed, with Mississippi in 1966 being the last state to do so.

Present-Day Regulation by Taxation

One immediate benefit of repealing Prohibition was the return of federal revenue from taxes on alcohol. Indeed, the impact on a struggling national economy hard hit by the Depression had been one of the arguments advanced by the repeal movement. In 1933 alone, such excise taxes brought in $500 million, which was used to finance social programs during the Depression.

The concept of collecting taxes on the basis of alcohol consumption dates back to the very beginning of the United States as a nation. In 1794, the newly formed U.S. Congress passed a law requiring an excise tax on the sale of whiskey. After a short-lived Whiskey Rebellion in which President Washington had to order federal militia to subdue Appalachian farmers who had refused to pay the new tax, the practice of taxing alcohol was accepted and has continued to the present day as a legal way of raising tax money.

Taxes on alcohol sales have been an indirect mechanism for regulating the consumption of alcohol by increasing its price, not unlike taxes on tobacco products (see Chapter 11). More than $8 billion each year is collected from federal excise taxes on alcohol. Total annual revenues exceed $18 billion, when additional excise taxes imposed by all U.S. states and some local communities are included. Today, alcoholic beverages are one of the most heavily taxed consumer products. Approximately 42 percent of the retail price of an average bottle of distilled spirits, for example, is earmarked for federal, state, or local taxes.[16]

It has been proposed that alcohol taxes be set high enough to begin to offset the total societal costs resulting from alcohol abuse. This approach would place a type of "user fee" on the consumption of alcohol. However, there is the possibility that raising alcohol prices by additional taxation might lead to the development of a black market for alcohol purchases, little change in alcohol consumption, and a net decline in tax revenues.[17]

Biological Effects of Chronic Alcohol Use

This section will deal with what we know about the consequences of long-term (chronic) consumption of alcohol over and above the acute effects that were discussed in the last chapter.

Tolerance and Withdrawal

As with other CNS depressants, alcohol consumption over a period of time will result in a tolerance effect. On a metabolic level, alcohol dehydrogenase activity during tolerance becomes higher in the stomach and liver, allowing the alcohol to leave the body somewhat faster; on a neural level, the brain is less responsive to alcohol's depressive effects.[18] Therefore, if alcohol consumption remains steady, the individual feels less of an effect.

As a result of tolerance and the tendency to compensate for it in terms of drinking a greater quantity, the chronic alcohol abuser is subject to increased physical risks. There are serious behavioral risks as well; for example, an alcohol-tolerant drinker may consider driving with a BAC level that exceeds the standard for drunk driving, thinking that he or she is not intoxicated and hence not impaired. A person's driving ability, under these circumstances, will be substantially overestimated.

An alcohol-dependent person's abrupt withdrawal from alcohol can result in a range of serious physical symptoms beginning from six to forty-eight hours after the last drink, but estimates vary as to how many people are typically affected. Among hospitalized patients, only 5 percent appear to show withdrawal symptoms, whereas other studies of alcoholics using outpatient facilities have estimated the percentage to be as high as 18. Although the exact incidence may be somewhat unclear, there is less

disagreement as to what takes place. Physical withdrawal effects are classified in two clusters of symptoms.

The first cluster, called the **alcohol withdrawal syndrome,** is the more common of the two. It begins with insomnia, vivid dreaming, and a severe hangover; these discomforts are followed by tremors (the "shakes"), sweating, mild agitation, anxiety (the "jitters"), nausea, and vomiting, as well as increased heart rate and blood pressure. In some patients, there are also brief tonic-clonic (grand mal) seizures, as the nervous system rebounds from the chronic depression induced by alcohol. The alcohol withdrawal syndrome usually reaches a peak from twenty-four to thirty-six hours after the last drink and is over after forty-eight hours.

The second cluster, called **delirium tremens (DTs),** is much more dangerous and is fortunately less common. The symptoms include extreme disorientation and confusion, profuse sweating, fever, and disturbing nightmares. Typically, there are also periods of frightening hallucinations, when the individual might experience seeing snakes or insects on the walls, ceiling, or his or her skin. These effects generally reach a peak three to four days after the last drink. During this time, there is the possibility of life-threatening events such as heart failure, dehydration, or suicide, so it is critical for the individual to be hospitalized and under medical supervision at all times. The current medical practice for treating individuals undergoing withdrawal is to administer antianxiety medication (see Chapter 15) to relieve the symptoms. After the withdrawal period has ended, the dose levels of the medication are gradually reduced and discontinued.[19]

Liver Disease

Chronic consumption of alcohol produces three forms of liver disease. The first of these is a **fatty liver,** resulting from an abnormal concentration of fatty deposits inside liver cells. Normally, the liver breaks down fats adequately, but when alcohol is in the body the liver breaks down the alcohol at the expense of fats. As a result, fats accumulate and ultimately interfere with the functioning of the liver. The condition is fortunately reversible, if the drinker abstains. The accumulated fats are gradually metabolized, and the liver returns to normal.

The second condition is **alcoholic hepatitis,** an inflammation of liver tissue causing fever, jaundice (a yellowing of the skin), and abdominal pain, resulting at least in part from a lower functioning level of the immune system. It is also reversible with abstinence, though some residual scarring may remain.

The third and most serious liver condition is **alcoholic cirrhosis,** characterized by the progressive development of

---

alcohol withdrawal syndrome: The more common of two general reactions to the cessation of alcohol consumption in an alcoholic. It is characterized by physiological discomfort, seizures, and sleep disturbances.

delirium tremens (DTs): The less common of two general reactions to the cessation of drinking in an alcoholic. It is characterized by extreme disorientation and confusion, fever, hallucinations, and other symptoms.

fatty liver: A condition in which fat deposits accumulate in the liver as a result of chronic alcohol abuse.

alcoholic hepatitis (AL-co-HAUL-ik hep-ah-TIE-tus): A disease involving inflammation of the liver as a result of chronic alcohol abuse.

alcoholic cirrhosis (AL-co-HAUL-ik seer-OH-sis): A disease involving scarring and deterioration of liver cells as a result of chronic alcohol abuse.

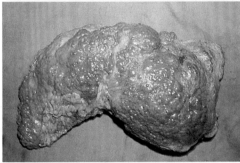

FIGURE 10.1

The dramatic difference between a healthy liver (top) and a cirrhotic liver (bottom).

scar tissue that chokes off blood vessels in the liver and destroys liver cells by interfering with the cell's utilization of oxygen. At an early stage, the liver is enlarged from the accumulation of fats, but at later stages it is shrunken as liver cells begin to degenerate (Figure 10.1). Though abstinence helps to prevent further liver degeneration when cirrhosis is diagnosed, the condition is not reversible except by liver transplantation surgery.

Prior to the 1970s, alcoholic cirrhosis was attributed to nutritional deficiencies that are often associated with an alcoholic's diet. We know now that, although nutritional problems play a role, alcohol itself is toxic to the liver. After a pattern of heavy alcohol consumption of many years, it is possible to develop cirrhosis, even when nutrition is adequate. A major cause of liver cell damage is the toxic accumulation of free radicals, molecule fragments that are by-products of acetaldehyde (Chapter 9).

Cirrhosis is ranked as the ninth leading cause of death in the United States, affecting approximately 30,000 each year. Most deaths occur in people forty to sixty-five years old. Daily drinkers are at a higher risk of developing cirrhosis than binge drinkers, though this risk may be the result of the relatively larger quantity of alcohol consumed over a long period of time. Generally, patients showing liver damage have been drinking for ten to twenty years. Only 10 to 20 percent of all heavy drinkers develop cirrho-

sis, however, in contrast to 90 to 100 percent who show evidence of either fatty liver or hepatitis. There may be a genetic predisposition for cirrhosis that puts a subgroup of alcoholics at increased risk.[20]

Cardiovascular Problems

About one in every four alcoholics develops cardiovascular problems owing to the chronic consumption of alcohol. The effects include inflammation and enlargement of the heart muscle, poor blood circulation to the heart, irregular heart contractions, fatty accumulations in the heart and arteries, high blood pressure, and stroke.[21]

Cancer

Chronic alcohol abuse is associated with the increased risk of several types of cancers—in particular, cancers of the pharynx and larynx. Nearly 50 percent of all such cancers are associated with heavy drinking. If alcohol abusers also smoke cigarettes, the increased risk is even more dramatic. An increased risk of liver cancer is also linked to chronic alcoholic abuse, whether or not cirrhosis is also present. In addition, an association has been made between alcohol consumption and breast cancer in women. There is either a weaker association or no association at all with cancers of the stomach, colon, pancreas, or rectum.

Alcohol is not technically considered a carcinogen (a direct producer of cancer), so why the risks are increased in certain cancer types is at present unknown. It is possible that the increased risk is a combined result of alcohol enhancing the carcinogenic effects of other chemicals and, as is true with the development of hepatitis, depressing the immune system. With a reduced immune response, the alcoholic may have a lowered resistance to the development of cancerous tumors.[22]

Dementia and Wernicke-Korsakoff Syndrome

Chronic alcohol consumption can produce longer-lasting deficits in the way an individual solves problems, remembers information, and organizes facts about his or her identity and surroundings. These cognitive deficits are commonly referred to collectively as **alcoholic dementia**

alcoholic dementia (AL-co-HAUL-ik dih-MEN-chee-ah): A condition in which chronic alcohol abuse produces cognitive deficits such as difficulties in problem solving and memory.

and are associated with structural changes in brain tissue. Specifically, there is an enlargement of brain ventricles (the interior fluid-filled spaces within the brain), a widening of fissures separating sections of cerebral cortex, and a loss of acetylcholine-sensitive receptors. The combination of these effects results in a net decrease in brain mass. CT and MRI scans, two imaging techniques that reveal the structural features of the brain, show that the degree of enlargement of the ventricles correlates with a decline in overall intelligence, verbal learning and retention, and short-term memory, particularly for middle-aged and elderly alcoholics.

Some 50 to 75 percent of all detoxified alcoholics and nearly 20 percent of all individuals admitted to state mental hospitals show signs of alcohol-related dementia. Through abstinence, it is possible to reverse some of the cognitive deficits and even some of the abnormalities in the brain, depending on the age of the alcoholic when treatment begins. As you might suspect, younger alcoholics respond better than older ones.[23]

A more severe form of cognitive impairment related to chronic alcohol consumption is a two-part disease referred to as **Wernicke-Korsakoff syndrome.** In *Wernicke's encephalopathy* or simply *Wernicke's disease,* the patient shows confusion and disorientation, abnormal eye movements, and difficulties in movement and body coordination. These neurological problems arise from a deficiency in Vitamin B$_1$ (**thiamine),** a necessary nutrient for glucose to be consumed by neurons in the brain. Extreme alcoholics may go days or weeks at a time eating practically nothing and receiving calories exclusively from drinking alcoholic beverages.

As a result of thiamine deficiency, large numbers of neurons die in areas of the brain specifically concerned with thinking and movement. About 15 percent of patients with Wernicke's disease, however, respond favorably to large amounts of thiamine supplements in combination with abstinence from alcohol, restoring their previous level of orientation, eye movements, and coordination.

Wernicke-Korsakoff syndrome (VERN-ih-kee KOR-sa-kof SIN-drohm): A condition resulting from chronic alcohol consumption, characterized by disorientation, cognitive deficits, amnesia, and motor difficulty.

thiamine (THY-ah-meen or THY-ah-min): Vitamin B$_1$.

confabulation: The tendency to make up elaborate past histories to cover the fact that long-term memory has been impaired.

fetal alcohol syndrome (FAS): A serious condition involving mental retardation and facial-cranial malformations in the offspring of an alcoholic mother.

teratogenic (TER-ah-tuh-JEN-ik): Capable of producing specific birth defects.

Many Wernicke's disease patients, whether or not they recover from confusion and motor impairments, also display a severe form of chronic amnesia and general apathy called *Korsakoff's psychosis.* Specifically, such patients cannot remember information that has just been presented to them and have only a patchy memory for distant events that occurred prior to their alcoholic state. They frequently attempt, through a behavior called **confabulation,** to compensate for their gaps in memory by telling elaborate stories of imagined past events, as if trying to fool others into thinking that they remember more than they actually do.

Thiamine deficiency is linked to Korsakoff's psychosis as well. About 20 percent of patients completely recover and 60 percent partially recover their memory after being treated with thiamine supplements. Yet the remaining 20 percent, generally the most severely impaired patients and those with the longest history of alcohol consumption, show little or no improvement and require chronic institutionalization.[24]

Fetal Alcohol Syndrome

The disorders just reviewed generally have been associated with consumption of large quantities of alcohol over a long period of time. In the case of the adverse effects of alcohol during pregnancy on unborn children, we are dealing with a unique situation. First of all, we need to recognize the extreme susceptibility of a developing fetus to conditions in the mother's bloodstream. In short, if the mother takes a drink, the fetus takes one, too. And to make matters worse, the fetus does not have sufficient levels of alcohol dehydrogenase to break down the alcohol properly; thus the alcohol stays in the fetus's system longer than in the mother's. In addition, the presence of alcohol coincides with a period of time in prenatal development when critical processes are occurring that are essential for the development of a healthy, alert child.

Although it has long been suspected that alcohol abuse among pregnant women might present serious risks to the fetus, a specific syndrome was not established until 1973, when Kenneth L. Jones and David W. Smith described a cluster of characteristic features in children of alcoholic mothers that is now referred to as **fetal alcohol syndrome (FAS).**[25] Their studies, and research conducted since then, have shown clearly that alcohol is **teratogenic;** that is, it produces specific birth defects in offspring by disrupting fetal development during pregnancy, even when differences in prenatal nutrition have been accounted for. Later in life, FAS children show deficits in short-term memory, problem solving, and attentiveness.

Present-day diagnoses of FAS are made on the basis

The face of a child with fetal alcohol syndrome, showing the wide-set eyes and other features that are characteristic of this condition.

of three groups of observations: (1) prenatal or post-natal growth retardation in which the child's weight or length is below the 10th percentile, (2) evidence of CNS abnormalities or mental retardation, and (3) a characteristic skull and facial appearance that includes a smaller-than-normal head, small wide-set eyes, drooping eyelids, a flattening of the vertical groove between the mouth and nose, a thin upper lip, and a short upturned nose. If only some of these characteristics are observed, the condition is referred to as possible **fetal alcohol effect (FAE).**

The incidence of FAS is approximately 0.5 to 3 cases per thousand live births in the general U.S. population, but the rates vary greatly within that population. Incidence is generally higher among Native Americans within the United States.[26]

We do not know at present how alcohol causes FAS or FAE, except that the greatest risk is in the first trimester of pregnancy, especially the third week of gestation when craniofacial formation and brain growth are prominent developmental milestones. Concentrated periods of drinking during this time appear to be very damaging to the fetus. For example, if two mothers consumed a similar overall quantity of alcohol during their pregnancies, but Mother A consumed one drink on each of seven days in a week and Mother B consumed all seven drinks on two weekend evenings, then Mother B would have incurred a far greater risk to her child than Mother A (Health Line, page 256).[27]

Although not all alcoholic mothers will give birth to babies with FAS or FAE, the research findings are clear: Risks are greatly increased when excessive drinking is taking place. Although an occasional drink may have minimal effects, no one has determined a "safe" level of drinking during pregnancy that would make this behavior risk-free. The objective of prevention, therefore, is to educate women to the dangers of drinking at any level and to encourage complete abstinence from alcohol (as well as other psychoactive drugs) during pregnancy. Since 1989, all containers of alcoholic beverages must contain two warning messages, one of which is that "according to the Surgeon General, women should not drink alcoholic beverages during pregnancy because of the risk of birth defects."

Fortunately, the public is aware of the problem and the number of women who consume alcohol during pregnancy has declined over the last twenty-five years. In some instances, it has been possible to reduce prenatal exposure to alcohol through broad social change. For example, in 1978, a change in social policy among members of a Southwestern Plains Native American tribe, shifting the distribution of mineral-rights income toward social programs on the reservation, resulted in the prevalence rate for FAS decreasing from fourteen per thousand live births to none at all. A combined prevalence rate of FAS and FAE decreased from twenty-seven per thousand live births to five. The potential influence of sociocultural factors in altering alcohol consumption patterns needs to be examined closely in all high-risk populations.[28]

The bad news, however, is that the rates of alcohol consumption among several other high-risk populations in the United States, such as pregnant smokers, unmarried women, women under the age of twenty-five, and women with the fewest years of education, remain substantial despite the fact that about 90 percent of women are aware of the potential harm. Ten percent of pregnant women nationwide continue to consume alcohol. Unfortunately, FAS and FAE continue to be the third leading cause of mental retardation not only in the United States but in the entire Western world, exceeded only by Down syndrome and spina bifida. The fact that the development of alcohol-related fetal defects is entirely preventable makes the incidence of these conditions all the more tragic.[29]

Patterns of Chronic Alcohol Abuse

When we consider the range of direct and indirect costs to society that result from chronic abuse of alcohol, the price we pay is enormous. These costs include the expense of treatment for alcoholism and of medical intervention for

fetal alcohol effect (FAE): A cognitive deficiency in the offspring of an alcoholic mother. It is regarded as less serious than fetal alcohol syndrome.

Health Line

The TWEAK Alcoholism Screening Instrument for Pregnant Women

One of the difficulties in getting information about possible alcoholic behavior is the tendency for the individual to deny that alcohol abuse is going on. It is especially important to find out whether pregnant women are engaging in this behavior. The following is a brief screening questionnaire, called the TWEAK, that provides personal information about drinking problems, without asking about them in a direct fashion. There are five basic questions (one question for each letter in the acronym TWEAK), with the first question presented in two alternative forms. The choice of whether to ask Question 1a or 1b is left to the health professional collecting the information.

1a. How many drinks does it take before you begin to feel the first effects of alcohol? (T—it asks about tolerance in terms of an initial state of intoxication)

1b. How many drinks does it take before the alcohol makes you fall asleep or pass out? Or, if you never drink until you pass out, what is the largest number of drinks you have? (T—it asks about tolerance in terms of an extreme level of intoxication)

2. Have your friends or relatives worried or complained about your drinking in the past year? (W—it asks about the extent of worry about one's drinking)

3. Do you sometimes take a drink in the morning when you first get up? (E—it refers to an "eye opener")

4. Are there times when you drink and afterward you can't remember what you did or said? (A—it refers to amnesia or a blackout episode)

5. Do you sometimes feel the need to cut down on your drinking? (K—it refers to the need to cut down on the level of alcohol consumption)

Three drinks or more is considered a positive answer to Question 1a; five drinks or more is considered a positive answer to Question 1b. Positive answers count for two points in Questions 1 and 2, and one point each for Questions 3, 4, and 5. A score of 3 or more, out of a maximum of 7, is interpreted as an indication of a possible alcohol problem.

Researchers have found that TWEAK scores can accurately identify up to 77 percent of women who are problem drinkers (an indication of the sensitivity of the questionnaire) and up to 93 percent of women who are not (an indication of the specificity of the questionnaire). Other short surveys are available, but they do not differentiate the two groups as well as the TWEAK. Using this instrument is a major step toward preventing FAS by identifying those women whose drinking during pregnancy will have potentially adverse effects on the developing fetus.

Sources: Bradley, Katharine A.; Boyd-Wickizer, Jodie; Powell, Suzanne H.; and Burman, Marcia L. (1998). Alcohol screening questionnaires in women: A critical review. *Journal of the American Medical Association, 280,* 166–171. Chan, W. K.; Pristach, E. A.; Welte, J. W.; and Russell, M. (1993). Use of the TWEAK test in screening for heavy drinking in three populations. *Alcoholism: Clinical and Experimental Research, 17,* 1188–1192. Copyright 1993 by Williams and Wilkins. Reprinted with permission. National Institute on Alcohol Abuse and Alcoholism (2002, April). Alcohol alert: Screening for alcohol problems—an update. No. 56. Rockville, MD: National Institute on Alcohol Abuse and Alcoholism.

alcohol-related diseases, lost productivity from absenteeism and decreases in worker performance, treatment for alcohol-related injuries, and the lost value of future earnings of individuals who die prematurely because of alcoholism. The total costs in the United States are estimated to be about $200 billion annually, even without taking into consideration the incalculable costs of human suffering that are involved in the estimated 125,000 alcohol-related deaths each year.[30]

The Demographics of Alcoholism

As mentioned earlier, alcoholics can be found in every age, gender, racial, ethnic, and religious group, and in all socioeconomic levels and geographic regions of the country. Nonetheless, large differences in prevalence exist within these categories. For example, men outnumber women in the incidence of alcoholism by about six to one, with men tending to be steadier from day to day in their consumption of alcohol and women tending to abstain from drinking for lengths of time and to binge once they start drinking again. Overall, women are more vulnerable to alcohol-related organ damage. Whether this higher risk is a result of differences in the pattern of drinking or in differences in the way alcohol is processed in a woman's body is at present unknown.[31]

Figure 10.2 shows a state-by-state analysis of alcohol problems as measured by alcohol consumption level.[32] Some of the other demographic differences have been examined in Chapter 9.

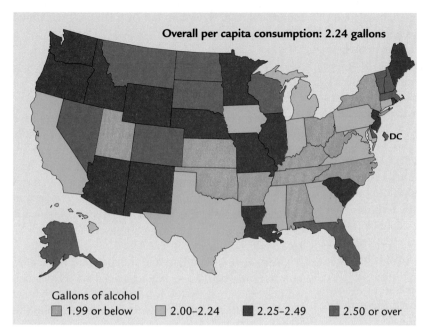

FIGURE 10.2

Annual per capita alcohol consumption in gallons for the U.S. population fourteen years and older by state in 2005.

Source: Lakins, Nekisha E., Williams, Gerald D., and Yi, Hsiao-ye. (2007, August). *Surveillance Report 82. Apparent per capita alcohol consumption: National, state and regional trends, 1977–2005.* Bethesda, MD: National Institute on Alcohol Abuse and Alcoholism, Division of Epidemiology and Prevention Research, Alcohol Epidemiologic Data System, Figure 5.

Alcohol Abuse among the Elderly

There is a widely held misconception that alcohol abuse is not much of a problem with the elderly. On the basis of careful studies addressing the problem of chronic alcohol abuse among the elderly, it has been estimated that approximately 9 percent of the elderly population have alcohol problems, as indicated by consuming four or more drinks in a single day or more than thirty per month. An analysis of Medicare records has indicated that more people over the age of sixty-five are hospitalized each year for alcohol-related problems than for heart attacks.[33]

One of the reasons for the underreporting of this problem is that we typically use the quantity of alcohol consumed as a primary index of alcoholism, and alcohol consumption does indeed decline with age. Yet, because of the changes in alcohol biotransformation over a lifetime, three drinks consumed at age sixty can be equivalent in their effects to four times as many drinks for someone at age twenty. In addition, the indications of social and occupational problems, traditionally part of the criteria for alcoholism, are often irrelevant for an elderly drinker. There would be no incidence of drunk driving if the person is no longer driving, no job supervisor to notice a decline in work performance, and frequently no spouse to complain of social difficulties. Finally, the occurrence of blackouts or symptoms of Wernicke-Korsakoff syndrome may be misdiagnosed simply as an indication of senility or the onset of Alzheimer's disease.

A number of problems particularly affect the elderly who chronically abuse alcohol. One problem is the risk of the alcohol interacting with the many medications that the elderly typically take. Another is the risk of complications for already existing medical conditions, such as gastrointestinal bleeding, hypertension and cardiac arrhythmias, osteoporosis, depression, and cognitive impairment–related disorders.

There is growing recognition that treatment programs for alcoholism ought to be tailored to the special needs of the elderly; frequently the traditional treatment programs that benefit much younger individuals do not work well with older people. Many seniors were brought up in an era when highly negative attitudes toward drinking prevailed, so if they are drinking themselves, they feel stigmatized and resist treatment. On a brighter note, however, it has been found that, when treatment programs are designed specifically with the elderly in mind, older alcoholics will often respond well to treatment.[34]

The Family Dynamics of Alcoholism: A Systems Approach

Alcoholism, like any form of drug abuse, is an especially traumatizing experience for the families involved. For every one person who has a problem with alcohol, there are, on average, at least four others who are directly affected on a day-to-day basis. It is therefore important to examine some of these effects on particular family members. Since the 1950s, a **systems approach** has advocated looking at how the alcoholic and other members of the family interact.[35] We discussed one of these aspects earlier in the chapter in connection with the adverse effects of enabling behavior on the alcoholic. Another important aspect related to an alcoholic's family is the possibility of codependency.

Beginning in the early 1980s, the concept of **codependency** has gained widespread attention as a way of understanding people who live on a day-to-day basis with an alcoholic or any individual with a drug dependence. Definitions vary but most identify four essential features. In members of the family of an alcoholic, therapists have observed (1) an overinvolvement with the alcoholic, (2) obsessive attempts to control the alcoholic's behavior, (3) a strong reliance upon external sources of self-worth, through the approval of others, and (4) an attempt to make personal sacrifices in an effort to improve the alcoholic's condition.[36]

If people in a relationship with a codependent act badly, the codependent believes that he or she is responsible for their behavior. Because codependency is considered to be a learned pattern of thinking rather than an innate trait, the goal of therapy is to teach the codependent person to detach himself or herself from the alcoholic and begin to meet his or her needs rather than to be controlled by the value judgments of others.[37]

Some professionals, however, have questioned the validity of the codependency concept. They have argued that by labeling a person a codependent, the therapist is promoting feelings of helplessness or victimization in these individuals that might not have existed before. Indeed, the idea of codependency might diminish the person's incentive to begin efforts to take control over his or her life by reinforcing the feeling that he or she is "doomed to suffer." Critics also have pointed out that actual patterns of codependency may not be specific to particular individuals but rather are common to practically everyone. Codependency simply may reflect the problems of living in modern society, only now we have found language to explain our own failures by blaming other people.[38]

Children of an Alcoholic Parent or Parents

Considering the immense impact that our parents have in our lives, it is understandable that an alcoholic family will have distinct negative consequences on the psychological development of the children in that family. As a result, **children of alcoholics (COAs)** have a higher statistical risk of becoming alcoholics than do children of nonalcoholics. Whether this increased risk is genetically or environmentally based is a complex issue that will be reviewed in the next section.

An equally important and independent risk factor, however, may be the specific behavioral and physiological reactions a person has to alcohol itself. Men who at age twenty have a relatively low response to alcohol, in that they need to drink more than other people to feel intoxicated, carry a higher risk of becoming alcoholic by the time they are thirty, regardless of their pattern of drinking at an earlier age and regardless of their parents' drinking. Sons of alcoholics having a low response to alcohol have a 60 percent chance of becoming alcoholics, compared with a 42 percent chance for sons of alcoholics in general. Sons of nonalcoholics having a low response to alcohol have a 22 percent chance of becoming alcoholics, compared with an 8 to 9 percent chance for sons of nonalcoholics in general.

The combination of these two risk factors—family history and a low response to alcohol—is obviously the worst scenario for a development of alcoholism, at least in males. Nonetheless, we should remember that a large proportion of people still *do not* become alcoholics, even with both risk factors present. The question of what protective factors may contribute to the resilience of high-risk individuals with regard to alcoholism is a major subject of current research.[39]

The Genetics of Alcoholism

For centuries, alcoholism has appeared to run in families. Today, this casual observation has led to a specific question: To what extent is alcoholism genetically determined (through the genes of the parents) and to what extent is it environmentally determined (through the living conditions in which the offspring have been brought up)? One approach is to examine the inheritance pattern in a family tree. It is impossible, however, to tease

systems approach: A way of understanding a phenomenon in terms of complex interacting relationships among individuals, family, friends, and community.

codependency: A concept that individuals who live with a person having an alcohol (or other drug) dependence suffer themselves from difficulties of self-image and social independence.

children of alcoholics (COAs): Individuals who grew up in a family with either one or two alcoholic parents.

out the separate genetic (nature) and environmental (nurture) factors from information of this kind.

For more precise answers, one option is to turn to cases of adoption in which children can be compared with either their biological or adoptive parents. In 1981, an extensive research study in Sweden looked at the adoption records of approximately three thousand children who had alcoholic biological parents but lived with nonalcoholic adoptive parents. The results showed that a larger percentage of these children become alcoholics than would be seen in the general population. The greater incidence was present even when the children had been raised by their adoptive parents immediately after being born, indicating that a strong genetic component was operating.

There were, however, two subgroups among those children who eventually became alcoholics. One subgroup, called *Type 1 alcoholics*, developed problem drinking later in life and generally functioned well in society. In addition to a genetic predisposition toward alcoholism, there was for this subgroup a strong environmental factor as well. Whether the child was placed in a middle-class or poor adoptive family influenced the final outcome. A second subgroup, called *Type 2 alcoholics*, developed alcoholism earlier in life and had significant antisocial patterns of behavior. A strong genetic component was operating in this subgroup, and because the socioeconomic status of the adoptive family made no difference in the outcome, we can conclude that environmental factors played a negligible role. Table 10.1 gives a more complete picture of the characteristics associated with Type 1 and Type 2 alcoholics.[40]

The study of twins is another source of information about the genetic and environmental influences in alcoholism. Probably the most important piece of data is the **concordance rate** for alcoholism in pairs of identical twins—that is, how likely one member of a pair is to be alcoholic if the other one is. The concordance rate has been found to be only 58 percent. If genetics were the whole story in determining the incidence of alcoholism, the concordance rate would have been 100 percent.

If we look closely at the type of alcoholic involved and whether the alcoholic is male or female, the data from twin studies are similar to those found in the adoption research. For example, the concordance rate for identical twins has been found to be significantly higher than the concordance rate for fraternal twins when one member of the pair is a male alcoholic whose drinking problems started in adolescence (in other words, a Type 2 alcoholic). For female and male alcoholics whose drinking problems started after adolescence (the Type 1 subgroup), a comparison of concordance rates shows that genetic factors played a lesser role.[41]

TABLE 10.1

Two types of alcoholics

CHARACTERISTICS	TYPE 1	TYPE 2
Usual age at onset	(late onset) after 25	(early onset) before 25
Inability to abstain	infrequent	frequent
Fights and arrests when drinking	infrequent	frequent
Psychological dependence (loss of control)	infrequent	frequent
Guilt and fear about alcoholism	frequent	infrequent
Novelty-seeking personality	low	high
Tendency to use alcohol to escape negative feelings	high	low
Tendency to use alcohol to achieve positive feelings	low	high
Gender	male and female	male only
Extent of genetic influences	moderate	high
Extent of environmental influences	high	low
Serotonin abnormalities in the brain	absent	present

Source: Updated from Cloninger, C. Robert (1987). Neurogenetic adaptive mechanisms in alcoholism. *Science, 236,* 410–416.

In the course of the continuing exploration of the human genome, a number of genes on several different chromosomes have been found to be involved in increasing the risk for alcohol dependence or influencing the tendency to consume alcohol in the first place. As these genes become more clearly identified, the expectation is that new drug-based treatments will be developed.[42]

The Concept of Alcoholism as a Disease

In contrast to the days when alcoholism was considered a moral failure or worse, the majority opinion today is

concordance rate: The likelihood that one member of a twin or family relation will have a condition if the other one has it.

that alcoholism is best characterized as a disease and that the alcoholic should be treated rather than punished. This viewpoint has evolved over the years, originating from the writings of E. M. Jellinek in the late 1940s. Jellinek proposed that alcohol dependence progressed through a natural sequence of stages, much as a physical illness develops.[43] In more recent interpretations, the disease concept has moved away from the idea that all alcoholics follow a common path (many of Jellinek's ideas have not been confirmed) to a more general focus on the biological factors that might differentiate alcoholics from nonalcoholics. In addition, the disease concept has led to the idea that the alcoholics are fundamentally out of control and that abstinence is the only answer to their recovery.[44]

Since 1957, the American Medical Association has defined alcoholism as a disease, and numerous other health organizations have adopted a similar position. As reasonable as this position might sound, the disease concept has created something of a dilemma among professionals concerned with the treatment of alcohol abuse. It places the burden on physicians to deal with the alcoholic through medical interventions, and unfortunately the medical profession is frequently ill equipped to help. A study in 2000, for example, found that 94 percent of a group of primary care physicians failed to make a correct diagnosis of early-stage alcohol abuse when presented with symptoms typical of this condition. Only a small percentage, approximately one out of five, considered themselves "very prepared" to diagnose alcoholism in the first place.[45]

Important legal considerations also cloud this issue. Can we say, for example, that an alcoholic is legally absolved from a crime or a legal obligation because he or she is afflicted with this disease? These and related issues will be explored later in the chapter in Health Line (page 264) and in Point/Counterpoint (pages 331–332).

Approaches to Treatment for Alcoholism

Alcoholism, as should be clear at this point, is a study in diversity, and it makes sense that there might be some advantage in matching alcoholics with certain characteristics to specific forms of treatment. One treatment program might be best suited for one subgroup, another for another subgroup. As reasonable as this hypothesis sounds, however, a major study begun in the late 1980s and completed in 1997 showed little or no benefit in patient–treatment matching. Apparently, no one treatment approach was overwhelmingly superior to others.[46] In this section, we will examine forms of alcoholism treatment as classified into two broad areas: biological interventions, which involve medications, and psychosocial interventions, such as Alcoholics Anonymous and other self-help programs.

Biologically Based Treatments

The use of **disulfiram** (brand name: Antabuse) is based on the idea that if a drug induces an aversive reaction in alcoholics when alcohol is consumed, then consumption will be avoided and the problems of alcoholism will be reduced. Disulfiram, taken orally as a pill once each day, inhibits alcohol dehydrogenase, allowing acetaldehyde to build up in the bloodstream. As a result, individuals who consume alcohol in combination with disulfiram experience a flushing of the face, rapid heart rate and palpitations, nausea, and vomiting. These effects occur not only by consuming alcoholic beverages but by ingesting alcohol in other forms such as mouthwashes, cough mixtures, and even by the absorption of aftershave lotions and shampoos through the skin.

Clearly the symptoms caused by a combination of disulfiram and alcohol can be a powerful short-term deterrent to alcoholic drinking, but the question is whether this kind of aversion therapy is an effective treatment over the long run. Careful studies in which disulfiram has been administered to large numbers of alcoholics indicate that it is not effective when it is the sole treatment. One major problem is that alcoholics must take the drug regularly every day, and because disulfiram does nothing to reduce the alcoholic's craving for alcohol, compliance rates are low. The consensus among professionals in this field is that disulfiram can be useful in a subgroup of higher-functioning alcoholics with exceptionally high motivation to quit drinking; for others, disulfiram can be useful as a transitional treatment until other support programs are in place.[47]

A more direct approach to treatment than aversion therapy is to reduce the actual craving for alcohol on a physiological level. As noted in Chapter 9, evidence suggests that alcohol dependence is related to neural activity in the same dopamine-releasing receptors in the nucleus accumbens that have been implicated in heroin craving as well as craving for cocaine and nicotine. Based upon

disulfiram (dye-SULL-fih-ram): A medication that causes severe physical reactions and discomfort when combined with alcohol. Brand name is Antabuse.

An anonymous group of men and women at a typical Alcoholics Anonymous meeting.

the association with heroin dependence, it makes sense that opiate receptor antagonists in this region of the brain, such as **naltrexone** (brand name: ReVia) and **nalmefene** (brand name: Revex), should be useful in alcohol-dependence treatment.

An extended-release injectable form of naltrexone (brand name: Vivitrol), administered on a monthly basis, was FDA-approved in 2006. The obvious advantage is that individuals do not have to remember to take their medication on a daily basis. Problems associated with individuals skipping their medication are eliminated, and there can be a more intensive concentration on the counseling component of recovery. The advantage of an extended-release naltrexone for treating alcohol dependence parallels that of extended-release formulations of buprenorphine (Subutex, Suboxone) for treating heroin abuse (Chapter 5).

An alternative approach in treating alcohol dependence has been to focus on the regulation of GABA, in a manner similar to the way gamma vinyl-GABA (Vigabatrin) is used for cocaine-abuse treatment (Chapter 4). **Acamprosate** (brand name: Campral) was FDA-approved in 2004 for this purpose. Recent studies have shown the usefulness of topiramate (brand name: Topamax), an antiepileptic and migraine-alleviating medication, for treating alcohol dependence, but its use for this purpose is not currently FDA-approved.

Still another approach has focused on the role of serotonin levels in the brains of alcoholics. Since early-onset (Type 2) alcoholism differs from late-onset (Type 1) alcoholism owing to its association with serotonin abnormalities in the brain (see Table 10.1), a drug that reduces serotonin levels such as **ondansetron** (brand name: Zofran), typically used as an antinausea medication, should be beneficial in treating this subgroup. This prediction has been confirmed. Among Type 2 alcoholics,

naltrexone (nal-TREX-ohn): A long-lasting opiate antagonist for the treatment of alcoholism. Brand name is ReVia. Brand name for an extended-release injectable form is Vivitrol

nalmefene (nal-MEH-feen): A long-lasting opiate antagonist for the treatment of alcoholism. Brand name is Revex.

acamprosate (A-cam-PRO-sate): A GABA-related drug for the treatment of alcoholism. Brand name is Campral.

ondansetron (on-DANS-eh-tron): A serotonin-related drug for the treatment of alcoholism. Brand name is Zofran.

Zofran has significantly reduced their drinking behavior and provided a longer period of abstinence.[48]

Alcoholics Anonymous

The best-known treatment program for alcoholism is **Alcoholics Anonymous (AA).** Founded in 1935, this organization has been conceived basically as a fellowship of alcoholics who wish to rid themselves of their problem drinking by helping one another maintain sobriety. The philosophy of AA is expressed in the famous Twelve Steps (Table 10.2). Members must have acknowledged that they were "powerless over alcohol" and that their lives became

Alcoholics Anonymous (AA): A worldwide organization devoted to the treatment of alcoholism through self-help groups and adherence to its principles.

unmanageable, and to have turned their will and their lives over "to the care of God *as we understood Him*." As the steps indicate, there is a strong spiritual component to the AA program, though the organization vigorously denies that any religious doctrine prevails (Portrait).

AA functions as a type of group therapy with each member oriented toward a common goal: the maintenance of abstinence from alcohol despite a powerful and continuing craving for it. All meetings are completely anonymous (only first names are used in all communications), and the proceedings are dominated by members recounting their personal struggles with alcohol, their efforts to stop drinking, and their support for fellow alcoholics in their own struggles. New members are encouraged to pair up with a sponsor, typically a more experienced AA member who has successfully completed the Twelve Steps and can serve as a personal source of support on a day-to-day basis. According to AA, no alcoholic is ever cured, only recovered, and the process of recovery continues throughout that person's life. Alcoholism, in its view, is a disease, and relapse from sobriety can occur at any moment (Health Line).

AA has grown to 114,000 groups and more than 2 million members in 180 countries, though it is difficult to get a precise count because the organization is deliberately structured very loosely. Perhaps more important than its size is the powerful impact it has made not only on the way we deal with alcoholism but also on the way we consider treatment for any compulsive behavior. Over the years, the twelve-step program has become a generic concept, as the precepts and philosophy of AA have been widely imitated. We now have Al-Anon for the spouses and family of alcoholics going through the AA program and Alateen as a specialized AA program for teenage alcoholics, as well as Gamblers Anonymous,

Nicotine Anonymous, Narcotics or Cocaine Anonymous, and Overeaters Anonymous.

Despite its stature as an approach to treatment, however, there are relatively few scientific appraisals of the overall effectiveness of AA. One of the principal problems is the anonymity that is guaranteed to all members, making it difficult to conduct well-controlled follow-up studies on how well AA members are doing. Nonetheless, AA is widely regarded in the field of alcohol rehabilitation as a beneficial self-help approach, particularly when it is combined with other treatments such as individual counseling and medical interventions.[49] It has been pointed out that AA employs four factors that are widely shown to be effective in preventing relapse in alcohol dependence: (1) the imposition of external supervision, (2) the substitution of dependence on a

---

Health Line
Is Controlled Drinking Possible for Alcoholics?

One of the most intensely debated questions in the field of alcoholism treatment has been whether it is possible for alcoholics to achieve a level of "controlled drinking" without falling back into a state of alcohol dependence.

On one side are well-entrenched organizations such as Alcoholics Anonymous (AA) and the National Institute on Alcohol Abuse and Alcoholism, as well as many other organizations that assert that alcoholism is an irreversible disease, that abstinence is the only answer, and that even the slightest level of alcohol consumption will trigger a cascade of problems that the alcoholic is constitutionally incapable of handling.

On the other side are groups, represented in greater numbers in Canada and Europe than in the United States, asserting that uncontrolled drinking is a reversible behavioral disorder and that for many alcoholics the promotion of total abstinence as a treatment goal is a serious obstacle to their success in rehabilitation. The organization Moderation Management (MM) is an example of this type of therapeutic approach.

Some of the early controlled-drinking studies had enough methodological flaws that the abstinence-only group were justified in denouncing them. But later research, using carefully randomized assignment of alcoholic subjects to either an abstinence-oriented treatment or a controlled-drinking one, has shown that long-term results are comparable for either group. This is not to say that the prospects are wonderful for either of them; the odds are still higher against long-term recovery from alcoholism than for it, no matter what

the treatment. But it does appear that controlled drinking can occur.

How many alcoholics can manage to achieve a continued level of nonproblem drinking? Percentages vary from 2 to 10 to 15, though the lower figure is probably more accurate for those individuals with severe alcoholic difficulties. Perhaps a more important point is that no one knows how to predict whether an alcohol abuser will be one of that small number of successful controlled drinkers. Obviously, most alcoholics are convinced that they will be the lucky ones. How does an alcoholism-treatment counselor handle this? A prominent expert offers one strategy:

> My own perspective is that there is little sense in losing a client by a standoff on this issue. . . . It has been my clinical experience that an unsuccessful trial at "controlled drinking" may be a more persuasive confrontation of the need for abstinence than any amount of argumentation between therapist and client.

Sources: Goode, Erich (1999). *Drugs in American society* (5th ed.). Boston: McGraw-Hill College, p. 194. Hester, Reid K., and Miller, William R. (1989). Self-control training. In Reid K. Hester and William R. Miller (Eds.), *Handbook of alcoholism treatment approaches.* New York: Pergamon Press, pp. 141–149. Miller, William R. (1989). Increasing motivation for change. In Reid K. Hester and William R. Miller (Eds.), *Handbook of alcoholism treatment approaches.* New York: Pergamon Press, pp 67–80. Quotation on p. 77. Sobell, Mark B., and Sobell, Linda C. (1978). *Behavioral treatment of alcohol problems: Individualized therapy and controlled drinking.* New York: Plenum.

Drugs...in Focus

The Non-Disease Model of Alcoholism and Other Patterns of Drug Abuse

Despite the "official" description of alcoholism as a disease by the American Medical Association and many international health organizations, the concept of alcoholism as a disease remains controversial and continues to attract vigorous criticism. As Erich Goode has put it, the non-disease theorists assert that alcoholics (as well as other drug abusers) are "... not 'sick,' but are rational, problem-solving human beings attempting to carve out a meaningful existence in a harsh and seemingly unyielding environment." Others have warned that the disease model encourages alcoholics to assume a passive stance, depending solely on the advances of modern medicine to save the day, and that acceptance of the disease model often leads to making excuses for one's behavior rather than changing it. As a one-liner expresses it, "There's nothing wrong with being an alcoholic, if you're doing something about it."

The "disease versus non-disease" debate has inevitable consequences for the ways in which we choose to respond to the problem. Non-disease theorists view the prevailing majority opinion as unfortunately leading to a marginalization of alcoholics, reducing them to a small group of afflicted, biologically predestined individuals, rather than seeing these people in the context of the way all of us behave to one degree or another. In the words of non-

disease advocate Stanton Peele, this attitude fosters a "coercive, one-size-fits-all...disease treatment system of hospitals, Alcoholics Anonymous, and the twelve steps, which are increasingly administered within the framework of the law enforcement system." He views the disease model as leading to the assumption that all drinking must cease (a position held by AA), instead of to encouragement of controlled levels of drinking, as advocated by Moderation Management (MM). He also argues that, without the disease model of alcoholism and other drug abuse, it is possible to focus on "the larger question of why some people seek to close off their experience through a comforting, but artificial and self-consuming relationship with something external to themselves. In itself, the choice of object is irrelevant to this universal process of becoming dependent."

Further discussion of the disease model of alcoholism can be found in the form of a simulated debate in Point/Counterpoint on pages 331–332.

Sources: Goode, Erich (1999). *Drugs in American society* (5th ed.). New York: McGraw-Hill College, quotation on p. 350. Kinney, Jean (2003). *Loosening the grip: A handbook of alcohol information* (7th ed.). St. Louis: Mosby, pp. 318–322. Peele, Stanton (1995). Assumptions about drugs and the marketing of drug policies. In W. K. Bickel and R. J. DeGrandpre (Eds.), *Drug policy and human nature.* New York: Plenum, pp. 199–220, first quotation on p. 214. Peele, Stanton, and Brodsky, Archie (1975). *Love and addiction.* New York: Taplinger Publishing, second quotation on p. 55.

---

group activity rather than drug-taking behavior, (3) the development of caring relationships, and (4) a heightened sense of spirituality.[50]

SMART Recovery

In contrast to AA, the self-help program **SMART Recovery** assumes that people do not need to believe they are "powerless over alcohol" or submit to "a Power greater than ourselves" (phrases taken from the Twelve Steps) to recover from alcoholism. Instead, the dominant

SMART Recovery: An alcoholism and other drug-abuse treatment program emphasizing a nonspiritual philosophy and a greater sense of personal control in the abuser. SMART stands for "Self-Management And Recovery Training."

philosophy is that individuals have the power themselves to overcome anything, including drinking. Unlike AA, SMART Recovery discourages labeling in general; a person is not required to call himself or herself an alcoholic to achieve success in recovery. The strategy is based on rational emotive behavior therapy (REBT), developed by the psychologist Albert Ellis, which emphasizes rooting out irrational thoughts, emotions, and beliefs that prevent the achievement of personal goals.

Another major difference is that SMART Recovery insists on professional involvement in its program, with a professional adviser (often a clinical psychologist) assisting members in learning the fundamentals of REBT. No reference is made to God or a higher power; the objective is "NHP (no higher power) sobriety." The goal is that within a year and a half members will be able to maintain sobriety without going to meetings. In contrast, AA members are encouraged to continue going to meetings for the rest of their lives.

Since 1990, there has been increased interest in secular (nonreligious) approaches to self-help alcoholism treatment such as that practiced by SMART Recovery. Other examples include Men for Sobriety (MFS), Women for Sobriety (WFS), Moderation Management (MM), and Secular Organization for Sobriety (SOS). Nonetheless, recent research has indicated that alcoholics benefit from participation in AA programs, regardless of their religious beliefs (Drugs... in Focus).[51]

Chronic Alcohol Abuse and Alcoholism in the Workplace

It has been estimated that about 10 percent of the people in the American work force (12.8 million workers) have been at work either under the influence of alcohol or with a hangover at least once in the previous 12 months. The prevalance rates of alcohol impairment at the workplace are higher among men than women, higher for white employees than minority employees, higher for younger than older employees, and higher for unmarried than married employees. Alcohol impairment is also most frequently reported by individuals in the arts/entertainment/sports/media industries, food preparation and service jobs, and building and grounds maintenance occupations. Individuals with jobs that would be seriously affected if alcohol impairment were present, such as workers in construction/extraction industries and transportation/material-moving industries, do not show a significantly higher prevalence rate of alcohol impairment at work than the work force at large.[52]

Given the adverse impact of chronic alcohol abuse on a range of workplace behaviors, it makes sense that corporations, hospitals, the armed services, and other large organizations should benefit by establishing workplace programs specifically tailored for employees who need help. Two major efforts address this problem. The first is employer-sponsored **employee assistance programs (EAPs),** and the second is union-supported **member assistance programs (MAPs).** EAPs have been established as a way of increasing the productivity of the organization, whereas MAPs are oriented toward enhancing the welfare of the individual worker.

In either case, a major thrust of workplace interventions has been to change the culture of drinking within the organization. For example, problems arise because employees tend to drink heavily in order to conform to workplace drinking norms. Within a heavy drinking culture, employees are more likely to use alcohol to cope with stress and feelings of alienation. Gender harassment, characterized by behaviors directed at female employees that convey hostile and degrading attitudes toward women, is associated with the proportion of male employees identified as heavy or "at-risk" drinkers, and the association is stronger when alcohol consumption is considered a common pattern of behavior during lunch or other meal breaks. In other words, a permissive, alcohol-oriented culture at work exacerbates an already serious workplace problem.

Workplace EAPs and MAPs will be examined in Chapter 17 in the larger context of treatment for the abuse of alcohol and other drugs.[53]

Quick Concept Check 10.2

Understanding Alcoholics Anonymous

Check your understanding of the principles and philosophy of Alcoholics Anonymous by checking off whether the following statements would be subscribed to by Alcoholics Anonymous.

1. I have always had the power to control my drinking. ☐ yes ☐ no

2. I must put myself in the hands of a Higher Power if I am to be sober for the rest of my life. ☐ yes ☐ no

3. It is possible to be cured of alcoholism. ☐ yes ☐ no

4. I am capable of having a drink once in a great while without slipping back into alcoholism. ☐ yes ☐ no

5. The more meetings I attend, the better chance I have of remaining sober. ☐ yes ☐ no

Answers: 1. no 2. yes 3. no 4. no 5. yes

---

employee assistance programs (EAPs): Corporate or institutional programs for workers or employees to help them with alcohol or other drug-abuse problems.

member assistance programs (MAPs): Institutional programs for workers or employees to help them with alcohol or other drug-abuse problems, set up by established unions within the organization and tailored for union members.

Summary

Alcoholism: Stereotypes, Definitions, and Criteria

- Alcoholism is a multidimensional condition that is typically defined in terms of four major criteria: (1) problems associated with a preoccupation with drinking, (2) emotional problems, (3) vocational, social, and family problems, and (4) physical problems. Not all criteria have to be met, however, for alcoholism to be diagnosed.

Alcohol Abuse and Alcohol Dependence

- According to health professionals, alcohol abuse is defined in terms of (1) persistent physical, social, or occupational problems that have become associated with alcohol use and (2) recurring use of alcohol in physically hazardous situations. Alcohol dependence is defined in terms of uncontrolled alcohol intake, unsuccessful efforts to reduce alcohol use, life problems, and alcohol tolerance and withdrawal.

- It is estimated that approximately 8.5 percent of U.S. adults can be classified as either alcohol abusers or as alcohol dependent.

The History of Efforts to Regulate Chronic Alcohol Abuse

- An appreciation of the adverse consequences of chronic alcohol abuse started in the late 1700s and took root in the United States as a temperance movement. This movement addressed its concerns primarily toward the drinking of distilled spirits.

- The differentiation among forms of alcohol drinking became blurred during the nineteenth century, as temperance advocates began to promote a total ban on alcohol consumption. National Prohibition was the law in the United States from 1920 to 1933.

- Since the end of Prohibition, government regulation has been carried out chiefly through education and the taxation of alcohol.

Biological Effects of Chronic Alcohol Abuse

- Physical effects of alcoholism include tolerance and withdrawal, liver disease, cardiovascular disease, cancer, and neurological disorders such as Wernicke-Korsakoff syndrome.

- A particular concern is the development of fetal alcohol syndrome (FAS) in the offspring of alcoholic mothers.

Patterns of Chronic Alcohol Abuse

- Alcoholics can be found in every age, gender, racial, ethnic, and religious group and in all socioeconomic and geographic categories. Nonetheless, men outnumber women in the incidence of alcoholism by about six to one, though women are more vulnerable to alcohol-related organ damage. The elderly tend to be an underreported group with respect to alcoholism.

- A systems approach to alcoholism examines the complex interacting relationships among individuals, family, friends, and community. The concept of codependency has helped shed light on the specific effects of alcoholism on spouses and other family members. The children of alcoholics (COAs) carry an increased risk of becoming alcoholic as a result of a vulnerability toward alcoholism that is genetically or environmentally based, or both.

The Genetics of Alcoholism

- Studies of adoptions and twins have provided information about the relative influences of genetics and environment on the development of alcoholism.

- A distinction has been made between a male or female alcoholic with drinking problems occurring late in life (Type 1) and a male alcoholic with drinking problems occurring in adolescence (Type 2). The latter subgroup appears to have a greater genetic component in the inheritance pattern.

The Concept of Alcoholism as a Disease

- The majority position with respect to alcoholism is that it should be considered a disease and that alcoholics should be treated rather than punished. Since 1957, the American Medical Association has supported this idea.

- Unfortunately, recent surveys of primary-care physicians indicate that the medical profession is frequently ill prepared to diagnose alcoholism or supervise effective treatment.

Approaches to Treatment for Alcoholism

- Approaches include biologically based treatments and psychosocial treatments such as the self-help programs of Alcoholics Anonymous (AA).

- Objections to certain aspects of the AA philosophy have promoted the growth of other self-help organizations, such as Moderation Management (MM) and SMART Recovery.

- Corporations and other large organizations have instituted employee assistance programs (EAPs), and unions have instituted member assistance programs (MAPs), to help workers with problems of alcohol abuse or other forms of drug abuse.

Key Terms

abstinence, p. 247
acamprosate, p. 261
alcohol abuse, p. 249
alcohol dependence, p. 249
alcoholic cirrhosis, p. 252
alcoholic dementia, p. 253
alcoholic hepatitis, p. 252
Alcoholics Anonymous
  (AA), p. 262
alcoholism, p. 245

alcohol withdrawal
  syndrome, p. 252
children of alcoholics
  (COAs), p. 258
codependency, p. 258
concordance rate, p. 259
confabulation, p. 254
delirium tremens (DTs),
  p. 252
disulfiram, p. 260

employee assistance
  programs (EAPs), p. 265
enablers, p. 248
fatty liver, p. 252
fetal alcohol effect (FAE),
  p. 255
fetal alcohol syndrome
  (FAS), p. 254
member assistance programs
  (MAPs), p. 265
nalmefene, p. 261

naltrexone, p. 261
ondansetron, p. 261
SMART Recovery, p. 264
symptomatic drinking,
  p. 245
systems approach, p. 258
teratogenic, p. 254
thiamine, p. 254
Wernicke-Korsakoff
  syndrome, p. 254

Endnotes

1. Goodwin, Donald W., and Gabrielli, William F. (1997). Alcohol: Clinical aspects. In Joyce H. Lowinson, Pedro Ruiz, Robert B. Millman, and John G. Langrod (Eds.), *Substance abuse: A comprehensive textbook.* Baltimore: Williams & Wilkins, pp. 142–148.

2. Hoff, Ebbe Curtis (1974). *Alcoholism: The hidden addiction.* New York: Seabury Press, pp. 75–88.

3. Hofmann, Frederick G. (1983). *A handbook on drug and alcohol abuse* (2nd ed.). New York: Oxford University Press, p. 99.

4. Hoff, *Alcoholism,* pp. 78–79.

5. Drobes, David J., and Thomas, Suzanne E. (1999). Assessing craving for alcohol. *Alcohol Research and Health, 23,* 179–186.

6. Conner, Kenneth R.; Yue, Li; Meldrum, Sean; Duberstein, Paul R.; and Conwell, Y. (2003). The role of drinking in suicidal ideation: Analysis of Project MATCH data. *Journal of Studies on Alcohol, 64,* 402–408. Schuckit, Marc A. (2000). *Drug and alcohol abuse: A clinical guide to diagnostic and treatment* (5th ed.). New York: Kluver Academic/Plenum, pp. 54–97.

7. Maiden, R. Paul (1997). Alcohol dependence and domestic violence: Incidence and treatment implications. *Alcohol Treatment Quarterly, 15,* 31–50. U.S. Department of Health and Human Services (1990). *Alcohol and health* (Seventh Special Report to the U.S. Congress). Rockville, MD: National Institute on Alcohol Abuse and Alcoholism, p. 174.

8. National Institute on Alcohol Abuse and Alcoholism (2000, April). Alcohol Alert: Imaging and alcoholism: A window on the brain. No. 47. Rockville, MD: National Institute on Alcohol Abuse and Alcoholism.

9. Fishbein, Diana H., and Pease, Susan E. (1996). *The dynamics of drug abuse.* Needham Heights, MA: Allyn and Bacon, pp. 122–124.

10. American Psychiatric Association (2000). *Diagnostic and statistical manual of mental disorders* (4th ed.). *Text Revision.* Washington DC: American Psychiatric Association, pp. 213–214.

11. Grant, Bridget F.; Stinson, Frederick S.; Dawson, Deborah A.; Chou, S. Patricia; Dufour, Mary C.; et al. (2004). Prevalence and co-occurrence of substance use disorders and independent mood and anxiety disorders. *Archives of General Psychiatry, 61,* 807–816. National Institute on Alcohol Abuse and Alcoholism (1995, October). Alcohol Alert: Diagnostic criteria for alcohol abuse and dependence. No. 30. Bethesda, MD: National Institute on Alcohol Abuse and Alcoholism.

12. Quoted in Sournia, Jean-Charles (1990). *A history of alcoholism.* Cambridge, MA: Basil Blackwell, p. 29.

13. Lincoln, Abraham (1842/1989). Address to the Washingtonian Temperance Society of Springfield, Illinois. *Speeches and writings, 1832–1858.* New York: Library of America, p. 84.

14. Lender, Mark E., and Martin, James R. (1982). *Drinking in America: A history.* New York: Free Press, p. 107.

15. Blocker, Jack S. (2006, February). Did Prohibition really work? Alcohol prohibition as a public health innovation. *American Journal of Public Health,* pp. 233–243. Lerner, Michael A. (2007). *Dry Manhattan,* Cambridge, MA: Harvard University Press. Musto, David F. (1996, April). Alcohol in American history. *Scientific American,* pp. 78–83. Sournia, *History of alcoholism,* p. 122.

16. *Standard and Poor's Industry Surveys* (2003, January 23). Alcoholic beverages and tobacco, p. 19. U.S. Department of Health and Human Services (2000). *Alcohol and health* (Tenth Special Report to the U.S. Congress). Rockville, MD: National Institute on Alcohol Abuse and Alcoholism, p. 370. *Standard and Poor's Industry Surveys* (1997, January 23). Alcoholic beverages and tobacco, p. 15. *Standard and Poor's Industry Surveys* (1997, September 11). Alcoholic beverages and tobacco, p. 16.

17. U.S. Department of Health and Human Services (2000). *Alcohol and health,* pp. 341–354.

18. Schuckit, *Drug and alcohol abuse,* pp. 79–80.

19. Sellers, Edward M., and Kalant, Harold (1982). Alcohol withdrawal and delirium tremens. In E. Mansell Pattison

and Edward Kaufman (Eds.), *Encyclopedic handbook of alcoholism.* New York: Gardner Press, pp. 147–166.

20. Ford, Richard, Hawkes, Nigel, and Elliott, Francis (2008, May 23). Alarm over the child drinkers with liver disease. *The Times (London),* pp. 1–3. Lieber, Charles S. (2001). Alcohol and hepatitis C. *Alcohol Research and Health,* 25, 245–254. National Institute on Alcohol Abuse and Alcoholism (1998, October). Alcohol Alert: Alcohol and the liver: Research update. No. 42. Rockville, MD: National Institute on Alcohol Abuse and Alcoholism.

21. Mukamal, Kenneth J.; Tolstrup, Janne S.; Friberg, Jens; Jensen, Gorm; and Gronbaek, Morton (2005). Alcohol consumption and risk of atrial fibrillation in men and women. *Circulation,* 112, 1736–1742.

22. Bagnardi, Vincenzo, Blangliardo, Marta, and LaVecchia, Carlo (2001). Alcohol consumption and the risk of cancer: A meta-analysis. *Alcohol Research and Health,* 25, 263–270. Smith-Warner, Stephanie A.; Spiegelman, Donna; Shiaw-Shyuan, Yuan; Van den Brandt, Piet A.; Folsom, Aaron R.; et al. (1998). Alcohol and breast cancer in women: A pooled analysis of cohort studies. *Journal of the American Medical Association,* 279, 535–540.

23. National Institute on Alcohol Abuse and Alcoholism (2001, July). Alcohol Alert: Cognitive impairment and recovery from alcoholism. No. 53. Rockville, MD: National Institute on Alcohol Abuse and Alcoholism. U.S. Department of Health and Human Services (1990). *Alcohol and health,* pp. 123–124.

24. McEvoy, Joseph P. (1982). The chronic neuropsychiatric disorders associated with alcoholism. In E. Mansell Pattison and Edward Kaufman (Eds.), *Encyclopedic handbook of alcoholism.* New York: Gardner Press, pp. 167–179.

25. Golden, Janet (2005). *Message in a bottle: The making of fetal alcohol syndrome.* Cambridge, MA: Harvard University Press. Jones, Kenneth L., and Smith, David W. (1973). Recognition of the fetal alcohol syndrome in early infancy. *Lancet,* 2, 999–1001. Sokol, Robert J., Delaney-Black, Virginia, and Nordstrom, Beth (2003). Fetal alcohol spectrum disorder. *Journal of the American Medical Association,* 290, 2996–2999.

26. Ma, Grace X.; Toubbeh, Jamil; Cline, Janette; and Chisholm, Anita (1998). Fetal alcohol syndrome among Native American adolescents: A model prevention program. *Journal of Primary Prevention,* 19, 43–55. Morbidity and Mortality Weekly Report (2002). Fetal alcohol syndrome— Alaska, Arizona, Colorado, and New York, 1995–1997. *Journal of the American Medical Association,* 288, 38–40. U.S. Department of Health and Human Services (2000). *Alcohol and health,* pp. 283–299.

27. National Institute on Alcohol Abuse and Alcoholism (2000, December). Alcohol Alert: Fetal alcohol exposure and the brain. No. 13. Bethesda, MD: National Institute on Alcohol Abuse and Alcoholism. U.S. Department of Health and Human Services (2000). *Alcohol and health,* pp. 300–322.

28. May, Philip A. (1991). Fetal alcohol effects among North American Indians. *Alcohol Health and Research World,* 15, 239–248. National Institute on Alcohol Abuse and Alcoholism (2004, July). Alcohol Alert: Alcohol—An important women's health issue. Bethesda, MD: National Institute on Alcohol Abuse and Alcoholism. U.S. Department of Health and Human Services (2000). *Alcohol and health,* pp. 323–336.

29. Carroll, Linda (2003, November 4). Alcohol's toll on fetuses: Even worse than thought. *New York Times,* pp. F1, F6. Centers for Disease Control and Prevention (2004, December 24). Alcohol consumption among women who are pregnant or who might become pregnant—United States, 2002. *Morbidity and Mortality Weekly Report,* 1178–1181. Ebrahim, Shahul H.; Diekman, Shane T.; Floyd, R. Louise; and Decoufle, Pierre (1999). Comparison of binge drinking among pregnant and nonpregnant women, United States, 1991–1995. *American Journal of Obstetrics and Gynecology,* 180, 1–7. Floyd, R. Louise; O'Connor, Mary J.; Sokol, Robert J.; Bertrand, Jacquelyn; and Cordero, José F. (2005). Recognition and prevention of fetal alcohol syndrome. *Obstetrics and Gynecology,* 106, 1059–1064.

30. U.S. Department of Health and Human Services (2000). *Alcohol and health,* pp. 364–372.

31. Cloninger, C. Robert (1987). Neurogenetic adaptive mechanisms in alcoholism. *Science,* 236, 410–416. National Institute on Alcohol Abuse and Alcoholism (1999, December). Alcohol Alert: Are women more vulnerable to alcohol's effects? No. 46. Rockville, MD: National Institute on Alcohol Abuse and Alcoholism.

32. Nephew, T. M.; Williams, G. D.; Hoy, A. K.; Stinson, F. S.; Sanchez, L. L.; et al. (2003, August). *Surveillance report 62: Apparent per capita alcohol consumption: National, state, and regional trends, 1977–2000.* Bethesda, MD: National Institute on Alcohol Abuse and Alcoholism.

33. Merrick, Elizabeth L.; Horgan, Constance M.; Hodgkin, Dominic; Garrick, Deborah W.; et al. (2008). Unhealthy drinking patterns in older adults: Prevalence and associated characteristics. *Journal of the American Geriatrics Society,* 56, 214–223.

34. Brody, Jane E. (2002, April 2). Hidden plague of alcohol abuse by the elderly. *New York Times,* p. F7. Fleming, Michael F.; Manwell, Linda B.; Barry, Kristen L.; Adams, Wendy; and Stauffacher, Ellyn A. (1999). Brief physician advice for alcohol problems in older adults: A randomized community-based trial. *Journal of Family Practice,* 48, 378–384. Graham, Kathryn; Della Clarke, Christine B.; Carver, Virginia; Dolinki, Louise; Smythe, Cynthia; et al. (1996). Addictive behaviors in older adults. *Addictive Behaviors,* 21, 331–348. Substance Abuse and Mental Health Services Administration (2007, January/February). Treatment for older adults: What works best? *SAMHSA News,* pp. 1–5.

35. DiNitto, Diana M., and McNeece, C. Aaron (1994). *Chemical dependency: A systems approach.* Englewood Cliffs, NJ: Prentice-Hall, pp. 214–239.

36. Doweiko, Harold E. (1993). *Concepts of chemical dependency* (2nd ed.). Pacific Grove, CA: Brooks-Cole, p. 265.

37. Whitfield, Charles L. (1997). Co-dependence, addictions, and related disorders. In Lowinson et al. (Eds.), *Substance*

abuse: A comprehensive textbook (3rd ed.). Baltimore: Williams & Wilkins, pp. 672–683.

38. Anderson, S. C. (1994). A critical analysis of the concept of codependency. *Social Work, 39*, 677–685. Doweiko, *Concepts of chemical dependency*, pp. 269–271, 282–284.

39. Erblich, Joel, and Earleywine, Mitchell (1999). Children of alcoholics exhibit attenuated cognitive impairment during an ethanol challenge. *Alcoholism: Clinical and Experimental Research, 23*, 476–482. Hussong, Andrea M., Curran, Patrick J., and Chassin, Laurie (1998). Pathways of risk for accelerated heavy alcohol use among adolescent children of alcoholic parents. *Journal of Abnormal Child Psychology, 26*, 453–466.

40. Cloninger, Neurogenetic adaptive mechanisms. Cloninger, C. Robert, Gohman, M., and Sigvardsson, S. (1981). Inheritance of alcohol abuse: Cross fostering analysis of adopted men. *Archives of General Psychiatry, 38*, 861–868.

41. McGue, Matt, Pickens, Roy W., and Svikis, Dace S. (1992). Sex and age effects on the inheritance of alcohol problems: A twin study. *Journal of Abnormal Psychology, 101*, 3–17.

42. National Institute on Alcohol Abuse and Alcoholism (2003, July). Alcohol Alert: The genetics of alcoholism. No. 60. Rockville, MD: National Institute on Alcohol Abuse and Alcoholism. Nurnberger, John I., and Bierut, Laura Jean. (2007, April). Seeking the connections: Alcoholism and our genes. *Scientific American*, pp. 46–53.

43. Jellinek, E. M. (1952). Phases of alcohol addiction. *Quarterly Journal of Studies in Alcohol, 13*, 672. Jellinek, E. M. (1960). *The disease concept of alcoholism*. New Haven, CT: Hillhouse Press. Vaillant, George E. (1995). *The natural history of alcoholism revisited*. Cambridge, MA: Harvard University Press.

44. George, William H., and Marlatt, G. Alan. (1983). Alcoholism: The evolution of a behavioral perspective. In Marc Galanter (Ed.), *Recent developments in alcoholism*. Vol. 1. New York: Plenum, pp. 105–138.

45. Maltzman, Irving (1994). Why alcoholism is a disease. *Journal of Psychoactive Drugs, 26*, 13–31. National Center on Addiction and Substance Abuse at Columbia University (2000, May). *Missed opportunity: National survey of primary care physicians and patients on substance abuse*. New York: National Center on Addiction and Substance Abuse at Columbia University.

46. Fuller, Richard K., and Hiller-Sturmhöfel, Susanne (1999). Alcoholism treatment in the United States. *Alcohol Research and Health, 23*, 69–77.

47. Banys, Peter (1988). The clinical use of disulfiram (Antabuse): A review. *Journal of Psychoactive Drugs, 20*, 243–261.

48. Flannery, B. A.; Poole, S. A.; Gallop, R. J.; and Volpicelli, J. R. (2003). Alcohol craving predicts drinking during treatment: An analysis of three assessment instruments. *Journal of Studies on Alcohol, 64*, 120–126. Johnson, Bankole A.; Rosenthal, Norman; Capece, Julie A.; Wiegand, Frank; Mao, Lian; et al. (2007). Topiramate for treating alcohol dependence: A randomized controlled trial. *Journal of the*

American Medical Association, 298, 1641–1651. Scott, Lesley J.; Figgitt, David P.; Keam, Susan J.; and Waugh, John (2005). Acamprosate: A review of its use in the maintenance of abstinence in patients with alcohol dependence. *CNS Drugs, 19*, 445–464. Substance Abuse and Mental Health Services Administration (2007, May/June). Treating alcohol dependence: Naltrexone advisory. *SAMHSA News*, p. 14.

49. Hopson, Ronald E., and Beaird-Spiller, Bethany (1995). Why AA works: A psychological analysis of the addictive experience and the efficacy of Alcoholics Anonymous. *Alcoholism Treatment Quarterly, 12*, 1–17. Morgenstern, Jon; Bux, Donald; LaBouvie, Erich; Blanchard, Kimberly A.; and Morgan, Thomas J. (2002). Examining mechanisms of action in a 12-step treatment: The role of 12-step cognitions. *Journal of Studies on Alcohol, 63*, 665–672. White, William H. (1998). *Slaying the dragon: The history of addiction treatment and recovery in America*. Bloomington, IL: Chestnut Health Systems, pp. 127–177.

50. Forcehimes, Alyssa A. (2004). *De Profundis*: Spiritual transformations in Alcoholics Anonymous. *Journal of Clinical Psychology/In Session, 60*, 503–517. How effective is Alcoholics Anonymous? (2003, December). *Harvard Medical Letter*, p. 7.

51. Ellis, Albert, and Velten, Emmett (1992). *When AA doesn't work for you: Rational steps to quitting alcohol*. Fort Lee, NJ: Barricade Press. Kaskutas, Lee A. (1996). A road less traveled: Choosing the "Women for Sobriety" program. *Journal of Drug Issues, 26*, 77–94. Schmidt, Eric (1996). Rational recovery: Finding an alternative for addiction treatment. *Alcoholism Treatment Quarterly, 14*, 47–57. SMART Recovery (2004). *SMART Recovery handbook*. Mentor, OH: SMART Recovery®. Winzelberg, Andrew, and Humphreys, Keith (1999). Should patients' religiosity influence clinicians' referral to 12-step self-help groups? Evidence from a study of 3,018 male substance abuse patients. *Journal of Consulting and Clinical Psychology, 67*, 790–794.

52. Frone, Michael R. (2006). Prevalence and distribution of alcohol use and impairment in the workplace: A U.S. national survey. *Journal of Studies on Alcohol and Drugs, 67*, 147–156.

53. Bachrach, Samuel B., Bamberger, Peter A., and McKinney, Valerie M. (2007). Harassing under the influence: The prevalence of male heavy drinking, the embeddedness of permissive workplace drinking norms, and the gender harassment of female coworkers. *Journal of Occupational Health Psychology, 13*, 232–250. National Institute on Alcohol Abuse and Alcoholism (1999, July). Alcohol Alert: Alcohol and the workplace. No. 44. Rockville, MD: National Institute on Alcohol Abuse and Alcoholism. Osilla, Karen C.; Zellmer, Steven P.; Larimer, Mary E.; Neighbors, Clayton; and Marlatt, G. Alan (2008). A brief intervention for at-risk drinking in an employee assistance program. *Journal of Studies on Alcohol and Drugs, 69*, 14–20.

chapter 11

Nicotine and Tobacco Use

Mark Twain is reported to have said that quitting smoking was easy and that he should know because he had done it a thousand times.

Well, I should know too. It seems that I've tried to quit a million times. I realize it's not good for me; I'm no fool. But you have to know that when I wake up in the morning, all I can think about is that first cigarette. Without it, my day doesn't begin.

Somehow I'm willing to suffer the indignity and inconvenience of standing out there in the rain and the cold, not to mention the disapproving glances of a lot of my friends, to have a cigarette. It's so hard to stop.

But I have to give it another try. I'll try.

—*Anonymous*

After you have completed this chapter, you will understand

- The story of tobacco through history
- The present-day tobacco industry
- The main culprits: carbon monoxide, tar, and nicotine
- Nicotine as a stimulant drug
- Nicotine and smoking dependence
- Adverse health consequences of smoking
- Patterns of tobacco use in the United States
- Global issues in the control of tobacco use
- Strategies for people who want to stop smoking

In some ways, our attitudes toward tobacco have not changed very much. In the sixteenth century, when tobacco was first introduced to the Western world, smoking behavior was considered personally objectionable, yet strangely alluring. The same is true today. And judging from the opening quotation, people in the twenty-first century have as much difficulty quitting as they did in Mark Twain's time.

In other ways, however, the times have definitely changed. For almost fifty years, until the middle 1960s, lighting up and smoking a cigarette was an unquestionable sign of sophistication. There was little or no public awareness that harm would come of it. It was an era before surgeon general's reports, National Smoke-out Days, and smoke-free restaurants and hotels.

Today, it is no longer a matter of debate that tobacco smoking is a major health hazard, not only to the person doing the smoking but also to society at large. These concerns are based not on public attitudes that can vacillate over time but on solid scientific fact. It is also no longer a matter of debate that the main psychoactive ingredient in tobacco, nicotine, is a major dependence-producing drug.

Yet, at the same time, we need to recognize that tobacco products are legally sanctioned commodities with an economic significance, both to the United States and to the world. How did we arrive at this paradoxical point, and what lies ahead? This chapter will explore what we now know about the effects of tobacco smoking and other forms of tobacco consumption, the impact these behaviors have had on U.S. society and the world, and the ways in which we have dealt with the issue of tobacco over the years. It also will consider current approaches toward helping people who choose to stop smoking, and prevention strategies for young people to avoid starting in the first place.

Tobacco Use through History

Shortly after setting foot on the small island of San Salvador on October 12, 1492, Christopher Columbus received from the inhabitants a welcoming gift of large, green, sweet-smelling tobacco leaves. Never having seen tobacco before, Columbus did not know what to make of this curious offering, except to observe in his journal that the leaves were greatly prized by the "Indians." In the first week of November, two members of the expedition ventured to the shores of Cuba, searching at Columbus's insistence for the great khan of Cathay (China). They found no evidence of the khan but did return with reports of natives who apparently were "drinking smoke." They rolled up tobacco leaves in the dried corn leaves or stuffed them into hollow reeds, lit them with fire, and then inhaled the smoke through the nose and mouth. It was a totally bizarre scene to these European observers; one interpretation was that the natives were perfuming themselves in some exotic ritual.

Before long, Columbus's men tried "tobacco drinking" themselves. One sailor in particular, Rodrigo de Jerez, became quite fond of the practice. He was, in fact, history's first documented European smoker, though he lived to regret it. When Rodrigo returned to Spain, he volunteered to demonstrate the newfound custom to his neighbors, who instead of being impressed thought that anyone who could emit smoke from the nose and mouth without burning had to be possessed by the Devil. A parish priest turned Rodrigo over to the Inquisition, which sentenced him to imprisonment for witchcraft. He spent several years in jail, presumably without a supply of tobacco. Rodrigo therefore also may be remembered as the first European smoker to quit cold turkey.[1]

In 1560, the year historians mark as the year tobacco was officially introduced to Europe, a Spanish physician brought some tobacco plants back from the New World and presented them to King Philip II of Spain. Meanwhile, in England, both Sir Francis Drake on his return from his voyage around the world and Sir Walter Raleigh on his return from the new colony of

by the numbers . . .

74	Percentage of American smokers who consider themselves addicted to cigarettes
4,000	On an average day in 2006, the number of adolescents in the United States, aged twelve to seventeen, who smoked a cigarette for the first time
100 million	The estimated number of people worldwide in the twentieth century who died prematurely of tobacco-related disease

Sources: Roper Center at the University of Connecticut (2005). Organization conducting the survey: The Gallup Organization. Substance Abuse and Mental Health Services Administration (2007). *A day in the life of American adolescents: Substance use facts.* Rockville, MD: Office of Applied Studies, Substance Abuse and Mental Health Services Administration. World Health Organization (2008). *The WHO report on the global tobacco epidemic 2008.* Geneva, Switzerland: World Health Organization.

Sir Walter Raleigh (1552–1618) relaxes with a long smoking pipe as his servant rushes in to extinguish the fire with a pail of beer. The risk of fire has always been associated with tobacco smoking.

Virginia championed the use of tobacco. Suddenly, the practice of smoking tobacco through long, elaborate pipes became fashionable among the aristocracy.

Not everyone was enthusiastic about this new fad of smoking. Predating a modern-day surgeon general's report by more than 350 years, King James I of England wrote in 1604, "A Counter-blaste to Tobacco," a lengthy treatise condemning tobacco use. Referring to tobacco as a "stinking weede," he characterized smoking as "a custom loathsome to the eye, hateful to the nose, harmful to the brain, [and] dangerous to the lung." In the first recorded comment on its potential for causing dependence, the king observed that "he that taketh tobacco saith he cannot leave it, it doth bewitch him."

Politics, Economics, and Tobacco

Elsewhere in the world, during the early seventeenth century, the condemnation of tobacco became extreme. In Russia, conservatives in power saw tobacco as a dangerous "Western" influence on the purity of Russian culture and established penalties for smoking that included whipping, mutilation, exile to Siberia, and death. Turkey, Japan, and China tried similar tactics, but, not surprisingly, tobacco use continued to spread.[2]

By the end of the seventeenth century even the fiercest opponents of tobacco had to concede that it was here to stay. A sultan of Turkey in 1648 became a

snuff: A quantity of finely shredded or powdered tobacco. Modern forms of snuff are available in either dry or moist forms.

snuffing: The ingestion of snuff either by inhalation or absorption through tissue in the nose.

smoker himself, and naturally, penalties for tobacco use vanished overnight; Czar Peter the Great in 1689 pledged to open up Russia to the West, and tobacco suddenly became a welcome symbol of modernism; Japan and China stopped trying to enforce a prohibition that citizens obviously did not want. Even England's James I put aside his personal dislike for tobacco and quickly recognized the attractive prospect of sizable revenue from taxes imposed on this popular new commodity.[3]

Snuffing and Chewing

One form of tobacco use observed by the early Spanish explorers was the practice of grinding a mixture of tobacco into a fine powder (**snuff**), placing or sniffing a pinch of it into the nose, and exhaling it with a sneeze. By the 1700s, this custom, called **snuffing,** overtook smoking as the dominant form of tobacco use. Among French aristocrats, both men and women, expensive snuffs, perfumed with exotic scents and carried in jeweled and enameled boxes, became part of the daily routine at the court in France and then in the rest of Europe. Sneezing was considered to clear the head of "superfluous humours," invigorate the brain, and brighten the eyes. In an era when bad smells were constant features of daily living, snuffing brought some degree of relief, not to mention a very effective way of sending nicotine to the brain (see Chapter 3).

Because of their dominance in the rapidly expanding tobacco market, the English colonies in America, particularly Virginia, prospered greatly. England enjoyed a profitable tobacco trade, but you might say that its development of colonial tobacco growing eventually backfired. In 1777, when Benjamin Franklin was sent as an envoy to France to gain support against the British in the American War for Independence, a key factor in his success was an offer to deliver prime Virginia tobacco in return for French money. The French agreed, and the rest is history. Had it not been for American tobacco, there might not have been a United States of America at all.[4]

In the United States, snuffing was soon replaced by a more rough-and-ready method for using tobacco: chewing. The practice was not totally new; early Spanish explorers had found the natives chewing tobacco as well as smoking it from the earliest days of their conquest, though North American tribes preferred smoking exclusively. Chewing tobacco had the advantage of freeing the hands for work, and its low cost made it a democratic custom befitting a vigorous new nation in the nineteenth century.

However, the need to spit out tobacco juices on a

regular basis raised the tobacco habit to unimaginable heights of gross behavior. It was enough to make the objections to smoke and of possible fire fade into insignificance; now the problem was a matter of public health. Tobacco spitting became a major factor behind the spread of infectious diseases such as tuberculosis. Adding to this unsavory picture was the likelihood that a man's accuracy in targeting the nearest spittoon was inevitably compromised by his level of alcohol consumption, which was setting all-time records during this period (see Chapter 9). Charles Dickens, on his travels through the United States, commented in 1842 that the demise of the once-handsome carpet in the U.S. Senate chamber was personally depressing:

> Washington may be called the head-quarters of tobacco-tinctured saliva. . . . In all the public places of America, this filthy custom is recognized. In the courts of law, the judge has his spittoon, the crier his, the witness his, and the prisoner his, while the jurymen and spectators are provided for.[5]

A present-day baseball dugout seems, by comparison, to be a model of decorum. The growth in the popularity of smokeless (chewing) tobacco since the 1970s will be examined in a later section.

Cigars and Cigarettes

By the time of the American Civil War, the fashion in tobacco use began to shift once more, as its overall popularity continued to soar. Although the plug of tobacco suitable for chewing was still a major seller and would remain so until the early twentieth century, two new trends emerged, particularly in the growing industrial cities.

The first trend was the popularity of smoking **cigars** (commonly known as "seegars"), tight rolls of dried tobacco leaves. New innovations in curing (drying) tobacco leaves had produced a milder and lighter-quality leaf that was more suitable for smoking than the older forms that had been around since the colonial period. North Carolina, with its ideal soil for cultivating this type of tobacco, began to dominate as the tobacco-growing center of the United States; it continues to do so today. With the advent of cigars, tobacco consumers could combine the feeling of chewing (since the cigar remained in the mouth for a relatively long period of time) and the effects of ingesting tobacco smoke. Pioneers heading west could indulge in foot-long cigars called "stogies," named after the Conestoga wagons that they rode during the long and tedious journey.

The second trend was the introduction of **cigarettes,** rolls of shredded tobacco wrapped in paper. They had become popular among British soldiers returning from

the Crimean War in 1856, who had adopted the practice from the Turks. Europe took to cigarettes immediately, but the United States proved a harder sell. Part of the problem was the opposition of a well-entrenched U.S. cigar industry, which did not look kindly on an upstart competitor. Cigar makers did not discourage the circulation of rumors that the cigarette paper wrapping was actually soaked in arsenic or white lead, that cigarette factory workers were urinating on the tobacco to give it an extra "bite," or that Egyptian brands were mixed with crushed camel dung.[6]

An even greater marketing challenge than unsubstantiated rumors was the effeminate image of cigarette smoking itself. A cigarette was looked upon as a dainty, sissy version of the he-man cigar; cigars were fat, long, and dark, whereas cigarettes were slender, short, and light. Well into the beginning of the twentieth century, this attitude persisted. This is what John L. Sullivan, champion boxer and self-appointed defender of American masculinity, thought of cigarettes in 1904:

> Who smokes 'em? Dudes and college stiffs—fellows who'd be wiped out by a single jab or a quick undercut. It isn't natural to smoke cigarettes. An American ought to smoke cigars. . . . It's the Dutchmen, Italians, Russians, Turks, and Egyptians who smoke cigarettes and they're no good anyhow.[7]

The public image of the cigarette eventually would change dramatically; until then, cigarette manufacturers had to rely instead on a powerful marketing advantage: low cost. In 1881, James Bonsack patented a cigarette-making machine that transformed the tobacco industry. Instead of producing at most 300 cigarettes an hour by hand, three machine operators could now turn out 200 a minute, or roughly 120,000 cigarettes a day. This is a snail's pace compared to the present state-of-the-art machines capable of producing more than 10,000 cigarettes a minute, but in those days, the Bonsack machine was viewed as an industrial miracle. Cigarette prices by the end of the 1800s were as cheap as twenty for a nickel.[8]

Tobacco in the Twentieth Century

At the beginning of the twentieth century, Americans could choose from a variety of ways to satisfy their hunger for tobacco. Cigars and pipes were still the dominant form of tobacco use. Plugs of chewing

cigars: Tightly rolled quantities of dried tobacco leaves.

cigarettes: Rolls of shredded tobacco wrapped in paper, today usually fitted at the mouth end with a filter.

Cigarette advertisements once drew heavily on an association with glamorous women, Hollywood celebrities, and baseball players.

tobacco were still enjoyed by many, and spittoons were still in evidence, but with the new emphasis on social manners and crackdowns by public health officials concerned with major epidemics of infectious diseases, their days were numbered in the big cities. Chewing remained popular, however, in rural towns of America, and present-day sales are concentrated in these regions.

The future seemed to favor the cigarette for two basic reasons. First, a growing number of women began to challenge the idea of masculine domination, and smoking tobacco was one of the privileges of men that women now wanted to share. Not that women smoking was met with immediate acceptance; in one famous case in 1904, a New York City woman was arrested for smoking in public. Nonetheless, as smoking among women became more common, the mild-tasting, easy-to-hold cigarette was the perfect option for them. By the 1920s, advertising slogans such as "Reach for a Lucky instead of a sweet" (a clever effort to portray cigarette smoking as a weight-control aid) as well as endorsements by glamorous celebrities were being designed specifically for the women's market. A second factor was World War I, during which time cigarettes were a logical form of tobacco to take along to war. Times of tension have always been times of increased tobacco use. When the war was over,

the cigarette was, in the words of one historian, "enshrined forever as the weary soldier's relief, the worried man's support, and the relaxing man's companion."[9]

Cigarettes really came into their own in the 1920s, with the introduction of heavily advertised brand names and intense competition among American tobacco companies. Some of the major brand names introduced during this period were Camel, Chesterfield, Lucky Strike, Philip Morris, and Old Gold. Cigarette sales in the United States increased from $45 billion in 1920 to $80 billion in 1925 and $180 billion by 1940.[10]

Health Concerns and Smoking Behavior

A combination of promotion through mass-media advertising and the implied endorsement of smoking by glamorous people in the entertainment industry and sports celebrities enabled the tobacco industry, now dominated by cigarettes, to increase its volume of sales from the 1940s to the 1980s by a steady 9 billion cigarettes each year. The peak in domestic sales was reached in 1981, when approximately 640 billion were sold. Owing to the increase in population, however, per capita consumption in the United States had peaked in 1963 at approximately 4,300 cigarettes per year (roughly twelve cigarettes per day).

Beginning in 1964, per capita consumption began a steady decline, with the present level at approximately 2,100 cigarettes per year (roughly six cigarettes per day). The year of the turnaround in per capita consumption is significant because it coincided with the U.S. surgeon general's first report on smoking and health. For the first time, the federal government asserted publicly what had been suspected for decades: that tobacco smoking was linked to cancer and other serious diseases.

From the standpoint of tobacco use in America, the surgeon general's report had three major effects. First, in the month or so immediately after the report was released, there was a dramatic drop (approximately 25 percent) in per capita consumption levels. Although succeeding months in 1964 showed a bounce upward, most likely reflecting the fact that many people who tried to quit had only temporary success, the long-term trend in U.S. tobacco consumption from that point on would never be upward again.

As evidence of health risks accumulated, restrictions on public consumption were instituted. In 1971, all television advertising for tobacco was banned, and in 1984, a rotating series of warning labels (already on all packages of tobacco products since 1966) was required on all print advertisements and outdoor billboards.[11]

A second major effect was the change in the types of cigarettes smoked by the average smoker. In the 1950s, more and more cigarette smokers chose to smoke filtered as distinct from unfiltered cigarettes, in an effort to ingest less of the toxins in tobacco. By the 1990s, about 95 percent of all smokers were using filtered brands.[12]

Unfortunately, the dominance of filtered cigarettes has not lessened the health consequences of smoking, only created the illusion of having done so. One problem is that when filtered cigarettes were introduced, the industry changed the formulation of the cigarette tobacco, substituting a stronger blend of tobacco with an increased tar content. Tar, as will be shown, represents a major factor in smokers' health problems, but it is also the primary source of a cigarette's flavor.

In short, a higher-tar blend of tobacco was used to satisfy the consumer, even though it essentially counteracted the point of using a filter in the first place or even made matters worse. As a result of a stronger "filter blend" formula in the cigarette, **sidestream smoke**, the smoke directly inhaled by a nonsmoker from a burning cigarette, ends up more toxic when originating from a

filtered cigarette than it is from an unfiltered one. In principle, a cigarette filter should allow a flow of air through small holes in the filter itself. Because a smoker typically holds the cigarette with the fingers covering these holes, however, little or no filtering is accomplished.

From the standpoint of profits, filtered cigarettes were a boon to the tobacco industry. Filters were only paper and therefore cost considerably less than filling the same space with tobacco. One prominent brand went one step further in the 1960s by advertising its recessed filter as "a neat, clean, quarter inch away," giving the further illusion of filtering away impurities but actually only creating air space.[13]

A third consequence was a direct response to the assertion by the surgeon general that tar and nicotine were specifically responsible for increased health risks from smoking. New cigarette brands were introduced that were low in tar and nicotine (T/N), and the Federal Trade Commission began to issue a listing of tar and nicotine levels in major commercial brands.

As later surgeon general's reports have indicated, however, smokers can essentially cancel out the benefits of switching to low T/N brands by varying the manner in which they smoke a low T/N cigarette. Smokers take more puffs, inhale more deeply, and smoke more of the cigarette when it has a lower T/N level so as to maintain the same amount of nicotine (the same number of nicotine "hits"). Moreover, a greater number of low T/N cigarettes have to be smoked in order to satisfy the smoker's needs. In 2003, Philip Morris announced that the designation of "lowered tar and nicotine" on packages of Marlboro Lights cigarettes would be dropped. Its decision was in response to a 2001 National Cancer Institute report that found no health benefits from smoking low T/N cigarettes instead of regular ones.

In 2007, the Harvard School of Public Health confirmed an earlier report that cigarette manufacturers had increased the nicotine concentrations in tobacco from 1997 to 2005 by 11 percent and also had modified certain design features of the cigarettes themselves to increase the number of puffs per cigarette during smoking. In the "medium/mild" market category, nicotine levels more than doubled from 1998 to 2005 in nonmetholated cigarettes and rose by 22 percent in mentholated cigarettes (Health Line, page 276).[14]

sidestream smoke: Tobacco smoke that is inhaled by nonsmokers from the burning cigarettes of nearby smokers. Also referred to as environmental tobacco smoke.

Tobacco Today: An Industry on the Defensive

The tobacco industry in the United States, since the early 1990s, has faced continuing challenges from federal governmental agencies, as well as individuals and groups who have sued tobacco companies for damages resulting from their ingestion of tobacco products. As a result, at the beginning of the new millennium, the legal and economic status of the tobacco industry has been altered significantly.

A number of major events occurred that would forever change the image of tobacco use in American society. In 1993, the U.S. Environmental Protection Agency (EPA) announced its conclusion from available

environmental tobacco smoke (ETS): Tobacco smoke in the atmosphere as a result of burning cigarettes; also called sidestream or secondary smoke.

research that **environmental tobacco smoke (ETS),** the sidestream smoke in the air that is inhaled by nonsmokers as a result of tobacco smoking, causes lung cancer. Since then, most U.S. states, cities, and communities have enacted laws mandating smoke-free environments in all public and private workplaces, unless ventilated smoking rooms have been provided. It is now commonplace for restaurants, hotels, and other commercial spaces to be completely smoke-free. In 1994, congressional hearings were held on allegations that during the 1970s tobacco companies had suppressed research data obtained in their own research laboratories regarding the hazards of cigarette smoking. Since then, the Philip Morris company has issued a statement, formally admitting that "there is overwhelming medical and scientific consensus that cigarette smoking causes cancer, heart disease, emphysema, and other serious diseases" and that "cigarette smoking is addictive, as that term is most commonly used today." This stance represented a complete reversal of the industry's 1994 congressional testimony regarding tobacco use.

In 1994, tobacco industry executives testified before a congressional committee in defense of cigarette smoking and other tobacco use. In 1999, the Phillp Morris company formally reversed its earlier position that smoking was not addictive.

The Tobacco Settlement

In 1998, the major American tobacco corporations entered into an agreement with all fifty U.S. states to resolve claims that the states should be compensated for the costs of treating people with smoking-related illnesses. Under the terms of the settlement, the tobacco industry agreed to pay the states approximately $246 billion in annual installments over twenty-four years. The tobacco industry also agreed to refrain from marketing tobacco products to those under eighteen and pay $24 million annually over ten years for a research foundation dedicated toward finding ways to reduce smoking among youths. In contrast to earlier proposed settlements, however, tobacco corporations under this agreement would not be penalized if levels of underage smoking did not decline over that period of time. In addition, the settlement did not prevent individuals or groups of individuals from suing tobacco corporations in separate actions.

Has the 1998 tobacco settlement had a specific impact on cigarette smoking among young people? As we will see later in this chapter, there has indeed been a substantial decline since 1998 in smoking levels among secondary school students, but several factors may have been at work. On the one hand, it is difficult to attribute this decline to the intended use of tobacco settlement money to finance tobacco-use prevention programs at the state level. By and large, compensation funds awarded to the states over the years since 1998 have been used to keep taxes down or pay off debt, not to support tobacco-use prevention programs. In 2007, only three states (Maine, Delaware, and Colorado) funded programs at the minimum levels recommended by the U.S. Centers

for Disease Control and Prevention. Seventeen states spent only about half of the minimum amount; thirty states spent less than half, despite studies showing that as the amount of settlement funds that a particular state invests, on a per capita basis, on tobacco use prevention among youths increases, the rate of cigarette smoking among youths in that state decreases.[15]

On the other hand, tobacco companies have increased their cigarette prices to help finance their settlement expenses, and several U.S. states have substantially increased their excise taxes on tobacco products, making cigarette purchases much more difficult for an age group with relatively little money to spend. Recent proposals in several states to increase excise taxes still further, if enacted, have the potential for making the financial burden even greater (Drugs . . . in Focus). It can be argued that cigarette smoking prevalence rates have gone down simply because cigarettes are now simply too expensive. In addition, the settlement has financed an increase in antismoking advertisements on television and other media outlets on a national level (see page 293) that have served to deglamorize the act of smoking, and it has required the removal of specific youth-oriented advertising images, such as Joe Camel, that had portrayed smoking as socially desirable. These developments appear to have been helpful in reducing the prevalence of cigarette smoking among teenagers.[16]

Tobacco Regulation and Global Economics

It should be noted that policy decisions regarding smoking in the United States concern tobacco products sold only within the United States. As will be discussed later in this chapter, many other nations have substantially higher prevalence rates for cigarette smoking, and their governments have taken far fewer steps toward instituting policies to reduce smoking behavior. For American tobacco corporations, an expanding global marketplace for American cigarettes has given them the opportunity for an increase in profits from foreign sales that has largely compensated for the financial losses from a decline in domestic sales. Moreover, in a larger sense, cigarette sales abroad represent a major component of overall U.S. foreign trade. In recent years, U.S. exports of tobacco products have exceeded imports by billions of dollars, creating a significant trade surplus. Therefore, the U.S. trade deficit (defined as an excess of imports over exports) would be worse than it is today were it not for the export of tobacco products to other nations.[17]

Drugs...in Focus

Cigarette Purchases on the Internet

The economic difference can be dramatic. A carton of Marlboro Full Flavor Kings, ordered online from a web site in Paducah, Kentucky, might cost approximately $35, including shipping. No state sales tax is charged, and the state excise tax amounts to 3 cents per pack. In New York City, the same carton would cost about $72, which includes at least $30 in city and state taxes *alone*.

The significant price difference has produced a rapidly expanding industry. In 2006, there were seven times as many Internet cigarette vendors as there were in 2000, and there is every indication that the upward trend has continued. From statistics gathered in 2005, the proportion of vendors from outside the United States reached 45 percent, a four-fold increase, in just two years. About two-thirds of domestic vendors were affiliated with Native American tribal communities.

Internet vendors outside the United States and Native American vendors claim special exemption from charging taxes on their cigarette sales. Other vendors largely ignore existing federal law that requires reporting any transaction across state boundaries to state tax authorities. As of 2006, thirty-four U.S. states have enacted provisions for the collection of excise tax on cigarettes purchased online. These regulations range from enforcing federal law to prohibiting the shipment or delivery of cigarettes to Internet consumers altogether.

The evasion of taxes on Internet cigarette sales has substantial adverse effects on both economic and social levels. First of all, public health programs are deprived of needed funds, since they are largely financed through government revenues. Second, the public health benefits of raising cigarette taxes to reduce smoking rates in high-tax states are undermined by the online availability of lower-cost, tax-free cigarettes. Third, the impact of regulations that serve to restrict cigarette sales to underage youths is diminished, since Internet cigarette vendors seldom do an effective job of checking the age of the purchaser. As access of underage youths to cigarettes becomes more limited in retail stores, more of them will turn to the Internet for this purpose. Youths who have been refused cigarette purchases at a retail outlet are three times more likely to purchase cigarettes online than youths who have successfully purchased cigarettes at a retail store.

Sources: Marcus, Dave, and Beja, Marc (2008, June 4). Smokers ignited over tax hike. *Newsday,* A16–A17. Phan, Monty (2003, June 19). Law smokes out online cigarette sales. *Newsday,* A46. Ribisi, Kurt M., Williams, Rebecca S., and Kim, Annice E. (2003). Internet sales of cigarettes to minors. *Journal of the American Medical Association, 290,* 1356–1359. Ribisi, Kurt M., and Williams, Rebecca S. (2007). Sales and marketing of cigarettes on the Internet: Emerging threats to tobacco control and promising policy solutions. In *Reducing tobacco use: Strategies, barriers, and consequences.* Washington DC: National Academy Press.

What's in Tobacco?

When a smoker inhales from a lit cigarette, the temperature at the tip rises to approximately 1,700 degrees Fahrenheit (926 degrees centigrade), as oxygen is drawn through the tobacco, paper, and other additives. This accounts for the bright glow as a smoker inhales from a cigarette. At

mainstream smoke: The smoke inhaled directly from cigarettes or other tobacco products.

particulate phase: Those components of smoke that consist of particles.

tar: A sticky material found in the particulate phase of tobacco smoke and other pollutants in the air.

this intense heat, more than four thousand separate compounds are oxidized and released through cigarette smoke. The smoker inhales the result as **mainstream smoke,** usually screened through the cigarette filter and cigarette paper. As mentioned earlier, the sidestream smoke that is released from the burning cigarette tip itself is unfiltered, and because it is a product of a slightly less intense burning process occurring between puffs, more unburned particles are contained in the smoke.

In general, we can speak of two components in tobacco smoke. The **particulate phase,** consisting of small particles (one micrometer or larger in diameter) suspended in the smoke, includes water droplets, nicotine, and a collection of compounds that will be referred to collectively as **tar.** The particles in tar constitute the primary source of carcinogenic compounds in tobacco. The second component is the **gaseous phase,** consisting of gas compounds in the smoke, including carbon dioxide, carbon monoxide, ammonia, hydrogen cyanide, acetaldehyde, and acetone. Among these gases, carbon monoxide is clearly the most toxic.

This diverse collection of physiologically active toxins is quite unique to tobacco. One way of putting it is that the fifty thousand to seventy thousand puffs per year that a one-pack-a-day cigarette smoker takes in amounts to a level of pollution far beyond even the most polluted urban environment anywhere in the world.[18] The following sections will focus on three of the most important compounds in tobacco smoke: carbon monoxide, tar, and nicotine.

Carbon Monoxide

As most people know, **carbon monoxide** is an odorless, colorless, tasteless, but extraordinarily toxic gas. It is formed when tobacco burns because the oxidation process is incomplete. In that sense, burning tobacco is similar to an inefficient engine, like a car in need of a tune-up. The danger in carbon monoxide is that it easily attaches itself to hemoglobin, the protein inside red blood cells, occupying those portions of the hemoglobin molecule normally reserved for the transport of oxygen from the lungs to the rest of the body. Carbon monoxide has about a two hundred times greater affinity for hemoglobin than does oxygen, so oxygen does not have much of a chance. Carbon monoxide is also more resistant to detaching itself from hemoglobin, so there is an accumulation of carbon monoxide over time.

The ultimate result of carbon monoxide is a subtle but effective asphyxiation of the body from a lack of oxygen. Generally, people who smoke a pack a day accumulate levels of carbon monoxide in the blood of 25 to 35 parts per million blood components (p.p.m.), with levels of 100 p.p.m. for short periods of time while actually smoking. Of course, greater use of tobacco produces proportionally higher levels of carbon monoxide. Carbon monoxide is the primary culprit in producing cardiovascular disease among smokers, as well as in causing deficiencies in physiological functioning and behavior.[19]

Tar

The quantity of tar in a cigarette varies from levels of 12 to 16 mg per cigarette to less than 6 mg. It also should be noted that the last third of each cigarette contains 50 percent of the total tar, making the final few puffs far more hazardous than the first ones.

The major problem with tar lies in its sticky quality, not unlike that of the material used in paving roads, which allows it to adhere to cells in the lungs and the airways leading to them. Normally, specialized cells with small, hairlike attachments called **cilia** are capable of removing contaminants in the air that might impede the breathing process. These cilia literally sweep the unwanted particles upward to the throat, in a process called the **ciliary escalator,** where they are typically swallowed, digested, and finally excreted from the body through the gastrointestinal system. Components in tar alter the coordination of these cilia so that they can no longer function effectively. The accumulation of sticky tar on the surface of the cells along the pulmonary system permits carcinogenic compounds that normally would have been eliminated to settle on the tissue. As will be discussed later, the resulting cellular changes produce lung cancer, and similar carcinogenic effects in other tissues of the body produce cancer in other organs.[20]

Nicotine

Nicotine is a toxic, dependence-producing psychoactive drug found exclusively in tobacco. It is an oily compound varying in hue from colorless to brown. A few drops of pure nicotine, about 60 mg, on the tongue would quickly kill a healthy adult, and it is commonly used as a major ingredient in insecticides and pesticides of all kinds. Cigarettes, however, contain from 0.5 to 2.0 mg of nicotine (depending on the brand), with about 20 percent being actually inhaled and reaching the bloodstream. This means that 2 to 8 mg of nicotine is ingested per day for a pack-a-day smoker, and 4 to 16 mg of nicotine for a smoker of two packs a day.[21]

Inhaled nicotine from smoking is absorbed extremely rapidly and easily passes through the blood-brain barrier, as well as through the blood-placental barrier in pregnant women, in a few seconds. The entire effect is over in a matter of minutes. By the time a cigarette butt is extinguished, nicotine levels in the blood have peaked, and its

---

gaseous phase: The portion of tobacco smoke that consists of gases.

carbon monoxide: An extremely toxic gas that prevents blood cells from carrying oxygen from the lungs to the rest of the body.

cilia: Small hair cells.

ciliary escalator: The process of pushing back foreign particles that might interfere with breathing upward from the air passages into the throat, where they can be swallowed and excreted through the gastrointestinal tract.

nicotine: The prime psychoactive drug in tobacco products.

breakdown and excretion from the body are well under-way. The elimination half-life of nicotine is approximately two to three hours.

The speed of nicotine absorption ordinarily would be much slower if it were not for the presence of ammonia as an additive in the tobacco blend. The combination of nicotine and ammonia changes the naturally acidic nicotine into an alkalinic free-base form that more easily passes from body tissues into the bloodstream. As a result, ammonia increases the availability of nicotine in the blood, much as the addition of alkaline materials like baking soda converts cocaine into crack cocaine (see Chapter 4). The information that ammonia had been introduced into the manufacture of cigarette tobacco during the 1970s, in an apparent effort to increase the "kick" of nicotine, came to light in 1995 and was confirmed by tobacco industry documents released in 1998.[22]

The primary effect of nicotine is to stimulate CNS receptors that are sensitive to acetylcholine (see Chapter 3). These receptors are called *nicotinic receptors* because they are excited by nicotine. One of the effects of activating them is the release of adrenalin, which increases blood pressure and heart rate. Another effect is to inhibit activity in the gastrointestinal system. At the same time, however, as most smokers will tell you, a cigarette is a relaxing factor in their lives. Part of this reaction may be due to an effect on the brain that promotes a greater level of clear thinking and concentration; another part may relate to the fact that nicotine, at moderate doses, serves to reduce muscle tone so that muscular tightness is decreased. Research has shown that cigarette smoking helps to sustain performance on monotonous tasks and to improve short-term memory. We can assume that it is the nicotine in cigarettes and other tobacco products that is responsible because nicotine tablets have comparable behavioral effects.[23]

The Dependence Potential of Nicotine

Historically, the dependence potential of nicotine has been demonstrated at times in which the usual availability of tobacco has suddenly been curtailed. In Germany following the end of World War II, for example, cigarettes were rationed to two packs a month for men and one pack a month for women. This "cigarette famine" produced dramatic effects on the behavior of German civilians. Smokers bartered their food rations for cigarettes, even under the extreme circumstances of chronic hunger and poor nutrition. Cigarette butts were picked from the dirt in the streets by people who admitted that they were personally disgusted by their desperate behavior. Some women turned to prostitution to obtain cigarettes. Alcoholics of both sexes testified that it was easier to abstain from drinking alcohol than it was to abstain from smoking.[24]

It is now known that nicotine stimulates the release of dopamine in the nucleus accumbens, the same area of the brain responsible for the reinforcing properties of opiates, cocaine, and alcohol.[25] In addition, several behavioral factors combine with this physiological effect to increase the likelihood that a strong dependence will be created. One of these factors is the speed with which smoked nicotine reaches the brain. The delivery time has been estimated as five to eight seconds. A second factor is the wide variety of circumstances and settings surrounding the act of smoking that later come to serve as learned rewards. A smoker may find, for example, that the first cigarette with a cup of coffee in the morning (a source of another psychoactive drug, caffeine) is strongly reinforcing. As a major researcher in this area has expressed it,

> Smoking . . . comes to be rewarded by the enjoyment of oral, manual, and respiratory manipulations involved in the process of lighting, puffing, and handling cigarettes, the pleasure and relaxation associated with using alcohol, finishing a good meal, . . . and the perceived diminution of unpleasant affective [emotional] states of anxiety, tension, boredom, or fatigue. . . . No other substance can provide so many kinds of rewards, is so readily and cheaply available, and can be used in so many settings and situations.[26]

A third factor is the sheer number of times the smoker experiences a dose of nicotine. When you consider that a smoker takes from one to two hundred puffs each day from the twenty cigarettes that represent a pack-a-day pattern of smoking, you realize that smoking is a highly practiced, overlearned behavior.[27]

The Titration Hypothesis of Nicotine Dependence

There is considerable evidence that smokers adjust their smoking behavior to obtain a stable dose of nicotine from whatever cigarettes they are smoking, an idea called the **titration hypothesis.** When exposed to cigarettes of decreasing nicotine content, smokers will

titration hypothesis: The idea that smokers will adjust their smoking of cigarettes so as to maintain a steady input of nicotine into the body.

smoke a greater number of them to compensate and will increase the volume of each puff. When they inhale more puffs per cigarette, a greater interval of time will elapse before they light up another one. If they are given nicotine gum to chew, the intensity of their smoking behavior will decline, even though they have not been told whether the gum contains nicotine or is a placebo. All these studies indicate that experienced smokers arrive at a consistent "style" of smoking that provides their bodies with a relatively constant level of nicotine.[28]

Tolerance and Withdrawal

First-time smokers often react to a cigarette with a mixture of nausea, dizziness, or vomiting. These effects typically disappear as tolerance develops in the nicotinic receptors in the brain. Other physiological effects, such as increases in heart rate, tremors, and changes in skin temperature, show weaker tolerance effects or none at all.

The strongest dependence-related effect of cigarette smoking can be seen in the symptoms of withdrawal that follow the discontinuation of smoking. Within about six hours after the last cigarette, a smoker's heart rate and blood pressure will decrease. Over the next twenty-four hours, common symptoms will include headache, an inability to concentrate, irritability, drowsiness, and fatigue, as well as insomnia and other sleep disturbances. Most striking of all are the strong feelings of craving for a cigarette. Ex-smokers can attest to cravings that slowly diminish but nonetheless linger on for months and, in some cases, for years.[29]

Nicotine dependence is the central factor in the continuation of smoking behaviors. The level of dependence is significant, even when compared with dependence levels of illicit drugs available on the street. In a study of people who smoked and were also in some form of drug-abuse treatment, 74 percent judged the difficulty of quitting smoking to be at least as great as the difficulty in stopping their drug of choice. One in three considered it "much harder" to quit smoking.[30]

Health Consequences of Tobacco Use

The adverse health consequences of tobacco use can be classified in three broad categories: cardiovascular disease, respiratory disease, and cancer. In addition, there are special health difficulties that smoking can bring to women and hazards from using smokeless tobacco. An enormous literature on the adverse effects

Health Line

Visualizing 400,000 to 450,000 Annual Tobacco-Related Deaths

The estimated annual death toll due to tobacco-related diseases is staggering but often difficult to visualize. In 2007, the following U.S. cities had populations in the neighborhood of this number. Imagine losing the entire community in any of these cities each year, or all of them in six years.

- Kansas City, Missouri (pop. 450,375)
- Cleveland, Ohio (pop. 438,042)
- Virginia Beach, Virginia (pop. 434,743)
- Omaha, Nebraska (pop. 424,482)
- Miami, Florida (pop. 409,719)
- Oakland, California (pop. 401,489)

Source: United States Census, 2007 estimates.

of tobacco use has grown steadily since the original surgeon general's report in 1964, though by that time more than thirty thousand research studies had been conducted on the question.

Beyond all the research reports are the sheer numbers of people who are affected. In the United States alone, of the estimated half-million deaths each year that are attributed to substance abuse of one kind or another, approximately 438,000 are specifically tied to tobacco use. This figure is higher than the total number of American casualties during World War II (Health Line). The public health community considers these deaths to be premature deaths because they are entirely preventable; these people would have been alive if their behaviors had been different.

The numbers are simple, and staggering: Smoking-related deaths account for nearly one out of every five deaths in the United States every year, about 1,200 deaths each day. A person's life is shortened by fourteen minutes every time a cigarette is smoked. Smoking two packs a day for twenty years reduces one's lifespan by approximately eight years.

An estimated 8.6 million persons in the United States have serious illnesses that are attributable to cigarette smoking. Unlike alcohol, which presents no significant health hazards when consumed in moderation, tobacco is a dangerous product *when used as intended* (Figure 11.1).[31]

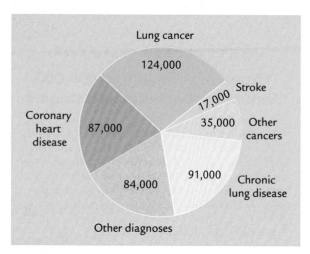

FIGURE 11.1

The distribution of approximately 438,000 U.S. deaths attributed each year to tobacco use.

Source: Centers for Disease Control and Prevention (2005, July 1). *Morbidity and Mortality Weekly Report.* Atlanta: Centers for Disease Control and Prevention.

Cardiovascular Disease

Cardiovascular disease includes a number of specific conditions. Some of these diseases are **coronary heart disease (CHD)**, in which damage to the heart is incurred due to the restriction of blood flow through narrowed or blocked coronary arteries; **arteriosclerosis,** in which the walls of arteries harden and lose their elasticity; **atherosclerosis,** in which fatty deposits inside arteries impede blood flow; and ischemic stroke, in which interruption or reduction in blood flow causes damage to the brain. In all these diseases, cigarette smoking increases the risk dramatically.

We know now that smoking is responsible for

---

coronary heart disease (CHD): Disease that damages the heart as a result of a restriction of blood flow through coronary arteries.

arteriosclerosis (ar-TEER-ee-oh-scluh-ROH-sis): A disease in which blood flow is restricted because the walls of arteries harden and lose their elasticity.

atherosclerosis (ATH-er-oh-scluh-ROH-sis): A disease in which blood flow is restricted because of the buildup of fatty deposits inside arteries.

chronic obstructive pulmonary disease (COPD): A group of diseases characterized by impaired breathing due to an abnormality in the air passages.

chronic bronchitis: A respiratory disease involving inflammation of bronchial tissue following a buildup of excess mucus in air passages.

---

approximately 30 percent of all CHD deaths. The risk of CHD doubles if you smoke and quadruples if you smoke heavily. On average, smoking also raises the risk of a sudden death (such as from a fatal heart attack) by two to four times, with the degree of risk increasing as a direct function of how many cigarettes are smoked per day. To put it even more boldly, it has been estimated that unless smoking patterns change dramatically in the future, about 10 percent of all Americans now alive may die prematurely from some form of heart disease as a result of their smoking behavior. Yet, strangely enough, only 29 percent of current smokers and only 39 percent of heavy smokers believe that they have a higher-than-average risk of a heart attack.[32]

These statistics are strengthened by the understanding we have of how cigarette smoking actually produces these dangerous cardiovascular conditions. The major villains are nicotine and carbon monoxide. Nicotine, as a stimulant drug, increases the contraction of heart muscle and elevates heart rate.

At the same time, nicotine causes a constriction of blood vessels, leading to a rise in blood pressure, and also increases *platelet adhesiveness* in the blood. As a result of a greater adhesiveness, platelets clump together and increase the risk of developing a blood clot. If a clot forms within coronary arteries, a heart attack can occur; a clot traveling into the blood vessels of the brain can produce a stroke. Finally, nicotine increases the body's serum cholesterol and fatty deposits, leading to the development of atherosclerosis.

While nicotine is doing its dirty work, carbon monoxide makes matters worse. A lack of oxygen puts further strain on the ability of the heart to function under already trying circumstances.[33]

Respiratory Diseases

The general term **chronic obstructive pulmonary disease (COPD)** refers to several conditions in which breathing is impaired because of some abnormality in the air passages either leading to or within the lungs. Although only 20 percent of smokers in the United States develop COPD, 80 to 90 percent of all COPD cases are the result of smoking. Historically, COPD has been viewed as "a man's disease," but since 1980 the death rate in women has tripled, and since 2000, more women than men have died or been hospitalized each year as a result of COPD. With the exception of a rare genetic defect, smoking is the only established cause of clinically significant COPD.

Two examples of COPD are **chronic bronchitis,** in which excess mucus builds up in air passages, leading to an inflammation of bronchial tissue, and **emphysema,** in which air sacs in the lungs are abnormally enlarged and the air sac walls either become inelastic or rupture, leading to extreme difficulty in inhaling oxygen and exhaling carbon dioxide. In the case of advanced emphysema, more than 80 percent of a patient's energy is required merely to breathe. These two diseases account for more than seventy thousand deaths each year, and many additional thousands are forced to lead increasingly debilitating lives, gasping and struggling each day to breathe:

> Many of [the thousands of people with COPD] are attached to oxygen tanks, imprisoned at home or in the hospital because they are too weak to breathe on their own. Often their friends or family members will pound on their backs, temporarily freeing the lungs of the yellow mucus that impedes their breathing every day.[34]

Pulmonary damage, however, is not limited to adults who have been smoking for many years. Cigarette smoking is also associated with airway obstruction and slower growth of lung function in younger populations. Adolescents who smoke five or more cigarettes a day are 40 percent more likely to develop asthma and 30 percent more likely to have symptoms of wheezing but not asthma than those who do not smoke. Among smokers, girls show a greater loss of pulmonary function than boys, even though boys report that they smoke more cigarettes.[35]

Lung Cancer

At the beginning of the twentieth century, lung cancer was a rare disease. Its steady increase in the United States as well as the rest of the world since then has occurred in direct proportion to the growing prevalence of cigarette smoking and other tobacco use. Today, nearly 90 percent of the more than approximately 213,000 new cases of lung cancer in the United States in 2007 have been determined by the American Cancer Society to be due to smoking. While there has been a steady decline in deaths due to lung cancer among American males since 1990, there remains an approximately 35 percent greater mortality rate among African American males due to smoking relative to white males. In general, males who are currently smoking incur a risk of lung cancer that is about twenty-two times higher than the risk for nonsmokers.

Another important change has occurred over the years with respect to the incidence of lung cancer among women. Like COPD, lung cancer was once considered to be limited largely to male smokers. More recently, however, increasing numbers of women have contracted lung cancer as a result of their increased level of cigarette smoking. The age-adjusted mortality rate for women is still about one-half that for men, but the decline in mortality rates seen among men since 1990 has yet to be realized among women. Since 1988, lung cancer has exceeded breast cancer as the leading cause of cancer deaths among women (Figure 11.2, page 284). In general, females who are currently smoking incur a risk of lung cancer that is about twelve times higher than that for nonsmokers.

These facts about lung cancer become even more tragic when you consider that the overall five-year survival rate after initial diagnosis of lung cancer (for all stages of cancer combined) is only 15 percent. Lung cancer patients have an approximately 50 percent chance of living five years when the disease is still localized at the time of diagnosis, but only 15 percent of lung cancers are diagnosed at this early stage.

As discussed earlier in the chapter, the exposure to tar in cigarette smoke disrupts the necessary action of ciliary cells in the bronchial tubes leading to the lungs. Without their protective function, the lungs are open to attack. Several carcinogenic compounds in the smoke can now enter the lungs and stimulate the formation of cancerous growths, **carcinomas,** in lung tissue. One of these compounds, *benzopyrene,* has been found to cause genetic mutations in cells that are identical to the mutations observed in patients who have developed carcinomas in their lungs. This finding is important because it establishes a causal link between a specific ingredient in tobacco smoke and human cases of cancer.[36]

Other Cancers

Certainly lung cancer is the best-known and most common example of smoking-related cancers; unfortunately, other organs are affected in a similar way. In the United States, approximately 30 percent of cancer deaths *of all types* have been linked to smoking. It has been estimated that smokers increase their risk by two to twenty-seven times for cancer of the larynx, thirteen times for mouth or lip cancer, two to three times for bladder cancer, two times for pancreatic cancer, and five times for cancers of the kidney or uterine cervix.[37]

---

emphysema (EM-fuh-SEE-mah): An enlargement of air sacs in the lungs and abnormalities in the air sac walls, causing great difficulty in breathing.

carcinomas (CAR-sih-NOH-mas): Cancerous tumors or growths.

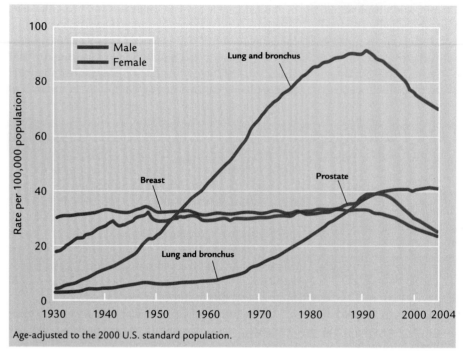

Despite a widespread belief to the contrary, using smokeless tobacco, in the form of chewing tobacco or snuff, does not prevent the user from incurring an increased risk of cancer. Continuing contact with tobacco in the mouth has been shown to produce precancerous cell changes, as revealed by **leukoplakia** (white spots) and **erythroplakia** (red spots) inside the mouth and nasal cavity. Even though smokeless tobacco obviously avoids the problems associated with tobacco smoke, it does not prevent the user from being exposed to carcinogens, specifically a class of compounds called **nitrosamines** that are present in all tobacco products. As a result of federal legislation enacted in 1986, all forms of smokeless tobacco must contain, on the package, a set of specific warnings that these products may cause mouth cancer as well as gum disease and tooth loss (Health Alert). To reinforce the idea that dangers are still present in smokeless tobacco, one of these warnings reads: "This product is not a safe alternative to cigarette smoking."

leukoplakia (LOO-koh-PLAY-kee-ah): Small white spots inside the mouth and nasal cavity, indicating precancerous tissue.
erythroplakia (eh-RITH-ro-PLAY-kee-ah): Small red spots inside the mouth and nasal cavity, indicating precancerous tissue.
nitrosamines (nih-TRAW-seh-meens): A group of carcinogenic compounds found in tobacco.

Special Health Concerns for Women

Tobacco use presents specific health risk concerns for women. Women who smoke have a more than three times greater risk of dying from stroke due to brain hemorrhaging and an almost two times greater risk of dying from a heart attack. Added to these concerns is the toxic interaction of tobacco smoke with birth control pills. If they are using birth control pills as well, the risk increases to twenty-two times and twenty times, respectively.

The higher risk of low birth weight and physical defects in the newborn due to the mother's smoking during pregnancy was discussed in Chapter 2. In addition, a recent study has shown a specific elevation in systolic blood pressure at about 2 months of age among infants whose mothers smoked during pregnancy.[38] Even though there has been a decline in smoking in recent years among pregnant women, more than one in six pregnant women (17 percent) have smoked in the past month, with more of them smoking in their first trimester of pregnancy (22 percent) than in their second or third trimester (14 percent and 15 percent, respectively).

The Hazards of Environmental Smoke

In the early days of development of methods for detecting the effects of nicotine in the bloodstream, scientists were puzzled to find traces of a nicotine metabolite in ing as much of it after one hour in a very smoky room as will a smoker after smoking ten to fifteen cigarettes.[39]

The U.S. surgeon general's report on involuntary exposure to tobacco smoke in 2006 has confirmed previous data on this question and extended its conclusions to the following:

- For nonsmoking adults, exposure to environmental smoke raises the risk of heart disease by 25 to 30 percent in both men and women. The risk of lung cancer is increased by 20 to 30 percent among nonsmokers who live with a smoker.
- Environmental smoke is a cause of sudden infant death syndrome (SIDS), accounting for 430 deaths per year in the United States. The risk is higher for children whose mothers were exposed to tobacco smoke during pregnancy and for children exposed during infancy.
- Among children of parents who smoke in the home, there is an increased risk of lower respiratory illnesses such as bronchitis, middle ear disease, wheezing, and childhood asthma.

It is estimated that environmental smoke exposure accounts for 46,000 premature deaths from heart disease and 3,000 premature deaths from cancer among adults in the United States each year. Although the proportion of nonsmokers has declined substantially as a result of publicity about the hazards of ETS and extensive smoking bans

nonsmokers. They suspected at first that there was some flaw in their analysis but later had to conclude that their measurements were indeed accurate. Nonsmokers testing positive had shared car rides or workplaces with smokers shortly before their tests. Today, a large body of evidence indicates not only the presence of tobacco smoke compounds in the bodies of nonsmokers but also the adverse consequences that such "involuntary smoking" can provoke. In other words, environmental tobacco smoke is a significant health hazard even to people who are not actively smoking.

Approximately 85 percent of the smoke in an average room where people are smoking cigarettes is generated by sidestream smoke, and about three-fourths of the nicotine originating from these cigarettes ends up in the atmosphere. In some cases, the carcinogens released in ETS are so potent that they are dangerous even in their diluted state. For example, N-nitrosamine (an example of a group of carcinogens mentioned earlier in connection with smokeless tobacco) is so much more concentrated in sidestream smoke than in mainstream smoke that nonsmokers will end up inhal-

Quick Concept Check   II.I

Understanding the Effects of Tobacco Smoking

Check your understanding of the effects of tobacco smoking by associating each of the following physical effects with (a) carbon monoxide, (b) tar, or (c) nicotine. It is possible to have a combination of two factors as the correct answer.

1. a decrease in oxygen in the body
2. physical dependence
3. cellular changes leading to cancer
4. cardiovascular disease
5. chronic bronchitis

Answers: 1. a   2. c   3. b   4. a and c   5. b

and restrictions, more than 126 million Americans remain subject to exposure at some time in their lives.[40]

Patterns of Smoking Behavior and Use of Smokeless Tobacco

In 1965, about 40 percent of all American teenagers and adults smoked cigarettes, and it is estimated that more than 50 percent did in the 1940s. In 2007, however, according to the National Survey on Drug Use and Health, approximately 24 percent of people aged twelve or older smoked a cigarette within the past month, qualifying as current smokers. Though this percentage is significantly less than it had been, we are still considering a very large number of people. Extrapolating to the U.S. population, a 24 percent prevalence rate corresponds to approximately 60 million Americans. American Indians and Alaska natives are more likely to smoke than any other group in the United States, with 34 percent of adults defined as smokers. In contrast, individuals of Asian descent are the least likely to smoke, with just 14 percent admitting to have smoked a cigarette in the past month.

A steady decline in the percentage of American adult smokers stopped around 1991, and the prevalence rate has declined only slightly since then. Among college students, thirty-day prevalence rates had been increasing from 1990 to 1999, but since then they have declined by 50 percent. In 2007, about 20 percent of college students had smoked cigarettes within the previous month, a lower proportion than the national average. About 14 percent of tenth graders in 2007 and 22 percent of high school seniors reported cigarette smoking within the previous month. It is unlikely that many tenth and twelfth graders will have begun smoking past this point in their lives.[41]

The Youngest Smokers

In the 2008 University of Michigan survey, approximately 21 percent of eighth graders reported that they had tried cigarettes in their lifetime and about 7 percent reported smoking at least once in the previous month. These figures are down substantially from the 49 and 21 percent figures, respectively, found in 1996. Approximately 3 percent of eighth graders smoked on a daily basis in 2008, and about 1 percent had smoked at least a half a pack a day, once again down substantially from 10 and 4 percent, respectively, in 1996.

In previous Michigan surveys, the peak years for starting to smoke have been reported to be in the sixth and seventh grade, though a significant number of eighth graders qualifying as regular smokers have said that they had started earlier. About 16 percent have reported that they had begun prior to the sixth grade; in fact, about 8 percent have reported that they had started prior to the fifth grade. In general, it has been estimated that between 80 and 90 percent of regular smokers began to smoke by the age of eighteen.[42]

Attitudes toward Smoking among Young People

Adolescent attitudes toward cigarette smoking have changed dramatically during the early years of the twenty-first century. In general, young people in middle and high school have become less accepting of cigarette smoking. About 87 percent of eighth graders, for example, reported in 2008 their disapproval of someone smoking a pack of cigarettes per day and 60 percent reported that such behavior would present "great risk" of harming themselves physically or otherwise.

Interestingly, adolescent attitudes toward the *social* aspects of smoking have become more negative as well. About half of tenth and twelfth graders agree with the statement "I strongly dislike being near people who are smoking." Between 75 and 80 percent of them prefer to date nonsmokers. About six out of ten view smoking as a behavior that reflects poor judgment on the part of those who smoke. The continuing disinclination toward dating smokers over recent years has been observed equally among males and females.[43] As Lloyd D. Johnston of the University of Michigan has observed:

> It now appears that taking up smoking makes a youngster less attractive to the great majority of the opposite sex, just the opposite of what cigarette advertising has been promising all these years. I think this is something that teens need to know, because it may be the most compelling argument for why they should abstain from smoking or, for that matter, quit if they have already started.[44]

In 1997, the FDA established eighteen as the national minimum age at which tobacco products could be purchased and required vendors to verify the ages of purchasers up to the age of twenty-seven as a means for reducing the access of young people to tobacco. In some U.S. states, efforts are under way to raise the minimum age for tobacco purchases to nineteen or twenty-one. This change would prevent high school seniors from buying cigarettes for their younger friends.

With regard to standards set in federal regulations on underage smoking, compliance rates on the part of tobacco retail vendors nationwide reached 80 percent in

Doonesbury

BY GARRY TRUDEAU

The nine-year Joe Camel advertising campaign ended in 1997 as opposition mounted against tobacco promotions targeting youth. Here is a parody from the early 1990s of the Camel campaign through the eyes of Garry Trudeau, creator of *Doonesbury*.

2006, which was substantially higher than the 60 percent rate reported in 1996. However, about 57 percent of eighth graders have said in 2008 that cigarettes were fairly easy or very easy to get. This percentage is significantly lower than percentages reported in the 1990s, but it still reflects relatively easy access.[45]

Use of Smokeless Tobacco

Smokeless tobacco is ingested, as the name implies, by absorption through the membranes of the mouth rather than by inhalation of smoke into the lungs (Table 11.1, page 288). The two most common forms are the traditional loose-leaf chewing tobacco (brand names include Red Man and Beech Nut) and moist, more finely shredded tobacco called **moist snuff** or simply snuff (brand names include Copenhagen and Skoal). Snuff, by the way, is no longer sniffed into the nose, as in the eighteenth century, but rather placed inside the cheek or alongside the gum under the lower lip. Some varieties of snuff are available in a small absorbent-paper sack (like a tea bag) so that the tobacco particles do not get stuck in the teeth. The practice is called "dipping."

In the national sample responding to the University of Michigan survey, about 4 percent of eighth graders, 5 percent of tenth graders, and 7 percent of high school seniors in 2008 had used smokeless tobacco within the previous thirty days. In general, smokeless tobacco use among teens is down substantially from the peak levels reported in the mid-1990s. More so than with respect to cigarette smoking, major demographic differences exist in the prevalence of

moist snuff: Damp, finely shredded tobacco, placed inside the cheek or alongside the gum under the lower lip.

smokeless tobacco use. Prevalence rates are substantially higher for males than for females, for eighth graders in the southern region of the United States than for those in the Northeast, Midwest, or West, and for white students than for African American and Latino students. In general, the greatest concentration of smokeless tobacco use is reported in nonmetropolitan areas of the nation.[46]

Currently, the form of smokeless tobacco showing the most consistent gains in recent sales is moist snuff, with some brands sold in cherry or wintergreen flavors. As with cigarette tobacco, variations in the alkalinity of different brands of moist snuff allow for different percentages of the nicotine in the tobacco to be absorbed through the membranes of the mouth. Thus, snuff users typically start with brands that release relatively low levels of nicotine, then "graduate" to more potent brands. The most potent brand on the current market, Copenhagen, is also the best-selling snuff in the United States.[47]

Cigarette smoking among minors is a continuing social problem.

TABLE 11.1

Forms of smokeless tobacco

TYPE	DESCRIPTION
Chewing tobacco	
Loose-leaf	Made of cigar-leaf tobacco, sold in small packages, heavily flavored or plain
Fine-cut	Similar to loose-leaf but more finely cut so that it resembles snuff
Plug	Leaf tobacco pressed into flat cakes and sweetened with molasses, licorice, maple sugar, or honey
Twist	Made of stemmed leaves twisted into small rolls and then folded
(Chewing tobacco is not really chewed but rather held in the mouth between the cheek and lower jaw.)	
Snuff	
Dry, moist, sweetened, flavored, salted, scented	
(A pinch of snuff, called a *quid*, is typically tucked between the gum and the lower lip. Moist varieties are currently the most popular.)	

Source: Adapted from Popescu, Cathy (1992). The health hazards of smokeless tobacco. In Kristine Napier (Ed.), *Issues in tobacco.* New York: American Council on Science and Health, pp. 11–12.

Despite continuing warnings that smokeless tobacco presents great risk to one's health, its popularity continues. As stated earlier, while smokeless tobacco presents no immediate danger to the lungs, there are substantial adverse effects on other organs of the body. At the very least, regular use of smokeless tobacco increases the risk of gum disease, damage to tooth enamel, and eventually the loss of teeth. More seriously, the direct contact of the tobacco with membranes of the mouth allows carcinogenic nitrosamines to cause tissue changes that can lead to oral cancer. Delay in the treatment of oral cancer increases the likelihood of the cancer spreading to the jaw, pharynx, and neck. When swallowed, saliva containing nitrosamines can produce stomach and urinary tract cancer. Moreover, all the negative consequences of ingesting nicotine during tobacco smoking are also present in the use of smokeless tobacco.[48]

Cigars and Flavored Cigarettes

For a brief time in the 1990s, there was a resurgence in the popularity of cigars, spurred on by images of media stars, both male and female, who had taken up cigar smoking as the tobacco use of choice. The cigar suddenly was fashionable.

By the end of the decade, however, the cigar-smoking craze had "gone up in smoke." While part of the problem related to changing market conditions for imported cigars, a major contributing factor was the increasing recognition that cigars could not be regarded as a safe alternative to cigarettes.[49] Cigar smoke is more alkaline than cigarette smoke, so the nicotine content in cigars can be absorbed directly through tissues lining the mouth rather than requiring inhalation into the lungs. In addition, due to the tar content, the risk of lung cancer is five times higher for those who smoke cigars, eight times higher for those smoking three or more cigars a day, and eleven times higher for those inhaling the smoke of cigars, relative to nonsmokers. Regular cigar smokers have a doubled risk, relative to nonsmokers, for cancers of the mouth, throat, and esophagus; they also incur a 45 percent higher risk of COPD and a 27 percent higher risk of coronary heart disease (Portrait). Major cigar manufacturers have now agreed to place warning labels on their products, alerting consumers to the risk of mouth and throat cancer, lung cancer and heart disease, and hazards to fertility and unborn children.[50]

More recently, another phenomenon in tobacco use is worth noting: the increasing popularity of flavored cigarettes. Hand-rolled cigarettes from India, flavored with cinnamon, orange, strawberry, or chocolate, called *bidis* (pronounced BEE-dees), and clove-flavored cigarettes from Indonesia, called *kreteks* (pronounced KRAY-teks) have become popular among teenagers. The annual prevalence rates among high school seniors for smoking bidis or kreteks in 2008 were 2 percent and 7 percent, respectively. These figures are substantially lower than those for regular cigarettes, but significant health concerns remain. Bidis and kreteks are unfiltered, contain higher nicotine and tar concentrations than traditional American brands, and require more vigorous puffing, thus pulling a greater amount of smoke into the lungs.[51]

Since 1999, flavored American-brand cigarettes have also become available. Kool cigarettes are marketed in Caribbean Chill, Midnight Berry, Mocha Taboo, and Mintrique varieties. Flavored versions of Camel cigarettes known as Exotic Camel Blends include Crema, Dark Mint, Mandarin Mint, and Bayou Blast (the latter marketed nationwide as a tie-in with Mardi Gras). Health professionals have criticized these new products as ways to appeal to young nonsmokers, an assertion that the tobacco industry denies.[52]

Sigmund Freud—Nicotine Dependence, Cigars, and Cancer

Probably the best-known photograph of Sigmund Freud, founder of psychoanalysis and one-time proponent of cocaine use (see Chapter 4), shows him with a cigar in hand. Given that Freud typically smoked twenty cigars each day, it is not surprising that he did not set it aside merely to have his picture taken. But there is a story behind this photograph, a lesson about the power of smoking over the will to stop and the tragic health consequences when the will succumbs.

In 1923, at the age of sixty-seven, Freud noted sores on his palate and jaw that failed to heal, a sign of oral cancer. Surgery was indicated and fortunately proved successful in removing the cancerous tissue. This would be only the first of thirty-three surgical operations on the jaw and oral cavity that Freud was to endure for the remaining sixteen years of his life. As the leukoplakia and finally genuine carcinomas returned to his mouth, he was repeatedly warned by specialists that his practice of smoking cigars was the root of his problems and that he must stop. Despite these warnings, Freud kept on smoking.

Freud tried very hard to stop; indeed, sometimes he would not smoke for a few weeks at a time. In addition to his problems with cancer, he suffered from chest pains called "tobacco angina." In 1936, the angina became acutely painful and as his biographer, Ernest Jones, has noted, "It was evidently exacerbated by nicotine, since it was relieved as soon as he stopped smoking."

By this time, Freud's jaw had been entirely removed and an artificial jaw substituted in its place. He was almost constantly in pain, often could not speak, and sometimes could not eat or swallow. Despite the agony, Freud still smoked a steady stream of cigars until he finally died at the age of eighty-three.

Here was a man whom many consider to be one of the intellectual giants of the twentieth century. Yet the giant was a slave to his cigars.

Source: Brecher, Ruth; Brecher, Edward; Herzog, Arthur; Goodman, Walter; Walker, Gerald; and the Editors of *Consumer Reports* (1963). *The Consumer Union's report on smoking and the public interest.* Mount Vernon, NY: Consumer Union, pp. 91–95.

Tobacco Use around the World

Since the seventeenth century, the practice of tobacco smoking has spread throughout the world, but until the 1980s the behavior itself had been largely independent of American tobacco corporations. Today, the picture has changed dramatically. Between 1985 and 1994 alone, U.S. cigarette exports to Japan increased 700 percent and to South Korea increased 1200 percent. In the late 1990s, American-made cigarettes moved into significant markets in Eastern Europe and Russia, where smoking prevalence rates are substantially higher than those in the United States (Figure 11.3, page 290). Presently, U.S. tobacco exports total more than $6 billion each year.

Unfortunately, the prevalence rate of smoking in many foreign countries far exceeds that of the United States, coupled with substantially less public concern for the consequences of smoking on health. In Japan, for example, 53 percent of all adult men smoke cigarettes. No-smoking sections in restaurants and offices are uncommon; approximately half a million outdoor vending machines allow minors to purchase cigarettes easily, though officially such sales are illegal; and there is little or no governmental opposition to smoking in general. The Japanese currently enjoy the longest life expectancy in the world, but health officials are concerned that this status is certain to change over the next twenty years. Deaths from lung, tracheal, and bronchial cancer among the Japanese have risen dramatically since 1980, and there is little indication that this trend will moderate in the future.[53]

Perhaps nowhere in the world is the impact of cigarette smoking on public health more evident than in present-day China. Because of its huge population, an estimated 300 to 340 million Chinese smokers, out of a population of 900 million adults, account for 30 percent of the world's total consumption of tobacco. Approximately 67 percent of all Chinese men smoke regularly. One million Chinese die each year from tobacco-related illnesses and, unless smoking patterns change, 3 million are expected to die by 2050.

Clearly, tobacco use on a global scale presents one of the most significant public health challenges we face in the twenty-first century. According to the World Health Organization (WHO), an estimated 5.4 million people worldwide die each year from tobacco-related diseases, and this figure is projected to increase to approximately 10 million by 2030. In the twentieth century, tobacco smoking contributed to the deaths of 100 million people worldwide. During the twenty-first century, the death toll could rise as high as a billion people.

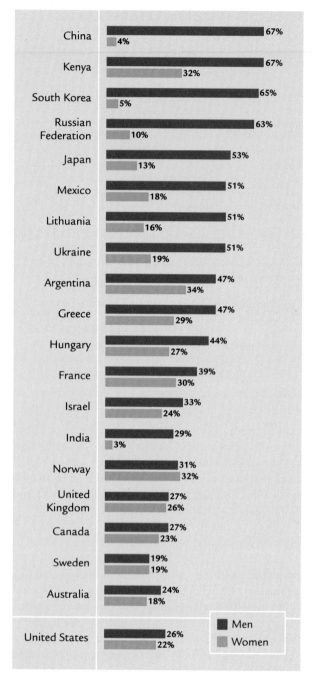

Country	Men	Women
China	67%	4%
Kenya	67%	32%
South Korea	65%	5%
Russian Federation	63%	10%
Japan	53%	13%
Mexico	51%	18%
Lithuania	51%	16%
Ukraine	51%	19%
Argentina	47%	34%
Greece	47%	29%
Hungary	44%	27%
France	39%	30%
Israel	33%	24%
India	29%	3%
Norway	31%	32%
United Kingdom	27%	26%
Canada	27%	23%
Sweden	19%	19%
Australia	24%	18%
United States	26%	22%

FIGURE 11.3

Smoking rates for men and women over fifteen years old in selected countries.

Source: Mackay, Judith, and Eriksen, Michael (2003). *The tobacco atlas.* Geneva, Switzerland: World Health Organization, Table A. Reprinted with permission.

Note: Percentages for the United States differ slightly from data in the National Household Survey on Drug Use and Health, due to differences in criteria and age range.

A young student enjoys a cigarette with friends before class outside his school in Perm, Russia. There are regulations against smoking in public places, but they are routinely ignored and rarely enforced. Smoking-related illnesses are among the reasons that the life expectancy for men in Russia dropped to fifty-nine years.

Making matters worse, global approaches to reducing the deadly effects of tobacco use are discouragingly weak or absent. Approximately 40 percent of countries in the world still allow smoking in hospitals and schools; only 5 percent of the world's population lives in a country that imposes a comprehensive national ban on tobacco advertising. Only 5 percent of the world's population lives in a country in which full services to treat tobacco dependence are widely available.[54]

In recognition of the enormous health crisis that exists at present and the potential calamity that looms in the future, a Framework Convention on Tobacco Control was unanimously adopted in May 2003 by the World Health Assembly at the WHO headquarters in Geneva, setting objectives for tobacco-use prevention and tobacco advertisements. By 2008, 150 nations out of the 192-nation membership had ratified the agreement. Progress, however, has not been easy. Governments around the world collect more than $200 billion dollars each year in taxes imposed on tobacco sales. In some cases, governments are dependent on these tax revenues to sustain their economies. In other cases, governments receive direct profits from state-owned tobacco corporations.[55]

Quitting Smoking: The Good News and the Bad

There is no question that tobacco use of any kind is harmful to your health as well as your wallet, and it is indeed hard to quit once you have started. But there's some good news with respect to the consequences of quitting.

The Good News: Undoing the Damage

Given the grim story of all the documented health risks associated with tobacco, it is at least reassuring to know that if a smoker does succeed in quitting, some of the damage can be undone. Here are the benefits:

- Within eight hours—Carbon monoxide levels in the blood drop to normal.
- Within twenty-four hours—Chances of a heart attack decrease.
- Within two weeks to three months—Circulation improves. Lung function increases by up to 30 percent.
- Within one to nine months—Coughing, sinus congestion, fatigue, and shortness of breath decrease. Cilia regain normal function in the lungs, increasing ability to handle mucus, clean the lungs, and reduce infection.
- Within one year—Excess risk of coronary heart disease is half that of a smoker.
- Within five to ten years—Risk of stroke is reduced to that of a nonsmoker.
- Within ten years—Lung cancer death rate is about half that of a continuing smoker.
- Within fifteen years—Risk of coronary heart disease is equal to that of a nonsmoker.[56]

The Bad News: How Hard It Is to Quit

The advantages of quitting are real and most people are aware of them, but the fact remains that, in the words of the surgeon general's report in 1988, "The pharmacologic and behavioral processes that determine tobacco addiction are similar to those that determine addiction to drugs such as heroin and cocaine."[57] It may be easy to quit smoking for a short while but it is very difficult to avoid a relapse, as any former or present smoker will tell you (Health Line).

About one-third of all smokers in the United States try to quit each year, the vast majority of them without any treatment, but only about 3 to 5 percent succeed with their initial attempt. Nonetheless, about half of all smokers do eventually manage to achieve long-term abstinence from the nicotine in tobacco products, but only after an average of eight attempts at quitting.

Research studies on smoking cessation indicate that there are no gender differences with regard to the likelihood that a person will quit smoking for one to four years, though men are more likely than women to have been abstinent for five years or more. The fact that a higher level of smoking is consistently related to a lower level of education and family income makes it vital that smoking-cessation programs be available to those who ordinarily would not be able to afford them.[58]

The options available to smokers who want to quit are numerous. In addition to behaviorally oriented social support groups (Smokers Anonymous, SmokeEn-

---

Health Line
Ten Tips on How to Succeed When Trying to Quit Smoking

- Choose a quit date and stick to it.
- Remember that you are dependent, physiologically and psychologically, on nicotine and that the first few days without cigarettes will be the hardest.
- Change the habits that are associated with smoking. If you have had a cigarette with your morning coffee, drink orange juice instead.
- Tell all the people you know that you are quitting and ask for their support.
- Drink lots of water and brush your teeth frequently to rid yourself of the taste of tobacco.
- Never carry matches or a lighter with you. Put away your ashtrays or fill them with something else.
- Spend time with people who don't smoke.
- Keep a supply of sugarless gum, celery sticks, or hard candy on hand to use as a cigarette substitute.

- If you have an uncontrollable urge to light up, take ten deep breaths instead. Hold the last breath, then exhale slowly, and tell yourself you have just had a cigarette.
- Think about all the money you are saving by not buying cigarettes. A simple calculation will convince you that the amount saved in five years from just a moderate level of smoking (say half a pack a day) can be more than $5,000.
- Get in touch with your local Department of Health Services or call the National Cancer Institute Quitline at 877-44U-QUIT.

Source: Information gathered from American Cancer Society (2008). Guide to quitting smoking. Atlanta, GA: American Cancer Society.

---

ders, Smoke-Stoppers), counseling either in person or through telephone "quitlines," hypnosis, acupuncture, and specific prescription drugs can help reduce the withdrawal symptoms and feelings of nicotine craving. One example is a sustained-release form of the antidepressant drug bupropion. Originally marketed as a treatment for depression under the name Wellbutrin, it was approved by the FDA in 1997 for use as an aid for smoking cessation and renamed Zyban when marketed for this purpose. It is recommended that Zyban be taken daily for a week prior to the last cigarette to allow drug levels to build up in the bloodstream and buffer the loss of nicotine when smoking stops. About 44 percent of individuals taking Zyban have refrained from smoking after seven weeks, and 23 percent remain smoke-free after one year, roughly twice the percentage of those who receive a placebo. Since 1999, the costs of all prescription medications and quit-smoking programs have been tax-deductible as medical expenses.[59]

In 2006, a twice-daily tablet called Chantix became available in the United States as a nicotine-free stop-smoking medication. Clinical trials of Chantix have shown that the rate of abstinence from tobacco is 22 percent, compared to 16 percent among those taking Zyban. Forty-eight percent of long-time, one-pack-per-day smokers quit after a twelve-week treatment with Chantix, compared to 33 percent among Zyban patients. Successful long-term abstinence may require multiple treatments. As a spokesperson for the American Cancer Society has remarked, "It's not going to be a revolution; it's going to be a substantial step forward."[60]

Nicotine Gums, Patches, Sprays, and Inhalers

The long-term goal in quitting smoking is to withdraw from dependence-producing nicotine altogether and to be totally free of any hazard associated with tobacco. In the meantime, however, it is possible to employ an alternative route of ingestion for nicotine that avoids inhaling carbon monoxide and tar into the lungs. Chewing gum containing nicotine (brand name: Nicorette), available since the early 1970s as a prescription drug, is now marketed on a nonprescription basis. Transdermal nicotine patches are marketed on a nonprescription basis as well. Prescription nicotine-substitute options include a nasal spray (brand name: Nicotrol NS) and an oral inhalation system (brand name: Nicotrol Inhaler) in which nicotine is inhaled from a cartridge through a plastic mouthpiece, and lozenges (brand name: Commit).[61]

A recent review of nicotine replacement methods for smoking cessation has confirmed the usefulness of nicotine replacement therapy (NRT) as a general strategy.[62] In an analysis of more than 40,000 people who were in the process of quitting, the following conclusions were reached:

- NRT increases the chances of quitting smoking by 50 to 70 percent, relative to quitting on one's own. However, if the baseline comparison is 3 to 5 percent, the use of NRT adds about only 2 or 3 percent to the success rate. If the baseline comparison is 15 percent (under more optimal circumstances), the use of NRT adds about 8 percent to the success rate.
- A combination of NRT products is better than one product alone.
- Smokers who use NRT, even while not trying to cut down, end up smoking less or reducing the level of nicotine intake from cigarettes.
- The effectiveness of NRT is largely independent of the intensity of behavioral support, although behavioral support in general raises the baseline chances of success to begin with.

The Role of Physicians in Smoking Cessation

Owing to the fact that tobacco use is the leading cause of preventable death in the United States, it is clear that physicians must play a critical role in addressing the issue of tobacco use in their patients as part of an intervention to help them quit smoking. Suggestions for a greater role of the physician in this regard have been dubbed the "Five A's":

- *Ask about tobacco use.* Identify and document tobacco-use status for every patient at every visit.
- *Advise to quit.* In a clear, strong, and personalized manner, urge every tobacco user to quit.
- *Assess willingness to make a cessation attempt.* Is the tobacco user willing to make a cessation attempt at this time?
- *Assist in cessation attempt.* For the patient willing to make a cessation attempt, use counseling and pharmacotherapy to help him or her quit.
- *Arrange follow-up.* Schedule follow-up contact, preferably within the first week after the cessation date.[63]

A recent study suggests that when physicians tell smokers their "lung age," as determined by the age of an

"Mind if I smoke?"

"Care if I die?"

Part of California's antismoking campaign, this billboard focuses on the dangers of environmental tobacco smoke. Researchers have found that an approach based on the potential decline in social attractiveness reduces the desire among adolescents to start smoking. In 2005, state health officials announced that smoking rates among adolescents and adults in California had declined sharply since the inception of the anti-tobacco campaign in 1990.

average healthy nonsmoker with a comparable level of breathing strength, smokers evidently get the message. They are twice as likely to quit, compared to smokers who are not informed of this fact. Unfortunately, however, the campaign to have physicians or other health professionals communicate any sort of quit-smoking information to patients has a long way to go. It has been estimated that as many as 42,000 additional lives in the United States would be saved each year if 90 percent of smokers were advised by a health professional to quit and were offered medication or other assistance to do so. Presently, only 28 percent of smokers receive such services.[64]

A Final Word on Quitting

When these efforts to quit on one's own have failed, alternative approaches need to be considered. Health professionals emphasize that if one treatment strategy does not work out, the smoker should try another. The long-term consequences of failure are just too great.

The best option, of course, is never to start in the first place, which brings us back to the teenage years, when virtually all adult smokers pick up the habit. The challenge at the beginning of the twenty-first century will be to maintain the communication of effective messages that prevent the initiation of cigarette smoking as well as other forms of tobacco use by young people (see Chapter 18).[65]

Your patients trust you.
They need your guidance.

DON'T BE SILENT ABOUT SMOKING
TalkToYourPatients.org

This is your greatest opportunity to save lives.

This advertisement is part of a media campaign to encourage more involvement among physicians in reducing the prevalence rates of smoking and other tobacco use. (Courtesy of the State of New York Department of Health. www.talktoyourpatients.org.)

Summary

Tobacco Use through History

- Tobacco use originated among the original inhabitants of North and South America, and its introduction to Europe and the rest of the world dates from the first voyage of Columbus. Europeans used tobacco initially in the form of pipe smoking and later in the form of snuff.

- In the nineteenth-century United States, the most popular form was tobacco chewing and later cigar smoking. It was not until the late nineteenth century and early twentieth century that cigarette smoking became popular.

Health Concerns and Smoking Behavior

- The 1964 surgeon general's report, the first official statement on the connection between smoking and adverse health consequences, produced a general reversal in the previously climbing per capita consumption of cigarettes.

- Since 1964, the surgeon general's reports have solidified the position that nicotine is a clearly addicting component of tobacco and that tobacco use, whether in a smoked or smokeless form, causes significant health risks.

- Since 1964, there has been increased use of filtered, low-tar, and low-nicotine cigarettes.

Tobacco Today: An Industry on the Defensive

- Since the early 1990s, most U.S. states, cities, and communities have enacted laws mandating smoke-free environments in all public and private workplaces. It is now typical for restaurants, hotels, and other commercial spaces to be at least partially smoke-free.

- Additional pressure on the tobacco industry has come from proposals to increase the federal excise tax on tobacco products.

- Increased public pressure since the mid-1990s has resulted in a greatly limited marketing approach for tobacco products, particularly with respect to sales to young people.

- In 1998, the major American tobacco corporations entered into a $246 billion settlement agreement with all fifty U.S. states to resolve claims that the states should be compensated for the costs of treating people with smoking-related illnesses.

What's in Tobacco?

- The principal ingredients consumed during the smoking of tobacco are nicotine, tar, and carbon monoxide.

- The smoker inhales smoke in the form of mainstream smoke (through the cigarette itself) and sidestream smoke (released from the cigarette tip into the air).

The Dependence Potential of Nicotine

- Nicotine ingestion produces both tolerance effects and physical withdrawal symptoms. A prominent feature of nicotine withdrawal is the strong feeling of craving for a return to tobacco use.

- Smokers typically adjust their smoking behavior to obtain a stable dose of nicotine.

Health Consequences of Tobacco Use

- Tobacco smoking produces an increased risk of cardiovascular disease such as coronary heart disease and stroke, lung cancer and other forms of cancer, and respiratory diseases such as chronic bronchitis and emphysema.

- In addition to the hazards to the smoker through the inhalation of mainstream smoke, there are hazards to the developing fetus when the mother is smoking and hazards to nonsmokers who inhale environmental tobacco smoke.

Patterns of Smoking Behavior and Use of Smokeless Tobacco

- In 2007, the past-month prevalence rate for cigarette smoking in the United States was approximately 24 percent.

- The peak years for starting to smoke are in the sixth and seventh grades of school.

- More than 25 percent of students think that cigarette smoking (one or more packs per day) does not present "great risk" to their health, despite well-publicized information regarding adverse effects.

- A steady increase in the prevalence of smoking among secondary school students during the 1990s has been reversed. As these young people get older, the prevalence rates for cigarette smoking among college students and young adults are likely to decline.

- A global trend of unabated smoking rates in Asia, Eastern Europe, Russia, and elsewhere threatens the future health of huge populations of people worldwide.

Quitting Smoking: The Good News and the Bad

- Research has clearly shown that when people quit smoking, many health risks diminish rapidly. Unfortunately, nicotine dependence is very strong, and it is difficult to quit smoking. Nonetheless, a wide range of smoking cessation treatments are available, and about 50 percent of smokers eventually succeed in quitting on a permanent basis.

● Present-day approaches toward smoking cessation include behavioral treatment programs, hypnosis, acupuncture, and prescription drugs to reduce withdrawal symptoms and craving, as well as a variety of nicotine substitutes.

Key Terms

arteriosclerosis, p. 282
atherosclerosis, p. 282
carbon monoxide, p. 279
carcinomas, p. 283
chronic bronchitis, p. 282
chronic obstructive
   pulmonary disease
   (COPD), p. 282

cigarettes, p. 273
cigars, p. 273
cilia, p. 279
ciliary escalator, p. 279
coronary heart disease
   (CHD), p. 282
emphysema, p. 283

environmental tobacco
   smoke (ETS), p. 276
erythroplakia, p. 284
gaseous phase, p. 279
leukoplakia, p. 284
mainstream smoke, p. 278
moist snuff, p. 287

nicotine, p. 279
nitrosamines, p. 284
particulate phase, p. 278
sidestream smoke, p. 275
snuff, p. 272
snuffing, p. 272
tar, p. 278
titration hypothesis, p. 280

Endnotes

1. Brooks, Jerome E. (1952). *The mighty leaf: Tobacco through the centuries*. Boston: Little, Brown, pp. 11–14. Fairholt, Frederick W. (1859). *Tobacco: Its history and associations*. London: Chapman and Hill, p. 13.

2. Brooks, *The mighty leaf*, pp. 74–80. White, Jason M. (1991). *Drug dependence*. Englewood Cliffs, NJ: Prentice-Hall, pp. 32–33.

3. Austin, Gregory A. (1978). *Perspectives on the history of psychoactive substance use*. Rockville, MD: National Institute on Drug Abuse, pp. 1–12.

4. Brooks, *The mighty leaf*, p. 181. Lehman Brothers (1955). *About tobacco*. New York: Lehman Brothers, pp. 18–20.

5. Quotation from Dickens, Charles (1842). *American notes*. Cited in Brooks, *The mighty leaf*, pp. 215–216.

6. Kluger, Richard (1996). *Ashes to ashes: America's hundred-year cigarette war, the public health, and the "unabashed" triumph of Philip Morris*. New York: Knopf, p. 14. Tate, Cassandra (1989). In the 1800s, antismoking was a burning issue. *Smithsonian*, 20(4), 111.

7. Quotation originally in Bain, John, and Werner, Carl (1905). *Cigarettes in fact and fancy*. Boston: H. M. Caldwell. Cited in Brooks, *The mighty leaf*, p. 259.

8. Kluger, *Ashes to ashes*, pp. 16–20. Lehman Brothers, *About tobacco*, pp. 24–27. Slade, John (1992). The tobacco epidemic: Lessons from history. *Journal of Psychoactive Drugs*, 24, 99–109.

9. Lehman Brothers, *About tobacco*, p. 30.

10. Ibid., p. 31.

11. U.S. Department of Health and Human Services (1991). *Strategies to control tobacco use in the United States: A blueprint for public health action in the 1990s* (NIH Smoking and Tobacco Control Monograph No. 1). Bethesda, MD: National Cancer Institute.

12. Federal Trade Commission Report to Congress (1992). Pursuant to the Federal Cigarette Labeling and Advertising Act, p. 31.

13. Short, J. Gordon (1990, fall). The golden leaf. *Priorities*, p. 10.

14. Connolly, Gregory N.; Alpert, Hillel R.; Wayne, Geoffrey F.; and Koh, Howard (2007, January). Trends in smoke nicotine yield and relationship to design characteristics among popular U.S. cigarette brands 1997–2005. A report of the Tobacco Research Program, Harvard School of Public Health, Boston. Nicotine in cigarettes increases significantly since 1998: DPH Report (2006, August 26). Department of Public Health, Commonwealth of Massachusetts, Boston. Gerstein, Dean R., and Levison, Peter K. (Eds.) (1982). *Reduced tar and nicotine cigarettes: Smoking behavior and health*. Washington DC: National Academy Press. Study: Low-tar cigarettes don't cut risks. (2004, January 9). *Newsday*, p. A28.

15. Campaign for Tobacco-Free Kids, American Heart Association, American Lung Association, and American Cancer Society Cancer Action Network (2007, December 17). *A broken promise to our children: The 1998 State Tobacco Settlement nine years later*. Washington DC: Campaign for Tobacco-Free Kids. Johnston, Lloyd D.; O'Malley, Patrick M.; Bachman, Jerald G.; and Schulenberg, John E. (2008, December 11). More good news on teen smoking: Rates at or near record lows. University of Michigan News Service, Ann Arbor, Figure 1.

16. Ochs, Ridgely (2000, December 28). An ounce of prevention? Little money from suit used to halt tobacco. *Newsday*, pp. A6, A62–A63. Tauras, John A.; Chaloupka, Frank J.; Farrelly, Matthew C.; Giovino, Gary A.; Wakefield, Melanie; et al. (2005). State tobacco control spending and youth smoking. *American Journal of Public Health*, 95, 338–344.

17. Alcoholic beverages and tobacco (1997, September 11). *Standard and Poor's Industry Surveys*, p. 10. Lok, Corie (2002, August 5). Hitting teen smokers where it hurts: In the wallet. *Newsweek*, p. 47. Wilgoren, Jodi (2002, July 17). Facing new costs, some smokers say "enough." *New York Times*, p. A14.

18. Centers for Disease Control and Prevention (2008). Smoking and tobacco use: Frequently asked questions. Atlanta,

GA: Centers for Disease Control and Prevention. Payne, Wayne A., and Hahn, Dale B. (1992). *Understanding your health.* St. Louis: Mosby Year Book, p. 270.

19. Schlaadt, Richard G. (1992). *Tobacco and health.* Guilford, CT: Dushkin Publishing, p. 41.

20. Gahagan, Dolly D. (1987). *Switch down and quit: What the cigarette companies don't want you to know about smoking.* Berkeley, CA: Ten Speed Press, p. 44. Payne and Hahn, *Understanding your health,* pp. 273–275.

21. Jacobs, Michael R., and Fehr, Kevin O'B. (1987). *Drugs and drug abuse: A reference text* (2nd ed.). Toronto: Addiction Research Foundation, pp. 417–425. Julien, Robert M. (2001). *A primer of drug action* (9th ed.). New York: Worth, p. 229.

22. Meier, Barry (1998, February 23). Cigarette maker manipulated nicotine, its records suggest. *New York Times,* pp. A1, A15. Pankow, J. F.; Mader, B. T.; Isabelle, L. M.; Luo, W. T.; et al. (1997). Conversion of nicotine and tobacco smoke to its volatile and available free-base form through the action of gaseous ammonia. *Environmental Science & Technology,* 31, 2428–2433.

23. Julien, *A primer of drug action,* p. 234. Phillips, Sarah, and Fox, Pauline (1998). An investigation into the effects of nicotine gum on short-term memory. *Psychopharmacology, 140,* 429–433. Schuckit, Marc A. (2000). *Drug and alcohol abuse: A clinical guide to diagnosis and treatment* (5th ed.). New York: Kluwer Academic/Plenum, pp. 262–264. Zhang, Hui, and Sulzer, David (2004). Frequency-dependent modulation of dopamine released by nicotine. *Nature Neuroscience,* 7, 581–582.

24. Brecher, Edward M., and the editors of *Consumer Reports* (1972). *Licit and illicit drugs.* Boston: Little, Brown, pp. 220–228. DiFranza, Joseph R. (2008, May). Hooked from the first cigarette. *Scientific American,* pp. 82–87.

25. Pontieri, Francesco E.; Tanda, Gianluigi; Orzi, Francesco; and DiChiara, Gaetano (1996). Effects of nicotine on the nucleus accumbens and similarity to those of addictive drugs. *Science, 382,* 255–257. Risso, Francesca; Parodi, Monica; Grilli, Massimo; Molfino, Francesca; et al. (2004). Chronic nicotine causes functional upregulation of ionotropic glutamate receptors medicating hippocampal noradrenaline and stratal dopamine release. *Neurochemistry International, 44,* 293–301.

26. Lichtenstein, Edward, and Brown, Richard A. (1980). Smoking cessation methods: Review and recommendations. In William R. Miller (Ed.), *The addictive behaviors: Treatment of alcoholism, drug abuse, smoking, and obesity.* New York: Pergamon Press, pp. 169–206. Quotation on p. 173.

27. Ibid., pp. 172–173. Brody, Jane E. (2008, February 12). In adolescents, addiction to tobacco comes easy. *New York Times,* p. F7.

28. Herning, Ronald I., Jones, Reese T., and Fischman, Patricio (1985). The titration hypothesis revisited: Nicotine gum reduces smoking intensity. In John Grabowski and Sharon M. Hall (Eds.), *Pharmacological adjuncts in smoking cessation* (NIDA Research Monograph 53). Rockville, MD: National Institute on Drug Abuse, pp. 27–41. Jarvik, Mur-ray E. (1979). Biological influences on cigarette smoking. In Norman A. Krasnegor (Ed.), *The behavioral aspects of smoking* (NIDA Research Monograph 26). Rockville, MD: National Institute on Drug Abuse, pp. 7–45.

29. Jarvik, Biological influences, pp. 25–29. Schuckit, *Drugs and alcohol abuse,* pp. 264–265.

30. Koslowski, Lynn T.; Wilkinson, Adrian; Skinner, Wayne; Kent, Carl; Franklin, Tom; and Pope, Marilyn. (1989). Comparing tobacco cigarette dependence with other drug dependencies. *Journal of the American Medical Association, 261,* 898–901.

31. Centers for Disease Control and Prevention (2003). Cigarette smoking-attributable morbidity—United States, 2000. *Morbidity and Mortality Weekly Report, 52,* 842–844. Centers for Disease Control and Prevention (2002). Annual smoking attributable mortality, years of potential life lost and economic costs—United States, 1995–1999. *Morbidity and Mortality Weekly Report, 51,* 300–303. Centers for Disease Control and Prevention (1997, May 23). *Fact sheet: Facts about cigarette mortality.* Atlanta, GA: Office of Communication, Centers for Disease Control and Prevention. Julien, *A primer of drug action,* p. 236. Roper, W. L. (1991). Making smoking prevention a reality. *Journal of the American Medical Association, 266,* 3188–3189.

32. Ayanian, John Z., and Cleary, Paul D. (1999). Perceived risks of heart disease and cancer among cigarette smokers. *Journal of the American Medical Association, 281,* 1019–1021. Howard, George; Wagenknecht, Lynne E.; Burke, Gregory L.; Diez-Roux, Ana; et al. (1998). Cigarette smoking and progression of atherosclerosis. *Journal of the American Medical Association, 279,* 119–124. U.S. Department of Health and Human Services, Public Health Service, Office of Smoking and Health (1983). *The health consequences of smoking: Cardiovascular disease* (A report of the surgeon general) Rockville, MD: U.S. Public Health Service, pp. 63–156.

33. Payne and Hahn, *Understanding your health,* pp. 272–273.

34. Grady, Denise (2007, November 29). From smoking boom, a major killer of women. *New York Times,* pp. A1, A22. Quotation in Schlaadt, *Tobacco and health,* p. 52

35. Gold, Diane R.; Wang, Xiaobin; Wypij, David; Speizer, Frank E.; Ware, James H.; et al. (1996). Effects of cigarette smoking on lung function in adolescent boys and girls. *New England Journal of Medicine, 335,* 931–937. U.S. Department of Health and Human Services, Public Health Service, Office of Smoking and Health (1984). *The health consequences of smoking: Chronic obstructive lung disease* (A report of the surgeon general). Rockville, MD: U.S. Public Health Service, pp. 329–360.

36. American Cancer Society (2008). *Cancer facts and figures 2007.* Atlanta, GA: American Cancer Society, pp. 2–3, 13–14. Denissenko, Mikhail F.; Pao, Annie; Tang, Moon-Shong; and Pfeifer, Gerd P. (1996). Preferential formation of benzopyrene adducts at lung cancer mutational hotspots in *P53. Science, 274,* 430–432. Landi, Maria T.; Dracheva, Tatiana; Rotunno, Melissa;, Figueroa, Jonine D.; et al. (2008). Gene expression signature of cigarette smoking and

its role in lung adenocarcinoma development and survival. *PLoS ONE*, published online February 20, 2008, by the Public Library of Science, San Francisco, CA.

37. Schuckit, *Drug and alcohol abuse*, p. 264.

38. Ebrahim, Shahul H.; Floyd, R. Louise; Merritt II, Robert K; Decoufle, Pierre; and Holtzman, David (2000). Trends in pregnancy-related smoking rates in the United States, 1987–1996. *Journal of the American Medical Association*, 283, 361–366. Geerts, Caroline C.; Grobbee, Diederick E.; van der Ent, Cornelis K; de Jong, Brita M.; et al. (2007). Tobacco smoke exposure of pregnant mothers and blood pressure in their newborns. *Hypertension*, 50, 572–578. Li, Yu-Fen; Langholz, Bryan; Salam, Muhammad T.; and Gilliland, Frank D. (2005). Maternal and grandmaternal smoking patterns are associated with early childhood asthma. *Chest*, 127, 1232–1241. U.S. Department of Health and Human Services, Public Health Service, Office of Smoking and Health (1980). *The health consequences of smoking for women* (A report of the surgeon general). Rockville, MD: U.S. Public Health Service, pp. 98–101.

39. Davis, Ronald M. (1998). Exposure to environmental tobacco smoke: Identifying and protecting those at risk. *Journal of the American Medical Association*, 280, 1947–1949. Ginzel, K. H. (1992). The ill-effects of second hand smoke. In Kristine Napier (Ed.), *Issues in tobacco*. New York: American Council on Science and Health, pp. 6–7.

40. Aligne, C. Andrew; Moss, Mark E.; Auinger, Peggy; and Weitzman, Michael (2003). Association of pediatric dental caries with passive smoking. *Journal of the American Medical Association*, 289, 1258–1264. Fielding, Jonathan E., and Phenow, Kenneth J. (1989). *Health effects of involuntary smoking*. Atlanta, GA: American Cancer Society. In France, adieu to smoking (2008, January). *Newsday*, p. A17. Kawachi, Ichiro; Colditz, Graham A.; Speizer, Frank E.; Manson, JoAnn E.; et al. (1997). A prospective study of passive smoking and coronary heart disease. *Circulation*, 95, 2374–2379. Nafstad, Per; Fugelseth, Drude; Qvigstad, Erik; Zahlsen, Kolbjørn; et al. (1998). Nicotine concentration in the hair of nonsmoking mothers and size of offspring. *American Journal of Public Health*, 88, 120–124. U.S. Department of Health and Human Services, Public Health Service, Office of Smoking and Health (2006). *The health consequences of involuntary exposure to tobacco smoke* (A report of the surgeon general). Rockville, MD: U.S. Public Health Service.

41. Johnston, O'Malley, Bachman, and Schulenberg (2008), More good news on teen smoking, Table 3. Johnston, Lloyd M.; O'Malley, Patrick M.; Bachman, Gerald G.; and Schulenberg, John E. (2008). *Monitoring the Future: National survey results on drug use, 1975–2007. Volume II. College students and adults ages 19–45, 2007.* Bethesda, MD: National Institute on Drug Abuse, Table 2-3. Substance Abuse and Mental Health Administration (2008). *Results from the 2007 National Survey on Drug Use and Health: Detailed tables.* Rockville, MD: Office of Applied Studies, Substance Abuse and Mental Health

Administration,. Tables 2-22A and 2-22B. Wechsler, Henry, Rigotti, Nancy A., and Gledhill-Hoyt, Jeana (1998). Increased levels of cigarette use among college students: A cause for national concern. *Journal of the American Medical Association*, 280, 1673–1678.

42. Centers for Disease Control and Prevention (2003). Tobacco use among middle and high school students—New Hampshire, 1995–2001. *Morbidity and Mortality Weekly Report*, 52, 7–9. Johnston, O'Malley, Bachman, and Schulenberg (2008), More good news on teen smoking, Table 1. Johnston, Lloyd D., O'Malley, Patrick M., and Bachman, Jerald G. (2002). *Monitoring the future: National results for adolescent drug use 1975–2001. Volume 1: Secondary school students 2001.* Bethesda, MD: National Institute on Drug Abuse, Table 6-1.

43. Johnston, O'Malley, Bachman, and Schulenberg (2008), More good news on teen smoking, Tables 2 and 3.

44. Johnston, Lloyd D., O'Malley, Patrick M., and Bachman, Jerald G. (2002, December 16). Teen smoking declines sharply in 2002, more than offsetting large increases in the early 1990s. University of Michigan News and Information Service, Ann Arbor, pp. 4–5. Quotation by Lloyd D. Johnston, p. 5.

45. Johnston, O'Malley, Bachman, and Schulenberg (2008), More good news on teen smoking, Table 2. Rigotti, Nancy A.; DiFranza, Joseph R.; Chang, YuChiao; Tisdale, Thelma; et al. (1997). The effect of enforcing tobacco-sales laws on adolescents' access to tobacco and smoking behavior. *New England Journal of Medicine*, 337, 1044–1057. Substance Abuse and Mental Health Services Administration (2007, October 5). SAMHSA news release: Federal/state program achieves dramatic national drop in tobacco sales to minors. Rockville, MD: Substance Abuse and Mental Health Services Administration.

46. Johnston, O'Malley, Bachman, and Schulenberg (2008), More good news on teen smoking, Tables 4, 9, 10, and 11.

47. Freedman, Alix M. How a tobacco giant doctors snuff brands to boost their "kick." (1994, October 26). *Wall Street Journal*, pp. A1, A14.

48. U.S. Department of Health and Human Services, Public Health Service, Office of Smoking and Health (1986). *The health consequences of smokeless tobacco* (A report of the advisory committee to the surgeon general). Rockville, MD: Public Health Service.

49. Hamilton, Kendall (1997, July 21). Blowing smoke. *Newsweek*, pp. 54–60.

50. Ackerman, Elise (1999, November 29). The cigar boom goes up in smoke. *Newsweek*, p. 55. Baker, Frank, et al. (2000). Health risks associated with cigar smoking. *Journal of the American Medical Association*, 284, 735–740. Substance Abuse and Mental Health Administration (2001, December 21). *The NHSDA report: Cigar use.* Rockville, MD: Office of Applied Studies, Substance Abuse and Mental Health Administration.

51. Johnston, Lloyd D.; O'Malley, Patrick M.; Bachman, Jerald G.; and Schulenberg, John E. (2008, December 11). Various stimulant drugs show continuing gradual declines

among teens in 2008, most illicit drugs hold steady. University of Michigan News Service, Ann Arbor, Table 2. Small Indian cigarettes light up teen smokers (1999, May 11). *Newsday*, p. A49. Watson, Clifford H.; Polzin, Gregory, M.; Calafat, Antonia M.; and Ashley, David, L. (2003). Determination of tar, nicotine, and carbon monoxide yields in the smoke of bidi cigarettes. *Nicotine and Tobacco Research*, 5, 747–753.

52. Ives, Nat (2004, March 9). Flavored Kool cigarettes are attracting criticism. *New York Times*, p. C11.

53. Sterngold, James (1993, October 17). When smoking is a patriotic duty. *New York Times*, Sect. 3, pp. 1, 6. Strom, Stephanie (2001, June 13). Japan and tobacco revenue: Leader faces difficult choice. *New York Times*, pp. A1, A14. Tagliabue, John (2005, September 8). The ash may finally be falling from the Gauloise. *New York Times*, p. A4. Watts, Jonathan (1999). Smoking, sake, and suicide: Japan plans a healthier future. *The Lancet*, 354, p. 843. Winter, Greg (2001, August 24). Enticing Third World youth. *New York Times*, pp. C1, C4.

54. Hampton, Tracy (2008, April 2). Global report highlights tobacco use, offers countermeasures for nations. *Journal of the American Medical Association*, 299, 1531–1552.

55. Marsh, Bill (2008, February 24). A growing cloud over the planet. *New York Times*, p. 4. Reeves, Hope (2000, November 5). Blowing smoke: What's one little worldwide antismoking treaty compared to the force of 1.1 billion nicotine-craving cigarette fiends? *New York Times Magazine*, p. 26. World Health Organization (2008). *WHO report on the global tobacco epidemic 2008: The MPOWER package*. Geneva, Switzerland: World Health Organization.

56. American Cancer Society, Atlanta. Cited in *The world almanac and book of facts 2000* (1999). Mahwah, NJ: Primedia Reference, p. 733.

57. U.S. Department of Health and Human Services, Public Health Service, Office of Smoking and Health (1988). *The health consequences of smoking: Nicotine addiction* (A report of the surgeon general). Rockville, MD: Public Health Service, p. 9.

58. American Legacy Foundation (2003). Factsheet: Quitting smoking. Washington DC: American Legacy Foundation. Ehrich, Beverly, and Emmons, Karen M. (1994). Addressing the needs of smokers in the 1990s. *The Behavior Therapist*, 17 (6), 119–122. Freudenheim, Milt (2007, October 26). Seeking savings, employers help smokers quit. *New York Times*, pp. A1, A18. Hughes, J. R., Keely, J., and Naud, S. (2004). Shape of the relapse curve and long-term abstinence among untreated smokers. *Addiction*, 99, 29–38. Munafò, Marcus R.; Clark, Taane G.; Johnstone, Elaine C.; Murphy, Michael F. G.; et al. (2004). The genetic basis for smoking behavior: A systematic review and meta-analysis. *Nicotine and Tobacco Research*, 6, 583–597. Schuckit, *Drug and alcohol abuse*, p. 267. U.S. Department of Health and Human Services, Public Health Service, Office of Smoking and Health (1990). *The health benefits of smoking cessation* (A report of the surgeon general). Atlanta, GA: Office of Smoking and Health, pp. 610–611.

59. Ahluwalia, Jasjit S.; Harris, Kari Jo; Catley, Delwyn; Okuyemi, Kolawole S.; and Mayo, Matthew S. (2002). Sustained-release bupropion for smoking cessation in African Americans: A randomized controlled trial. *Journal of the American Medical Association*, 288, 468–474. Benowitz, Neal L. (1997). Treating tobacco addiction—Nicotine or no nicotine? *New England Journal of Medicine*, 337, 1230–1231. Jain, Anjali (2003). Treating nicotine addiction. *British Medical Journal*, 327, 1394–1395. Smoking treatments deductible (1999, June 11). *Newsday*, p. A66. Zickler, Patrick (2003). Genetic variation may increase nicotine craving and smoking relapse. *NIDA Notes*, 18(3), 1, 6.

60. High hopes for new stop-smoking pill (2006, May 12). *Newsday*, p. A36. Quotation on p. A36. Nides, Mitchell; Oncken, Cheryl; Gonzales, David; Rennard, Stephen; Watsky, Eric J.; et al. (2006). Smoking cessation with varenicline, a selective alpha-4-beta-2 nicotinic receptor partial agonist. *Archives of Internal Medicine*, 166, 1561–1568.

61. Franzon, Mikael, Gustavsson, Gunnar, and Korberly, Barbara H. (2002). Effectiveness of over-the-counter nicotine replacement therapy. *Journal of the American Medical Association*, 288, 3108–3110. Mathias, Robert (2001). Nicotine patch helps smokeless tobacco users quit, but maintaining abstinence may require additional treatment. *NIDA Notes*, 16(1), 8–9. Shiffman, Saul, Dresler, Carolyn M., and Rohay, Jeffrey M. (2004). Successful treatment with a nicotine lozenge of smokers with prior failure in pharmacological therapy. *Addiction*, 99, 83–92.

62. Stead, L. F; Perera, R.; Bullen, C.; Mant, D.; and Lancaster, T. (2008). Nicotine replacement therapy for smoking cessation (Review). *Cochrane Database of Systematic Reviews*, Issue 1, Article Number CD000146.

63. Fiore, Michael C., Hatsukami, Dorothy K., and Baker, Timothy, B. (2002). Effective tobacco dependence treatment. *Journal of the American Medical Association*, 288, 1768–1771. Spangler, John G.; George, Geeta; Foley, Kristie Long; and Crandall, Sonia J. (2002). Tobacco intervention training: Current efforts and gaps in U.S. medical schools. *Journal of the American Medical Association*, 288, 1102–1109.

64. Parkes, Gary; Greenhaigh, Trisha; Griffin, Mark; and Dent, Richard (2008). Effect of smoking quit rate on telling patients their lung age: The Step2quit randomized controlled trial. *British Medical Journal*, 336, 598–600. Partnership for Prevention (2008). New study: Boosting five preventive services would save 100,000 lives each year. Washington DC: Partnership for Prevention, National Commission on Prevention Priorities.

65. Goldman, Lisa K., and Glantz, Stanton A. (1999). Evaluation of antismoking advertising campaigns. *Journal of the American Medical Association*, 279, 772–777. Raising kids who don't smoke (2003), created by Philip Morris USA Youth Smoking Prevention. Story, Louise (2007, January 2). Kicking an addiction, with real people. *New York Times*, p. C7. Two questions to identify future smokers (2008, July 15). *New York Times*, p. F6.

chapter 12

Caffeine

For a while, Steve couldn't understand why he was suffering those headaches. Every Sunday afternoon, sometimes earlier in the day, he would get a pounding headache and feel grumpy and out of sorts. Steve would notice that he felt achy, as though he were coming down with the flu.

Then it occurred to him. On the weekends at home, he was able to sleep late and drank decaffeinated coffee instead of his regular brew at the office. He realized that he was going through caffeine withdrawal. I had better cut down, he said to himself, or stick with regular on the weekends.

After you have completed this chapter, you will understand

● Examples of stimulant compounds called xanthines: caffeine, theobromine, and theophylline

● The sources of caffeine: coffee, tea, chocolate, soft drinks, and medications

● How coffee is decaffeinated

● The effects of caffeine on the body

● The effects of caffeine on human behavior and performance

● Health considerations when consuming caffeine

● The medical uses of theophylline

● The effects of caffeine on kids

If you enjoy a cup of caffeinated coffee or caffeinated tea, a piece of chocolate, or a can of "regular" Coke or Pepsi, you may be surprised to know that you are engaging in the most popular form of drug-taking behavior in the world. To varying degrees, all these products contain caffeine, a psychoactive stimulant drug. It should be added, however, that you need not be overly concerned. Among the range of psychoactive stimulants that exist (the major ones were examined in Chapters 4 and 11), caffeine is considerably weaker than most and the research shows that caffeine consumption is relatively benign. Nonetheless, as will be shown, caffeine can be a dependence-producing drug, and several precautions against its use should be heeded.

Caffeine belongs to a family of stimulant compounds called **xanthines.** Two other major examples of xanthines, **theobromine** (found in chocolate) and **theophylline** (found in small amounts in tea), also have stimulating effects. In general, theophylline and caffeine have approximately equal stimulatory effects; theobromine is only about one-tenth as strong. The focus of this chapter will be on what we know about caffeine itself, beginning with a look at three natural sources of caffeine: coffee, tea, and chocolate.

Coffee

We do not know exactly when coffee drinking began, but we do know that the plant *Coffea arabica*, from which coffee beans were first harvested, originated in Ethiopia, and its cultivation spread to Yemen and Arabia at some time between the eleventh and the fifteenth centuries. Coffee has been called "the wine of Islam," suggesting that it was viewed as a substitute for alcoholic beverages, which are forbidden by the Koran.

---

caffeine: A xanthine stimulant found in coffee, tea, chocolate, soft drinks, and several medications.

xanthines (ZAN-theens): A family of CNS stimulant drugs that includes caffeine, theophylline, and theobromine.

theobromine (THEE-oh-BROH-meen): A xanthine stimulant found in chocolate.

theophylline (thee-OFF-ill-lin): A xanthine stimulant found in small amounts in tea. It is used as an anti-asthma medication.

Coffea arabica (KOFF-ee-uh air-RAB-beh-ka): A type of coffee bean native to the Middle East but now grown principally in South America. It is typically referred to simply as arabica.

A popular legend concerning the beginnings of coffee drinking has it that a young Yemenite or Ethiopian goatherd named Khaldi, while tending his flock, noticed that his goats were unusually hyperactive and unable to sleep after nibbling some red berries in the field. Khaldi tried some himself and, on feeling as exhilarated as his goats, took the berries to the local Islamic monastery. The chief holy man there prepared a beverage from these berries and found the effect to be so invigorating that he was able to stay awake during a long night of prayers in the mosque. According to this legend, the fame of the "wakeful monastery" and its remarkable potion spread through the whole kingdom and to other countries of the region.[1]

At first, coffee was banned on religious grounds because some Islamic clerics considered it to be as much an intoxicant as an alcoholic beverage, but these ecclesiastic disputes were eventually settled and coffee drinking became a fixture of daily life. In the words of one historian, "The growth of coffee and its use as a national beverage became as inseparably connected with Arabia as tea is with China."[2]

Coffee in Britain and North America

The practice of coffee drinking reached England in the middle of the seventeenth century, just in time to be associated with one of the most turbulent periods of political, social, economic, and religious unrest in its history. It was in establishments specializing in the sale of coffee, known as coffee houses, that intellectuals met and argued their respective points of view. Until the end of the eighteenth century, when tea began to replace coffee

---

by the numbers . . .

80   Milligrams of caffeine in an 8.3-ounce can of Red Bull, the leading "energy drink" in the U.S. market. The caffeine content in a 12-ounce serving is approximately $3\frac{1}{3}$ times that in a 12-ounce can of Coca-Cola Classic.

260   Milligrams of caffeine in a 12-ounce Starbucks Tall coffee, approximately $7\frac{1}{2}$ times that of a 12-ounce can of Coca-Cola Classic.

65   Percentage of U.S. public middle schools with exclusive soft-drink (primarily caffeinated soft-drink) contracts for vending machines in 2005. The percentage in 2000 was 26 percent.

Sources: Energyfiend.com, 2008. U.S. Government Accountability Office (2005, September). Survey of public middle schools in the federal school lunch program. Washington DC: U.S. Government Accountability Office.

---

as the dominant British drink, coffee was the principal alternative social beverage to alcohol. The British coffee house enjoyed the reputation of being a place where men (women rarely frequented them, though they often managed them) could socialize with one another and enjoy a nonintoxicating beverage in sober company.

The emphasis was on keeping a clear head, which was certainly not likely after an hour or two at the local tavern. In fact, historians have credited coffee houses with helping to moderate the widespread drunkenness that was rampant as a result of the "gin epidemic" in England during the 1700s (see Chapter 9). A popular nickname for coffee houses was "penny universities," since the conversation there was considered to be as stimulating as a university education and a lot cheaper.[3]

Coffee houses in colonial America served a similar purpose. One such political gathering place, the Green Dragon in Boston, was the setting for the meetings of John Adams, Samuel Adams, Paul Revere, and their compatriots as they planned their strategy against the British. After the Revolutionary War, coffee emerged as the American national drink, especially after 1830 when alcohol consumption began to decline (see Chapter 9). During the settling of the American frontier, coffee was an indispensable provision for the long trek westward. By 1860, Americans were consuming three-fourths of the world's entire production of coffee.

Today, the United States remains the world's top importer of coffee, with about one-half originating in Brazil and Colombia. However, U.S. per capita coffee consumption barely ranks in the top twenty among nations of the world, behind most European countries. Since roughly 1960, coffee consumption has gradually declined as American drinking habits have shifted to an increased consumption of colas, particularly among young adults. In the meantime, the types of coffee that Americans consume have become more and more sophisticated. As one writer has put it:

> We no longer boil grounds campfire style or percolate them genteel style in the pot. And we have a taster's dream choice of beans, roasts, grinds, and brewing equipment. Even our lingo has changed—from "Gimme a cuppa joe" to "Give me an iced short schizo skinny hazelnut cappuccino with wings." (Translation: a small iced hazelnut coffee with one shot of regular and one of decaf, plus skim milk with foam, to go.)[4]

Major Sources of Coffee

Two species of coffee beans dominate the world market. *Coffea arabica*, the original coffee bean as far as West-

Expert coffee tasters in a German coffee company sample the possibilities before deciding on a particular blend.

erners are concerned, is grown mostly in Brazil and Colombia, having been brought to South America by the French in the early 1700s. Another major species, *Coffea robusta*, is grown primarily in formerly Dutch plantations on the Indonesian island of Java (hence, the phrase "a cup of Java" for a cup of coffee); some is also produced in Brazil and the Ivory Coast and other countries in Africa. *Coffee arabica* beans represent about 70 percent of the world's coffee production.

Coffee blends are generally combinations of these two types of beans, with the ratio dictated by local tastes and economic concerns. Robusta beans are considered by coffee experts to be inferior to arabica beans because of their harsher taste, but robusta beans have approximately twice the caffeine content and are cheaper to buy.

The Caffeine Content in Coffee

The caffeine content in a "standard" 5-ounce cup of coffee can range from about 57 to 145 milligrams (mg) depending on the method of brewing, the amount of coffee used, the brand of coffee, and the brewing time. Roughly speaking, the caffeine content in coffee can be estimated to be about 100 mg (20 mg per ounce). Comparable amounts of instant coffee have about 60 mg

Coffea robusta (KOFF-ee-uh row-BUS-tah): A type of coffee bean grown principally in Indonesia, Brazil, and Africa.

Why There Are No (Live) Flies in Your Coffee

Chemical compounds found naturally in plants are generally there for a purpose, though it may take a while for scientists to figure out what that purpose may be. In the case of plants containing xanthines, the benefit lies in the area of insect control.

We now know that xanthines interfere with an insect's ability to feed on a plant because they increase the level of octopamine, an excitatory chemical in the nervous system of invertebrates. As a result, contact with xanthine-containing plants causes insects to become overly stimulated and die.

Fortunately, octopamine plays little or no role in mammalian nervous systems. One extra benefit in knowing how xanthines affect insects is the possibility in the future of developing xanthine-based pesticides that are effective on cockroaches but a good deal safer for human beings.

Sources: Hirashima, Akinori; Morimoto, Masako; Kuwane, Eiichi; and Eto, Morifusa (2003). Octopaminergic agonists for the cockroach neuronal octopamine receptor. *Journal of Insect Science, 3,* 1–9. Nathanson, James A. (1984). Caffeine and related methylxanthines: Possible naturally occurring pesticides. *Science, 226,* 184–187.

---

of caffeine (12 mg per ounce).[5] Bear in mind, however, that a regular-size mug holds about 8 ounces, and a 12- to 24-ounce cup is often the preferred serving size. Caffeine is the only xanthine found in coffee (Drugs . . . in Focus).

Tea

By the standard of historical records, tea is the world's oldest caffeine-containing beverage. The legendary Chinese emperor Shen Nung is credited with its discovery in 2737 B.C., along with other stimulants such as the antiasthma medication we now know as ephedrine (see Chapter 4) and marijuana (see Chapter 7). Tea is a brew of leaves from the *Camellia sinensis* (tea plant), a large evergreen tree that is typically trimmed back to look more like a bush. The Latin word *sinensis* refers to its origin in China.[6]

Dutch traders brought tea from Asia to Western Europe in the early 1600s, where it was met with mixed reviews. The Germans tried tea drinking for a while but then returned to beer; the French also tried it but then returned to coffee and wine. The Chinese traded directly with the Russians, who loved it and made tea drinking a national pastime, sipping hot tea from glasses through a sugar cube held between the teeth. Giant tea urns, called *samovars*, kept tea available for drinking throughout the day.

Camellia sinensis (ka-MEE-yah sin-EHN-sis): The plant from which tea leaves are obtained.

Tea in Britain and North America

The principal Dutch success with tea in Europe was in Britain, where it eventually became the national drink. Chinese tea, as noted in Chapter 5, was in such great demand by the British that the Chinese were forced to trade their tea in exchange for opium imported by the British into their own country. By 1842, the problems with this odd arrangement escalated into the Opium War, pitting China against Britain and later France and the United States.

By the end of the nineteenth century, however, China was no longer the principal source for British tea. Tastes had changed, away from the subtle flavor of Chinese green tea leaves and toward a stronger, blacker tea that was being grown in India and Ceylon (now Sri Lanka). It also did not hurt that a greater number of cups could be made from a pound of Indian or Ceylonese tea, making it more economical for the average consumer. Today's teas are blends of black tea leaves, chiefly from India, Sri Lanka, and Indonesia, though there is a growing market for green tea from China and Kenya.[7]

We do not know whether the gentlemen at the Green Dragon coffee house in Boston were drinking coffee or tea during the months of growing unrest and resentment against the British prior to the beginning of the Revolutionary War, but it is quite likely that much of the talk concerned tea. In 1773, the British government had decided to allow British agents to sell cheap tea directly to the American colonies, bypassing American tea merchants in the process. In the eyes of the Americans, the policy was another instance of British tyranny and one more reason why the colonies should be independent.

An engraving depicting American colonists at the Boston Tea Party, 1773.

We do know what happened next. On the night of December 16, 1773, while three British ships loaded with chests of British tea lay at anchor in Boston Harbor, fifty to sixty colonists, some of them dressed as Mohawk Indians, boarded the vessels and proceeded to break open the tea chests and dump the contents into the water. Thus, the Boston Tea Party entered the pages of history. Strangely enough, the initial reaction to this event in British newspapers focused not on the political ramifications but rather on the pharmacological effect of the tea on the unfortunate fish in Boston Harbor. One report said that the fish "had contracted a disorder not unlike the nervous complaints of the body." Assuming this story is true, we can only conclude that all that tea had given the fish a large dose of caffeine and theophylline.[8]

Largely as a result of continuing anti-British sentiment during the early history of the United States, drinking tea was viewed to be unpatriotic, and coffee became the preferred beverage. Today, American consumption of tea is only approximately one-eighth that of Ireland and Great Britain, who lead the world, as you might suspect, in per capita tea drinking. More than 80 percent of all tea consumed in the United States is in the form of iced tea, a beverage that was introduced at the Louisiana Purchase Exposition in St. Louis in the summer of 1904.

The Chemical Content in Tea

Tea contains two xanthines, caffeine and theophylline. The caffeine content of a 5-ounce cup of tea is approximately 60 mg. This estimate, however, applies to a medium brew of tea. If the tea is a strong brew, the caffeine content approaches that of regular coffee, especially if the tea is produced in Britain rather than the United States. A strong brew of Twining's English Breakfast tea, for example, contains approximately 107 mg of caffeine.[9]

The other xanthine found in tea, theophylline, is found in much smaller concentrations than caffeine. As will be noted later, its bronchodilating effect is clinically useful for the treatment of asthma and other respiratory problems.

A group of nonxanthine chemicals in tea, called *polyphenols*, appears to have beneficial effects in the prevention of heart disease, inflammatory disorders, and some forms of cancer. Polyphenols are plentiful in green tea and, to a lesser degree, black or pekoe tea. Although both types of tea are harvested from the *Camellia sinensis* plant, they are processed differently. Black tea leaves are fermented prior to drying, whereas green tea leaves are not. During the fermentation process, black tea loses most of its polyphenols and therefore its potential health benefits.[10]

Chocolate

Chocolate comes from **cocoa bean pods** growing directly on the trunk and thick main branches of cacao trees. Cacao trees are native to Mexico and Central America, but now they are grown in tropical regions of the Caribbean, South America, Africa, and Asia. The leading exporters of cocoa beans to the United States are the Ivory Coast, Ghana, and Indonesia.[11]

According to a popular legend, chocolate was a gift from the Aztec god Quetzalcoatl to give humans a taste of paradise. At the time of Hernando Cortés's expedition to Mexico in 1519, chocolate (*xocoatl or chocolatl* as the Aztecs called it) was a prized beverage, to be enjoyed only by the rulers and the upper classes of society. The Aztec emperor Montezuma II drank a cocoa-derived mixture flavored with spices and presumably liked it so much that he consumed fifty cups daily. But it was very different from the chocolate we know today. The original version was a cold, thick, frothy, souplike concoction that was eaten with a spoon. Most significant, it was bitter in taste and had to be flavored with vanilla and other spices, since Aztecs had no knowledge of sugarcane. Reluctantly, Cortés took some cocoa bean pods back to Spain in 1528.

Once home, Cortés prepared chocolate as he had learned it from the Aztecs, but with an important difference: the addition of sugar. Now, in a sweetened form called *molinet*, chocolate became an instant success, and a closely guarded secret of the Spanish emperor Charles V and his royal court. Inevitably, however, word

cocoa bean pods (COH-coh): Parts of the cacao tree that are the raw material for cocoa and chocolate. Not to be confused with coca, the source of cocaine.

leaked out to the other royal courts of Europe that the Spanish were enjoying an exotic new drink that came from the New World.

The official unveiling of sweet chocolate coincided with a royal wedding. When the fourteen-year-old Spanish princess arrived in Paris to marry the fourteen-year-old Louis XIII of France in 1615, she carried with her a betrothal gift of Spanish chocolate. It was the beginning of the traditional connection of chocolate with romance. Later, in 1660, a similar betrothal gift at the wedding of another Spanish princess and Louis XIV of France sealed its reputation as the gift of love. It also has not hurt chocolate's image that the eighteenth-century Italian lover Casanova credited his considerable sexual prowess to a habit of drinking chocolate each morning.

Chocolate took its place in England not so much as a symbol of romance but as simply another good-tasting

cocoa butter: The fat content of the cocoa bean.

chocolate liquor (lih-KOOR): A deep-colored paste made when roasted cocoa beans are heated so that the cocoa butter in the beans melts.

beverage that could be sold in the growing number of coffee houses in English cities. From the beginning, chocolate was sold in shops rather than hidden away behind palace walls. It was not cheap, but at least it was available to all who could afford to buy it. By 1700, the specialty chocolate house rivaled the coffee house as a place to gather and discuss current events.

How Chocolate Is Made

From the days of pre-Columbian America to the early part of the nineteenth century, the method for preparing chocolate did not fundamentally change, except for the addition of such ingredients as sugar. In 1828, however, something did change. To appreciate what transpired, it is important to understand the nature of chocolate itself and the ways it can be processed.

Once cocoa beans are roasted, they can be heated in a machine to such temperatures that the natural fat within the beans, called **cocoa butter,** melts. The result is a deep-colored chocolaty-smelling paste called **chocolate liquor.** When it later cools and hardens, the

---

Health Line
Chocolate and Heart Disease: Some Good News

Are we running any risk to our health by indulging in our obvious love for chocolate? It is true that chocolate is rich in saturated fatty acids, villains when it comes to raising cholesterol and clogging our coronary arteries. Yet the particular saturated fatty acid in the cocoa butter of chocolate turns out to be quite benign. The main component of cocoa butter is a fatty acid known as stearic acid, which is rapidly converted in the liver to oleic acid, a monounsaturate that neither raises nor lowers serum cholesterol.

One study found that healthy young men on a twenty-six-day diet in which a total of 37 percent of calories came from fat and 81 percent of those fat calories came from cocoa butter had no increase in their serum cholesterol, and their cholesterol levels were no higher than if they had been on a comparable diet in which the fat came from olive oil (see Chapter 1).

Recent evidence suggests that chocolate may even *protect* arteries from disease. Cocoa powder, it has been discovered, has a concentration of compounds called *flavonoids* that are known to function as antioxidants of the bloodstream. The greater the level of antioxidants, the lower the probability that artery-clogging cells will develop. Dark chocolate has twice the antioxidants of milk chocolate, but both forms of chocolate have several times greater antioxidant

properties than prunes, raisins, blueberries, blackberries, and leafy vegetables.

This is not to say that chocolate should be considered a substitute for fruits and vegetables, foods that have obvious nutritional virtues. Nor should chocolate be viewed necessarily as a health food. Milk chocolate contains by definition (and by law) a minimal amount of milk-derived butterfat in addition to cocoa butter. Some chocolates also contain palm oil or coconut oil, two saturated fats that *do* raise cholesterol levels. And no one should expect to lose weight on a chocolate diet. Even so, nutritionists are concluding that there is little harm in eating two or three chocolate bars a week, which is welcome news for chocolate lovers everywhere.

Sources: Brody, Jane E. (2002, February 12). Valentine to dark chocolate, but go easy. *New York Times,* p. F7. Ding, Eric L.; Hutfless, Susan M.; Ding, Xin; and Girotra, Saket (2006). Chocolate and prevention of cardiovascular disease: A systematic review. *Nutrition and Metabolism,* accessed from www.nutritionandmetabolism.com/content/3/1/2. Raloff, Janet (2000, March 18). Chocolate hearts: Yummy and good medicine? *Science News,* pp. 188–189. Waterhouse, Andrew J., Shirley, Joseph R., and Donovan, Jennifer I. (1996). Antioxidants in chocolate. *Lancet,* 348, 834.

---

paste is often called **baking chocolate.** As chocolate, it is as pure as you can get, but since it has an "extra-bittersweet" flavor, it is not yet good enough to eat.

The real innovation in chocolate processing came in 1828, when a Dutch chemist, Coenraad van Houten, invented a screw press to squeeze the cocoa butter out of the hardened chocolate liquor. Surprisingly, pure cocoa butter is not brown but white in color; in fact, "white chocolate" is essentially pure cocoa butter with added ingredients. What is left after the cocoa butter has been removed from the chocolate liquor is a dry, dark-colored, cakelike substance that can be crushed into a powder. This powder can be mixed with sugar and other flavorings, and hot milk or water can be added to make cocoa.

To make chocolate as we know it, several additional processing steps are required, many of which were developed by the Swiss chocolatier Rodolphe Lindt in 1879. A ratio of cocoa liquor and cocoa butter is combined with milk, sugar, and vanilla to make milk chocolate. Just how much cocoa butter is added depends on the type of chocolate that is wanted—the more cocoa butter, the sweeter the result. Fortunately, unlike other fats, cocoa butter almost never goes rancid. In other words, milk chocolate keeps. It might turn white after a while, but that simply means that the cocoa butter is starting to separate from the mixture. It is all right to eat, though chocolate connoisseurs would surely disagree. All that is needed to produce commercial chocolate is to refine the texture to achieve that degree of smoothness the world has come to know and love (Health Line).[12]

The Chocolate Industry Today

Present-day domestic sales of chocolate bars in the United States are dominated by Hershey Chocolate USA and M&M/Mars, together holding approximately 85 percent of a $18 billion annual market (see Portrait). Overall, the annual per capita consumption of chocolate in the United States is approximately 12 pounds, which puts the country eleventh among chocolate-loving nations of the world. The champion, not surprisingly, is Switzerland, where the per capita consumption of chocolate is more than 22 pounds per year.[13]

> **baking chocolate:** A hardened paste, consisting of chocolate liquor, produced by heating roasted cocoa beans.

PORTRAIT

Milton S. Hershey and the Town Built on Chocolate

When Milton Hershey made a decision in 1893 to go into the chocolate business, he was already an experienced confectioner with a prosperous caramel company in Lancaster, Pennsylvania, to his credit. But he could see that the future was in chocolate. New German-built machinery was now available to mass-produce milk chocolate. Hershey wanted to be in the business on the ground floor.

He bought the equipment and started to experiment on a special recipe, using fresh milk from the local dairy farms instead of powdered milk. The proportion of milk and sugar, the blend of cocoa beans, and the roasting time are secrets to this day. All we know is that somehow Hershey figured out a recipe that was a winner. The new Hershey bar was an instant hit.

By 1903, the Hershey chocolate business had become so successful that it needed a new factory. Defying conventional wisdom, however, Hershey did not look for a town or city for the factory but rather went into the surrounding countryside. He bought a thousand acres of prime Pennsylvania Dutch farmland, built his factory, then decided to build a town around it.

By 1930, the town of Hershey had grown to include residents beyond the six thousand factory workers. The Hershey business was now worldwide, with its chocolate kisses and chocolate syrup in addition to other products. During hard economic times, to maintain employment, Hershey went on a construction spree. He built the famous Hershey Hotel, Hershey Gardens, a football stadium and sports arena, and a convention center. Because he was childless, he turned his attention to building a Milton Hershey school for orphaned boys and girls.

Milton Hershey died in 1945 at the age of eighty-eight, but his corporate heirs continued in his spirit. Today, there is the Milton S. Hershey Medical Center of the Pennsylvania State University, endowed by the Hershey Company. And of course there is Hersheypark, a continuation of an old amusement park Hershey had built in 1905, all powered by a best-selling chocolate bar and a man with a very sweet dream.

Sources: D'Antonio, Michael (2006). *Hershey: Milton S. Hershey's extraordinary life of wealth, empire, and utopian dreams.* New York: Simon and Schuster. Morton, Marcia, and Morton, Frederic (1986). Chocolate: *An illustrated history.* New York: Crown Publishers, pp. 89–125.

The Xanthine Content in Chocolate

The amounts of xanthines are much smaller in chocolate than in coffee or tea. A typical 1-ounce piece of milk chocolate, for example, contains about 6 mg of caffeine and about 44 mg of theobromine. With theobromine packing about one-tenth the stimulant power of caffeine, we can approximate the total effect of this quantity of chocolate to be roughly equivalent to 10 mg of caffeine. Of course, eating more than 1 ounce will change these figures (a typical chocolate bar is approximately 1.5 ounces), but even so, it is unlikely that chocolate will keep you up at night.[14]

Soft Drinks

The fourth and final major source of caffeine in our diet is soft drinks. Table 12.1 shows the caffeine content of prominent soft-drink brands. Although most of the caffeinated drinks are colas, it is possible for a noncola to be caffeinated as well. The reason is that more than 95 percent of the caffeine in caffeinated soft drinks is added by the manufacturer during production; less than 5 percent actually comes from the West African kola nut, from which cola gets its name.

TABLE 12.1

Caffeine levels and domestic U.S. market share of leading brands of soft drinks

BRAND NAME	PERCENTAGE OF MARKET (2006)	CAFFEINE CONTENT (MG/12 OZ.)
Coca-Cola Classic	17.3	34
Pepsi-Cola	11.0	38
Diet Coke	9.8	46
Mountain Dew	6.6	55
Diet Pepsi	6.0	36
Dr Pepper	5.8	41
Sprite	5.7	none
Fanta	1.8	none
Diet Dr Pepper	1.5	4.1
Diet Mountain Dew	1.5	55
Others (cola, citrus, orange, root beer, etc.)	33.0	—

Sources: Energyfiend.com. Sales figures from *Market share reporter,* Volume 1 (2008). Farmington Hills, MI: Thomson Gale, p. 158.

In general, the United States leads the world in per capita consumption of soft-drink products, nearly 53 gallons annually or the equivalent of two to three 8-ounce servings each day. Beverages with high levels of caffeine, either citrus-flavored noncolas (such as Mountain Dew), colas (such as Jolt), or a wide array of new energy-drink products (see Table 12.3, page 313), constitute a relatively small proportion of total soft-drink sales, but they have been the fastest-growing segment of the beverage industry since 2001. The concern that these beverages might be a problem for young drinkers who are attracted to them as stimulants will be explored in a later section.[15]

Caffeine from OTC Drugs and Other Products

Caffeine is sold purely as a stimulant in over-the-counter (OTC) drugs such as NoDoz and Vivarin tablets and as one of several ingredients in a number of other products ranging from pain relievers and cold remedies to diuretics and weight-control aids. As Table 12.2 shows, the equivalent caffeine level in these products ranges approximately from that of one-third cup to two cups of regular coffee.

The availability of caffeine in OTC drugs has recently been supplemented by novelty products such as

TABLE 12.2

Caffeine content in common over-the-counter medications

MEDICATION	CAFFEINE PER TABLET OR CAPSULE (in milligrams)	CAFFEINE PER RECOMMENDED DOSAGE (in milligrams)
Stimulants		
NoDoz	100	200
Vivarin	200	200
Pain relievers		
Anacin	32	64
Excedrin	65	130
Midol	32	64
Vanquish	33	66
Cold remedies		
Coryban-D	30	30
Dristan	16	32
Triaminicin	30	30
Diuretics		
Aqua-Ban	100	200

Note: Caffeine is also found in prescription remedies for migraines (Cafergot and Migral) and in pain relievers (Darvon Compound and Fiorinol).

Source: Updated from Gilbert, Richard J. (1986). *Caffeine: The most popular stimulant.* New York: Chelsea House Publishers, p. 51.

caffeinated lip balm, caffeinated sunflower seeds, caffeinated beer, and even caffeinated soap (promoted as waking you up while the coffee is brewing).[16]

The Era of Decaffeination

Public concerns about adverse effects of caffeine and a general increase in consciousness about health have led to a steady increase in decaffeinated consumer products, particularly coffee. Since 1960, decaffeinated coffee's share of total coffee sales has risen dramatically, though it remains smaller than that of caffeinated coffee.

Unfortunately, decaffeination can reduce coffee flavor. One of the reasons for the loss in flavor is the choice of beans being decaffeinated. Typically only the robusta species of coffee bean is decaffeinated, not only because it costs less but also because its harsher flavor can better withstand the decaffeination process.[17]

Another reason stems from the major technique employed in decaffeination, known as the *water method*. In this technique, the beans are first steamed and then soaked in water. The soaking removes the caffeine but also all the other solids in the coffee beans that give them a rich flavor. The water is removed, the caffeine is removed from the water, and the remaining water is returned to soak the still-wet beans, in an effort to reintroduce some of the lost flavor. Most coffee experts consider the coffee bean that has been "naturally decaffeinated" in this way to bear only a pale resemblance to its former self. Coffee manufacturers tend to roast the decaffeinated beans longer (some say that they are then overroasted) to produce extra body and flavor.

A newer technique has been developed in which carbon dioxide loosens the chemical bonds that hold caffeine to the coffee bean. Decaffeinated coffee produced in this way is available in a few selected brands. Its flavor is significantly superior to the flavor of coffee that has been decaffeinated by the water method.

Future decaffeination techniques may work on the basis of the coffee bean plant itself. It is technically feasible to genetically alter the plant, through a technique called RNA interference, so that it produces less of the enzyme that produces caffeine. Whether this strategy can eliminate as much as 97 percent of the caffeine in coffee, the current standard for commercial decaffeination, remains to be determined.

Genetic engineering, however, may someday not be necessary to achieve the perfect decaffeinated cup of coffee. In 2004, a naturally decaffeinated arabica coffee plant was discovered in Ethiopia. It might be feasible in the future to transfer this characteristic feature to commercial varieties of arabica coffee plants through hybridization techniques.[18]

Caffeine as a Drug

When ingested orally, caffeine is absorbed in about thirty to sixty minutes. Caffeine levels peak in the bloodstream in one hour, and reactions in the central nervous system peak in about two hours. Many coffee drinkers notice a boost of energy, or "buzz," almost immediately, but this effect is attributable either to the sugar in the coffee or to a conditioned learning effect, not to the caffeine itself. From three to seven hours after caffeine is consumed, approximately half of it still remains in the bloodstream.

The biotransformation of caffeine and the time it takes to eliminate it vary according to a number of factors. For example, women in late stages of pregnancy and those using oral contraceptives eliminate caffeine from their systems more slowly than either men or women in general. Infants and the elderly also show a slower elimination of caffeine. In contrast, smokers eliminate caffeine about 100 percent more quickly than nonsmokers. As a result, smokers on average experience the effect of the caffeine they consume for a relatively shorter period of time; it is possible that smokers tend to drink more caffeinated coffee than nonsmokers to compensate for their faster elimination of caffeine.[19]

Effects of Caffeine on the Body

The stimulant effects of caffeine, as well as those of the other xanthines, are a result of its ability to block the effects of an inhibitory neurotransmitter called **adenosine.** Normally, adenosine binds to receptors on the surface of cells and, consequently, produces sleepiness, dilation of blood vessels, and constriction of bronchial passageways. It also protects the body against seizures, slows down the body's reaction to stress, and lowers heart rate, blood pressure, and body temperature.

By inhibiting the effects of adenosine, caffeine and other xanthines cause the opposite responses to occur, though the actual results are complex. In general, peripheral blood vessels are dilated, while cerebral blood vessels in the head are constricted. Because dilated blood vessels in the head can frequently result in headache pain, caffeine can help headache sufferers, and that is why it is found in many over-the-counter pain relievers. Heart rate is slightly elevated when caffeine is consumed, but the effect is dose-dependent and often is not observed at all.

The fact that caffeine has a bronchodilating effect makes it helpful in treating asthmatic conditions in which the bronchial passageways are abnormally constricted. Theophylline, however, has a stronger bronchodilating effect than caffeine and as a result can be prescribed at lower doses. Caffeine is effective, but patients often report unpleasant side effects of "jitteriness" before their asthmatic condition improves.[20]

Effects of Caffeine on Behavior

A major effect of caffeine as well as other xanthines is to excite neuronal activity in the brain. As the dose increases, the effects expand from the cerebral cortex downward to

lower systems in the brain and finally to the spinal cord. The behavioral consequence of this excitation is a feeling of mental alertness and lack of fatigue.

On the basis of these effects, you might expect that caffeine would also improve human performance, but reports in this regard are quite mixed. Subjects in controlled experimental settings feel stimulated and more alert, but whether their performance improves after caffeine depends on the type of task, their personal characteristics, and even the time of day when the experiment is conducted. In a recent study of possible performance-enhancing effects among competitive cyclists, it was found that caffeine administration increased their performance during timed trials overall, but the effect was greater when the cyclists were (falsely) informed that they had not ingested it![21]

Nonetheless, it is possible to make some generalizations about caffeine's effect on performance. In general, caffeine increases vigilance and attentiveness in tasks at which subjects become easily bored, and it decreases the response time to simple visual or auditory signals. For more complex tasks in which subjects need to make decisions or in situations that require motor coordination, however, caffeine either has little effect or can be disruptive. Most reports of improvements under caffeine involve conditions in which the subject is already either bored or fatigued. In these circumstances, caffeine helps either to maintain a level of performance that would otherwise have declined or to restore performance from a state degraded by boredom or fatigue. Caffeine, therefore, can serve to support a moderate level of arousal and attention that is optimal for the task at hand.[22]

Caffeine is typically most effective to ward off sleep and improve performance on tedious tasks, both at home and in the workplace.

adenosine (a-DEN-oh-seen): An inhibitory neurotransmitter that is blocked, or neutralized, by caffeine and other xanthines. The action on adenosine receptors in the body is the basis for the stimulant properties of these drugs.

The best-known effect, however, is the impact on sleep. Coffeine lengthens the time it takes to fall asleep and reduces the quality of sleep once it comes. Generally, studies investigating caffeine effects have involved coffee drinking, and the sleep effects are seen more strongly in nondrinkers of coffee than in habitual heavy coffee drinkers.[23]

As a final note, it is important to understand what interacting effects caffeine may or may not have on alcohol intoxication. First of all, caffeine does *not* have ability to sober up a person recently intoxicated with alcohol. Despite the widespread notion that a cup of strong black coffee will help someone who is drunk, the evidence is simply not there. If anything, the behavioral consequences of alcohol intoxication can worsen (see Health Line, page 236). Second, the ingestion of highly caffeinated energy drinks (see Table 12.3, page 313) as mixers with alcohol at bars and clubs will not reduce alcoholic intoxication, as measured by objective tests. The combination reduces a person's perception of intoxication, leading them to believe that they are more in control than they actually are. As a result, caffeinated energy drinks can make it more likely that greater amounts of alcohol will be consumed.[24]

Potential Health Benefits

In 2000, an intriguing connection was found between caffeine consumption and a lower risk of developing Parkinson's disease. In a follow-up of about eight thousand Japanese American men in Honolulu, the incidence of Parkinson's disease was about one-fifth in men who consumed at least 28 ounces of coffee per day, compared to those who consumed none at all. A lower risk of Parkinson's disease was observed no matter what the source of the caffeine and independent of intake levels of milk and sugar.

A second study in 2001 involving a larger sample of men confirmed this relationship, but it is presently uncertain whether the same relationship exists in women. In studies in which a lower risk is found in women, there is a U-shaped function for women, with either low or high consumption levels being less protective than moderate ones; for men, the higher the caffeine intake, the better the protection. The gender differences may ultimately be due to hormonal factors—perhaps caffeine's interaction with estrogen. A recent study has shown that caffeine reduces the risk of Parkinson's disease among postmenopausal women who do not take replacement estrogen; for those women

who do take this therapy, caffeine increases the risk of the disorder.

Caffeine consumption, in the form of coffee or tea drinking, has also been reported to reduce the risk of oral, pharyngeal, and esophageal cancer and the risk of Type 2 diabetes mellitus. However, the degree to which caffeine is beneficial in these cases is relatively small, and the quantities of consumption need to be considerably greater than typical levels of caffeine intake. An exception is a recent finding that as little as two cups of coffee a day lowers the risk of liver cirrhosis by almost one-half, after adjusting for sex, age, and alcohol use.[25]

Potential Health Risks

Studies investigating the potential adverse health consequences of caffeine consumption have been conducted for more than a century, and the conclusions have varied considerably. In some cases, earlier concerns have been determined to be unfounded. For example, a 1971 study indicated an association between caffeine consumption and urinary tract cancer, and a 1981 study indicated an association with pancreatic cancer. In both studies, however, the conclusions were compromised by methodologically flawed designs. At present, the medical consensus is that caffeine consumption is not causally related to these or other types of cancer.[26]

Cardiovascular Effects

Because it is known that caffeine stimulates cardiac muscle as well as skeletal muscle throughout the body, it is only natural to be concerned with the possibility that caffeine consumption would be a risk factor for a heart attack or cardiac arrhythmia (irregular heart beat). In 1973, a great deal of publicity was generated by a study called the Boston Collaborative Drug Surveillance Program in which a large number of individuals at Boston metropolitan hospitals were surveyed as to their use of many different drugs, including caffeine, and the incidence of various disease states. The researchers reported that the consumption of more than six cups of caffeinated coffee a day more than doubled the risk of a heart attack. Further studies, however, have failed to find any connection at all between caffeine and heart attacks.[27]

What do we do when the medical literature is so inconclusive and contradictory? First of all, in caffeine studies that show some cardiovascular health risk, the consumption levels are rather high (five to six cups or more a day). Drinking less caffeine has not been identified as a risk factor. Even so, potential health problems associated with caffeine consumption have to be considered in the context of other behaviors. As a pharmacologist has put it,

> In both males and females without heart disease, the use of caffeinated coffee and the total daily intake of caffeine do not appreciably increase the risk of coronary artery disease or stroke.... Coffee consumption is strongly associated with cigarette smoking, and increased rates of coronary heart disease in heavy coffee drinkers who smoke occur as a result of the cigarette smoking, not the caffeine consumption.[28]

At the same time, we should be aware that a four-year-old child drinking a 20-ounce cola drink is consuming a very high dose of caffeine per body weight, and we should not be surprised that marked behavioral and physiological effects will follow (Health Line).

Osteoporosis and Bone Fractures

A 1990 study analyzing caffeine consumption and incidence of hip fractures among more than three thousand elderly men and women found that those who reported drinking 2.5 to 3 cups of caffeinated coffee or 5 to 6 cups of caffeinated tea per day had a 69 percent greater risk of osteoporosis (bone loss and brittleness) than caffeine abstainers. Those who reported drinking more than 3.5 cups of caffeinated coffee or 7 cups of caffeinated tea had an 82 percent greater risk. Because one of the effects of caffeine is to increase the urinary excretion of calcium and to inhibit the absorption of calcium from the diet in the elderly, it makes sense that there might be an adverse effect on bone tissue in this age group.[29]

Breast Disease

A 1981 report indicated a relationship between caffeine consumption and the formation of benign (that is, noncancerous) lumps in the breasts called *fibrocystic lesions*. However, the study was severely criticized as not being based on randomized sampling nor having methodological controls that would shield the researchers from imposing their bias in observing fibrocystic lesion cases. Subsequent studies that were more carefully executed showed no relationship between the incidence of this frequently painful condition and caffeine consumption.[30] There is disagreement about whether women who already have fibrocystic lesions might show improvement by abstaining from caffeinated products; a 1985 report indicates that abstinence is helpful, whereas subsequent reports indicate that there is no benefit.[31]

Health Line
Coffee, Genes, and Heart Attacks

The known stimulant effect of caffeine on cardiac muscle has raised suspicions about the potential risk of a heart attack due to coffee intake. As described in this chapter, the medical findings are often confusing, and a number of explanations have been advanced to explain contradictions in the data.

A major study points to the role of an enzyme that controls the metabolism of caffeine in the body. Researchers studied 2,000 patients who had suffered heart attacks and 2,000 healthy subjects. Analysis of their DNA revealed a gene sequence that allowed caffeine to break down up to four times more slowly than normally. Individuals with the relatively "slow" version of this gene had an increased risk of a heart attack with as little as two cups of coffee per day. However, those individuals with the relatively "fast" version had no increased risk, even with four or more cups per day. Indeed, for individuals younger than 50 years of age who had the fast version of the gene, the consumption of one to three cups per day was associated with a *lower* risk. In other words, for this particular group, caffeine had a protective effect with respect to a potential heart attack.

The stimulant effect of caffeine on the nervous system is not related to this particular gene sequence, so whether individuals had the slow or fast version did not change their behavioral response to coffee. Nonetheless, the increasing attention toward genomic variations among individuals is certain to shed light on previously inconclusive medical research concerning the health risks of various orally administered drugs (see Chapter 3).

Source: Cornelis, Marilyn C.; El-Sohemy, Ahmed; Kabagambe, Edmond K.; and Campos, Hannia (2006). Coffee, CYP1A2 genotype, and risk of myocardial infarction. *Journal of the American Medical Association, 295,* 1135–1141.

Effects during Pregnancy and Breastfeeding

At one time, caffeine use was suspected to be linked to infertility in women. A study in 1990 reported that women who consumed three cups of coffee a day reduced their chances of getting pregnant by 25 percent. A more recent study in 1998, however, has found no relationship between caffeine intake and infertility.[32]

Nonetheless, there can be potential problems later in pregnancy. Caffeine consumption (more than three or four cups of coffee a day) during the first three months of pregnancy is related to a greater incidence of low birth weight in the newborn, though the incidence of premature birth or birth defects is not increased. There is also a relationship between very high levels of caffeine consumption (more than six cups of coffee per day) during pregnancy and an increased risk of miscarriage. Therefore, the cautionary advice of the FDA is warranted: Women should abstain from caffeine if at all possible during pregnancy.[33]

Afterward, in the case of breastfeeding, it is also a good idea to continue a caffeine-free diet. Enzymes that normally break down caffeine in the liver are not present in the liver of a newborn baby, and as a consequence the elimination half-life of caffeine is much longer than in the adult, up to eighty-five hours. Though there is no evidence of specific harm from having a stimulant such as caffeine in the nervous system for such intervals of time, it seems to be a situation that might well be avoided.[34]

Panic Attacks

Consumption of caffeine equivalent to about four to five cups of coffee a day has been associated with the onset of panic attacks in those individuals suffering from a panic disorder. This finding is consistent with the known effects of caffeine as a CNS stimulant. Any person with a history of panic attacks should be careful to avoid caffeine, and mental health professionals should be aware of the possibility that caffeine consumption could trigger a panic episode.[35]

Dependence, Acute Toxicity, and Medical Applications

More than 85 percent of people in the United States consume caffeine in one form or another each day. In 1985, 401 men and women, all employees of the state of New York, were asked about their caffeine consumption over the previous seventy-two-hour period, including all foods, beverages, and medications that might contain caffeine. Only eleven of them did not consume any caffeine at all, and the average caffeine consumption level was about 400 mg.[36] This was neither a random nor a large sample, but the results nonetheless illustrate the basic point made at the opening of this chapter: Caffeine consumption is a cultural norm in the United States and the rest of the world. The fact that caffeinated beverages in particular are embedded in the diet of this country makes it difficult to think of caffeine as a drug, much less one that could cause dependence. "People say they're addicted to caffeine and laugh," a prominent caffeine researcher has said. "They wouldn't say the same thing about heroin."[37]

Tolerance

When individuals who do not usually use caffeine are administered repeated doses equivalent to amounts that would ordinarily be acquired from the diet, the initial increases in heart rate and blood pressure start to decline after approximately seventy-two hours.[38] In other words, with respect to the cardiovascular effects of caffeine, a classic tolerance effect, as defined in Chapter 2, can be observed.

With respect to the behavioral and psychological effects of caffeine, tolerance effects are more difficult to evaluate, despite the fact that most of us have noticed at some time in our lives that caffeine was having a progressively smaller effect on us as we started to be habitual caffeine consumers. The problem appears to be that once we are in a laboratory setting, most of us are already tolerant to the effects of caffeine. Recent studies that have specifically controlled for variations in the subject's recent dietary intake of caffeine have shown tolerance effects for dosage levels as low as 100 mg, the equivalent of one to two cups of coffee.

Withdrawal

A stronger case for caffeine being a drug that produces physical dependence is contained in the research findings concerning withdrawal. As you may have encountered yourself, a sudden cessation in the intake of coffee or other caffeinated products results in symptoms of headache, impaired concentration, drowsiness, irritability, muscle aches, and other flu-like symptoms. A headache is a typical withdrawal symptom, usually appearing from twelve to eighteen hours after the last dose of caffeine, peaking over the next two days or so, and persisting in some individuals for up to a week. This pain is associated with an increase in blood flow to the brain, at levels above what a person normally experiences. As you might expect, a reintroduction of caffeine causes the pain and other withdrawal symptoms to disappear. One study on the pattern of withdrawal symptoms from coffee found significant symptoms even when subjects had been consuming as little as 100 mg per day.[39]

Craving

The case for physical dependence is clear; the case for psychological dependence, however, is presently uncertain. We do not know if the tendency to have that next cup of coffee or other caffeinated product is a matter of desiring to have it or an effort to avoid withdrawal symptoms that would ensue if we did not have it.

Acute Toxicity of Caffeine

Too much caffeine can produce toxic effects on the body, but the amount that might do so is substantial and generally beyond what we typically consume. Approximately 1,000 mg of caffeine (equivalent to about ten cups of caffeinated coffee), consumed over a short period of time, results in extreme nervousness and agitation, muscle hyperactivity and twitching, profound insomnia, heart palpitations and arrhythmias, gastrointestinal upset, nausea, and diarrhea. The condition is referred to as **caffeinism.** In a few individuals, particularly those who do not typically ingest caffeine, these symptoms might arise from a much lower dose level. There is also growing concern that caffeine use might magnify emotional difficulties in mental health patients and reduce the benefits of medications that they are taking.

While caffeinism is not officially recognized as a psychological disorder by the American Psychiatric Association, the DSM-IV-TR manual defines a condition called *acute caffeine intoxication*, resulting from a caffeine intake in excess of 250 mg and producing caffeinism-like symptoms that cause "significant distress or impairment in social, occupational, or other important areas of functioning." It is admittedly unusual to observe such behaviors from a caffeine level equivalent to two or three cups of coffee, but as the dose rises above this level, the probability of observing a toxic reaction can be expected to increase.[40]

---

caffeinism: A dangerous state of overstimulation from a very large dose of caffeine.

The adult lethal dose is approximately 5 to 10 grams (5,000 to 10,000 mg), which is equivalent roughly to somewhere between fifty and one hundred cups of caffeinated coffee. The lowest caffeine dose known to have been fatal in an adult is 3.2 grams (3,200 mg), administered mistakenly by a nurse who believed the syringe contained another drug. Lethal doses for children are lower, and a number of accidental deaths have resulted from eating large quantities of caffeine-containing medications.[41]

Prescription Drugs Based on Xanthines

Owing to the superiority of theophylline over caffeine in its ability to relax smooth muscle, theophylline has been used medically to treat a number of clinical conditions. Its application as a bronchodilator for asthmatics has been mentioned earlier. One particular medication, aminophylline, combines theophylline with methylediamine, an inert compound that increases the absorption of theophylline and enhances its clinical benefit. Because theophylline also stimulates cardiac muscle, it is sometimes prescribed for patients with congestive heart disease.

Kids and Caffeine: A Special Concern

There is little doubt that caffeine consumption among young people in the United States under the age of eighteen has risen significantly in the last decade or so. One reason has to do with the consumption of caffeinated soft drinks. It has been estimated that teenagers consume about sixty-four gallons of soft drinks each year, largely in caffeinated forms. Mega-sized soft drinks, sometimes with free refills, are standard offerings in fast-food restaurants and convenience stores; soft-drink vending machines that provide 20-ounce bottles, instead of 12-ounce cans, are not uncommon. You might recall a similar issue in Chapter 9 in calculating the total amount of alcohol in a given number of alcoholic "drinks."

Another major opportunity for caffeine consumption in this age group comes from patterns of coffee drinking at coffee bars, where highly caffeinated espresso drinks served sweet, cold, and in "grande" quantities are increasingly popular. Although the level of caffeine intake in multiple soft drinks and coffee may be equivalent to levels experienced by many adults, the

TABLE 12.3

Current leading "energy drinks" in the U.S. market

BRAND	PERCENTAGE MARKET SHARE BASED ON DOLLAR SALES	CAFFEINE CONTENT (mg)	SERVING QUANTITY (oz)	CAFFEINE (mg/oz)*
Red Bull	43	80	8.3	9.6
Monster	14	160	16	10.0
Rockstar	11	160	16	10.0
Full Throttle	7	144	16	9.0
Sobe No Fear	5	174	16	10.9
Amp	4	75	8.4	8.9
Sobe Adrenaline Rush	3	79	8.3	9.5
Tab Energy	2	95	10.5	9.0

Note: Some brands also contain taurine, guarana, or bitter orange. All of these ingredients have stimulant properties and have the potential for elevating heart rate and blood pressure. Checking the list of ingredients is a good idea, even though manufacturers are not required to specify the milligram quantities.

*Comparable caffeine content in Coca-Cola Classic is 2.9 mg/oz.

Sources: Sevenson, Kim (2006, June 19). Energy drinks are fueling concerns. *New York Times*, p. F9. www.energyfiend.com, 2008.

physiological and behavioral effects are actually greater, since body weight in a younger population is only one-half to two-thirds that of an adult. In other words, the dosage level of caffeine, expressed as milligrams per kilogram (mg/kg), ends up exceeding levels typically ingested by adults (Table 12.3). In some European countries (United Kingdom, Sweden, and Finland) per capita caffeine consumption among young people exceeds that in the United States.

The extent of caffeine consumption in this population raises some significant health concerns. Drinking caffeinated beverages instead of milk can result in obesity as well as deficient levels of calcium and phosphorus, minerals that are needed for normal bone growth during adolescence. While research is presently lacking as to whether significant caffeine consumption in the early years will lead to osteoporosis in adulthood, the research showing an increased risk among the elderly suggests that a similar risk might exist for younger people as well. Finally, the evidence is quite clear that soft-drink consumption and the substantial calorie intake associated with it have significant adverse metabolic effects, resulting in obesity and increased risk of Type 2 diabetes. Indeed, soft-drink consumption is widely viewed as a factor in the increased prevalence of childhood obesity in American youth. Unfortunately, a recent study found that the proportion of students whose schools permit the soft-drink bottler to advertise in the school and to sponsor school events increases with declining socioeconomic status (SES) of the student population.[42]

On a behavioral level, there are concerns about insomnia, nervousness, and anxiety among young people who ingest large amounts of caffeine. On the other hand, some evidence suggests that moderate levels of caffeine consumption may reduce hyperactivity and impulsiveness associated with attention deficit/hyperactivity disorder (ADHD). In this sense, caffeine acts as a CNS stimulant in a way similar to the stronger stimulant medications, such as methylphenidate (Ritalin) or amphetamine, that are prescribed for this disorder (Chapter 4).[43]

The large doses of caffeine ingested by young people on a daily basis have raised health concerns.

Summary

- Caffeine belongs to a family of stimulant drugs called xanthines. It is found in coffee, tea, chocolate, many soft drinks, and some medications.
- Other xanthines are theophylline (found in tea) and theobromine (found in chocolate).

Coffee

- Coffee drinking originated in the Middle East and later was introduced to England in the seventeenth century. Coffee houses in Britain and in colonial America sprang up as establishments where political and social discussions could be held.
- Today's coffee comes from a mixture of arabica and robusta beans, imported largely from Brazil, Colombia, Indonesia, and several nations in Africa.
- On average, a 5-ounce cup of coffee contains roughly 100 mg of caffeine, with the actual level determined by the type of coffee beans used and the method of brewing.

Tea

- Tea drinking originated in China and later was introduced to Europe by Dutch traders in the early seventeenth century. It became most popular in Britain and Russia. Today, tea consumption is greatest in Britain and Ireland.
- On average, a 5-ounce cup of tea contains roughly 60 mg of caffeine, with the actual level determined by the method of brewing and brand.

Chocolate

- Chocolate originated in pre-Columbian Central America and was introduced to Europe by the return of Cortés to Spain in 1528. Its popularity spread across Europe in the seventeenth century. By the 1880s, techniques for producing present-day milk chocolate had been perfected.
- The caffeine level in chocolate is relatively low, roughly 6 mg per ounce.

Soft Drinks

- Caffeinated colas have most of the caffeine content added to the beverage during production. Levels of caffeine in these beverages are approximately 38–45 mg per 12 ounces.

Caffeine from Medications

- Like drugs, caffeine and other xanthines are stimulants of the CNS and of peripheral musculature. Theophylline, in particular, has a strong bronchodilating effect and is useful for treating asthmatic conditions.

Caffeine as a Drug

- The behavioral effects of caffeine can be characterized principally as a reduction in fatigue and boredom, as well as a delay in the onset of sleep.
- Recent evidence suggests that caffeine might lower the risk of developing Parkinson's disease in men. A comparable protective role in women is currently uncertain.
- Health risks from moderate consumption of caffeine are not clinically significant, except for the adverse effects on fetal development during pregnancy, the development of bone loss among the elderly, possibly an adverse effect on the cardiac condition of patients already suffering from cardiovascular disease, and the aggravation of panic attacks among patients with this disorder.
- Continued consumption of caffeine produces tolerance effects; when caffeine consumption ceases, withdrawal symptoms are observed. High levels of caffeine consumption can produce toxic effects, though deaths are extremely rare.

Kids and Caffeine

- Young people in the United States ingest increasingly large quantities of caffeine through the drinking of caffeinated soft drinks and coffee. The actual dosage level is substantial, since body weight is less than that of an adult.
- Health concerns regarding caffeine consumption in this population include potential deficiencies in calcium and phosphorus for normal bone growth as well as behavioral problems such as insomnia, nervousness, and anxiety.

Key Terms

adenosine, p. 308
baking chocolate, p. 305
caffeine, p. 300
caffeinism, p. 312
Camellia sinensis, p. 302
chocolate liquor, p. 304
cocoa bean pods, p. 303
cocoa butter, p. 304
Coffea arabica, p. 300
Coffea robusta, p. 301
theobromine, p. 300
theophylline, p. 300
xanthines, p. 300

Endnotes

1. Austin, Gregory A. (1978). *Perspectives on the history of psychoactive substance use.* Rockville, MD: National Institute on Drug Abuse, p. 50. Jacob, Heinrich E. (1935). *Coffee: The epic of a commodity.* New York: Viking Press, pp. 3–10.

2. Robinson, Edward F. (1893). *The early history of coffee houses in England.* London: Kegan Paul, p. 26. Cited in Edward M. Brecher, and the editors of *Consumer Reports* (1972), *Licit and illicit drugs.* Boston: Little, Brown, p. 197.

3. Ukers, William H. (1935). *All about coffee.* New York: Tea and Coffee Trade Journal Co., p. 61. Wellman, Frederick L. (1961). *Coffee: Botany, cultivation, and utilization.* New York: Interscience Publishers, p. 22 or 23.

4. Fussell, Betty (1999, September 5). The world before Starbucks. *New York Times Book Review,* p. 26, quotation on p. 26. International Coffee Organisation, London, 2008. Pendergrast, Mark (1999). *Uncommon grounds: The history of coffee and how it transformed our world.* New York: Basic Books. Starbird, Ethel A. (1981, March). The bonanza bean: Coffee. *National Geographic Magazine,* pp. 398–399.

5. Barone, J. J., and Roberts, H. (1984). Human consumption of caffeine. In Peter B. Dews (Ed.), *Caffeine: Perspectives from recent research.* Berlin: Springer-Verlag, pp. 60–63.

6. Shalleck, Jamie (1972). Tea. New York: Viking Press. www.energyfiend.com/the_caffeine_database.

7. MacFarlane, Alan, and MacFarlane, Iris (2003). *The empire of tea: The remarkable history of the plant that took over the world.* New York: Overlook. Maitland, Derek (1982). *5000 years of tea: A pictorial companion.* Hong Kong: CFW Publications Limited, pp. 80–89.

8. Gilbert, Richard (1986). *Caffeine: The most popular stimulant.* New York: Chelsea House, p. 23.

9. Grosser, Daniel S. (1978). A study of caffeine in tea. *American Journal of Clinical Nutrition, 31,* 1727–1731.

10. Haqqi, Tariq M.; Anthony, Donald D.; Gupta, Sanjay; Ahmad, Nihal; Lee, M.-S.; et al. (1999). Prevention of collagen-induced arthritis in mice by a polyphenolic fraction from green tea. *Proceedings of the National Academy of Sciences, 96,* 4524–4529. The major polyphenol from green tea may contribute to preventing carcinogenesis (2004, January 19).

11. *Health and Medicine Week,* pp. 116–117. Food and Agriculture Organization (FAO) of the United Nations, 2008.

12. Morton, Marcia, and Morton, Frederic (1986). *Chocolate: An illustrated history.* New York: Crown Publishers, pp. 77–87. Nelson, Bryn (2003, June 24). Uncovering an early taste for chocolate: Maya, Aztec cultures show a rich history. *Newsday,* pp. A29, A31.

13. Information for 2006 courtesy of the Chocolate Manufacturers' Association and the CAOBISCO Secretariat, Brussels.

14. Apgar, Joan L., and Tarka, Stanley M. (1998). Methylxanthine composition and consumption patterns of cocoa and chocolate products. In Gene A. Spiller (Ed.), *Caffeine.* Boca Raton, FL: CRC Press, pp. 163–192. Spiller, Gene A. (1984). *The methylxanthine beverages and foods: Chemistry, consumption, and health effects.* New York: A. R. Liss, pp. 171–172.

15. Barboza, David (1997, August 22). More hip, higher hop. *New York Times,* pp. D1, D5. Noonan, David (2001, May 14). Red Bull's good buzz. *Newsweek,* p. 39. Warner, Melanie (2006, March 6). Soda sales are showing their age. *New York Times,* pp. C1, C6. Winter, Greg (2001, May 1). Red to the rescue: PepsiCo looks to a new drink to jolt soda sales. *New York Times,* p. C1.

16. Kuchment, Anna (2007, July 30). Make that a double: Our desire for caffeinated "energy" products is soaring. *Newsweek,* p. 48. Shute, Nancy (2007, April 23). Over the limit: Americans young and old crave high-octane fuel and doctors are jittery. *Newsweek,* pp. 60–68.

17. Kummer, Corby (1990, July). Is coffee harmful? *Atlantic, 266,* pp. 92–96.

18. DeMers, John (1986). *The community kitchen's complete guide to gourmet coffee.* New York: Simon and Schuster, pp. 85–89. Kummer, Is coffee harmful? pp. 92–96. Making beans less jumpy. Study: New method to decaffeinate coffee (2003, June 19). *Newsday,* p. A39. Silvarolla, Maria B., Mazzafera, Paulo, and Fazuoli, Luiz C. (2004). Plant biochemistry: A naturally decaffeinated arabica coffee. *Nature, 429,* 826.

19. Fredholm, Bertil B.; Bättig, Karl; Homén, Janet; Nehlig, Astrid; and Zvartau, Edwin E. (1999). Actions of caffeine in the brain with special reference to factors that contribute to its widespread use. *Pharmacological Reviews, 51,* 83–133. Gilbert, *Caffeine,* pp. 76–79. Julien, Robert M. (2001). *A primer of drug action* (9th ed.). New York: Worth, p. 222. Quinlan, Paul, Lane, Joan, and Aspinall, Laurence (1997). Effects of hot tea, coffee and water ingestion on physiological responses and mode: The role of caffeine, water, and beverage type. *Psychopharmacology, 134,* 164–173. Reid, T. R. (2005, January). Caffeine. *National Geographic Magazine,* pp. 2–32.

20. Davis, A. Mark; Zhao, Zuowei; Stock, Howard S.; Mehl, Kristen A.; et al. (2003). Central nervous system effects of caffeine and adenosine on fatigue. *American Journal of Physiology, 53,* R399. Schiwall, S. I. (1986, November). Asthma relief that's brewed by the cup. *Prevention, 38,* 127. Spiller, Gene A. (1998). Basic metabolism and physiological effects of the methylxanthines. In Gene A. Spiller (Ed.), *Caffeine.* Boca Raton, FL: CRC Press, pp. 225–231.

21. Foad, Abigail J., Beedie, Christopher, J., and Coleman, Damian A. (2008). Pharmacological and psychological effects of caffeine ingestion in 40-km cycling performance. *Medicine and Science in Sports and Exercise, 40,* 158–165. Yun, Anthony J., Doux, John D., and Daniel,

Stephanie M. (2007). Brewing controversies: Darwinian perspective on the adaptive and maladaptive effects of caffeine and ethanol as dietary autonomic modulators. *Medical Hypotheses, 68,* 31–36.

22. Brice, Carolyn, and Smith, Andrew (2001). The effects of caffeine on simulated driving, subjective alertness, and sustained attention. *Human Psychopharmacology: Clinical and Experimental, 16,* 523–531. Snel, Jan, Lorist, Monicque M., and Tieges, Zoë (2004). Coffee, caffeine, and cognitive performance. In Astrid Nehlig (Ed.), *Coffee, tea, chocolate, and the brain.* Boca Raton, FL: CRC Press, pp. 53–71. Watters, Paul A., Martin, Frances, and Schreter, Zoltan (1997). Caffeine and cognitive performance: The nonlinear Yerkes-Dodson Law. *Human Psychopharmacology: Clinical and Experimental, 12,* 249–257.

23. Curatolo, Peter, and Robertson, David (1983). The health consequences of caffeine. *Annals of Internal Medicine, 98,* 641–653. Snel, Jan, Lorist, Monicque M., and Tieges, Zoë (2004). Effects of caffeine on sleep and wakefulness: An update. In Astrid Nehlig (Ed.), *Coffee, tea, chocolate, and the brain.* Boca Raton, FL: CRC Press, pp. 13–33.

24. Fillmore, Mark T., Roach, Emily, L., and Rice, Julietta T. (2002). Does caffeine counteract alcohol-induced impairment? The ironic effects of expectancy. *Journal of Studies on Alcohol, 63,* 745–754. Mason, Michael (2006, December 12). The energy-drink buzz is unmistakable. The health impact is unknown. *New York Times,* p. F5.

25. Ascherio, Alberto; Zhang, Shumin M.; Hernan, Miguel A.; Kawachi, Ichiro; et al. (2001). Prospective study of caffeine consumption and risk of Parkinson's disease in men and women. *Annals of Neurology, 50,* 56–63. Schwarzschild, Michael A., and Ascherio, Alberto (2004). Caffeine and Parkinson's disease. In Astrid Nehlig (Ed.), *Coffee, tea, chocolate, and the brain.* Boca Raton, FL: CRC Press, pp. 147–163. Tavani, Alessandra; Bertuzzi, Michaela; Talamini, Renato; Gallus, Silvano; Parpinel, Maria; et al. (2003). Coffee and tea intake and risk of oral, pharyngeal, and esophageal cancer. *Oral Oncology, 39,* 695–670. Tverdal, Aage, and Skurtveil, Svetlana (2003). Coffee intake and mortality from liver cirrhosis. *Annals of Epidemiology, 13,* 419–423. Van Dam, Rob M., and Hu, Frank B. (2005). Coffee consumption and risk of Type 2 diabetes. *Journal of the American Medical Association, 294,* 97–104.

26. Curatolo and Robertson, Health consequences of caffeine. Michels, Karin B.; Willett, Walter C.; Fuchs, Charles S.; and Giovannucci, Edward (2005). Coffee, tea, and caffeine consumption and incidence of colon and rectal cancer. *Journal of the National Cancer Institute, 97,* 282–292. International Food Information Council Foundation (2008, March). IFIC Review: Caffeine and health: Clarifying the controversies. Washington DC: International Food Information Council Foundation.

27. Jick, Hershel; Miettinen, Olli S.; Neff, Raymond K.; Shapiro, Samuel; Heinonen, Olli; et al. (1973). Coffee and myocardial infarction. *New England Journal of Medi-*

cine, 289, 63–67. Myers, Martin G. (1992, November). Caffeine under examination—A passing grade. *The Western Journal of Medicine,* pp. 586–587.

28. Bonita, Jennifer S.; Mandarano, Michael; Shuta, Donna; and Vinson, Joe (2007). Coffee and cardiovascular disease: *In vitro,* cellular, animal, and human studies. *Pharmacological Research, 55,* 187–198. Julien, Robert M. (1998). *A primer of drug action* (8th ed.). New York: Freeman. Quotation on p. 163.

29. Bruce, Bonnie, and Spiller, Gene A. (1998). Caffeine, calcium, and bone health. In Gene A. Spiller (Ed.), *Caffeine.* Boca Raton, FL: CRC Press, pp. 345–356. Kiel, Douglas P.; Felson, David T.; Hannan, Marian T.; Anderson, Jennifer J.; and Wilson, Peter W. F. (1990). Caffeine and the risk of hip fracture: The Framingham study. *American Journal of Epidemiology, 132,* 675–684.

30. Levinson, Wendy, and Dunn, Patrick M. (1986). Nonassociation of caffeine and fibrocystic breast disease. *Archives of Internal Medicine, 146,* 1773–1775. Minton, John P.; Foecking, M. K.; Webster, J. T.; and Matthews, R. H. (1979). Caffeine, cyclic nucleotides, and breast diseases. *Surgery, 86,* 105–109. Russell, Linda C. (1989). Caffeine restriction as initial treatment for breast pain. *Nurse Practitioner, 14,* 36–37.

31. Julien, *A primer of drug action* (8th ed.), p. 162.

32. Caan, Bette, Quesenberry, Charles P., and Coates, Ashley, O. (1998). Differences in fertility associated with caffeinated beverage consumption. *American Journal of Public Health, 88,* 270–274. Joesoef, M. Riduan; Beral, V.; Rolfs, Robert T.; Aral, Sevgio O.; and Cramer, Daniel W. (1990). Are caffeinated beverages risk factors for delayed conception? *Lancet, 335,* 136–137.

33. Fenster, Laura; Eskenazi, Brenda; Windham, Gayle C.; and Swan, Shanna H. (1991). Caffeine consumption during pregnancy and fetal growth. *American Journal of Public Health, 81,* 458–461. Grady, Denise (2008, January 21). Pregnancy problems tied to caffeine. *New York Times,* p. A10. Klebanoff, Mark A.; Levine, Richard J.; DerSimonian, Rebecca; Clemens, John D.; and Wilkins, Diana G. (1999). Maternal serum paraxanthine, a caffeine metabolite, and the risk of spontaneous abortion. *New England Journal of Medicine, 341,* 1639–1644. Nawrot, P.; Jordan, S.; Eastwood, J.; Rotstein, J.; et al. (2003). Effects of caffeine on human health. *Food Additives and Contaminants, 20,* 1–30. Signorello, Lisa B., and McLaughlin, Joseph K. (2004). Maternal caffeine consumption and spontaneous abortion: A review of the epidemiologic evidence. *Epidemiology, 15,* 229–239. Weng, Xiaoping, Odouli, Roxana, and Li, De-Kun (2008). Maternal caffeine consumption during pregnancy and the risk of miscarriage: A prospective cohort study. *American Journal of Obstetrics and Gynecology, 198,* 279e1–279e8.

34. Gilbert, *Caffeine,* pp. 78–79.

35. Charney, Dennis S., Heniger, George R., and Jatlow, Peter L. (1985). Increased anxiogenic effects of caffeine in panic disorders. *Archives of General Psychiatry, 42,*

233–243. Clay, Rebecca A. (1996, August). Coffee's jittery high can thwart treatment plans. *APA Monitor* (American Psychological Association, Washington DC), p. 12.

36. Knight, C. A.; Knight, I.; Mitchell, D. C.; and Zepp, J. E. (2004). Beverage caffeine intake in U.S. consumers and subpopulations of interest: Estimates from the Share of Intake Panel survey. *Food and Chemical Toxicology, 42,* 1923–1930. Weidner, Gerdi, and Istvan, Joseph (1985). Dietary sources of caffeine. *New England Journal of Medicine, 313,* 1421.

37. DeAngelis, Tori (1994, February). People's drug of choice offers potent side effects. *APA Monitor.* (Washington DC: American Psychological Association), p. 16. Quotation by Dr. John Hughes.

38. Robertson, David; Wade, Dawn; Workman, Robert; and Woosley, Raymond L. (1981). Tolerance to the humoral and hemodynamic effects of caffeine in man. *Journal of Clinical Investigation, 67,* 1111–1117.

39. Fredholm, Bättig, Holmén, Nehlig, and Zvartau, Actions of caffeine, Sections VI–XII. Griffiths, Roland R., and Woodson, Phillip P. (1988). Caffeine physical dependence: A review of human and animal laboratory studies. *Psychopharmacology, 94,* 437–451. Nehlig, Astrid (2004). Dependence upon coffee and caffeine: An update. In Astrid Nehlig (Ed.), *Coffee, tea, chocolate, and the brain.* Boca Raton, FL: CRC Press, pp. 133–145.

40. American Psychiatric Association (2000). *Diagnostic and statistical manual of mental disorders (DSM-IV)* (4th ed.). *Text Revision.* Washington DC: American Psychiatric Association, p. 232. Greden, John F., and Walters, Adale (1997). Caffeine. In Joyce H. Lowinson, Pedro Ruiz, Robert B. Millman, and John G. Langrod (Eds.), *Substance abuse: A comprehensive textbook* (3rd ed.). Baltimore: William & Wilkins, pp. 294–307.

41. Gilbert, *Caffeine,* pp. 108–109.

42. Dhingra, Ravi; Sullivan, Lisa; Jacques, Paul F.; Wang, Thomas J.; Fox, Caroline S.; et al. (2007). Soft drink consumption and risk of developing cardiometabolic risk factors and the metabolic syndrome in middle-aged adults in the community. *Circulation, 116,* 480–488. Johnston, Lloyd D., Delva, Jorge, and O'Malley, Patrick M. (2007). Soft drink availability, contracts, and revenues in American secondary schools. *American Journal of Preventive Medicine, 33,* S209–S225.

43. Cordes, Helen (1998, April 27). Generation wired. *The Nation,* pp. 11–16. Finnegan, Derek (2003). The health effects of stimulant drinks. *British Nutrition Foundation, Nutrition Bulletin, 28,* 147–155. Heatherley, Susan V., Hancock, Katie M. F., and Rogers, Peter J. (2006). Psychostimulant and other effects of caffeine in 9- to 11-year-old children. *Journal of Child Psychology and Psychiatry, 47,* 135–142. McManis, Sam (2002, December 8). New drug of choice for teens. Even high school kids have trouble kicking the caffeine habit. *San Francisco Chronicle,* p. E5. Pollak, Charles P., and Bright, David (2003). Caffeine consumption and weekly sleep patterns in U.S. seventh-, eighth-, and ninth-graders. *Pediatrics, 111,* 42–46.

chapter 13

Glues, Solvents, and Other Inhalants

"I remember," Julio says, taking quick, nervous puffs from his cigarette, "when I was a little kid, maybe eight or nine, and I used to take the garbage out for my mother, I'd always see tubes from airplane glue under the stairwell in our apartment house and in the alley out back. At first, glue just meant building models to me. But I'd see people sniffing it, under the stairwell. I was curious, and one day I tried it. It made me feel like I was in a trance. It wasn't really exciting, but I did it again and again until we moved, and in the new neighborhood people weren't into glue and I didn't see the empty tubes to remind me anymore."[1]

Sometimes, psychoactive drugs do not need to be acquired in a pharmacy, a convenience store, a liquor store, or on the street. They can be found under the sink, in kitchen or bathroom cabinets, in the basement, or in the garage. Ordinary household products frequently have the potential for giving euphoriant effects if they are sniffed or inhaled. When you consider that these substances are readily available to anyone in a family, including its youngest members, the consequences of their abuse become particularly troubling. This chapter will concern itself with glues, solvents, and other inhalant products as dangerous recreational drugs.

Inhalants through History

The mind-altering effects of substances inhaled into the lungs have been known since the beginnings of recorded history. Burnt spices and aromatic gums were used in acts of worship in most parts of the ancient world; exotic perfumes were inhaled during Egyptian worship as well as in Babylonian rituals. Inhalation effects also figured prominently in the famous rites of the oracle at Delphi in ancient Greece, where trances induced by the inhaling of vapors led to mysterious utterances that were interpreted as prophecies. We know now, from archeological studies, that limestone faults underneath the temple at Delphi once caused petro-chemical fumes to rise to the surface. The oracle was probably inhaling ethylene, a sweet-smelling gas that produces an out-of-body sense of euphoria.[2]

It was not until the latter part of the eighteenth century that reports about the inhalation of specific drugs began to appear. The two most prominent examples

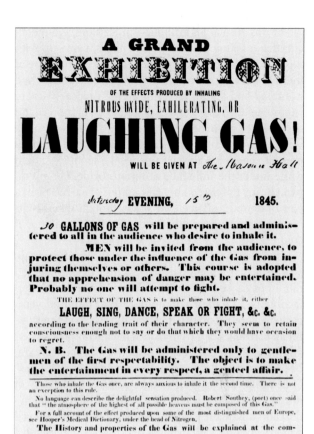

Public demonstrations of nitrous oxide ("laughing gas") inhalation were popular entertainments in the first half of the nineteenth century.

were cases involving nitrous oxide and ether. These anesthetic drugs were first used as surgical analgesics in the 1840s, but they had been synthesized decades earlier. From the very start, the word spread of recreational possibilities.

Nitrous Oxide

The British chemist Joseph Priestley synthesized the gas **nitrous oxide** in 1775. By the 1790s, the recreational possibilities of this "laughing gas" became widely known, and nitrous oxide parties were common both in England and in the United States. In the 1840s, public demonstrations were held in cities and towns, as a traveling show, by entrepreneurs eager to market the drug commercially.

nitrous oxide (NIGH-trus OX-ide): An analgesic gas commonly used in modern dentistry. It is also referred to as laughing gas.

---

by the numbers . . .

16	Percentage of eighth-graders in 2008 who reported that they had used inhalants to get high at some previous time in their lives
1,000's	The estimated number of household products containing toxic substances that can be ingested through inhalation

Source: Johnston, Lloyd D.; O'Malley, Patrick M.; Bachman, Jerald G.; and Schulenberg, John E. (2008, December 11). Various stimulant drugs show continuing gradual declines among teens in 2008, most illicit drugs hold steady. University of Michigan News Service, Ann Arbor, Table 1.

It was at such an exhibition in Hartford, Connecticut, that a young dentist, Horace Wells, came up with the idea for using nitrous oxide as an anesthetic. One of the intoxicated participants in the demonstration had stumbled and fallen, receiving in the process a severe wound to the leg. Seeing that the man showed no evidence of pain despite his injury, Wells was sufficiently impressed to try out the anesthetic possibilities himself. The next day, he underwent a tooth extraction while under the influence of nitrous oxide. He felt no pain during the procedure, and nitrous oxide has been a part of dental practice ever since, though recently its role as a routine anesthetic has become a matter of controversy.[3]

During the 1960s, nitrous oxide inhalation reappeared as a recreational drug. Tanks of compressed nitrous oxide were diverted for illicit use, and health professionals, like their counterparts one hundred years earlier, were reportedly hosting nitrous oxide parties. Small cartridges of nitrous oxide called **whippets**, generally used by restaurants to dispense whipped cream, became available through college campus "head shops" and mail-order catalogs. The customary pattern of nitrous oxide abuse was to fill a balloon from these cylinders and inhale the gas from the balloon. The result was a mild euphoric high that lasted for a few minutes and a sense of well-being that lingered for several hours. Sometimes, there would be a loss of consciousness for a few seconds and an experience of "flying." Once consciousness returned, there was the possibility of sensory distortions, nausea, or vomiting. Ordinary cans of commercial whipped cream, in which nitrous oxide is the propellant gas, currently provide easy access to this inhalant.

Nitrous oxide itself is a nontoxic gas, but its inhalation presents serious risks. As with any euphoriant drug, the recreational use of nitrous oxide can be extremely dangerous when a person is driving under its influence. In addition, if nitrous oxide is inhaled through an anesthetic mask and the mask is worn over the mouth and nose, without the combination of oxygen, the consequences can be lethal. Nitrous oxide dilutes the air that a person breathes. Unless there is a minimum of 21 percent oxygen in the mixture, reproducing the 21 percent oxygen content in the air, a lack of oxygen (called **hypoxia**) will produce suffocation or irreversible brain damage.[4]

Ether

As was true of nitrous oxide, **ether** came into use well before its anesthetic effects were appreciated by the medical profession. It was introduced by Friedrich Hoffmann at the beginning of the 1700s, under the name Anodyne, as a liquid "nerve tonic" for intestinal cramps, toothaches, and other pains. Whether it was swallowed or inhaled (it evaporated very quickly), ether also produced effects that resembled intoxication from alcohol. In fact, during the mid-1800s, when the combination of a heavy tax on alcohol and an anti-alcohol temperance campaign in England and Ireland forced people to consider alternatives to alcoholic beverages, both ether drinking and ether inhalation became quite popular. It was used for the same purpose later in the United States during the Prohibition years and in Germany during World War II when alcohol was rationed. Ether's flammability, however, made its recreational use highly dangerous.[5]

Glue, Solvent, and Aerosol Inhalation

The abuse of nitrous oxide and ether may have a relatively long history, but the more familiar reports of inhalation abuse involving glue and solvent chemicals have appeared only since the late 1950s. Table 13.1 lists some of the common products that have been subject to abuse, including glues, paint thinners, lighter fluid, and stain removers. In addition, many aerosol products are inhalable: hair sprays, deodorants, vegetable lubricants for cooking, and spray paints. Unfortunately, new products are continually being introduced for genuinely practical uses, with little awareness of the consequences should someone inhale their ingredients on a recreational basis (Table 13.2).

There are also significant problems associated with occupational exposure to solvent vapors. In a major study of 125 pregnant women who had been exposed to solvent products at the workplace over a nine-year period, there was a thirteen times greater risk of birth defects among the exposed group, relative to controls. Occupations of these women included factory workers, laboratory technicians, artists, printing industry workers, chemists, and painters.[6]

---

whippets: Small canisters containing pressurized nitrous oxide.

hypoxia (high-POX-ee-ah): A deficiency in oxygen intake.

ether (EE-ther): An anesthetic drug, first introduced to surgical practice by William T. Morton in the 1840s. It is highly flammable.

TABLE 13.1

Common household products with abuse potential as inhalants

Gasoline

Hobby glues and cements

Paint thinners

Lacquers and enamels

Varnishes and varnish removers

Cigarette or charcoal lighter fluid

Fingernail polishes and polish remover

Stain removers, degreasers, and other dry-cleaning products

Upholstery protection spray products (e.g., Scotchgard*)

Windshield de-icers

Disinfectants

Fire extinguishing volatile chemicals

Typewriter correction fluid

Permanent felt marker ink

Aerosol hair sprays

Vegetable frying pan lubricants

Spray deodorants

Spray paints

Whipped cream propellants

Freon

Note: The above is a partial list. New products are continually being introduced.

*Scotchgard is a registered product of the 3M Corporation. In 2000, while continuing to market its well-known fabric-protection product, 3M phased out a formulation of Scotchgard that had contained perfluorooctane sulfonate (PFOS), a chemical that the U.S. Environmental Protection Agency had determined to be toxic. In late 2003, a reformulation of Scotchgard, based on a variation of PFOS considered to be safe when used as directed, was introduced.

Source: Bjorhus, Jennifer (2003, May 28). 3M looks to rebuild Scotchgard business. *Saint Paul (Minnesota) Pioneer Press,* p.C1.

TABLE 13.2

Household products with abuse potential and their ingredients

HOUSEHOLD PRODUCT	POSSIBLE INGREDIENTS
Glues, plastic cements, and rubber cements	Acetates, acetone, benzene, hexane, methyl chloride, toluene, trichloroethylene
Cleaning solutions	Carbon tetrachloride, petroleum products, trichloroethylene
Nail polish removers	Acetone
Lighter fluids	Butane, isopropane
Paint sprays, paint thinners, and paint removers	Acetone, butylacetate, methanol, toluene, methyl chloride
Other petroleum products	Acetone, benzene, ether, gasoline, hexane, petroleum, tetraethyl lead, toluene
Typewriter correction fluid	Trichloroethylene, trichlorethane
Hair sprays	Butane, propane
Deodorants, air fresheners	Butane, propane
Whipped cream propellants	Nitrous oxide

Sources: Schuckit, Marc A. (2000). *Drug and alcohol abuse: A clinical guide to diagnosis and treatment.* New York: Kluwer Academic/Plenum, p. 222. Sharp, Charles W., and Rosenberg, Neil L. (1997). Inhalants. In Joyce H. Lowinson, Pedro Ruiz, Robert B. Millman, and John G. Langrod (Eds.), *Substance abuse: A comprehensive textbook* (3rd ed.). Baltimore: Williams & Wilkins, p. 248.

The Abuse Potential of Inhalants

Commercial glues, solvents, and aerosol sprays are prime candidates for drug abuse for a number of reasons. First, because they are inhaled into the lungs, the feeling of intoxication occurs more rapidly than with orally administered alcohol. "It's a quicker drunk," in the words of one solvent abuser.[7] The feeling is often described as a "floating euphoria," similar to the effect of alcohol but with a shorter course of intoxication. The high is over in an hour or so, and the hangover is considered less unpleasant than that following alcohol consumption. Second, the typical packaging of inhalant products makes them easy to carry around and conceal from others. Even if they are discovered, many of the products are so common that it is not difficult to invent an excuse for having them on hand.

Finally, most inhalants are easily available in hardware stores, pharmacies, and supermarkets, where they can be bought cheaply or stolen. Among some inhalant abusers, shoplifting these products from open shelves is not just routine but expected. Inhalants are even more widely available than alcohol in poor households; liquor may be in short supply but gasoline, paints, or aerosol products are usually around the house or garage.[8] All these factors contribute to the considerable potential for inhalant abuse.

Acute Effects of Glues, Solvents, and Aerosols

The fumes from commercial inhalant products fall into the general category of depressant drugs, in that the central nervous system is inhibited after they are inhaled. Brain waves, measured objectively through an electroencephalograph (EEG), slow down. Subjectively, the individual feels intoxicated within minutes after inhalation. The most immediate effects include giddiness, euphoria, dizziness, and slurred speech, lasting for fifteen to forty-five minutes. This state is followed by one to two hours of drowsiness and sometimes a loss of consciousness. Along with these effects are occasional experiences of double vision, ringing in the ears, and hallucinations.[9]

The Dangers of Inhalant Abuse

We should realize that inhalant abuse often involves concentrations of glue and solvent products that are usually fifty to a hundred times greater than the maximum allowable concentration of exposure in industry. The health of the inhalant abuser, therefore, is obviously at risk (Health Alert).

The dangers of inhalant abuse lie not only in the toxic effects of the inhaled compound on body organs but in the behavioral effects of the intoxication itself. Inhalant-produced feelings of euphoria include feelings of recklessness and omnipotence. There have been instances of young inhalant abusers leaping off rooftops in an effort to fly, running into traffic, lying on railroad tracks, or incurring severe lacerations when pushing their hand through a glass window that has been perceived as open. The hallucinations that are sometimes experienced carry their own personal risks. Walls may appear to be closing in or the sky may seem to be falling. Ordinary objects may be perceived to be changing their shape, size, or color. Any one of these delusions easily can lead to impulsive and potentially destructive behavior.[10]

There are also significant hazards that are related to the ways in which inhalants are administered. While solvents are sometimes inhaled from a handkerchief or from the container in which they were originally acquired ("huffing"), glues and similar vaporous compounds are often squeezed into a plastic bag and inhaled while the bag is held tightly over the nose and mouth ("bagging"). Potentially, a loss of consciousness can result in hypoxia and asphyxiation. Choking can occur if there is vomiting while the inhaler is unconscious. In an early investigation in the 1960s of nine documented deaths attributed to glue inhalation, at least six were caused specifically by a lack of oxygen.[11] Another danger lies in the inhalation of Freon, a refrigerant gas so cold that the larynx and throat can be frozen upon contact.

The toxic effects of inhalant drugs themselves depend on the specific compound, but the picture is

---

HEALTH ALERT!

The Signs of Possible Inhalant Abuse

- Headaches and dizziness
- Light sensitivity (from dilation of the pupils)
- Reddened, irritated eyes and rash around the mouth
- Double vision
- Ringing in the ears (tinnitus)
- Sneezing and sniffling
- Coughing and bad breath
- Nausea, vomiting, and loss of appetite
- Diarrhea
- Chest pains
- Abnormal heart rhythm (cardiac arrhythmia)
- Muscle and joint aches
- Slurred speech and unsteady muscle coordination

- Chemical odor or stains on clothing or body
- Rags, empty aerosol cans and other containers
- Plastic and paper bags found in closets and other hidden places

Where to go for assistance:
www.inhalant.org
www.inhalants.org

These web sites are sponsored by the Alliance for Consumer Education, Washington DC, and the National Inhalant Prevention Coalition, Chattanooga, Tennessee, respectively.

Sources: Fox, C. Lynn, and Forbing, Shirley E. (1992). *Creating drug-free schools and communities.* New York: HarperCollins, p. 37. Schuckit, Marc A. (1995). *Drug and alcohol abuse: A clinical guide to diagnosis and treatment* (4th ed.). New York: Plenum Medical Book Co., p. 219.

complicated by the fact that most products subject to inhalant abuse contain a variety of compounds and in some cases the list of ingredients on the product label is incomplete. Therefore, often we do not know if the medical symptoms resulted from a particular chemical or its interaction with others. Nonetheless, there are specific chemicals that have known health risks. The most serious concern involves sudden-death cases, brought on by cardiac dysrhythmia, that have been reported following the inhalation of propane and butane, commonly used as a propellant for many commercial products.

Besides butane and propane, other inhalant ingredients that present specific hazards are *acetone, benzene, hexane, toluene,* and *gasoline.*

- *Acetone:* **Acetone** inhalation causes significant damage to the mucous membranes of the respiratory tract.
- *Benzene:* Prolonged exposure to **benzene** has been associated with carcinogenic (cancer-related) disorders, specifically leukemia, as well as anemia. Benzene is generally used as a solvent in waxes, resins, lacquers, paints, and paint removers.
- *Hexane:* The inhalation of **hexane,** primarily in glues and other adhesive products, has been associated with peripheral nerve damage leading to muscular weakness and muscle atrophy. There is a latency period of a few weeks before the symptoms appear.
- *Toluene:* **Toluene** inhalation through glue sniffing has been associated with a reduction in short-term memory, anemia, and a loss of hearing, dysfunctions of the cerebellum that result in difficulties in movement and coordination and an overall reduction in brain activity. Toluene also has been implicated as a principal factor in cases of lethal inhalation of spray paints and lacquers, though it is difficult to exclude the contribution of other solvents in these products.
- *Gasoline:* Concentrated vapors from gasoline can be lethal when inhaled. Medical symptoms from gasoline inhalation are also frequently attributed to gasoline additives that are mixed in the fuel. The additive **triorthocresyl phosphate (TCP),** in particular, has been associated with spastic muscle disorders and liver problems. Lead content in gasoline is generally linked to long-term CNS degeneration, but fortunately leaded gasoline is no longer commonly available in the United States. On the other hand, present-day gasoline mixtures contain large amounts of toluene, acetone, and hexane to help achieve the "anti-knock" property that lead had previously provided.[12]

Patterns of Inhalant Abuse

Among all the psychoactive drugs, inhalants are associated most closely with the young and often the very young. For those who engage in inhalant abuse, these compounds frequently represent the first experience with a psychoactive drug, preceding even alcohol or tobacco. Overall, inhalant abuse ranks as the fourth highest incidence of drug experimentation among secondary school students, surpassed only by alcohol, tobacco, and marijuana (in that order). Most of these drug abusers, however, are younger than secondary school age: often they are between eleven and thirteen years old. Inhalants are the only class of drugs for which

A group of abandoned Brazilian children inhale glue from bags in Rio de Janeiro. The dazed expression is a typical sign of inhalant intoxication.

acetone (ASS-eh-tone): A chemical found in nail polish removers and other products.

benzene: A carcinogenic (cancer-producing) compound found in many solvent products, representing a serious health risk when inhaled.

hexane: A dangerous compound present in many glues and adhesive products. Inhalation of these products has been associated with muscular weakness and atrophy.

toluene (TOL-yoo-ene): A compound in glues, cements, and other adhesive products. Inhalation of these products results in behavioral and neurological impairments.

triorthocresyl phosphate (TCP) (tri-OR-thoh-CREH-sil FOS-fate): A gasoline additive. Inhalation of TCP-containing gasoline has been linked to spastic muscle disorders and liver problems.

the incidence of usage in the eighth grade significantly exceeds the incidence in the tenth and twelfth grades.

Evidently, awareness of this form of drug-taking activity is quite extensive in the later elementary and middle school student population. According to a recent survey, almost two-thirds of ten- to seventeen-year-olds know the meaning of "huffing" and report that they were about twelve years of age when they first knew of classmates abusing inhalants.[13]

In other cultures and under different circumstances, inhalant abuse affects even younger children and a wider proportion of that age group. In Mexico City, among street children as young as eight or nine who live without families in abandoned buildings, rates of inhalant abuse are extremely high, with 22 percent reporting some form of solvent inhalation on a daily basis. Inhalant abuse is reported to be commonplace among street children in Rio de Janeiro and other major cities in Central and South America as well as Asia (Drugs . . . in Focus).[14]

Inhalant abuse, on an experimental basis, is not restricted by social or geographic boundaries (Portrait). Chronic inhalant abuse, however, is overrepresented among the poor and those youths suffering emotional challenges in their lives and seeking some form of escape. Studies of young inhalant abusers show high rates of delinquency, poor school performance, and emotional difficulties. They often come from disorganized, multi-problem homes in which the parents are actually or effectively absent or else engage themselves in abuse of alcohol or some other substance.[15] The diversity of ethnic sub-groups showing high prevalence rates for inhalant abuse include such disparate groups as Latino children in a rural community in the Southwest, Native American children on U.S. reservations, and white children in an economically disadvantaged neighborhood in Philadelphia.

Whatever the ethnic identity of the chronic inhalant abuser, a critical factor is peer influence. Most studies indicate that glue, solvent, or aerosol inhalation is generally experienced in small groups, often at the urging of friends or relatives. Young inhalant abusers tend to be more alienated than others at this age, and the feelings of alienation can be an important factor in leading a youth to others who are also alienated, thus creating a cluster of peers who engage in this form of drug-taking behavior. One survey among Native American youth, for example, found that when friends strongly encouraged inhalant use or would

Drugs...in Focus

Resistol and *Resistoleros* in Latin America

In the cities of Central and South America, the street children are referred to as *resistoleros*, a name derived from their frequent habit of sniffing a commercial brand of shoemaker's glue called Resistol. Granted, many cases of inhalant abuse among the hundreds of thousands of children in Latin America do not specifically involve Resistol; nevertheless, the frequency of Resistol abuse and the fact that Resistol dominates the market in commercial solvent-based adhesives have focused attention on the company that manufactures it, the H. B. Fuller Company of St. Paul, Minnesota.

Concern for the welfare of these children has also spotlighted a thorny ethical issue: Should a corporation accept the social responsibility when widespread abuse of its product exists, either in the United States or elsewhere in the world? Testor Corporation in 1969 added a noxious ingredient to discourage abuse of its model glue; in 1994,

a German chemical company marketing a Resistol rival stopped its distribution in this region. For its part, Fuller did modify the formulation of Resistol in 1992, replacing the sweet-smelling but highly toxic toluene with a slightly less toxic chemical, cyclohexane. However, it continues to sell Resistol, claiming that its legitimate uses benefit the economies of regions where it is marketed. Moreover, the company has funded community programs for homeless children throughout Central America and has restricted its Resistol marketing efforts to large industrial customers rather than small retailers. Unappeased, foes continue to press Fuller to discontinue the product entirely.

Note: There is no association between Resistol glue and Resistol Western Hats or any corporation-related sponsorships such as the Resistol Arena in Mesquite, Texas.

Source: Henriques, Diana B. (1995, November 26). Black mark for a "good citizen." Critics say H. B. Fuller isn't doing enough to curb glue-sniffing. *New York Times*, Section 3, pp. 1, 11.

On a secluded beach in south Florida, a group of friends would meet on a weekend and pass around the $5 spray can of Scotchgard, a substance that is sprayed on upholstery and carpets to prevent stains from spills. A saturated washcloth held against the mouth for a few seconds was all it would take to get a few minutes of tingling and intoxication. There would be no worry about beer cans or liquor bottles that their parents might discover, no need for a fake ID to buy it, and no telltale signs to give them away.

"That's all that you really needed to get high," Courtney Knief, a fifteen-year-old girl from Fort Pierce, later recalled. She doesn't, however, sniff Scotchgard anymore.

"It killed my boyfriend and my best friend. I had no idea somebody could die from it. I wish I would have had the sense to open my eyes and say hey this is stupid."

Courtney's boyfriend was sixteen-year-old Scott Pecor of nearby Port St. Lucie, who had died of heart failure from a large dose of inhaled Scotchgard. His older brother had

found him unconscious in his backyard and had found the near-empty can on the family's couch. Scott and Courtney had been "huffing" Scotchgard for about three months; they had gotten high three days before he died.

Scott was a soccer player and honors student in his high school, with aspirations to be an architect. He wasn't an angry or rebellious kid, his parents say. Without any signs of overt drunken behavior or obvious aftereffects, Scott's inhalant abuse went totally unnoticed by them.

From 1989 to 1991, the local medical examiner had recorded three teenage deaths in three nearby counties. One boy died after inhaling butane lighter refills, another from inhaling paint thinner. Scott was the first casualty from Scotchgard itself, though the manufacturer, the 3M Company of Minneapolis, reported that from 1989 to 1991, more than twenty people died from inhaling the fabric protector. A 1990 school district survey in a Florida county immediately south of where Scott

lived had found that 10 percent of seventh graders regarded inhalants as not harmful, and between 8 and 10 percent of them reported having used them. Scotchgard and Freon were current favorites.

The hazards of inhalant abuse among adolescents are as real today as they were more than twenty years ago. Reports of teenage "huffing" and "bagging" deaths continue in all parts of the United States. In the University of Michigan survey in 2008, 16 percent of eighth graders reported inhalant use sometime in their lifetime, 9 percent reported use within the past year, and 4 percent reported use within the past thirty days.

Source: Hiaasen, Rob (1991, March 29). The newest deadly high. *Palm Beach Post*, p. 1D. Johnston, Lloyd D.; O'Malley, Patrick M.; Bachman, Jerald G.; and Schulenberg, John E. (2008, December 11). Various stimulant drugs show continuing gradual declines among teens in 2008, most illicit drugs hold steady. University of Michigan News Service, Ann Arbor, Tables 1, 2, and 3.

not try to stop it, 84 percent of the sample reported having tried inhalants and 41 percent reported having used them recently. In contrast, when friends discouraged inhalant use or were perceived as applying strong sanctions against it, only 19 percent reported having tried inhalants and only 3 percent had used them recently.[16]

Chronic Inhalant Abuse

The long-term effects of inhalant abuse are not well documented, owing to the fact that inhalant abuse frequently does not extend over more than a year or two in a person's life and may occur only sporadically. There have been reports of cases showing a tolerance to the euphoriant effects of glues and gasoline. Although it is difficult to determine the dosages that are involved with these tolerance effects, it appears that individuals exposed only to low concentrations for brief periods of

time or high levels occasionally do not show tolerance to the inhalants.

Inhalant dependence occurs frequently. Inhalant abusers have been reported as feeling restless, irritable, and anxious when prevented from inhaling glues, solvents, or aerosols. Physiological withdrawal symptoms are only rarely observed among inhalant abusers but are frequently observed among animals in laboratory studies, so the question of whether physical dependence exists has yet to be definitively answered.[17]

A Gateway for Future Drug Abuse?

The young age at which inhalant abuse occurs leads to the question of whether there is a causal link between inhalant abuse and later abuse of other drugs. Without a doubt, some youths will subsequently replace inhalants with alcohol, marijuana, and other recreational drugs, but the experience of inhalants cannot be considered to lead on a pharmacological level to other drug experimentation or long-term abuse. This is how one expert has put it:

> The socially and emotionally healthy juvenile casually experimenting with solvent sniffing does not bear any greater potential for heroin addiction than had he not sniffed solvents. Conversely, the disturbed youth from a broken home, who is frequently exposed to pushers, probably bears the same high risk of ultimate narcotic abuse whether or not he sniffs glue. Regardless of surrounding circumstances, however, any significant resort to intoxicating substances in childhood should be carefully noted as a potential warning of a growing emotional disturbance or as a predictor of a future drug-dependent personality.[18]

A similar "gateway argument" with respect to marijuana was presented in Chapter 7.

Responses of Society to Inhalant Abuse

> Sniffing gasoline or paint is a grubby, dirty, cheap way to get high. Inhalant users are, therefore, likely to be the social rejects, the emotionally disturbed, the disadvantaged minorities, the maladjusted, as well as angry and alienated. There is nothing attractive, exciting, or appealing about inhalant use or inhalant users. . . .[19]

Certainly, the concern about inhalant abuse takes a backseat to more widely publicized concerns about cocaine, methamphetamine, and heroin abuse, or the abuse of club drugs. Despite the relatively low priority given to inhalant abuse, however, steps have been taken to reduce some of its hazards. One major approach has been to restrict the availability and sales of glues to young people, a strategy that, as you might predict, has met with mixed success. Some U.S. cities have restricted sales of plastic cement unless it is purchased with a model kit, but such legislation is largely ineffective when model kits themselves are relatively inexpensive. As with the official restriction of sales of alcohol and tobacco to minors, young people can find a way around these laws.

More direct action has been taken since 1969 by the Testor Corporation, a leading manufacturer of plastic cement for models, by incorporating **oil of mustard** into the formula. This additive produces severe nasal irritation similar to the effect of horseradish, while not affecting its use as a glue or the effect on the user who does not inhale it directly. Other brands of glues and adhesives, however, may not contain oil of mustard and as a result could still be available for abuse, and additives in general would not be desirable for certain products that are used for cosmetic purposes.

In an additional step taken to reduce inhalant abuse, concentrations of benzene in many household products sold in the United States have been reduced or eliminated, though it is difficult to determine the exact composition of solutions merely by inspecting the label. Standards for products manufactured and sold in foreign countries are typically far less stringent.[20]

Beyond the difficulty in identifying the toxicity of specific solvent compounds, there is the overriding general problem of the enormous variety and easy availability of solvent-containing products. As one researcher

SNIFFING CORRECTION FLUID CAN STOP YOUR HEART.

Poster images represent a growing national effort to prevent inhalation abuse.

oil of mustard: An additive in Testor brand hobby-kit glues that produces nasal irritation when inhaled, thus reducing the potential for inhalant abuse.

has lamented, "If sales of gold paint or paint thinner are curtailed, people may choose to use typewriter correction fluid, or shoe polish or nail polish remover, or hundreds of other items that have legitimate uses in everyday life."[21]

Ultimately, some sort of educational strategy must be coordinated that is targeted at children in the elementary grades in school and their parents at home. Different countries have differing educational approaches, ranging from nonalarmist, low-key programs to those urging absolute abstinence, and it is not clear which strategy is most effective in controlling inhalant abuse. A National Inhalants and Poisons Awareness Week is currently held each year in March, to promote greater efforts to inform the public about this problem. On the treatment side, special guidelines are currently being developed for a variety of inhalant-abuse populations—not only the adolescents engaging in transient inhalant abuse but also those individuals who are twenty to twenty-nine years old, have a five-year or longer history of inhalant exposure, and have sustained possible brain damage as a result.[22]

In the meantime, attention has been directed toward the abusive inhalation of two specific products, amyl nitrite and butyl nitrite, affecting a different population from the one traditionally associated with glue, solvent, or aerosol inhalants. Like nitrous oxide and ether, these nitrites have been around for some time, but their abuse has been relatively recent.

Amyl Nitrite and Butyl Nitrite Inhalation

Amyl and butyl nitrites were first identified in the nineteenth century. When inhaled, they produce an intense vasodilation, a relaxation of smooth muscle, a fall in blood pressure, and a reflex increase in heart rate. Since 1867, **amyl nitrite** has been used medically, on a prescription basis, in the treatment of angina pain in heart patients and as an antidote to cyanide poisoning. **Butyl nitrite** produces similar therapeutic effects but has never been used on a clinical basis.

News of the recreational potential of nitrite inhalation began to spread in the 1960s and reached a peak in the 1970s, particularly within the gay community, as it was recognized that the vasodilation of cerebral blood vessels produced a euphoric high, anal sphincter muscles were relaxed, and vasodilation of genital blood vessels enhanced sexual pleasure (Table 13.3). By 1979, more than 5 million people in the United States were using amyl or butyl nitrites more than once a week.

TABLE 13.3	
A chronology of nitrite inhalation abuse	
DATE	**EXAMPLE OF INHALATION**
1859	Flushing of skin with amyl nitrite first described
1867	First therapeutic use of amyl nitrite for angina pain
1880s	Butyl nitrite studied but not used clinically
1960	Amyl nitrite prescription requirement eliminated by FDA
1963	First reports of recreational use of nitrites
1960s	Widespread recreational use of nitrites among young adults
1969	Amyl nitrite prescription requirement reinstated
1970	Street brands of butyl nitrite beginning to be widely available
1974	Popper craze beginning
1976	$50 million sales reported in nitrites in one U.S. city
1977	Nitrite inhalation predominant among gay men
1979	More than 5 million people estimated to have used nitrites more than once per week
	19 cases of Kaposi's sarcoma found in retrospect
1980	56 cases of Kaposi's sarcoma reported
1981	Increased suspicions of a link between nitrite use and Kaposi's sarcoma
1985	Concerns about AIDS and HIV infection beginning to receive widespread media attention
1990s to present	Alleged association between nitrite inhalation and Kaposi's sarcoma is discredited
	Nitrite inhalation abuse greatly reduced among heterosexual populations

Source: Updated from Newell, Guy R., Spitz, Margaret R., and Wilson, Michael B. (1988). Nitrite inhalants: Historical perspective. In Harry W. Haverkos and John A. Dougherty (Eds.), *Health hazards of nitrite inhalants* (NIDA Research Monograph 83). Rockville, MD: National Institute of Drug Abuse, p. 6.

amyl nitrite (AY-mil NIGH-trite): An inhalant drug that relaxes smooth muscle and produces euphoria. Clinically useful in treating angina pain in cardiac patients, it is also subject to abuse.

butyl nitrite (BYOO-til NIGH-trite): An inhalant drug similar in its effects to amyl nitrite. It is commonly abused because it induces feelings of euphoria.

Since then, there has been a substantial decline in their popularity. By 1986, the University of Michigan survey of young adults between nineteen and twenty-eight years of age found that only 2 percent reported having abused nitrites within the previous year, and by 1994 the percentage had declined to one-third of 1 percent.[23]

Patterns of Nitrite Inhalation Abuse

Amyl nitrite is often referred to as "poppers" or "snappers" because it is commonly available in a mesh-covered glass ampule and there is a popping sound as the ampule is broken and the vapors of the nitrite are inhaled as they are released into the air. It is quick-acting, with vasodilatory

TABLE 13.4		
"Brand names" for butyl nitrite		
Aroma of Men	Hardware	Mama Poppers
Ban Apple Gas	Heart On	Oz
Bang	Highball	Quick Silver
Bullet	Jac Aroma	Rush
Climax	Lightning Bolt	Satan's Scent
Crypt Tonight	Liquid Increase	Thrust
Discorama	Locker Room	Toilet Water

Source: Maickel, Roger P. (1988). The fate and toxicity of butyl nitrites. In Harry W. Haverkos and John A. Dougherty (Eds.), *Health hazards of nitrite inhalants* (NIDA Research Monograph 83). Rockville, MD: National Institute on Drug Abuse, p. 16.

Quick Concept Check 13.1

Understanding the History of Inhalants

Check your understanding of the history of inhalant drugs by indicating whether a particular substance was used (a) first recreationally, then as an application in medicine; (b) first as an application in medicine, then recreationally; or (c) recreationally, with no known application in medicine.

1. amyl nitrite
2. hexane
3. nitrous oxide
4. toluene
5. ether
6. benzene

Answers: 1. b   2. c   3. a   4. c   5. a   6. c

effects appearing within thirty seconds. Light-headedness, a flushing sensation, blurred vision, and euphoria last for about five minutes, followed by headache and nausea. Butyl nitrite follows a similar time course in its effects and is available in pornography shops and mail-order catalogs. Many of the various "trade names" for butyl nitrite (Table 13.4) have referred to its supposed sexual benefits as well as the fact that its vapors emit a strong odor resembling that of sweaty socks.

Cases of nitrite inhalation have also been found among both heterosexual and gay adolescents, for whom the primary attraction is a feeling of general euphoria. The University of Michigan survey began looking at prevalence rates for nitrite inhalation in 1979. In that year, approximately 11 percent of high school seniors reported having tried nitrite inhalants at least once in their lifetime. In 2008, the rate had dropped substantially to less than 1 percent.[24]

Summary

Inhalants through history

- Nitrous oxide was discovered in 1798 and became a major recreational drug in the 1800s. It is still used recreationally, but its primary application is as a routine anesthetic in dentistry.
- Ether is another anesthetic drug, first introduced in the 1840s. It has also been used as a recreational drug, particularly in times when alcohol availability has been severely reduced.

Glue, Solvent, and Aerosol Inhalation

- Present-day inhalant abuse involves a wide range of commercial products: gasoline, glues and other adhesives, household cleaning compounds, aerosol sprays, and solvents of all kinds.
- These products are usually cheap, readily available, and easily concealable, and their intoxicating effects when inhaled are rapid. All of these factors make inhalants prime candidates for abuse.

- The principal dangers of inhalant abuse lie in the behavioral consequences of intoxication and in the possibility of asphyxiation when inhalants are administered by an airproof bag held over the nose and mouth.
- Specific toxic substances contained in inhalant products include acetone, benzene, hexane, toluene, and gasoline.

Patterns of Inhalant Abuse

- Inhalant abuse respects no social or geographic boundaries, though prevalence rates are particularly high among poor and disadvantaged populations.
- Research studies indicate the presence of psychological dependence rather than physical dependence in inhalant abuse behavior.
- Tolerance effects are seen for chronic inhalant abusers when the inhalant concentration is high and exposure is frequent.

Responses of Society to Inhalant Abuse

- Concern about the dangers of inhalant abuse has led to restriction of the sale of model-kit glues to minors and a modification of the formulas for model-kit glue in an attempt to lessen the popularity of deliberate inhalation.
- There are so many products currently on the open market that contain volatile chemicals that a universal restriction of abusable inhalants is practically impossible. Therefore, prevention efforts regarding inhalant abuse are critical elements in reducing this form of drug-taking behavior.

Amyl Nitrite and Butyl Nitrite Inhalation

- Two types of inhalants, amyl nitrite and butyl nitrite, appeared on the scene in the 1960s, reaching a peak in the late 1970s. Although they are often identified with gay men, populations of heterosexual adolescents and young adults have also engaged in this form of inhalant abuse.

Key Terms

acetone, p. 323
amyl nitrite, p. 327
benzene, p. 323
butyl nitrite, p. 327

ether, p. 320
hexane, p. 323
hypoxia, p. 320

nitrous oxide, p. 319
oil of mustard, p. 326
toluene, p. 323

triorthocresyl phosphate (TCP), p. 323
whippets, p. 320

Endnotes

1. Quotation from Silverstein, Alvin, Silverstein, Virginia, and Silverstein, Robert (1991). *The addictions handbook.* Hillside, NJ: Enslow Publishers, p. 51.
2. Broad, William J. (2002, March 19). For Delphic oracle, fumes and visions. *New York Times*, pp. F1, F4. Preble, Edward, and Laury, Gabriel V. (1967). Plastic cement: The ten cent hallucinogen. *International Journal of the Addictions*, 2, 271–281.
3. Gillman, Mark A., and Lichtigfeld, Frederick J. (1997). Clinical role and mechanisms of action of analgesic nitrous oxide. *International Journal of Neuroscience*, 93, 55–62. Nagle, David R. (1968). Anesthetic addiction and drunkenness. *International Journal of the Addictions*, 3, p. 33.
4. Julien, Robert M. (2001). *A primer of drug action* (9th ed.). New York: Worth, pp. 121–122. Layzer, Robert B. (1985). Nitrous oxide abuse. In Edmond I. Eger (Ed.), *Nitrous oxide/N_2O*. New York: Elsevier, pp. 249–257. Morgan, Roberta (1988). *The emotional pharmacy.* Los Angeles: Body Press, pp. 212–213.
5. Nagle, Anesthetic addiction and drunkenness, pp. 26–30.
6. Khattak, Sohail; K-Moghtader, Guiti; McMartin, Kristen; Barrera, Maru; Kennedy, Debbie; and Koren, Gideon (1999). Pregnancy outcome following gestational exposure to organic solvents. *Journal of the American Medical Association*, 281, 1106–1109.
7. Cohen, Sidney (1977). Inhalant abuse: An overview of the problem. In Charles W. Sharp and Mary Lee Brehm (Eds.), *Review of inhalants: Euphoria to dysfunction* (NIDA Research Monograph 15). Rockville, MD: National Institute on Drug Abuse, p. 7.
8. Ibid., pp. 6–8.
9. Schuckit, Marc A. (1995). *Drug and alcohol abuse: A clinical guide to diagnosis and treatment* (4th ed.). New York: Plenum Medical Book Co., pp. 217–225. Sharp, Charles W., and Rosenberg, Neil L. (1997). Inhalants. In Joyce H. Lowinson, Pedro Ruiz, Robert B. Millman, and John G. Langrod (Eds.), *Substance abuse: A comprehensive textbook*. Baltimore: Williams & Wilkins, pp. 246–264.
10. Abramovitz, Melissa (2003, October). The dangers of inhalants. *Current Health 2*, pp. 19–21. Winger, Gail,

Hofmann, Frederick G., and Woods, James H. (1992). *A handbook on drug and alcohol abuse: The biomedical aspects* (3rd ed.). New York: Oxford University Press, pp. 90–91.

11. Brecher, Edward M., and the editors of Consumer Reports (1972). *Licit and illicit drugs.* Boston: Little, Brown, p. 331.

12. Brands, Bruna, Sproule, Beth, and Marshman, Joan (1998). *Drugs and drug abuse: A reference text.* Toronto: Addiction Research Foundation, pp. 469–471. Bruckner, James V., and Peterson, Richard G. (1977). Toxicology of aliphatic and aromatic hydrocarbons. In Charles W. Sharp and Mary L. Brehm (Eds.), *Review of inhalants: Euphoria to dysfunction* (NIDA Research Monograph 15). Rockville, MD: National Institute on Drug Abuse, pp. 124–163. Garriott, James C. (1992). Death among inhalant abusers. In Charles W. Sharp, Fred Beauvais, and Richard Spence (Eds.), *Inhalant abuse: A volatile research agenda* (NIDA Research Monograph 129). Rockville, MD: National Institute on Drug Abuse, pp. 171–193. Whitten, Lori (2008, June). Animal studies elaborate toluene's effects. *NIDA Notes,* pp. 14–15.

13. Anderson, Carrie E., and Loomis, Glenn A. (2003). Recognition and prevention of inhalant abuse. *American Family Physician, 68,* 869–874. Edwards, Ruth W., and Oetting, E. R. (1995). Inhalant use in the United States. In Nicholas Kozel, Zili Sloboda, and Mario De La Rosa (Eds.), *Epidemiology of inhalant abuse: An international perspective* (NIDA Research Monograph 148). Rockville, MD: National Institute on Drug Abuse, pp. 8–28. Johnston, Lloyd D., O'Malley, Patrick M., Bachman, Jerald G., and Schulenberg, John E. (2004, December 21). Overall, teen drug use continues gradual decline, but use of inhalants rises. University of Michigan News and Information Services, Ann Arbor, Tables 1, 2, and 3. Johnston, Lloyd D.; O'Malley, Patrick M.; Bachman, Jerald G.; and Schulenberg, John E. (2008, December 11). Various stimulant drugs show continuing gradual declines among teens in 2008, most illicit drugs hold steady. University of Michigan News Service, Ann Arbor, Tables 1, 2, and 3. Substance Abuse and Mental Health Services Administration (2008, March 13). Inhalant use across the adolescent years. *The NSDUH Report.* Rockville, MD: Substance Abuse and Mental Health Services Administration. Preboth, Monica (2000, February 15). Prevalence of inhalant abuse in children. *American Family Physician,* p. 1206.

14. Howard, Matthew O.; Walker, R. Dale; Walker, Patricia S.; Cottler, Linda B.; and Compton, Wilson M. (1999). Inhalant use among urban American Indian youth. *Addiction, 94,* 83–95. Kin, Foong, and Navaratnam, Vis (1995). An overview of inhalant abuse in selected countries of Asia and the Pacific region. In Nicholas Kozel, Zili Sloboda, and Mario De La Rosa (Eds.), *Epidemiology of inhalant abuse: An international perspective* (NIDA Research Monograph 148). Rockville, MD: National Institute on Drug Abuse, pp. 29–49. Leal,

Hermán; Mejía, Laura; Gómez, Lucila; and Salina de Valle, Olga (1978). Naturalistic study on the phenomenon of inhalant use in a group of children in Mexico City. In Charles W. Sharp and L. T. Carroll (Eds.), *Voluntary inhalation of industrial solvents.* Rockville, MD: National Institute on Drug Abuse, pp. 95–108. Medina-Mora, María Elena, and Berenzon, Shoshana (1995). Epidemiology of inhalant abuse in Mexico. In Nicholas Kozel, Zili Sloboda, and Mario De La Rosa (Eds.), *Epidemiology of inhalant abuse: An international perspective* (NIDA Research Monograph 148). Rockville, MD: National Institute on Drug Abuse, pp. 136–174. Surratt, Hilary L., and Inciardi, James A. (1996). Drug use, HIV risks, and prevention/intervention strategies among street youths in Rio de Janeiro, Brazil. In Clyde B. McCoy, Lisa R. Metsch, and James A. Inciardi (Eds.), *Intervening with drug-involved youth.* Thousand Oaks, CA: Sage Publications, pp. 173–190.

15. Hofmann, Frederick G. (1983), *A handbook on drug and alcohol abuse: The biomedical aspects* (2nd ed.). New York: Oxford University Press, p. 134. Howard, Matthew O., and Jenson, Jeffrey M. (1998). Inhalant use among antisocial youth: Prevalence and correlates. *Addictive Behaviors, 24,* 59–74. Mackesy-Amiti, Mary Ellen, and Fendrich, Michaeal (1999). Inhalant abuse and delinquent behavior among adolescents: A comparison of inhalant users and other drug users. *Addiction, 94,* 555–564.

16. Oetting, E. R., Edwards, Ruth W., and Beauvais, Fred (1988). Social and psychological factors underlying inhalant abuse. In Raquel A. Crider and Beatrice A. Rouse (Eds.), *Epidemiology of inhalant abuse: An update* (NIDA Research Monograph 85). Rockville, MD: National Institute on Drug Abuse, pp. 172–203.

17. Hofmann, *Handbook on drug and alcohol abuse,* pp. 138–139. Karch, *The pathology of drug abuse,* p. 432. Korman, Maurice (1977). Clinical evaluation of psychological factors. In Charles W. Sharp and Mary Lee Brehm (Eds.), *Review of inhalants: Euphoria to dysfunction* (NIDA Research Monograph 15). Rockville, MD: National Institute on Drug Abuse, pp. 30–53. National Institute on Drug Abuse (2005, March). Inhalant abuse. Research report series. Rockville, MD: National Institute on Drug Abuse.

18. Hofmann, *Handbook on drug and alcohol abuse,* p. 134.

19. Oetting, Edwards, and Beauvais, Social and psychological factors, p. 197.

20. Sharp, Charles W. (1977). Approaches to the problem. In Charles W. Sharp and Mary Lee Brehm (Eds.), *Review of inhalants: Euphoria to dysfunction* (NIDA Research Monograph 15). Rockville, MD: National Institute on Drug Abuse, pp. 226–242.

21. Kerner, Karen (1988). Current topics in inhalant abuse. In Raquel A. Crider and Beatrice A. Rouse (Eds.), *Epidemiology of inhalant abuse: An update* (NIDA Research Monograph 85). Rockville, MD: National Institute on Drug Abuse, p. 20.

22. Draft of National Inhalant Prevention Coalition guidelines for inhalant abuse treatment (2003). Information

courtesy of the National Inhalant Prevention Coalition, Austin, Texas. Office of National Drug Control Policy (2003, February). *Inhalants: Drug Policy Information Clearinghouse fact sheet.* Washington DC: White House Office of National Drug Control Policy. Substance Abuse and Mental Health Services Administration (2003). *Inhalants: Substance abuse treatment advisory.* Rockville, MD: Center for Substance Abuse Treatment, Substance Abuse and Mental Health Services Administration.

23. Johnston, Lloyd D., O'Malley, Patrick M., and Bachman, Jerald D. (2001). *Monitoring the future: National survey results on drug use, 1975–2000. Volume II: College students and young adults ages 19–40.* Bethesda, MD: National Institute on Drug Abuse, Table 5-2. Newell, Guy R., Spitz, Margaret R., and Wilson, Michael B. (1988). Nitrite inhalants: Historical perspective. In Harry W. Haverkos and John A. Dougherty (Eds.), *Health hazards of nitrite inhalants* (NIDA Research Monograph 83). Rockville, MD: National Institute on Drug Abuse, pp. 1–14.

24. Johnston, O'Malley, Bachman, and Schulenberg (2008). Various stimulant drugs show continuing gradual declines, Table 1.

PART THREE
Legal Drugs in Our Society

POINT/COUNTERPOINT

Should Alcoholism Be Viewed as a Disease?

The following viewpoints on whether alcoholism is a disease represent both sides of this controversial issue. Read them with an open mind. Don't think you have to come up with the final answer, nor should you necessarily agree with the last argument you read. Many of the ideas in this feature come from the sources listed.

POINT
Alcohol abuse has recently been defined by the National Institute of Alcohol Abuse and Alcoholism (NIAAA) as having three criteria: a preoccupation with drinking alcohol, a pattern of compulsive use despite the adverse consequences, and a pattern of relapse to alcohol use. Alcoholics cannot control their drinking; that is their disease. Give a drink to a person who is genetically vulnerable to alcohol and the consumption of alcohol will make that person an alcoholic, just as a person infected with a type of bacteria might acquire an infectious disease.

COUNTERPOINT
First of all, you're taking considerable liberties with the bacterial infection argument. The research on alcoholism does not show that everyone who acquires the behaviors of alcohol abuse was genetically disposed to it. Controlled drinking is attainable for at least some alcoholics. How do you separate the alcoholics who respond less to genetic factors than to environmental ones and seem to retain some degree of control over their drinking from those individuals who do not? Besides, we are not talking about alcohol as some invisible bacteria floating around, waiting to "infect" people without their knowledge. Alcoholics become alcoholic because they consume a substance that later on they no longer can handle. At one time in their lives, they chose to have that first drink; no one person or thing made them do it.

POINT
We accept the fact that the alcoholic is responsible for "that first drink," but we assert that the consequences are not voluntary. The alcoholic is powerless over alcohol, not over his or her alcoholism. The situation is similar to a diabetic being in control over whether a treatment of insulin injections should be taken. The alcoholic can seek treatment.

COUNTERPOINT
You can't have it both ways. Being responsible for the treatment of the disease is not the same as being powerless in the face of alcoholism (one of the main assumptions of Alcoholics Anonymous). Even the Supreme Court has trouble wrestling with the issue. In 1988, it ruled that two alcoholics could not be excluded from claiming

educational benefits normally accorded to veterans just because their alcoholism prevented them from applying in the time allowed. The Veterans Administration had refused them, claiming that alcoholism, without physical or mental disorders, is an example of "willful misconduct."

POINT

Not exactly. The Court ruled that the source of the "willful misconduct" was the disease of alcoholism. In doing so, it actually reconfirmed the concept of alcoholism as a disease. The courts typically do not excuse the alcoholic from the consequences of the condition. Instead, they give the person a choice of being punished for his or her offenses or accepting a program of rehabilitation. We cannot go back to the days when drinking too much was considered a moral deficiency.

COUNTERPOINT

If alcoholism is a disease, then it's a very strange one. It may be in a category all its own.

Critical Thinking Questions for Further Discussion

1. Suppose that the evidence were overwhelming that moderate alcohol intake was a health-promoting activity and that there were social programs promoting moderate alcohol use through society. How would this work and would you envision any unanticipated consequences? What would be the effect on efforts to prevent and treat alcohol abuse?

2. Suppose you are an alcohol abuser and have attended several meetings of Alcoholics Anonymous (AA), to no avail. Programs that permit a moderate but nonzero level of alcohol consumption have not worked for you either. What options do you have, assuming you want to stop drinking? Do you go back to AA?

Sources: Holden, Constance (1987). Is alcoholism a disease? *Science, 238,* 1647. Levinthal, Charles F. (2003). *Point/Counterpoint: Opposing perspectives on issues of drug policy.* Boston: Allyn and Bacon, Chapters 5 and 6. Maltzman, Irving (1994). Why alcoholism is a disease. *Journal of Psychoactive Drugs, 26,* 13–31. Miller, Norman, and Toft, Doug (1990). *The disease concept of alcoholism and other drug addiction.* Center City, MN: Hazelden Foundation.

chapter 14

Prescription Drugs, Over-the-Counter Drugs, and Dietary Supplements

After you have completed this chapter, you will understand

- The distinction between prescription and OTC drugs, as opposed to dietary supplements
- The evolution of U.S. drug regulations
- FDA procedures for approving new drugs
- Prescription drugs changing to OTC drugs
- Safety issues with respect to prescription drugs
- Types of OTC analgesic drugs
- Sleep aids and cough-and-cold remedies
- The pharmaceutical industry today
- Dietary supplements

The little English graveyard contained a dozen or so monuments, their inscriptions nearly worn away by more than two centuries of wind and rain. Each epitaph told a bit about a life remembered. One was in rhyme:

> Here lies the body of Mary Ann Lauders,
> died of drinking Cheltenham waters.
> If she had stuck to Epsom salts,
> she wouldn't be lying in these here vaults.

I wondered what Mary's family might have done today. Would they have sued Cheltenham for promoting a pharmaceutical product that was neither safe nor effective? Would the British equivalent of the FDA have shut them down? And who says that Epsom salts would have been more effective? Where are the clinical trials?

The next time you are in a pharmacy or drugstore, take a minute to look around you. Besides the overwhelming variety of soaps, cosmetics, shaving creams, toothpastes, deodorants, and all the other products that have become part of our daily lives, notice the three broad categories of products that are available for purchase as medicines.

The first group of medicinal products, a few thousand of them, placed mostly out of view and behind the pharmacist's counter, are **prescription drugs.** Their purchase and use require the submission of a written prescription form with an appropriate signature (or a doctor's phone call) that certifies that you are taking one of these drugs for a medical condition and at a dosage level appropriate for that condition. The amount of the drug that you are allowed to purchase at any one time is specified, and a limit on the number of prescription refills offers some control over that drug's use over an extended period of time. By law, only licensed physicians or dentists are permitted to write (or call in) prescriptions for their patients, and only registered pharmacists are permitted to fill these prescriptions and dispense these drugs to the consumer.

The second group of products, more than 100,000 of them, are **over-the-counter (OTC) drugs,** encompassing about 800 significant active ingredients. In contrast to prescription drugs, OTC drugs are available to you right off the shelves that line the aisles of the store, and their use is limited only by your ability to pay for them. With OTC drugs, you are your own physician. In most cases, you have diagnosed the ailment yourself and determined the course of treatment. Recommended doses are clearly printed on the label, and you may get some guidance from the pharmacist; however, there is no direct medical supervision over the dosage level that you actually consume at any given time. No one will tell you when to stop using these drugs or whether they were appropriate to take in the first place. Given the almost total absence of supervision over the personal use of OTC drugs, some basic safeguards are needed. Are the

by the numbers . . .

40 Percentage of American doctors who received no instruction in medical school in prescribing controlled substances

55 Percentage of American doctors who received no instruction in medical school in identifying prescription drug abuse or dependence

43 Percentage of American doctors who do not inquire about prescription drug abuse when taking a medical history of a patient

Sources: National Center on Addiction and Substance Abuse at Columbia University (2005). *Under the counter: The diversion and abuse of controlled prescription drugs in the U.S.* New York: National Center on Addiction and Substance Abuse, pp. 130–131, 138.

drugs safe to use if taken at the dosage levels listed on the package? Are they effective in helping you in the way they claim?

In the United States, the regulation of both prescription and OTC drugs has been assigned to the U.S. Food and Drug Administration (FDA). The FDA is responsible for determining whether an existing prescription drug should continue to be available for public use and whether a newly developed drug can pass established standards of safety and effectiveness to be marketed as a prescription drug. The agency also oversees the safety and effectiveness of OTC drugs. By necessity, according to FDA standards, the strength and concentration of active ingredients in OTC drugs must have a greater margin of safety than active ingredients in prescription drugs to justify their wide availability to the general public under such unsupervised circumstances.

No drug, however, is totally free of potentially toxic effects, despite extensive efforts to ensure the safety of prescription and OTC drugs. The potential for misuse of OTC drugs is a particular concern. It is important, therefore, to review three major classes of OTC drugs for which a potential for misuse exists: analgesics, sleep aids, and cough-and-cold remedies.

In contrast to prescription drugs and OTC drugs, a third group of products called **dietary supplements** are relatively new, but they have been occupying an increasing amount of shelf space in recent years. Dietary supplements are generally available to the public in the form of vitamin or herbal preparations. While they are marketed in a similar manner as OTC drugs, there is an important difference. As defined by the Dietary Supplement Health and Education Act in 1994, dietary supplements do not have to be proved safe and effective, as prescription and

prescription drugs: Drugs available to the public only when approved by a medical professional and dispensed by a licensed pharmacist.

over-the-counter (OTC) drugs: A class of medicinal drugs available to the public without the requirement of a prescription. They are often referred to as nonprescription drugs.

dietary supplements: Products (other than tobacco), distributed with the intention of supplementing the diet, that contain a vitamin, mineral, amino acid, herb or other botanical product, enzyme, organ tissue, metabolites, or any combination of these substances.

Pharmacists are specially trained to dispense approximately 2,500 different prescription drugs, although only about 50 of them account for 95 percent of retail pharmacy sales.

OTC drugs do, although as of 2010, manufacturers must show that the purity, strength, and composition of these products have been tested and that the labels are accurate descriptions of the contents. Federal regulations stipulate that dietary supplement labels must specify that the product has *not* been evaluated by the FDA and that the claims of benefit from using the product are limited only to helping certain common physical conditions associated with different stages of life (adolescence, pregnancy, menopause, and aging). Dietary supplement manufacturers are not allowed to claim benefits with respect to the diagnosis, treatment, cure, or prevention of more uncommon conditions or diseases.[1] Two prominent dietary supplements marketed for psychoactive applications, ginkgo biloba and ginseng, will be reviewed in this chapter.

How the Regulation of Prescription and OTC Drugs Began

We take for granted that the ingredients in drugs commercially available to us through drugstores, pharmacies, and supermarkets are pure and unadulterated. We assume that they will not harm us when we use them as directed and

that they will reliably produce the benefits stated on the package or accompanying information packet.

Prior to 1906, no assumption of any kind could have been made. The consumer of any of the fifty thousand or so patent medicines available for purchase had no guarantee about what he or she was getting. Consumers could order, for example, the White Star Secret Liquor Cure from the 1897 Sears, Roebuck catalog (see Chapter 5) and not be told that they would be consuming opium. The manufacturer was under no obligation to inform the buyer of that fact, or anything else for that matter.

As a response to public outcry over the unregulated patent medicines flooding the market, as well as publicity about the terrible conditions in the meatpacking industry, Congress enacted the Pure Food and Drug Act in 1906. This legislation set out to ensure that all foods and drugs in the United States would be inspected for purity and consistency. In addition, all active ingredients in drugs had to be clearly and accurately identified on the label. The 1906 act did not, however, guarantee any more protection than that. Until 1938, drugs could still be useless and/or dangerous as long as the label listed the ingredients in a correct manner.

As often happens, it took a major national crisis to generate further regulatory action. In September 1937, a syrup for sore throats called Elixir Sulfanilamide, manufactured in a small factory in Tennessee, was found to be the cause of 107 deaths throughout the United States. Many of those affected were children. The reason for the tragic results was quickly determined to be the fact that the sulfanilamide component (in itself a useful antibiotic) had been dissolved in a solution containing diethylene glycol, a close relative to present-day antifreeze. Obviously, the product had not been adequately tested for safety.

Luckily, the FDA was able to seize the entire stock, and it was taken off the market before any more deaths occurred. But the FDA acted not because Elixir Sulfanilamide had been judged unsafe (under the 1906 law, the FDA would not have been able to act on these grounds) but because *the preparation had been mislabeled.* Technically, an elixir had to contain some quantity of ethyl alcohol (see Chapter 9), and Elixir Sulfanilamide had none. Hence, the law had been broken![2]

After this incident, the American public sent a clear message to Washington that they would no longer tolerate the marketing of unsafe drugs. President Roosevelt signed into law the Federal Food, Drug, and Cosmetic (FDC) Act, which has served to the present day as the basic food and drug law in the United States. Taking effect in 1938, this law mandated that all ingredients in cosmetic products had to be accurately identified, and drug companies were henceforth required to

PORTRAIT

In October 1961, a new medical officer at the FDA's Division of New Drugs, Dr. Frances Kelsey, was assigned the task of supervising the approval for a new drug called thalidomide. Introduced by a German pharmaceutical company in 1958, the drug had been hailed as "the tranquilizer of the future." Even massive doses of thalidomide couldn't kill you. Virtually all the countries of the world had accepted thalidomide for marketing within their own borders; only France, Israel, and the United States were holding out. At that time, the FDA had to reject the application for a new drug in sixty days or automatically allow it to be approved and marketed. Merrell Pharmaceuticals had sponsored the application for thalidomide and was anxiously awaiting the results. But Kelsey kept on stalling; after each sixty-day period, she would routinely reject the application as "incomplete."

As Kelsey studied the data, something seemed wrong about thalidomide. One of its side effects, of minor importance by itself, was a mild neuritis, or "tingling of the nerves." It reminded her of research she had conducted fifteen years earlier in which she had observed that neuritis of this type in pregnant animals resulted in deformed offspring. None of the experimental animal data, however, had shown anything even resembling birth defects. It remained simply her gut instinct to wait a little longer, just to be sure.

In retrospect, seldom had a wait been more worthwhile. Within a year of thalidomide's introduction in Germany, an extremely rare birth deformity began to appear. Babies were born with short, finlike flaps instead of normal arms and legs, victims of a disorder called *phocomelia*. The number of cases of phocomelia had mysteriously increased from 12 in 1959, to 83 in 1960, to 302 in 1961. A German pediatrician offered the theory that these horrible deformities were tied to the taking of thalidomide by pregnant women. By 1962, it was clear that the drug was indeed the culprit.

It has been estimated by the FDA that more than ten thousand babies in twenty countries were victims of thalidomide. But American children never had to experience this tragedy, thanks to one woman who listened to her suspicions and was brave enough to say no. In 1962, President John F. Kennedy awarded Kelsey the President's Gold Medal for Distinguished Service, in honor of her heroic stance.

Today, thalidomide (brand name: Thalomid) is used only in extremely restricted applications and is never given to fertile women. Ironically, this highly teratogenic (birth-defect-causing) drug is one of the few treatments available for Hansen's disease (formerly known as leprosy). It is also used in the treatment of multiple myeloma, a form of bone-marrow cancer, and rare disorders of the immune system.

Sources: Editorial: Thalidomide— A revival story (1999). *New England Journal of Medicine, 341,* 1606–1609. Patrick, William (1988). *The Food and Drug Administration.* New York: Chelsea House, pp. 41–42. Stephens, Trent, and Brynner, Rock (2001). *Dark remedy: The impact of thalidomide and its revival as a vital medicine.* Boulder, CO: Perseus Books.

demonstrate by research studies that new drugs were safe (when used as directed) before they could be marketed commercially. A 1951 amendment to the FDC Act established a clear distinction between prescription and OTC drugs. By that point, the FDA had grown in stature and power as the official guardian of the public interest with regard to food, drugs, and cosmetics.

The final element of governmental control took effect in 1962, once again as a reaction to a well-publicized health emergency. In the late 1950s, a drug called **thalidomide** had been marketed by a West German pharmaceutical company and used by thousands of pregnant women in Europe, Canada, Australia, and South America as a sedative and treatment for the discomforts of morning sickness. Within the United States, however, despite pressure to do so, the FDA refused to approve the drug. Scattered reports had been noted of the incidence of deformities among babies of mothers who had been taking thalidomide. By 1962, Americans learned of the enormity of the tragedy and how close they had come to being affected themselves. Thousands of babies around the world were born armless, legless, or both because of this drug (Portrait).

Though the Kefauver-Harris Amendment of 1962 was a direct consequence of the thalidomide crisis, the FDA had in fact been acting on the basis of statutes that already existed. The safety of new drugs had to be ensured by an FDA approval process, which is precisely what the FDA carried out. Nonetheless, the American public, anxious that it had come so near to a major catastrophe, was insistent that the FDA be given broader powers. As a result of the 1962 amendment, drug companies were required

---

thalidomide (tha-LID-oh-mide): A highly teratogenic (birth-defect producing) drug. Brand name is Thalomid.

TABLE 14.1

Major regulatory laws of the FDA since 1938

ACT OR AMENDMENT	YEAR	EFFECT
Color Additive Amendment	1960	Regulated the safe use of color additives in drugs and food
Hazardous Substances Labeling Act	1960	Required warning labels on all products intended for home use
Kefauver-Harris Amendment	1962	Required that new drugs be effective as well as safe
Child Protection Act	1966	Regulated the safety of toys sold across state lines
Medical Device Amendment	1976	Required that any health care product or device be effective and safe
Instant Formula Act	1980	Regulated the contents of baby-formula preparations
Anti-tampering Act	1983	Required tamper-resistant packaging for all OTC products
Orphan Drug Act	1983	Allowed drug companies to take tax credits for developing new drugs with low potential for profits
Prescription Drug User Fee Act	1992	Increased FDA efficiency in the review of new drug applications
Dietary Supplement Health and Education Act	1994	Set guidelines for the marketing of vitamin and herbal preparations
FDA Modernization Act	1997	Streamlined procedures for approval of new drugs, food labels, and medical devices

Source: Patrick, William (1988). *The Food and Drug Administration.* New York: Chelsea House, pp. 37–49. Updated with information from the U.S. Food and Drug Administration, Washington DC.

to prove that new drugs were *effective* as well as safe. The only concern until then had been with regard to safety.

An important additional feature of the new regulations, however, did affect the maintenance of drug safety. Once new drugs were approved, drug companies were now required to send reports to the FDA on a regular basis, informing the agency of any adverse reactions experienced by their users. As a result, any unforeseen difficulties with FDA-approved drugs could be recognized and appropriate measures could then be taken.

The FDA continues to prosecute violators of the drug laws, but enforcement is no longer its sole mission. Regulations since 1938 have allowed the FDA a more active role in preventing problems from arising in the first place (Table 14.1).[3] A major part of this preventive approach is the set of procedures required for the approval of new prescription drugs and the setting of standards for OTC drugs.

Procedures for Approving Prescription and OTC Drugs

The current process for introducing a new prescription drug on the market consists of a number of stages or phases of approval required by the FDA. It begins in the laboratories of the drug companies themselves, with the identification of the composition of a new compound,

a purification of its active ingredients, and a preliminary determination of any possible toxic effects. Extensive tests in two or more species of laboratory animals are carried out to establish the LD50 dosage of the compound, the concentration that leads to death in 50 percent of the animals studied (see Chapter 2). Specific tests are also made on pregnant animals to determine whether administration of the compound might produce birth defects. If the intention is to market the compound as a drug for chronic disorders, the toxicity studies need to be extended over a period of time that simulates the projected duration that the drug might be used by human patients.

After these preliminary studies are completed and the new drug has been determined to be safe with animals, the drug company then notifies the FDA, through an application known as a Notice of Claimed Investigational Exemption for a New Drug (IND), that this compound has promise as a new prescription drug and that permission is now requested to conduct testing in humans.

Phases of Clinical Testing for Prescription Drugs

At this point, drug-testing procedures focus on the question of whether the compound will be effective as a medicinal drug, although safety considerations are noted as well. A sequence of four stages of clinical testing is now begun, with each stage dependent on the success of the preceding one.

- In the first stage of clinical studies, called **Phase 1 trials,** about ten to one hundred healthy volunteers (frequently prison inmates or medical students) are administered the drug, and certain pharmacological questions are answered. How quickly is the new drug absorbed and eliminated? Are any side effects observed? What range of dosages is safe for use? Do any specific schedules for administration (one large dose per day versus three small ones) minimize any adverse effects?

Phase 1 trials: The first stage of clinical testing, in which an experimental drug is administered to healthy volunteers to check on possible side effects and to determine patterns of absorption and elimination.

Phase 2 trials: The second stage of clinical testing, in which an experimental drug is given to a small population of patients having the medical condition for which the drug is considered a possible treatment.

Phase 3 trials: The third stage of clinical testing, in which an experimental drug is given to a large population of patients, through which issues of safety, effectiveness, and proper dosage levels are finalized.

- In the second stage of clinical studies, called **Phase 2 trials,** the new drug is tested on one hundred to five hundred patients who have the medical condition or illness that the drug is intended to treat. Researchers are careful to select only those patients who are free of other health problems so that any improvements will be identified as a genuine effect on the illness in question. It should not be surprising that all these clinical studies are conducted in a double-blind fashion. Neither the researchers nor the patients are aware of whether the new drug or a look-alike placebo (see Chapter 3) is being administered. As a result, positive effects (if any) are attributed to the therapeutic properties of the drug, free of any expectations or biases that the researchers or patients may have had.

- If these two trials have been successful, the third clinical stage, called **Phase 3 trials,** is undertaken. At this testing point, the safety, effectiveness, and proper dosage levels are investigated in a population of one thousand to three thousand patients. A closer examination of possible side effects (some of which may be observed only rarely) is carried out, and further fine-tuning is made in the recommended usage of the drug (Health Line).

Health Line

Widening the Population during Drug Testing

Traditionally, clinical trials for potential new drugs have been conducted on young men. In 1977, the FDA banned women from taking part in most of the clinical trials for new drugs on the grounds that there might be harm to the fetus if a woman became pregnant during testing. Since 1993, however, the ban has been lifted. Possible risks for pregnant women are still a matter of great concern, but equal consideration is now directed to the need for gender-specific data on a future drug. As a result, it is now possible to know about any adjustment in dosage or administration that might optimize the drug's effect for women, as well as men.

A related matter is the smaller amount of attention that has been paid to the possibility that either elderly or very young patients might have responses to a prescription drug substantially different from those of young adults. It is not simply a matter of giving a lower level of the recommended "adult dose" to these populations. The elderly and children often metabolize drugs in unique ways, so some prescription drugs may not be appropriate for them at any dose level. Since 1999, drug manufacturers must conduct prescription drug testing in children if the medication is to be used by a significant number of

young patients. In addition, drug companies are required to conduct new studies of some drugs already in wide use among children.

While some progress has been made in widening the population included in clinical trials, more remains to be done in this area. The elderly are represented in nearly 40 percent of all heart attack cases in the United States, but the inclusion of the elderly in clinical trials of new heart disease medications from 1966 to 2000 rose from 2 percent to no more than 9 percent. Similarly, the inclusion of women in these clinical trials rose from 20 percent to 29 percent, even though women account for 43 percent of heart attack patients.

Sources: Editorial: Drug safety for children (1999, January 1). *New York Times,* p. A18. Kluger, Jeffrey (2003, November 3). Medicating young minds. *Time,* pp. 48–54. Lee, Patrick Y.; Alexander, Karen P.; Hammill, Bradley G.; Pasquali, Sara K.; and Peterson, Eric D. (2001). Representation of elderly persons and women in published randomized trials of acute coronary syndromes. *Journal of the American Medical Association, 286,* 708–713. Testing drugs in older people (1990, November). *FDA Consumer,* pp. 24–27.

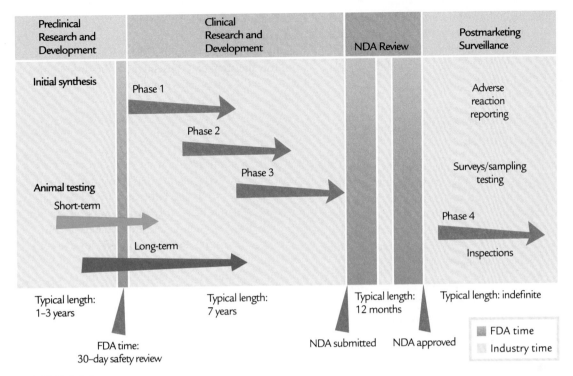

FIGURE 14.1

Development of new prescription drugs and the FDA approval process. In 2006, the FDA approved an accelerated procedure in which drug companies are permitted to test experimental compounds on fewer than twelve human subjects before animal studies are complete.

Sources: FDA OKs new ways to test drugs (2006, January 13). *Newsday,* p. A57. U.S. Food and Drug Administration (2001, March–April). Making medical progress: A look at FDA approvals in 2000. *FDA Consumer,* pp. 7–8. Zivin, Justin A. (2003, April). Understanding clinical trials. *Scientific American,* pp. 69–75.

■ After all three stages of clinical trials have been completed, a process that takes three years or more (Figure 14.1), and the drug company considers the results to be satisfactory, a New Drug Application (NDA) is submitted for approval by the FDA. This application includes all the data on the animal testing and clinical trials. Less than 30 percent of all compounds that drug companies consider worthy of human clinical trials will have made it this far. Under usual circumstances, the FDA then has six months to review the application and to either accept or reject the new drug for commercial marketing, though the entire FDA review process at this stage takes up to a year or more.

By the time a new drug is FDA-approved for prescription use, it is likely that several years will have elapsed since the compound was first synthesized and considered promising enough to warrant clinical testing. The research and development costs to pharmaceutical companies now exceed $30 billion each year. Since 1997, fewer than forty original new drugs (excluding variations on existing drugs and new medical applications for existing drugs) have been FDA-approved each year, a tiny fraction of the original number that had been synthesized in the laboratory.[4]

Even after release for commercial use, a new drug is still monitored for any unforeseen side effects or toxic reactions, in a stage called **Phase 4 trials.** At this point, physicians throughout the United States are instructed, through a federal program called MedWatch, to report to the FDA any instances of adverse effects resulting from the use or misuse of the new drugs by their patients. In cases in which significant adverse drug reactions are reported, a special notice is placed in the *Physicians' Desk Reference for Prescription Drugs* (an annual publication

Phase 4 trials: The fourth stage of clinical testing, in which possible adverse reactions to a drug that is already available to the public are monitored by physicians who have prescribed it.

that includes detailed information on all FDA-approved prescription medications), referred to as a "black box warning," so that these reactions can be avoided. In extreme cases, FDA approval is rescinded and the drug is withdrawn from the market.[5]

Patents and Generic Forms of Prescription Drugs

Approval by the FDA gives the drug company exclusive rights to manufacture and sell the new drug under its own brand name (beginning with a capital letter and often accompanied by a small, circled letter R just to the right of it, signifying that the name is a registered trademark). All other companies are forbidden by law to sell the compound under that brand name or any other name.

patent: The exclusive right of a drug company to market a particular drug. The duration of a patent is twenty years.

bioequivalence: A characteristic of two drugs in which all pharmacological and physiological effects are identical.

These rights, called a **patent,** have a fixed duration of twenty years. The clock starts, however, at the time the original IND is submitted to the FDA, not when the drug hits the market. Consequently, the drug company may, in reality, have patent protection for a prescription drug for only ten to twelve years. After that, the drug "goes off patent" and generic forms of it can be manufactured and sold to the public.

After the patent expires, the original drug company frequently continues to market the drug under its brand name, but now the consumer has the option of having it prescribed and purchased either as a brand drug or as a generic (and much less expensive) version. In some cases, when a particular patent expires, a drug company might decide to apply for FDA approval for its prescription drug to be marketed as an OTC drug (as was the case with Claritin in 2002 and Prilosec in 2003), rather than compete with producers of generic versions.[6]

Since 1984, the FDA has required that all generic drugs demonstrate **bioequivalence** with respect to the original, brand-name drug, meaning that both versions must be shown to be chemically and pharmacologic-

---

Health Line

Bioequivalence and Bioavailability

Bioequivalence refers to a characteristic of two drug products in which both contain the same active compound in the same amount. In effect, bioequivalent drugs are expected to produce equivalent drug concentrations in blood and tissues, within a margin of difference of plus or minus 20 percent.

Bioequivalence is not the whole story, however, in establishing an "equivalent" physiological response. A key element to be considered is the possible differences in the bioavailability of the two drugs. Bioavailability is the extent to which (or the rate at which) a drug enters the circulation and reaches the site of action for that drug. For example, relative to a comparison drug, an orally administered drug might be absorbed more quickly or absorbed more slowly.

Therefore, two bioequivalent drugs might not be the same in their respective levels of bioavailability. Unfortunately, this possibility presents significant complications in ensuring that generic drugs have the same therapeutic effects as their prescription counterparts. In the case of antiepileptic (antiseizure) medications, the tolerance limits for effectiveness are quite narrow. As a result, bioavailability issues are very important.

Differing levels of bioavailability from person to person also help explain why the same identical drug might have different therapeutic effects in two individuals. An increasing understanding of the basis for variations in bioavailability will be undoubtedly useful in future drug development. It may be possible someday to "tailor" the dosage level of specific medications for a given individual to attain optimal therapeutic benefits. It is conceivable that future patients might undergo genetic screening to determine their individualized enzymatic profile and, in turn, their levels of bioavailability that ensure the best results for the medications they are taking.

Sources: Bioavailability (2006). *Merck Manual of Diagnosis and Therapy.* Section 22: Clinical Pharmacology. Chapter 298 : Drug Input and Disposition. De Leon, J., Armstrong, S. C., and Cozza, K. L. (2006). Clinical guidelines for psychiatrists for the use of pharmacogenetic testing for CYP450 2D6 and CYP450 2C19. *Psychosomatics, 47,* 75–85. Pollack, Andrew (2005, November 8). A special drug just for you, at the end of a long pipeline. *New York Times,* pp. F1, F6. Rosenthal, Jessica; Kong, Brian; Jacobs, Leslie; and Katzman, Martin (2008). Did a switch to a generic antidepressant cause relapse? *Journal of Family Practice, 57,* 109–114.

ally identical. However, there may still be differences in the clinical effects of these generic versions (Health Line).

Speeding Up the FDA Approval Process

Since the 1990s, not all drugs have had to travel this long and arduous road to reach the marketplace. Under special circumstances, the process can be accelerated. In 1987, the FDA authorized the use of a "treatment IND" application, specially designed for new drugs that show promise for certain seriously ill patients. Without compromising the standards for safety and effectiveness, a streamlined approval procedure now makes it possible for a novel drug treatment to reach patients who can benefit from it in a matter of months instead of years. Medical conditions for which drugs have been approved in this way include AIDS, infection associated with kidney transplants, Alzheimer's disease, Parkinson's disease, and forms of advanced cancers. One particular drug to treat AIDS and related conditions was approved in 1995 in an agency record-setting ninety-seven days.

Ultimately, the limiting factor in much of the approval process is the number of scientists and administrators assigned to examine test data from the thousands of new drugs evaluated each year. Since 1992, the FDA

has been permitted to charge drug companies user fees to support the hiring of chemists, microbiologists, and pharmacologists, as well as other professionals and support staff at the agency. A recent trend has been for drug companies to hire independent contract research organizations specifically to conduct clinical trials for a drug in development. Efficiency is increased because these organizations have the capacity to test multiple drugs simultaneously. Their trustworthiness is assured because they do not profit from the sales of future drugs (avoiding an obvious conflict of interest), and their reputations are maintained to the extent to which their trials stand up to FDA standards (Table 14.2).[7]

Procedures for Approving OTC Drugs

When the Kefauver-Harris Amendment took effect in 1962, its aim was to ensure that all drugs sold in the United States were both safe and effective. Two governmental study groups were established for this purpose. The Drug Efficacy Study Investigation (DESI) examined all existing prescription medicines, and the Over-the-Counter Review (OTC Review) examined all existing nonprescription medicines. Whether it was in a prescription or nonprescription category, every drug was to be judged as GRAS (generally regarded as safe), GRAE (generally regarded as effective), and GRAHL (generally

TABLE 14.2		
The top ten leading brands of prescription drugs based on U.S. sales, 2007		
BRAND NAME (MANUFACTURER)	MEDICAL APPLICATIONS	RETAIL SALES (in billions of dollars)
Lipitor* (Pfizer)	Elevated cholesterol	$6.17
Nexium (Astrazeneca)	Acid reflux, heartburn	4.36
Advair Diskus (GlaxoSmithKline)	Asthma	3.39
Prevacid* (TAP)	Acid reflux, heartburn, stomach ulceration	3.32
Plavix (Bristol-Myers Squibb)	Excessive blood clotting	3.08
Singulair (Merck)	Asthma, allegies	2.86
Seroquel (Astrazeneca)	Bipolar disorder, schizophrenia	2.52
Effexor XR* (Wyeth)	Depression	2.46
Lexapro (Forest)	Depression, anxiety	2.30
Actos (Tekeda)	Type 2 diabetes	2.23

*Patent expirations: Effexor XR (2008), Prevacid (2009), Lipitor (2010).

Note: Pharmaceutical industry analysts predict that, from 2008 to 2012, prescription drugs that generate a total of $67 billion of annual revenue will have lost patent protection and will have quickly lost market share to cheaper generic versions.

Sources: Tesoriero, Heather Won (2008, February 21). Drug prices surge, despite criticisms on campaign trail. *Wall Street Journal*, p. B1. Top 200 brand drugs by retail dollars in 2007. Reprinted with permission from *Drug Topics*, March 10, 2008. Drug patent expirations for 2008–2009. *Drug Topics*, April 14, 2008. *Drug Topics* is a copyrighted publication of Advanstar Communications, Inc. All rights reserved.

TABLE 14.3

A partial listing of former prescription drugs now sold on an over-the-counter (OTC) basis

OTC BRAND NAME	GENERIC NAME	CLINICAL USE
Actifed	triprolidine	Antihistamine
Aleve	naproxen	Analgesic and anti-inflammatory
Benadryl	diphenhydramine	Antihistamine
Claritin, Alavert	loratadine	Antihistamine
Dimetane, Dimetapp	brompheniramine	Antihistamine
Monistat	miconazole	Treatment for vaginal yeast infections
Motrin, Advil, Nuprin	ibuprofen	Analgesic and anti-inflammatory
Pepcid AC	famotidine	Heartburn relief
Prilosec	omeprazole	Heartburn relief
Tagamet HB	eimetidine	Heartburn relief
Zantac	ranitidine	Heartburn relief

Sources: Information courtesy of the Nonprescription Drug Manufacturers Association, Washington DC. *Physicians' desk reference* (62nd ed.) (2008). Montvale, NJ: Medical Economic Company. *Physicians' desk reference for nonprescription drugs, dietary supplements, and herbs* (29th ed.) (2007). Montvale, NJ: Thomson HealthCare.

regarded as honestly labeled). If a drug failed to meet any one of these criteria, the drug manufacturer had six months to convince the FDA otherwise or else the drug would no longer be permitted to be marketed across state lines within the United States.

The OTC Review has produced three important changes in OTC drugs available to the consumer. First, the professional committees examining present-day OTC drugs have recommended and the FDA has approved an increase in the recommended dosage for certain OTC drugs. OTC-type antihistamines, for example, are stronger than in previous years as a result. Second, several prescription drugs have been determined to be safe enough to warrant use on an OTC basis, and consequently a growing number of prescription drugs are available for purchase on a nonprescription basis. Table 14.3 lists some of the present-day OTC drugs that had formerly been available only on a prescription basis. Third, new regulations require that OTC drugs have consumer-friendly labels so that individuals can easily determine the symptoms that might be relieved by the medications and the safety precautions that must be heeded in their use. Some of these precautions include warnings about possible adverse reactions ("Ask a doctor before use if you have. . . .") and possible side effects ("When using this product you may get. . . .").[8]

Are FDA-Approved Drugs Safe?

The answer to the safety question for FDA-approved drugs, unfortunately, is yes and no. On the one hand, the FDA approval process is designed to prevent the introduction of any new drug or the continued availability of any present drug if there is a serious question about its safety when consumed in the recommended dosage for the treatment of certain specified medical disorders.

On the other hand, there is no guarantee that some drugs might slip through the approval process without enough scrutiny and cause problems after it has been introduced and available to the public.

The Issue of Speed versus Caution

It has always been necessary to balance the need to provide in an expeditious manner drugs for people suffering from a variety of physical and mental disorders with the cautious deliberation required to screen out drugs that may be potentially harmful. In recent years, however, the pendulum has swung in the direction of caution as opposed to speed. According to many public health officials, this new approach is largely due to the FDA decision in 2004 to withdraw the arthritis medication Vioxx from the market after the discovery of a link between the drug and a doubling of the risk of heart attack or stroke. In 2007, the FDA approved only seventeen new drugs with active ingredients that had never previously been marketed in the U.S., the lowest number in five years. In 2007, 64 percent of applications were approved by the FDA, in contrast to 73 percent in 2006.[9]

In the future, a spirit of caution is likely to be influenced by two recent developments. The U.S. Supreme Court ruled in 2008 that medical-device manufacturers could not be sued by persons alleging that they had been injured by a defectively designed medical device that the FDA had approved to be safe and effective after a full review. Whether this "preemption" ruling can be applied to FDA-approved drugs remains to be determined, though it is certain that the 2008 decision will be argued as a legal precedent in future cases. Second, in a 2008 study examining FDA drug approvals between 1950 and 2005, it was found that drugs that had been approved just prior to the deadline for doing so were more likely to present safety problems after their introduction than those drugs that had received approval with more time to spare. One of the authors of the study has commented that "FDA staffers by their own admission feel very much under the gun as these deadlines loom. If they're forced to make decisions prematurely, they may not make the right decisions."[10]

Misuse of Prescription Drugs

No drug is without side effects. Some of these side effects are quite minor, but others can be severe if the drug is taken by individuals with specific health problems. A quick look at the full disclosure statement that is packaged with commercially available drugs will indicate to you the wide range of possible adverse effects (Health Alert, page 344).

The safety issue is further complicated when individuals misuse prescription drugs by either ignoring the manufacturer's precautionary advice or by exceeding (deliberately or accidentally) the recommended dosage levels. In these cases, there is a risk of a medical emergency, resulting in a drug-related ED visit.

Three important points should be made, however, when considering ED visits that are associated with prescription drugs alone. First, drug-related ED visits in this category are far eclipsed by ED visits involving cocaine, marijuana, heroin, or other opiate drugs, and alcohol-in-combination (see Chapter 2). Second, prescription drugs are frequently the agents for a suicide attempt. According to the Drug Abuse Warning Network (DAWN) report, more than half (about 58 percent) of suicide attempts in 2006 involved the misuse of drugs used for the treatment of anxiety and/or depression, and slightly less than half (about 45 percent) involved the misuse of analgesic drugs (pain relievers). Obviously, the doses in these cases far exceeded recommended levels. Third, most ED visits associated with prescription drugs involve the combination of multiple drugs, typically a mix of a psychotherapeutic medication, pain reliever, and alcohol. In some cases, the ingestion of a single prescription drug by itself would not have been problematic. For example, the antianxiety drug diazepam (brand name: Valium) is much more likely to produce a medical emergency or even a life-threatening condition when it is combined with alcohol than when it is ingested alone, even in substantial quantities (see Chapter 15). The tendency to combine drugs with alcohol (categorized as "alcohol-in-combination" in the DAWN statistics) substantially raises the risks of acute toxicity for drugs that are licit as well as those that are illicit.[11]

Unintentional Drug Misuse through Prescription Errors

Dangers can come from unintentional misuse as well, particularly in specific populations. The increasing number of prescription drugs on the market and the growing numbers of elderly patients taking multiple medications on an outpatient basis for various disorders have recently become subjects of great concern. Due largely to prescribing errors on the part of physicians, an estimated 500,000 preventable adverse reactions, ranging from

HEALTH ALERT!

Side Effects of Common Medications

This Health Alert is a cautionary note on the side effects that may occur from the use of *medicinal* drugs at recommended dosages. Physicians often warn their patients that a stimulant drug might cause some sleep disturbance, or another might produce some gastrointestinal distress or sexual potency problems, but few of them routinely mention possible effects on the mouth, eyes, ears, or skin. Here are some common prescription and OTC drugs that can produce these types of side effects.

A Drying of the Mouth or Reduction in Saliva, as Well as a Reduction in Tear Flow in the Eyes

- Lasix, Hydrodiuril, Dyrenium (diuretic drugs)
- Aldomet, Catapres, Minipress (antihypertensive drugs)
- Tofranil, Elavil (antidepressant drugs)
- Compazine, Haldol, Thorazine (antipsychotic drugs)
- Artane, Larodopa (anti-Parkinson's disease drugs)

Eye Problems

- corticosteroids, which can trigger the growth of a cataract
- digitalis (a heart stimulant), which can disrupt color vision
- sulfa drugs and diuretics, which can cause blurred vision
- antipsychotic drugs, which can cause a feeling of burning
- oral contraceptives, which can cause bleeding in the eye

Hearing and Equilibrium Problems

- aspirin, which can cause a ringing in the ears and deafness
- neomycin (antibiotic), which can cause auditory damage

Increased Skin Sensitivity to the Sun

- many antipsychotic drugs and antidepressant drugs
- tetracycline, sulfa drugs (antibiotics)
- Lasix, thiazides (diuretic drugs)
- oral contraceptives

> **Where to go for assistance:**
> www.drugs.com/sfx
>
> An extensive inventory of drug side effects from this authoritative online drug information resource.

Sources: Brody, Jane E. (1992, February 26). Personal health: Unsuspected common drugs can wreak havoc. *New York Times*, p. C13. *Physicians' desk reference: Companion guide* (59th ed.) (2005). Montvale, NJ: Thomson HealthCare, pp. 1153–1409.

---

relatively mild symptoms of nausea to life-threatening kidney failure, are suffered by elderly patients in the United States alone each year. This problem has arisen in part because it is extremely difficult for physicians to monitor the complex array of potential drug interactions among their patients. From the perspective of the pharmacist, handwritten prescriptions from health care professionals can be easily confused, leading to the inappropriate medication being dispensed (Health Line).[12]

Even in the more controlled settings of hospitals and clinics, prescription errors have occurred with alarming frequency, affecting patients of all ages. In 2006, an FDA regulation went into effect, mandating the use of bar-coded identifications, similar to those on commercial products, for all prescription and OTC drugs administered in a health care facility. Each patient admitted to a hospital receives a bar-coded identification bracelet linked to his or her individual

The elderly often have to contend with a multitude of medications, many of which may interact with one another.

Health Line

The Possibility of Death by Prescription Error

Look carefully at the two prescriptions shown below. The one on the left is for Accupril, a drug used to treat high blood pressure; the one on the right is for Accutane, a drug to treat severe acne. The distinction between the two drugs is by no means trivial. If Accutane is taken instead of Accupril, the patient carries not only an increased risk of stroke from untreated hypertension but also (if the patient is a pregnant female) an increased risk of birth defects in an unborn child.

Even so, the prescriptions look disturbingly similar. This is the essence of the problem facing physicians, pharmacists, and patients in today's world of prescription drugs. Estimates of deaths due to medication errors within the United States range from about four hundred (about one per day) to seven thousand per year.

It is not simply a matter of prescription handwriting. Pharmaceutical companies have increasingly introduced brand names for new drugs that are very difficult to distinguish from each other. In 2008, the United States Pharmacopeia identified 3,370 pairs of drug brand names that either looked or sounded alike—nearly double the number it had identified in 2004.

Here are some examples of how prescription errors might arise from the similarity of prescription brand names. The disorders for which these drugs are prescribed are indicated in parentheses:

Celebrex (arthritis pain), Celexa (depression), Cerebyx (seizures)

Levadopa (Parkinson's disease), Methyldopa (hypertension)

Norflex (muscle spasms), Norfloxacin (bacterial infection)

Procrit (anemia), Proscar (enlarged prostate), ProSom (insomnia), Prozac (depression)

Ranitidine (stomach ulcers), Rimantadine (influenza)

Selegline (Parkinson's disease), Serentil (schizophrenia), Seroquel (bipolar disorder, schizophrenia), Sertraline (depression)

Xanax (anxiety), Zocor (high cholesterol), Zofran (nausea, vomiting), Zoloft (depression), Zytec (allergies)

Sources: Commonly confused drug pairs. *Drug Topics*, accessed March 10, 2008. Medication mishaps (1997, July–August). *FDA Consumer*, pp. 19–21. Friedman, Richard, A. (2002, December 17). Curing and killing: The perils of a growing medicine cabinet. *New York Times*, p. F6. Ricks, Delthia (2008, February 4). Sorting out drug names. *Newsday*, p. A34. Ricks, Delthia (2001, March 19). Poison in prescription: Illegible writing can lead to dangerous medication errors. *Newsday*, pp. A2–A3, A22.

**2612 NORTH THIRD STREET
HARRISBURG, PENNSYLVANIA 17110**

DEA Reg No. _____

Lic. no. MD-032491-L

NAME _____ AGE _____

ADDRESS _____ DATE _____

℞ *Accupril*

☐ LABEL

REFILL _____ TIMES

SUBSTITUTE PERMISSIBLE _____ , M.D.

IN ORDER FOR A BRAND NAME PRODUCT TO BE DISPENSED, THE PRESCRIBER MUST HAND-
WRITE "BRAND NECESSARY" OR "BRAND MEDICALLY NECESSARY" IN THE SPACE BELOW.

**2612 NORTH THIRD STREET
HARRISBURG, PENNSYLVANIA 17110**

DEA Reg No. _____

Lic. no. MD-032491-L

NAME _____ AGE _____

ADDRESS _____ DATE _____

℞ *Accutane*

☐ LABEL

REFILL _____ TIMES

SUBSTITUTE PERMISSIBLE _____ , M.D.

IN ORDER FOR A BRAND NAME PRODUCT TO BE DISPENSED, THE PRESCRIBER MUST HAND-
WRITE "BRAND NECESSARY" OR "BRAND MEDICALLY NECESSARY" IN THE SPACE BELOW.

---

medical records. When the patient receives his or her medication, the bar codes on the bracelet and the medication container are checked against the patient's medical chart to make sure that the right amount of the right medication is being given at the right time.

The FDA estimates that over a period of 20 years, the barcode-based medication administration system will have prevented 500,000 adverse drug events and achieved a 50 percent reduction in the likelihood of medication errors.[13]

Major OTC Analgesic Drugs

Four classes of OTC drugs currently constitute the non-prescription analgesic market: aspirin, acetaminophen, ibuprofen, and naproxen. Of these, aspirin, ibuprofen, and naproxen are often referred to as **nonsteroidal anti-inflammatory drugs (NSAIDs)**. This name identifies them as useful in reducing the swelling and pain that often results from injury or illness (anti-inflammatory) but unrelated to the cortisone-based steroids often prescribed for this purpose (nonsteroidal). Acetaminophen, as we will see, is an effective analgesic, but because it does not reduce inflammation, it is not classified as an NSAID.

NSAIDs are not limited to OTC drugs. Prominent prescription NSAIDs, used primarily for the treatment of arthritic pain, are celecoxib (brand name: Celebrex) and diclofenac (brand name: Voltaren). The latter became available in 2008 as an analgesic patch (brand name: Flector). Rofecoxib (brand name: Vioxx) and valdecoxib (brand name: Bextra) were withdrawn from the market in 2004.

Aspirin

When American pioneers traveled west in the nineteenth century, they encountered Native American tribes who were treating pain and fever by chewing willow bark, reminiscent of a remedy that had been popular in Europe from as early as 400 B.C. It turns out that willow bark contains an analgesic compound called **salicylic acid,** named from *Salix*, the botanical name for willow.

The beneficial effect of pure salicylic acid on pain, however, was for a long time limited by the fact that most digestive systems could not handle it easily. In 1898, Felix Hoffman, a chemist at the Bayer Company in Germany, found that by adding an acetyl group (making the result **acetylsalicylic acid,** or **ASA**), this side effect was reduced without lessening its therapeutic power. To arrive at a name that was easier to say, company officials noted that salicylic acid also came from spirea plants: thus the name **aspirin** was born.[14]

In 1918, following World War I, Sterling Products (later Sterling Winthrop and now Bayer Corporation) bought the trademark rights to the name *aspirin*. Later, a U.S. federal judge ruled that the name was common enough to be treated generically. To this day, Bayer Corporation markets its aspirin as "Genuine Bayer Aspirin," though the ASA contained in it is identical to that in any other ASA product. In the United States, Britain, and France, aspirin is the common name for ASA, and any company marketing ASA can use the name to describe its product. In approximately seventy other countries, aspirin is a registered trademark of Bayer AG, Germany. In Canada, aspirin is a registered trademark name used exclusively to identify ASA manufactured and distributed by Bayer Corporation. In this chapter, the terms aspirin and ASA are used interchangeably.[15]

The three principal medical applications of aspirin are well known. It is an effective *analgesic* drug for mild to moderate pain (hence, its use in treating headaches), an **anti-inflammatory** drug in that it relieves inflammation and tenderness in joints of the body (hence, its use in treating rheumatoid arthritis), and an **antipyretic** drug in that it lowers elevated body temperature when the body is fighting infection (hence, its use in treating fever). A recommended adult dosage of 325 to 650 mg (one to two tablets or capsules), taken every four hours, is considered to be adequate for these purposes, with a recommended limit of 3,900 mg (twelve tablets or capsules) per day.[16]

Until the early 1970s, the therapeutic effects of aspirin were largely a mystery. A prominent magazine had even called aspirin "the wonder drug nobody understands."[17] The answer surfaced in a surprising way. Aspirin was found to work as an analgesic, not on a CNS level (like morphine or other opiate drugs) but rather on a peripheral level by blocking the synthesis of **prostaglandins,** a group of hormone-like chemicals normally produced by every body cell when some injury to that cell has occurred. Prostaglandins, when released following injury, also encourage inflammation in the joints.

---

nonsteroidal anti-inflammatory drug (NSAID): Any of a group of OTC analgesics (including aspirin, ibuprofen, and naproxen) or prescription analgesics (Celebrex) that are unlike cortisone-based drugs but nonetheless reduce pain and swelling caused by injury or disease.

salicylic acid (SAL-ih-SIL-ik ASS-id): A drug developed in the nineteenth century to treat mild to moderate pain, though it was extremely irritating to the stomach.

acetylsalicylic acid (ASA) (a-SEE-til-SAL-ih-SIL-ik ASS-id): A modification of salicylic acid that makes the drug less irritating to the stomach without lessening its analgesic powers.

aspirin: Any analgesic drug containing acetylsalicylic acid (ASA).

anti-inflammatory: Having an effect that reduces inflammation or soreness.

antipyretic: Having an effect that reduces body temperature and fever.

prostaglandins (PROS-tah-GLAN-dins): Hormone-like substances that are blocked by many OTC analgesic drugs.

Finally, prostaglandins act on the hypothalamus of the brain to elevate body temperature, so a blocking of prostaglandins here has a fever-reducing effect. Therefore, a combination of antiprostaglandin effects, in both the central and peripheral nervous systems, explains the three therapeutic actions of aspirin.[18]

Other physiological effects of aspirin can produce serious problems, however, and as a result three specific cautions about the use of aspirin are in order.

- First, aspirin-treated patients have a higher risk of developing gastric bleeding because the drug has a direct erosive effect on the stomach wall. Anyone with a history of stomach ulcers or related stomach problems should avoid taking aspirin. To reduce these symptoms, some forms of aspirin are either buffered with a coating of an antacid or "enteric-coated" so that absorption is delayed until the aspirin has moved past the stomach and into the upper intestine. These forms of aspirin alleviate the gastric problems, but they also delay the pain-reducing and other therapeutic effects.

- The second caution is that aspirin increases the time it takes for blood to clot. Ordinarily, prostaglandins promote the clumping of blood platelets that is part of the normal clotting process. Therefore, when there is a reduction in the action of prostaglandins, the ability of blood to clot is reduced as well. Surgical patients should not have their bleeding time increased, so they are frequently advised *not* to take aspirin a week to ten days prior to surgery.

  A reduction of clotting can be beneficial, however, for individuals who are susceptible to small clots that can potentially block either coronary arteries leading to a heart attack, or blood vessels in the brain, which could lead to an ischemic (blood flow–interrupting) stroke. On the other hand, aspirin increases the risk of a hemorrhagic (bleeding) stroke, because the normal clotting process is diminished. In addition, the anticlotting nature of aspirin can have serious adverse effects for women in the late stages of pregnancy, leading to prolonged labor and bleeding during delivery.[19]

- The third caution involves children who have contracted a viral infection such as chicken pox or the flu. Aspirin has been found to be related to the development of **Reye's syndrome,** a rare but highly dangerous condition marked by lethargy, nausea and severe vomiting, disorientation, and coma. Approximately 26 percent of Reye's syndrome cases are fatal. Since 1985, a warning has been required on the labels of all aspirin products indicating that "children and teenagers should not take aspirin for chicken pox or flu symptoms before a doctor is consulted." Because it is difficult to tell if even a common cold may be the beginning of the flu, it is advisable to refrain from giving aspirin to anyone under the age of twenty. There has been a significant decrease in the incidence of Reye's syndrome in the United States since these warnings were instituted.[20]

Acetaminophen

Since the 1950s, **acetaminophen** (brand names: Tylenol, Datril, Anacin-3, and Panadol, among others) has been available as an OTC drug, but it is only since the 1970s that it has been a popular alternative to aspirin for analgesic and antipyretic purposes. You may notice that an anti-inflammatory purpose has been left out. Acetaminophen does not reduce inflammation and, except for reducing the associated pain, does not help in the treatment of arthritis. However, acetaminophen does not produce gastric distress nor does it interfere with the clotting process, so there are significant benefits for those individuals adversely affected by aspirin.

The fact that acetaminophen has an effect on pain equivalent to that of aspirin without some of the prominent aspirin-related side effects has made acetaminophen the leading form of OTC pain reliever in the United States.[21]

This is not to say that acetaminophen is completely benign. Three areas of concern have been addressed with respect to its use.

- A serious problem is its relatively high potential for causing liver damage. About 7,500 mg of acetaminophen (equivalent to fifteen 500-mg tablets of Extra-Strength Tylenol) can produce liver damage, and the combination of acetaminophen with alcohol greatly increases the risk of such a toxic reaction. In 1993, an FDA advisory panel recommended that warnings on acetaminophen labels refer to the particular risk of combining acetaminophen with alcohol. It has been recommended that individuals having up to two drinks a day restrict their intake of acetaminophen to 2,000 mg per day (equivalent to four extra-strength tablets or about six regular-strength

Reye's syndrome (RYES SIN-drohm): A rare but highly dangerous childhood disorder that has been associated with the administration of ASA-type analgesic drugs for the treatment of certain viral infections.

acetaminophen (a-SEE-tuh-MIN-oh-fen): A type of OTC analgesic drug. A major brand name is Tylenol.

Safety-sealed, tamper-resistant packaging became a fact of life for consumers of OTC drugs following the 1982 Tylenol poisoning crisis, when several deaths were attributed to cyanide in packages of Tylenol that had been tampered with.

tablets). The normal maximal recommended dose per day is 4,000 mg.

Anyone who has taken acetaminophen in this dosage range in combination with alcohol should seek medical attention immediately, prior to the appearance of symptoms related to liver disease. As an emergency medical procedure, an injection of acetyl-cysteine (brand name: Mucosil) can be used as an antidote for acetaminophen overdose, but this treatment is successful only if begun immediately. It may take as long as forty-eight to ninety-six hours before the symptoms of acetaminophen overdose appear, and by this time liver damage will have reached an advanced stage. Approximately one hundred people in the United States have died and more than two thousand are hospitalized each year as a result of liver damage from unintentional overdoses of aceta-minophen. As a result of this evidence, the FDA in 2002 mandated a strongly worded warning on nearly two hundred OTC products containing aceta-minophen that taking more than the recommended dose could cause liver damage.[22]

- A second concern is the risk of kidney damage as a result of heavy average use or moderate cumulative use of acetaminophen. The risk of kidney failure

ibuprofen (EYE-buh-PRO-fin): A type of OTC analgesic drug. Major brand names include Advil, Motrin, and Nuprin.

naproxen (na-PROX-sin): An analgesic drug, formerly available only by prescription (brand names: Naprosyn and Anaprox). It is now available as an OTC drug under the brand name Aleve.

doubles in people who have taken more than 365 acetaminophen pills over a year's time (averaging one per day) or 1,000–5,000 pills over a lifetime. Aspirin use has not been found to increase the chances of kidney damage, though, as noted earlier, aspirin has its own health risks.[23]

- A third concern with acetaminophen is the risk of enhancing the effect of prescription anticlotting medications such as warfarin (brand name: Coumadin). While a reduction of clotting is often indicated for patients who suffer from clogged arteries, acetaminophen creates a situation in which the reduction of clotting is excessive, leading to hemorrhage. To this extent, acetaminophen shares the same interactive effect as aspirin and other NSAIDs.[24]

In the United Kingdom and other nations outside North America, generic acetaminophen is referred to as paracetamol (brand name: Panadol).

Ibuprofen

Ibuprofen is marketed as an OTC drug under a variety of brand names, most prominently as Advil, Mediprin, Midol, Motrin, and Nuprin. It is effective in reducing pain, inflammation, and elevated temperature due to fever. In addition, ibuprofen has been found to be particularly effective in the treatment of menstrual cramps. As with aspirin, the mechanism behind ibuprofen's effects is to block the production of prostaglandins.

The recommended adult dosage of ibuprofen is 200 mg (one tablet) every four to six hours. Two tablets may be used but no one should exceed 1,200 mg (six tablets) in a twenty-four-hour period. There is less gastric irritation in taking ibuprofen than when taking aspirin, though some discomfort can be experienced and the warning label suggests that milk or food be consumed when taking the drug. An additional concern is the potential for kidney damage or kidney failure. As a result, it is not advisable for individuals who have a history of kidney disease to take ibuprofen. In general, ibuprofen shares the anticlotting feature associated with aspirin, though recent evidence indicates that it interferes with aspirin's ability to protect against recurring heart attacks.[25]

Naproxen

The newest OTC analgesic drug, **naproxen,** is actually a well-known prescription drug that has been FDA-approved since 1994 for nonprescription use. When it was marketed as a prescription drug, it was known under the brand names Naprosyn and Anaprox. As an OTC drug, naproxen is available at a slightly lower dosage under the brand name Aleve.

Naproxen has analgesic, anti-inflammatory, and antipyretic effects, with a duration of action of eight to twelve hours, substantially longer than the other types of OTC analgesic drugs. The principal problem with naproxen is gastrointestinal irritation. Chronic naproxen treatment may cause gastric bleeding, ulceration, or perforation. It is important to be alert to signs of these problems while taking naproxen and to discontinue its use if any difficulties arise. It also has anticlotting effects.[26]

OTC Analgesic Drugs and Attempted Suicide

If you were to combine the four categories of OTC analgesic drugs, they would be represented in approximately one in four drug-related ED visits involving a suicide attempt in 2006. In the overwhelming number of cases, the circumstance includes the ingestion of alcohol. As noted with respect to prescription drug overdoses, combinations with alcohol are far more dangerous than when OTC analgesic drugs are taken alone.[27]

Other Major Classes of OTC Drugs

In addition to analgesic products, a number of other product categories play a major role in the overall OTC market. Two of them will be considered here: sleep aids and cough-and-cold remedies.

Sleep Aids

The only FDA-approved active ingredients in OTC sleep aids are **diphenhydramine,** an antihistamine to be taken in either a 25 mg or 50 mg dosage once a day (also available in various types of Benadryl), and **doxylamine succinate,** another antihistamine to be taken in a 25 mg dosage once a day. Brand names of such sleep aids containing diphenhydramine include Nytol QuickCaps and Sleepinal Night-time Sleep Aid; Unisom is the brand name for a sleep aid containing doxylamine succinate. Some of these products are also marketed in combination with acetaminophen as a "sleep-aid pain-relief formula" medication (Tylenol PM, for example). Individuals taking this kind of medication should be aware that they are dealing with a CNS depressant, and any combination with other depressants, such as alcohol or antihistamines contained in cough-and-cold remedies, can inadvertently enhance the overall effect.[28]

Cough-and-Cold Remedies

As we all know, a cold can be a miserable experience. It can be frustrating as well because it is a viral infection and no antiviral drug (or any other drug for that matter) has yet been discovered that can prevent a cold, cure a cold, or even reduce the length of time that we have to endure a cold. All we can do is attempt to reduce its symptoms. This is where OTC remedies come into the picture.

Choosing a cough-and-cold remedy (along with similar medications that treat allergic symptoms) depends

diphenhydramine (DYE-fen-HIGH-druh-meen): One of two FDA-approved active ingredients in OTC sleep-aid products, such as Nytol and Sleepinal.

doxylamine succinate (DOX-il-a-meen SUK-sih-nate): One of two FDA-approved active ingredients in OTC sleep-aid products, such as Unisom.

on the symptoms that are present. Basic ingredients can include an *antitussive agent*, or cough suppressant, for the control of a cough; an *expectorant* to reduce the thickness of mucus in the throat and pharynx (making it easier to cough up); a *decongestant* to widen blocked nasal passages and sinuses; an *antihistamine* to relieve the itching, sneezing, teary eyes, and runny nose; and finally an *analgesic* and *antipyretic* drug to reduce the sinus pain, headache, or fever. Most cough-and-cold medications combine these ingredients in various proportions, so it is important to read the labels carefully to identify the specific product that is best suited for a particular combination of symptoms.

Potential problems can occur as a result of four major factors in current cough-and-cold medications.

- The first problem is that antihistamines are CNS depressants. Though antihistamines can sometimes act paradoxically in young children (just as stimulants can act paradoxically as depressants; see Chapter 4), they produce drowsiness and sleep in most adults. This effect might be fine for bedtime, but it is very important to refrain from driving a car, or engaging in any task that requires full attention, while taking an antihistamine product.

- The second problem concerns the quantity of alcohol in several cough-and-cold remedies. With levels of alcohol sometimes reaching 25 percent, these cough-and-cold remedies can function essentially as alcoholic beverages. This factor will combine additively to the antihistamine effect and make a person even drowsier than he or she would have been with the antihistamine alone. A person should take care not to consume alcoholic beverages while being treated with an antihistamine medication.

- Due to the alcohol content, there is a potential for abuse of cough-and-cold remedies by young people who use them to get drunk. While this form of alcohol consumption is undoubtedly less than pleasant, some may see these products as an opportunity to bypass present restrictions on alcohol sales to underage customers. Mouthwashes also have this potential for alcohol-related abuse.

- Cough-and-cold medications, particularly those containing the nasal decongestant pseudoephedrine, present health risks in young children. On the advice of the U.S. Centers for Disease Control and Prevention and the American College of Chest Physicians, manufacturers in 2008 changed their products' labels to say that they should not be used in children under age 4.

Fortunately, most cough-and-cold products include specific warnings on the labels that refer to potential difficulties that might arise if the individual is diabetic, has high blood pressure, or suffers from heart or thyroid disease. Women who are pregnant or nursing should consult their physicians or other health professionals before taking any cough-and-cold remedy.[29]

The Pharmaceutical Industry Today

Pharmaceutical companies clearly are profitable enterprises, but like other businesses they are only as successful as the products they sell. In an extremely competitive marketplace, diversification is a key factor for continued growth. For example, a pharmaceutical company best known for a particular type of analgesic drug more than likely manufactures and distributes other types as well. Bayer Corporation is best identified with Bayer Aspirin, but the company also markets an acetaminophen product (Panadol), a combination of aspirin, acetaminophen, and caffeine (Vanquish), an ibuprofen product (Bayer Select Ibuprofen), and naproxen (Aleve).

In the new millennium, major pharmaceutical companies are facing increasing strains and pressures not only within their own industry but also from governmental agencies and the public at large. They have been criticized for runaway prescription drug prices, excessive corporate profits, commercial ties to physicians and scientists conducting drug research, and an apparent willingness to spend nearly as much on advertising and promotion as on research and development (see Point/Counterpoint on pages 393–394).

A prescription drug mail-order kiosk in Tulsa, Oklahoma, to assist in the shipping of drugs from Canada. In 2003, Rx Depot was ordered by a U.S. federal court to cease operations. The question of prescription drug importation remains a hotly debated issue. Many consumer advocacy groups are in favor of importation, while the U.S. government and the pharmaceutical industry are opposed.

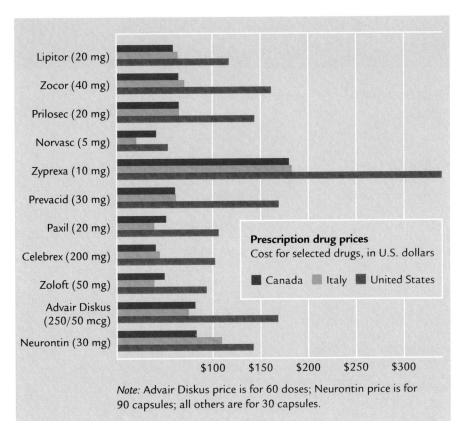

FIGURE 14.2

A comparison of retail prices for eleven major prescription medications in Canada, Italy, and the United States.

Source: Harris, Gardiner (2003, November 16). If Americans want to pay less for drugs, they will. *New York Times,* p. 4. Copyright © 2003 by the New York Times Company. Reprinted by permission.

Note: Advair Diskus price is for 60 doses; Neurontin price is for 90 capsules; all others are for 30 capsules.

The costs of prescription medications in the United States are a particular concern when viewed in terms of the economic burden placed on the elderly. They typically require a substantially greater proportion of drugs than do younger subpopulations, and, to make matters worse, they are frequently ineligible to receive reimbursements for outpatient pharmaceutical expenses. As a result, the practice of skipping doses of medication or splitting pills to extend the duration of a prescription for financial reasons has become a major problem. The fight to contain the high cost of prescription drugs, sometimes called "the other drug war," as well as the high cost of health care in general, is certain to continue (Figure 14.2) (Health Alert, page 352).[30]

Dietary Supplements

There are well over one hundred dietary supplements currently available to the public. Of these, approximately seventy are herbal preparations.[31] In Chapter 8, two supplements (androstenedione and creatine) were discussed in the context of athletic performance; in Chapter 16, one supplement (St. John's wort) will be covered in the con-

text of treating depression. In this chapter, two supplements, ginkgo biloba and ginseng, will be discussed in the context of improving cognitive function.

Ginkgo Biloba

Ginkgo biloba, commonly called ginkgo, is extracted from the Ginkgo tree, indigenous to Europe, Asia, and North America; its medicinal use has been recorded in Chinese texts dating back to about 3000 B.C. In its modern form, ginkgo extracts produced in Europe have been standardized to contain approximately 24 percent flavonoids and 6 percent terpenoids. These molecules are classified as antioxidants, a class of agents that inhibit platelets in the blood from sticking together. Blood circulation is improved and, presumably, the circulation of blood to the brain is enhanced. As a result, the most frequent application of ginkgo has been to improve memory or cognitive function.

Ginkgo extract has been shown to produce modest, but statistically significant, improvements in cognitive

ginkgo biloba (GINK-goh bih-LOH-bah): An herb-based dietary supplement considered to improve blood circulation and possibly increase mental alertness.

The Risks of Web Pharmacies/The Allure of Foreign Drugs

A fifty-three-year-old Chicago man dies after taking Viagra, ordered over the Internet. He didn't see a doctor and was not advised that Viagra could be dangerous for individuals at risk for heart disease. A twenty-two-year-old New York man dies after taking a bodybuilding drug that has been banned by the FDA since the 1930s for its toxicity, again ordered over the Internet. These cases are examples of a growing trend related to the dispensing of medications—some of them legitimate prescription drugs, but others no longer available through legitimate channels.

Currently, hundreds of drug-dispensing web sites are in operation. On the one hand, they offer opportunities for consumers to obtain prescription drugs more cheaply. On the other hand, consumers are vulnerable to exploitation by those who dispense these drugs without prescriptions or licenses. The National Association of Boards of Pharmacy has begun a process of certifying legitimate online pharmacies, so it is advisable to check whether certification has been secured before purchasing medications in this manner. It has been proposed that the FDA be given the power to review and certify these establishments and impose heavy fines when regulations are violated. Obviously, the Internet has opened up a whole new world of e-commerce, and the prescription drug industry is not immune to these new developments.

In the meantime, mail-order businesses selling prescription drugs from Canada and Mexico, in addition to Americans purchasing these drugs directly in towns just outside U.S. borders, are becoming a fact of life. The dramatically lower cost of medications when they are imported from other countries is a powerful incentive for people who do not have health insurance to cover their pharmaceutical expenses.

> **Where to go for assistance:**
>
> www.pueblo.gsa.gov/cic_text/health/buyperscript-online/guide.htm
>
> A series of consumer-safety "do's and don'ts" when buying prescription medicines online, presented by the Federal Citizen Information Center, a division of the U.S. Food and Drug Administration, Center for Drug Evaluation and Research.

Sources: Kessler, Robert E. (2001, September 25). Arrest in fatal Internet deal. *Newsday,* p. A17. Luhby, Tami (2002, November 3). Strategies in lowering your drug tab. *Newsday,* pp. F2–F3. Plan: Regulate web pharmacies (1999, December 29). *Newsday,* p. A3. Weiner, Tim (2001, August 14). In Tijuana, a new kind of peril: Low prices for unregulated prescription drugs lure Americans. *New York Times,* p. A7.

---

functioning in Alzheimer's disease patients, but studies of ginkgo involving normal individuals generally show no benefits. While ginkgo is considered relatively safe when taken in standard dosages, the anticlotting effect makes it dangerous for individuals who are taking blood-thinning medications, such as warfarin (brand name: Coumadin) or NSAIDs.[32]

Ginseng

Ginseng is extracted from the ginseng root, grown in Asia as well as the United States. In general, Asian ginseng is considered to be of better quality than ginseng grown domestically. The active molecules in ginseng are referred to as *ginsenosides*, which function as antioxidants. While not necessarily having the same anticlotting effect as does ginkgo, ginsenosides have been reported to have caused uterine bleeding in postmenopausal women. More generally, ginseng effects can include elevations in blood pressure, nervousness, and insomnia, especially in individuals taking large dosages.

The traditional application has been for improved mental alertness and concentration among the elderly, but more recently there have been claims that ginseng can benefit cognitive function in younger populations, as well as produce an enhanced sense of well-being. The research literature, however, has been difficult to evaluate, since ginsenoside amounts in ginseng products have not been standardized.[33]

ginseng (JIN-SENG): An herb-based dietary supplement with possible applications that include an improvement in mental alertness among the elderly.

Summary

- Three categories of medicinal products are available for purchase: prescription drugs (which require medical approval) and over-the-counter (OTC) drugs and dietary supplements (which are available without any restrictions).
- The U.S. Food and Drug Administration (FDA) is responsible for setting the standards of safety, effectiveness, and honesty in labeling for the first two categories.

How the Regulation of Prescription and OTC Drugs Began

- A series of federal laws, put into effect since 1906, have established the FDA as the authority for safeguarding the public health with regard to prescription and OTC drugs, as well as food products, cosmetics, and medical devices.

Procedures for Approving Prescription and OTC Drugs

- The FDA process for the approval of new prescription drugs begins with animal studies to determine their safety limits and relative toxicity. If these standards are met, clinical trials, first with healthy human volunteers and later with actual patients, are conducted to identify the optimal dosage levels and degree of effectiveness.
- Only a small proportion of new compounds developed by drug companies make it successfully through these clinical trials and are eventually approved by the FDA for marketing as new prescription drugs. The process often takes several years.
- Since 1962, all prescription and OTC drugs have been required by the FDA to be generally recognized as safe (GRAS), effective (GRAE), and honestly labeled (GRAHL).

Are FDA-Approved Drugs Safe?

- There is considerable concern that although prescription and OTC drugs are FDA-approved for use when taken in the recommended dosages and under the recommended circumstances, their misuse can result in medical emergencies and fatalities.
- Prescription drug misuse, whether intentional or unintentional (through prescription errors), is a growing public health problem as the number of available medications increases.

Major OTC Analgesic Drugs

- Acetylsalicylic acid (aspirin), acetaminophen, ibuprofen, and naproxen are four types of OTC analgesic drugs available to the public.
- Because each of these types has its benefits *and* hazards, it is strongly urged that recommended dosage levels be observed and anyone with specific health problems be aware that analgesic drugs may be harmful.

Other Major Classes of OTC Drugs

- Two other classes of OTC drugs can be highlighted in terms of their use and potential for misuse. The first is the variety of sleep aids, with the active ingredient of either diphenhydramine or doxylamine succinate. The second is the variety of cough-and-cold remedies that generally contain some combination of antihistamine and decongestant.
- Careful use of all of these products is advised.

The Pharmaceutical Industry Today

- In the present-day pharmaceutical industry, companies have diversified their prescription and OTC products to maintain their share of a highly competitive market.
- Pharmaceutical companies are also under pressure to reduce the prices of their products as a component of controlling overall health care costs, particularly for patients who lack adequate insurance to cover their pharmaceutical expenses.

Dietary Supplements

- A large number of products, referred to as dietary supplements, are available to the public. Unlike OTC preparations, dietary supplements have not been evaluated by the FDA for safety and efficacy. Therefore, claims of medical benefits are often difficult to verify, and caution should be exercised when using them.
- Of the herbal varieties of dietary supplements, ginkgo biloba and ginseng have been promoted as enhancing aspects of cognitive functioning such as mental alertness, concentration, and memory. Well-controlled studies of these herbs have shown either negative or inconclusive resuts in normal individuals.

Key Terms

acetaminophen, p. 347

acetylsalicylic acid (ASA),
p. 346

anti-inflammatory, p. 346

antipyretic, p. 346

aspirin, p. 346

bioequivalence, p. 340

dietary supplements, p. 334

diphenhydramine, p. 349

doxylamine succinate, p. 349

ginkgo biloba, p. 351

ginseng, p. 352

ibuprofen, p. 348

naproxen, p. 348

nonsteroidal anti-
inflammatory drug
(NSAID), p. 346

over-the-counter (OTC)
drugs, p. 334

patent, p. 340

Phase 1 trials, p. 338

Phase 2 trials, p. 338

Phase 3 trials, p. 338

Phase 4 trials, p. 339

prescription drugs, p. 334

prostaglandins, p. 346

Reye's syndrome, p. 347

salicylic acid, p. 346

thalidomide, p. 336

Endnotes

1. F.D.A. approves vitamin rules (2007, June 23). *New York Times*, p. A8. *Physicians' desk reference* (62nd ed.) (2008). Montvale, NJ: Thomson HealthCare. Center for Drug Evaluation and Research, U.S. Food and Drug Administration, Washington DC.

2. Hilts, Philip J. (2003). *Protecting America's health: The FDA, business, and one hundred years of regulation.* New York: Knopf. Patrick, William (1988). *The Food and Drug Administration.* New York: Chelsea House, pp. 29–49.

3. Burkholz, Herbert (1994). *The FDA follies.* New York: Basic Books. Patrick, *The Food and Drug Administration*, p. 40.

4. Berenson, Alex (2006, January 11). Drugs in '05: Much promise, little payoff. *New York Times*, pp. C1, C4. Julien, Robert M. (1995). *A primer of drug action* (7th ed.). New York: Freeman, p. 47. Zivin, Justin A. (2003, April). Understanding clinical trials. *Scientific American*, pp. 69–75.

5. Lasser, Karen E.; Allen, Paul D.; Woolhandler, Steffie J.; Himmelstein, David U.; Wolfe, Sidney M.; et al. (2002). Timing of new black box warnings and withdrawals for prescription medications. *Journal of the American Medical Association*, 287, 2215–2220. Temple, Robert J., and Himmel, Martin H. (2002). Safety of newly approved drugs: Implications for prescribing. *Journal of the American Medical Association*, 287, 2273–2275.

6. Ruling gives drug makers up to three extra years on patents (1995, May 26). *New York Times*, pp. D1, D7. Sail, Stephanie (2007, August 8). More generics slow the surge in drug prices. *New York Times*, pp. A1, A17. Yorke, Jeffrey (1992, September). FDA ensures equivalence of generic drugs. *FDA Consumer*, pp. 11–15.

7. FDA's approval of drugs gains speed (1996, January 20). *New York Times*, p. 24. Als-Nielsen, Bodil; Chen, Wendong; Gluud, Christian; and Kjaergard, Lise L. (2003). Association of funding and conclusions in randomized drug trials. *Journal of American Medical Association*, 290, 921–928. Henkel, John (1993, October). User fees to fund faster reviews. *FDA Consumer*, pp. 19–21. Zivin, Understanding clinical trials.

8. Brass, Eric P. (2001). Changing the status of drugs from prescription to over-the-counter availability. *New England Journal of Medicine*, 345, 810–816. Nightingale, Stuart L. (1999). From the Food and Drug Administration: New easy-to-understand labels for OTC drugs. *Journal of the American Medical Association*, 281, 1164.

9. Schmit, Julie (2008, February 9). FDA drug approvals fall to a five-year low. Analysts say the agency has been more cautious after having to pull Vioxx, others from market. *USA Today*, p. A1.

10. Carpenter, Daniel, Zucker, Evan James, and Avorn, Jerry (2008). Drug-review deadlines and safety problems. *New England Journal of Medicine*, 358, 1354–1361. Glantz, Leonard H., and Annas, George J. (2008). The FDA, preemption, and the Supreme Court. *New England Journal of Medicine*, 358, 1883–1885. Quotation by Jerry Avorn in RedOrbit News, www.Redorbit.com, May 1, 2008.

11. Substance Abuse and Mental Health Administration (2008). *Drug Abuse Warning Network, 2006: National estimates of drug-related emergency department visits.* Rockville, MD: Office of Applied Studies, Substance Abuse and Mental Health Administration, Table 16.

12. Gurwitz, Jerry H.; Field, Terry S.; Harrold, Leslie R.; Rothschild, Jeffrey; Debellis, Kristin; et al. (2003). Incidence and preventability of adverse drug events among older patients in the ambulatory setting. *Journal of the American Medical Association*, 289, 1107–1116. Ricks, Delthia (2001, March 19). Poison in prescription: Illegible writing can lead to dangerous medication errors. *Newsday*, pp. A2–A3, A21.

13. Lyall, Sarah (2001, December 20). More deaths in England, due to error, report says. *New York Times*, p. A6. McNeil, Donald G., Jr. (2003, March 14). To cut errors, F.D.A. orders drug bar codes. *New York Times*, pp. A1, A22. NEPS reduces hospital medication errors (2008, April 16). News release, NEPS LLC, Salem, New Hampshire. Poison in prescription, *Newsday*, pp. A2–A3, A21.

14. Krantz, John C. (1974). Felix Hoffman and aspirin. *Historical medical classics involving new drugs.* Baltimore: Williams & Wilkins, pp. 37–41. Levinthal, Charles F. (1988). *Messengers of paradise: Opiates and the brain.* New York: Anchor Press/Doubleday, p. 112.

15. Levinthal, *Messengers of paradise*, p. 211. Mann, Charles C., and Plummer, Mark L. (1991). *Aspirin wars.* New York: Knopf, p. 4.

16. *Physicians' desk reference for nonprescription drugs, dietary supplements, and herbs* (29th ed.) (2007). Montvale, NJ: Thomson HealthCare, pp. 617–618, 620–629.

17. Boehm, George A. W. (1966, September 11). Aspirin doesn't cure disease—It is the wonder drug nobody understands. *New York Times Magazine*, p. 56.

18. Stix, Gary (2007, January). Better ways to target pain. *Scientific American*, pp. 84–86.

19. He, Jiang; Whelton, Paul K.; Vu, Brian; and Klag, Michael J. (1998). Aspirin and risk of hemorrhagic stroke: A meta-analysis of randomized controlled trials. *Journal of the American Medical Association, 280,* 1930–1935.

20. *Physicians' desk reference for nonprescription drugs, dietary supplements, and herbs,* p. 620. Zamula, Evelyn (1990, November). Reye's syndrome: The decline of a disease. *FDA Consumer,* pp. 21–23.

21. Top analgesics 2004 (2005, June 3). *Chain Drug Review,* p. 95.

22. Acetaminophen warning (1993, June 30). *New York Times,* p. C14. Schiødt, Frank V.; Rochling, Fedja A.; Casey, Donna L.; and Lee, William M. (1997). Acetaminophen toxicity in an urban county hospital. *New England Journal of Medicine, 337,* 1112–1117. Stolberg, Sheryl G. (2002, September 20). Warning sought for popular painkiller: F.D.A. panel says many used toxic doses of acetaminophen. *New York Times,* p. A25.

23. Perneger, Thomas V., Whelton, Paul K., and Klag, Michael J. (1994). Risk of kidney failure associated with the use of acetaminophen, aspirin, and nonsteroidal anti-inflammatory drugs. *New England Journal of Medicine, 331,* 1675–1679.

24. Hylek, Elaine M.; Heiman, Heather; Skates, Steven J.; Sheehan, Mary A.; and Singer, Daniel E. (1998). Acetaminophen and other risk factors for excessive warfarin anticoagulation. *Journal of the American Medical Association, 279,* 657–662.

25. Ibuprofen interferes with aspirin's benefits (2003, April). *Health News,* p. 6. *Physicians' desk reference for nonprescription drugs, dietary supplements, and herbs,* pp. 668–673. Whelton, Andrew; Stout, Robert; Spilman, Patricia; and Klassen, David (1990). Renal effects of ibuprofen, piroxicam, and sulindac in patients with asymptomatic renal failure. *Annals of Internal Medicine, 112,* 568–576.

26. *Physicians' desk reference for nonprescription drugs, dietary supplements, and herbs,* p. 749.

27. Substance Abuse and Mental Health Services Administration, *Drug Abuse Warning Network,* Table 18.

28. *Physicians' desk reference for nonprescription drugs and dietary supplements* (24th ed.) (2003). Montvale, NJ: Thomson HealthCare, pp. 503–523.

29. Gunn, Veronica L.; Taha, Samina H.; Leibelt, Erica L; and Serwint, Janet R. (2001). Toxicity of over-the-counter cough and cold medications. *Pediatrics, 108,* p. e52. Harris, Gardiner (2008, October 8). Cold drugs for children will carry new warning. *New York Times,* p. A17. *Physicians' desk reference for nonprescription drugs, dietary supplements, and herbs,* pp. 736–746. Schneider, Mellissa K.; Shehab, Nadine; Cohen, Adam L.; and Budnitz, Daniel S. (2008). Adverse events attributable to cough and cold medications in children. *Pediatrics, 121,* 783–787. Willis, Judith L. (1991, November). Using over-the-counter medications wisely. *FDA Consumer,* pp. 35–37.

30. Carlat, Daniel (2007, November 25). Dr. drug rep. *New York Times Magazine,* pp. 64–69. Joyce, Geoffrey F.; Escarce, José J.; Solomon, Matthew, D.; and Goldman, Dana P. (2002). Employer drug benefit plans and spending on prescription drugs. *Journal of the American Medical Association, 288,* 1733–1739. Hidden drug payments at Harvard (2008, June 10). *New York Times,* p. A22. Langreth, Robert (2003, March 31). The new drug war. *Forbes,* pp. 85–90. Noonan, David (2000, September 23). Why drugs cost so much. *Newsweek,* pp. 24–30. Simon, Bernard (2004, January 14). Pfizer moves to try to stop drugs from Canada. *New York Times,* pp. W1, W7.

31. Karch, Steven B. (1999). *The consumer's guide to herbal medicine.* Hauppauge, NY: Advanced Research Press, pp. 25–179.

32. Gold, Paul E., Cahill, Larry, and Wenk, Gary L. (2003, April). The lowdown on ginkgo biloba. *Scientific American,* pp. 87–91. *Physicians' desk reference for nonprescription drugs and dietary supplements.* Sierpina, Victor; Wollschlaeger, Bernd; and Blumenthal, Mark (2003). Ginkgo biloba. *American Family Physician, 68,* 923–926. Solomon, Paul R.; Adams, Felicity; Silver, Amanda; Zimmer, Jill; and DeVeaux, Richard (2002). Ginkgo for memory enhancement: A randomized controlled trial. *Journal of the American Medical Association, 288,* 835–840.

33. Karch, *The consumer's guide to herbal medicine,* pp. 99–101. Ochs, Ridgely (1999, November 30). Conclusion: Uncertain. Studies worldwide—from echinacea to ginseng—yield few definitive answers on risks and results. *Newsday,* pp. C8–C14. *Physicians' desk reference for nonprescription drugs and dietary supplements.*

chapter 15

Sedative-Hypnotics and Antianxiety Drugs

Jennie never expected to be addicted to a prescription drug. After all, weren't the really dangerous drugs the ones you got on the streets? It started with stress and anxiety, an engagement that didn't work out, trouble with the boss at work. The doctor gave her the prescription to help her fall asleep, to calm her down and get her through the day. And the drug worked—all too well. She was frightened of the thought of stopping. After several months, when she was embarrassed to ask for the fifth refill, she found another doctor who didn't ask any questions. So it went, from doctor to doctor, pharmacist to pharmacist, until she started to realize she was in trouble.

After you have completed this chapter, you will understand

- The development of barbiturates as sedative-hypnotic drugs

- The acute and chronic effects of barbiturates

- The search for the perfect nonbarbiturate sedative-hypnotic drug

- The nature of anxiety

- The development of benzodiazepines as antianxiety drugs

- Newly developed sedative-hypnotics and antianxiety drugs

- Present-day concerns about gamma hydroxybutyrate (GHB)

Just as cocaine, amphetamines, and other stimulants bring us up, depressants bring us down. Just as there is a desire to be stronger, faster, and more attuned to the world, there is also the desire to move apart from that world, reduce the stresses and anxieties of our lives, and fall asleep more easily. Historically, the prime psychoactive depressant drug has been alcohol. As was discussed in Chapter 9, practically every culture in the world has discovered in one way or another the effects of alcohol on the body and the mind. This chapter, however, focuses on a group of depressant drugs called **sedative-hypnotics,** so named since they calm us down and produce sleep (from the Greek word *hypnos,* meaning "to sleep"). There are several types of depressants that promote sedation and sleep, ranging from drugs that were introduced a hundred years ago to others that have become available only recently.

This chapter also looks at drugs that provide specific relief from stress and anxiety without sedating us. These drugs have often been referred to as *tranquilizers* by virtue of their ability to make us feel peaceful or tranquil, but we will call them by their more current name, **antianxiety drugs.**

Unfortunately, sedative-hypnotics and antianxiety drugs have been subject not only to legitimate medical use but to misuse and abuse as well. Although they are available as prescription medications, many of them can be obtained from illicit sources as street drugs and are consumed for recreational purposes. The psychological problems and physical dangers associated with the misuse and abuse of these depressants are of particular concern.

by the numbers . . .

70 million	Approximate number of Americans who suffer from insomnia
$2.7 billion	Sales in 2007 of anti-insomnia drugs, supported by $619 million in advertising and promotion
$4.4 billion	Projected world market in 2010 for the short-term treatment of insomnia and other sleep disorders

Sources: LeadDiscovery Ltd. (2005, September). The world sleep disorders market 2005–2010: A market with high growth potential. East Sussex, UK: LeadDiscovery Ltd. National Institutes of Health, Bethesda, MD. Press release: U.S. sleep aids market grows to $23 billion, as Americans battle insomnia, sleep disorders (2008, June 6). Marketdata Enterprises, Inc., Tampa, FL.

of a class of drugs called **barbiturates.** Barbituric acid itself has no behavioral effects, but if additional molecular groups combine with the acid, depressant effects are observed. In 1903, the first true barbiturate, diethylbarbituric acid, was created and marketed under the name Veronal. Over the next thirty years, several major barbiturate drugs were introduced: **phenobarbital** (marketed in generic form), **amobarbital** (brand name: Amytal), **pentobarbital** (brand name: Nembutal), and **secobarbital** (brand name: Seconal).

Categories of Barbiturates

Barbiturates all share a number of common features. They are relatively tasteless and odorless, and at sufficient

Barbiturates

In 1864, the German chemist Adolf von Baeyer combined a waste product in urine called urea and an apple extract called malonic acid to form a new chemical compound called barbituric acid. There are two often told stories about how this compound got its name. One story has it that von Baeyer had gone to a local tavern to celebrate his discovery and encountered a number of artillery officers celebrating the feast day of St. Barbara, the patron saint of explosives handlers. Inspired by their celebration, the name "barbituric acid" came to mind. The other story attributes the name to a relationship with a certain barmaid whose name was Barbara.[1]

Whichever story is true (if either is), von Baeyer's discovery of barbituric acid set the stage for the development

sedative-hypnotics: A category of depressant drugs that provide a sense of calm and sleep.

antianxiety drugs: Drugs that make the user feel more peaceful or tranquil; also called tranquilizers.

barbiturate (bar-BIT-chur-rit): A drug within a family of depressants derived from barbituric acid and used as a sedative-hypnotic and antiepileptic medication.

phenobarbital (FEEN-oh-BAR-bih-tall): A longacting barbiturate drug, usually marketed in generic form.

amobarbital (AY-moh-BAR-bih-tall): An intermediateacting barbiturate drug. Brand name is Amytal.

pentobarbital (PEN-toh-BAR-bih-tall): A short-acting barbiturate drug. Brand name is Nembutal.

secobarbital (SEC-oh-BAR-bih-tall): A short-acting barbiturate drug. Brand name is Seconal.

dosages they reliably induce sleep, although the quality of sleep is a matter that will be discussed later. Because they slow down the activity of the central nervous system, barbiturates are also useful in the treatment of epilepsy.

The principal difference among them lies in how long the depressant effects last; a rough classification of barbiturates is based on this factor. Barbiturates are categorized as *long-acting* (six or more hours), *intermediate-acting* (four to six hours), or *short-acting* (less than four hours).

Bear in mind, however, that these groups are relative only to one another. All other factors being equal, injectable forms of barbiturates are shorter-acting than orally administered forms of the same drug, since it takes longer for the drug to be absorbed when taken by mouth and longer for it to be eliminated from the body. Naturally, a higher dose of any drug lasts longer than a lower dose because it takes longer for all of the drug to be eliminated from the body (Table 15.1).

The barbiturates used in surgical anesthesia, such as thiopental (brand name: Pentothal) and methohexital (brand name: Brevital), take effect extremely rapidly (within seconds) and last only a few minutes. For this reason, they are referred to as *ultra-short-acting barbiturates*. Because these features are undesirable to a person seeking a recreational drug, ultra-short-acting barbiturates are not commonly abused.

Acute Effects of Barbiturates

You can visualize the effects of barbiturates on the body and the mind as points along a scale ranging from mild

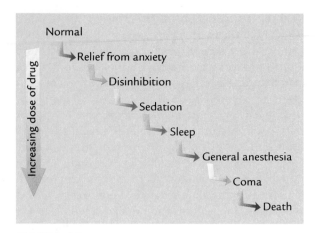

FIGURE 15.1

The downward continuum of arousal levels, as induced by depressants.

Source: Julien, Robert M. (1998). *A primer of drug action* (8th ed). Copyright © 1998 by W. H. Freeman and Company. Reprinted with permission.

relaxation on one end to coma and death on the other (Figure 15.1). In this sense, barbiturate effects are the same as the effects of depressants in general. The particular point that is achieved depends on the dose level that is taken.

At very low doses, the primary result of oral administrations of a barbiturate is relaxation and, paradoxically, a sense of euphoria. These effects derive chiefly from a disinhibition of the cerebral cortex, in which normal inhibitory influences from the cortex are reduced. You

TABLE 15.1

Major barbiturates

GENERIC NAME	BRAND NAME	DURATION OF ACTION	RELATIVE POTENTIAL FOR ABUSE
phenobarbital	generic*	long	low
mephobarbital	Mebaral	long	low
butalbarbital	Pheniline Forte†	intermediate	moderate
amobarbital	Amytal	intermediate	high
secobarbital and amobarbital	Tuinal	short, intermediate	high
pentobarbital	Nembutal	short	high
secobarbital	Seconal	short	high

Note: Short-acting barbiturates begin to take effect in about fifteen minutes, intermediate-acting barbiturates in thirty minutes, and long-acting barbiturates in one hour.

*Phenobarbital is also available in combination with hyoscyamine, atropine, and scopolamine under the brand name Donnatal.

†Several brands combine butalbarbital with acetaminophen.

Sources: Henningfield, Jack E., and Ator, Nancy A. (1986). *Barbiturates: Sleeping potion or intoxicant?* New York: Chelsea House, p. 24. *Physicians' desk reference* (62nd ed.) (2008). Montvale, NJ: Thomson HealthCare.

Drugs...in Focus

Is There Any Truth Regarding "Truth Serum"?

The idea that a sedative-hypnotic drug such as amobarbital (Amytal, or "sodium amytal") may function as a "truth serum" is not at all new. It has been known for centuries that depressants can produce remarkable candor and freedom from inhibition. The oldest example is simple alcohol, whose effect on loosening the tongue has led to the Latin proverb *in vino veritas* ("in wine, there is truth").

Whether we are guaranteed truthfulness under any of these circumstances, however, is another matter entirely. Courts have ruled that expert opinion in criminal cases based *solely* on drug-assisted testimony cannot be admitted as evidence. Controlled laboratory studies have shown that individuals under the influence of Amytal, when pressed by questioners, are as likely to give convincing renditions of fabrications (outright lies) or fantasies as they are to tell the truth. So, perhaps, Amytal might be better described as a "tell anything serum."

Recently, the question of whether Amytal or other depressant drugs should be used to gain information has come up with regard to the interrogation of captured al Qaeda prisoners following the September 11, 2001, attacks. The United States has determined that such individuals are unlawful combatants, a designation that excludes them from protection under the Geneva Convention guidelines prohibiting such practices for prisoners of war. When speaking on the record, U.S. officials deny that drugs are being used to gain information from captives under American jurisdiction. It is possible that this practice is in effect in other countries to which captives have been transferred.

The lack of evidence that truthful information may be gained through the use of depressant drugs has not changed, however. Nonetheless, military and intelligence experts point to the potential for gaining some relevant information that might be buried in drug-induced ramblings.

Source: CBS News (2003, April 23). Truth serum: A possible weapon. www.cbsnews.com. Michaells, James I. (1966). Quaere, whether "in vino veritas": An analysis of the truth serum cases. *Issues in Criminology, 2* (2), 245–267.

---

might recognize these symptoms as similar to the inebriating or intoxicating effects that result from low to moderate doses of alcohol (Drugs . . . in Focus).

As the dose level increases, lower regions of the brain become affected, specifically the reticular formation (Chapter 3). At therapeutic doses (one 100 mg capsule of secobarbital, for example), barbiturates make you feel sedated and drowsy. For this reason, patients are typically warned that barbiturates can impair the performance of driving a car or operating machinery. At higher doses, a hypnotic (sleep-inducing) effect will be achieved.

Historically, the primary use of barbiturates has been in the treatment of insomnia. One of the reasons that barbiturates have fallen from favor is that the sleep induced by these drugs turns out to be far from normal. Barbiturates tend to suppress rapid eye movement (REM) sleep, a phase of everyone's sleep that represents about 20 percent of the total sleep time each night. REM sleep is associated with dreaming and general relaxation of the body. If barbiturates are consumed over many evenings and then stopped, the CNS will attempt to catch up for the lost REM sleep by producing longer REM periods on subsequent nights. This **REM-sleep rebound** effect produces vivid and upsetting nightmares, along with a barbiturate hangover the next day, during which the user feels groggy and out of sorts. In other words, barbiturates may induce sleep, but a refreshing sleep it definitely is not.[2]

The most serious acute risks of barbiturate use involve the possibility of a lethal overdose either from taking too high a dose level of the drug alone or from taking the drug in combination with alcohol, as when a barbiturate is taken after an evening of drinking. In these instances, sleep can all too easily slip into coma and death, since an excessive dose produces an inhibition of the respiratory centers in the medulla. The mixture of barbiturates with alcohol produces a synergistic

REM-sleep rebound: A phenomenon associated with the withdrawal of barbiturate drugs in which the quantity of rapid eye movement (REM) sleep increases, resulting in disturbed sleep and nightmares.

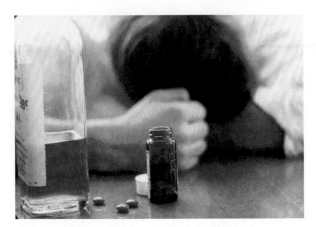

Barbiturates and alcohol have frequently been combined in attempts to commit suicide.

effect (see Chapter 3), in which the combined result is greater than the sum of the effects of each drug alone (Health Alert).

> Half of the lethal dose of secobarbital combined with ¼ the lethal dose of alcohol can kill in a synergistic double whammy. In another typical case of accidental overdose, a person takes a sleeping pill and awakens drugged and confused a few minutes later, annoyed at being aroused. The person then forgetfully takes another pill, or several, from the nightstand, and goes to sleep forever. This is called "drug automatism," a good reason not to keep medications within reach of the bed.[3]

During the period between 1973 and 1976, barbiturates were implicated in more than half of all drug-related deaths labeled as suicide by medical examiners.[4]

Chronic Effects of Barbiturates

The use of barbiturates as sleep medications often initiates a cycle of behavior that leads to dependence. Even after brief use of barbiturates, anxiety may be temporarily increased during the day and there may be an even greater degree of insomnia than before. In addition, because a barbiturate-induced sleep typically leaves a person feeling groggy the next morning, it is tempting to take a stimulant drug during the day to feel completely alert. At bedtime, the person still feels the stimulant effects and is inclined to continue taking a barbiturate to achieve any sleep at all. To make matters worse, the brain builds up a pharmacological tolerance to barbiturates quite quickly, requiring increasingly higher doses for an equivalent effect.

HEALTH ALERT!

In Case of a Barbiturate Overdose Emergency...

What to Do

- Keep the patient awake and moving, if possible.
- If the patient cannot be kept awake, make him or her warm and elevate the feet.
- Send for emergency help immediately.

What Not to Do

- Do not give stimulants such as coffee; they may worsen convulsions later.

Likely Emergency Department Procedures

- Patient will be put on life support and artificially respirated until the barbiturates are metabolized.
- Drugs may be administered to speed up urination.
- Hemodialysis (machine-assisted filtering of the blood) may be employed to help remove the barbiturate from the bloodstream.

> Where to go for assistance:
>   www.drugs.com/enc/barbiturate-intoxication-and-overdose.html
> A valuable review of the symptoms and treatment strategies for cases of barbiturate overdose.

Source: Palfai, Tibor, and Jankiewicz, Henry (1991). *Drugs and human behavior.* Dubuque, IA: W. C. Brown, p. 212.

Withdrawal symptoms, observed when barbiturates are discontinued, indicate a strong physical dependence on the drug. A person may experience a combination of tremors (the "shakes"), nausea and vomiting, intense perspiring, general confusion, convulsions, hallucinations, high fever, and increased heart rate. The barbiturate withdrawal syndrome closely resembles that of withdrawal after chronic alcohol abuse (see Chapter 10).

Professionals in the treatment of drug dependence often view the effects of barbiturate withdrawal as the most distressing as well as the most dangerous type of drug withdrawal. From a medical perspective, the withdrawal process is potentially life-threatening unless it is carried out in gradual fashion in a hospital setting. Without medical supervision, abrupt withdrawal from barbiturates carries approximately a 5 percent chance of death.[5]

Current Medical Uses of Barbiturates

Considering the problems of barbiturate use in the treatment of insomnia, it should not be surprising that the clinical use of barbiturates for this problem is essentially "obsolete."[6] Nonetheless, barbiturates continue to play an important role in the treatment of epileptic seizures. Phenobarbital and mephobarbital (two long-acting barbiturates) are prescribed to prevent convulsions. Dose levels need to be monitored carefully, because the concentration must be high enough to control the development of seizures (despite the tendency for tolerance effects to occur over time) without being so high as to produce drowsiness.

Patterns of Barbiturate Abuse

There are clear indications that taking barbiturate drugs is positively reinforcing. Laboratory animals will eagerly press a lever to deliver intravenous injections of barbiturates, particularly for the short-acting types, at rates that are equal to those for cocaine. When given the choice between pentobarbital and a nonbarbiturate depressant and given no knowledge as to the identity of the drugs, human drug abusers reliably select an oral dose of pentobarbital.[7]

Barbiturate abuse reached its peak in the 1950s and 1960s, later to be overshadowed by abuses of heroin, hallucinogens, nonbarbiturate depressants, amphetamines, and, more recently, abuses of cocaine, crack, and various stimulants and hallucinogens (Table 15.2). The principal reason was that barbiturates became less widely available as prescription drugs.

Despite their decline as major drugs of abuse, however, barbiturates are still being abused. The 2008 University of Michigan survey of high school seniors found that 9 percent of them had used some form of barbiturates during their lifetime, down from 17 percent in 1975, and 6 percent had taken them within the past year, down from 11 percent in 1975.[8]

Nonbarbiturate Sedative-Hypnotics

As the hazards of barbiturate use became increasingly evident, the search was on for sedative-hypnotic drugs that

TABLE 15.2
Street names for various barbiturates

TYPE OF BARBITURATE	STREET NAME
pentobarbital (Nembutal)	abbotts, blockbusters, nebbies, nembies, nemmies, yellow bullets, yellow dolls, yellow jackets, yellows
amobarbital (Amytal)	blue angels, bluebirds, blue bullets, blue devils, blue dolls, blue heavens, blues
secobarbital (Seconal)	F-40s, Mexican reds, R.D.s, redbirds, red bullets, red devils, red dolls, reds, seccies, seggies, pinks
secobarbital and amobarbital (Tuinal)	Christmas trees, double trouble, gorilla pills, rainbows, tootsies, trees, tuies
barbiturates in general	downers, down, goofballs, G.B.s, goofers, idiot pills, King Kong pills, peanuts, pink ladies, sleepers, softballs, stumblers

Note: Like any other street drug, illicit barbiturate capsules often contain an unknown array of other substances, including strychnine, arsenic, laxatives, or milk sugars. Any yellow capsule may be "marketed" as Nembutal, any blue capsule as Amytal, or any red capsule as Seconal.

Source: Henningfield, Jack E., and Ator, Nancy A. (1986). *Barbiturates: Sleeping potion or intoxicant?* New York: Chelsea House, p. 82.

were not derivatives of barbituric acid and, it was hoped, had fewer undesirable side effects. One such drug, **chloral hydrate,** had been first synthesized as early as 1832. As a depressant for the treatment of insomnia, it has the advantage of not producing the REM-sleep rebound effect or bringing on the typical barbiturate hangover. A major disadvantage, however, is that it can severely irritate the stomach. Like other depressants, it is also highly reactive when combined with alcohol. In the nineteenth century, a few drops of chloral hydrate in a glass of whiskey became the infamous Mickey Finn, a concoction that left many an unsuspecting sailor unconscious and eventually "shanghaied" onto a boat for China.

The development of **methaqualone** (brand names:

chloral hydrate: A depressant drug once used for the treatment of insomnia. It is highly reactive with alcohol and can severely irritate the stomach.

methaqualone (MEH-tha-QUAY-lone): A nonbarbiturate depressant drug once used as a sedative. Brand name is Quaalude.

Quaalude, Sopor), first introduced in the United States in 1965, was a further attempt toward achieving the perfect sleeping pill. In 1972, methaqualone had become the sixth-best-selling drug for the treatment of insomnia. During the early 1970s, recreational use of methaqualone (popularly known as "ludes" or sopors) was rapidly spreading across the country, aided by the unfounded reputation that it had aphrodisiac properties.

The problem with methaqualone was compounded by the extensive number of prescriptions written by physicians who mistakenly saw the drug as a desirable alternative to barbiturates. On the street, quantities of methaqualone were obtained from medical prescriptions or stolen from pharmacies. In 1984, this drug's legal status changed to that of a Schedule I drug, the most restricted classification, which indicates a high potential for abuse and no medical benefits.[9] Though no longer manufactured by any pharmaceutical company, methaqualone is still available as an illicit drug. It is either manufactured in domestic underground laboratories or smuggled into the country from underground laboratories abroad.

The Nature of Anxiety

As Figure 15.2 shows, feelings of anxiety are positioned along a continuum of emotions that range in magnitude from a complete lack of concern to moderate apprehension, to justified or unjustified anxiety, finally to outright panic. Some of these emotional states have a genuine adaptive purpose. That is, we would be less able to survive in a hostile and potentially dangerous world if we were not on our guard and capable of anticipating or responding to possible hazards surrounding us. Our highly developed sympathetic autonomic nervous system (see Chapter 3) has evolved to mobilize the resources of our bodies to deal with threats and challenges.

Given the importance of some level of anxiety to our survival as a species, it should not be surprising that mechanisms in the brain have developed that concern themselves specifically with this emotion. In that sense, we can view therapeutic drugs for anxiety in terms of

anxiety disorders: A variety of psychological conditions dominated by excessive worry, sympathetic autonomic activity, and maladaptive behavior. Six types of anxiety disorders are panic disorder, obsessive-compulsive disorder, post-traumatic stress disorder, social anxiety disorder, specific phobias, and generalized anxiety disorder.

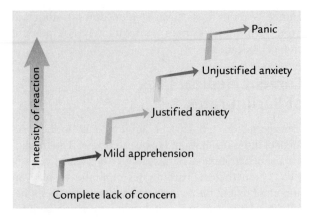

FIGURE 15.2

Levels of anxiety and stress.

Source: Julien, Robert M. (1995). *A primer of drug action* (7th ed.). Copyright © 1995 by W. H. Freeman and Company.

their ability to manage a normal physiological process that has essentially gotten out of control.

It is when anxiety interferes with our daily lives, or when it causes us great personal distress, that an adaptive emotion has become maladaptive. We refer to these conditions as **anxiety disorders.** It has been estimated that 19 million Americans between the ages of eighteen and fifty-four suffer from an anxiety disorder each year and that as many as 40 million people have been affected at some time in their lives.[10]

Anxiety disorders can be classified in six basic types.

- *Panic disorder.* People with panic disorder have feelings of terror that strike suddenly and repeatedly with no warning. They cannot predict when an attack will occur, and many individuals develop intense anxiety between episodes, worrying when and where the next one will strike. During a panic attack, symptoms may include a pounding heart, sweatiness, weakness, dizziness, tingling hands, nausea, or chest pressure. Some individuals who suffer from panic disorder genuinely believe they are having heart attacks, losing their minds, or on the verge of death.

- *Obsessive-compulsive disorder.* Individuals who have obsessive-compulsive disorder (OCD) experience persistent, unwelcome thoughts or images, or have the urgent need to engage in certain rituals. They may continually think about germs or dirt and consequently wash their hands over and over, or they may be filled with doubt and feel the need to check things repeatedly. The disturbing thoughts or images are called *obsessions,* and the behavioral rituals that are performed to try to prevent or get rid of them are called

A person's job and other aspects of modern-day life are often sources of enormous stress and anxiety.

compulsions. Typically, no pleasure is felt in carrying out the rituals, only a sense of temporary relief from the anxiety that is felt when they are not performed.

- *Post-traumatic stress disorder.* Individuals with post-traumatic stress disorder (PTSD) have persistent frightening thoughts and memories of a previously experienced terrifying event. These events might include violent attacks such as mugging, rape or torture, child abuse, serious accidents, natural disasters, or experiences of terrorism or warfare. Whatever the source of the problem, some people with PTSD repeatedly relive the trauma in the form of nightmares and disturbing recollections during the day, or else they feel detached or numb, are easily startled, or lose interest in pleasurable everyday events. Of course, not every traumatized person gets full-blown PTSD or experiences PTSD at all. In those who do develop the disorder, symptoms usually begin within three months of the trauma and the course of the illness varies.

- *Social anxiety disorder.* Individuals with social anxiety disorder (also called social phobia) have an overwhelming level of anxiety and excessive self-consciousness in everyday social situations. They have a persistent, intense, and chronic fear of being watched and judged by others and of being embarrassed or humiliated by their own actions. Their fear may be so severe that it interferes with work, school, or other ordinary activities. While many people with social phobia recognize that their fear of being around (or in front of) people may be excessive or unreasonable, they are unable to overcome it. They often worry for days or weeks in advance of a dreaded social situation.

- *Specific phobias.* A specific phobia is an intense fear of something that poses little or no actual danger. Some of the more common specific phobias center on closed-in places, heights, escalators, tunnels, highway driving, water, flying, dogs, and injuries involving blood. Such phobias should not be confused with extreme fear; they are irrational fears about a particular thing.

- *Generalized anxiety disorder.* In this condition, the individual has a level of anxiety that far exceeds the normal anxiety that people experience day to day. The anxiety is chronic and fills one's day with exaggerated worry and tension, even though little or nothing occurs to provoke it. Having this disorder means always anticipating disaster, often worrying excessively about health, money, family, or work. Sometimes, the source of the worry is hard to pinpoint. Simply the thought of getting through the day provokes anxiety.[11]

The Development of Antianxiety Drugs

If historians consider the 1950s "the age of anxiety," then it is appropriate that this period would also be marked by the development of drugs specifically intended to combat that anxiety. These drugs were originally called *minor tranquilizers*, to distinguish them from other drugs regarded as *major tranquilizers* and developed at about the same time to relieve symptoms of schizophrenia. This terminology is no longer used today, for we now know that the difference between the two drug categories is more than simply a matter of degree. Anxious people (or even people who are not bothered by anxiety) are not affected by drugs designed to treat schizophrenia. The current, and more logical, practice is to refer to drugs in terms of a specific action and purpose. The minor tranquilizers are now called *antianxiety drugs.* The major tranquilizers are now called *antipsychotic drugs*; they will be reviewed in Chapter 16.

The first antianxiety drug to be developed was **meprobamate** (brand name: Miltown), named in 1955 for a New Jersey town near the headquarters of the pharmaceutical company that first introduced it. Miltown became an immediate hit among prescription drugs, making its name a household word and essentially a synonym for tranquilizers in general.

meprobamate (MEH-pro-BAYM-ate): A nonbarbiturate antianxiety drug and sedative. Brand name is Miltown.

Even though meprobamate was the first psychoactive drug in history to be marketed as an antianxiety medication, most pharmacologists have identified the effects of this drug more in terms of sedation than of relief from anxiety.[12] Meprobamate reduces the activity of acetylcholine at the nicotinic synapses where the motor nerves innervate the body's skeletal muscles (see Chapter 3). As a result, muscle contractions are weaker and general relaxation follows. Motor reflexes are diminished, making driving more hazardous. People often complain of drowsiness, even at dose levels that should only be calming them down.

Meprobamate can also produce both physical and psychological dependence, at slightly more than twice the normal recommended daily dose.[13] This is not a very wide margin for possible abuse, and as a result meprobamate is classified as a Schedule IV drug, requiring limits on the number of prescription refills. Meprobamate is still occasionally prescribed for anxiety and insomnia, but by 1960, it had been far eclipsed by a different class of antianxiety drugs called benzodiazepines.

Benzodiazepines

The introduction of a new group of drugs, called **benzodiazepines,** was a dramatic departure from all earlier attempts to treat anxiety. For the first time, there were drugs that had a *selective* effect on anxiety itself, instead of producing a generalized reduction in the body's overall level of functioning. It was their tranquilizing effects, rather than their sedative effects, that made benzodiazepines so appealing to mental health professionals. It is important, however, to distinguish between the well-publicized virtues of benzodiazepines when they were first introduced in the 1960s and the data that accumulated during the 1970s as millions of people experienced these new drugs. Although certainly very useful in the treatment of anxiety and other stress-related problems, long-acting benzodiazepines are no longer recognized as the miracle drugs they were promoted to be when they first entered the market.

---

benzodiazepines (BEN-zoh-dye-AZ-eh-peens): A family of antianxiety drugs. Examples are diazepam (Valium), chlordiazepoxide (Librium), and triazolam (Halcion).

chlordiazepoxide (CHLOR-dye-az-eh-POX-ide): A major benzodiazepine drug for the treatment of anxiety. Brand name is Librium.

diazepam (dye-AZ-eh-pam): A major benzodiazepine drug for the treatment of anxiety. Brand name is Valium.

TABLE 15.3

The leading benzodiazepines on the market

TRADE NAME	GENERIC NAME	ELIMINATION HALF-LIFE (in hours)
Long-acting benzodiazepines		
Valium	diazepam	20–80
Librium	chlordiazepoxide	24–48
Limbitrol	chlordiazepoxide and amitriptyline (an antidepressant)	24–48
Dalmane	flurazepam	74–160
Tranxene	clorazepate	40–50
Intermediate-acting benzodiazepines		
Ativan	lorazepam	10–24
Klonopin	clonazepam	30–40
Restoril	temazepam	8–35
ProSom	estazolam	13–35
Short-acting benzodiazepines		
Versed	midazolam	2–5
Halcion	triazolam	2–6
Xanax	alprazolam	6–12

Note: Generic formulations are available.

Sources: Julien, Robert M. (1998). *A primer of drug action* (8th ed.). New York: Freeman, p. 99. *Physicians' desk reference* (63rd ed.) (2008). Montvale, NJ: Thomson HealthCare.

Medical Uses of Benzodiazepines

The first marketed benzodiazepine, **chlordiazepoxide** (brand name: Librium), was introduced in 1960, followed by **diazepam** (brand name: Valium) in 1963. Table 15.3 lists the major benzodiazepine drugs currently on the market. They are all chemically related, but their potencies and time courses vary considerably. Valium, for example, is five to ten times stronger than Librium and takes effect about one hour sooner. The relatively quicker response from Valium is a principal factor in making it more popular than Librium.

The variations in benzodiazepine effects have led to different recommendations for their medical use. Oral administrations of the relatively long-acting benzodiazepines, in general, are recommended for relief from anxiety, with the effects beginning thirty minutes to four hours after ingestion. Besides Librium and Valium, other examples of this type include flurazepam (brand name: Dalmane) and clorazepate (brand name: Tranxene).

When a very quick effect is desired, an injectable form of diazepam is used either to reduce the symptoms of agitation that follow alcohol withdrawal (delirium tremens, or the DTs), as an anticonvulsant for epileptic patients, or as a preanesthetic drug to relax the patient just prior to surgery. In general, shorter-acting oral benzodiazepines are recommended for sleeping problems because their effects begin more quickly and wear off well before morning. Examples of this type include triazolam (brand name: Halcion), midazolam (brand name: Versed), and temazepam (brand name: Restoril).

How effective are benzodiazepines for the treatment of anxiety? In randomized double-blind studies (Chapter 3), Valium is observed to be helpful for about 70 to 80 percent of people with an anxiety disorder. Approximately 25 to 30 percent of them, however, are helped by the placebo alone, so it is also evident that psychological factors play a significant role in the final outcome.[14]

Interestingly, benzodiazepines work best when the physician prescribing the medication is perceived as being warm, has a positive attitude toward use of antianxiety drugs, and believes that the patient will improve (Table 15.4).[15] The positive impact of such factors on the outcome of treatment underscores the importance of the physician–patient relationship, along with the genuine antianxiety effects of the drugs themselves. This phenomenon also reinforces the idea discussed in Chapter 3 that the context of drug-taking behavior plays a significant role in an individual's response to a particular drug. Predictions of a therapeutic outcome in the case of psychoactive medications are dependent on factors that go beyond the pharmacological aspects of the drug itself.

Acute Effects of Benzodiazepines

In general, benzodiazepines are absorbed relatively slowly into the bloodstream, so their relaxant effects last longer and are more gradual than those of barbiturates. The primary reason is that benzodiazepines are absorbed from the small intestine rather than the stomach, as is the case with barbiturates. The relatively greater water-solubility, and by implication the relatively lower fat-solubility, of benzodiazepines is also a factor.

The major advantage that benzodiazepines have over barbiturates is their higher level of safety. Respiratory centers in the medulla are not affected by benzodiazepines, so it is rare that a person will die of respiratory failure from an accidental or intentional overdose. Even after taking fifty or sixty times the therapeutic dose, the person will still not stop breathing. It is almost always possible to arouse a person from the stupor that such a

---

Source: Rickels, Karl (1981). Benzodiazepines: Clinical use patterns. In Stephen I. Szara and Jacqueline P. Ludford (Eds.), *Benzodiazepines: A review of research results 1980* (NIDA Research Monograph 33). Rockville, MD: National Institute on Drug Abuse, p. 46.

---

drug quantity would produce. In contrast, doses of barbiturates or nonbarbiturate sedatives that are ten to twenty times the therapeutic dose are lethal. Yet, we should understand that this higher level of safety assumes that *no alcohol or other depressant drugs are being taken at the same time.*[16]

Nonetheless, despite the relative safety of Valium and other benzodiazepines, this drug family poses a number of medical risks for special populations. For elderly patients, for example, the rate of elimination of these drugs is slowed down significantly, resulting in the risk of a dangerously high buildup of benzodiazepines after several doses. In the case of a long-acting benzodiazepine such as Valium or Librium, the elimination half-life is for them as long as ten days. An elderly patient with this rate of elimination would not be essentially drug-free until two months had passed.

The continued accumulation of benzodiazepines in the elderly can produce a type of drug-induced dementia in which the patient suffers from confusion and loss of memory. Without understanding the patient's medication history, these symptoms can be easily mistaken for the onset of Alzheimer's disease or other forms of dementia. A prominent pharmacologist has remarked that his eighty-five-year-old grandmother began to experience forgetfulness and disorientation while taking Valium. "Two months after discontinuation of the drug, her dementia disappeared and she remained lucid until her death ten years later." It is for this reason that long-acting benzodiazepines are no longer recommended for this age group, and those who are currently taking these drugs are being encouraged to switch to shorter-acting forms or alternative antianxiety therapies.[17]

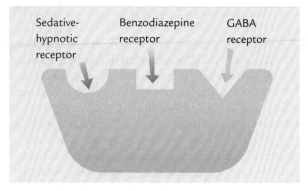

FIGURE 15.3

A simplified view of the benzodiazepine receptor.

Chronic Effects of Benzodiazepines

The benzodiazepines were originally viewed as having few if any problems relating to a tolerance effect or an acquired dependence. We now know that the *anxiety-relieving* aspects of benzodiazepines show little or no tolerance effects when the drugs are taken at prescribed dosages, but there is a tolerance to the *sedative* effects. In other words, if the drugs are taken for the purpose of relieving anxiety, there is no problem with tolerance, but if they are taken for insomnia, more of the drug may be required in later administrations to induce sleep.[18]

We also now know that physiological symptoms appear when benzodiazepines are withdrawn, an indication of benzodiazepine dependence (Chapter 2). In the case of Valium and other long-acting benzodiazepines, the slow rate of elimination delays the appearance of withdrawal symptoms until between the third and sixth day following drug withdrawal. The first signs include an anxiety level that may be worse than the level for which the drug was originally prescribed. Later, there are symptoms of insomnia, restlessness, and agitation. In general, however, withdrawal symptoms are less severe than those observed after barbiturate withdrawal, occur only after long-term use, and are gone in one to four weeks.[19]

How Benzodiazepines Work in the Brain

The key factor in the action of benzodiazepines is the neurotransmitter gamma aminobutyric acid (GABA), which normally exerts an inhibitory effect on the nervous system (see Chapter 3). When benzodiazepines are in the vicinity of GABA receptors, the actions of GABA are increased. The antianxiety drugs attach themselves to their own receptors on the membrane of neurons and in doing so heighten the effect of GABA. The facilita-

tion of GABA produces a greater inhibition and a decreased activity level in the neurons involved.[20]

The receptor described here is a large protein molecule that has multiple binding locations, arranged like docking sites for different kinds of boats. As shown in Figure 15.3, the receptor consists of three binding sites: one for sedative-hypnotics (including the barbiturates), one for benzodiazepines (and alcohol), and one for GABA. When GABA attaches to its binding site, there is greater inhibition if the benzodiazepine sites are also occupied at the time by a benzodiazepine drug than if they are not occupied.[21] A successful binding of a chemical at one site facilitates the binding at the others.

It is not difficult to imagine how cross-tolerance and cross-dependence among various depressant drugs would occur. As discussed in Chapter 3, if two depressant drugs were to bind to the same receptor, the receptor would not be able to "tell the difference" between them. As far as the receptor is concerned, the effect would be the same. Evidently, sedative-hypnotics and benzodiazepines share this feature: an ability to lock into a common receptor with multiple binding locations.

Where are the receptors for depressant drugs? They are understood to be localized primarily in the limbic system and the cerebral cortex. It is believed that receptors in the limbic system underlie the antianxiety action of benzodiazepines (remember that the limbic system is involved with emotionality), while receptors in the cortex underlie their sedative actions. Teasing apart the neuronal actions of benzodiazepines, by delineating the most relevant subtype of GABA receptor, is the key to the future development of better medications for anxiety.[22]

Patterns of Benzodiazepine Misuse and Abuse

Benzodiazepines do not present the same potential for abuse that cocaine, alcohol, or the barbiturates do, for two primary reasons. First, benzodiazepines are only weak reinforcers of behavior. When trained to press a lever for an injection of Valium, for example, laboratory animals will self-administer the drug but at far less robust levels than they would show for self-administering pentobarbital or methaqualone. Studies with normal college student volunteers show that, when given the choice between a placebo and Valium and the true identity of neither choice is known, the placebo is actually preferred. For these individuals, presumably nondrug abusers and relatively anxiety free, the results show no indication of a positive Valium reaction.[23] Second, the slow onset of a benzodiazepine effect prevents the sudden "rush" feeling that is characteristic of many abused drugs such as cocaine, heroin, and amphetamines.

The foregoing is *not* to say, however, that benzodiazepines fail to be abused. It is simply that their abuse exists in the context of abusing other drugs as well, often referred to as multiple substance abuse or polydrug abuse. Alcoholics, for example, sometimes take benzodiazepines at work, in an attempt to relax and to avoid having the smell of alcohol on their breath. Heroin abusers may take benzodiazepines to augment their euphoria and reduce their anxiety when the opiate levels in their blood begin to fall. Cocaine abusers may take the drugs to soften the crashing feeling that is experienced as the cocaine starts to wear off.[24]

Therefore, the principal social problems surrounding the taking of benzodiazepine drugs, since their introduction in the 1960s, have arisen more from their *misuse* than from their *abuse* (see Chapter 1). The greatest concern during the 1960s and 1970s was the enormous quantity of benzodiazepine prescriptions that were being written. In 1972, Valium ranked first (and Librium third) among the most frequently prescribed drugs of any type. At the height of their popularity in 1975, more than 100 million such prescriptions were processed around the world, with 85 million in the United States. In Western Europe and North America, it was estimated that 10 to 20 percent of adults were taking benzodiazepines on a fairly regular basis.[25]

Benzodiazepine use and misuse have since declined substantially in psychiatric practice, as newer approaches to anxiety disorders have been pursued. Nonetheless, benzodiazepines remain widely prescribed drugs throughout the world, particularly for people over

the age of sixty-five years, to treat problems of insomnia and anxiety. While they are useful for short-term use, unfortunate adverse side effects can arise when benzodiazepines are taken over a long period of time. The potential for cognitive impairment among elderly people and the issue of benzodiazepine dependence in general were discussed earlier in this chapter. There is also an increased risk of falls and hip fractures among the elderly, due to the disorientation that can sometimes be experienced. These possibilities are a particular problem in European countries where wine is consumed on a regular basis and, as a consequence, benzodiazepines are often combined with alcohol.[26]

In recent years, considerable publicity has focused on the social and personal concerns surrounding the abuse of a specific benzodiazepine, flunitrazepam (brand name: Rohypnol); it is not legally available in the United States but is accessible as a club drug through illicit channels (Health Alert, page 368).

Nonbenzodiazepine Sedative-Hypnotics and Antianxiety Drugs

Just as benzodiazepines represented a great advance over barbiturates, the development of new nonbenzodiazepine drugs has provided better opportunities to treat sleep disorders and anxiety. Prominent examples of this new generation of medications are zolpidem, eszopiclone, buspirone, beta blockers, and, strangely enough, antidepressants.

Zolpidem and Eszopiclone

Zolpidem (brand name: Ambien) is not a benzodiazepine drug, but it binds to a specific subtype of GABA receptors. This is probably why it produces only some of the effects usually associated with benzodiazepines, with particular usefulness in the short-term treatment of insomnia. Its strong but transient sedative effects (with a half-life of about two hours) have led to the marketing of zolpidem, since its introduction in 1993, as a sedative-hypnotic rather than an antianxiety agent. Little or no muscle relaxation is experienced.

zolpidem (ZOL-pih-dem): A nonbenzodiazepine sedative-hypnotic drug, first introduced in 1993, for the treatment of insomnia. Brand name is Ambien.

The Dangers of Rohypnol as a Date-Rape Drug

Flunitrazepam (brand name: Rohypnol) is a long-acting benzodiazepine, not unlike diazepam (Valium) except that it is approximately ten times stronger. Because of its extreme potency and the fact that it is highly synergistic with alcohol, Rohypnol is not legally available in the United States. It is, however, approved for medical use in Europe and South America, where it is marketed by Hoffmann-La Roche Pharmaceuticals as a treatment for sleep disorders and as a surgical anesthetic. The U.S. supply of Rohypnol is smuggled into the country from Mexico and South America and sold for recreational use, frequently in its original bubble packaging.

The abuse potential of Rohypnol surfaced in the mid-1990s, when the number of pills seized by the U.S. Customs Service increased by 400 percent from 1994 to 1995 alone. Under such street names as "roofies," "rope," "wolfies," "roches," "R2," and "Mexican Valium," this drug has been promoted as an alcohol enhancer and as a strategy for getting drunk without having a blood-alcohol concentration level that would be defined as legal intoxication. Rohypnol has also been involved in numerous date-rape cases in which victims had been unknowingly slipped the drug, causing them to pass out—the ultimate vulnerable situation. The disinhibition of behavior and the subsequent memory loss of the experience are similar to an alcohol-induced blackout (see Chapter 9).

At one time, Rohypnol was odorless, colorless, and tasteless, so it could be easily combined with an alcoholic beverage without detection. Recently, in response to instances of abuse, Hoffmann-La Roche has taken steps to reformulate the drug so that it turns blue when dissolved in a clear liquid. This helps to make Rohypnol somewhat more noticeable to an unsuspecting drinker, but it is important to realize that some alcoholic beverages may not show a discernible change in color, particularly under the dim illumination conditions of a typical bar.

Since 1996, U.S. federal law provides for a twenty-year sentence for the use of Rohypnol in connection with rape or other violent crime. Unfortunately, Rohypnol is an increasingly accessible illicit drug. According to one law-enforcement official in Miami, "It may be easier for teenagers to obtain flunitrazepam (Rohypnol) than alcohol." A recent study has found that a variety of benzodiazepines, all marketed by Hoffmann-La Roche, are being abused and linked to sexual assaults. Because these drugs all bear the same Roche imprint on the tablets, they are collectively known as "roches."

Rohypnol is an example of a group of present-day "club drugs" that have a dangerous potential for abuse as date-rape drugs. Other examples include MDMA or Ecstasy (see Chapter 4) and GHB (to be discussed later in this chapter).

> **Where to go for assistance:**
>
> www.4woman.gov/faq/rohypnol.htm
>
> This web site is sponsored by the National Women's Health Information Center, a service of the U.S. Department of Health and Human Services dedicated to women's health issues.

Sources: Community Epidemiology Work Group (1996). *Epidemiologic trends in drug abuse,* Volume 1: *Highlights and executive summary.* Rockville, MD: National Institute on Drug Abuse, pp. 8, 64. Quotation on p. 64. Drug Enforcement Administration, U.S. Department of Justice, Washington DC, 1997. Office of National Drug Control Policy (2003, February). *ONDCP Drug Policy Clearing-house fact sheet: Rohypnol.* Washington DC: Executive Office of the President.

Introduced in 2004, **eszopiclone** (brand name: Lunesta, formerly known as Estorra) is also a nonbenzodiazepine drug that is prescribed for the treatment of insomnia. As a result of successful clinical trials lasting six months, the FDA has approved Lunesta for an interval of treatment that is longer than the recommended treatment with Ambien. Because its half-life of six hours is longer than that of Ambien, Lunesta has been helpful for people who have difficulty in staying asleep during the night as well as difficulty in falling asleep (Drugs . . . in Focus).[27]

eszopiclone (es-ZOP-eh-clone): A nonbenzodiazepine sedative-hypnotic, first introduced in 2005, for the treatment of insomnia. Brand name is Lunesta.

buspirone (BYOO-spir-rone): A nonbenzodiazepine antianxiety drug, first introduced in 1986. Brand name is BuSpar.

Buspirone

Since 1986, a new type of antianxiety drug has been available called **buspirone** (brand name: BuSpar), with a number of remarkable features. It has been found to be

Drugs...in Focus

Ambien versus Lunesta—The Sleeping Pill War

The evidence is clear that Americans and others around the world have turned to sleep medications in dramatically increasing numbers, due to heavy marketing in the late 1990s of Ambien and its prominent rival, Lunesta. Although these products offer a greater amount of safety in their treatment of sleep disorders than had been the case with barbiturates and benzodiazepines, public health officials are worried that, as an editorial in the *New York Times* in 2006 expressed it, "the pills will be overused by people who don't really need them or that doctors may reflexively prescribe pills while ignoring underlying conditions that may be responsible for sleeplessness." If this happens, widespread overuse would be a historical repeat of the 1950s (with barbiturates) and the 1970s (with benzodiazepines).

Adding fuel to the marketing fire were reports in 2006 of bizarre behavior in some patients taking Ambien that involves dangerous driving and other behaviors while "sleepwalking." In Wisconsin between the years 1999 and 2004, for example, Ambien was in the top ten list of drugs found in the bloodstreams of 187 drivers arrested for impaired driving. Having collided into trees and engaged in erratic driving, these individuals had no memory of getting behind the wheel. In other cases, Ambien patients have found themselves in the morning engorged with food after a night of raiding the refrigerator. These effects appear to have affected no more than 1 percent of Ambien users, but with more than 26 million prescriptions of Ambien filled in 2006 in the United States alone, the potential for widespread emergences was frightening.

An additional problem for Ambien marketers was that the patent period for the drug was nearing its end. The introduction of Ambien CR (a controlled-release version) in 2005 extended the patent protection for the Ambien formulation; the patent for the original version of Ambien had expired. However, in 2007, generic substitutes (zolpidem) caused Ambien sales to plummet, and Ambien CR itself would be scheduled to go off patent in 2009. At this point, Lunesta appears dominant in terms of market share, although the picture tends to change quickly from year to year. With a worldwide sales market for sleep medications of $4.4 billion projected for 2010, the marketing war for sleeping pills should continue to be intense.

Sources: Barrett, Jennifer (updated 2006, March 16). Wake-up call. *Newsweek,* MSNBC.com. LeadDiscovery Ltd. (2005, September). The world sleep disorders market 2005–2010: A market with high growth potential. East Sussex, UK: LeadDiscovery Ltd. Saul, Stephanie (2006, March 8). Some sleeping pill users range far beyond bed. *New York Times,* pp. C1, C5. Quotation from sleeping pill wars: Editorial (2006, February 18). *New York Times,* p. A14. Saul, Stephanie (2006, March 14). To sleep, perchance to eat. Is it the pills? *New York Times,* pp. C1, C6. Sepracor hikes price of Lunesta sleep drug—analyst (2007, June 14). Thomson Reuters, www.reuters.com.

---

equivalent to Valium in its ability to relieve anxiety. Yet, unlike the benzodiazepines in general, buspirone shows no cross-tolerance or cross-dependence with alcohol or other depressants and no withdrawal symptoms when discontinued after chronic use. When compared with benzodiazepines, side effects are observed less frequently and are less troublesome to the patient; 9 percent report dizziness and 7 percent report headaches. Animals do not self-administer buspirone in laboratory studies, and human volunteers indicate an absence of euphoria.

Buspirone also fails to show the impairments in motor skills that are characteristic of benzodiazepines. In other words, the relief of anxiety is attainable without the accompanying feelings and behavioral consequences of sedation. Perhaps anxiety and sedation do not necessarily have to be intertwined after all. Unlike benzodiazepines, buspirone does not affect GABA receptors in the brain but rather acts on a special subclass of serotonin receptors. Evidently, the influence of buspirone on serotonin produces the antianxiety effects.

Despite its virtues, however, buspirone has a distinct disadvantage: a very long delay before anxiety relief is felt. It may take weeks for the drug to become completely effective. While this feature makes buspirone clearly inappropriate for relieving acute anxiety conditions, patients suffering from long-term generalized anxiety disorder find it helpful as a therapeutic drug. An extra benefit of the delay in the action of buspirone is that it becomes highly undesirable as a drug of abuse. Do not expect to see news headlines in the future warning of an epidemic of buspirone abuse (Table 15.5).[28]

TABLE 15.5

The advantages of buspirone over other means to reduce anxiety

FACTOR FOR POSSIBLE ABUSE	ALCOHOL	BARBITURATES	BENZODIAZEPINES	BUSPIRONE
Euphoria	++	+++	+	0
Rapid action	+++	++	+	0
Unsupervised use	++++	++	++	0
Social encouragement	++++	++	+	0
Tolerance	++	++	+	0
Physical dependence	++++	+++	++	0
Cross-tolerance	+++	+++	+++	0
Cross-dependence	+++	+++	+++	0
Total	25	20	14	0

Note: Each plus sign indicates a degree of abuse potential. The greater the total number of plus signs, the greater the overall abuse potential for each drug. A zero indicates that the drug has no value with regard to a particular factor.

Source: Modified from Lickey, Marvin E., and Gordon, Barbara (1991). *Medicine and mental illness.* New York: Freeman, p. 324.

Beta Blockers

The traditional medical uses of beta-adrenergic-blocking drugs, commonly known as **beta blockers,** include slowing the heart rate, relaxing pressure on the walls of blood vessels, and decreasing the force of heart contractions. The combination of a beta blocker drug and a diuretic is a frequent treatment for the control of high blood pressure. These drugs are also prescribed for individuals facing an anxiety-producing event, such as performing on the stage or giving a speech. Examples of beta blockers include atenolol (brand name: Tenormin), metoprolol (brand name: Lopressor), and propanolol (brand name: Inderal).

Antidepressants

A recent development in the treatment of panic disorder, post-traumatic stress disorder, and social anxiety disorder has been the use of antidepressant medications—specifically, selective serotonin reuptake inhibitors (SSRIs) such as sertraline (brand name: Zoloft), paroxetine (brand names: Paxil, Asima), and others. A more extensive discussion of this subcategory of antidepressants will be found in Chapter 16.[29]

---

beta blockers: Medicinal drugs that are traditionally used to treat cardiac and blood pressure disorders. They are also prescribed for individuals who suffer from "stage fright" or anxiety regarding a specific event. Examples include atenolol (brand name: Tenormin), metoprolol (brand name: Lopressor), and propanolol (brand name: Inderal).

Quick Concept Check 15.1

Understanding the Abuse Potential in Drugs

Each of the following statements describes a particular attribute of a new drug. Based on material in this chapter, judge whether each description, when taken by itself, either increases or decreases the abuse potential of the drug.

1. Drug fails to produce euphoria at any dose levels.

2. Drug acts very quickly.

3. Drug is cross-tolerant to barbiturates and alcohol.

4. Drug is not available to the public.

5. There are tolerance effects when taking this drug.

6. The drug can be used without the need for medical supervision of dose or dosage schedule.

Answers: 1. decreases 2. increases 3. increases
4. decreases 5. increases 6. increases

A Special Alert: The Risks of GHB

Of all the much-publicized club drugs to emerge in recent years, perhaps the most notorious is the CNS depressant **gamma hydroxybutyrate (GHB).** First synthesized in the 1960s, GHB was found to be produced naturally in the body in very small amounts, but no one has discovered its function. At one time, GHB was sold in health-food stores and similar establishments. It was considered to have steroid-enhancing and growth-hormone-stimulating effects, leading to interest among body builders (see Chapter 8). Other promotions focused on GHB as a sedative.

By 1990 numerous reports of GHB-related seizures and comas led the FDA to remove GHB as an available ingredient in dietary supplements, and it became a Schedule I controlled substance in 2000. However, since 2002, GHB (brand name: Xyrem) has been FDA-approved for the treatment of symptoms of muscle weakness and paralysis that often accompany narcolepsy. For treatment purposes, it is classified as a Schedule III drug (see Chapter 2), while retaining its Schedule I status for all other circumstances.

Acute Effects

Present-day GHB abuse focuses on its ability to produce euphoria, an "out-of-body" high, with an accompanying lowering of inhibitions. Frequently, a combination of GHB and alcohol can produce a lack of consciousness in about fifteen minutes and subsequent amnesia about the experience. The notoriety of GHB as a date-rape drug stems from its being colorless, odorless, and virtually tasteless. As a result, it can be easily slipped into alcoholic beverages without the knowledge of the drinker.[30]

Protective Strategies for Women

The vulnerability of women to being drugged with GHB while consuming alcohol in a club or bar is considerable (Portrait). Nonetheless, a number of protective strategies can be employed to minimize the risk.

- Watch the person who pours you a drink, even if it is a friend or a bartender. Even better, do not drink what you cannot open or pour yourself. Avoid punch bowls and shared containers. Never accept a drink offered to you by a stranger.
- Do not leave a drink alone—not while you are dancing, using the restroom, or making a telephone call. If you have left it alone, it is better to toss the beverage.
- Appoint a designated "sober" friend to check up on you at parties, bars, clubs, and other social gatherings.
- If a friend seems extremely drunk or sick after a drink and has trouble breathing, call 911 immediately.

gamma hydroxybutyrate (GHB) (GAM-ma heye-DROX-ee-BYOO-tih-rate): A powerful CNS depressant, often abused to induce euphoria and sedation. When slipped in an alcoholic beverage without the knowledge of the drinker, GHB has been employed as a date-rape drug.

PORTRAIT — Patricia White, GHB, and the "Perfect" Crime

Patricia White, a forty-seven-year-old mother of three, was at a party celebrating the birthday of her boss, Lorenzo Feal. According to testimony later given by White, as she was about to leave the party, Feal handed her a bottle of water. She took a gulp. A few hours later, White woke up in Feal's bed, naked and nauseated. She had been drugged and raped. Doctors at the emergency department of the local hospital found traces of GHB in her system, and Feal was eventually convicted of using an anesthetic substance in carrying out White's rape.

A prosecuting attorney has called GHB "ideal for predators and tough for prosecutors" because it is so easily concealed in a drink. Without toxicological evidence, it is difficult to prove that the rape victim had not given consent to sex. Perhaps GHB should really be called an "acquaintance- and date-rape drug."

In 1994, when GHB was relatively new, only 56 GHB-related emergency department visits were reported in the United States. By 2001, that number had grown to 3,340. Colleges and universities, as well as commercial bars, have become justifiably alarmed. The Drug Enforcement Administration (DEA) has collaborated with the Rape, Abuse, and Incest National Network (RAINN) in an effort to promote a heightened awareness of GHB and other "predatory" drugs such as Rohypnol. Patricia White now counsels GHB rape victims and speaks out publicly about her personal story. In the case of GHB, the more you know about this drug, the safer you are.

Sources: Office of Women's Health (2008, December 8). Date rape drugs. Washington DC: U.S. Department of Health and Human Services. Smalley, Suzanne (2003, February 3). "The perfect crime": GHB is colorless, odorless, leaves the body within hours—and is fueling a growing number of rapes. *Newsweek*, p. 52.

- If you have been slipped GHB, the drug will take effect within ten to thirty minutes. Initially, you will feel dizzy or nauseous or develop a severe headache. You can be incapacitated rapidly. This is the time when having a nondrinking friend nearby is crucial.

- If you wake up in a strange place and believe you have been sexually assaulted while under the influence of GHB, do not urinate until you have been admitted to a hospital. There is an approximately twelve-hour window of opportunity to detect GHB through urinanalysis.

A test strip created by Drink Safe Technology is now available that can detect not only GHB but also Rohypnol and ketamine. A straw can be used to place a few drops of one's drink on the test strip. If the liquid turns blue, there is a positive result. Unfortunately, when the drink contains dairy products, an accurate detection cannot be made. Bar coasters have been developed that incorporate this particular test strip. *Be aware, however, of the fact that the original and all-time leading date-rape drug is simply alcohol.*[31]

This commercially available bar coaster is used to test for the presence of GHB in an alcoholic beverage.

Summary

Barbiturates

- Introduced in 1903 and in use until approximately 1960, the primary sedative-hypnotics (drugs that produce sedation and sleep) belonged to the barbiturate family of drugs.

- Barbiturates are typically classified by virtue of how long their depressant effects are felt, from long-acting (example: phenobarbital) to intermediate-acting (examples: butalbarbital and amobarbital) to short-acting (examples: pentobarbital and secobarbital).

- A major disadvantage of barbiturates is the potential of a lethal overdose, particularly when combined with other depressants such as alcohol. In addition, barbiturate withdrawal symptoms are very severe and require careful medical attention.

Nonbarbiturate Sedative-Hypnotics

- Methaqualone (Quaalude) was introduced in the 1960s as an alternative to barbiturates for sedation and sleep. Unfortunately, this drug produced undesirable side effects and became subject to widespread abuse. It is no longer available as a licit drug.

The Nature of Anxiety

- Anxiety is a common and necessary element of our survival, enabling us to anticipate and contend with possible challenges and hazards. Anxiety disorders are essentially conditions in which this adaptive emotion has become maladaptive.

- Anxiety disorders include panic disorder, obsessive-compulsive disorder, post-traumatic stress disorder, social anxiety disorder, specific phobias, and generalized anxiety disorder.

The Development of Antianxiety Drugs

- Beginning in the 1950s, a major effort was made by the pharmaceutical industry to develop a drug that would relieve anxiety (tranquilize) rather than merely depress the CNS (sedate).

- Meprobamate (Miltown) was introduced in 1955 for this purpose, though it is now understood that the effects of this drug result more from its sedative properties than its ability to relieve anxiety.

Benzodiazepines

- The introduction of benzodiazepines, specifically diazepam (Valium) and chlordiazepoxide (Librium), in the early 1960s, was a significant breakthrough in the development of antianxiety drugs. These drugs selectively affect specific receptors in the brain instead of acting as general depressants of the nervous system.

- In general, benzodiazepines are safer drugs than barbiturates, when taken alone. When taken in combination with alcohol, however, dangerous synergistic effects are observed.

- Benzodiazepines produce their effects by binding to receptors in the limbic system and cerebral cortex in the brain that are sensitive to the inhibitory neurotransmitter gamma aminobutyric acid (GABA).

- Social problems concerning the taking of benzodiazepine drugs during the 1970s centered on the widespread misuse of the drug. Prescriptions were written too frequently and for excessive dosages.

Nonbenzodiazepine Sedative-Hypnotics and Antianxiety Drugs

- Recently developed nonbenzodiazepines have provided better opportunities to treat sleep disorders and anxiety. Three examples are zolpidem, eszopiclone, and buspirone.

- Zolpidem (brand name: Ambien) and eszopiclone (brand name: Lunesta) have been useful as sedative-hypnotics in the treatment of insomnia. They have strong but transient sedative effects and produce little or no muscle relaxation.

- Buspirone (brand name: BuSpar) has been useful as an antianxiety medication that does not cause sedation.

- Beta blockers, traditionally used to treat cardiac and blood pressure disorders, have been prescribed for individuals who are facing an anxiety-producing event, such as performing on the stage or speaking in public.

- Certain antidepressants called selective serotonin reuptake inhibitors (SSRIs) have been successful in treating a variety of anxiety disorders.

The Risks of GHB

- Gamma hydroxybutyrate (GHB) is a CNS depressant, first used by body builders because of the possibility that it had growth-hormone-stimulating effects. Today, GHB is an underground drug, available only through clandestine channels.

- As with Rohypnol, the depressant effects of GHB have made it attractive as a club drug. Its involvement as a potential date-rape drug has raised very serious concerns.

Key Terms

amobarbital, p. 357
antianxiety drugs, p. 357
anxiety disorders, p. 362
barbiturate, p. 357
benzodiazepines, p. 364
beta blockers, p. 370

buspirone, p. 368
chloral hydrate, p. 361
chlordiazepoxide, p. 364
diazepam, p. 364
eszopiclone, p. 368

gamma hydroxybutyrate (GHB), p. 371
meprobamate, p. 363
methaqualone, p. 361
pentobarbital, p. 357

phenobarbital, p. 357
REM-sleep rebound, p. 359
secobarbital, p. 357
sedative-hypnotics, p. 357
zolpidem, p. 367

Endnotes

1. Palfai, Tibor, and Jankiewicz, Henry (1991). *Drugs and human behavior.* Dubuque, IA: W. C. Brown, p. 203.

2. Jacobs, Michael R., and Fehr, Kevin O'B. (1987). *Drugs and drug abuse: A reference text* (2nd ed.). Toronto: Addiction Research Foundation, pp. 183–194.

3. Palfai and Jankiewicz, *Drugs and human behavior*, p. 213.

4. Jacobs and Fehr, *Drugs and drug abuse*, p. 189.

5. Kauffman, Janice F., Shaffer, Howard, and Burglass, Milton E. (1985). The biological basics: Drugs and their effects. In Thomas E. Bratter and Gary G. Forrest (Eds.), *Alcoholism and substance abuse: Strategies for clinical intervention.* New York: Free Press, pp. 107–136.

6. Sleeping pills and antianxiety drugs (1988). *The Harvard Medical School Mental Health Letter,* 5 (6), 1–4.

7. Griffiths, Roland R., Bigelow, George, and Liebson, Ira (1979). Human drug self-administration: Double-blind comparison of pentobarbital, diazepam, chlorpromazine, and placebo. *Journal of Pharmacology and Experimental Therapeutics, 210,* 301–310. Griffiths, Roland R.; Lukas, Scott E.; Bradford, L. D.; Brady, Joseph V.; and Snell, Jack D. (1981). Self-injection of barbiturates and benzodiazepines in baboons. *Psychopharmacology, 75,* 101–109.

8. Johnston, Lloyd D.; O'Malley, Patrick M.; Bachman, Jerald G.; and Schulenberg, John E. (2008, December 11). Various stimulant drugs show continuing gradual declines among teens in 2008, most illicit drugs hold steady. University of Michigan News Service, Ann Arbor, Tables 1 and 2.

9. Carroll, Marilyn, and Gallo, Gary (1985). *Quaaludes: The quest for oblivion.* New York: Chelsea House.

10. Cowley, Geoffrey (2003, February 24). Our bodies, our fears. *Newsweek,* 42–49. National Institute of Mental Health (2001, October). *Facts about anxiety disorders.* Bethesda, MD: National Institute of Mental Health.

11. National Institute of Mental Health (2002). *Anxiety disorders.* Bethesda, MD: National Institute of Mental

Health. O'Connor, Anahad (2004, January 27). Panic spells are traced to chemical in the brain. *New York Times*, p. F6.

12. Julien, Robert M. (2001). *A primer of drug action* (9th ed.). New York: Worth, p. 54.

13. Berger, Philip A., and Tinklenberg, Jared R. (1977). Treatment of abusers of alcohol and other addictive drugs. In Jack D. Barchas, Philip A. Berger, Roland D. Caranello, and Glen R. Elliott (Eds.), *Psychopharmacology: From theory to practice*. New York: Oxford University Press, pp. 355–385.

14. Leavitt, Fred (1982). *Drugs and behavior* (2nd ed.). New York: Wiley.

15. Rickels, Karl (1981). Benzodiazepines: Clinical use patterns. In Stephen I. Szara and Jacqueline P. Ludford (Eds.), *Benzodiazepines: A review of research results 1980* (NIDA Research Monograph 33). Rockville, MD: National Institute on Drug Abuse, pp. 43–60.

16. Lickey, Marvin E., and Gordon, Barbara (1991). *Medicine and mental illness*. New York: Freeman, p. 280. Tanaka, Einosuke (2002). Toxiological interactions between alcohol and benzodiazepines. *Journal of Toxicology—Clinical Toxicology*, 40, 69–75.

17. Julien, *A primer of drug action*, p. 161. Salzman, Carl (1999). An 87-year-old woman taking a benzodiazepine. *Journal of the American Medical Association*, 281, 1121–1125.

18. Rickels, Karl; Case, W. George; Downing, Robert W.; and Winokur, Andrew (1983). Long-term diazepam therapy and clinical outcome. *Journal of the American Medical Association*, 250, 767–771.

19. Julien, *A primer of drug action*, pp. 153–163. Longo, Lance P., and Johnson, Brian (2000). Addiction: Part I. Benzodiazepines—Side effects, abuse risk and alternatives. *American Family Physician*, 61, 2121–2128.

20. Mohler, H., and Okada, T. (1977). Benzodiazepine receptors in rat brain: Demonstration in the central nervous system. *Science*, 198, 849–851. Squires, Richard F., and Braestrup, Claus (1977). Benzodiazepine receptors in rat brain. *Nature*, 266, 732–734.

21. Lickey and Gordon, *Medicine and mental illness*, p. 291. Nelson, John, and Chouinard, Guy (1996). Benzodiazepines: Mechanisms of action and clinical indications. In Andrius Baskys and Gary Remington (Eds.). *Brain mechanisms and psychotropic drugs*. Boca Raton, FL: CRC Press, pp. 213–238.

22. Löw, Karin; Crestani, Florence; Keist, Ruth; Benke, Dietmar; Brünig, Ina; et al. (2000). Molecular and neuronal substrate for the selective attenuation of anxiety. *Science*, 290, 131–134.

23. Griffiths, Roland R., and Ator, Nancy A. (1981). Benzodiazepine self-administration in animals and humans: A comprehensive literature review. In Stephen I. Szara and Jacqueline P. Ludford (Eds.), *Benzodiazepines: A review of research results, 1980* (NIDA Research Monograph 33). Rockville, MD: National Institute on Drug Abuse, pp. 22–36.

24. Julien, Robert M. (1998). *A primer of drug action* (8th ed.). New York: Freeman, pp. 106–107.

25. Lickey and Gordon, *Medicine and mental illness*, p. 278.

26. Lagnaouli, Rajaa; Moore, Nicholas, Dartigues, Jean François; Fourrier, Annie; and Bégaud, Bernard (2001). Benzodiazepine use and wine consumption in the French elderly. *British Journal of Clinical Pharmacology*, 52, 455–456. Pimlott, Nicholas J. G.; Hux, Janet E.; Wilson, Lynn M.; Kahan, Meldon; Li, Cindy; and Rosser, Walter W. (2003). Educating physicians to reduce benzodiazepine use by elderly patients: A randomized controlled trial. *Canadian Medical Association Journal*, 168, 835–839.

27. Gershell, Leland (2006). From the analyst's couch: Insomnia market. *Nature Reviews and Drug Discovery*, 5, 15–16.

28. Julien, *A primer of drug action* (9th ed.), pp. 169–171.

29. Julien, *A primer of drug action* (9th ed.), p. 172. Julien, Robert M. (1988). *Drugs and the body*. New York: Freeman, pp. 80–81. Kent, J. M., Coplan, J. D., and Gorman, J. M. (1998). Clinical utility of the selective serotonin reuptake inhibitors in the spectrum of anxiety. *Biological Psychiatry*, 44, 812–824.

30. Dyer, J. E. (2000). Evolving abuse of GHB in California: Bodybuilding drug to date-rape drug. *Journal of Toxicology—Clinical Toxicology*, 38, 184. Office of National Drug Control Policy (1998, October). *ONDCP Drug Policy Information Clearinghouse fact sheet: Gamma hydroxybutyrate (GHB)*. Washington DC: Executive Office of the President.

31. Adams, Genetta M. (2003, January 5). A safety test for a night on the town. *Newsday*, p. D2. Information regarding bar coasters courtesy of Drink Safe Technology, Wellington, FL. Office of National Drug Control Policy, *ONDCP Drug Policy Information Clearinghouse fact sheet: Gamma hydroxybutyrate (GHB)*.

chapter 16

Drugs for Treating Schizophrenia and Mood Disorders

It was getting pretty weird. My thoughts were completely paralyzed. Dr. Thompson's great-great-grandmother last month told me herself that I better be on my guard about those paralyzing thoughts. Now lately, I suppose the medicine has killed off that stuff. That old woman's voice doesn't visit me anymore. I'm a lot calmer now. My brain works better.

That's how it seems to me. I reckon the medicine just took those bad thoughts away. Don't ask me how it did it, 'cause I don't know. But it did.

—A schizophrenia patient under Thorazine

Many drugs have the potential to liberate the mind from symptoms of mental illness, either moderate or severe in degree. Chapter 15 dealt, in part, with the use of drugs in the treatment of anxiety disorders. This chapter will look at a special class of psychoactive drugs that can relieve severe emotional distress, reduce intense personal suffering, and enable deeply troubled people to lead relatively normal lives. The primary focus will be on medications used for the treatment of two major forms of mental illness: schizophrenia and mood disorders such as depression or mania. All drugs used in treating mental illness are often referred to as **psychiatric drugs,** because they are generally prescribed and supervised by psychiatrists. An alternative term, **psychotropic medication,** refers to the fact that their pharmacological effects move the patient closer to a normal state of mind (*trop,* meaning "to turn toward").

The development of psychiatric drugs has brought about nothing short of a revolution in the quality of mental-health care, as well as a major insight into the biochemical nature of mental illness. Millions of individuals suffering from schizophrenia, depression, or mania have benefited from psychiatric drugs.

The Biomedical Model

Using the term *mental illness* to describe the symptoms of disorders such as schizophrenia, depression, or mania implies that we are viewing abnormal psychological and behavioral symptoms as being no different from symptoms arising from a physical disease such as pneumonia or a stroke. This viewpoint, commonly referred to as the **biomedical model,** holds that abnormal thoughts and behaviors are results of abnormal biochemical processes in the brain. According to this model, the effectiveness of psychiatric drugs in changing such symptoms is a function of altering these biochemical processes toward a more normal state.

Not everyone believes wholeheartedly in the biomedical model, and some mental-health professionals have considered alternative points of view. It is possible

---

by the numbers . . .

11 Percentage of noninstitutionalized adults (one in nine) in the United States who have been prescribed a psychotropic medication, in a survey of more than 12,000 individuals conducted in 1999–2002. This percentage is nearly twice the percentage reported in 1988–1994.

283 million Number of prescriptions for psychotropic medications written in the United States in 2006.

8 Percentage of noninstitionalized adults (one in twelve) in the same survey who have been prescribed an antidepressant medication. This percentage is a three-fold increase over 1988–1994.

124 million Number of prescriptions for antidepressant medications written in the United States in 2006.

Sources: Munsey, Christopher (2008, February). At least one in ten Americans are prescribed psychotropics. *Monitor on Psychology,* pp. 52–53. Paulose-Ram, Ryne; Safran, Marc A.; Jonas, Bruce S.; Gu, Qiuping; and Orwig, Denise (2007). Trends in psychotropic medication use among U.S. adults. *Pharmacoepidemiology and Drug Safety, 16,* 560–570.

---

that adverse sociological factors, psychodynamic factors, or behavioral and cognitive factors also play a role in producing abnormal thoughts and behaviors. The fact remains, however, that for many patients the administration of psychiatric drugs is an effective means for treating schizophrenia and mood disorders. Because these drugs are affecting the functioning of neurons in the brain, the inference is inescapable that the improvements observed in such patients are directly related to the biochemical changes that the drugs produce. In other words, from the perspective of developing therapeutic approaches toward these patients, the biomedical model seems to work.

We can also look at the genetic and epidemiological evidence in favor of the biomedical model, particularly in the case of patterns of schizophrenia. For example, the concordance rate for schizophrenia in pairs of identical twins (corresponding to the probability of one twin becoming schizophrenic if the other twin already is) has been estimated to be 46 percent, compared to a concordance rate of 15 percent in pairs of fraternal twins. Given the essentially equivalent environmental

---

psychiatric drugs: Medications used to treat forms of mental illness.

psychotropic medication: An alternative term for psychiatric drugs.

biomedical model: A theoretical position that mental disorders are caused by abnormal biochemical processes in the brain.

---

influences on identical and fraternal twins, the difference in the two concordance rates indicates a strong genetic component. In addition, the incidence of schizophrenia shows a remarkable stability throughout the world, across such widely separated and diverse cultures and societies as those of Swedes, Eskimos, and West African tribal peoples. If a common biological factor were not operating, it is unlikely that we would be seeing such a consistent pattern. Indeed, recent evidence indicates that specific genes predispose individuals to the development of schizophrenia as well as other major psychiatric disorders.[1]

Antipsychotic Drugs and Schizophrenia

Drugs specifically intended to treat schizophrenia are traditionally referred to as **antipsychotic drugs.** Before considering these drugs in detail, however, it is helpful first to take a careful look at the often misunderstood symptoms of schizophrenia itself.

The Symptoms of Schizophrenia

The name **schizophrenia** literally means "split-mind," a term that unfortunately has led to a widespread misconception about how schizophrenic patients typically think and behave. *Schizophrenia patients do not have a split or multiple personality. Such psychiatric conditions exist, but they are referred to as dissociative disorders.* The accurate

A woman with catatonic schizophrenia displays the classic symptoms of immobility and unusual body posture.

way of viewing a schizophrenia patient is in terms of an individual being "split off" or "broken off" from a firm sense of reality. The presence of **delusions** (beliefs not rooted in reality) leading to feelings of persecution or paranoia and the presence of auditory hallucinations, commonly in the form of "voices," often torment the patient on a daily basis.

This is not to say that all schizophrenia patients have delusions or hallucinations. Some may display a significant "split" in the connections that normally exist among the processes of thinking, emotion, and action. The expression of emotion may be dulled or altogether absent; verbal expressions or mannerisms may be entirely inappropriate to a given situation; odd postures may be assumed for long periods of time (a condition called **catatonia**). Given the wide diversity in schizophrenic behaviors, it is possible that we may be dealing with a cluster of disorders collectively known as schizophrenia rather than simply one singular psychiatric condition (Health Line, page 378).

Overall, the prevalence of schizophrenia is approximately 1 percent of the U.S. adult population, representing more than 2 million people; as mentioned earlier, the incidence rate is roughly uniform throughout the world. While schizophrenia affects men and women with equal frequency, the disorder often appears earlier in men, usually in their late teens or early twenties, than in women, who generally begin to show symptoms in their twenties or early thirties.[2]

The Early Days of Antipsychotic Drug Treatment

To appreciate the impact antipsychotic drugs have made on the treatment of schizophrenia, we have to go back to the mid-1950s. Prior to that time, the principal methods of dealing with schizophrenia patients included the heavy administration of barbiturates and neurosurgical interventions such as prefrontal lobotomies. The side effects of these treatments included apathy and a loss of emotional expression. By 1955, the total population of

antipsychotic drugs: Medications used to treat symptoms of schizophrenia.

schizophrenia: A major mental illness, characterized by being "cut off" from a sense of reality. Symptoms of schizophrenia may include hallucinations and delusional thinking.

delusions: Ideas that have no foundation in reality.

catatonia (CAT-ah-TONE-yah): A symptom displayed by some schizophrenic patients, characterized by a rigid, prolonged body posture.

Health Line

Mercury Poisoning: On Being Mad as a Hatter

Everyone knows the Mad Hatter character, the eccentric host of the tea party in Lewis Carroll's *Alice in Wonderland*. What is not widely known is that the expression "mad as a hatter" originates from a commonly observed phenomenon in the nineteenth century. Most hats during this period were made of felt and derived from either beaver or rabbit pelts. To soften and mat the hair, hatmakers used a toxic solution of mercurous nitrate. Without proper ventilation or protection, fumes from this mercury compound would be inhaled and the mercury itself would be absorbed through the fingers.

Over an extended period, mercury levels in the hatmakers would rise in the bloodstream and eventually in the brain. The result was symptoms of drooling, trembling, memory loss, and psychotic behavior. In Danbury, Connecticut, a leading center of hatmaking in the United States, the condition became known as the "Danbury Shakes." Another common source for mercury poisoning in the nineteenth century was a popular patent medicine called *blue mass* (see Drugs . . . in Focus on page 383).

The neurological symptoms resulting from mercury poisoning are commonly observed in a range of modern-day psychiatric conditions, referred to as *occupational organic solvent neurotoxicity*, in which symptoms include fatigue, irritability, depression, anxiety, and dementia. These conditions result from chronic exposure to solvents used in industry in paints, glues, adhesives, and cleaning agents (Chapter 13) and in the production of plastics, textiles, and dyes. Continual updating of safety standards in industry has reduced the incidence of these problems, but in the cases of elderly individuals whose exposure earlier in their lives predated these protections, the adverse effects are still being observed today.

Sources: Ogden, Jenni A. (2005). *Fractured minds: A case-study approach to clinical neuropsychology* (2nd ed.). New York: Oxford University Press, pp. 222–236. The phrase "mad as a hatter." (2008). Edited guide entry, www.bbc.co.uk.

---

hospitalized psychiatric patients in the United States (of which schizophrenia patients represented the majority) had risen to about 560,000, roughly 50 percent of all those hospitalized for *any* reason. The demand for facilities to house psychiatric patients was quickly reaching crisis proportions.[3]

With the introduction of antipsychotic drugs around 1955, the tide turned. For the first time, symptoms of a major mental disorder such as schizophrenia were genuinely alleviated. Many schizophrenia patients could now be successfully treated on an outpatient basis:

> While virtually all symptoms decreased with use of antipsychotics, the decrease in symptoms of confusion and disorganization was the greatest. For example, incoherent speech became coherent. Personal hygiene improved, patients dressed themselves, washed, combed their hair, and used the toilet. Patients who had not spoken or responded to others became responsive to questions and requests. . . . Antipsychotics do not always eliminate delusions and hallucinations, but the drugs usually permit the patient to recognize hallucinations and delusions as such and to know that they are symptoms of disease.[4]

Over the next thirty years, the resident population in U.S. mental hospitals decreased by 80 percent, a result of

two principal factors. The first was the beneficial effect of antipsychotic medications on approximately half the schizophrenia patient population, allowing them to lead relatively normal lives outside a mental hospital (Portrait). The second was a policy of deinstitutionalization, in which psychiatric patients of all types were admitted to mental hospitals only for limited periods of time. The social consequences of deinstitutionalization will be considered later in this chapter.[5]

The Nature of Antipsychotic Drug Treatment

For most schizophrenia patients, antipsychotic drugs are administered orally in daily doses. In a few cases, i.v. or i.m. injections are given when a highly agitated patient has to be subdued quickly. When administered orally, the benefits appear slowly over a period of a few weeks. During the initial days of treatment, patients usually feel sedated, but the degree of sedation generally declines as the antipsychotic effects begin to appear. In general, activity levels tend to become normal, with agitated patients becoming more relaxed and withdrawn patients becoming more sociable. When receiving the proper dosage, patients remain reasonably alert. Because they do not produce euphoria, tolerance, or psychological

PORTRAIT

As a result of the Academy Award–winning 2001 motion picture *A Beautiful Mind*, directed by Ron Howard, the public not only is acquainted with the remarkable life of a mathematical genius, John Forbes Nash, Jr. (portrayed in the film by actor Russell Crowe, above right photo), but also has some insight into the harrowing world of mental illness—specifically, paranoid schizophrenia. The onset and eventual remission of Nash's psychotic symptoms is an inspiring tale of personal courage, both on screen and in real life.

An eminent colleague has called Nash (above left photo) "the most remarkable mathematician of the second half of the century." His creative insights ranged from discoveries in pure mathematics to a formulation of economic game theory (for which he won the Nobel Prize for economics in 1994) that has been applied to everything from interpersonal rivalry and labor negotiations to international diplomacy. Students of mathematical logic and game theory today encounter the concept of the "Nash equilibrium" as one of the major cornerstones in this area of research.

Yet, in the 1950s, Nash's brilliant and rational mind descended into mental disturbance and irrationality. He became increasingly withdrawn from his colleagues and friends. He developed extreme delusional behavior, believing at one point that newspaper articles contained encrypted messages from aliens of another galaxy that only he could decipher, and auditory hallucinations that convinced him that he was the Emperor of Antarctica.

As Nash would express it, "My head is as if a bloated windbag, with Voices which dispute within." These hallucinations (portrayed in visual instead of auditory terms for cinematic effect in the film) and the schizophrenia in general became severe. Nash was treated by psychiatrists during the 1960s with now-obsolete insulin shock therapy and antipsychotic medications that were available at the time, primarily Stelazine. (His treatment came prior to the introduction of second-generation antipsychotic drugs.)

Nash would personally claim that he recovered by the sheer strength of will, but most mental-health professionals disagree. It is difficult to ascertain all the components that make a mentally ill individual well again, but as Sylvia Nasar, author of his biography *A Beautiful Mind*, has pointed out:

> . . . the only periods when he was relatively free of hallucinations, delusions, and the erosion of will were the periods following either insulin treatment or the use of antipsychotics. In other words, rather than reducing Nash to a zombie, medication seemed to have reduced zombielike behavior.

Fortunately, Nash refrained from long-term exposure to these "first-generation" medications, thus avoiding their adverse side effects.

The transformations in the life of John Forbes Nash, Jr., have been remarkable in the extreme. Nasar has called it a story "in three acts: genius, madness, reawakening." This is how she ends her biography:

> When John met Russell Crowe, who plays him in the movie inspired by his life, he told me that his first words to the Australian actor were, "You're going to have to go through all these transformations!" . . . The [factual] transformations in Nash's life have been as remarkable as any that will be portrayed on screen.

Sources: Milnor, John (1998). John Nash and "A Beautiful Mind." *Notices of the American Mathematics Society, 45,* 1329–1332. Nasar, Sylvia (1998). *A beautiful mind: The life of mathematical genius and Nobel laureate John Nash.* New York: Simon and Schuster. Quotations on pp. 12, 22, 328, 353, and 390.

---

dependence, antipsychotic drugs have a low potential for misuse or abuse. They also are quite safe from the risks of accidental overdose because even massive doses do not impair breathing.[6]

To minimize side effects, the customary practice is to administer gradually increasing doses of antipsychotic medication until symptoms appear to moderate. Once the patient is responding well to a particular level of the drug, it is then customary to lower the dose to determine the least amount of drug required to achieve a beneficial effect.[7]

The currently available, FDA-approved antipsychotic medications can be classified in three major "generational" groups (Table 16.1, page 380). We will begin with the first generation of drugs for schizophrenia treatment, which were introduced in the mid-1950s.

First-Generation Antipsychotic Drugs

The earliest medications for schizophrenia included chlorpromazine (brand name: Thorazine), haloperidol (brand name: Haldol), thiothixene (brand name: Navane), thioridazine (brand name: Mellaril), and trifluperazine (brand name: Stelazine). While they have been demonstrated to significantly reduce hallucinatory and delusional behavior that is characteristic of many schizophrenia patients, these agents are less effective in reducing "less active" problems such as social withdrawal, apathy, and disorientation. A number of adverse side effects also arise with their long-term use. In fact, the side effects of first-generation drugs are so predictable (that is, typical) that the medications have frequently been referred to as **typical antipsychotic drugs.**

The adverse side effects of first-generation drugs range from relatively minor inconveniences to severe neurological difficulties. Patients may develop a dry mouth, blurred vision, dizziness, or weight gain. The skin can become oversensitized to the sun so that burning occurs even after a minimum of exposure. More significant reactions, however, include a severe disturbance in movement-control systems in the brain (see Chapter 3). Patients may develop a stiff, shuffling walk, a lack of spontaneity, restlessness, a fixed facial expression, and loss of coordinated movements such as the free swinging of the arms during walking. These problems are called **Parkinson's-like symptoms** because they resemble many of the features of Parkinson's disease. In fact, some types of anti-Parkinson's medication, such as trihexyphenidyl (brand name: Artane), benztropine (brand name: Cogentin), and procyclidine (brand name: Kemadrin), are frequently given along with antipsychotic drugs to reduce the incidence of these particular side effects. Strangely, administration of the original drug developed to relieve Parkinson's disease symptoms, L-Dopa, makes matters worse rather than better.[8]

A related side effect associated with first-generation antipsychotic drugs is a condition called **tardive dyskinesia,** a neurological syndrome that may appear after two or more years of continual drug treatment. Tardive dyskinesia, which literally means "a movement disorder arriving late," consists of jerky, tic-like movements of the lips, tongue, jaw, and face. Patients may smack their lips or flick their tongues in and out as frequently as twenty times in thirty seconds; their walking may become progressively unsteady, or they may rock back and forth while seated. It has been estimated that the likelihood of developing tardive dyskinesia as a result of long-term

typical antipsychotic drugs: A majority of available antipsychotic medications, all of which are associated with the possibility of Parkinson's-like side effects.

Parkinson's-like symptoms: Side effects of typical antipsychotic drugs, involving a fixed facial expression and difficulty walking.

tardive dyskinesia (TAR-div DIS-keh-NEEZ-ee-ah): A serious side effect affecting approximately 15 percent of schizophrenic patients who have undergone chronic treatment with first-generation (typical) antipsychotic drugs.

TABLE 16.1

Currently available, FDA-approved antipsychotic medications

GENERIC NAME	BRAND NAME*	RANGE OF DAILY ORAL DOSAGE (in milligrams)
First-generation drugs (typical antipsychotic drugs)		
chlorpromazine	Thorazine	100–500[†]
fluphenazine	Prolixin	5–20[†]
haloperidol	Haldol	1–12[†]
mesoridazine	Serentil	100–300[†]
perphenazine	Trifalon, Etrafon[‡]	12–24[†]
pimozine	Orap	1–2
prochlorperazine	Compazine	50–150[†]
thioridazine	Mellaril	150–600
thiothixene	Navane	10–30[†]
trifluoperazine	Stelazine	10–30[†]
Second-generation drugs (atypical antipsychotic drugs)		
clozapine	Clozaril	300–900
loxapine	Loxitane	20–60[†]
molindone	Moban	100–225
olanazapine	Zyprexa	10
paliperidine	Invega	Extended release
quetiapine	Seroquel	50–400
risperidone	Risperdal	1–3
ziprasidone	Geodon	20–160[†]
Third-generation drugs (newer atypical antipsychotic drugs)		
aripiprazole	Abilify	10–30

*Many of these medications, particularly those in the first-generation category, have been off-patent for many years and are prescribed in generic form, though they are often still referred to by their original brand names.

[†]Also available in injectable forms.

[‡]Etrafon is a combination of perphenazine and amitriptyline (an antidepressant).

Source: U.S. Food and Drug Administration, Washington DC.

treatment with first-generation antipsychotic drugs is about 15 to 20 percent. Women and elderly patients show a higher incidence than men and younger patients in general.[9]

Second-Generation Antipsychotic Drugs

A second generation of antipsychotic drugs, developed in the 1980s, has allowed for more complete treatment of schizophrenic symptoms without the potential for Parkinson's-like side effects. Because this particular problem is minimized or absent altogether, these medications are often referred to as **atypical antipsychotic drugs.**

Second-generation antipsychotic drugs have, in general, outperformed first-generation drugs in treating a wider spectrum of schizophrenic symptoms without inducing undesirable movement difficulties, but they are not without adverse side effects of their own. For example, clozapine (brand name: Clozaril) is effective in treating many schizophrenia patients who have not been helped by chlorpromazine, haloperidol, or other drugs in that category. Parkinson's-like symptoms and tardive dyskinesia are rare. However, a unique feature of Clozaril is the 1 to 2 percent chance of developing a potentially lethal blood disease called **agranulocytosis,** a condition involving the loss of white blood cells and a decline in the immune system as a result. If early signs of agranulocytosis are detected, Clozaril can be withdrawn and the patient will recover. As a safeguard, Clozaril-treated patients must undergo regular blood tests for the entire time they are under treatment. The need for blood testing has made Clozaril treatment far more expensive than traditional treatment with first-generation antipsychotic drugs.

More recently developed second-generation drugs share Clozaril's wide spectrum of effectiveness in treating schizophrenia as well as its very low incidence of Parkinson's-like symptoms and tardive dyskinesia. They include olanzapine (brand name: Zyprexa), risperidone (brand name: Risperdal), quetiapine (brand name: Seroquel), and ziprasidone (brand name: Geodon). Fortunately, none of these drugs is linked to agranulocytosis, so there is no need for frequent blood tests.

However, patients taking Zyprexa, Risperdal, and related antipsychotic medications experience considerable weight gain. In addition, there is an increased risk of hyperglycemia (high blood sugar) and the development of diabetes. The FDA now issues a strong warning that Zyprexa, Risperdal, and related drugs should not be administered to treat psychotic symptoms related to dementia among elderly individuals, as these medications nearly double the risk of death due to heart-related problems or respiratory infections such as pneumonia. In light of these problems, the question remains whether the new medications are more advantageous in the treatment of schizophrenia than older medications such as Thorazine and Haldol.[10]

Third-Generation Antipsychotic Drugs

The newest atypical antipsychotic drugs, referred to as third-generation medications for schizophrenia, are currently arriving on the scene. Aripiprasole (brand name: Abilify), available since 2002, has been shown to be an effective treatment for schizophrenia, without the risk of Parkinson's side effects, tardive dyskinesia, agranulocytosis, weight gain, or diabetes. Due to the absence of the undesirable side effects, the discontinuance rate (that is, the percentage of patients who no longer wish to take the drug) is only approximately 9 percent, a very low level when compared to the discontinuance rate for antipsychotic drugs in general. As we will see shortly, Abilify is categorized as a third-generation antipsychotic drug on the basis of its unique mechanism of action in the brain.[11]

Effects of Antipsychotic Drugs on the Brain

When the first antipsychotic drugs were introduced in the 1950s, the question of how they worked at a neuronal level in the brain was a total mystery. In those days, drugs were "discovered" quite accidentally. Chlorpromazine, for example, was first administered as a treatment for severe vomiting (which remains one of its applications today) and as a sedative for presurgical patients. Only later was it recognized as having beneficial effects on certain schizophrenic symptoms.

As haphazard as the development of psychiatric drugs was at that time, a common thread frequently connected them, suggesting that a common mechanism might be responsible for their actions. In the case of antipsychotic drugs, there was an unmistakable connection between the improvement in schizophrenic symptoms and the often observed signs of Parkinson's-like motor problems. Could this connection provide a clue as to the underlying biochemistry of schizophrenia?

By 1963, the biochemical nature of Parkinson's disease was beginning to be understood. Essentially, its symptoms were found to be a result of a deficiency in

atypical antipsychotic drugs: Antipsychotic medications that, unlike earlier medications used for treating schizophrenia, do not produce Parkinson's-like side effects. Clozaril, Risperdal, Zyprexa, Geodon, and Abilify are examples.

agranulocytosis (A-GRAN-yoo-loh-sigh-TOH-sis): A potentially lethal blood disorder associated with the antipsychotic drug clozapine (brand name: Clozaril).

dopamine-releasing neurons in an area of the midbrain called the substantia nigra (see Chapter 3).[12] One result was the development of new treatment drugs that helped Parkinson's patients by boosting the activity of dopamine systems in the brain.

The second result was an insight into the mechanism behind antipsychotic drugs. The reasoning was that if Parkinson's-like symptoms were appearing when patients' schizophrenic symptoms were improving and if Parkinson's disease was due to a dopamine deficiency, then perhaps the antipsychotic drugs were actually reducing the activity level of dopamine in the brain. By implication, schizophrenia would be tied to an excessively high level of dopamine activity, and treating it would be a matter of bringing that level down.

Evidence for a dopamine involvement in schizophrenia comes from a variety of sources. You would predict that an overdose of L-Dopa, an anti-Parkinson's drug that elevates the activity of dopamine systems in the brain, would produce schizophrenic-like behavior, and it does. Parkinson's patients need to be careful about the dose levels of their medication to avoid displaying signs of disorientation, disturbed thinking, paranoia, or catatonia. Another prediction is that the mechanism behind the action of antipsychotic drugs would be specifically associated with a decline in dopamine activity. It turns out that all the typical antipsychotic drugs block the stimulation of dopamine-sensitive receptor sites. In fact, the drugs that are most effective in blocking dopamine are the very same drugs that are most effective in treating schizophrenia. Likewise, drugs that are relatively weak blockers of dopamine are relatively ineffective in treatment.

Other evidence, however, points to the possibility that the dopamine connection might be only a first step toward understanding schizophrenia. Researchers know that dopamine-sensitive receptors in the brain can be broken down into subtypes, and in some cases subtypes within subtypes. At least six major subtypes of dopamine receptors (called D_1 through D_6) have been identified so far.

Understanding distinctions within neurotransmitter receptors has provided some insight into the effectiveness of various drugs as well as side effects that might or might not occur. For example, first-generation (typical) antipsychotic drugs block D_2 receptors to varying degrees. The incidence of Parkinson's-like side effects and tardive dyskinesia is considered to be linked to the reduction in D_2 receptor activity, without the protection that might be provided by changes in other neurotransmitters.

Second-generation (atypical) antipsychotic drugs operate in a somewhat different way. Clozaril, for example, blocks D_4 receptors to a greater extent than it inhibits D_2 receptors, which helps to explain why motor difficulties do not arise, but there is a linkage to an increased risk of agranulocytosis. Geodon, Risperdal, and Zyprexa block D_2 receptors but evidently the Parkinson's-like side effects and tardive dyskinesia are avoided because these drugs also block a special subtype of serotonin receptor.

Third-generation (also atypical) antipsychotic drugs are unique in that D_2 receptors are not necessarily blocked as with other medications, but rather are modulated. Abilify increases the functioning of D_2 receptors when the neural pathways are hypodopaminergic (that is, when dopamine activity is too low) and decreases it when neural pathways are hyperdopaminergic (that is, when dopamine activity is too high). In other words, Abilify stabilizes the activity at this subtype of dopamine receptors. The additional feature of blocking certain serotonin receptors (the same ones that are involved in second-generation drugs) appears to be helpful in avoiding Parkinson's-like side effects and tardive dyskinesia.[13]

Drugs Used to Treat Depression

Severe and debilitating depression, usually referred to as major depression, is the most common form of mood disorder. It has been estimated that one in six Americans will be severely depressed at some time in their lives and one in sixteen will be severely depressed in any given year. The disorder strikes both young people and adults, both rich and poor. Not surprisingly, a large number of famous men and women in history—from the Roman emperor Tiberius and Queen Victoria to Peter Tchaikovsky, Fyodor Dostoevski, Abraham Lincoln, and Sigmund Freud—suffered depressive symptoms (Drugs...in Focus).

Major depression is an emotional state far beyond ordinary feelings of sadness, grief, or remorse. Many depressed individuals have turned to alcohol for relief. As we know, however, the depressant action of alcohol on the nervous system not only makes matters worse but also sets the stage for alcohol dependence and alcoholism (see Chapter 10).

A more immediate concern, obviously, is the risk of suicide. Although not all people who either attempt or actually commit suicide are depressed, the inclination toward depression increases the risk substantially. On the one hand, only about 15 percent of depressed people are suicidal; on the other, most suicide-prone people are or have been depressed. Ironically, the likelihood of a suicide attempt is increased in the initial phase of an upswing in mood after a deep period of depression. When the depression is at its most intense, the depressed individual has little energy to carry out suicidal feelings and thoughts.[14]

Drugs...in Focus

Abraham Lincoln, Depression, and Those "Little Blue Pills"

It is well known to historians that Abraham Lincoln suffered from long bouts of melancholy, a condition that would today be diagnosed as major depression. He suffered two major depressive episodes early in his life, in 1835 and 1841. What is less known is that Lincoln had been advised by his physician in the late 1850s to take what he called his "little blue pills" to help him raise his mood. A few months into his presidency, in 1861, however, Lincoln stopped taking these pills, complaining that they made him "cross." During the late 1850s, Lincoln had experienced episodes of bizarre behavior that included towering rages and mood changes that appeared out of nowhere or were responses to innocuous and sometime trivial circumstances. It is reasonable to assume that the symptoms were, as Lincoln himself surmised, due to the "little blue pills."

It is a good thing that Lincoln made this decision. The medication he was taking was a common nineteenth-century remedy for depression called *blue mass*. It consisted of licorice root, rosewater, honey, sugar, and rose petals. But the main ingredient in these blue-colored pills, about the size of peppercorns, was approximately 750 micrograms of mercury, a highly toxic substance. At the common dosage level of two or three pills per day, individuals ingested nearly nine thousand times the amount of mercury that is considered safe by current health standards.

If Lincoln had continued to take blue mass for his depression, he undoubtedly would have continued to experience the behavioral and neurological symptoms common to chronic mercury poisoning (see Health Line on page 378) as he led the nation during the Civil War. Fortunately, the symptoms of mercury poisoning in Lincoln's case were reversible after he stopped taking blue mass. Lincoln would suffer from severe bouts of depression until his death in 1865, but America was spared what might have been a catastrophe of historic proportions.

Source: Hirschhorn, Norbert, Feldman, Robert G., and Greaves, Ian (2001, Summer). Abraham Lincoln's blue pills: Did the 16th president suffer from mercury poisoning? *Perspectives in Biology and Medicine,* pp. 315–322. Shenk, Joshua W. (2005). *Lincoln's melancholy: How depression challenged a president and fueled his greatness.* New York: Houghton Mifflin.

Drugs used to treat major depression are referred to as **antidepressants**. As with the antipsychotic drugs discussed earlier, these medications can be classified in terms of three generations of drug development.

First-Generation Antidepressant Drugs

Like the earliest antipsychotic medications, the first-generation antidepressants were discovered accidentally, with their applications frequently having little to do with psychological disorders. One early antidepressant was originally intended for the treatment of tuberculosis. It was soon recognized that the improvement in the patient's spirits was not merely a matter of reduced symptoms of this disease. When depressed but otherwise healthy individuals were given the drug, a significant improvement in mood was observed. Eventually, it was discovered that other chemically similar drugs were also effective antidepressants. The key factor connecting them all was their ability to inhibit the enzyme **monoamine oxidase (MAO)**—hence their classification as **MAO inhibitors**. Two MAO inhibitors are currently marketed for the treatment of depression: phenelzine (brand name: Nardil) and tranylcypromine (brand name: Parnate).

Despite their benefits in the treatment of depression, MAO inhibitors are safely administered only to patients whose dietary habits can be carefully supervised or who can be relied on to observe certain specific dietary restrictions. The problem is that MAO inhibitors inhibit MAO not only in the brain but elsewhere in the body as well. In the liver, MAO serves a useful function in breaking down

antidepressants: Drugs prescribed and used for the treatment of depression.

monoamine oxidase (MAO) (MON-oh-AY-meen OX-ih-dace): An enzyme that breaks down dopamine, norepinephrine, or serotonin at their respective synapses in the brain.

MAO inhibitors: A class of first-generation antidepressants that reduce the effects of monoamine oxidase (MAO) in the brain.

a chemical called *tyramine*. Too high a level of tyramine produces a highly toxic reaction by elevating the blood pressure and increasing the chances of a stroke. Therefore, although MAO inhibitors are useful at the level of the brain, they remove the individual's natural safety barrier against the harmful effects of excessive tyramine. Ordinarily, this action would not be a problem, except for the fact that tyramine is contained in many foods and drinks.

Because any food product or drink that involves fermentation or aging in its processing contains high levels of tyramine, combining one with an MAO inhibitor can be highly dangerous. Therefore, any such food or drink must be avoided by patients on MAO-inhibitor antidepressants. MAO inhibitors continue to be an option in the treatment of depression, but the difficulty in maintaining this kind of restricted diet for long periods of time has until recently been a major problem for many patients.[15]

Another set of first-generation antidepressants all have a three-ring portion in their molecular structure. They are referred to as **tricyclic antidepressants** for this reason. The most prominent examples are amitriptyline (brand name: Elavil), nortriptyline (brand name: Parmelor), desipramine (brand name: Norpramin), and imipramine (brand name: Tofranil). Because tricyclic drugs do not operate specifically on MAO, the problems inherent in a potentially high level of tyramine are not an issue and dietary restrictions are unnecessary. As a result, depressed patients being treated on an outpatient basis can be given these types of antidepressants more safely. Those patients with cardiovascular problems, however, need to be monitored regularly because high doses of tricyclic drugs can produce an irregular or elevated heart rate. Some patients with cardiovascular disease cannot be treated with tricyclic drugs at all.

Second-Generation Antidepressant Drugs

A second generation of antidepressants became available in the late 1980s that bore no chemical similarity to either MAO inhibitors or tricyclic drugs. These antidepressants are referred to as **selective serotonin reuptake inhibitors**

(SSRIs), owing to the fact that the reuptake of serotonin from its receptors at the synapse is slowed down. The net effect is to prolong the action of serotonin at receptors that are sensitive to it. SSRI antidepressants include citalopram (brand name: Celexa), escitalopram (brand name: Lexapro), fluoxetine (brand name: Prozac), paroxetine (brand name: Paxil), and sertraline (brand name: Zoloft). Prozac was the first SSRI to become available and, as a result, it has attracted the most attention.

By all accounts, Prozac (along with other second-generation antidepressants) has been viewed as a genuine breakthrough in the treatment of major depression. Introduced in 1987, it has quickly become the number one antidepressant medication on the strength of its effectiveness in reducing depressive symptoms with comparatively few side effects. In particular, Prozac is safe for cardiovascular patients who would have difficulty with tricyclic medications, and many patients whose feelings of depression have not been reduced by other antidepressants respond well to Prozac.[16]

Unfortunately, Prozac has significant adverse side effects, as do all SSRIs to varying degrees. Some patients report agitation and a feeling of nausea, as well as sexual dysfunction. There is an increased risk of seizures, though this side effect can be controlled either by lowering the dose or by combining the drug with antiseizure medication. Another source of concern is the tendency for Prozac and other SSRIs to be overprescribed, not only as a treatment for major depression but also for milder episodes of depression and related ailments that might have been better treated by traditional psychotherapy or counseling (Health Alert).

Long-term effects are unknown. A potential problem is that Prozac and other SSRIs may simply be too good; patients may be reluctant to withdraw from it because they fear the return of depressive feelings. The potential for this form of psychological dependence remains an important concern with Prozac as well as other psychiatric drugs. There is, however, no evidence for tolerance or physical withdrawal symptoms with Prozac or other SSRIs.[17]

Third-Generation Antidepressant Drugs

The newest generation of antidepressants include duloxetine (brand name: Cymbalta), mirtazepine (brand name: Remeron), venlafaxine (brand name: Effexor), and desvenlafaxine (Pristiq). Like SSRIs, these medications act upon serotonin in the brain but not exclusively so. As we will see in the next section, third-generation antidepressants affect the activity level of norepinephrine as well as serotonin. For this reason, these medications

---

tricyclic antidepressants: A class of first-generation antidepressant drugs. Brand names include Elavil, Norpramin, and Tofranil.

selective serotonin reuptake inhibitors (SSRIs): A group of antidepressants that slow down the reuptake of serotonin at synapses in the brain. Prozac, Celexa, Lexapro, Paxil, and Zoloft are prominent examples.

SSRI Antidepressants and Elevated Risk of Suicide among Children and Adolescents

In September 2004, a federal advisory committee recommended to the FDA that "black box" warnings be issued to physicians, indicating that SSRI antidepressants may cause some children and adolescents to become suicidal and may indeed not be effective in reducing depressive symptoms. Such warnings on standard drug references and information sheets are printed in boldface type with a black border around it and positioned at the top of the warning label of these drugs. Although the incidence of suicide is roughly twice as high as when a placebo is administered, the overall risk of taking SSRIs is low. The likelihood of suicide would be 2 or 3 percent higher among patients taking SSRIs than those taking a placebo. Considering the increased practice of prescribing antidepressant medication to this age group in recent years, the precaution has been deemed necessary. Physicians are still permitted to prescribe these drugs but have to be careful in doing so.

Concerns that SSRI antidepressants might cause a small number of patients to develop suicidal thoughts have been raised since the early introduction of Prozac in the late 1980s. In 1991, the question seemed to be settled when an FDA panel concluded that there was no convincing evidence linking increased suicide risk to Prozac itself. Nonetheless, later studies reawakened the controversy, particularly with respect to a young population and the wider availability of different forms of SSRI medications. The FDA issued a second warning in July 2005 that physicians prescribing SSRI antidepressants should carefully monitor their depressed patients of all ages at early stages of SSRI treatment or when dosage levels are adjusted upward or downward.

Where to go for assistance:

http://www.fda.gov/CDER/Drug/antidepressants/default.htm

This web site is sponsored by the U.S. Food and Drug Administration (FDA) and is specifically designed to address potential adverse effects of SSRI antidepressants in adolescent patients.

Sources: Carey, Benedict, and Harris, Gardiner (2006, May 12). Antidepressants may raise young adult suicide risk. *New York Times*, p. A26. Grady, Denise, and Harris, Gardiner (2004, March 24). Overprescribing prompted warning on antidepressants. *New York Times*, p. A13. Harris, Gardiner (2004, September 15). F.D.A. panel urges stronger warning on antidepressants. *New York Times*, pp. A1, A19.

---

are referred to as **serotonin-norepinephrine reuptake inhibitors (SNRIs)**.

Effects of Antidepressant Drugs on the Brain

When MAO inhibitors were discovered to be effective in reducing symptoms of depression, theories concerning the mechanism behind the action of these drugs turned to the properties of MAO itself. As enzymes, MAO molecules were known to inactivate dopamine, norepinephrine, and serotonin (collectively referred to as monoamines) at the synapses where these neurotransmitters operate. We can think of a drug as producing a double-negative effect on these neurotransmitters. By inhibiting MAO, we are inhibiting an inhibitor, and the net result will be a rise in the activity level of dopamine, norepinephrine, or serotonin. If so, then it would be logical to theorize that depression is associated with a lower-than-normal level of any one of these neurotransmitters or some combination of the three.

With the discovery of tricyclic antidepressants, it has been possible to focus on a more specific biochemical theory. Unlike MAO inhibitors, tricyclic drugs do not act on enzymes in the synapse. Instead, they slow down the reuptake of norepinephrine and serotonin at their respective synapses. Since the reuptake process allows neurotransmitter molecules to be reabsorbed from the receptor sites back to the neuron that released them in the first place (see Chapter 3), a slowing down means that these neurotransmitter molecules now remain in the receptor site for a longer period of time. When the neurotransmitter stays in the receptors longer, the receptors are stimulated more intensely. In other words, the effect of tricyclic drugs is to increase the activity level of norepinephrine and serotonin. Following the line of reasoning presented earlier, depression would be associated with a lower-than-normal level of activity with respect to these neurotransmitters.

serotonin-norepinephrine reuptake inhibitors (SNRIs): A group of antidepressants that slow down the reuptake of serotonin and norepinephrine at synapses in the brain. Remeron, Cymbalta, and Effexor are prominent examples.

Prozac was unique in that it was not "discovered" as much as it was designed with a specific purpose in mind. The intent was to identify a chemical that slowed down the reuptake of serotonin alone, hence its eventual designation as a selective serotonin reuptake inhibitor (SSRI). Since its introduction, Prozac has been joined by other SSRIs that share this pharmacological feature. On a theoretical level, the successful development of Prozac and other SSRIs as effective antidepressants has provided strong evidence for the involvement of serotonin in providing the optimal level of mood in a person's life.

This fact does not necessarily mean, however, that serotonin is the exclusive neurotransmitter system in the regulation of mood. As noted earlier, a sizable proportion of depressive patients benefit from the administration of drugs such as tricyclic drugs, implying that a norepinephrine system is involved as well. Third-generation antidepressants, such as Effexor, Pristiq, and Remeron, are desirable for some patients because they affect both neurotransmitters. Effexor and Pristiq, for example, slow the reuptake of both norepinephrine and serotonin. In this respect, Effexor and Pristiq resemble tricyclic antidepressants, but their chemical structure and effects on other neurotransmitters are different. As a result, treatment with Effexor and Pristiq make it possible to avoid the adverse side effects associated with tricyclic medications. In the case of Remeron, greater amounts of norepinephrine and serotonin are allowed to be released at their respective synapses. At the same time, only certain subtypes of serotonin receptors are involved.[18]

The Effectiveness of Specific Antidepressant Drugs

Approximately 65 percent of patients taking any antidepressant drug will show significant improvement in their mood, compared to about 35 percent who will feel improvement with a placebo. This finding is sufficient to warrant the use of antidepressants in general, but the question remains as to which antidepressant is best. Comparative studies of various antidepressants indicate that roughly the same percentage of patients show improvements, no matter which antidepressant is used. However, substantial

---

mania: A mood disorder characterized by agitation, bursts of energy, and impulsiveness.

bipolar disorder: A mood disorder in which the patient swings back and forth between feelings of depression and mania.

lithium (LITH-ee-um) carbonate: A psychiatric drug used in the treatment of mania or bipolar disorder.

---

individual differences in responsiveness have been noted. As expressed in the *Harvard Mental Health Letter* in 2000,

> *If 100 depressed patients are given the tricyclic, imipramine [Tofranil], 65 are likely to get significant relief. If the same patients are given an SSRI, 65 will also respond, but not the same 65. Moreover, the effect will range from no benefit at all to total recovery.*[19]

It may be the case that depression is expressed in different neurochemical ways in different people. The key to future success in treating depression in the most effective way will be to find a way of determining, ahead of time, which patients are likely to respond to which neurochemical manipulation and, in turn, to which medication. One group of patients might respond best to a higher level of norepinephrine activity; another group might respond to a higher level of serotonin activity; and a third group might respond to a higher level of serotonin activity but only at specific subtypes of serotonin receptors.

Drugs for Other Types of Mental Disorders

In addition to drugs designated specifically for the treatment of schizophrenia and depression, there exists a range of psychotropic drugs that are useful in dealing with other mental disorders. Two examples are described here.

Mania and Bipolar Disorder

A mood disorder can encompass forms other than simple depression. Some individuals may display symptoms of **mania** that are as disruptive to themselves and their families as depression. Symptoms of mania include sleeplessness, impulsiveness (a manic patient with a credit card is a dangerous combination), irritability, and feelings of grandeur. Others may display mood swings back and forth between depression and mania (a condition referred to as **bipolar disorder,** formerly known as manic-depression). Until recently, the primary psychiatric drug for the treatment of either mania or bipolar disorder has been **lithium carbonate.** Unfortunately, lithium carbonate is effective for only 50 percent of patients showing these symptoms, and those who respond well to it must undergo periodic blood testing to avoid potential toxic effects to the thyroid gland and kidneys.[20]

The drug valproate (brand name: Depakote) has now been found to help patients suffering from either mania or bipolar disorder, as an alternative to lithium carbonate. Recently, it has been found also to be useful in conjunction with antipsychotic medication when

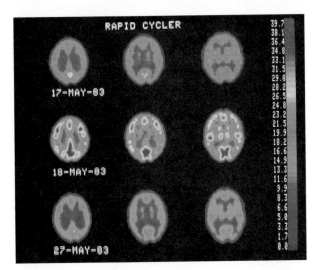

These PET scans show significant differences in the neural activity (yellow and red areas being the highest) of a bipolar disorder patient during times of alternating depression (top and bottom rows) and hypomania, a mild form of mania (middle row). Similar scans have identified differences in neural activity between normal and schizophrenic individuals.

psychotic symptoms are accompanied by an instability of mood. Valproate was originally introduced for the treatment of epilepsy, for which it continues to be prescribed. The mechanism by which it is effective in the treatment of a variety of psychiatric disorders is unclear.[21]

Since 2005, a number of second-generation antipsychotic medications have been FDA-approved for the treatment of bipolar disorder. These medications include Risperdal, Geodon, Seroquel, and a combination of Zyprexa with Prozac (brand name: Symbyax). However, they presently carry a "black box" warning (see Chapter 14) that they should not be administered to elderly patients with dementia, on the basis of evidence showing an elevated risk of death from cardiovascular disease or infections such as pneumonia.[22]

Autism

Autism is a complex developmental disability that typically appears during the first three years of life and impairs the social connectedness that a person shares with others. In some cases, behavioral problems among autistic individuals include aggressiveness, severe temper tantrums, and self-injury. In 2006, the FDA approved Risperdal as a treatment for these behavioral problems in autistic children and adolescents. There are indications that Abilify might be helpful in controlling aggressive behavior in this population as well, although FDA approval for this purpose has not yet been secured.[23]

Off-Label Usage of Psychotropic Medications

Increasingly, psychotropic medications have been used for purposes other than those specified by the FDA when they were first approved. This practice, referred to as **off-label usage,** is common not only for psychotropic medications but for prescription drugs in general. By law, physicians are given considerable latitude to prescribe drugs for their patients that they consider appropriate for a specific set of symptoms, even if there is no official sanction for that particular application.[24]

autism: A form of developmental disability, typically appearing during the first three years of life, that affects the normal development of the brain in areas of social communication and communication skills. Autistic children and adults have difficulties in verbal and nonverbal communication and emotional responses.

off-label usage: The practice of prescribing the use of a particular medication, even if the drug in question has not been FDA-approved for that purpose.

In circumstances of mental-health treatment, some antidepressants may be useful in the treatment of anxiety and some antianxiety medications may be useful in the treatment of depression. In some instances, official changes are made by the FDA to widen the possible applications from those originally designated when the drug was introduced. In general, this kind of "cross-over" pharmacotherapy is on the rise and is part of the challenge we face in our attempt to understand biochemical bases for normal as well as abnormal behavior.[25]

St. John's Wort: An Herbal Alternative for Treating Depression

It is believed that ancient Greeks used an extract from a yellow-flowered plant, now known as **St. John's wort** (*Hypericum performatum*), to drive away evil spirits and banish sadness. Since the early 1980s, St. John's wort has been a popular remedy in Europe for depression. A 1994 study tracking the herb's effect in more than three thousand depressed patients found that 80 percent either reported feeling less depressed than before or completely recovered. *Hypericum* extract is known to inhibit serotonin and norepinephrine uptake, consistent with its antidepressant action.

In randomized controlled trials of St. John's wort, however, consensus has emerged that it is not more effective than placebo for moderate to severe depression. In studies involving mild to moderate depressive symptoms, however, St. John's wort appears to be helpful, relative to a placebo. Nevertheless, even for this population, no convincing evidence exists that the herb is superior to SSRI antidepressants or other medications available for depression.

Fortunately, adverse side effects of St. John's wort are relatively few. Mild gastrointestinal symptoms, fatigue, and sensitivity to light appear to be the major adverse reactions, though there can be significant adverse interactions with other medications that a person is taking (Health Alert). Experts in the field of herbal medicine caution that depressed patients should

St. John's wort: A dietary supplement, derived from an herbal extract, that has potential as a treatment for mild to moderate depressive symptoms.

deinstitutionalization: The social policy of encouraging mentally ill individuals to be treated in community-based programs rather than in large mental hospitals.

consult with a physician before switching to St. John's wort from an existing prescription antidepressant or self-medicating themselves in the first place.

Because it is derived from a natural herb, St. John's wort is available commercially in the United States without restriction, as a dietary supplement. Consequently, there is a lack of standardization in St. John's wort products. Until recently, the herbal compound *hypericin* was considered to be the active ingredient in St. John's wort for depression, and supplement products have pegged their potency claims to its content. Now the focus has shifted to another compound, *hyperforin*, as the active ingredient. Whether this revision will make a difference in the rigorous assessments of St. John's wort for the treatment of depression remains to be seen.[26]

Psychiatric Drugs, Social Policy, and Deinstitutionalization

Prior to the 1960s, the dominant approach to treating severely impaired psychiatric patients was institutionalization in large state-supported mental hospitals. In such places, the treatment of choice, medication, could be controlled by psychiatrists and hospital staff. During the 1960s, the policy toward treating the mentally ill started to change. A 1960 U.S. Supreme Court decision, later to form the basis for the mental-health policy known as the "least restrictive alternative," established that involuntary admission to psychiatric hospitals was permitted only if there were no other feasible means of treatment that would allow more freedom to patients. As a result, responsibility for treatment largely shifted from centralized institutions to decentralized community mental-health clinics. Patient advocates argued that these smaller centers could provide a more humane setting for psychiatric treatment. The process of **deinstitutionalization** was greatly accelerated by the expansion of federal Medicaid and Medicare programs, enabling thousands of patients to sustain themselves financially in the community.

Today, the concept of deinstitutionalization is the subject of considerable ambivalence. When large numbers of institutionalized patients were released, theories about psychiatric rehabilitation were largely untested and not enough planning was conducted to anticipate and meet the needs of people with serious mental illnesses in the community at large. Community mental-health centers failed to live up to their promise to provide comprehensive mental-health care, particularly for the patients with substance-abuse problems. The large numbers of

HEALTH ALERT!

The Risks of Interactions between St. John's Wort and Prescription Drugs

While the direct side effects of St. John's wort are relatively mild, there is increasing concern about its interacting effects with certain prescription drugs. The herbal antidepressant reduces blood levels of indinavir (brand name: Crixivan), a major drug used in HIV treatment. Other evidence indicates that St. John's wort reduces levels of digoxin (brand name: Lanoxin), used for treating congestive heart failure; bronchodilator drugs for treating asthma; carbamazepine (brand name: Tegretol), used for treating epilepsy; and warfarin (brand name: Coumadin), used as a blood thinner. These herbal supplement/drug interactions are potentially dangerous, since the benefits of major life-saving drugs may be reduced as a result. You may recall that another herbal supplement, ginkgo biloba, has the opposite effect on blood-thinning medications, increasing their effects rather than decreasing them. The additive interaction on blood-thinning medications is also shared by some OTC analgesic products (see Chapter 14).

Unfortunately, many people do not think taking an herbal supplement is important information they should tell their physician when being prescribed medication. Recently, the FDA has disallowed dietary supplements from being promoted for common pregnancy-related conditions like morning sickness and leg swelling, pending new studies regarding their safety.

There is concern over the increase in dietary supplements being taken by the elderly. Two specific supplements, ginkgo biloba and St. John's wort, are currently marketed as aids in reducing memory loss and depression, respectively. The elderly are particularly drawn to these products as possible remedies, in part as a convenience to them and as a response to the increasing costs of prescription medication. Since individuals in this population typically take a sizable number of medicines for their particular medical conditions, the probability of an adverse interaction is increased.

Where to go for assistance:

http://nccam.nih.gov/health/stjohnswort/
sjwataglance.htm

This web site is sponsored by the National Center for Complementary and Alternative Medicine, a service of the National Institutes of Health, Bethesda, MD. It covers questions regarding the use of St. John's wort in treating depression.

Sources: Henney, Jane E. (2000). Risk of drug interactions with St. John's wort. *Journal of the American Medical Association, 283,* 1679. Lantz, Melinda S., Buchalter, Eric, and Giambanco, Vincent (1999). St. John's wort and antidepressant drug interactions in the elderly. *Journal of Geriatric Psychiatry and Neurology, 12,* 7–10. Stolberg, Sheryl G. (2000, February 10). FDA bars marketing of supplements to pregnant women. *New York Times,* p. A28.

---

homeless young adults, displaying obvious signs of disorientation and distress, received considerable media attention.

Where has the policy of deinstitutionalization left psychiatric patients? With court decisions upholding the illegality of involuntary commitment (requiring a patient to be hospitalized against his or her will) for more than a limited period of time unless there is a clear danger to society, many patients have ended up drifting in and out of mental-health facilities, no longer supervised carefully enough to take their medication regularly or attend to their personal needs. Estimates are that between one-third and one-half of all homeless adults have been diagnosed with a severe mental disorder. It has been said that, at its worst, deinstitutionalization moved some psychiatric patients from the back wards of mental hospitals to the back alleys of our slums. In addition, more than 250,000 patients with severe mental illness are in jails or prisons, where psychiatric treatment is often unavailable to them. More than 400,000 elderly individuals in nursing homes suffer from some form of severe mental illness, and these facilities are so hard-pressed in dealing with their physical needs that mental-health treatment is often poor or nonexistent (Drugs . . . in Focus).

Nonetheless, despite the very real problems, it can be argued that most mentally ill patients lead better lives now than their counterparts in the days of institutionalized care. About two-thirds of these people who are provided with a comprehensive range of services, including social support, can live outside of mental hospitals. Patients themselves overwhelmingly prefer living in the community than in a mental hospital. The challenges that lie ahead involve addressing more effectively the needs of those patients who are "falling through the cracks" in the system. It is unlikely that anyone will be advocating a return to the era of massive institutionalized care.[27]

Drugs...in Focus

Psychiatric Drugs and the Civil Liberties Debate

Let's imagine that you are a hospitalized psychiatric patient, either voluntarily or involuntarily committed to a mental-health facility on the basis of a diagnosis of schizophrenia. You are handed your daily medication that has been prescribed by a staff psychiatrist. There has been a careful diagnosis of your mental illness and a determination that the medication is appropriate and effective in reducing your symptoms. Can you refuse to take it? Do you even have to give a reason for your refusal? If you are asked to participate in a study in which a new experimental drug is being tested against a placebo, should you be required to do so? If you signed an informed consent form, are you mentally competent to know what you are agreeing to do? If you state that you are mentally competent but have been diagnosed as a schizophrenic, would your self-assessment be considered valid?

These are a few of the difficult questions currently being faced in mental-health treatment facilities and in the development of new therapeutic drugs. Few of them have been totally resolved. In the late 1960s in Minnesota and New York, physicians were successfully sued for *not* medicating committed, drug-refusing patients. However, in 1975 in Massachusetts, physicians were successfully sued *for* medicating drug-refusing patients. Court decisions since 1979 regarding a patient's right to refuse medication have generally been in the patient's favor, though the decision as to the mental competence of an individual patient is frequently left to a judge's ruling.

Another controversy has arisen surrounding the rights of patients in the development of new drugs, particularly with regard to the treatment of schizophrenia. Should these patients participate in clinical testing trials for experimental antipsychotic medications? On the one hand, as a research psychiatrist has put it, "We must figure out this disease. . . . Unfortunately, there are no animal models for hallucinations and thought disorders. There is no substitute for studying humans." On the other hand, as a civil rights attorney has said, "Persons with severe psychiatric disabilities cannot be made guinea pigs for the greater good of humanity."

What do you think?

Sources: Amarasingham, Lorna R. (1980). Social and cultural perspectives on medication refusal. *American Journal of Psychiatry, 137,* 353–358. Applebaum, P. D. (1988). Antipsychotic medications: Retrospect and prospect. *American Journal of Psychiatry,* 145, 413–419. Gutheil, Thomas G. (1980). In search of true freedom: Drug refusal, involuntary medication, and "Rotting with your rights on." *American Journal of Psychiatry, 137,* 327–328.

Summary

- The development of psychiatric drugs to treat major mental illnesses such as schizophrenia and mood disorders has both revolutionized the field of mental health and provided insights into the biochemical basis for mental illness.

- As effective as psychiatric drugs might be for the mentally ill, none is without side effects. The perfect drug has yet to appear on the scene.

The Biomedical Model

- The biomedical model, the prevailing viewpoint among mental-health professionals, asserts that abnormal thoughts and behaviors are results of biochemical processes in the brain.

Antipsychotic Drugs and Schizophrenia

- Therapeutic medications for schizophrenia patients are classified as first-generation, second-generation, and third-generation antipsychotic drugs. First-generation drugs include chlorpromazine (brand name: Thorazine) and haloperidol (brand name: Haldol). Second-generation drugs include clozapine (brand name: Clozaril) and risperidone (brand name: Risperdal). The newest third-generation drugs include apiprazadole (brand name: Abilify).

- First-generation antipsychotic drugs have been effective in reducing symptoms for many patients, but they also carry with them the potential for the development of severe movement-related motor problems.

- Second-generation and third-generation antipsychotic medications do not produce this particular side effect.
- Antipsychotic medications are believed to be clinically effective and involve the fewest number of adverse side effects by virtue of a combination of actions upon subtypes of dopamine and serotonin receptors in the brain.

Drugs Used to Treat Depression

- First-generation antidepressant drugs can be divided in two groups: MAO inhibitors and tricyclic antidepressants.
- The MAO inhibitors were the first group to be developed for the treatment of depression. Although they are effective, patients need to be on a restricted diet to avoid serious adverse side effects.
- Tricyclic antidepressants do not require dietary restrictions, but their effects on the cardiovascular system make them undesirable for certain patients.
- Second-generation antidepressants include the well-known drug fluoxetine (brand name: Prozac) and similar drugs that slow down the reuptake of serotonin. Collectively, they are referred to as selective serotonin reuptake inhibitors (SSRIs).
- Third-generation antidepressants slow down the reuptake of both serotonin and norepinephrine in the brain.

Drugs for Other Types of Mental Disorders

- Mania and extreme mood swings between mania and depression (bipolar disorder) are two mood disorders that have been treated successfully with lithium carbonate or valproate (brand name: Depakote), as well as antipsychotic medications such as risperidone (brand name: Risperdal) and ziprasidone (brand name: Geodon), or a combination of antipsychotic and antidepressant medications (brand name: Symbyax).
- Risperidone (brand name: Risperdal) has been approved as a treatment for symptoms of autism in children and adolescents.

St. John's Wort

- Increasing attention has focused on the application of St. John's wort in the treatment of depressive symptoms. Widely used in Europe, this herbal extract has been found in randomized controlled trials conducted in the United States to be effective (relative to a placebo) in the treatment of mild to moderate depression. Caution is advised as to possible adverse interactions with certain prescription medications.

Psychiatric Drugs, Social Policy, and Deinstitutionalization

- Since the 1960s, a growing number of psychiatric patients have been treated outside a centralized hospital or institution and placed in treatment-care clinics in the community. While the policy of deinstitutionalization has sparked great debate and significant social problems remain, there is a growing consensus that mental-care treatment implemented in this manner is superior to institutionalization.

Key Terms

agranulocytosis, p. 381
antidepressants, p. 383
antipsychotic drugs, p. 377
atypical antipsychotic drugs, p. 381
autism, p. 387
biomedical model, p. 376
bipolar disorder, p. 386
catatonia, p. 377

deinstitutionalization, p. 388
delusions, p. 377
lithium carbonate, p. 386
mania, p. 386
MAO inhibitors, p. 383
monoamine oxidase (MAO), p. 383
off-label usage, p. 387

Parkinson's-like symptoms, p. 380
psychiatric drugs, p. 376
psychotropic medication, p. 376
St. John's wort, p. 388
schizophrenia, p. 377
selective serotonin reuptake inhibitors (SSRIs), p. 384

serotonin-norepinephrine reuptake inhibitors (SNRIs), p. 385
tardive dyskinesia, p. 380
tricyclic antidepressants, p. 384
typical antipsychotic drugs, p. 380

Endnotes

1. Cahill, Larry (2005, May). His brain, her brain. *Scientific American*, pp. 40–47. Law, Amanda J.; Lipska, Barbara K.; Weickert, Cynthia S.; Hyde, Thomas M., et al. (2006). Neuregulin 1 transcripts are differentially expressed in schizophrenia and regulated by 5'SNPs associated with the disease. *Proceedings of the National Academy of Sciences, 103*, 6747–6752. Murphy, Jane M. (1976). Psychiatric labeling in cross-cultural perspective. *Science, 191*, 1019–1028. Swaminathan, Nikhil (2008, March 28). A new, genetic model for schizophrenia. www.Sciam.com. Walsh, Tom; McClellan, Jon M.; McCarthy, Shane E.; Addington, Angené; et al. (2008). Rare structural variants disrupt multiple genes in neurodevelopmental pathways in schizophrenia. *Science, 320*, 539–543. Wilffert, B., Zaal, R., and Brouwers, J. R. (2005). Pharmacogenetics as a tool in the therapy of schizophrenia (2005, February). *Pharmacy World and Science*, pp. 20–30.

2. American Psychiatric Association (1994). *Diagnostic and statistical manual* (4th ed.). Washington DC: American Psychiatric Association, pp. 278–290. National Institute of Mental Health (1999, revised 2002). *Schizophrenia.* Bethesda, MD: National Institute of Health.

3. Levinthal, Charles F. (1988). *Messengers of paradise: Opiates and the brain.* New York: Anchor Press/Doubleday, pp. 60–61. Snyder, Solomon H. (1974). *Madness and the brain.* New York: McGraw-Hill, pp. 19–21.

4. Lickey, Marvin E., and Gordon, Barbara (1991). *Medicine and mental illness: The use of drugs in psychiatry.* New York: Freeman, p. 92.

5. Hollister, Leo E. (1983). *Clinical pharmacology of psychotherapeutic drugs* (2nd ed.). New York: Churchill Livingston, pp. 110–171.

6. Davis, John M. (1980). Antipsychotic drugs. In Harold I. Kaplan, Arnold M. Freedman, and Benjamin J. Saddock (Eds.), *Comprehensive textbook of psychiatry.* Vol. 3. Baltimore: Williams & Wilkins, pp. 2257–2289.

7. Baron, Robert A. (1992). *Psychology* (2nd ed.). Boston: Allyn and Bacon, p. 593. Meltzer, Herbert Y. (1993). New drugs for treatment of schizophrenia. *Psychiatric Clinics of North America, 16,* 365–385.

8. Honigfeld, Gilbert, and Howard, Alfreda (1973). *Psychiatric drugs: A desk reference.* New York: Academic Press, p. 37. Silverstone, Trevor, and Turner, Paul (1978). *Drug treatment in psychiatry* (2nd ed.). London: Routledge and Kegan Paul, pp. 106–108.

9. Lickey and Gordon, *Medicine and mental illness,* pp.132–133.

10. Antipsychotic drugs not advised for Alzheimer's (2005, October 25). *Newsday,* p. B17. Chou, James C.-Y., and Serper, Mark R. (1998). Ziprasidone—A new highly atypical antipsychotic. *Essentials of Psychopharmacology, 2,* 463–485. Essig, Maria G. (2003, March 14). Antipsychotic drugs that induce weight gain reviewed. *Drug Week,* pp. 71–72. Schneider, Lon S., Tariot, Pierre N., Dagerman, Karen S., et al. (2006). Effectiveness of atypical antipsychotic drugs in patients with Alzheimer's Disease. *New England Journal of Medicine, 355,* 1525–1538. Janssen Pharmaceutica, Inc. (2004, July 21). Important correction of drug information with respect to Risperdal. U.S. Food and Drug Administration (2004, March 1). Medwatch: 2004 safety alert: Zyprexa (olanzapine). Washington DC: U.S. Food and Drug Administration. Lieberman, Jeffrey A.; Stroup, T. Scott; McEvoy, Joseph P.; Swartz, Marvin S., et al. (2005). Effectiveness of antipsychotic drugs in patients with chronic schizophrenia. *New England Journal of Medicine, 353,* 1209–1223.

11. Burris, Kevin D.; Molski, Thaddeus F.; Xu, Cen; Ryan, Elaine; Tottori, Katsura; et al. (2003). Aripiprazole, a novel antipsychotic, is a high-affinity partial agonist at human dopamine D_2 receptors. *Journal of Pharmacology and Experimental Therapeutics, 302,* 381–389. Carey, Benedict (2006, June 6). Use of antipsychotics by young people in U.S. rose fivefold in decade, researchers report. *New York Times,* p. A18.

12. Duvoisin, Roger C. (1991). *Parkinson's disease: A guide for patient and family* (3rd ed.). New York: Raven Press. Hornykiewicz, Oleh (1974). The mechanisms of L-dopamine in Parkinson's disease. *Life Sciences, 15,* 1249–1259.

13. Butcher, James (2000). News: Dopamine hypothesis gains more support. *Lancet, 356,* 140. Plotkin, Steven G.; Saha, Anutosh R.; Kujawa, Mary J.; Carson, William H.; Ali, Mirza; et al. (2003). Aripiprazole, an antipsychotic with a novel mechanism of action, and risperidone vs. placebo in patients with schizophrenia and schizoaffective disorder. *Archives of General Psychiatry, 60,* 681–690. Rivas-Vazquez, Rafael A. (2003). Aripiprazole: A novel antipsychotic with dopamine stabilizing properties. *Professional Psychology: Research and Practice, 34,* 108–111.

14. Kessler, Ronald C.; Berglund, Patricia; Demler, Olga; Jin, Robert; Koretz, Doreen; et al. (2003). The epidemiology of major depressive disorder. *Journal of the American Medical Association, 289,* 3095–3105. Lefton, Lester A. (1994). *Psychology* (5th ed.). Boston: Allyn and Bacon, p. 481. Wingert, Pat, and Katrowitz, Barbara (2002, October 7). Young and depressed. *Newsweek,* pp. 52–61.

15. Julien, Robert M. (2005). *A primer of drug action* (10th ed.). New York: Worth, pp. 271–272.

16. Geoffrey Cowley (1990, March 26). The promise of Prozac. *Newsweek,* p. 39.

17. Cramer, Peter D. (1993). *Listening to Prozac.* New York: Viking. Glenmullen, Joseph (2000). *Prozac backlash: Overcoming the dangers of Prozac, Zoloft, Paxil, and other antidepressants with safe, effective alternatives.* New York: Simon and Schuster. Goode, Erica (1999, July 27). Some still despair in a Prozac nation. *New York Times,* pp. F1, F7. Kantrowitz, Barbara, and Winsert, Pat (2005, November 28). Sex, drugs, and hope. *Newsweek,* p. 48.

18. Jacobs, Barry L. (2004). Depression: The brain finally gets into the act. *Current Directions in Psychological Science, 13,* 103–106. Julien, *A primer of drug action,* pp. 253–305. Levinthal, Charles F. (1990). *Introduction to physiological psychology* (3rd ed.). Englewood Cliffs, NJ: Prentice-Hall, pp. 174–177. Maas, James W. (1975). Biogenic amines of depression. *Archives of General Psychiatry, 32,* 1357–1361. Rosack, Jim (2006). Protein discovery may lead to new psychiatric drugs. *Psychiatric News, 41,* 18.

19. SSRIs: Prozac and company—Part I (2000, October). *Harvard Mental Health Letter,* p. 2.

20. Bower, Bruce (1991). Manic depression: Success story dims. *Science News, 139,* 324–325.

21. Johnson, F. Neil (1984). *The history of lithium therapy.* New York: Macmillan. Shelton, Richard C. (1999). Mood-stabilizing drugs in depression. *Journal of Clinical Psychiatry, 60* (Suppl. 5), 37–40.

22. FDA issues public health advisory for antipsychotic drugs used for the treatment of behavioral disorders in elderly patients (2005, April 11). *FDA Talk Paper.* Keck, Paul E., Jr.; Marcus, Ronald; Tourkodimitris, Stavros; Ali, Mirza; Liebeskind, Amy; et al. (2003). A placebo-controlled, double-blind study of the efficacy and safety

of aripiprazole in patients with acute bipolar mania. *American Journal of Psychiatry, 160,* 1651–1658. Waring, E. W.; Dewan, V. K.; Cohen, D.; and Grewal, R. (1999). Risperidone as an adjunct to valproic acid. *Canadian Journal of Psychiatry, 44,* 189–190.

23. McCracken, James T.; McGough, James; Shah, Bhavik; Cronin, Pegeen; Hong, Daniel; et al. (2002). Risperidone in children with autism and serious behavioral problems. *New England Journal of Medicine, 347,* 314–321. McDougle, Christopher J.; Stigler, Kimberly A.; Erickson, Craig A.; and Posey, David J. (2006). Pharmacology of autism. *Clinical Neuroscience Research, 6,* 179–188.

24. Beck, James M., and Azari, Elizabeth D. (1998). FDA, off-label drug use, and informed consent: Debunking myths and misconceptions. *Food and Drug Law Journal, 53,* 71–104.

25. Barlow, David H.; Gorman, Jack M.; Shear, M. Katherine; and Woods, Scott W. (2000). Cognitive-behavioral therapy, imipramine, or their combination for panic disorder. *Journal of the American Medical Association, 283,* 2529–2536. Brady, Kathleen; Pearlstein, Teri; Asnis, Gregory M.; Baker, Dewleen; Rothbaum, Barbara; et al. (2000). Efficacy and safety of sertraline treatment of posttraumatic stress disorder. *Journal of the American Medical Association, 283,* 1837–1844. Gelenberg, Alan J.; Lydiard, R. Bruce; Rudolph, Richard L.; Aguiar, Loren; Haskins, J. Thomas; et al. (2000). Efficacy of venlafaxine extended-release capsules in nondepressed outpatients with generalized anxiety disorder: A 6-month randomized controlled trial. *Journal of the American Medical Association, 283,* 3082–3088.

26. Butterweck, Veronika (2003). Mechanism of action in St. John's wort in depression. *CNS Drugs, 17,* 539–562. De Smet, Peter A. G. M. (2002). Herbal remedies. *New England Journal of Medicine, 347,* 2046–2056. Formichelli, Linda (2002, July/August). The decline of St. John's wort: Is our favorite herb a dud? *Psychology Today,* p. 16.

27. Doyle, Rodger (2002, December). Deinstitutionalization: Why a much maligned program still has life. *Scientific American,* p. 38. Grob, Gerald N. (1995, July/August). The paradox of deinstitutionalization. *Society,* pp. 51–58. Krieg, Randall G. (2001). An interdisciplinary look at the deinstitutionalization of the mentally ill. *Social Science Journal, 38,* 367–380.

PART FOUR
Medicinal Drugs

POINT/COUNTERPOINT

Should Prescription Drugs Be Advertised to the Public?

The following discussion of viewpoints represents the opinions of people on both sides of the controversial issue of prescription drug advertisement. Read them with an open mind. Don't think you have to come up with the final answer, nor should you necessarily agree with the argument you read last. Many of the ideas in the feature come from sources listed.

POINT

You have seen the DTC (direct-to-consumer) prescription drug advertising images on TV and in practically every magazine you read: good-looking people, apparently in superb health, enjoying the outdoors under an azure sky—all because they had taken Flonase, a prescription drug that could only have been obtained with a doctor's assent. It is as if the consumer now exclaims, "Wow, this Flonase must really be good. Besides, it makes me realize I have hay fever!" This is blatant manipulation. Why does a prescription drug have to be advertised to the public when the public couldn't obtain it legally on its own?

COUNTERPOINT

You obviously don't understand the evolving pharmaceutical marketplace. The more information presented to the patient, the better the health care system will be. Without advertising, you don't have a choice in your health care, and television is the most efficient outlet. Health care consumers should make choices for themselves.

POINT

Wait a minute. Since the FDA relaxed the rules on DTC advertising in 1997, things have gotten out of hand. Every major prescription drug available now has been promoted to the public through the media, and lately this use of the media has been extended to the advertising of medical devices. (One commercial that aired during a Thanksgiving Day football game in 2007 promoted a new coronary stent used in angioplasty surgery!) The American Medical Association gave up trying to ban the practice in 2006. Shouldn't it be the physician who makes the decision about a pharmaceutical treatment for his or her patients? Drug ads are not-so-subtle ways of getting patients to bring up the subject (and the drug they had heard about) when they see a doctor. And these ads are very big business with huge advantages to the pharmaceutical companies. It's been estimated that every dollar spent on DTC advertising yields more than four dollars in drug sales. Obviously, the patient inquiries stimulated by this advertising are working on the physicians. A study in 2005 showed that women who went to their physician pretending to have major depression were prescribed an antidepressant 53 percent of the time if they specifically mentioned that they had seen a Paxil ad on TV, compared to 31 percent of the time if no drug was mentioned—a whopping 74 percent increase in antidepressant sales. And this was from patients who only *pretended* to be depressed!

COUNTERPOINT
Patients are encouraged to speak to their physician for truly appropriate health care. FDA regulations require that consumers receive a balanced and clear description of a drug's potential application, as well as its effectiveness, major side effects, and overall risks.

POINT
Pharmaceutical companies have a cagey way of abiding by these regulations. What about the following tag line for Adderall XR, an extended-release version of the popular psychostimulant treatment for attention deficit disorder? "Talk to your doctor to see if the all-day symptom control of Adderall XR can add new mean-

ing to your child's life." The headline reads "Already Done with My Homework, Dad!"—a play on the letters ADHD. It's as if a prescription drug is being marketed like breakfast cereal.

COUNTERPOINT
The viewing audience can tell the difference between medicine and cereal. DTC advertising in a thirty-second or sixty-second television spot or on a full page of a magazine simply empowers consumers to make informed decisions about their drug therapy when they go to a health care professional. People aren't dummies.

POINT
What you call "empowerment" amounts to $4.8 billion spent on DTC advertising in a single year (2006 figures, double the expenditure in 2000), just for promotional purposes. This is money that could have been directed toward the actual costs of research into new drugs that could save lives. Advertising costs have to be picked up by the consumer in terms of exorbitantly high prescription drug prices. Some people simply can't afford these drugs.

COUNTERPOINT
People don't complain that they now can't afford food because all the grocery stores advertise. Ironically, advertising lowers costs. Pharmaceutical companies can't add the advertising cost on top of the product if there are other competi-

tively priced alternatives already on the market. The health insurance companies will see to it that they don't. It is the high costs for research and development that are to blame for high prescription drug prices, not the expense of advertising.

Critical Thinking Questions for Further Debate

1. You are a physician, and your patient comes to you with the name of a prescription medication heard on TV in a drug commercial. The drug in question is equivalent to the drug the patient is currently taking for a certain disorder. Do you switch the prescription to the new drug, in light of your patient's feeling that it might be more effective? How would the placebo effect figure into your debate about this question?

2. You are a physician, and your patient comes to you with the name of a prescription medication heard on TV in a drug commercial. The patient believes that he or she has the symptoms that this drug is designed to treat. The patient also hints that if you do not supply a written prescription for this drug, he or she will consult another physician. Do you prescribe the drug to the patient, even though you have some reservations about whether the patient really has the symptoms in question?

Sources: Boden, William E., and Diamond, George A. (2008). DTCA for PTCA—Crossing the line in consumer health education. *New England Journal of Medicine, 358,* 2197–2200. Kaiser Family Foundation (2001, November). Impact of direct-to-consumer advertising on prescription drug spending. Menlo Park, CA: Kaiser Family Foundation. Kravitz, Richard L.; Epstein, Ronald M.; Feldman, Mitchell D.; Franz, Carol E.; et al. (2005). Influence of patient's requests for direct-to-consumer advertised antidepressants. *Journal of the American Medical Association, 293,* 1995–2002. Rados, Carol (2004, July–August). Truth in advertising: Rx drug ads come of age. *FDA Consumer,* pp. 20, 27. Salazar, Veronica (2008, May 15). Our view on pharmaceutical advertising: Can you believe what you see on TV? Ask your doctor. *USA Today.* http://blogs.usatoday.com/oped/2008/05/edit15.html. Thomaselli, Rich (2006). AMA gives up push to ban DTC drug ads. *Advertising Age, 77,* p. 4.

chapter **17**

Intervention and Treatment: Strategies for Change

I would lie about everything, and I lied to everybody. It was so easy to do. My parents were in major denial, and I played off of that. What is all that drug stuff in my room? Oh, I'm just holding it for a friend. It would get me so angry that the lies worked so well with them. They would never call me on anything. It became a way of life. But after a while I got sick and tired of all the lying. And I started to think about the possibility that I might be dead at an early age. Half of my friends are now dead; the other half are in jail.

That's why I'm here to get help. I had to change somehow. It really just came down to that.

—A seventeen-year-old recovering drug abuser, explaining why he came to Daytop Village

After you have completed this chapter, you will understand

- The three major levels of intervention in drug-abuse prevention
- The biopsychosocial approach to drug-abuse treatment
- Prison-alternative and prison-based treatment programs
- Drug courts in the criminal justice system
- Efforts to create a drug-free workplace in the United States
- Stages of change in substance-abuse recovery
- Issues related to the personal decision to seek treatment
- The importance of family dynamics in drug abuse and treatment
- Considerations when deciding on a particular treatment program or facility
- The continuing need for drug-abuse treatment

Consider for a moment the goal of preventing the misuse and abuse of psychoactive drugs in our society. Everyone is obviously in favor of prevention; no one questions that the personal damage and social havoc wrought by the sale, distribution, and consumption of illicit drugs are devastating. As political leaders continually remind us, we have to "do something" if this monster is to be slain. At the same time, we are appalled by the magnitude of preventable disease and death associated with *licit* drugs such as alcohol and nicotine. It is imperative that we reduce the risks to our health and the health of our families and friends.

Yet, as unanimous as we may be in the necessity for some prevention strategy, the issues are complex and the answers have been elusive. It has been a challenge to create programs that have a significant and long-lasting positive impact on an individual's inclination to use drugs. In these final two chapters, we turn to an examination of drug-abuse prevention in our society.

Levels of Intervention in Drug-Abuse Prevention

It has been customary to divide efforts to prevent the abuse of drugs into three levels of intervention: primary, secondary, and tertiary. Each intervention has its own target population and goals.

In **primary prevention,** efforts are directed to those who have not had any experience with drugs or those who have been only minimally exposed. The objective is to prevent drug abuse from starting in the first place, "nipping the problem in the bud" so to speak. Targets in primary prevention programs are most frequently elementary school or middle school youths, and intervention usually occurs within a school-based curriculum or specific educational program. For example, a primary prevention

---

primary prevention: A type of intervention in which the goal is to forestall the onset of drug use by an individual who has had little or no previous exposure to drugs.

secondary prevention: A type of intervention in which the goal is to reduce the extent of drug use in individuals who have already had some exposure to drugs.

tertiary (TER-shee-eh-ree) prevention: A type of intervention in which the goal is to prevent relapse in an individual following recovery in a drug-treatment program.

---

by the numbers . . .

23.2 million	Estimated number of individuals aged twelve or older in the United States needing treatment for an alcohol or illicit drug-use problem in 2007
3.9 million	Estimated number of individuals receiving treatment in 2007
$4 to $7	Estimated reduction in the cost of drug-related crime, criminal justice costs, and theft alone for every $1 invested in substance-abuse treatment programs. When savings related to health care are included, total savings exceed costs by a ratio of 12 to 1.

Source: National Institute on Drug Abuse (2000, July). *Principles of drug addiction treatment: A research-based guide.* Rockville, MD: National Institute on Drug Abuse, p. 21. Substance Abuse and Mental Health Services Administration (2008). *Results from the 2007 National Survey on Drug Use and Health: National findings.* Rockville, MD: Office of Applied Studies, Substance Abuse and Mental Health Services Administration, pp. 77, 80.

---

program would include teaching peer-refusal skills that students can use when they are offered marijuana, alcohol, or cigarettes (that is, ways to say no).

In **secondary prevention,** the target population has already had some experience with drugs. The objective is to limit the extent of drug abuse (reducing it, if possible), prevent the spread of drug abuse to substances beyond the drugs already encountered, and teach strategies for the responsible use of licit drugs such as alcohol. Ordinarily, those receiving secondary-prevention efforts are older than those involved in primary-prevention programs. High school students who are identified as alcohol or other drug users may participate in a program that emphasizes social alternatives to drug-taking behavior. College students may focus on the skills necessary to restrict their behavior to the moderate use of alcohol, the dangers of combining drinking and driving, and the signs of chronic alcohol abuse.

In **tertiary prevention,** the objective is to ensure that an individual who has entered treatment for some form of drug-abuse problem becomes drug-free, without reverting to former patterns of drug-taking behavior. Successful prevention of relapse is the ultimate indication that the treatment has taken hold.

This chapter concentrates on tertiary-prevention efforts, specifically those treatment interventions intended to rescue an individual from a life of drug abuse. On an annual basis, approximately 1.8 million Americans are admitted to treatment for abuse of alcohol or drugs in a facility that is licensed or certified to provide substance-abuse treatment programs (Figure 17.1).[1] Chapter 18 will focus on primary- and secondary-prevention efforts, primarily the array of school- and community-based educational programs available at the present time.

A Biopsychosocial Strategy for Treatment

Treatment programs for abusers of specific drugs have been reviewed in earlier chapters. In some cases, a treatment program is uniquely tailored for individuals seeking help in dealing with a certain form of drug abuse. A methadone maintenance program or buprenorphine treatment (see Chapter 5), for example, is not appropriate for a cocaine abuser or an alcoholic, since the intent is to substitute an illicit, unpredictable opiate (heroin) with an opiate that can be medically supervised (methadone or buprenorphine). The use of disulfiram (Antabuse) is restricted to the treatment of alcoholism (see Chapter 10) because it is a specific inhibitor of enzymes involved in the breakdown of alcohol and its effects are not felt if alcohol is not in the system.

However, some treatments can cut across different forms of drug abuse. We have seen how so-called twelve-step programs have been useful not only for alcohol abusers in the traditional Alcoholics Anonymous format but also for individuals seeking help with heroin abuse (Narcotics Anonymous) or cocaine abuse (Cocaine Anonymous). You may recall that one particular location in the brain, the nucleus accumbens, is known to be stimulated by a variety of dependence-producing drugs (opiates, cocaine, alcohol, and nicotine). The current use of naltrexone (brand names: ReVia, Vivitrol) and nalmefene (brand name: Revex), both opiate antagonists, in the treatment of alcoholism (see Chapter 10) as well as heroin abuse (see Chapter 5) is a good example of the cross-over value of

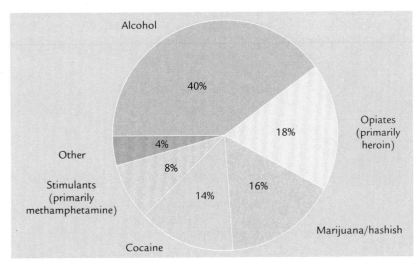

FIGURE 17.1

Five substances of abuse account for 96 percent of all reasons for treatment in facilities licensed or certified to provide treatment programs.

Source: Substance Abuse and Mental Health Services Administration (2008). *Treatment Episode Data Set (TEDS) highlights: 2006. National admissions to substance abuse treatment services.* Rockville, MD: Office of Applied Studies, Substance Abuse, and Mental Health Services Administration, Table 1b.

current drug treatment strategies. Given the evidence for a common neural and neurochemical basis for drug dependence in general, it makes sense that a common approach should work in its treatment.[2]

The consideration of a common treatment approach is dictated also by a fact of life regarding drugs in our society today. The reality is that not one but several types of drugs, either licit or illicit, are often involved in an individual's "dependence profile." *It is an uncommon individual who abuses only a single drug.* An abuser of heroin will also frequently smoke marijuana and tobacco, drink alcohol, or dabble in any of a variety of available street drugs. These individuals, referred to as **polydrug abusers,** benefit most from a treatment program that acknowledges the fact that more than one form of drug dependence exists at the same time. In such cases, the most effective program is one that addresses a host of *multiple substance abuse* problems. For these reasons, as we review approaches toward tertiary prevention in this chapter, keep in mind that the term *drug abuse* is meant to include the possible abuse of a wide range of substances.

In addition, an effective treatment program must consider the reality that many drug-abuse clients are contending with co-occurring mental health conditions such as depression, anxiety, or other types of serious psychological distress. Roughly one-half of all abusers of alcohol or other drugs have had a serious mental disorder in their lifetime. These individuals are often referred to as *dual-diagnosis patients or clients.* It is possible, for example, that drug abuse is a form of "self-medication" undertaken to reduce feelings of depression, or that drug-taking behavior might be making the depression worse. In these circumstances, a psychiatrist, psychologist, or clinical social worker plays a crucial role in finding the most appropriate mix of pharmacological and behavioral treatment.[3]

Inevitably, success in drug-abuse treatment rests upon the recognition that there are multiple pathways to drug abuse and dependence. For each individual, there is a specific combination of biological, psychological, and social factors that has played a role in getting that person to the point at which treatment is necessary. This integrated approach to treatment has often been called the **biopsychosocial model** (Figure 17.2). Un-

polydrug abusers: Individuals whose drug-taking behavior involves the abuse of two or more licit or illicit drugs simultaneously. Also referred to as *multiple substance abusers.*

biopsychosocial model: A perspective on drug-abuse treatment that recognizes the biological, psychological, and social factors underlying drug-taking behavior and encourages an integrated approach, based on these factors, in designing an individual's treatment program.

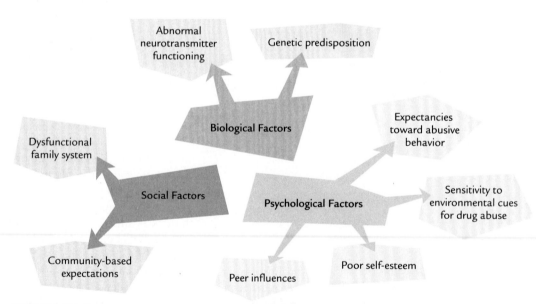

FIGURE 17.2

The biopsychosocial model asserts that there are multiple pathways to drug abuse.

Source: Modified from Margolis, Robert D., and Zweben, Joan E. (1998). *Treating patients with alcohol and other drug problems: An integrated approach.* Washington DC: American Psychological Association, pp. 76–87.

fortunately, through much of the history of drug-abuse treatment in the United States, there has been a tendency to view the problems of drug abuse, particularly illicit drug abuse, through a limited perspective. The next section reviews intervention and treatment efforts in the context of law enforcement and punishment.

Incarceration and Other Punitive Measures in the United States

A natural response to the presence of an individual whose behavior poses a significant threat to society is to remove that individual from society and provide some form of containment or **incarceration** in a prison, jail, or other secure environment. Besides protecting society at large, incarceration is intended to be preventive in the long run by (1) reducing the likelihood that the individual will behave in a similar way in the future, after the sentence is completed, and (2) conveying the message to others who might contemplate engaging in similar behavior that a comparable punishment would apply to them as well. The first goal is referred to as **rehabilitation;** the second goal is referred to as **deterrence.**

Prevention through Law Enforcement

Drug-control laws in general have been formulated over the years according to the philosophy that punitive measures such as incarceration or financial penalties (fines) lead to rehabilitation on a personal level and deterrence on a societal level. The five categories or schedules of controlled substances, adopted by the Comprehensive Drug Abuse Prevention and Control Act of 1970, were designed not only to set up limitations in public access to different types of drugs but also to establish different levels of criminal penalties for unauthorized behavior related to these drugs, based on their potential for abuse.

Specifically, the law defined **drug trafficking** as the unauthorized manufacture, distribution by sale or gift, or possession with intent to distribute any controlled substance (Table 17.1, pages 400 and 401). The severity of the penalties that were established by federal laws enacted in 1970, and revised in 1986 and 1988, has varied according to the schedule of the controlled substance involved, with Schedule I violations being the most severely punished and Schedule V violations being the least (Chapter 2). As a result of the Anti-Drug-

Police officers arrest drug offenders in a drug bust.

Abuse Acts of 1986 and 1988, a number of special circumstances also are considered in arriving at the penalty imposed:

- Penalties are doubled for first-offense trafficking of Schedule I or II controlled substances if death or bodily injury results from the use of such substances.
- Penalties for the sale of drugs by a person over twenty-one years old to someone under the age of eighteen are increased to up to double those imposed for sale to an adult.
- Penalties for the sale of drugs within 1,000 feet of an elementary or secondary school are increased to up to double those imposed when the sale is made elsewhere.
- Fines for companies or business associations are generally $2\frac{1}{2}$ times greater than for individuals. In either case, penalties include the forfeiture of cars, boats, or planes that have been used in the illegal conveyance of controlled substances.
- If a family is living in public housing, the entire family can be evicted if a family member is convicted of criminal activity, including drug trafficking, on or near the public-housing premises.

incarceration: Imprisonment for a fixed length of time.

rehabilitation: A process of change through which there is a reduced likelihood that a pattern of problematic behavior will recur.

deterrence: The reduced likelihood that a person might engage in a pattern of problematic behavior in the future.

drug trafficking: The unauthorized manufacture of any controlled substance, its distribution by sale or gift, or possession of such a substance with intent to distribute it.

TABLE 17.1

Current federal penalties for drug trafficking, according to each of five controlled substance schedules (CSS)

CSS	2ND-OFFENSE PENALTY	1ST-OFFENSE PENALTY	QUANTITY	DRUG	QUANTITY	1ST-OFFENSE PENALTY	2ND-OFFENSE PENALTY
I and II	Not less than 10 years. Not more than life. If death or serious injury, not less than life. Fine of not more than $4 million individual, $10 million other than individual.	Not less than 5 years. Not more than 40 years. If death or serious injury, not less than 20 years. Not more than life. Fine of not more than $2 million individual, $5 million other than individual.	10–99 g or 100–999 g mixture	Metham-phetamine	100 g or more or 1 kg* or more mixture	Not less than 10 years. Not more than life. If death or serious injury, not less than 20 years. Not more than life. Fine of not more than $4 million individual, $10 million other than individual.	Not less than 20 years. Not more than life. If death or serious injury, not less than life. Fine of not more than $8 million individual, $20 million other than individual.
			100–999 g mixture	Heroin	1 kg or more mixture		
			500–4,999 g mixture	Cocaine	5 kg or more mixture		
			5–49 g mixture	Cocaine base	50 g or more mixture		
			10–99 g or 100–999 g mixture	PCP	100 g or more or 1 kg or more mixture		
			1–10 g mixture	LSD	10 g or more mixture		
			40–399 g mixture	Fentanyl	400 g or more mixture		
			10–99 g mixture	Fentanyl Analogue	100 g or more mixture		

CSS	DRUG	QUANTITY	1ST-OFFENSE PENALTY	2ND-OFFENSE PENALTY
	Others†	Any	Not more than 20 years. If death or serious injury, not less than 20 years, not more than life. Fine $1 million individual, $5 million not individual.	Not more than 30 years. If death or serious injury, life. Fine $2 million individual, $10 million not individual.
III	All	Any	Not more than 5 years. Fine not more than $250,000 individual, $1 million not individual.	Not more than 10 years. Fine not more than $500,000 individual, $2 million not individual.
IV	All	Any	Not more than 3 years. Fine not more than $250,000 individual, $1 million not individual.	Not more than 6 years. Fine not more than $500,000 individual, $2 million not individual.
V	All	Any	Not more than 1 year. Fine not more than $100,000 individual, $250,000 not individual.	Not more than 2 years. Fine not more than $200,000 individual, $500,000 not individual.

(continued)

*Law as originally exacted states 100 g. Congress requested technical correction to 1 kg.

†Does not include marijuana, hashish, or hash oil.

Note: Trafficking penalties distinguish between Schedule I drugs excluding marijuana (above) and marijuana itself (page 401).

Federal penalties for **simple possession,** defined as having on one's person any illegal or nonprescribed controlled substance in *any* of the five schedules for one's own use, are much simpler. First-offense violators face a maximum of one year imprisonment and a fine of between $1,000 and $5,000. Second-offense violators face a minimum of fifteen days up to a maximum of two years and a fine of up to $10,000 (Drugs . . . in Focus, page 402).[4]

simple possession: Having on one's person any illegal or nonprescribed controlled substance for one's own use.

TABLE 17.1 *(continued)*

Current federal penalties for drug trafficking of marijuana

QUANTITY	DESCRIPTION	1ST-OFFENSE PENALTY	2ND-OFFENSE PENALTY
1,000 kg or more; or 1,000 or more plants	Marijuana Mixture containing detectable quantity‡	Not less than 10 years, not more than life. If death or serious injury, not less than 20 years, not more than life. Fine not more than $4 million individual, $10 million other than individual.	Not less than 20 years, not more than life. If death or serious injury, not less than life. Fine not more than $8 million individual, $20 million other than individual.
100 kg to 1,000 kg; or 100–999 plants	Marijuana Mixture containing detectable quantity‡	Not less than 5 years, not more than 40 years. If death or serious injury, not less than 20 years, not more than life. Fine not more than $2 million individual, $5 million other than individual.	Not less than 10 years, not more than life. If death or serious injury, not less than life. Fine not more than $4 million individual, $10 million other than individual.
50 to 100 kg	Marijuana	Not more than 20 years. If death or serious injury, not less than 20 years, not more than life. Fine $1 million individual, $5 million other than individual. Not more than 5 years. Fine not more than $250,000, $1 million other than individual.	Not more than 30 years. If death or serious injury, life. Fine $2 million individual, $10 million other than individual. Not more than 10 years. Fine $500,000 individual, $2 million other than individual.
10 to 100 kg	Hashish		
1 to 100 kg	Hashish oil		
50–99 plants	Marijuana		
Less than 50 kg	Marijuana		
Less than 10 kg	Hashish		
Less than 1 kg	Hashish oil		

‡Includes hashish and hashish oil.

Source: Drug Enforcement Administration, U.S. Department of Justice. Penalties established by the 1986 Anti-Drug-Abuse Act.

Federal penalties set the standard for the punishment of drug offenses in the United States, but most drug-related offenses are prosecuted at the state rather than the federal level, and state regulations for simple possession and drug trafficking can vary widely. In cases of simple possession of small amounts of marijuana, some U.S. states might be more lenient (see Chapter 7), whereas in cases of heroin possession some states might be more stringent. Certain aspects of drug-taking behavior, such as the day-to-day regulation of alcohol sales and distribution, are regulated primarily by state and local municipalities, unless interstate commerce is involved. States and local municipalities have also taken on regulatory authority with regard to **drug paraphernalia,** products whose predominant use is to administer, prepare, package, or store illicit drugs. Nearly all U.S. states have statutes making it unlawful to sell these items to minors, unless they are accompanied by a parent or legal guardian. In addition, the importation, exportation, and advertising of drug paraphernalia are prohibited.[5]

A look at the inmate population at federal and state levels gives us an idea of how drug enforcement responsibilities in the United States have been distributed. Drug-related offenses represent the reason for the incarceration of approximately 53 percent of all inmates in federal prisons.

Yet it is more likely that a drug offender is serving his or her time in a state prison because state inmates in general outnumber federal inmates by more than eight to one. Drug offenses represent no more than 20 percent of the sentences among inmates in state prisons, but the fact that the state inmate population is about seven times larger than the federal inmate population more than compensates for the lower percentage. The bottom line is this: Of every four drug offenders presently incarcerated, three are in a state prison and one is in a federal prison.[6]

What happens to these people who are arrested and convicted of drug-law violations? Does the criminal justice system provide a deterrent against drug abuse by

drug paraphernalia: Products that are considered to be used to administer, prepare, package, or store illicit drugs.

Drugs...in Focus

Penalties for Crack versus Penalties for Cocaine: New Developments in Criminal Prosecution

You may have noticed in Table 17.1 the distinction between penalties for cocaine itself (the powdered form) and those for cocaine base (crack) under the 1986 Anti-Drug-Abuse Act. Though the effects of both drugs are very similar, a mandatory minimum prison sentence of five years is imposed upon conviction of possessing more than 500 grams of powder forms of cocaine, whereas the possession of as little as 5 grams of crack can result in the same penalty. In 1988, the federal penalty for possession of more than 5 grams of cocaine powder was set at a minimum of one year in prison; the penalty for possessing an equivalent amount of crack was set at a minimum of five years.

This "100-to-1" disparity, according to critics of this policy, has resulted in far more African Americans than white drug offenders in prison for five years or more. Why? Statistics show that whites are more likely to snort or inject cocaine, whereas African Americans are more likely to smoke cocaine in its cheaper crack form. The differential effects of drug-law enforcement for the two forms of cocaine are reflected in a drug-offense inmate population that is currently divided along racial lines. In 2006, for example, African Americans represented 81 percent of drug offenders convicted in federal court for crack cocaine possession, but only 27 percent of drug offenders for powder cocaine possession. Moreover, it is more common for offenses relating to the possession of powder cocaine to be prosecuted under state regulations, under which mandatory minimum sentences frequently do not apply.

Fortunately, as a result of recent judicial decisions, the enormous disparity in crack and cocaine offense penalties may be diminishing. In 2007, the United States Sentencing Commission, a government panel in charge of recommending appropriate federal prison terms, established new guidelines that would reduce the average sentence for crack cocaine possession from ten years one month to eight years ten months, to be applied retroactively to approximately 19,500 inmates presently incarcerated for this offense. Putting this in perspective, this number of inmates represents about one-fourth of all defendants sentenced in federal court in 2006 and one-tenth of the entire federal prison population. At the same time, the U.S. Supreme Court ruled that federal district judges could, in the future, exert broad discretion to impose what they think are reasonable sentences, even if federal guidelines call for more lengthy ones. This decision has been viewed as a major step toward a restoring of flexibility for trial judges in drug cases.

Sources: Greenhouse, Linda (2007, December 11). Justices restore judges' control over sentencing. *New York Times*, pp. A1, A28. Hatsukami, Dorothy K., and Fischman, Marian W. (1996). Crack cocaine and cocaine hydrochloride: Are the differences myth or reality? *Journal of the American Medical Association, 276,* 1580–1588. Liptak, Adam (2007, December 11). Given the latitude to show leniency, judges may not. *New York Times*, p. A28. Stout, David (2007, December 12). Retroactively, panel reduces drug sentences. *New York Times*, pp. A1, A31.

others in society? We will defer an examination of this question to the discussion of primary and secondary prevention in Chapter 18. A more immediate question at this point is the extent to which the criminal justice system offers opportunities for rehabilitation.

Prison-Alternative and Prison-Based Treatment Programs

A large number of drug offenders who could potentially be incarcerated are instead offered treatment as an alternative to imprisonment or other punitive measures. Approximately 50 percent of all individuals who enter a publicly funded drug treatment program have done so because of direct or indirect legal pressure. Since the late 1980s, it has been common for arrestees demonstrating drug dependence to be "steered" toward drug treatment as a condition for having prosecution postponed, a prison sentence reduced or avoided, or some form of probationary status approved.

While most U.S. states presently make provisions, in some manner, for a treatment option in the drug-offense sentencing, some states have gone further. In 2000, California enacted a law that *requires* judges to offer non-violent drug offenders probation with substance-abuse treatment instead of incarceration for their first two offenses. The judge may choose from diverse state-licensed treatment programs and require community service, literacy training, family counseling, and vocational training as conditions for probation. The benefits of this approach have been indicated by follow-up studies in Arizona, a state that instituted a similar policy in 1996. Results showed that 75 percent of its participants remained drug-free in the program's first year, saving the state approximately $2.5 million.[7]

For those drug offenders who *are* sentenced to prison, a previous history of drug abuse or dependence continues to present difficulties that do not go away just because the inmate is now behind bars. A substantial percentage of male arrestees test positive for one or more illicit drugs at the time of arrest, regardless of the reason for their arrest.

Since the mid-1980s, the Stay'n Out program has become a model for the application of therapeutic community principles (similar to those of Daytop Village or Samaritan Village) to a correctional setting. Established as a separate unit within the prison, Stay'n Out makes use of group and individual counseling sessions that help inmates explore issues of personal development. It is a demanding experience, and many inmates choose to return to traditional prison cells after only a few weeks. Nonetheless, for those individuals spending nine to twelve months in the program, fewer than 23 percent have been found to have violated parole or returned to prison in the three years after release. This figure should be compared to more than 50 percent who would have done so if no treatment had been provided or if standard counseling had been offered.

Other treatment programs modeled after Stay'n Out have shown a comparable level of effectiveness. Unfortunately, however, it has been estimated that less than 20 percent of prisoners with drug-abuse problems in the United States receive any kind of treatment program while incarcerated. The potential for prison-based rehabilitation is there, but the resources available for effective interventions are currently far from adequate.[8]

Drug Courts

A growing presence in the criminal justice system has been the establishment of specialized judicial proceedings called **drug courts** in which adult, nonviolent drug offenders are provided intensively supervised treatment as a "sentence" instead of being incarcerated. More than 2,000 drug courts presently operate in the United States.[9]

The initial step in drug-court programs begins with defense attorneys, probation officers, or prosecutors referring a potential candidate to the drug court itself. Candidates must be judged to be serious drug abusers, cannot be on parole, and cannot have a prior conviction for a serious or violent felony. Upon accepting a drug-court procedure,

the candidate waives his or her right to a jury trial and enters a treatment program for a year, during which he or she is subject to random drug tests. Participants are supervised by a probation officer to ensure that they adhere to program rules. In many cases, a therapeutic community approach, such as Daytop Village, Samaritan Village, or a similar organization (Portrait, page 404) is chosen as the placement for treatment.

Numerous studies have shown that drug-court programs are successful in providing effective rehabilitation. First of all, they decrease the rate of criminal recidivism (repeated arrests). In a study sampling approximately 17,000 drug-court graduates nationwide within one year of their graduation from the program, only 16 percent had been rearrested and charged with a felony offense—approximately one-third the level of recidivism observed in drug offenders not participating in a drug court. Second, drug-court programs are cost-effective. Approximately $250 million in incarceration costs has been saved each year in New York State alone by diverting 18,000 nonviolent drug offenders into treatment. Third, drug courts increase the length of time an individual remains in treatment. The coercive power of the criminal justice system with respect to getting into treatment and staying in treatment is dramatic. Ordinarily, between 40 percent and 80 percent of drug abusers drop out of treatment within ninety days, and between 80 percent and 90 percent drop out within twelve months. In sharp contrast, more than two-thirds of drug-court participants complete a treatment program lasting a year or more. The benefits of drug-court programs have been demonstrated in nonurban as well as urban communities.[10]

According to experts in the field of drug-abuse treatment, the mandated treatment approach in drug-court programs is more likely to result in a successful outcome than in circumstances where the decision to go into treatment is made on a voluntary basis. One man in a Boston drug court expressed his feelings in this way:

> Drug court at first was just getting in the way of my using. But I think without drug court, I probably would never have went to Gaven House, got me a program, got me in line for getting sober. I didn't want to be here, but at the same time, now that it's almost over I'm kind of grateful for it, because I probably would not have stopped or even wanted to. You know? So I'm grateful for drug court.[11]

drug court: Specialized court system that handles adult, nonviolent offenders of drug laws, incorporating a supervised treatment program instead of standard criminal sentencing.

In 1957, Monsignor William O'Brien was a simple parish priest in Tuckahoe, New York, a quiet suburban town north of New York City. He was quite unprepared for the gritty facts of life on urban streets when he was assigned to serve at St. Patrick's Cathedral in the center of Manhattan. For the first time, he came face to face with the desperate and the despondent victims of drug abuse. Both crushed and touched, he wanted to help them as a priest and counselor, but he soon discovered how difficult such cases can be. In his own words,

> *I reached out for two years to help drug addicts and I was the biggest disaster in New York. Because it's just the thing you can't do with alcoholics and drug addicts. They'd go in the parish house bathroom and shoot up behind your back. . . . I discovered a hard discovery. I first had to deal with the human before I could go to the divine. Otherwise, I was building a house on sand.*

In 1963, Monsignor O'Brien helped establish a small center in New York, based on a then-unique concept of drug-treatment intervention: an intensive, therapeutic community where drug-dependent people could relearn how to live their lives, could move toward a drug-free way of thinking. The center was called Daytop (short for Drug Addicts Yielding to Persuasion) Village, and it was the beginning of what is today the oldest and largest drug-free, therapeutic community program for AOD (alcohol and other drugs) dependence in the United States. Since the 1980s, Daytop Village has expanded beyond its twenty-nine centers in this country to more than sixty-six locations around the world.

More than 93,000 individuals have participated in Daytop, and the overwhelming majority of them have reclaimed their lives as a result of its programs. As a reflection of the growing levels of drug use among young people in the 1990s, it is not surprising

that teenagers, who once accounted for scarcely 25 percent of the Daytop client population, now represent half the total. Referrals to Daytop increase steadily and an extensive waiting list for new entrants has no end. Monsignor O'Brien continues to direct Daytop Village through its expansion. He also continues, in the face of budgetary cutbacks at the federal and state levels, to be an eloquent spokesman for therapeutic communities, and AOD treatment in general, as a strategic weapon in our society's ongoing war on drugs.

Sources: Marriot, Michel (1989, November 13). A pioneer in residential drug treatment reaches out. *New York Times,* p. B2. Nieves, Evelyn (1996, August 25). Wresting a life from the grip of addiction. *New York Times,* p. 41. O'Brien, William B., and Henican, Ellis (1993). *You can't do it alone.* New York: Simon and Schuster. Daytop Village, Inc., New York, NY, 1997.

Clearly, the drug-court movement represents a shift away from a criminal justice policy oriented toward punishing illicit drug users to a policy that focuses on treatment and recovery. Since the early 1990s, a number of problem-solving court programs, modeled after drug courts, have been created to foster treatment for other psychosocial difficulties. Mental-health courts, for example, provide a means for mentally ill defendants who have committed nonviolent criminal offenses to receive psychiatric evaluation and treatment. Driving-under-intoxication (DUI) courts and courts addressing problems of domestic violence have been developed as well.

Prevention and Treatment in the Workplace

The workplace has been recognized as an important focus for drug prevention and treatment. The 1988 Drug-free Workplace Act requires that all companies and businesses

receiving any U.S. federal contracts or grants provide a drug-free workplace. Specifically, organizations must initiate a comprehensive and continuing program of drug education and awareness. Employees must also be notified that the distribution, possession, or unauthorized use of controlled substances is prohibited in that workplace and that actions will be taken against any employee violating these rules. Supervisors are advised to be especially alert to changes in a worker that might signal early or progressive stages in the abuse of alcohol and or other drugs. These signals include chronic absenteeism, a sudden change in physical appearance or behavior, spasmodic work pace, unexpectedly lower quantity or quality of work, partial or unexplained absences, a pattern of excuse-making or lying, the avoidance of supervisors or coworkers, and on-the-job accidents or lost time from such accidents.

Employee Assistance Programs

By executive order of President Reagan in 1986, all U.S. federal agencies were directed to establish an employee assistance program (EAP) for governmental employees. Nongovernmental organizations have since been encouraged (but not required) by the 1988 Act to establish EAP services as well, so as to identify and counsel employees with personal problems that are connected to drug abuse or dependence and to provide referrals to community agencies where these individuals can get further help. Though not technically required to do so, steadily increasing numbers of American businesses have set up EAPs and are becoming committed to prevention and treatment. Of the approximately 115 million full-time workers aged eighteen to sixty-four in the United States, nearly 60 percent are currently employed in a workplace setting that has ongoing EAP services, and nearly 80 percent report that they are aware of a written policy about drug and alcohol use in the workplace. Traditionally, the emphasis in EAPs (as well as in union-supported member assistance programs, MAPs) has been on problems resulting from alcohol abuse, understandable given that this category represents such a large proportion of drug abuse in general

It's amazing how Dave's car broke down for the fifth straight Monday.

Dave doesn't really have a car problem. He has a drug problem. And if he works for you, it's your problem. Drug users have almost double the normal absentee rate, which you certainly can't afford.

So call **1-800-843-4971** for a free guide on how to set up a drug-free workplace.

It's surprisingly easy. And a lot cheaper than Dave's car problem.

DRUGS DON'T WORK

1-800-843-4971
Partnership for a Drug-Free America

Drug and alcohol problems are major sources of worker absenteeism and decreased productivity.

(Chapter 10). This emphasis remains, but there is a growing awareness that the range of drug-abuse problems is wider than alcoholism.[12]

Drug Testing in the Workplace

The 1986 Executive Order also mandated preemployment drug screening of all federal employees as well as periodic, random schedules of drug testing afterward. Assuming the most commonly available EMIT urinalysis were used (see Chapter 8), drug testing refers to a screening for opiates, amphetamines, cocaine, benzodiazepines, and marijuana. (It is not known whether the president at the time or subsequent presidents since 1986 have been included in this requirement.)

As with the policy regarding EAPs under the 1988 Drug-free Workplace Act, statutes do not require drug testing for employees other than those working for the federal government. Nonetheless, in 2004, according to a survey conducted by the American Management Association, approximately 62 percent of all companies tested for illicit drugs; 55 percent conducted testing as part of the job application process, and 44 percent conducted testing among current employees on a periodic basis.[13]

While it is easy to understand the rationale for drug testing in the workplace in the overall scheme of drug prevention, the procedure has raised a number of important issues regarding individual rights. Is the taking of a urine sample a violation of a person's freedom from "unreasonable search and seizure" as guaranteed by the Fourth Amendment to the U.S. Constitution? It turns out that if the government requires it, the decision rests on the question of whether there is reasonable or unreasonable cause for the drug testing to occur. In cases in which a threat to public safety is involved, the cause has been ruled as reasonable. However, if a private business requires it, the legal rights of employees are somewhat murky. An employee typically accepts his or her job offer with the assumption and agreement that periodic monitoring of drug use will take place, but whether this understanding is a form of implied coercion is an open question.

If you lose your job as a result of testing positive in a drug test, has there been a violation of your right to "due process" as guaranteed by the Fifth Amendment? The courts have ruled that this right would be violated only if the method of drug screening were unreliable, if the analysis and reporting were carried out in an unreliable manner, or if it could not be shown that the presence of any one of the screened substances had a relationship to job impairment. In general, screening methods are not perfectly reliable, the handling of drug tests is not perfectly controlled, and the relationship between drug use and a decline in job performance is not perfectly clear, but drug tests have nonetheless been judged to have met reasonable standards and the practice is allowed. The bottom line is that drug testing, despite its obvious infringements on individual privacy, has become a fact of life in corporate America.[14]

Nonetheless, despite the increasing acceptance of drug testing as a tool for drug-abuse prevention in the workplace, there will always be questions about the impact on workers themselves. For example, the possibility of false positives (when an individual tests positive but has not been using a particular drug) or false negatives (when an individual who, on the basis of prior drug use, should test positive for a particular drug, does not do so) during drug testing can present unfortunate consequences. Consider this possible preemployment screening scenario:

> *Suppose that the EMIT test were 100 percent effective in spotting drug users (it is not) and that it has a false-positive rate of 3 percent (which is not unreasonable). In a group of 100 prospective employees, one person has recently taken an illegal drug. Since the test is 100 percent effective, that person will be caught, but three other people (the 3 percent false-positive rate) will also. Therefore, 75 percent of those who fail the test are innocent parties.*[15]

Another problem is that companies are not required to follow up a positive EMIT test result with another more sensitive method, such as one using the GC/MS procedure (Chapter 8). Some companies allow for retesting in general, but most do not.

The Prevalence and Economic Costs of Alcohol and Other Drug Abuse in the Workplace

When considering the scope of drug-abuse problems in the workplace, it is all too easy to look at high-profile instances of on-the-job accidents involving the effects of either illicit drugs or alcohol. In 1991, a New York subway operator crashed his train near a station in lower Manhattan, resulting in five deaths and 215 injuries. The operator admitted that he had been drinking prior to the crash, and his BAC level was measured at 0.21 percent, more than twice the legal limit of 0.10 percent in New York at that time. In 1987, a Conrail train brakeman and an engineer were found to be responsible for a collision that resulted in sixteen deaths and 170 injuries. Drug testing revealed traces of marijuana in their systems,

though it was not clear if they were intoxicated at the time of the accident.

While these conspicuous examples are frequently used to justify the need for workplace testing, they do not accurately reflect the impact of alcohol and other drug abuse in the workplace for a number of reasons. First, the likelihood of an adverse effect is not adequately reflected in news reports, any more than the impact of drug toxicity on our society can be assessed by reading the news stories of public figures and celebrities who have died of drug overdoses (Chapter 2). Second, in many cases, we are limited in determining the extent to which we can connect drug use with the tragic consequences of an accident because some drugs leave metabolites in the system long after they have stopped producing behavioral effects. In the case of the Conrail incident, the continued presence of marijuana metabolites for weeks after marijuana use can make the positive test results irrelevant. Nonetheless, we are greatly influenced in our thinking by the media coverage of such events.

Obviously, we must turn to estimates gathered from other sources of information. Unfortunately, these estimates are "soft," having large margins of error. Even so, they leave little doubt that the abuse of alcohol and other drugs has a major impact on workplace productivity. On the basis of its own studies, the federal Center for Substance Abuse Prevention (CSAP) estimates that, relative to nonabusers, abusers of alcohol and other drugs

- are 5 times more likely to file a workers' compensation claim
- are 2.5 times more likely to be absent from work for eight days or more
- are 3.6 times more likely to be involved in an accident on the job
- are 5 times more likely to be personally injured on the job
- are 3 times more likely to be late for work
- are 2.2 times more likely to request early dismissal from work or time off
- use 16 times more sick leave

Overall, the estimated costs from productivity lost as a result of such behavior amount to $60–$100 billion each year.[16]

The Impact of Drug-Free Workplace Policies

Given the adverse effects of drug abuse on productivity, we should expect to see substantial economic and personal benefits when drug-free workplace policies are in place. In one well-documented case, a program developed by the Southern Pacific Railroad Company in the 1980s, extensive drug testing was required for all employees who had been involved in a company accident or rule violation. As a result, the annual number of accidents decreased from 911 to 168 in three years and the financial losses from such accidents decreased from $6.4 million to $1.2 million. During the first few months of the new testing program, it was found that 22–24 percent of employees who had experienced some human-factor-related accident tested positive for alcohol or other drugs, a figure that fell to 3 percent three years later.[17]

It makes sense that drug-abuse prevention programs would have the greatest impact in companies within the transportation industry, owing to the close relationship between drug-induced impairments in performance and the incidence of industrial accidents. Beyond this application, however, it is widely recognized that a similar impact, if not one as dramatic in magnitude, can be demonstrated in any business setting. The reasons relate to the basic goals of prevention, as discussed earlier: deterrence and rehabilitation. The practice of testing for illicit drug use in the workplace functions as an effective deterrent among workers because the likelihood is strong that illicit drug use will be detected. In addition, EAP services can function as an effective rehabilitative tool because those workers who might otherwise not receive help with drug-abuse problems of all kinds now will be referred to appropriate agencies for treatment services.[18]

The Personal Journey to Treatment and Recovery

Individuals who seek help in a treatment program have typically been "jolted" by some external force in their lives. They may have no other option except imprisonment for drug offenses; they may be at risk of losing their job because their supervisor has identified an unproductive pattern of behavior; a spouse may have threatened to leave if something is not done; a friend may have died from a drug overdose or a drug-related accident. Any of these crises or others similar to them can force the question and the decision to seek treatment.

The prospect of entering a treatment program is probably the most frightening experience the abuser has ever had in his or her life. Treatment counselors frequently hear the questions "Couldn't I just cut down?" or "Couldn't I just give up drugs temporarily?" or "How will I be able to take the pain of withdrawal?" or "How

will I be able to stand the humiliation?" Far from stalling tactics, these questions represent real obstacles to taking the crucial first steps to recovery.[19]

Rehabilitation and the Stages of Change

Rehabilitation from drug abuse and dependence has three major goals. First, the long decline in physical and psychological functioning that has accumulated over the years must be reversed. Drugs take a heavy toll on the user's medical condition and his or her personal relationships. Second, the use of all psychoactive substances must stop, not simply the one or two that are causing the immediate problem and not merely for a limited period of time. Thus the motivation to stop using alcohol and other drugs and to remain abstinent on a permanent basis must be strong, and stay strong. Third, a life-style free of alcohol and other drugs must be rebuilt, from scratch if necessary. This frequently means giving up the old friends and the old places where drugs were part of an abuser's life, and finding new friends and places that reinforce a drug-free existence. A determination to stay clean and sober requires avoiding high-risk situations, defined as those that increase the possibility of relapse.[20]

We can understand the journey toward rehabilitation by examining five separate stages through which the recovering individual must pass.[21] These stages are (1) precontemplation, (2) contemplation, (3) preparation, (4) action, and (5) maintenance. Rather than thinking of these stages as a linear progression, however, it is more accurate to think of them as points along a spiral (Figure 17.3); more than likely, a person will recycle through the stages multiple times before he or she is totally rehabilitated. Unfortunately, relapse is the rule rather than the exception in the process of recovery. The following is an examination of each stage in detail.

- *Precontemplation.* Individuals who are in the **precontemplation stage** may *wish* to change but lack the serious intention to undergo change in the foreseeable future or may be unaware of how significant their problems have become. They may be entering treatment at this time only because they perceive that a crisis is at hand. They may even demonstrate a

precontemplation stage: A stage of change in which the individual may wish to change but either lacks the serious intention to undergo change in the foreseeable future or is unaware of how significant his or her problem has become.

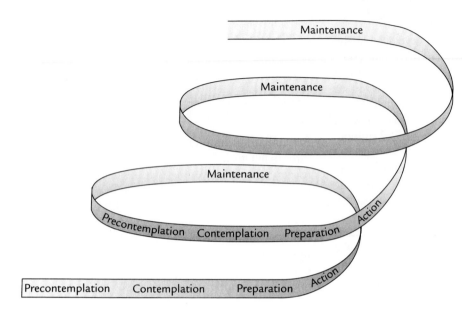

FIGURE 17.3

A spiral model of the stages of change in the recovery from drug abuse and dependence.

Source: Prochaska, James O., DiClemente, Carlo C., and Norcross, John C. (1992). In search of how people change: Applications to addictive behaviors. *American Psychologist, 47,* p. 1104. Copyright © 1992 by the American Psychological Association. Adapted with permission.

change in behavior while the pressure is on, but once the pressure is off, they revert to their former ways. It is often difficult for a counselor to deal with a drug abuser during the precontemplation stage because the abuser still feels committed to positive aspects of drug use. A principal goal at this point is to induce inconsistencies in the abuser's perception of drugs in general.

■ *Contemplation.* In the **contemplation stage,** individuals are aware that a problem exists and are thinking about overcoming it but have not yet made a commitment to take action. At this point, drug abusers may struggle with the prospect of the tremendous amount of effort and energy needed to overcome the problem. Counselors can help them by highlighting the negative aspects of drug use, making reasonable assurances about the recovery process, and building the self-confidence necessary to change.

contemplation stage: A stage of change in which the individual is aware that a problem exists and is thinking about overcoming it but has not yet made a commitment to take action.

preparation stage: A stage of change in which the individual seriously considers taking action to overcome a problem in the next thirty days and has unsuccessfully taken action over the past twelve months.

action stage: A stage of change in which the individual actually modifies his or her behavior and environment to overcome a problem.

maintenance stage: A stage of change in which the individual has become drug-free for a minimum of six months and has developed new skills and strategies that reduce the probability of relapse.

■ *Preparation.* Individuals in the **preparation stage** are defined as those who are seriously considering taking action in the next thirty days and have unsuccessfully taken action over the past twelve months. Alcohol abusers or tobacco smokers may at this point set a "quit date," or a heroin abuser may make a firm date to enter a therapeutic community within the next month. Because drug abusers are fully capable of stating a clear commitment to change at the preparation stage, counselors can begin to discuss the specific steps in the recovery process, strategies for avoiding problems or postponements, and ways to involve friends and family members.

■ *Action.* The **action stage** is the point at which individuals actually modify their behavior, their experiences, and their environment in an effort to overcome their problem. Drug use has now stopped. This is the most fragile stage; abusers are at a high risk for giving in to drug cravings and experiencing mixed feelings about the psychological costs of staying clean. If they successfully resist these urges to return to drug use, the counselor should strongly reinforce their restraint. If they slip back to drug use temporarily and then return to abstinence, the counselor should praise their efforts to turn their life around. An important message to be conveyed at this stage is that a fundamental change in life-style and a strong support system of friends and family will reduce the chances of relapse.

■ *Maintenance stage.* Individuals in the **maintenance stage** have been drug-free for a minimum of six months. They have developed new skills and strategies to avoid backsliding and are consolidating a life-style free of drugs. Here, the counselor must simultaneously acknowledge the success that has been achieved and emphasize that the struggle will never be totally over. The maintenance stage is ultimately open-ended, in that it continues for the rest of the ex-user's life. Therefore, it may be necessary to have booster sessions from time to time so that the maintenance stage is itself maintained.

Stages of Change and Other Problems in Life

If these stages of change seem vaguely familiar to you, with or without a drug-related problem, it is no accident. Problems may take many different forms, but the difficulties that we face when we confront these problems have a great deal in common. We may wish to lose weight, get more exercise, stop smoking, end an unhappy relationship, seek out a physician to help a medical condition, or any of a number of actions that might lead toward a healthier and more productive life. We only have to witness the popularity of New Year's Eve resolutions to appreciate the fact that our desire to take steps to change is part of simply being human. And yet, we often feel frustrated when our intentions do not prevail and those resolutions are left unfulfilled. You may find it helpful to look at your own personal journey toward resolving a problem in your life in terms of the five stages of change.[22]

The Importance of Family Systems in Prevention and Treatment

Family members of a drug abuser can be highly resistant to becoming involved in the treatment process, often abdicating any responsibility for the problems that abuse has produced. Their embarrassment, shame, and personal feelings of inadequacy in the face of the abuser's drug-dominated life-style are overwhelming. Resistance to change may also come from a family's assumption that they must assume the responsibility when the drug abuser has not. This second scenario results in a pattern of enabling behavior.

Family Dynamics in Drug Abuse

Learning how the family has coped with having a drug abuser as a family member is crucial not only in understanding the origins of the abuse but also in maximizing

the chances of successful treatment (Health Alert). A prominent therapist and author has put it this way:

The alcoholic/addict family system could be compared with an unbalanced toy top, one so top-heavy that when it tries to spin in a functional pattern, it instead swerves to one side and skids in a diagonal direction until it stops. The individuals in this system are all compensating in different yet similar ways. It's as if they are walking around with a heavy weight on one shoulder; they have to either lean to one side to walk properly or use all their energy to try to compensate and look as if they are walking upright. Both positions require a great deal of energy.[23]

Coping with a Child's Abuse of Alcohol or Other Drugs: What Parents Should and Should Not Do

The negative impact of enabling behaviors on anyone's path to recovery is particularly evident in the interactions between a parent and a child. Beyond simply recognizing the process of enabling, parents (and other family members as well) should learn the skills necessary to "disenable" or disengage from the ongoing abuse. It is a critical step to take to establish a family climate in which treatment and rehabilitation can advance. Here are some guidelines:

You Should Avoid

feeling hurt or guilty when your child turns his or her anger on you

nagging your child about the destructive effects of drug abuse; it will merely provoke your child to continue the abusive behavior in a more surreptitious way

hiding your child's abuse from other family members or friends or making excuses to them about your child's behavior

making threats you neither mean nor can effectively enforce

You Should Never

confront your child when you are angry

use physical or verbal abuse toward your child

be the janitor for your child's messes by paying fines, repairing property damage, and so on

You Should

remember that your responsibility lies in helping your son or daughter recover from a sickness

---

Where to go for assistance:

www.theantidrug.com

The "Parents: The antidrug" web site is sponsored by the National Youth Anti-Drug Media Campaign, partnering with the Substance Abuse and Mental Health Services Administration (SAMHSA), U.S. Department of Health and Human Services. It contains advice and information for parents of teenage children with regard to drug use and abuse.

Source: Schaefer, Dick (1987). *Choices and consequences: What to do when a teenager uses alcohol/drugs.* Minneapolis, MN: Johnson Institute Books, pp. 82–84.

The pattern of family reactions to the conditions of drug abuse in many ways resembles the stages people go through when grieving the loss of a loved one.

Treatment for drug-related problems is optimized when there is positive involvement from the family.

- *Denial.* Feelings of denial help family members avoid feelings of humiliation and shame, not to mention their own sense of responsibility. They might rationalize that their family is no different from most others. If they talk with people outside the family system, it is typically done to reinforce their denial. They want assurance that their denial of problems is not a delusion.

- *Anger.* Expressed verbally or physically, anger is a strategy for avoiding feelings of shame by blaming others in the family for the problem. Causing a fight at home is sometimes a way for the abuser to get out of the house and to escape to a place where the abuse of alcohol or other drugs is more easily tolerated. Needless to say, the pattern of family interaction can be confused and unpredictable.

- *Bargaining.* When a major crisis ensues, family members can no longer deny the problem or react in anger. Implicit agreements are made that if a pattern of drug abuse will stop, the family will respond in a positive way. Conversely, a bargain might be struck that if the family tolerates the continuation of drug abuse, then the abuser will continue to support the family financially.

- *Feeling.* Earlier reactions, now exhausted, are replaced by a pervasive anxiety and obsessiveness toward the entire situation. Family members may cry at the slightest provocation or find themselves immobilized in carrying out their daily lives.
- *Acceptance.* Denial, anger, and bargaining have failed, and feelings have become too disruptive. The family is forced to seek help; they realize that they have a problem, and they are ready to do whatever is necessary to overcome or resolve it. It is at this point that the contemplation and preparation stages of change begin.[24]

Enabling Behaviors as Obstacles to Rehabilitation

The adverse impact of enabling on the life of an alcoholic was discussed in Chapter 10, but it should be evident that applications hold for all forms of drug abuse. In general, enablers take on themselves the responsibility that has been rejected by someone else. In effect, they try to cushion the consequences that inevitably occur as a result of that other person's irresponsibility. This pattern of behavior can take several forms.[25]

- *Avoiding and shielding.* Enablers make up excuses to avoid social situations where drug abuse is going on and keep up appearances when among friends or neighbors. They may stay away from home as much as they can to avoid dealing with the family situation.
- *Attempting to control.* Enablers might buy gifts in an attempt to divert the abuser from dealing with his or her problems. They might threaten to injure themselves in an attempt to get the family member to stop.
- *Taking over responsibilities.* Enablers might assume the responsibility of waking the abuser of alcohol or other drugs in time for work in the morning. They might take second jobs to cover the bills that have piled up because money has been squandered on alcohol and other drugs.
- *Rationalizing and accepting.* Enablers might communicate the belief that the episodes of drug abuse were only isolated and sporadic, that family members were not *really* endangered, or that there was a positive side to the drug-taking behavior, such as the relief of depression or anxiety.
- *Cooperation and collaborating.* At an extreme level, enablers might facilitate the process of drug abuse by

helping to clean and purify drugs, drinking along with an alcoholic, or lending money to purchase street drugs or alcohol so that stealing money is not necessary.

Survival Roles and Coping Mechanisms

The problems of growing up in a dysfunctional family system were examined in Chapter 10 in the case of children of alcoholic parents. Not surprisingly, the interpersonal problems within the family unit are similar for any situation in which drug abuse or dependence is involved. Sharon Wegscheider-Cruse has been an influential theorist in pointing out specific ways of coping with this difficult circumstance. In her view, there are five dysfunctional roles that a family member may assume. While each of these roles eventually works to the detriment of the individual, understanding them helps the family during the process of counseling and facilitates the eventual reconstruction of family relationships.[26]

- *Chief Enabler.* In this role, the chief enabler takes on the principal responsibility for the family member involved in alcohol or other drug abuse. These responsibilities include shielding and denying the extent of dysfunctionality in the family, controlling the abuser's life, and rationalizing the negative effects on others in the family.
- *Family Hero.* As a compensation for the failures of the family, the family hero will strive to be the model child, escaping the dysfunctional system through personal achievement. This individual will be outwardly successful but feel like an overachiever and a fraud, undeserving of success and happiness.
- *Family Scapegoat.* This is an effort to divert attention away from real problems within the family through antisocial behavior. The family scapegoat role often results in delinquency in school and elsewhere.
- *The Lost Child.* This is a role that is intended to reduce the pain and suffering within the family, by isolating oneself from family dynamics and denying one's own feelings and needs. Often, the lost child "fades into the woodwork," becoming disconnected emotionally and physically from the family.
- *Family Mascot.* Through humor and self-disparaging behavior, the family mascot strives to divert attention away from the dysfunctionality of the family. As a result, however, the price paid for calm and emotional relief is a lack of maturity and a diminished sense of personal self-esteem.

Resistance at the Beginning, Support along the Way

Given the variety of possible dysfunctional interactions within the family, it is not surprising that it is difficult to get a person to seek help in a meaningful way. Abusers might feel protective of their families, not wishing to add more pain and anguish to what they have already suffered. For their part, families might reinforce these protective feelings by being appreciative that the abuser is thinking of them. Abusers might feel that involving the family in treatment may uncover their own communication of inaccurate or distorted information to the counselor. There is also the fear that if counselors criticize family members for sharing the responsibility for drug abuse, family members might later retaliate by making domestic life even worse than it is.

Whatever the difficulties in family dynamics at the onset of treatment, there is no doubt that family support is crucial as treatment progresses. Counselors frequently emphasize that family members and friends should not feel the burden of responsibility for the problem itself, nor are they responsible for the abuser's decision to enter (or reject) treatment. Instead, their responsibility is to support the abuser along the way to recovery by changing as well. In the case of alcoholism, the establishment of sobriety does not always ensure a smooth, placid relationship within the family. As a therapist has expressed it, the entire family needs to "reestablish communication, work through old resentments, develop trust, and strive to produce a comfortable and rewarding relationship."[27] A drug-free family is more than a family without drugs in their lives; it is a family that is completely different from what it has been before.

Finding the Right Drug-Abuse Treatment Program

Seeking treatment in general may be difficult enough, but there are also the decisions that must be made regarding the type of program that is best suited for a given individual. Health professionals recommend a comprehensive drug-abuse treatment, based upon a combination of therapies and other services that have been tailored to specific needs (Figure 17.4).

Certain general guidelines can help in this process.

- First, outpatient treatment should be given preference over inpatient treatment; among the advantages, an outpatient approach is less costly and concentrates on the adjustment to a drug-free life in the context of functioning in the "real world." Consider inpatient treatment (1) when outpatient treatment has failed, (2) when medical or psychiatric problems require hospitalization, (3) when outpatient treatment facilities are a great distance from home, or (4) when problems are so severe so as to warrant a removal from the current environment for a length of time. If inpatient treatment is chosen, the program should be kept as short as possible, usually two to four weeks, as longer inpatient care has not been demonstrated to be any more effective.

- Second, a pharmacological approach (such as methadone maintenance or naltrexone treatment) should be combined with psychotherapy or behavioral counseling whenever possible. A multipronged approach is usually the most effective one.

- Third, self-help groups such as Alcoholics Anonymous (AA) and similar organizations should be considered; they cost nothing and are helpful not only in the action stage of change but also in the maintenance stage that follows.

- Fourth, contact should be continued with the treatment facility for at least six to twelve months. This ongoing connection minimizes the possibility of dropping out of the program or relapse during maintenance.

- Fifth, drug abusers with few sources of social support should consider a half-way or recovery house for three to six months.[28]

Judging the Quality of the Treatment Facility

Claims that sound "too good to be true" are never made by a high-quality drug-abuse treatment facility, and advertisements give only a superficial impression of what the program might really entail. A good idea is to interview key people at the facility in person. Some good questions to ask are the following:

- Does the program accept your insurance? If not, will the facility staff work with you on a payment plan or find other means of support for you?

- Is the program run by state-accredited, licensed, and/or trained professionals? Is the facility accredited by the Joint Commission for the Accreditation of Healthcare Organizations (JCAHO)?

- Is the facility clean, organized, and well run?

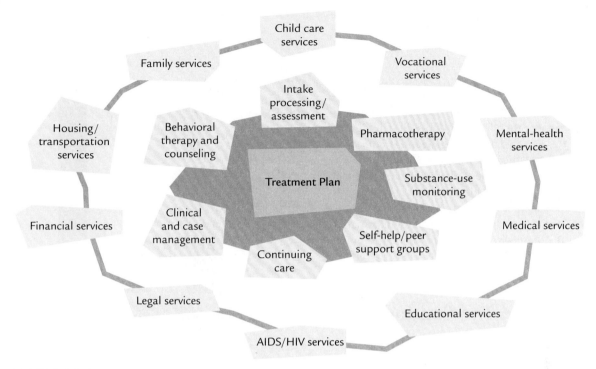

FIGURE 17.4

Components of a comprehensive treatment program for drug abuse.

Source: Modified from National Institute on Drug Abuse (1999), *Principles of drug addiction treatment: A research-based guide.* Rockville, MD: National Institute on Drug Abuse, p. 14.

- Does the program encompass the full range of needs of the individual (e.g., medical, including infectious diseases; psychological, including coexisting mental illness; social; vocational; legal)?

- Does the treatment program address sexual orientation and physical disabilities as well as provide age-, gender-, and culturally appropriate treatment service?

- Is long-term aftercare support and/or guidance encouraged, provided, and maintained?

- Is there ongoing assessment of an individual's treatment plan to ensure that it meets changing needs?

- Does the program employ strategies to engage and keep individuals in longer-term treatment, increasing the likelihood of success?

- Does the program offer counseling (individual or group) and other behavioral therapies to enhance the individual's ability to function in the family/community?

- Does the program offer medication as part of the treatment regimen, if appropriate?

- Is there ongoing monitoring of possible relapse to help guide patients back to abstinence?

- Are services or referrals offered to family members to ensure that they understand the nature of substance dependence and the recovery process, to help them support recovering individuals?[29]

Information Resources

Information about treatment options in your community can be found in newspapers and classified sections (yellow pages) of telephone directories, under Alcoholism or Drug Abuse and Addiction Treatment. Web sites on the Internet are also very helpful. Probably the most comprehensive source is the National Clearinghouse for Alcohol and Drug Information (NCADI). Materials on topics covered in this chapter and regarding virtually any aspect of drug use, misuse, or abuse can be ordered free by calling 800-729-6686 or by accessing the NCADI web site at http://www.health.org.

The locations of more than 11,000 alcohol- or drug-abuse treatment facilities in the United States, Guam, U.S. Virgin Islands, and Puerto Rico are now searchable through a comprehensive directory database, sponsored by the Substance Abuse and Mental Health Services Administration (SAMHSA), through its web site at http://findtreatment.samhsa.gov. For residents of Canada, the Canadian Drug Rehab Centres web site (www.canadiandrugrehabcentres.com) provides a list of treatment facilities for alcohol and drug abuse. For residents of the United Kingdom, the web site www.addaction.org.uk describes the largest specialist drug- and alcohol-treatment charity in the country. To protect visitors' personal privacy, information entered into these directories is permanently erased after the search has been completed.

A Final Note: The Continuing Need for Drug-Abuse Treatment

According to U.S. government estimates, in 2007, approximately 7.5 million people aged twelve or older needed treatment for an illicit drug problem, but only 18 percent of them received drug-abuse treatment at a specialty substance-abuse facility in the past twelve months. With respect to those identified as having a need for alcohol-abuse treatment, the picture was even worse. In 2007, approximately 19.3 million people aged twelve or older needed treatment for an alcohol problem, but only 8 percent of them received it. Figure 17.5 shows, in visual terms, the wide gap between treatment needed and treatment received.

The reasons that people gave for not having received treatment even though treatment was needed are illuminating. For the approximately 6.2 million individuals who needed treatment for *an illicit drug problem* but did not receive it, only about 550,000 of them (9 percent) personally felt a need to seek help. The major reasons people in this latter group gave for failing to receive treatment included not having adequate insurance coverage or not being about to afford treatment costs on their own, not being ready to stop illicit drug use, or fearing the negative impact in their community or their workplace if they sought treatment. For the approximately 17.7 million individuals who needed treatment for *an alcohol use problem* but did not receive it, only about 860,000 of them (5 percent) personally felt a need to seek help. About three-fourths

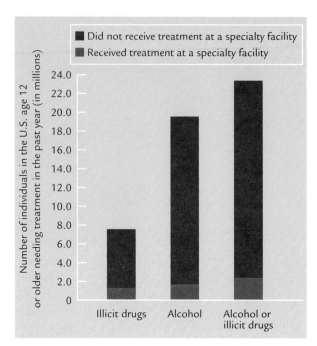

FIGURE 17.5

The gap between treatment needed and treatment received among individuals in the United States over the age of twelve.

Source: Substance Abuse and Mental Health Services Administration (2008). *Results from the 2007 National Survey on Drug Use and Health: National findings.* Rockville, MD: Office of Applied Studies, Substance Abuse and Mental Health Services Administration, pp. 80, 83.

of the people in this latter group made no effort at all to receive treatment.[30]

The future challenges for providing effective treatment for individuals with substance abuse are two-fold. First, more work must be done to increase the number of substance abusers who recognize that they need to seek treatment and that, should they do so, it would not have a negative impact in their lives. Second, more work must be done to provide accessible and affordable substance-abuse treatment for those individuals who want it and are willing to seek it out. Fortunately, affordable substance-abuse treatment in the United States took a major step forward recently when the Mental Health Parity and Addiction Equity Act of 2008 was passed by the U.S. Congress. As a result, individuals seeking treatment for substance use or a mental-health disorder will no longer face unfair and arbitrary restrictions on their benefits coverage, relative to coverage for other forms of health treatment, effective January 2010. It is estimated that approximately 113 million Americans will be affected by this new legislation.

Summary

Levels of Intervention in Drug-Abuse Prevention

- Drug-abuse prevention efforts fall into three basic levels of intervention: primary, secondary, and tertiary.

- Primary prevention focuses on populations that have had only minimal or no exposure to drugs. Secondary prevention focuses on populations whose drug experience has not yet been associated with serious long-term problems. Tertiary prevention focuses on populations who have entered drug treatment; the goal is to prevent relapse.

A Biopsychosocial Strategy for Treatment

- Because many individuals experience problems stemming from polydrug abuse, treatment programs must consider common difficulties associated with a range of alcohol and other drugs.

- Chances of success in drug-abuse treatment can be increased by looking at the combination of biological, psychological, and social factors leading to drug abuse. This is referred to as the biopsychosocial model.

Incarceration and Other Punitive Measures in the United States

- Federal laws since 1970 have established a hierarchy of criminal penalties for drug trafficking, depending on the schedule of the controlled substance, amounts that are involved, and special circumstances under which violations have been committed.

- In some cases, abusers of illicit drugs who are arrested for violating drug-control laws are given the option of a treatment program rather than prosecution and imprisonment. For those who are sentenced to a prison term, a limited number of opportunities for drug treatment exist within the prison system.

Prevention and Treatment in the Workplace

- Since the mid-1980s, a growing number of companies and other businesses have adopted measures to encourage a drug-free workplace. This involves, in part, the establishment of educational programs that increase workers' awareness of alcohol abuse, the abuse of illicit drugs, and the impact of these behaviors on productivity and the quality of the workers' lives.

- One element of most drug-free workplace programs is an employee assistance program (EAP), serving to help workers with abuse problems. Where unions exist, member assistance programs (MAPs) supplement and complement the work of EAPs. Another element is a policy of drug testing, serving to reduce illicit drug use among workers and employment applicants.

- Although employee assistance programs and drug testing have been readily accepted among U.S. businesses, questions about the extent to which drug testing violates personal privacy and individual rights still remain.

The Personal Journey to Treatment and Recovery

- The road to recovery can be understood in terms of five stages of change: precontemplation, contemplation, preparation, action, and maintenance. It is possible to recycle through these stages multiple times in a kind of spiraling pattern before long-term recovery is attained.

- The five stages of change are applicable to the resolution of any life problems, not just those associated with drug abuse.

The Importance of Family Systems in Prevention and Treatment

- It is critical to examine the family dynamics surrounding a drug abuser not only to understand the situational problems that have developed but also to anticipate and deal with the obstacles that might derail treatment. Family units typically pass through the stages of denial, anger, bargaining, feeling, and finally acceptance as treatment is at first rejected and then sought.

- One major way that family systems can jeopardize successful treatment is through enabling behavior, in which family members assume many of the responsibilities that are rejected by the drug abuser. Enabling can take several forms.

- Family support is crucial for a treatment program to be successful and for relapse to be avoided, though the responsibility always remains with the abuser.

Finding the Right Drug-Abuse Treatment Program

- It is important to consider the goals and objectives of a treatment program to find the one best suited to the person seeking help. Decisions must be made regarding the inpatient/outpatient format for treatment or whether a pharmacological intervention is indicated.

- It is also important to inspect the treatment facility in person. The ability for the treatment program to address the full range of individual needs, the availability to offer diverse forms of treatment, and the licensure and/or accreditation status of the facility are among the major criteria to be weighed.

The Continuing Need for Drug-Abuse Treatment

● According to U.S. government estimates, more than 7 million people, aged twelve or older, need treatment for an illicit drug problem; more than 19 million people need treatment for an alcohol problem. A small fraction, however, have received treatment at a specialized facility in the past twelve months.

● Of those individuals who have needed treatment for illicit drug or alcohol use problems but have not received it, fewer than 10 percent personally felt the need to seek it out. Major reasons for not seeking treatment include the lack of financial means to pay for treatment services, an unwillingness to stop using illicit drugs or alcohol, and the perceived negative impact that might result from entering treatment.

Key Terms

action stage, p. 408
biopsychosocial model, p. 398
contemplation stage, p. 408
deterrence, p. 399

drug court, p. 403
drug paraphernalia, p. 401
drug trafficking, p. 399
incarceration, p. 399
maintenance stage, p. 408

polydrug abusers, p. 398
precontemplation stage, p. 407
preparation stage, p. 408
primary prevention, p. 396

rehabilitation, p. 399
secondary prevention, p. 396
simple possession, p. 400
tertiary prevention, p. 396

Endnotes

1. Foxhall, Kathryn (2001, June). Preventing relapse: Looking at data differently led to today's influential relapse prevention therapy. *Monitor on Psychology*, pp. 46–47. Substance Abuse and Mental Health Services Administration (2005). Substance Abuse and Mental Health Service Administration (2008). *Treatment Episode Data Set (TEDS) highlights—2006: National admissions to substance abuse treatment services*. Rockville, MD: Office of Applied Studies, Substance Abuse and Mental Health Services Administration, p. 1. Swisher, John D. (1979). Prevention issues. In R. L. DuPont, A. Goldstein, and J. O'Donnell (Eds.). *Handbook on drug abuse*. Washington DC: National Institute on Drug Abuse, pp. 423–435.

2. Julien, Robert M. (2001). *A primer of drug action* (9th ed.). New York: Worth, pp. 371–377. Nestler, Eric J., and Malenka, Robert C. (2004, March). The addicted brain. *Scientific American*, pp. 78–85.

3. Substance Abuse and Mental Health Services Administration (2006). Emergency department visits involving patients with co-occurring disorders. *The New DAWN Report*. Rockville, MD: Substance Abuse and Mental Health Services Administration. Substance Abuse and Mental Health Services Administration (2003). 22 million Americans suffer from substance dependence or abuse. *SAMHSA News, 11* (3).

4. Drug Enforcement Agency, U.S. Department of Justice. Statutes of the Controlled Substances Act of 1970, as amended and revised in 1986 and 1988.

5. Healey, Kerry (1988). *State and local experience with drug paraphernalia laws*. Washington DC: U.S. Government Printing Office, pp. 69–73.

6. Sabol, William J., Couture, Heather, and Harrison, Paige M. (2007, December). Prisoners in 2006. *Bureau of Justice Statistics Bulletin*. Washington DC: Bureau of Justice Statistics, U.S. Department of Justice, pp. 1 and 9. Sabol, William, and Couture, Heather (2008, June). Prison inmates at midyear 2007. *Bureau of Justice Statistics Bulletin*. Washington DC: Bureau of Justice Statistics, U.S. Department of Justice, 1.

7. California drug courts: A methodology for determining costs and avoided costs (2004, May). *Journal of Psychoactive Drugs*, SARC Supplement 2, 147–156.

8. Burdon, William M.; Farabee, David; Prendergast, Michael L.; Messina, Nena P.; and Cartier, Jerome (2002). Prison-based therapeutic community substance abuse programs: Implementation and operational issues. *Federal Probation, 66*, 3–5. Center for Substance Abuse Treatment (1997). *50 strategies for substance abuse treatment*. Rockville, MD: Substance Abuse and Mental Health Services Administration. National Center on Addiction and Substance Abuse at Columbia University (1998, January). Behind bars: Substance abuse and America's prison population. Bureau of Justice Statistics, Special Report.

9. Office of National Drug Control Policy (2005, February). The President's National Drug Control Strategy. Washington DC: Office of National Drug Control Policy. Substance Abuse and Mental Health Services Administration (2006, March/April). Incarceration vs. treatment: Drug courts help substance abusing offenders. *SAMHSA News*, pp. 1–3, 4.

10. Gottfredson, D.C., Najaka, S.S., and Kearley, B. (2003). Effectiveness of drug treatment courts: Evidence from a randomized trial. *Criminology and Public Policy, 2*, 401–426. Huddleston, C. West, Freeman-Wilson, Karen, and Boone, Donna L. (2004, May). *Painting the current picture: A national report card on drug courts and other*

problem solving court programs in the United States. Alexandria, VA: National Drug Court Institute. Office of Justice Programs (2006, June). *Drug courts: The second decade. NIJ Special Report.* Washington DC: U.S. Department of Justice.

11. Goldkamp, John S. (2001). Do drug courts work? Getting inside the drug court black box. *Journal of Drug Issues, 31,* 27–73. Huddleston, Freeman-Wilson, and Boone (2005), *Painting the current picture.* Quotation from Home Box Office (2007, March). Mandated treatment. www.hbo.com/addiction.

12. Larson, Sharon L.; Eyerman, Joe; Foster, Misty S.; and Gfroerer, Joseph C. (2007). *Worker substance use and workplace policies and programs.* Rockville, MD: Substance Abuse and Mental Health Services Administration, p. 2.

13. American Management Association (2004). *AMA 2004 workplace testing survey: Medical testing.* New York: American Management Association, p. 3. French, Michael T., Zarkin, Gary A., and Bray, Jeremy W. (1995). A methodology for evaluating the costs and benefits of employee assistance programs. *Journal of Drug Issues, 25,* 451–470. Substance Abuse and Mental Health Services Administration (2008, March 15). *Making your workplace drug-free: A kit for employers.* Rockville, MD: Substance Abuse and Mental Health Services Administration.

14. Comerford, Anthony W. (1999). Work dysfunction and addiction. *Journal of Substance Abuse Treatment, 16,* 247–253. Normand, J., Lempert, R., and O'Brien, C. (Eds.) (1994). *Under the influence? Drugs and the American work force.* Washington DC: National Academy Press.

15. Avis, Harry (1996). *Drugs and life* (3rd ed.). Dubuque, IA: Brown and Benchmark, p. 256.

16. Center for Substance Abuse Prevention (1994). *Making the link: Alcohol, tobacco, and other drugs in the workplace.* Rockville, MD: Center for Substance Abuse Prevention. Substance Abuse and Mental Health Services Administration.

17. National Transportation Safety Board (1988). *Alcohol/drug use and its impact on railroad safety: Safety study.* Washington DC: U.S. Department of Transportation.

18. Blum, Terry C., and Roman, Paul M. (1995). *Cost-effectiveness and preventive implications of employee assistance programs.* Rockville, MD: Substance Abuse and Mental Health Services Administration.

19. Connors, Gerard J., Donovan, Dennis J., and DiClemente, Carlo C. (2001). *Substance abuse treatment and the stages of change: Selecting and planning interventions.* New York: Guilford Press. DiClemente, Carlo C., Bellino, Lori E., and Neavins, Tara M. (1999). Motivation for change and alcoholism treatment. *Alcohol Research and Health, 23,* 86–92. Schuckit, Marc A. (1995). *Educating yourself about alcohol and drugs: A people's primer.* New York: Plenum Press, pp. 131–153.

20. Schuckit, *Educating yourself,* pp. 186–216.

21. Dijkstra, Arie, Roijackers, Jolanda, and DeVries, Hein (1998). Smokers in four stages of readiness to change. *Addictive Behaviors, 23,* 339–350. Prochaska, James O.,

DiClemente, Carlo C., and Norcross, John C. (1992). In search of how people change. *American Psychologist, 47,* 1102–1114.

22. Norman, Gregory J.; Velicer, Wayne F.; Fava, Joseph L.; and Prochaska, James O. (1998). Dynamic typology clustering within the stages of change for smoking cessation. *Addictive Behaviors, 23,* 139–153. Prochaska, James O. (1994). *Changing for good.* New York: William Morrow. Velicer, Wayne F.; Norman, Gregory J.; Fava, Joseph L.; and Prochaska, James O. (1999). Testing 40 predictions from the transtheoretical model. *Addictive Behaviors, 24,* 455–469.

23. Fields, Richard (2007). *Drugs in perspective: A personalized look at substance use and abuse* (6th ed.). New York: McGraw-Hill, p. 155.

24. Ibid., pp. 165–171.

25. Ibid., pp. 160–165. Margolis, Robert D., and Zweben, Joan E. (1998). *Treating patients with alcohol and other drug problems: An integrated approach.* Washington DC: American Psychological Association. Nelson, Charles (1988). The style of enabling behavior. In David E. Smith, and Donald Wesson (Eds.), *Treating cocaine dependence.* Center City, MN: Hazelden Foundation.

26. Wegscheider-Cruse, Sharon (1981). *Another chance: Hope and health for the alcoholic family.* Palo Alto, CA: Science and Behavior Books. Wegscheider-Cruse, Sharon; Higby, Kathy; Klontz, Ted; and Rainey, Ann (1994). *Family reconstruction: The Living Theater Model.* Palo Alto CA: Science and Behavior Books.

27. Schuckit, *Educating yourself,* pp. 229–230.

28. Schuckit, Marc A. (1995). *Drug and alcohol abuse: A clinical guide to diagnosis and treatment* (4th ed.). New York: Plenum Press, pp. 306–308. Sorensen, James L.; Rawson, Richard A.; Guydish, Joseph; and Zweben, Joan E. (2003). *Drug abuse treatment through collaboration: Practice and research partnerships that work.* Washington DC: American Psychological Association. Substance Abuse and Mental Health Services Administration, *50 strategies for substance abuse treatment.*

29. Center for Substance Abuse Treatment (2006). *Detoxification and substance abuse treatment.* Treatment Improvement Program (TIP) Series 45. Rockville, MD: Substance Abuse and Mental Health Services Administration. Adapted from Donatelle, Rebecca J., and Davis, Lorraine G. (2000). *Access to health* (6th ed.). Needham Heights, MA: Allyn and Bacon, p. 219. Guidelines for finding effective alcohol and drug treatment, courtesy of the Center for Substance Abuse Treatment, Substance Abuse and Mental Health Services Administration.

30. Markel, Howard (2003, October 21). Treatment for addiction meets barriers in the doctor's office. *New York Times,* pp. F5, F8. Substance Abuse and Mental Health Services Administration (2008). *Results of the 2007 National Survey on Drug Use and Health: National findings.* Rockville, MD: Office of Applied Studies, Substance Abuse and Mental Health Services Administration, pp. 76–84.

chapter 18

Prevention and Education: Schools, Community, and Family

Your daughter is pretty and popular. She's the homecoming queen and the editor of the school paper. So you think you're safe. You're not. Your son is on the swimming team, a star athlete. He's talking about going to medical school. So you think you're safe. You're not. That's what brings me here: I'm just like you. I thought I was safe too. What a kid needs today is self-esteem, right? Something to make him feel good about himself. A stable home life. And you'll get by. Wrong. . . .

Drugs are everywhere and they're everybody's problem. They're in big cities and in small rural communities. They strike troubled families and families whose children are seeming achievers, good students, athletes, prom queens.

—*Beth Polson,* Not my kid: A parent's guide to kids and drugs

The ruinous impact of illicit drugs on young people in the United States is one of the most emotion-laden social issues of our day. Perhaps the most disturbing aspect of statistical reports regarding the incidence of drug use concerns the youngest age category studied: eighth graders who are thirteen or fourteen years old. The need for effective prevention and education programs to reduce drug use and abuse among young people is a deeply personal issue, and we ask ourselves: What can be done?

This final chapter focuses on the efforts we are making in the area of primary and secondary prevention. In the case of primary prevention, we are assuming that the target population for these interventions may have been exposed to drug-taking behavior in other people but have not had drug experiences of their own. We recognize that the potential for young people to engage in drug use themselves is substantial, and only through an effective primary prevention can we keep that potential from turning into reality.

It is increasingly clear that the age of onset for drug-taking behavior of any kind is a key factor in determining problems later in life, particularly with respect to licit drugs. For example, a young person who begins drinking before the age of fifteen is twice as likely to develop a pattern of alcohol abuse and four times as likely to develop alcohol dependence than an individual who begins drinking at the age of twenty-one. In general, if the age of onset can be delayed significantly, there is the possibility of reducing the incidence of drug-taking abuse or dependence.[1]

In the case of secondary prevention, we are concentrating on the life-style of a somewhat older population, and our goal is to minimize the problems associated with drug-taking behavior, assuming that some level of that behavior already exists. As mentioned in Chapter 17, emphasis is placed on social alternatives to behaviors involving alcohol and other drugs among high school students. At the college level, the moderate use of alcohol, and particularly the avoidance of alcohol binging, as well as education about the personal risks of some of the newer club drugs and the nonmedical use of prescription medications, are all elements in a program of secondary prevention.

Whether we are addressing issues of primary or secondary prevention, however, we must remain fully aware that the entire range of drug-taking behaviors needs to be considered. This range encompasses not only illicit drug use but also the drinking of alcohol, the inappropriate use of medications, and the consumption of tobacco products. As a consequence, it will be useful in this chapter to adopt a somewhat awkward but

necessary phrase *alcohol, tobacco, and other drug (ATOD) prevention* to describe our society's response in this regard. As we all know, a conspicuous target behavior within the overall mission of prevention and education in recent years has been tobacco use among young people.

ATOD Prevention: Strategic Priorities, Goals, and Resilience

The U.S. federal agency specifically charged with the prevention of alcohol, tobacco, and other drug abuse is the Center for Substance Abuse Prevention (CSAP). According to CSAP guidelines, ATOD prevention is accomplished through two major efforts. The first is the promotion of constructive life-styles and norms that discourage ATOD use. The second is the development of social and physical environments that facilitate ATOD-free life-styles.

You may recall from Chapter 1 that two groups of factors play a major role in predicting the extent of ATOD use in a particular individual: risk factors that increase the likelihood of ATOD use and protective factors that decrease it. You can think of the two components of prevention in those terms. On one hand, it is a matter of minimizing the impact of risk factors in an individual's life. On the other hand, it is a matter of maximizing the impact of protective factors. The number of "developmental assets" (see Chapter 1) increases the chances that ATOD prevention and education efforts will be successful.

Resilience and Primary Prevention Efforts

Successful primary prevention programs are built around the central idea that an individual is less inclined to engage in ATOD use if the protective factors in his or her life are enhanced and the risk factors are diminished. Only then can a young person be resilient enough to overcome the temptations of alcohol, tobacco, and other drugs. **Resilience,** defined as the inclination to resist the effect of risk factors through the action of protective factors, can be a make-or-break element in his or her social development. The promotion of positive social and personal skills, and the encouragement of a proactive rather than a passive approach to problem solving, enhance the "buffering effect" of protective factors with respect to ATOD use and other forms of deviant behavior. To be most effective, it is necessary to incorporate aspects of a young person's environment beyond the school itself in the fight against ATOD use. In a later section, we will turn to primary prevention efforts that involve the community at large.[2]

National Drug-Control Strategy Priorities

The overall national policy for the control of drug use in the United States is coordinated by the White House Office of National Drug Control Policy (ONDCP). In the current formulation of this policy, three priorities are set as components of a national strategy.[3]

- *Priority I—Stopping drug use before it starts.* Primary prevention programs, to be reviewed in this chapter, are essentially the first line of defense against drug-abuse problems among young people. The key characteristic of effective programs is their basis on research ("research based" programs). That is, the

outcome measures of individuals who have participated in the program are directly compared to those of individuals who have not participated in the program (the control group). If drug use among eighth graders has declined as a result of a prevention program, for example, but this decline is not greater than a decline among eighth graders in the control group, then the prevention program is essentially ineffective. As we will see, effective school-based prevention programs do exist, but the overall effectiveness is enhanced when there is a combination of education and community action.

- *Priority II—Healing America's drug users.* Tertiary prevention programs, accomplished through intervention and drug-abuse treatment, were reviewed in Chapter 17. As with primary prevention programs, treatment programs are judged effective based on the comparison of program outcome measures (the period of time during which individuals remain drug-free, for example) to measures for individuals in appropriate control groups. In 2003, a new federal "voucher program" was instituted for people in need of treatment for services that can be obtained in a variety of contexts, including emergency departments in hospitals, health clinics, the criminal justice system, schools, or the faith community. In addition, drug court programs were expanded to provide treatment, mandatory drug testing, and vigorous aftercare services to help sustain recovery from drug abuse.

- *Priority III—Disrupting the market.* Attacking the economic basis of the drug trade, from the cultivation of raw materials for illicit drugs and drug trafficking on domestic and international levels to the sale of illicit drugs at the local level, form the "supply side" approach to the drug-abuse problem. Chapter 2 specifically addressed attempts to reduce the influx and distribution of illicit drugs. Chapters 9 and 11 addressed efforts to reduce the sale of alcohol and tobacco to individuals below legally defined age limits.

The Public Health Model of ATOD Prevention

It is important to recognize that an ATOD-free life constitutes a major element in a healthy life and, in turn, a healthy society. Figure 18.1 shows dramatically how ATOD-taking behaviors impact upon the nation's health in general. As you can see, about one-half of all preventable deaths in the United States are accounted for by

resilience: The inclination to resist the negative impact of risk factors in a person's life through the positive impact of protective factors.

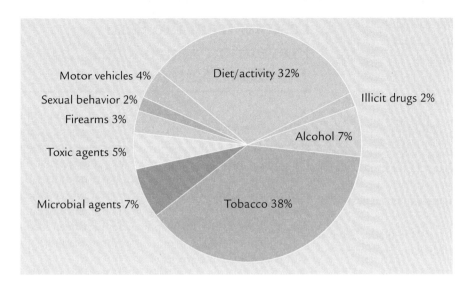

FIGURE 18.1

The relative incidence of causes of preventable death in the United States.

Source: Mokdad, Ali H.; Marks, James S.; Stroup, Donna F.; and Gerberding, Julie L. (2004). Actual causes of death in the United States, 2000. *Journal of the American Medical Association, 291,* 1238–1245.

the abuse of either alcohol products (7 percent), tobacco products (38 percent), or illicit drugs (2 percent). Each year, an estimated 537,000 deaths are attributed to these three circumstances (Health Line).[4]

It should not be surprising that when the U.S. Public Health Service established in 2000 a comprehensive, national health promotion and disease prevention agenda in a program called Healthy People 2010,

---

Health Line

The Public Health Model and the Analogy of Infectious Disease Control

The idea that reducing the negative consequences of drug-taking behavior is a desirable goal for the enhancement of the overall health of society is often referred to as the Public Health Model. As Avram Goldstein, a prominent drug-abuse researcher and policy analyst, has pointed out, the problems of reducing drug-taking behavior have many similarities to wresting control over an infectious disease. A virus, for example, infects some people who are relatively more susceptible than others (in other words, there are risk factors), while some people will be relatively immune (in other words, there are protective factors). Public health measures can be established to reduce or eradicate the virus (just as we attempt to reduce the supply of illicit drugs from reaching the consumer); specific vaccinations can be discovered to increase a person's resistance to the virus (just as we search for effective primary prevention programs in drug abuse).

We can carry the analogy further. Medical treatment for an infectious disease is considered uncontroversial and necessary for two reasons. First, we are alleviating the suffering of the infected individual; second, we are reducing the pool of infection to limit the spread to others. Analogously, drug-abuse treatment is desirable to relieve the negative consequences of drug abuse, as well as reduce the social influence of drug abusers on nondrug abusers in our society.

Goldstein asks a provocative question:

There are individuals who contribute to the AIDS epidemic by having promiscuous sexual contacts without taking elementary precautions. Are those behaviors, which contribute to the spread of infectious disease, really different in principle from that of pack-a-day cigarette smokers who will not try to quit, despite all the evidence of physical harm to themselves and their families?

There is certainly no consensus on how the problem of drug abuse should be conceptualized. Some have objected to the implications of the Public Health Model, arguing that it ignores the moral and ethical choices that are made in establishing a pattern of drug-taking behavior. You may recognize a similar controversy, discussed in Chapter 10, regarding the question of whether alcoholism should be considered a disease.

Sources: Goldstein, Avram (1994). *Addiction: From biology to drug policy.* New York: Freeman. Quotation on p. 10. Jonas, Steven (1997). Public health approaches. In Joyce H. Lowinson, Pedro Ruiz, Robert B. Millman, and John G. Langrod (Eds.), *Substance abuse: A comprehensive textbook.* Baltimore, MD: Williams & Wilkins, pp. 775–785.

a major component was devoted to ATOD use among young people aged twelve to twenty-five years.[5] Healthy People 2010 included the following goals with respect to ATOD use among adolescents:

- Reducing the proportion of twelve- to seventeen-year-olds who engage in binge drinking of alcoholic beverages from 7.7 percent (based on 1998 figures) to 2 percent
- Reducing among twelve to seventeen-year-olds the use of marijuana over the past thirty days from 8.2 percent (based on 1998 figures, later revised to 2002 figures) to 0.7 percent
- Reducing tobacco use by adolescents in grades nine through twelve from 40 percent (based on 1999 figures) to 21 percent.

As of the Midcourse Review of the program, published in 2005, only 14 percent of the targeted change in binge drinking had been achieved and only 4 percent of the targeted change in marijuana use had been achieved. However, 68 percent of the targeted change in tobacco use had been achieved. Unless major progress has been made among adolescents in the second half of the Healthy People 2010 program, it is likely that the final report in 2010 will be a mixture of moderate successes and significant failures.[6] As Figure 18.2 shows, the picture looks bleak with respect to meeting 2010 goals in tobacco use among adults.

Lessons from the Past: Prevention Approaches That Have Failed

When deciding how to solve a problem, it always helps to look at what has *not* worked in the past. That way, we can avoid wasting time, effort, and money on nonsolutions. In the general opinion of health professionals and researchers, the following efforts have been largely unsuccessful with regard to primary prevention, when positioned as the major thrust of a particular program. Nonetheless, some of these approaches have been incorporated successfully as one of several components within an overall effective package.

Reducing the Availability of Drugs

It is reasonable to expect that the problems of illicit drug abuse would diminish if the availability of these drugs were reduced or eliminated altogether. This is essentially the "supply/availability" argument in drug prevention, and you will recall that Priority III of the National Drug Control Strategy concerned the reduction of the manufacture and distribution of illicit drugs into and within the United States. As noted in Chapter 2, a huge amount of governmental resources is spent on reducing the supply or availability of these substances.[7]

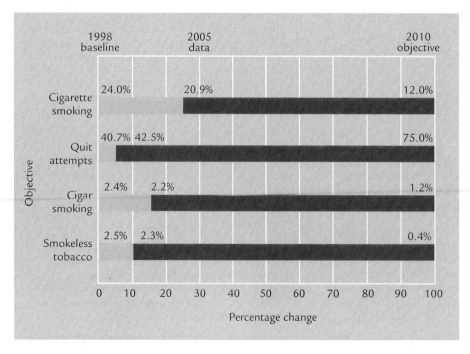

FIGURE 18.2

Percentage change in 2005 toward achieving four tobacco-use health objectives for adults in Healthy People 2010.

Source: Centers for Disease Control and Prevention (2006, October 27). Tobacco use among adults—United States, 2005. *Mortality and Morbidity Weekly Report,* pp. 1145–1148.

According to the economic principle of supply and demand, however, a decline in supply or availability works to produce an increase in value and an increase in demand. If one accepts the first viewpoint, then reductions in supply or availability should help prevent drug-taking behavior; if one accepts the second viewpoint, then such reductions should exacerbate the situation. Which theoretical viewpoint is operating with respect to illicit drugs (or with respect to alcohol, tobacco, and other licit drugs) is a point of controversy among health professionals both inside and outside the government.

Given the fact that the United States has adopted the policy of reducing the supply or availability of illicit drugs as part of an overall national strategy, how successful have we been? Have we been able, for example, to reduce the production of illicit drugs around the world and their influx into the United States? Unfortunately, drug cultivation (such as the harvesting of opium, coca leaves, and marijuana) and the exportation of processed illicit drugs from their points of origin are so deeply entrenched in many regions of the world and the resourcefulness of drug producers is so great that our global efforts have been frustratingly inadequate. As was pointed out in Chapter 2, a production crackdown in one region merely serves to create a marketing vacuum that another region quickly fills. Moreover, efforts to control international drug smuggling have been embarrassingly unsuccessful, despite well-publicized drug busts, arrests, and seizures. It is estimated that only a small fraction of illicit drugs is interdicted at U.S. borders.[8]

With respect to alcohol, a strategy of reduced availability has been implemented on a nationwide basis since 1984 for a specific age group, by prohibiting alcohol to young people under the age of twenty-one (see Chapter 9). Prior to this time, some states had adopted this policy, while neighboring states had not, allowing for comparisons in alcohol consumption rates and the incidence of alcohol-related automobile accidents. In one study, the percentage of teenage, nighttime, single-vehicle accident fatalities in Massachusetts was found to have declined in 1979 (the year the legal drinking age in that state was raised to twenty-one) to a significantly greater degree than in New York, which at that time still had a minimum drinking age of eighteen. That was the good news.

The bad news was that levels of alcohol consumption in this age range stayed the same. Therefore, although one particular consequence of immoderate alcohol use (drunk driving) was reduced as a secondary prevention intervention, the prevalence of alcohol use itself as a result of a primary prevention intervention was unaffected. As we are all aware, underage drinking still is widespread; minors still find opportunities to drink and to drink in excess. The fact that minimum-age requirements have only a limited effect on drinking among minors reinforces the complexity of dealing with primary prevention, whether we are considering licit or illicit drugs.[9]

Punitive Measures

In the last chapter, the question of deterrence was raised with respect to the preventive role of law-enforcement and judicial policies toward drug offenders. The expectation from such policies is that an individual would be less inclined to use and abuse illicit drugs for fear of being arrested, prosecuted, convicted, and incarcerated. The available statistics show that this deterrent factor has failed to take hold. The enticements of many psychoactive drugs are extremely powerful, and the imposition of harsh penalties has frequently been delayed or inconsistent. Mandatory minimum-sentencing laws (see Chapter 17) have resulted in a clogged judicial system and vastly overcrowded prisons, without any noticeable dent in the trafficking in or consumption of illicit drugs. Although the enforcement of these penalties may be defended in terms of an overall social policy toward illicit drugs, it has evidently failed as a means for either primary or secondary prevention. Whether a current trend toward greater flexibility in sentencing guidelines for drug offenses will result in more positive effects remains to be determined.[10]

Scare Tactics and Negative Education

In the late 1960s, the suddenly widespread use of marijuana, amphetamines, barbiturates, LSD, and other hallucinogens, first among students on college campuses and later among youth at large, spawned a number of hastily designed programs based on the arousal of fear and exaggerated or blatantly inaccurate information about the risks involved. They were the products of panic rather than careful thought.

As might be imagined, such efforts turned young people *off* precisely at the time when they were turning themselves *on* to an array of exotic and seemingly innocuous drug-taking experiences. Professionals have called it the "reefer madness approach," an allusion to the government-sponsored movie of the 1930s that attempted to scare people away from experimenting with marijuana (see Chapter 7). These programs accomplished little, except to erode even further the credibility of the adult presenters in the eyes of youths who often knew (or thought they knew) a great deal more about drugs and their effects than their elders.[11]

Objective Information Approaches

At the opposite end of the emotional spectrum are programs designed to present information about drugs and their potential dangers in a straightforward, nonjudgmental way. Unfortunately, evaluations of this "just the facts, ma'am" approach have found that youths exposed to such primary prevention programs are no less likely to use drugs later in their lives and sometimes are *more* likely to use them. These programs tend to increase their curiosity about drugs in general, obviously something the program planners want to avoid.[12]

Despite these failures, however, it would be a mistake to dismiss the informational aspect of any ATOD prevention program completely out of hand, particularly when the information is presented in a low-fear atmosphere.[13] The overall value of an informational approach appears to depend on whether the target population consists of high-risk or low-risk children:

> Providing information to low-risk youth on the health and legal implications of using illegal drugs often is enough incentive for them to avoid using drugs. When low-risk young people really understand the dangers of drugs, they choose to remain drug-free. High-risk youth may not be so easily dissuaded from using drugs, and for them additional intervention is necessary.[14]

Magic Bullets and Promotional Campaigns

A variety of antidrug promotional materials such as T-shirts, caps, rings, buttons, bumper stickers, posters, rap songs, school assembly productions, books, and brochures are available and frequently seen as "magic bullets" that can clinch success in an ATOD prevention program. Their appeal lies in their high visibility; these items give a clear signal to the public at large, eager for signs that the drug-abuse problem might easily go away, that something is being done. Yet, although they may be helpful in deglamorizing ATOD use and providing a forum for young people to express their feelings about drugs, promotional items are inadequate by themselves to reduce ATOD abuse overall. They do, however,

affective education: An approach in ATOD prevention programs that emphasizes the building of self-esteem and an improved self-image.

values clarification: An approach in ATOD prevention programs that teaches positive social values and attitudes.

Designations of drug-free pledges are prominent features of many school-based drug prevention programs.

remain viable components of more comprehensive programs that will be examined later in the chapter.[15]

Self-Esteem Enhancement and Affective Education

In the early 1970s, several ATOD prevention programs were developed that emphasized the affective or emotional component of drug-taking behavior rather than specific information about drugs. In the wake of research that showed a relationship between drug abuse and psychological variables such as low self-esteem, poor decision-making skills, and poor interpersonal communication skills, programs were instituted that incorporated role-playing exercises with other assignments designed to help young people get in touch with their own emotions and feel better about themselves.

This effort, called **affective education,** was an attempt to deal with underlying emotional and attitudinal factors rather than specific behaviors related to ATOD use (in fact, alcohol, tobacco, and other drugs were seldom mentioned at all). Affective education was based on the observation that ATOD users had difficulty identifying and expressing emotions such as anger and love. In a related set of programs called **values clarification,** moral values were actively taught to children, on the assumption that ATOD users frequently have a poorly developed sense of where their life is going and lack the moral "compass" to guide their behavior.

Difficulties arose, however, when parents, community leaders, and frequently educators themselves argued that the emphasis of affective education was inappropriate for public schools. In regard to values clarification, there was concern that a system of morality was being imposed on students without respecting their individual backgrounds and cultures. This kind of instruction, it was felt, was more suited for faith-based education settings.[16]

Beyond these social considerations, the bottom line was that neither affective education nor values clarification was effective in preventing ATOD use. Some researchers have recently questioned the basic premise that self-esteem is a major factor at all. As a result, affective issues are no longer viewed as central considerations in primary or secondary prevention. Nonetheless, they can be found as components in more comprehensive prevention programs, discussed later, that have been more successful.[17]

Hope and Promise: Components of Effective School-Based Prevention Programs

One of the major lessons to be learned from evaluations of previous ATOD prevention efforts is that there is a far greater chance for success when the programs are multifaceted than when they focus on only a single aspect of drug-taking behavior. We need to remember that success can be measured in various ways. A school-based ATOD program, for example, might be considered successful if it enjoys support from parents, administrators, and teachers. It might be considered successful if there is evidence of a change in a child's view toward ATOD use or in the child's stated inclination to engage in ATOD use in the future.

However gratifying these effects may be to the community, they do not impact on the core issue: Is the prevalence of ATOD use reduced? *The goal of any prevention program aimed at young people is to lower the numbers of new ATOD users or to delay the first use of alcohol and tobacco toward an age at which they are considered adults.* To be considered "research-based," prevention programs must be evaluated against a control group that did not receive the intervention; otherwise, it

is impossible to determine whether the effect of the program itself was greater than doing nothing at all.

Evaluations of ATOD prevention programs frequently have looked only at the "exit results" in the form of short-term effects, such as changes in how young people feel after the program has ended or how they think they will act in the future, rather than long-term effects such as actual ATOD use over an extended period of time. Obviously, we are far more interested in the latter measure. With these considerations in mind, it is useful to examine the components of programs that have been judged effective. The following are elements of school-based, ATOD prevention programs that have been shown to work.

Peer-Refusal Skills

A number of school-based programs, developed during the 1980s, have included the teaching of personal and social skills as well as techniques for resisting various forms of social pressure to smoke, drink, or use other drugs (often referred to as **peer-refusal skills**). The emphasis is directed toward an individual's relationships with his or her peers and the surrounding social climate. Rather than simply prodding adolescents to "just say no," these programs teach them *how* to do so when placed in often uncomfortable social circumstances. Health Line lists some specific techniques that have been taught to help deflect peer pressure regarding ATOD use.

Primary prevention programs using peer-refusal skill training have been shown to reduce the rate of tobacco smoking, as well as alcohol drinking and marijuana smoking, by 35 to 45 percent. With respect to tobacco smoking, this approach has been even more effective for young people identified as being in a high-risk category (in that their friends or family smoked) than for other students.[18]

Anxiety and Stress Reduction

Adolescence can be an enormously stressful time, and ATOD use is frequently an option chosen to reduce feelings of anxiety, particularly when an individual has inadequate coping skills to deal with that anxiety. It is therefore useful to learn techniques of self-relaxation and stress management and to practice the application of these techniques to everyday situations.

peer-refusal skills: Techniques by which an individual can resist peer pressure to use alcohol, tobacco, or other drugs.

Social Skills and Personal Decision Making

Peer-refusal skills are but one example of a range of assertiveness skills that allow young people to express their feelings, needs, preferences, and opinions directly and honestly, without fearing that they will jeopardize their friendships or lose the respect of others. Learning assertiveness skills not only helps advance the goals of primary prevention but also fosters positive interpersonal relationships throughout life. Tasks in social skills training have included the ability to initiate social interactions (introducing oneself to a stranger), offer a compliment to others, engage in conversation, and express feelings and opinions. Lessons generally involve a combination of instruction, demonstration, feedback, reinforcement, behavioral rehearsal, and extended practice through behavioral homework assignments.

A related skill is the ability to make decisions in a thoughtful and careful way. Emphasis is placed on the identification of problem situations, the formulation of goals, the generation of alternative solutions, and the consideration of the likely consequences of each. Lessons also focus on identifying persuasive advertising appeals and exploring counterarguments that can defuse them. Primary prevention programs using a social skills training approach have been shown to reduce the likelihood that a young person will try smoking by 42 to 75 percent and the likelihood that a nonsmoker will be a regular smoker in a one-year follow-up by 56 to 67 percent.[19]

A Model School-Based Prevention Program: Life Skills Training

One of the most successful efforts in school-based ATOD prevention has been the Life Skills Training (LST) program, developed by Gilbert Botvin at the Cornell University Medical College in New York City. Three LST programs have been designed with developmentally appropriate content for young people in elementary school, middle school, or high school. The elementary school program can be taught either during the third grade or over the course of the fourth, fifth, and sixth grades. The middle school program is taught over the course of the seventh, eighth, and ninth grades. The high school program is taught in one year, either as a stand-alone program or as a maintenance program in conjunction with earlier sessions in middle school.[20]

The major elements include the following:

- A *cognitive component* designed to provide information concerning the short-term consequences of alcohol, tobacco, and other drugs. Unlike traditional prevention approaches, LST includes only minimal information concerning the long-term health consequences of ATOD use. Evidently, it is not useful to tell young people about what might happen when they are "old." Instead, information is provided concerning immediate negative effects, the decreasing social acceptability of ATOD use, and actual prevalence rates among adults and adolescents. This last element of the lesson is to counter the myth that ATOD use is the norm in their age group, that "everyone's doing it."

- A *decision-making component* designed to facilitate critical thinking and independent decision making. Students learn to evaluate the role of the media in behavior as well as to formulate counterarguments and other cognitive strategies to resist advertising pressures.
- A *stress-reduction component* designed to help students develop ways to lessen anxiety. Students learn relaxation techniques and cognitive techniques to manage stress.
- A *social skills component* designed to teach social assertiveness and specific techniques for resisting peer pressure to engage in ATOD use.
- A *self-directed behavior-change component* designed to facilitate self-improvement and encourage a sense of personal control and self-esteem. Students are assigned to identify a skill or behavior that they would like to change or improve and to develop a long-term goal over an eight-week period and short-term objectives that can be met week by week.

Originally designed as a smoking-prevention program, LST presently focuses on issues related to the entire spectrum of ATOD use, as well as on risky behaviors in general. Over a period of as long as six years following exposure to the program, participants have been found to have a 50 to 75 percent lower incidence of alcohol, tobacco, and marijuana use, a 66 percent lower incidence of multiple-drug use, a 25 percent lower incidence of pack-a-day cigarette smoking, and a lower incidence of inhalant, opiate, and hallucinogen use, relative to controls.[21] Reductions in ATOD use have been seen among inner-city minority students as well as among white middle-class youths, an encouraging sign that these primary prevention strategies can have a positive influence on adolescents from varying social backgrounds. As Botvin has expressed it, ATOD prevention interventions exist that can be used "in cities and towns and villages across the United States without having to develop separate intervention approaches for each and every different population."[22]

In recent studies, LST programs have demonstrated positive influences in a number of high-risk social behaviors beyond simply ATOD use. Reductions in violence and delinquency have been observed among sixth-grade LST participants, relative to controls. There has also been a reduction in risky driving behaviors among adolescent participants. Young adults who have participated in LST programs have a reduced level of HIV-risk behaviors, as indicated by multiple sex partners, frequency of intercourse while drunk or high, and recent high-risk substance use (for example, administration by needle injection). These studies illustrate the long-term protective results of effective ATOD prevention for a range of life decisions.[23]

Drug Abuse Resistance Education (DARE)

The Drug Abuse Resistance Education program, commonly known as DARE, is undoubtedly the best-known school-based ATOD prevention program in the United States and perhaps the world. It was developed in 1983 as a collaborative effort by the Los Angeles Police Department and the Los Angeles United School District to bring uniformed police officers into kindergarten and elementary grade classrooms to teach basic drug information, peer-refusal skills, self-management techniques, and alternatives to drug use.

Quite rapidly, the DARE program expanded until today it has been established in all fifty U.S. states, in all Native American schools administered by the Bureau of Indian Affairs, the U.S. Department of Defense schools worldwide, and in school systems in many foreign countries. There are also teacher-orientation sessions, officer–student interactions at playgrounds and cafeterias, and parent-education evenings.[24]

Responses to Project DARE from teachers, principals, students, and police officers are typically enthusiastic, and it is clear that the program has struck a responsive chord over the years for a public that has pushed for active prevention programs in the schools. Part of this enthusiasm can be seen as coming from the image of police departments shifting their emphasis from exclusively "supply reduction" to a larger social role in "demand reduction."

Yet, despite its success in the area of public relations, the evidence supporting the effectiveness of DARE in achieving genuine reductions in ATOD use is weak. In general, children who participated in the DARE program have a more negative attitude toward drugs one year later than children who did not, as well as a greater capability to resist peer pressure and a lower estimate of how many of their peers smoked cigarettes. However, there were no significant differences between DARE and non-DARE groups in the level of ATOD use itself. Recent studies show few differences in drug use, drug attitudes, or self-esteem when young people are measured ten years after the administration of the DARE program.[25]

The DARE program has also been criticized for advocating that children be questioned about possible drug offenders in their families. A DARE lesson called

"The Three R's: Recognize, Resist, Report" encourages them to tell friends, teachers, or police if they find drugs at home. Critics of DARE have viewed this and related elements of the program as a mechanism for turning young children into informants.[26]

Why DARE remains popular when its effectiveness and questionable practices have been consistently challenged is an interesting question. Some health professionals in this field theorize that the popularity of DARE is, in part, a result of the perception among parents and DARE supporters that it *appears* to work, through a process of informally comparing children who go through DARE against an imagined perception of those children who do not:

> The adults rightly perceive that most children who go through DARE do not engage in problematic drug use. Unfortunately, these individuals may not realize that the vast majority of children, even without any intervention, do not engage in problematic drug use. . . . That is, adults may believe that drug use

among adolescents is much more frequent than it actually is. When the children who go through DARE are compared to this "normative" group of drug-using teens, DARE appears effective.[27]

In 2001, in response to the criticism leveled against its lack of impact on drug use, the DARE program was modified to become "enhanced DARE." In this new approach, more emphasis has been placed on student interaction, providing more opportunities for children to participate rather than being lectured by police officers.[28] In effect, DARE administrators have adopted many of the basic components of effective school-based prevention programs such as LST. The Point/Counterpoint debate, following this chapter, examines the continuing controversy of the effectiveness of the DARE program.

Community-Based Prevention Programs

Community-based prevention programs offer several obvious advantages over those restricted to schools. The first is the greater opportunity to involve parents and other family members, religious institutions, and the media as collaborative agents for change. The most important factor here is the comprehensive nature of such programs. They draw on multiple social institutions that have been demonstrated to represent protective factors in an individual's life, such as the family, religious groups, and community organizations. In addition, corporations and businesses can be contributing partners, in both a financial and nonfinancial sense. Undoubtedly, we are in a better position to tackle the complexities of ATOD use through the use of multiple strategies rather than a single approach.

Components of an Effective Community-Based Program

Typically, many of the prevention components that have been incorporated in the schools are also components in community-based programs, such as the dissemination of information, stress management, and life skills training. Other approaches can be handled better in a community setting. For example, although schools can promote the possibility of alternative student activities that provide positive and constructive means for addressing feelings of boredom, frustration, and powerlessness (activities such as Midnight Basketball and Boys and Girls Clubs), the community is in a better position than the schools to actually provide these activities.

There is also a greater opportunity in the community to elicit the involvement of significant individuals to act as positive role models, referred to as **impactors**, and to enlist the help of the mass media to promote antidrug messages in the press and on television. In addition, community-based programs can be more influential in promoting changes in public policy that foster opportunities for education, employment, and self-development.[29]

Alternative-Behavior Programming

It should not be surprising that it is easier to say no to drugs when you can say yes to something else. In community-based prevention programs, a major effort is made to provide the activities and outlets that steer people away from the high-risk situations associated with ATOD use. Owing to the fact that adolescents spend a majority of their time outside school, and it is outside school that the preponderance of ATOD use occurs, community programs have the best chance of providing the necessary interventions. In fact, adolescents at highest risk of engaging in ATOD use are the least likely even to be attending school on the days that prevention efforts are delivered.[30]

Table 18.1 on page 430 gives a sampling of alternative behaviors corresponding to a particular individual's interests and needs. One way of thinking about alternative-behavior programming is that a person is trading a negative dependence (on alcohol, tobacco, or other drugs) that causes harm on a physical or psychological level for a positive dependence that causes no harm and taps into pleasures from within.

In a 1986 review of its effectiveness based on well-controlled research studies, alternative-behavior programming was identified as being highly successful for at-risk adolescents such as ATOD users, juvenile delinquents, and students having problems in school. On the basis of these evaluations, the general view is that alternative-behavior programming can work and deserves to have a place in comprehensive prevention programs.[31]

The Influence of Media

In the words of a major 2005 study analyzing the life-styles of eight- to eighteen-year-olds, young people today live "media-saturated lives, spending an average of nearly $6\frac{1}{2}$ hours a day with media." Since about one-fourth of the time they are engaged in media multitasking (reading, listening to music, text messaging with friends, for example), they are actually crowding $8\frac{1}{2}$ hours of media into each day—the equivalent of a full-time job. These individuals (dubbed "Generation M" to reflect the dominance of media in their lives) are the first generation to have grown up with easy access to computers and particularly the Internet.[32]

Because of the unprecedented media access available at home (frequently in the privacy of their bedrooms), it is important to evaluate the impact of ATOD information on drug-taking behavior in their lives and the potential for media exposure to promote primary prevention. Earlier in this chapter, we noted that young people are exposed to more than 80 explicit references to substance use per day, in the course of listening to popular music. A relationship has been identified between the amount of exposure among young people ten to fourteen years old to alcohol drinking in popular movies and early-onset teen drinking, even after controlling for variables such as socioeconomic status, personality characteristics, school performance, and gender. In other words, exposure to movie alcohol use can be viewed as an independent risk factor for drinking behavior in this population.[33]

Traditionally, anti-drug messages have been largely confined to public-service announcements, brief commercials, and limited program series. Even so, the potential impact can be substantial. A prominent example is a series of memorable and persuasive anti-drug advertisements on TV, on the radio, in print, and other media sources, sponsored by the Partnership for a Drug-Free America (PDFA), a nonprofit coalition of professionals in the communications industry whose mission is to reduce demand for drugs in America. In the early 1990s, a number of PDFA spots targeted inner-city youths living in high-risk drug-use environments, and a 1994 study indicated that these messages had a significant effect in promoting increasingly anti-drug attitudes, particularly among African American children attending schools in areas where many families had incomes below the poverty line.[34]

Unfortunately, despite the intensified efforts to publicize anti-drug information in the media, several factors have the potential to undermine these efforts. There are a rapidly growing number of Internet web sites devoted to information about marijuana cultivation, drug paraphernalia, and illicit drug use in general. These pro-drug outlets have proliferated since the advent of online services.[35]

A Model Community-Based Prevention Program: CASASTART

An intensive and coordinated program of preventive services and community-based law enforcement has been

impactors: Individuals in the community who function as positive role models to children and adolescents in ATOD prevention programs.

TABLE 18.1

Alternative behaviors to drug use: Needs and motives

LEVEL OF EXPERIENCE	NEEDS AND MOTIVES	ALTERNATIVES
Physical	Physical satisfaction, more energy	Athletics, dance/exercise, hiking, carpentry, or outdoor work
Sensory	Stimulation of sensory experience	Sensory awareness training, sky diving, experiencing
Emotional	Relief from anxiety, mood elevation, emotional relaxation	Individual counseling, group therapy
Interpersonal	Peer acceptance, defiance of authority figures	Confidence training, sensitivity groups, helping others in distress
Social/environmental	Promotion of social change or Identification with a subculture	Social service; community action; helping the poor, aged, handicapped; environmental activism
Intellectual	Escape from boredom, curiosity, or Inclination to explore one's own awareness	Reading, creative games, memory training, discussion groups
Creative/aesthetic	Increase in one's creativity or enjoyment of images and thoughts	Nongraded instruction in visual arts, music, drama, crafts, cooking, gardening, writing, singing
Philosophical	Discovery of the meaning of life, organization of a belief system	Discussions, study of ethics or other philosophical literature
Spiritual/mystical	Transcendence of organized religion, spiritual insight or enlightenment	Study of world religions, meditation, yoga
Miscellaneous	Adventure, risk taking, "kicks"	Outward Bound survival training, meaningful employment

Source: Adapted from Cohen, Allan Y. (1972). The journey beyond trips: Alternatives to drugs. In David E. Smith and George R. Gay (Eds.), *It's so good, don't even try it once: Heroin in perspective.* Englewood Cliffs, NJ: Prentice-Hall, pp. 191–192.

designed by the National Center on Addiction and Substance Abuse at Columbia University in New York, called CASASTART (the first part of the acronym refers to the center that designed it, and the latter part stands for "Striving Together to Achieve Rewarding Tomorrows"). The target population for the program is defined as children between eight and thirteen years of age who have at least four risk factors for substance abuse problems. These risk factors may involve school (such as poor academic performance, in-school behavior problems, or truancy), family (such as poverty, violence at home, or a family member involved with gangs, drug use or sales, or a criminal conviction within five years), or the individual child (such as a history of known or suspected drug use or sales, past arrest, gang membership, or being a victim of child maltreatment).

In the CASASTART program, a case manager serving fifteen children and their families coordinates a variety of services, including social support, family and educational services, after-school and summer activities, mentoring, incentives, and juvenile justice intervention. The objective is to build resilience in the child, strengthen families, and make neighborhoods safer for children and their families. Relative to controls, CASASTART children have been found to be 60 percent less likely to sell drugs, 20 percent less likely to use drugs in the past thirty days, 20 percent less likely to commit a violent act, and more likely to be promoted to the next grade in school.[36]

Family Systems in Primary and Secondary Prevention

It can be argued that family influences form the cornerstone of any successful ATOD prevention program, just as we have seen the impact of the family on alcohol and drug-abuse treatment (see Chapter 17). In effect, the family is the first line of defense against alcohol, tobacco, and other drugs (Figure 18.3). Reaching the parents or guardians of youths at greatest risk, however, is a difficult task. Too often, ATOD prevention programs are attended by those parents or guardians who do not really need the information; those who need the information the most—parents who are either in denial, too embarrassed, or too

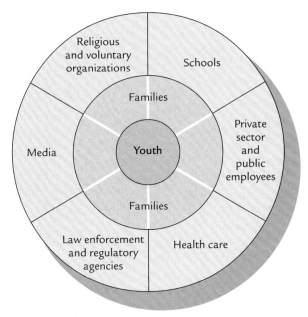

FIGURE 18.3

A schematic of various factors that impact upon families, and youth in turn, in ATOD prevention.

Source: Adapted from Fields, Richard (1998). *Drugs in perspective* (3rd ed.). Dubuque, IA: WCB McGraw-Hill, p. 309. Reprinted with permission of The McGraw-Hill Companies.

The power of a Grandpa.

Children have a very special relationship with Grandma and Grandpa. That's why grandparents can be such powerful allies in helping keep a kid off drugs.

Grandparents are cool. Relaxed. They're not on the firing line every day. Some days a kid hates his folks. He never hates his grandparents. Grandparents ask direct, point-blank, embarrassing questions you're too nervous to ask:

"Who's the girl?"

"How come you're doing poorly in history?"

"Why are your eyes always red?"

"Did you go to the doctor? What did he say?"

The same kid who cons his parents is ashamed to lie to Grandpa. Without betraying their trust, a loving, understanding grandparent can discuss the danger of drugs openly with the child he adores. And should.

• The average age of first-time drug use among teens is 13. Some kids start at 9.

• 1 out of 4 American kids between 9 and 12 is offered illegal drugs. 22% of these kids receive the offer from a friend. And 10% named a family member as their source.

• Illegal drugs are linked to increased violence in many communities, to AIDS, to birth defects, drug-related crime, and homelessness.

As a grandparent, you hold a special place in the hearts and minds of your grandchildren. Share your knowledge, your love, your faith in them. Use your power as an influencer to steer your grandchildren away from drugs.

If you don't have the words, we do. We'll send you information on how to talk to your grandkids about drugs. Just ask for your free copy of *Keeping Youth Drug-Free*. Call 1-800-788-2800 or visit our websites, www.projectknow.com or www.drugfreeamerica.org.

Grandma, Grandpa. Talk to your grandkids. You don't realize the power you have to save them.

Office of National Drug Control Policy
Partnership for a Drug-Free America

Communication between grandparents and grandchildren can be an important tool in ATOD prevention.

out of control themselves—are notably absent. Other parents or guardians may need and genuinely want to participate, but they may have difficulty attending because of lack of child care at home, lack of transportation, scheduling conflicts with their employment, or language differences. Several of the factors that prevent their attendance are the same factors that increase the risk of ATOD use among their children.[37]

Special Role Models in ATOD Prevention

Although obstacles exist, comprehensive ATOD prevention programs strive to incorporate parents or guardians, as well as other family members, into the overall effort. The reason lies in the variety of special roles they play in influencing children with regard to ATOD use:

- As role models, parents or guardians may drink alcoholic beverages, smoke, or drink excessive amounts of caffeinated coffee, not thinking of these habits as ATOD use. They can avoid sending their children signals about ATOD abstinence that are inconsistent at best, hypocritical at worst.

- As educators or resources for information, they can help by conveying verbal messages about health risks that are accurate and sincere.

- As family policymakers and rule setters, they can convey a clear understanding of the consequence of ATOD use. If a parent or guardian cannot or will not back up family rules with logical and consistent consequences, the risk increases that rules will be broken.

- As stimulators of enjoyable family activities, parents or guardians can provide alternative-behavior programming necessary to steer youth away from high-risk situations.

- As consultants against peer pressure, parents or guardians can help reinforce the peer-refusal skills of their children. Children and adolescents frequently report that a strongly negative reaction at home was the single most important reason for their refusing alcohol, tobacco, and other drugs from their peers.

Dysfunctional Communication within the Family

One further aspect of parenting deserves special mention as it pertains to ATOD prevention: the tendency to engage in enabling behaviors. As was noted in Chapter 17,

Sarah
First drink age 14.

START TALKING
BEFORE THEY
START DRINKING
www.stopalcoholabuse.gov

Kids who drink before age 15
are 5 times more likely to have
alcohol problems when they're adults.

SAMHSA
Substance Abuse & Mental Health
Services Administration

Ad
Council

An outdoor public-service announcement urges parents to begin a dialogue early about the short-term and long-term dangers of underage drinking. Parents generally underestimate the extent of alcohol use in their children and find it hard to decide how or when to begin this important conversation.

enabling behaviors on the part of a spouse, family member, or friend can inadvertently aggravate problems associated with alcohol and other drug abuse, and serve as a major obstacle to recovery. In the context of primary and secondary prevention, enabling behaviors on the part of a parent or guardian can have an equally detrimental influence. Enabling behaviors give children the message that it is all right to engage in ATOD use. They also make it easier for children to engage in these behaviors by protecting them from the negative consequences of ATOD use.

In recognition of the importance of parental communication in efforts to reduce ATOD use, the program "Parents: The Antidrug" has been a dominant feature in public-service announcements in recent years.[38] The need for better lines of communication between parents and teenagers is illustrated in a PDFA survey. When asked whether they talked to their teenagers about drugs at least once, 98 percent of parents reported that they had done so, but only 65 percent of teenagers recalled such a conversation. Barely 27 percent of teenagers reported learning at lot at home about the risks of drug use, even though virtually all of their parents said they had discussed the topic. Justifiably, anti-drug media campaigns have focused on parent–child communication skills, specifically on the difficulty many parents have in talking to their children about sensitive subjects like drugs and the role of drug-taking behavior in their children's social lives.[39] Drugs . . . in Focus examines an option that may be necessary when family communication breaks down.

The Triple Threat: Stress, Boredom, and Spending Money

ATOD prevention in young people can sometimes be simpler and more straightforward than we realize. A recent survey of teenagers aged twelve to seventeen measured the effects of three circumstances on the likelihood that a teenager might engage in some form of ATOD abuse: (1) the degree of stress they feel they are under, (2) the frequency with which they are bored, and (3) the amount of money they have to spend in a typical week. High-stress teens (one-fourth of teens interviewed) were twice as likely as low-stress teens (a little more than one-fourth of teens interviewed) to smoke, drink, get drunk, and use illicit drugs. Teens reporting that they were frequently bored were 50 percent more likely than not-often-bored teens to engage in these behaviors. Teens with $25 or more a week in spending money were nearly twice as likely as teens with less spending money to smoke, drink, and use illicit drugs, and they were more than twice as likely to get drunk. Combining two or three of these risk factors (high stress, frequent boredom, and too much spending money) made the risk of smoking, drinking, and illicit drug use *three times higher* than when none of these characteristics was present.[40]

Multicultural Issues in Primary and Secondary Prevention

In the case of ATOD prevention efforts, it is important to remember that information intended to reach individuals of a specific culture passes through a series of **sociocultural filters.** Understanding this filtering process is essential to maximize the reception and acceptance of ATOD prevention information.

Prevention Approaches among Latino Groups

A good example of the need to recognize sociocultural filters is the set of special concerns associated with communicating ATOD information to Latinos, a diverse group of nearly 48 million people living throughout the United States.[41] The following insights concerning elements of the Latino community have a strong bearing on an ATOD prevention program's chances of succeeding.

- Because of the importance Latinos confer on the family and religious institutions, prevention and treatment efforts should be targeted to include the entire family and, if possible, its religious leaders. Prevention efforts will be most effective when counselors reinforce family units and value them as a whole.

- Prevention programs are needed to help Latino fathers recognize how important their role or example is to their sons' and daughters' self-image regarding alcohol and other drugs. Because being a good father is part of *machismo,* it is important that the men become full partners in parenting. Mothers should be encouraged to learn strategies for including their husbands in family interactions at home.

- Because a Latina woman with alcohol or other drug problems is strongly associated with a violation of womanly ideals of purity, discipline, and self-sacrifice, educational efforts should concentrate on reducing the shame associated with her reaching out for help. One particular web site that addresses the needs of the Latino community is sponsored by the National Latino Council on Alcohol and Tobacco Prevention (NLCATP).

Prevention Approaches among African American Groups

Another set of special concerns exist with regard to communicating ATOD information in African American communities.[42] Some basic generalizations have proven helpful in optimizing the design of ATOD prevention programs.

---

sociocultural filters: A set of considerations specific to a particular culture or community that can influence the reception and acceptance of public information.

Yes, You: ATOD Prevention and the College Student

In turning to the subject of ATOD prevention among college students, we first need to recognize that we are hardly speaking of a homogeneous population. U.S. college students represent all racial, ethnic, and socio-economic groups and are likely to come from all parts of the world. They include undergraduate and graduate students, full-time and part-time students, residential students and commuters, students of traditional college age and students who are considerably older.

In particular, there are marked differences in the objectives of a prevention program between those under twenty-one years of age and those who are older. In the former group, the goal may be "no use of" (or abstinence from) alcohol, tobacco, and other drugs, whereas in the latter group the goal may be the low-risk (that is, responsible) consumption of alcohol and no use of tobacco and other drugs. The term "low-risk consumption" refers to a level of use restricted by considerations of physical health, family background, pregnancy risk, the law, safety, and other personal concerns.

With respect to alcohol, secondary prevention guidelines might stipulate that pregnant women, recovering alcoholics or those with a family history of alcoholism, people driving cars or heavy machinery, people on medications, or those under the age of twenty-one should not drink alcohol at all. Although the distinction between under-twenty-one and over-twenty-one preventive goals is applicable in many community-oriented programs, it is an especially difficult challenge for prevention efforts on a college campus when the target population contains both subgroups so closely intermingled.[43]

Changing the Culture of Alcohol and Other Drug Use in College

A major challenge with regard to prevention programs at colleges and universities comes from the widely regarded expectation that heavy alcoholic drinking, as well as some illicit drug use, during the college years represents something of a rite of passage. College alumni (and potential benefactors) frequently impede the implementation of drug and alcohol crackdowns, arguing that "we did it when we were in school."[44] Moreover, national surveys in 2008 indicate that by the end of high school about 72 percent of all students have consumed alcoholic beverages, 55 percent have been drunk at least

INHALANTS...
(Sprays / Aerosols / Glues)

EVIL SPIRITS THAT BREAK THE BONDS BETWEEN OURSELVES AND OUR ELDERS, DISRUPT THE CIRCLE OF OUR FAMILY SYSTEM, DESTROY THE HARMONY BETWEEN US AND ALL CREATION.

FOR OUR OWN SURVIVAL, THE SURVIVAL OF OUR FAMILY, OUR TRIBE AND THE INDIAN NATION, WE MUST RESIST THESE SPIRITS OF DEATH.

This ATOD prevention message focuses on inhalant abuse among Native American children, adolescents, and young adults through the sociocultural filter of their community.

- African American youths tend to use drugs other than alcohol after they form social attitudes and adopt behaviors associated with delinquency. The most common examples of delinquency include drug dealing, shoplifting, and petty theft. With regard to the designing of media campaigns, it is the deglamorization of the drug dealer that appears to be most helpful in primary prevention efforts among African American youths.

- Drug use and social problems are likely to be interrelated in primarily African American neighborhoods. The effects of alcohol and other drug use are intensified when other factors exist, such as high unemployment, poverty, poor health care, and poor nutrition.

- Several research studies have shown that most African American youths, even those in low-income areas, do manage to escape from the pressures to use alcohol and other drugs. The protective factors of staying in school, solid family bonds, strong religious beliefs, high self-esteem, adequate coping strategies, social skills, and steady employment all build on one another to provide resilience on the part of high-risk children and adolescents. As noted before, prevention programs developed with protective factors in mind have the greatest chance for success.

once, and 43 percent have smoked marijuana. Therefore, we cannot say that use of these drugs is a new experience for many college students.[45] Given this base of prior exposure, it is not surprising that further experimentation and more extensive patterns of ATOD use will occur. There is a compelling argument for secondary and tertiary prevention programs to be in place at this point.

The emphasis on most campuses is on the prevention and control of alcohol problems (Health Line, page 436). However, it is less common for college administrators to focus on the problems associated with drugs other than alcohol. Although alcohol-abuse programs are virtually certain to be found on college campuses, attention directed toward comparable programs related specifically to drugs other than alcohol lags behind. Frequently, the only policy in place involves a procedure of punitive action if a student-athlete tests positive for an illicit drug. While no-smoking campuses are the norm, few if any programs are in place to help reduce the level of tobacco use among college students.

Prevention Approaches on College Campuses

On the positive side, college campuses have the potential for being ideal environments for comprehensive ATOD prevention programs because they combine features of school and community settings. Here are some suggested strategies for ATOD prevention on the college campus:

- Develop a multifaceted prevention program of assessment, education, policy, and enforcement. Involve students, faculty, and administrators together to determine the degree of availability and demand for alcohol and other drugs on campus and in the surrounding community and initiate public information and education efforts.

- Incorporate alcohol and other drug education into the curriculum. Faculty members can use drug-related situations as teachable moments, include drug topics in their course syllabi, and develop courses or course projects on issues relating to alcohol and other drugs.

- Ensure that hypocrisy is not the rule of the day. ATOD prevention is not a goal for college students only but is a larger issue that affects all members of the academic community, including faculty and administration.

- Encourage environments that lessen the pressures to engage in ATOD use. Foster more places where social and recreational activities can take place spontaneously and at hours when the most enticing

This ad, sponsored by the American Medical Association (AMA), appeared in college newspapers in 2004 in a campaign to discourage binge drinking, just prior to Spring Break. In 2007, the AMA called on the National Collegiate Athletic Association (NCAA) to eliminate alcohol advertising during radio and television broadcasts of college sports. The NCAA currently limits alcohol-related commercials to one minute per broadcast and encourages "responsibility themes and messages."

alternative may be the consumption of alcohol and other drugs. A recent promising sign is the growing popularity of drug-free dormitories on many college campuses, where student residents specifically choose to refrain from alcohol, tobacco, and other drugs.[46]

The seriousness of the issue of ATOD use on college campuses could not be demonstrated more clearly than in the context of alcohol drinking among members of college fraternities. A statement in a 1994 decision of

Health Line

Alcohol 101 on College Campuses

A familiar experience among many students entering college for the first time is referred to by public health officials as the "college effect"—defined as an increase in drinking and negative behaviors associated with it (Chapter 9). One increasingly popular approach intended to minimize this phenomenon is a three-hour web-based online course called AlcoholEdu, developed by Outside the Classroom, Inc. More than 500 colleges and universities nationwide are currently participating in this program.

AlcoholEdu is oriented toward responsible drinking behavior rather than abstinence. Topics include an understanding of blood alcohol concentrations, activities that increase the likelihood of blacking out, discredited remedies for hangovers, as well as an appreciation of the alcohol beverage industry's role in fostering the image of alcohol consumption as a means for advancing social and interpersonal relationships. Participants are given an exam that tests their knowledge of the information provided in the course.

Colleges and universities have varying policies regarding students taking AlcoholEdu. Some require students to complete and pass the course with a minimum score on the exam prior to the first day of classes or prior to registering for the next semester. Others convey an expectation that the AlcoholEdu should be completed and warn that severe consequences will be imposed for those students who fail to finish the course and commit an alcohol violation in the future. There are early indications that student participation in AlcoholEdu results in

significantly fewer negative consequences of drinking, such as missing class, attending class with a hangover, blacking out, and abusive behavior. Intensive studies of effectiveness, both short-term and long-term, however, need to be carried out.

In the meantime, additional programs addressing a wider range of alcohol problems on campuses have been developed. AlcoholEdu for Sanctions is an intervention program suited for students who have violated academic policies on alcohol, aimed at reducing recidivism rates. Alcohol Innerview is a brief motivational intervention tool for students who have experienced alcohol problems or are in alcohol-abuse counseling. AlcoholEdu for Parents is designed to support parents with college-age children in fostering conversations that can help shape healthy decisions about alcohol use at college.

Recent developments in online prevention programs by Outside the Classroom, Inc. include MentalHealthEdu, raising campus community awareness of college student mental-health issues, and SexualAssaultEdu, focusing on relationships and decision making to reduce the incidence of sexual assaults on campus.

Sources: Fact sheet on alcohol issues, University of Colorado at Boulder (2004, August 11). Boulder, CO: Office of News Services, University of Colorado. Kesmodel, David (2005, November 1). Schools use web to teach about booze. *Wall Street Journal Online.* Outside the Classroom (2008), www.outsidetheclassroom.com.

---

the Arizona Supreme Court expressed the concern in no uncertain terms:

> We are hardpressed to find a setting where the risk of an alcohol-related injury is more likely than from under-age drinking at a university fraternity party the first week of the new college year.[47]

Since 2000, when one in five fraternity chapters in the United States began to phase in a policy forbidding alcohol of any kind anywhere in the fraternity house, even in rooms of members who were of legal drinking age, there has been a steady upward trend in the number of alcohol-free fraternity (and sorority) houses around the country.[48]

Where You Can Go for Help

Throughout our lives, we will need to confront the reality that licit and illicit substance abuse represents a major factor in our personal health and the public health of our communities. From everything that has been reviewed in this introduction to drug-taking behavior in today's society, it is clear that as decision makers we need all the help we can get.

Fortunately, information or guidance is all around us (Portrait). For local referral sources, check out the yellow pages of your telephone book under Alcoholism Information or Drug Abuse and Addiction Information. There are also numerous web sites on the Internet that are specifically designed to provide assistance with any problem associated with alcohol, tobacco, and other drug abuse.

As mentioned at the end of Chapter 17, the most comprehensive source in the United States is the National Clearinghouse for Alcohol and Drug Information (NCADI). Prevention and educational materials regarding virtually any aspect of drug use, misuse, or abuse can be ordered free by calling 800-729-6686 or accessing NCADI's web site at www.health.org. For residents of Canada, the Canadian Centre on Substance Abuse is a useful source of help; it can be reached by calling 613-235-4048 or accessing its web site at www.ccsa.ca. For residents of the United Kingdom, the following web sites are available: www.talktofrank.com and www.drugs.homeoffice.gov.uk/drug-strategy.

Good luck.

PORTRAIT

Meredith Poulten—A Counselor on the Front Lines

Since 1987, in the high school in Medway, Massachusetts, a quiet suburban town outside Boston, young people have had a place to go for help, for a referral, for a sympathetic ear, or just to sit and relax for a few minutes from the pressures of school, parents, and peers. It is called a Walk-in Center, with entrances both within the school and directly from the outside, and Meredith Poulten, its director and counselor, has been its driving force since its inception. The center deals with contemporary issues of teen suicide, depression, family conflicts, sexuality, alcohol and other drugs, self-esteem, physical health, and personal hygiene—not from a distance but as the daily reality of today's adolescents.

Out of an average of 150 student contacts per week in this center, more than half concern alcohol or other drug involvement at some level. Before the center was established, such students were essentially on their own, "self-medicating" their problems, in the words of Poulten, rather than learning to handle the stresses of their lives. The school guidance department was oriented toward academic needs rather than day-to-day student problems, and many students have said that there was too great a stigma attached to talking to the school psychologist. As one student has expressed it, "I talk to Mrs. P. every day. She's more of a friend than a counselor. I can talk to her about anything." Another student admitted that were it not for the center, he would have been dead in less than a month.

The functioning of Poulten's Walk-in Center illustrates that the problems of today's youth do not fit into neat categories. They live in a world where drugs and sex are readily available and the pressure to indulge in both is high. The presence of alcohol and other drugs has become "normalized" at parties and social gatherings. Ecstasy ("X") is pervasive, as are Adderall ("Addies"), OxyContin ("Oxy"), and Percocet ("Perks").

At the same time, society equates success with being first and being second-best with failure. For many students, communication with parents is next to impossible. Even when parents are open-minded about their child's circumstances, "You don't want to talk to your parents about your problems," says a student, "because you always want to please them."

Sources: Graham, Fiona (1989, October 11). A place to call their own. *The Country Gazette* (Medway, MA), pp. 1, 14. Hudson, Ted (1991, February 20). Letter to the Editor: Medway High Walk-in Center must be spared. *The Country Gazette* (Medway, MA), p. 3. Meredith Poulten, personal communication, 2008.

Summary

ATOD Prevention: Strategic Priorities, Goals, and Resilience

- The overall strategy for alcohol, tobacco, and other drug (ATOD) prevention and education is to minimize the risk factors in a person's life with respect to ATOD use and maximize the protective factors. The inclination to resist the effects of risk factors for ATOD use through the action of protective factors is referred to as resilience.

- The overall national policy for the control of drug use in the United States is coordinated by the White House Office of National Drug Control Policy (ONDCP). In a recent formulation of this policy, three priorities have been established as components of a national strategy: stopping drug use before it starts through primary prevention, healing America's drug users through tertiary prevention, and disrupting the market through efforts to reduce the availability of illicit drugs.

- In 2000, the federal program, Healthy People 2010, set specific objectives to be reached by 2010 regarding aspects of personal health, including those that pertain to ATOD use.

Lessons from the Past: Prevention Approaches That Have Failed

- Several strategies have been largely unsuccessful in meeting the goals of ATOD prevention. They include the reliance on supply/availability reduction, punitive judicial policies, scare tactics, objective information, and affective education.

Hope and Promise: Components of Effective School-Based Prevention Programs

- Effective school-based programs have incorporated a combination of peer-refusal skills training, relaxation and stress management, and training in social skills and personal decision making.
- The Life Skills Training program is a model for programs incorporating school-based components for effective ATOD prevention.

Community-Based Prevention Programs

- Community-based programs make use of a broader range of resources, including community leaders and public figures as positive role models, opportunities for alternative-behavior programming, and the mass media.
- Recent efforts by the media have had a major impact on the image of ATOD use in both high-risk populations and others in the community.
- CASASTART is a model for programs incorporating intensive community-wide components of ATOD prevention.

Family Systems in Primary and Secondary Prevention

- Community-based prevention programs are increasingly mindful of the importance of the family, particularly parents, as the first line of defense in ATOD prevention efforts.
- A major emphasis in ATOD prevention has been on the special roles of parents, grandparents, guardians, and other family members. Improved lines of communication within the family are crucial elements.

Multicultural Issues in Primary and Secondary Prevention

- Special cultural considerations need to be made when communicating with specific subgroups such as Latino and African American individuals.

Yes, You: ATOD Prevention and the College Student

- On college campuses, ATOD prevention programs are incorporating features of both school-based and community-based approaches. There is a compelling argument for the need to change the culture of alcohol and other drug use in college. There is the perception that heavy alcoholic drinking, as well as some illicit drug use, during the college years represents something of a rite of passage.
- ATOD prevention programs should involve faculty and administrators, as well as students, in an overall comprehensive strategy. Recently, online prevention and education programs have served to address the issue of alcohol use on college campuses. College fraternities have taken important strides toward an alcohol ban in fraternity houses, even in rooms where members are of legal drinking age.

Key Terms

affective education, p. 424
impactors, p. 429

peer-refusal skills, p. 425
resilience, p. 420

sociocultural filters, p. 433
values clarification, p. 424

Endnotes

1. Grant, Bridget F., and Dawson, Deborah A. (1997). Age at onset of alcohol use and its association with DSM-IV alcohol abuse and dependence: Results from the National Longitudinal Alcohol Epidemiological Survey. *Journal of Substance Abuse, 9,* 103–110. Grant, Bridget F., and Dawson, Deborah A. (1998). Age of onset of drug use and its association with DSM-IV drug abuse and dependence: Results from the National Longitudinal Alcohol Epidemiological Survey. *Journal of Substance Abuse, 10,* 163–173.

2. Brook, Judith S., and Brook, David W. (1996). Risk and protective factors for drug use. In Clyde B. McCoy, Lisa R. Metsch, and James A. Inciardi (Eds.), *Intervening with drug-involved youth.* Thousand Oaks, CA: Sage Publications, pp. 23–44. Catalano, Richard F.; Kosterman, Rick; Hawkins, J. David; Newcomb, Michael D.; and Abbott, Robert D. (1996). Modeling the etiology of adolescent substance use: A test of the social development model. *Journal of Drug Issues, 23,* 429–455. Glantz, Meyer D., and Johnson, Jeannette, L. (Eds.) (2003). *Resilience and development: Positive life adaptations.* New York: Kluwer Academic/Plenum. Joseph, Joanne M. (1994). *The resilient child: Preparing today's youth for tomorrow's world.* New York: Plenum Press, pp. 25–43. Wills, Thomas A., and Yaeger, Alison M. (2003). Family factors in adolescent substance abuse: Models and mechanisms. *Current Directions in Psychological Science, 12,* 222–226.

3. Biglan, Anthony; Mrazek, Patricia J.; Carnine, Douglas; and Flay, Brian R. (2003). The integration of research and practice in the prevention of youth problem behaviors. *American Psychologist, 58,* 433–441. Office of National Drug Control Policy (2008, February). *National drug control strategy: FY 2009 Budget Summary.* Washington DC: White House Office of National Drug Control Policy.

4. Mokdad, Ali H.; Marks, James S.; Stroup, Donna F.; and Gerberding, Julie L. (2004). Actual causes of death in the United States, 2000. *Journal of the American Medical Association, 291,* 1238–1245. Mokdad, Ali H.; Marks, James S.; Stroup, Donna F.; and Gerberding, Julie L. (2005). Correction: Actual causes of death in the United States, 2000. *Journal of the American Medical Association, 293,* 298.

5. Marwick, Charles (2000). Healthy People 2010 initiative launched. *Journal of the American Medical Association, 283,* 989–990. Public Health Service (2000). *Healthy People 2010: National health promotion and disease prevention objectives: Conference edition.* Bethesda, MD: Public Health Service.

6. Public Health Service (2005). *Healthy People 2010 midcourse review.* Bethesda, MD: Public Health Service, Figures 26.1 and 27.1.

7. Office of National Drug Control Policy, *National drug control strategy,* p. 4.

8. Goode, Erich (2008). *Drugs in American society* (7th ed.). New York: McGraw-Hill College, pp. 400–403.

9. Hingson, Ralph W.; Scotch, Norman; Mangione, Thomas; Meyers, Allan; Glantz, Leonard; et al. (1983). Impact of legislation raising the legal drinking age in Massachusetts from 18 to 21. *American Journal of Public Health, 73,* 163–170.

10. Goode, *Drugs in American society,* pp. 385–417. Greenhouse, Linda (2007, December 11). Justices restore judges' control over sentencing. *New York Times,* pp. A1, A28. Steinberg, Neil (1994, May 5). The law of unintended consequences. *Rolling Stone,* pp. 33–34.

11. Funkhouser, Judith E., and Denniston, Robert W. (1992). Historical perspective. In Mary A. Jansen (Ed.), *A promising future: Alcohol and other drug problem prevention services improvement* (OSAP Prevention Monograph 10). Rockville, MD: Office of Substance Abuse Prevention, pp. 5–15.

12. Flay, Brian R., and Sobel, Judith L. (1983). The role of mass media in preventing adolescent substance abuse. In Thomas J. Glynn, Carl G. Leukenfeld, and Jacqueline P. Ludford (Eds.), *Preventive adolescent drug abuse.* Rockville, MD: National Institute on Drug Abuse, pp. 5–35.

13. Williams, R., Ward, D., and Gray, L. (1985). The persistence of experimentally induced cognitive change: A neglected dimension in the assessment of drug prevention programs. *Journal of Drug Education, 15,* 33–42.

14. Meeks, Linda, Heit, Philip, and Page, Randy (1994). *Drugs, alcohol, and tobacco.* Blacklick, OH: Meeks Heit Publishing, p. 201.

15. Ibid., p. 202.

16. McBride, Duane C., Mutch, Patricia B., and Chitwood, Dale D. (1996). Religious belief and the initiation and prevention of drug use among youth. In Clyde B. McCoy, Lisa R. Metsch, and James A. Inciardi (Eds.), *Intervening with drug-involved youth.* Thousand Oaks, CA: Sage Publications, pp. 110–130.

17. Schroeder, Debra S., Laflin, Molly T., and Weis, David L. (1993). Is there a relationship between self-esteem and drug use? Methodological and statistical limitations of the research. *Journal of Drug Issues, 22,* 645–665. Yuen, Francis K. O., and Pardeck, John T. (1998). Effective strategies for preventing substance abuse among children and adolescents. *Early Child Development and Care, 145,* 119–131.

18. Best, J. Allan; Flay, Brian R.; Towson, Shelagh M. J.; Ryan, Katherine B.; et al. (1984). Smoking prevention and the concept of risk. *Journal of Applied Social Psychology, 14,* 257–273.

19. Botvin, Gilbert J., and Botvin, Elizabeth M. (1992). School-based and community-based prevention approaches. In Joyce H. Lewisohn, Pedro Ruiz, and Robert B. Millman (Eds.), *Substance abuse: A comprehensive textbook* (2nd ed.). Baltimore: Williams & Wilkins, pp. 910–927. Orlandi, Mario A. (1986). Prevention technologies for drug-involved youth. In Clyde B. McCoy, Lisa R. Metsch, and James A. Inciardi (Eds.), *Intervening with drug-involved youth.* Thousand Oaks, CA: Sage Publications, pp. 81–100. Schinke, Steven P., and Gilchrist, Lewayne D. (1983). Primary prevention of tobacco smoking. *Journal of School Health, 53,* 416–419.

20. Botvin, Gilbert J., and Tortu, Stephanie (1988). Preventing adolescent substance abuse through life skills training. In Richard M. Price, Emory L. Cowen, Raymond P. Lorion, and Julia Ramos-McKay (Eds.), *Fourteen ounces of prevention: A casebook for practitioners.* Washington DC: American Psychological Association, pp. 98–110. www.lifeskillstraining.com

21. Botvin, Gilbert J.; Baker, Eli; Dusenbury, Linda; Botvin, Elizabeth M.; and Diaz, Tracy (1995). Long-term follow-up results of a randomized drug abuse prevention trial in a white middle-class population. *Journal of the American Medical Association, 273,* 1106–1112. Botvin, Gilbert J.; Epstein Jennifer A.; Baker, Eli; Diaz, Tracy; and Ifill-Williams, Michelle (1997). School-based drug abuse prevention with inner-city minority youth. *Journal of Child and Adolescent Substance Abuse, 6,* 5–19.

22. Mathias, Robert (1997, March/April). From the 'burbs to the 'hood . . . This program reduces student's risk of drug use. *NIDA Notes,* pp. 1, 5–6. Quotation on p. 6.

23. Botvin, Gilbert J., Griffin, Kenneth W., and Nichols, Tracy D. (2006). Preventing youth violence and delinquency through a universal school-based prevention approach. *Prevention Science, 7,* 403–408. Griffin, Kenneth W., Botvin, Gilbert J., and Nichols, Tracy D. (2006). Effects of a school-based drug abuse prevention program for adolescents on HIV risk behaviors in young adulthood. *Prevention Science, 7,* 103–112. Griffin, Kenneth W., Botvin, Gilbert J., and Nichols, Tracy D. (2004). Long-term follow-up effects of a school-based drug abuse prevention program on adolescent risky driving. *Prevention Science, 5,* 207–212.

24. Cavazos, Lauro F. (1989). *What works: Schools without drugs.* Washington DC: U.S. Department of Education, p. 38.

25. Clayton, Richard R., Cattarello, Anne M., and Johnstone, Bryan M. (1996). The effectiveness of Drug Abuse Resistance Education (Project DARE): 5-year follow-up results. *Preventive Medicine, 25,* 307–318. Lynam, Donald R.; Milich, Richard; Zimmerman, Rick; Novak, Scott P.; Logan, T. K.; et al. (1999). Project DARE: No effects at 10-year follow-up. *Journal of Consulting and Clinical Psychology, 67,* 590–593.

26. Miller, Joel (2004). *Bad trip: How the war against drugs is destroying America.* New York: Nelson Thomas.

27. Lynam, Project DARE, p. 593.

28. Zernike, Kate (2001, February 15). Antidrug program says it will adopt a new strategy. *New York Times,* pp. A1, A29.

29. Wandersman, Abraham, and Florin, Paul (2003). Community interventions and effective prevention. *American Psychologist, 58,* 441–448. Winick, Charles, and Larson, Mary Jo (1997). Community action programs. In Joyce H. Lowinson, Pedro Ruiz, Robert B. Millman, and John G. Langrod (Eds.), *Substance abuse: A comprehensive textbook* (3rd ed.). Baltimore: Williams & Wilkins, pp. 755–764.

30. Rhodes, Jean E., and Jason, Leonard A. (1991). The social stress model of alcohol and other drug abuse: A basis for comprehensive, community-based prevention. In Ketty H. Rey, Christopher L. Faegre, and Patti Lowery (Eds.), *Prevention research findings: 1988* (OSAP Prevention Monograph 3). Rockville, MD: Office of Substance Abuse Prevention, pp. 155–171.

31. Tobler, Nancy S. (1986). Meta-analysis of 143 adolescent drug prevention programs: Quantitative outcome results of program participants compared to a control group. *Journal of Drug Issues, 16,* 537–567.

32. Ridout, Victoria, Roberts, Donald F., and Foehr, Ulla G. (2005, March). *Generation M: Media in the lives of 8–18-year-olds: Executive summary.* Menlo Park, CA: Kaiser Family Foundation. Quotation on page 6.

33. Masten, Ann S.; Faden, Vivian B.; Zucker, Robert A.; and Spear, Linda P. (2008). Underage drinking: A developmental framework. *Pediatrics, 121,* S235–S251. Primack, Brian; Dalton, Margaret A.; Carroll, Mary V.; Agarwal, Aaron A.; and Fine, Michael J. (2008). Content analysis of tobacco, alcohol, and other drugs in popular music. *Archives of Pediatric and Adolescent Medicine, 162,* 169–175. Sargent, James D.; Wills, Thomas A.; Stoolmiller, Mike; Gibson, Jennifer; and Gibbons, Frederick X. (2006). Alcohol use in motion pictures and its relation with early-onset teen drinking. *Journal of Studies in Alcohol, 67,* 54–65.

34. Partnership for a Drug-Free America (1994, July 12). Press release: New study shows children in NYC becoming more anti-drug, bucking national trends. Partnership for a Drug-Free America, New York.

35. Center for Media and Public Affairs. Cited in Sussman, Steve; Stacy, Alan W.; Dent, Clyde W.; Simon, Thomas R.; and Johnson, C. Anderson (1996). Marijuana use: Current issues and new research directions. *Journal of Drug Issues, 26,* p. 714. Office of National Drug Control Policy (2006, July 21). Media campaign fact sheets: Teens and technology fact sheet. National Youth Anti-drug Media Campaign, Office of National Drug Control Policy, Washington DC. Partnership for a Drug-Free America, New York.

36. Information courtesy of the Substance Abuse and Mental Health Services Administration, Rockville, MD.

37. National Center on Addiction and Substance Abuse at Columbia University (1999). No safe haven: Children of substance-abusing parents. New York: National Center on Addiction and Substance Abuse. Kumpfer, Karol L., and Alvarado, Rose (2003). Family-strengthening approaches for the prevention of youth problem behaviors. *American Psychologist, 58,* 457–465. Seizas, Judith S., and Youcha, Geraldine (1999). *Drugs, alcohol, and your children: What every parent needs to know.* New York: Penguin Books.

38. The Ad Council. (2008, March/April). Underage drinking prevention: Alcohol initation rates highest during summer. *PSA Bulletin,* p. 1. Wooldridge, Leslie Quander (2007, March/April). Ads, billboards highlight younger children. *SAMHSA News,* p. 11.

39. The National Center on Addiction and Substance Abuse at Columbia University (2005, September). The importance of family dinners II. New York: National Center on Addiction and Substance Abuse at Columbia University. The National Center on Addiction and Substance Abuse at Columbia University (2006, August). National Survey of American Attitudes on Substance Abuse XI: Teens and parents. New York: National Center on Addiction and Substance Abuse at Columbia University. Partnership for a Drug-Free America (1998). Partnership attitude tracking survey: Parents say

they're talking, but only 27% of teens—1 in 4—are learning a lot at home about the risk of drugs. Partnership for a Drug-Free America (1999). Partnership attitude tracking survey: More parents talking with kids about drugs more often, and appear to be having an impact. Information courtesy of Partnership for a Drug-Free America, New York.

40. The National Center on Addiction and Substance Abuse at Columbia University (2003, August). National Survey American Attitudes on Substance Abuse VIII: Teens and parents. New York: National Center on Addiction and Substance Abuse at Columbia University.

41. Hernandez, Lawrence P., and Lucero, Ed (1996). La Familia community drug and alcohol prevention program: Family-centered model for working with inner-city Hispanic families. *Journal of Primary Prevention, 16*, 255–272. Office of Substance Abuse Prevention (1990). *The fact is . . . reaching Hispanic/Latino audiences requires cultural sensitivity.* Rockville, MD: National Clearinghouse for Alcohol and Drug Information, National Institute on Drug Abuse. U.S. Census Bureau (2008, June). *The Hispanic population in the United States.* Washington DC: U.S. Department of Commerce.

42. Hahn, Ellen J., and Rado, Mary (1996). African-American Head Start parent involvement in drug prevention. *American Journal of Health Behavior, 20*, 41–51. Office of Substance Abuse Prevention (1990). *The fact is . . . alcohol and other drug use is a special concern for African American families and communities.* Rockville, MD: National Clearinghouse for Drug and Alcohol Information, National Institute on Drug Abuse.

43. Castro, Ralph J., and Foy, Betsy D. (2002). Harm reduction: A promising approach for college health. *Journal of American College Health, 51*, 89–91. Lewis, David C.

(2001). Urging college alcohol and drug policies that target adverse behavior, not use. *Journal of American College Health, 50*, 39–41. Weitzman, Elissa R.; Nelson, Toben F.; Lee, Hang; and Wechsler, Henry (2004). Reducing drinking and related harms in college: Evaluation of the "A Matter of Degree" program. *American Journal of Preventive Medicine, 27*, 187–196.

44. Freedman, Samuel G. (2007, September 12). Calling the folks about campus drinking. *New York Times*, p. B6. National Institute on Alcohol Abuse and Alcoholism (2002, October). Changing the culture of campus drinking. *Alcohol Alert*, No. 58. Rockville, MD: National Institute on Alcohol Abuse and Alcoholism.

45. Johnston, Lloyd D.; O'Malley, Patrick M.; Bachman, Jerald G.; and Schulenberg, John E. (2008, December 11). Various stimulant drugs show continuing gradual declines among teens in 2008, most illicit drugs hold steady. Ann Arbor, MI: University of Michigan News Service, Table 1.

46. Office of Educational Research and Improvement (1990). *A guide for college presidents and governing bodies: Strategies for eliminating alcohol and other drug abuse on campuses.* Washington DC: U.S. Department of Education.

47. Denizet-Lewis, Benoit (2005, January 9). Band of brothers. *New York Times Magazine*, pp. 32–39, 52, 73. Quotation on page 35. Office of Educational Research and Improvement, *A guide for college presidents.*

48. Crump, Sarah (2008, March 6). Fraternity life without keg parties safer, saner, say Phi Delta Theta guys. www.cleveland.com/lifestyles/2008. Schackner, Bill (2000, August 18). Fraternity houses turn off the taps and sober up. www.post-gazette.com.

PART FIVE
Treatment, Prevention, and Education

POINT/COUNTERPOINT

Should We DARE or Shouldn't We?

The following discussion of viewpoints presents the opinions of people on both sides of the controversial issues regarding the Project DARE prevention program. Don't think you have to come up with the final answer, nor should you necessarily agree with the argument you read last. Many of the ideas in this feature come from sources listed.

POINT

No program in recent years has had the success of Project DARE in reaching millions of schoolchildren with an ATOD prevention message. DARE is now the primary educational program in our war on drugs in America. Every year, in school district after school district, police officers from the community serve to administer DARE sessions, and all of them have received eighty hours of training for the job, at no cost to the educational districts that receive this service.

COUNTERPOINT

No one questions the success of DARE, but how effective is it in reducing ATOD use among the children it serves? At least fifteen evaluation studies of the long-term effects of DARE have been conducted by reputable researchers or research centers since the early 1990s, and the results are remarkably consistent. When DARE programs are compared with control groups, the studies show little or no differences in the level of ATOD use or onset of use among adolescents.

POINT

That position continues on and on. It's quite possible the researchers don't know how to measure things. There is more at stake here than good statistics. If those researchers could just see the kids' faces during the DARE sessions, they'd know how much good it's doing. Besides, a DARE police officer in the classroom is a symbol that the community at large is involved in ATOD prevention, that law enforcement is on the side of the kids, that it is not just a matter of reducing the supply of drugs but reducing the demand for them at the grass-roots level.

COUNTERPOINT

But don't you think there would be some indication of effectiveness among all these studies? It's true that students, teachers, administrators, parents, police, and political leaders feel good about DARE because it means something is being done about substance abuse, but we are talking about a program budget of approximately $750 million a year with $600 million coming from federal, state, and local sources. A publicly funded program like DARE, therefore, ought to be accountable for what it achieves. How can DARE maintain this standard of accountability?

POINT

First of all, there were positive effects in the studies you referred to. There was a significant increase in the level of self-esteem among children in the DARE program. Second, those evaluation studies were working with the DARE program before it was substantially revised. DARE sessions are now much more interactive than they had been in the past. In other words, the whole curriculum has been redesigned.

COUNTERPOINT

To coin a phrase, show me the data. The latest studies in 1999 show no advantages gained from the DARE program after a six-year and ten-year follow-up. The results simply aren't there. In the meantime, given the situation as it stands now, why should DARE remain the dominant ATOD prevention program in the United States?

POINT

Granted that evaluations of the DARE program have been less than positive, but we now have an enhanced DARE program that addresses the criticisms that have been directed at it. The revised program is more interactive than instructional, more active-learning oriented than passive. The early evaluation results are positive.

COUNTERPOINT

Yes, DARE has changed to a new and improved DARE, but in doing so the program has simply co-opted the components of other school-based programs that we know are effective. Besides, because the enhanced DARE program is so new, the long-term positive effects you refer to remain to be determined. In the meantime, given the situation as it stands now, why should DARE still retain its exalted position as the dominant ATOD prevention program in the United States? Why not simply substitute it for a prevention program with a track record of research-based success?

Critical Thinking Questions for Further Debate

1. DARE seems like such a good idea. Why do you think it fails to reduce drug use?
2. Suppose you are a sixteen-year-old teenager using illicit drugs as well as smoking cigarettes. What program back in the fifth or sixth grade, do you think, would have prevented this from happening? Suppose you are a sixteen-year-old teenager not engaging in this behavior. Did DARE make a difference in your life?

Sources: Lynam, Donald R.; Milich, Richard; Zimmerman, Rick; Novak, Scott P.; Logan, T. K.; et al. (1999). Project DARE: No effects at 10-year follow-up. *Journal of Consulting and Clinical Psychology, 67,* 590–593. Toy, Vivian S. (2004, February 1). DARE program: Sacred cow or fatted calf? *New York Times,* Section 14, pp. 1, 5. Wysong, Earl, and Wright, David W. (1995). A decade of DARE: Efficacy, politics, and drug education. *Sociological Focus, 28,* 283–311. Zernike, Kate (2001, February 15). Antidrug program says it will adopt a new strategy. *New York Times,* pp. A1, A29.

INDEX

Crack cocaine (*continued*)
  pregnancy and, 45
  systemic violence and, 49–50
  use across life span, 19
  use among American youth, 16
  withdrawal from, 48
Craving for caffeine, 312
Creatine, 24, 204–5, **204**
Creativity
  LSD and, 151
  marijuana and, 173
Crime, 46–50
  crack cocaine and, 99
  heroin abuse and, 123, 131
  LSD use and, 152
  methadone maintenance and reduction of, 133
  meth-related, 109
  OxyContin abuse and, 137
  Prohibition and, 251
Criminal organizations, Prohibition and, 11
"Criss-crossing," 130
Crixivan (indinavir), 389
Crohn's disease, 183
Cross-dependence, 67, 80–81, 366, 369, 370
"Cross-over" pharmacotherapy, 388
Cross-tolerance, 67, 80–81, 366, 369
  from benzodiazepines, 366, 369, 370
  between LSD and psilocin, 153
Crowe, Russell, 379
Crystal meth (ice), 108–9
CSAP (Center for Substance Abuse Prevention), 406, 419
Curare, 77
Curcumin, 5
Customs and Border Patrol Agency, U.S., 52
Cyanosis, 155
Cycling pattern of steroid abuse, 201
Cyclohexane, 324
Cymbalta (duloxetine), 384

Dalmane (flurazepam), 364
Damasio, Hanna, 82
d-amphetamine, 106, 107, 111
Danazol, 193
"Danbury Shakes," 378
Danocrine capsules (danazol), 193
DARE, 427–28, 441–42
Darvocet-N (propoxyphene), 119, 136
Darvon (propoxyphene), 119, 132, 136, 208
Date-rape drugs, 162, 368, 371, 372
Datril (acetaminophen), 347
Datura stramonium, 145, **160**
DAWN. *See* **Drug Abuse Warning Network (DAWN)**
Daytop Village, 403, 404
DEA, 52, 53, 157, 184, 186, 200, 371
Deadly nightshade, 159, 160
Dean, James, 12
Death(s)
  from alcohol, 38
  associated with ATOD use, 420–21
  from cancers, age-adjusted rates for, 284
  from cocaine, 38
  DAWN statistics on, 36–37
  drug-related (1962-2008), 34
  from heroin, 38
  from inhalants, 322–23, 325

  lethal dose, 32, **32,** 39, 40
  from medication errors, 345
  from morphine, 38
  from tobacco, 38, 281–82, 283
Deca-Durabolin IM (nandrolone decanoate), 193
Decaffeination, 307
Decision making, training in, 426, 427
Decongestant, 350
Decriminalization, 185
  of marijuana, 185–87
Defense, Department of, 52
Deinstitutionalization, 378, 388–89, **388**
Delatestryl IM, 193
Delirium tremens (DTs), 252, 365
Delta-9-tetrahydrocannabinol (THC), 169, 172–79. *See also* **Marijuana**
Deltasone (prednisone), 231
Delusions, 377
Dementia
  alcoholic, 253–54, **253**
  benzodiazepines and, 365–66
Demerol (meperidine), 68, 119, 136
Demographics, DAWN statistics on, 37
Dendrites, 74, 75
Denial
  of alcoholism, 248
  family reaction of, 410
Depakote (valproate), 386
Dependence, 40–42. *See also* **Physical dependence; Psychological dependence**
  alcohol, 249, **249**
  on barbiturates, 360
  on benzodiazepines, 366
  on caffeine, 311–12
  cross–, 67, 80–81, 366, 369, 370
  on heroin, 131–32
  on inhalants, 325
  LSD and, 150
  on marijuana, 176
  on meprobamate, 364
  on nicotine, 280–81, 289
  on opiates, 122–26
  physical, 360
  on steroids, 201–3
  substance, 43–44, **43**
Dependence profile, 398
Depressants, synthetic, 161. *See also* **Sedative-hypnotics**
Depression, 376, 382–86
  alcohol and, 247, 382
  MAO inhibitors for, 383–84, **383,** 385
  selective serotonin reuptake inhibitors for, 370, 384, **384,** 386, 388
  suicide and, 382
  tricyclic antidepressants for, 384, 385, 386
DeQuincey, Thomas, 121
DESI, 341
Designer drugs, 125, 156–57
  PCP variations, 161–62
Desipramine, 68, 384
Deterrence, 399, 423
Detoxification, 132, 133
Developmental assets, 21, 22
Deviance-prone pattern of behavior, 181
Deviant behavior, 48
Deviant subculture, 20
Devil Harvest (film), 172

Dexedrine (d-amphetamine), 106, 111
Dextroamphetamine (d-amphetamine), 106, 107, 108, 111
Dextromethorphan, 25, **135,** 158
Diabetes mellitus, Type 2, 309, 313
Diagnostic and Statistical Manual, Text Revision, fourth edition (DSM-IV-TR), 43–44, 249, 312
  criteria for substance dependence and abuse in, 43, 44
Dianabol (methandrostenolone), 193
Diarrhea, opiates for treatment of, 135
Diazepam, 7, 67, 343, **364,** 365, 367, 368, 369
  for LSD panic, 151
  withdrawal, 366
Dickens, Charles, 273
Diclofenac, 346
Dietary Guidelines for Americans (2000), 238
Dietary Supplement Health and Education Act (1994), 24, 334–35, 337
Dietary supplements, 22–24, **22,** 334–35, **334,** 351–52
  for depression, 388
  as ergogenic aids, 204–5
  taken by the elderly, 389
Diethylbarbituric acid, 357
Digitalis, side effects of, 344
Digoxin, 68, 389
Dilantin (phenytoin), 45, 231
Dilaudid (hydromorphone), 119, 136, 208
Dimetane (brompheniramine), 342
Dimetapp (brompheniramine), 342
2,5, -Dimethoxy-4-methylamphetamine (DOM or STP), 144, 145, 155–56, **156**
Dimethyltryptamine (DMT), 144, **154**
Diphenhydramine, 342, **349**
Dipping, 287
Disease
  alcoholism as, 259–60, 331–32
  distinction between non-disease and, 24
Disinhibition theory, 234
Dissociative anesthetic hallucinogens, 161, 162
Dissociative disorders, 377
Distillation, 218, 218
Distilled spirits, 218, **218,** 219
Disulfiram, 231, **260,** 397
Diuretic effects of alcohol, 230
Diuretics, 231
  caffeine in, 307
  side effects of, 344
Diuril, 231
DMT, 10
DNA, naturally occurring gene mutations in, 195
Dr. Agnew's Catarrh Powder, 11
Dole, Vincent, 133
"Doll's eyes," 161
Dolorphine (methadone), 136
DOM, 144, 145, 155–56, **156**
Domestic violence, alcoholism and, 247
Doors of Experience, The (Osmond), 146
Dopamine, 76, **77,** 79
  amphetamines and, 106
  cocaine and, 97
  L-Dopa as precursor of, 80
  molecular structure of, 106
  nicotine and release of, 280
  psychological dependence and, 81